IN/SECURITY

Canada in the Post-9/11 World

IN/SECURITY

Canada in the Post-9/11 World

Edited by Alexander Netherton,
Allen Seager, and Karl Froschauer

Centre for Canadian Studies
Simon Fraser University

IN/SECURITY: CANADA IN THE POST-9/11 WORLD

Chapter 5 has been previously published in the *Osgoode Hall Law Journal*, vol. 41; Number 2,3 (Summer/Fall 2003), 211–240. Reprinted by permission. A later version of the paper comprising Chapter 9 appeared as "'Economic Security is Not So Cheap as the December 2001 Canada–U.S. Smart Border Declaration Would Imply: Suggestions for Moving Beyond the Post-9/11 Rhetoric on Borders" in the *Journal of Borderlands Studies*, vol 17, issue 2, Fall 2003.

Library and Archives Canada Cataloguing in Publication Data

In/Security: Canada in an International World (2002 : Simon Fraser University)
In/security: Canada in the post-9/11 world / edited by Alexander Netherton, Allen Seager, and Karl Froschauer.

Papers delivered at the conference In/Security: Canada in an International World, held Nov. 7, 2002 at Simon Fraser University.
Includes bibliographical references.
ISBN 0-86491-277-3

1. National security--Canada. 2. Terrorism--Canada--Prevention. 3. Canada--Foreign relations--Middle East. 4. Middle East--Foreign relations--Canada. 5. Canada--Foreign relations--United States. 6. United States--Foreign relations--Canada. 7. National security--United States.
I. Netherton, Alex, date- II. Seager, Allen III. Froschauer, Karl, 1946-
IV. Centre for Canadian Studies (Burnaby, B.C.) V. Title.
HV6433.C3I57 2005 303.6'25'0971 C2005-904364-4

Printed in Canada by Hignell Book Printing
Cover Art: Miller Brittain, *Night Target, Germany* 1946. Oil and tempera on canvas, 76.5 x 61.0 cm. Canadian War Museum, AN19710261-1436.

Cover Design, Book Design, Typesetting: Robert D. MacNevin

Centre for Canadian Studies, Simon Fraser University, 8888 University Drive, Burnaby, British Columbia, V5A 1S6, Canada
www.sfu.ca/cns/

Contents

List of Tables

Preface

This book is the result of an interdisciplinary conference entitled *In/Security: Canada in an International World* in November 2002, hosted by the interdisciplinary conference program of the Centre for Canadian Studies at Simon Fraser University, in the wake of the September 11, 2001 (9/11) terrorist attacks on major targets in the United States.

The main aims of the Centre's program are to provide a forum for Canadianists (those who make Canada their primary society of inquiry) for academic exchange on contemporary Canadian issues and questions and to publish edited volumes or journal articles of their proceedings. Rather than addressing issues from a single academic perspective, the Centre's program promotes interdisciplinary inquiry where scholars can bring to bear the different viewpoints of their respective disciplines to illuminate and interpret Canadian responses to major events.

The immediate American response to 9/11 and subsequent "war against terrorism" constituted a significant turning point for Canada, leading to new legislation as well as changes in foreign affairs, security policies, trade relations, and human rights considerations. The conference provided a forum for intellectual reassessment, emerging perspectives, and a research agenda for a critical analysis of Canada's post-9/11 changes in policy and discourses.

The program of the conference was conceived and organized by Allen Seager (then the director of the Centre) and Alex Netherton. Together they have edited the proceedings, which were then revised by their authors before they appeared as working papers on the *In/Security* website and prepared for final publication in this volume. Given the rapid progress of events that led to the war in Iraq shortly after the conference and resulted in further security measures, some authors made additions in their revisions to deal with the war on Iraq, while others maintained their primary focus on the first year after the air strikes.

Since I took on the position of Director of the Centre for Canadian Studies in January, 2004 I agreed to become involved in editing the proceedings and the introduction, and to supervise all stages of the book's preparation, co-ordinating my co-editors' work with the light copy-editing, book design, and layout by Robert MacNevin. I am grateful to them for supporting my selection of the indelible image of true terror in and from the skies for the cover image—Miller Brittain's *Night Target, Germany* (1946), which was included in the exhibit *Canvas of War: Masterpieces from the Canadian War Museum* in the Vancouver Art Gallery (28 February 2004). As Allen Seager wrote: "Miller Brittain was a romantic left and avant-garde figure of the 1930s who 'did his bit' during WW II by volunteering as a war artist for the Royal Canadian Air Force. *Night Target* is really no different from Brittain's take on Canada in his painting *Workers Arise!* (1936). His pictures were meant to raise questions about patriotism, popular frontism, political violence, and not to hammer the viewer with a sledgehammer blow of propaganda, and to that extent, they stand the test of time."

In addition to the discussants, authors, co-editors, and the designer, I would like to thank the key funding institutions, Simon Fraser University, and numerous individuals, without the support of whom neither the conference on *In/Security* nor the publication of this edited volume would have been possible. A Social Sciences and Humanities Research Council of Canada (SSHRC) grant helped fund the attendance of the core participants. Internal university support came from the Centre for Canadian Studies, the office of the Vice-President, Academic, and the Boag Foundation of Vancouver. In addition, I would like to acknowledge John Pierce, Dean of Arts for his support of the Canadian Studies Program, Stephen McBride, then Chair of the Political Science Department, for his departmental support, John Whatley for his publishing advice, Penny Southby for her conference organization skills, Colette Sauro for her assistance with accounts and correspondence, John Marriott for proofreading, Jane Cowan for copy-editing, and the War Museum of Canada for allowing the use of the image *Night Target*.

Karl Froschauer — Director of the Centre for Canadian Studies

IN/SECURITY

Canada in the Post-9/11 World

Introduction: Framing In/Security

Alexander Netherton and Allen Seager

On September 11th, 2001, then-unknown assailants made terrifying strategic and symbolic attacks using hijacked domestic aircraft on centres of global capitalism, military prowess, and governance in the United States. For Americans, these attacks were a turning point, defining the moment when collective and personal securities were shattered. The first major "successful" air attack by foreign forces on the American mainland, it signalled that terrorism did not simply occur "out there" in parts of the world where political violence against civilians was a cruel daily reality. They were not alone in feeling the impact. Common borders, significant economic integration, and political alliances meant that Canada was immediately affected and became integrally involved, as did the other members of NATO.

In the following weeks, both the media and politicians began to use a political lexicon that named al-Qaida, the Taliban, and Osama bin Laden as the primary enemies. President George W. Bush declared he would lead a global "war on terror," a war clearly based upon the insecurity and vulnerability represented by September 11th. Canada has participated in that war from the start. Initial fears (eventually proved groundless) that the September 11th terrorists had slipped into the United States from the north politicized border security. In the months following the attacks, "security" became not simply an "add on" to conventional policy areas, but rather a concern that reshaped several national and international Canadian policies. For instance, a new security policy would be implemented to serve domestic needs and also to prove to alliance partners that Canada was doing her share.

The articles that follow are the revised proceedings of the Centre for Canadian Studies' conference *In/Security: Canada in an International World,* held at Simon Fraser University in November, 2002, a gathering of scholars who sought to explore how security-related perspectives and policies, broadly defined, changed in Canada during the year after September 11th.[1] Accordingly, the purpose of the authors who contributed to this collection is to analyze Canada's changed perspectives on security and the policy initiatives that tried to re-establish security in North America and abroad. As the papers show, society cannot be completely secure, and trade-offs that place more emphasis on one aspect of security may well jeopardize another.

This introduction first sketches out the context of September 11, then it describes the major Canadian policy responses to the terrorist attacks against the United States, and, finally, it presents the emerging reseach agenda evident in the analytical approaches and research questions raised in the papers. We have subdivided this agenda into five sections and conclude the introduction with comments on the advancement of the research agenda.

The Context of September 11

The attacks of September 11th did not occur in a vacuum, nor were the groups named as enemies completely unknown. In the 1990s, the continuing disorder in the Middle East saw the U.S. taking action against Muslim groups and countries it had tacitly or actively supported — Iraq after it invaded Kuwait and the Taliban who had been instrumental in driving Soviet troops from Afghanistan but increasingly restricted the freedoms of the country's citizens. However, the postwar UN sanctions imposed on Iraq following the first Gulf War (1990–91) proved to be unstable, inhumane, and corrupt, and weapons inspection regimes in Iraq failed to verify disarmament, their principal goal. Also in the Middle East, following the "first intifada" (1987–93), the hopes raised for a settlement between Israelis and Palestinians by the 1993 Oslo Accords completely collapsed, revealing that there was neither an international consensus on the nature of this conflict nor an international mechanism to end hostilities.

If terrorism is the use of violence and intimidation against civilian populations to attain political objectives, then the significant thing about September 11th is not that it happened, but rather its location, timing, and scale. Given that acts of terror against the U.S. targets in the 1990s had increased, intellectuals had warned of a coming "clash of civilizations" between the West and Islam.[2] For instance, in 1992, a group closely linked to bin Laden's al-Qaida had bombed the World Trade Center. In addition, al-Qaida itself, already known to be training Mujahideen, first in the Sudan and then in Afghanistan, was held responsible for the havoc wreaked on civilians by the bombing of American embassies in East African capitals in 1998 and a suicide attack on the USS *Cole* in Yemen in 2000, its operatives apparently unaccountable to international law and out of reach of the U.S. military.

After the fall of the Soviet bloc trading system and the strengthening of the North American and European economies, the 1990s also witnessed the apogee of neo-liberal globalization in the West[3] represented by the continuation of a global trade regime headed by the World Trade Organization (WTO). In North America, the Canada-United States Free Trade Agreement (FTA) and then the North America Free Trade Agreement (NAFTA) represented significant steps in furthering the Americanization of the Canadian economy. To offset this process, Canada began in the mid-1990s to stake out a multilateral foreign policy niche as a middle power that would accomplish specific objectives within a revitalized international system. Lisa Ferrari outlines how then Foreign Affairs Minister Lloyd Axworthy turned towards "Human Security," as opposed to military security, and began to focus foreign policy on multilateral initiatives and international law. Illustrations of Canada's multilateralism are the sponsorship of the Ottawa Convention to eliminate anti-personnel mines, the ratification of the Kyoto Accord to reduce global warming, and its involvement in establishing the International Criminal Court in The Hague to bring perpetrators of war crimes, genocide, and crimes against humanity to justice. These approaches oriented towards human security, however, were taking place in a period when the Canadian state had weakened its military power. After two decades of substantial deficits, the harsh 1990s neoliberal fiscal discipline included cuts to military and security spending. At the same time, as several authors remark, the process of economic integration had been so rapid and extensive that Canadian policy before September 11th centred on streamlining the process of cross-border trade. As a result, the heightened U.S. concern with border security after September 11th threatened Canada's economic security.

In contrast, in the 1990s the U.S. continued to increase military spending and weapons innovations, which produced a substantial gap in military power between the U.S. and its allies. Learning its lessons from terrorism in that decade, the United States developed a concept (and embryonic regime) of "homeland security" measures to protect the United States from non-traditional security risks. In addition, U.S. President George W. Bush's new Republican Administration adopted a commitment to pursue a specifically American international agenda, one that turned its back on older multilateral commitments. Increasingly, the U.S. showed that unilateral thinking affected its policies on international justice, disarmament, and global warming, whereas Canada took a more multilateral approach to these foreign policy domains. September 11th, then, occurred at a point in which the foreign policies of the two states differed in substantial ways.

Canada's Response to September 11th

Canada's immediate response to the al-Qaida attacks was to help the United States with air defence. When U.S. authorities closed national airspace to incoming international flights, Canada agreed to allow all U.S.-bound planes (carrying a total of 33,000 passengers and crew) to land at its airports such as Gander, Newfoundland, where a third of them were accommodated, and Canada co-operated with the U.S. to guard against any further hijacked passenger jets. When NATO invoked "Article 5," Canada and the other members proclaimed that the attack on the United States was the equivalent to an attack on all of them. In October 2001, the U.S. led the NATO attack on the Taliban regime and al-Qaida in Afghanistan. "Operation Apollo," Canada's military contribution, included modest ground forces (one battle group with regular aznd special forces) and a significant naval task force with a long-range patrol and a tactical airlift detachment.[4]

Though the invasion of Afghanistan quickly removed the Taliban from power, it did not destroy al-Qaida, its leadership, or that of the Taliban. Military efforts then centred on consolidation of the new government, the destruction of remaining Taliban and al-Qaida forces, and, especially, the capture of Osama bin Laden. Operation Apollo wound down in 2003, and Canadian forces continued participation in the UN/NATO International Security Assistance Force (ISAF) in Afghanistan when U.S./UK-led forces invaded Iraq. NATO allies were divided on the invasion of Iraq. While the UK was a willing partner to the invasion, Canada, like France and Germany, did not endorse or participate in the war on Iraq, despite extensive U.S. pressure to do so. One reason frequently given for the disagreement was that UN weapons inspectors had not completed their task — and that no significant caches of weapons of mass destruction had been found. But as Desmond Morton and Douglas Ross explain, there was also an increasingly wide gap between U.S. military capacity and defence doctrine and that of its major NATO allies. The new U.S. doctrine of "pre-emptive" war used to claim the invasion was legitimate had little support in Ottawa, and efforts to rally public opinion behind the American cause by sections of the media had little effect. On the domestic front, the Canadian government sought more powers and the institutional capacity to assure the Americans that there was no weakening of resolve to fight terrorism. The U.S. government quickly enacted sweeping anti-terrorist legislation, the *Patriot Act* (an acronym for the last part of the official title: Uniting and Strengthening America by Providing Appropriate Tools Required to Intercept and Obstruct Terrorism), and Canada followed with the introduction of two major pieces of legislation intended to stave off terrorism and improve security.

Canada's *Anti-Terrorism Act* contained a broad definition of terrorism, increased police powers, substantially changed the immigration process, and contained new identification procedures. Its *Public Safety Act* also allowed officials to use and share confidential information about airline passengers without their consent. Early versions of these Acts generated controversies. As Hassan-Yari and Ousman, and Patrick J. Smith indicate, opponents did not believe that to combat terrorism effectively it was necessary to suspend provisions in the *Canadian Charter of Rights and Freedoms*. In fact, the public security legislation underwent continual change and refinement until the House of Commons finally passed the current *Public Safety Act* in May, 2004.[5] In the same year, the government published *Securing an Open Society, Canada's National Security Policy*.

In December 2003, the Government of Canada combined new security responsibilities with traditional "natural" emergency responsibilities within the Department of Public Safety and Emergency Preparedness (PSEP). Related institutional developments included the creation of a Cross-Cultural Roundtable on Security, an Advisory Council on National Security, and a Federal-Provincial Forum on Security. Canada's legislative and institutional responses will doubtless continue to change in light of international obligations, policy exigencies, and domestic pressures.

Since 2001, the new security agenda has been intended to be instrumental in reshaping and stabilizing Canada–U.S. relations, which, at the same time, have been plagued by select U.S. protectionism and trade disputes over particular commodities, such as softwood lumber and cattle. A key concern of the Canadian state was and is to preserve open borders for travel and trade in the face of protectionism and barriers created by U.S. homeland security measures. Both governments attempted to find ways to ensure that border crossings could handle the increased trade and prevent road and rail blockages. Following September 11, 2001, the U.S. government deployed well-armed federal officials to screen southbound passengers and freight, which symbolized American pressure on Canada to re-examine its own border security and also to harmonize policy fields such as anti-terrorist security and intelligence, transportation regulation, refugee acceptance, and customs policy. In its fullest expression, policy harmonization with the Americans was expected to be part of a common "North American Security Perimeter," a Republican grand plan for continental integration that emerged from American Homeland Security thinking.

Washington's "North American Security Perimeter" did not materialize, but governments did undertake controversial and strategic incremental steps to harmonize policy (see the contributions of Matthew S. Mingus, Darren Prokop, and Louis-Blaise Dumais-Lévesque and

Anne-Marie Durocher). Of particular importance were the ways mutual trade and security objectives were met in the Canada–U.S. Smart Border Declaration signed in December 2001 and its related "Action Plan." For instance, the Canada Border Services Agency, created in 2003, has the responsibility for the coordination and administration of traditional and nontraditional border-related services. As in the case of military security, incremental harmonization of border management, security, trade, and immigration policy are subject to further change in the light of competing political pressures.[6]

The Research Agenda

Contributors to this multi-authored volume have pursued a variety of perspectives, research questions, and analytical approaches to the post-September 11 sense of insecurity, security problems, and policy responses that represent an emerging research agenda. To examine the sense of insecurity and security-related policies developed after these events, they propose that readers view this field of inquiry from a number of different perspectives. Some authors have analyzed Canada's responses to September 11 historically, looking at policy continuity and change over time; others ask readers to consider the the subject within a larger conceptualization of events and broader theoretical syntheses; and still others approach security by employing contemporary public policy analysis and by examining controversial debates.

The preferences and self-directed research orientations of the contributing authors are evident in the questions they raise about security-related post-9/11 problems and their critiques and careful review of American and Canadian policy responses. Their research contributions resulted in an emerging research agenda with analytical preferences that we have subdivided into five sets of questions that guide their inquiries and set out in the subsections that follow (Parts I to V below).

The first set of questions deal with the war on terrorism, weapons of mass destruction, forms of insecurity, and understanding policy responses. How is Canada to participate in an asymmetric war on terrorism? (Desmond Morton). How can defence policy analysts and advisers to the Canadian government on Defence and Security Policy best understand the changes in policy since September 11th, 2001?

(Houchang Hassan-Yari and Abdelkérin Ousman). What have been the American and Canadian political, military, and North American home-security policy responses to threats posed by a terrorism that has recourse to weapons of mass destruction? (Douglas Ross). What is the ontology of a post-September 11 form of insecurity that serves a public psychology of fear? (Samir Gandesha).

The second set deals with security problems, political policing, balancing security and rights, torture warrants, and the utility of anti-terrorist legislation. What were the origins of political policing in the contexts of class, the law, and the Burden of Empire? (Andrew Parnaby and Gregory S. Kealey). In the aftermath of September 11, has Canada's policy discourse maintained an appropriate balance between security and rights? (Patrick J. Smith). Should Canada allow torture warrants for the interrogation of alleged terrorists? (David MacAlister). Would we be better off without an Anti-Terrorism Act? (Avery Plaw).

The third set deals with economic security, enforcement and technology at borders, and the privatization of security. Can economic security exist so long as current forces are aligned to maintain the concentrated flow of trade through so few tunnels and bridges? (Mathew Mingus). Is there a distinction between safe borders and smart borders? (Darren Prokop). How can we assess the trends and manage the issues of the continued privatization of security services after September 11 in Canada? (Christopher Spearin).

The fourth set concerns Canada's Middle Eastern policy and its policy on human security. The contributors ask: Is Canada's Middle East policy in the post-September 11 era going to be an authentic expression of what is vitally important to Canadians, and will it reflect Canada's long-term interests under the new circumstances? (Ayla Kiliç). Are the Ottawa Convention's concerns about "human security" still timely after September 11? (Lisa Ferrari). Has Canada's policy towards the Arab world and Israel been balanced and unbiased, and, if not, how does Canada have to change its Middle Eastern policy in response to the events of September 11? (Shaun Narine).

The fifth set deals with Canada's post-September 11 foreign policy transformations, the Canadian response, customs and monetary union, and perspectives of the Canadian elite and raises additional questions. Although Canadian policy responses are still in flux, we can ask: What transformations of foreign policy have taken place? (Karl Kresl). Can the Canadian response to the events of September 11 be seen as a model? (Louis-Blaise Dumais-Lévesque and Anne-Marie Durocher). In Canada's desire to secure access to the American market, do the discussions and proposals point more towards a customs and monetary union in North America? (Denis Michaud). Did the Canadian media and political élite move towards a more nationalist perspective after September 11? (Stephen McBride). In the five sections that follow, we summarize the contributors' answers to these sets of questions.

Part I: Post-9/11 Perspectives on Terrorism, Defence, Security, and Insecurity

The four essays on security matters in the post-September 11 years in Part I address Canada's participation in the asymmetrical war against terrorism, how best to analyze Canadian military and security policy, the inadequacies of these policies in light of a terrorism that can employ weapons of mass destruction, and the roots of the post-September 11 form of insecurity that perpetuates the public psychology of fear.

In the first essay, Desmond Morton argues for the separation of the controversial issues of the underfunding of the Canadian Armed Forces from questions of global terrorism and participation in America's "asymmetrical" wars. Canada, he argues, has no real enemies and no defence problem save for security issues vis-à-vis the United States. Since they have a similar understanding, Canadian policymakers have looked at the military in opportunistic terms: the main objective of defence policy has always turned on the question of convincing the United States that Canada is doing "enough," the challenge being, of course, to determine just how much is enough. Morton does not think that the traditional political formula is working in the present security crisis and questions the link between military investment and the fight against terror. Fighting terrorists, he believes, is essentially police work, and the modernization of the Canadian Armed Forces could be achieved with a very modest shopping list — as long as anti-terrorism and defence are appropriately separated from each other.

In their comprehensive overview of Canadian defence and security policy processes and Canadian–American military relations, Houchang

Hassan-Yari and Abdelkérim Ousman also caution against "reinventing the wheel" in response to al-Qaida or U.S. pressure. Instead, they defend the cautious Canadian defence and security processes as an incremental policy-making model that differs markedly from the "rational choice" decision-making that has characterized U.S. policy. They argue that the rational choice model conflicts with the dynamics of the Canadian constitution, where the judiciary protects *Charter* rights by examining the extent to which the state infringes on an individual's legally defined rights, not on its making efficient policies. "It is our view [they write] that Canada's process of defence and security change exemplifies a process of incrementalism that is more in keeping with Canada's Constitution and the *Charter of Rights and Freedoms* than the rational calculation of the likely costs and benefits of policy options that are designed to please or displease the current the U.S. Administration."

Nevertheless, the authors describe a policy process that is fraught with complex trade-offs and does not necessarily translate into good policy content. Bill C-36, for example, defined terrorism in such broad terms that it was not clear whether normal political dissent would be tolerated or whether the legislation would pass a judicial test of proportionality. With respect to the issue of Canada's participating in the U.S. National Missile Defence initiative, Hassan-Yari and Ousman pose the trade-offs starkly in terms of "sovereignty, liberties, and freedoms," on one hand, and "safety, defence, and economic well-being," on the other.

Douglas A. Ross presents a provocative critique of Canadian defence and security policy that runs counter to much left/liberal nationalist thinking before and after September 11th. Ross argues that Canada has fundamentally misunderstood the American security dilemma and that disdain for President George W. Bush and his neo-conservative project masks the real failure of the Canadian government as a credible player in international security issues. Chronic underfunding of the military has become a *de facto* national policy, effectively making Canada a habitual "free rider" with neither freedom of action nor a positive role to play.

Ross firmly accepts that the U.S. concern that "rogue states" may use weapons of mass destruction is valid, as is the possibility that such weapons may spread to terrorist arsenals. He argues that because such weapons are so accessible, they are a real threat to Canada as well, for it is both a close and proximate ally of the U.S. Ross argues that Bush's doctrine of pre-emptive war is based upon rational assumptions and, indeed, that it may be impossible to protect an open society against the use weapons of mass destruction by terrorist groups. For Ross, the reality is that the fear of proliferation of weapons of mass destruction lies at the core of U.S. strategic thinking and that "there is no liberal alternative to U.S. unilateralism." He identifies a shopping list of security and defence priorities needed for Canada to "survive the twenty-first century battlefields" but doubts that Ottawa will act on them.

Stepping away from policy analyses, Samir Gandesha addresses the post-September 11th form of insecurity and fear by employing an ontological perspective. Drawing on the work of Anthony Giddens, he argues that the politics of fear and insecurity derive from the historical processes of modernization, particularly its contemporary manifestation in globalization.[7] This process fragments solidarity and therefore provides the conditions in which a right-wing populism that often targets marginal segments of society can grow. Such right-wing groups oppose the higher levels of immigration that are integral to globalization with arguments that they are defending traditional social and national identities. September 11th events have exacerbated such pre-existing anti-immigration trends in Western Europe and North America, but Canadian multicultural communities have responded to them in ways that deserve comparative attention.

Part II: Post-9/11 Reponses to Terrorism, Torture, Rights, and Anti-Terrorism Acts

The authors whose work is summarized in this section show their post-September 11 research interests by examining the historical origins of political policing that has served class, law, and empire; the policy discourses that show an imbalance between security and rights; the question of whether Canada should allow torture warrants; and whether an Anti-Terrorism Act is legally prudent.

In their review of the historical record of political policing, Andrew Parnaby and Gregory S. Kealey probe the origins of Canada's security services in periods of tension that were influenced by the pull of Empire, fear of outsiders, concerns about constitutional governance, and specific crises that arose in the years between 1860 and 1914. Starting in the 1860s, the chief purpose of the small Canadian secret service that was organized in the United States during the U.S. Civil War was to monitor the actions of the Fenian Brotherhood in order to defend against cross-border raiders. Later, Canadian operatives worked within a network of immigrants and British India agents to root out potential radicals. In both cases, the security services reported directly to the executive, were not accountable to Parliament, and used unscrupulous, sometimes brutal, tactics that occasionally backfired. The Canadian state, we learn, had no qualms in using intelligence services to pursue a narrowly defined "national interest" and was more than willing to bend its services for Empire.

Patrick J. Smith uses a different approach in his comparison of discourses that have defined security and rights since the 1980s. He analyzes two discourses by comparing one from the 1980s during the formation of Canada's contemporary intelligence regime, the Canadian Security and Intelligence Service (CSIS) and the Canadian Security Review Committee (CSRC), with another discourse in the 2001–2 period that defined the post-September 11th security regime. Concerns for civil liberties and mechanisms of political accountability clearly dominated the formative discourse for CSIS and CSRC, successors to the scandal-scarred Royal Canadian Mounted Police (RCMP) Security Services of the 1970s, with the debates on the *Anti-Terrorism Act* of 2001—Canada's equivalent of the *USA Patriot Act*. However, Smith argues that the balance turned towards collective security at the expense of individual rights. Although the Canadian government had not yet finalized its anti-terrorism proposals when he wrote his article, he substantiates his argument with findings from a detailed analysis of relevant inquiries, debates, and reviews. Questions like the status of individuals and organizations on a confidential "List of Terrorists" created substantial backlash from human rights groups informed by the *Charter* and from legal experts within Parliament. In acknowledging the substance of these concerns, amendments provided a five-year "sunset clause" for the expanded police powers and commitments to legislative review of the Act in three years, thus guaranteeing that exceptional powers are subject to democratic review and do not establish so much bureaucratic inertia that they become written in stone. Smith suggests that the initial versions of the *Public Safety Act* (2002) were withdrawn, not because of the vocal dissent but because the legislation would not have stood up to a legal challenge under the *Charter of Rights and Freedoms*. The idea of special "military control zones" in which normal rights of protest and dissent were prohibited, for example, read like a recipe to rid the government of anti-globalization protesters during summit diplomacy.

Avery Plaw goes somewhat further on the problem of "imbalance" between security and rights by asking the question "Would we be better off without an Anti-Terrorism Act?" Plaw would prefer not only that terrorism and terrorists' acts be treated within established criminal law, and not under an Anti-Terrorism Act, but also that governments concentrate on providing security forces with the resources to do their job. In particular, Plaw analyzes and critiques the controversial legal definitions of terrorism that divided government and the policy community during the uneasy passage of the *Anti-Terrorism Act*. Definitions of terrorism as a crime embedded in political, religious or ideological motivation are central to his argument. Criminal law has long focused on behaviour rather than intent for the good reason that intent is difficult, even impossible, to prove. The judiciary cannot enter the territory of motivation without making subjective judgements about what is a good ("acceptable") intent and what is a bad ("unacceptable") intent. Plaw predicts that attempts to focus on motivation will cause more and more obscurity—and will bring the administration of Canadian justice into disrepute.

In the final essay in Part II, David MacAlister tackles legal questions about "torture warrants" by arguing against advocates who suggest torture is a legitimate means of information gathering. MacAlister's comprehensive rebuttals of their arguments touch on a key American debate that is of importance to Canada, the United Kingdom, and other democratic states about whether torture is justified.[8]

Part III: Post-9/11 Examinations of Trade Security, Border Security, and Privatized Security

The authors in this section explore the effects of September 11th on Canada–U.S. relations by focusing on security when Canada–U.S. trade is concentrated at a few major border crossings, on the analysis of the burden of safe (enforced) and smart (high-tech) borders, and the continued privatization and subcontracting of the provision of security. For instance, the *Smart Borders Declaration* and similar highly touted measures of Canada–U.S. co-operation demonstrate the aim to harmonize U.S. security concerns with such business strategies as "Just in Time" production that is integrated across borders.

How does the post-September 11th regime handle these trade-offs? Matthew Mingus provides a preliminary analysis of the effects of the geography of trade along the Canada–U.S. border. Mingus demonstrates how cross-border trade is concentrated at six to eight crossings. Unfortunately, he argues, the new security regime has distorted the flow of trade by intensifying this concentration. Much of the new security regime is comprised of ideas discussed but not implemented during the 1990s. The high-profile "common security perimeter" concept (often assumed to be a post-September 11th innovation) was proposed by the American ambassador to Canada well before the attacks and was "weeded out" in the wake of the travel and trade emergency of 2001. Among the most important unintended side effects of bilateral trade that uses such few major crossings is its increasing vulnerability to terrorist attacks.

Darren Prokop examines the effects of trade and security measures on various transportation modes (air, water, and road). Through policy harmonization, American and Canadian policies try to ensure that security measures are initiated at points on the supply chain well before goods reach the border, part of the objective being to shift the burden of security regulation and enforcement from the government to producers and shippers. If large firms want to maintain integrated transnational production, they will have to invest heavily in new information technologies that allow for electronic manifests and monitoring of cargo. Prokop asks whether the new policies encourage shippers and carriers to become "free riders" on the security efforts of others, particularly in the mammoth trucking sector. The new "harmonized" security regime institutionalizes a multi-tiered system where small shippers and carriers who transport mixed cargoes face significantly more border delays than the larger carriers transporting for single shippers, providing further support for the trend towards corporate concentration rather than the idealized open and competitive free market championed by

Canadian neo-liberals. Christopher Spearin examines border security from the perspective of the new public administration model where the state takes responsibility for the provision of a service but uses private contractors to deliver it. After a decade of deficits, cutbacks, and downsizing, Spearin asks if the first Canadian "security" budget, one that allocated over $7 billion towards improving security, would reverse this trend. His analysis shows that this was emphatically not the case, that several factors, including declining troop strength, have compelled the governments to rely more heavily than ever on private contractors for security services. This reliance poses critical public policy problems, and Spearin suggests ways in which the issues associated with this new private/public sector mix might be addressed. Clearly, the contemporary security strategy will not lead Canada back to the patterns of the past, though the final form of this neo-liberal mix has yet to be determined.

Part IV: Post-9/11 Reviews of Middle East Policy and Human Security

Much of the post-September 11th security crisis stemmed from a single source: Western involvement in the Middle East. The research agenda pursued by three authors who examined Canada's Middle East policy follows several paths of inquiry: a historical review of rationales in Canada's Middle East policies with a reference to post-September 11, an examination of the issue whether the Ottawa Convention's concerns about human security (such as those created by land mines) are still timely, and a consideration of whether the potential imbalances between Canadian policies towards Arab countries and Israel may have to change.

Ayla Kiliç's historical review outlines why Canada has always had difficulty formulating a coherent policy for the Middle East. Kiliç outlines a typology of policies, some classified in terms of roles, such as "helpful fixer" or "honest broker," that portray Canada's strategy towards the Middle East in different periods of the twentieth century. The preferred "honest broker" approach to the conflict associated with tilts and shifts of activist diplomacy, Kiliç notes, did not please Israeli, Palestinian, or other Arab actors in the region. A policy of benign neglect or disengagement, on the other hand, is impossible because there are highly motivated domestic constituencies, both pro-Israeli and, through immigration, growing pro-Arab and Islamist groups, who work to influence Canada's Middle East policy. A "domestic stability" or constituency approach leads to competition between the promotion of Canadian values abroad and responses to U.S. policy interests. Acknowledging that the war against terrorism has changed the relative balance among these domestic and external variables, she concludes that Canadian policy towards the Middle East may well move back and forth between opposing poles.

For Lisa Ferrari, who examines Canada's diplomatic role in light of the so-called "Axworthy Doctrine" or Human Security foreign policy, the negative results of the "war on terror" are clear. The apex of Canada's human security agenda was represented by the Ottawa Convention, a 1997 international convention that aimed to ban the use of land mines in much the same spirit that Canada has supported any number of disarmament measures since the era of the League of Nations. The accord also had a broader objective — to establish (or re-establish) the principles of international "conventions" that would supersede the terms of state to state treaties. By mid-2004, 149 states had signed and ratified the accord. Still, forty states had not, including the Russian Federation, the United States, and all of the principal states in the Middle East.

Ferrari argues that Operation Apollo eroded the human security agenda in various ways, ranging from the use of cluster bombs in Afghanistan to the diversion of scarce Canadian resources from human security to military and border security objectives. Furthermore, it consumed intellectual resources and forced Canada to confine the Ottawa Accord to its specific legal framework rather than to extend its scope and principles to other fields of endeavour. In short, the more the Canadian state participates in the "war on terror," the less emphasis is placed upon human security as a signature foreign policy and the heavier the burden on interested non-governmental organizations becomes.

Shaun Narine examines attempts by the Canadian government to implement the Axworthy Doctrine within the domain of the Arab (Palestinian)-Israeli conflict, drawing a similar conclusion: without an active and constructive role in the conflict, particularly the commitment of more resources, the pursuit of human security strategy becomes a marginal form of "pulpit diplomacy." In the present situation, efforts to mediate between Israeli and Palestinian positions, given the polarized political and military alliances, also makes Canadian policy look like a mixture of idealism and political expediency. He offers hope that there is room for Canada's human security agenda — once great power diplomacy has determined the contours of a peace settlement. Assessing reasons for Canada's timidity in defining a clear Middle East strategy, Narine does not seek explanation in the influence of the Canada–Israel Committee, its Arab and Muslim counterparts, or the predominance of the United States in the region. He suggests that, at root, the Canadian government simply has a history of ambivalence in the region.

Part V: Post-9/11 Evaluations of Foreign Policy, Canadian Responses, Economic Union, and Elite Nationalism

The agenda set by the fifth group of researchers shows a preference for inquiries that assess whether the September 11 events have brought transformations in Canadian foreign policy, whether Canada's response can be seen as model or "organized hypocrisy," whether economic security can be attained through customs or monetary union between Canada and the U.S., and whether the Canadian media and political élite moved towards a more nationalist perspective.

Peter Karl Kresl argues that all three pillars of Canada's stated foreign policy, the promotion of peace, trade, and culture, have been changed in subtle ways as emphasis shifts to the politics of multilateral institutions and continental security regimes and cultural nationalism is challenged by the promotion of universal "Western" values and culture. Although Kresl does not use George Grant's term "homogenous state," their arguments runs along parallel lines: the more Canadian policy and culture reflect the exigencies of "the West," the more nationalism is subjected to the pull of a universalizing American liberal empire.

Denis Michaud's paper on monetary and customs union returns to the questions of borders and economic integration that were at the centre of Canadian public policy before September 11th. Increased levels of economic integration and international monetary instability during the closing years of the millennium opened up policy debates on the establishment of a North American Monetary Union (NAMU). Michaud describes the emergence of a carefully managed debate amongst economists, members of leading think tanks, leaders of financial institutions, and parliamentarians, a debate, he remarks, that ended by creating ideas for greater structural integration at a later date.

Louis-Blaise Dumais-Lévesque and Anne-Marie Durocher argue that the Canadian government played a game of "organized hypocrisy" in response to the backlash over American pressure on the proposed North American Security Perimeter. Drawing on the works of Nils Brunsson and Stephen Krasner, they define organized hypocrisy as a political behaviour in which states may have to "talk in a way that satisfies one demand, to decide in a manner that satisfies another, and to supply the products in a manner that satisfies a third." In this case, they argue that Canada gave the United States what it wanted but in a way that masked the loss of sovereignty to Canadian nationalists and thus protected free trade for Canadian business.

The ambivalence of Canadian nationalism in the post-September 11th world is neatly framed by Stephen McBride's essay "The Long Goodbye." McBride's analysis is in two parts. In the first, he presents the historical argument that Canadian élites have progressively abandoned the pursuit of an independent national path of development. Then, in the second, he illustrates his argument with an analysis of the élites' responses to September 11th. He presents two kinds of data: documents and publications of business élites and think tanks and content analysis of selected media coverage. In his analysis of the Canadian media élites' editorials, columns, and op-ed pieces discussing Canada–U.S. relations after September 11, McBride identifies a wide range of arguments, but the most popular was one that McBride termed "self-criticism, self-flagellation." The common thread in the media and political élites' statements is that Canadians had somehow failed Americans through lax immigration and border security policies, underfunding the military, or providing an anaemic response to September 11th. Above all, there was a perceived need to be better friends to the Americans. McBride's conclusions amplify the theme of retreat from nationalist positions during the security crisis, magnifying longstanding élite trends.

Part VI: Plenary Discussions

In the first plenary session of the In/Security Conference, several distinguished individuals discussed the politics of security. Chaired by Dave Barrett, former MP and premier of British Columbia, the panel reflected the wide range of opinion on September 11th, the war against terrorism, and the impending invasion of Iraq.

John Brewin, a former New Democratic Party MP and labour lawyer, argued that the post September 11th security politics had touched the fault lines in all the main federal political parties.[9] The NDP itself was torn between its historical pacifism and commitments to collective security. Brewin placed himself in the latter camp and, thus, among those who supported Tony Blair's policy of solidarity with military actions in Iraq. Peter Stursberg, who has received the Order of Canada for his decades of work as a war correspondent and political journalist, picked up on the quandary identified by Desmond Morton — that conventional armies were not good tools for fighting terrorism or guerrilla wars. Such "police actions" tend to be very costly in the long run and have unintended consequences for those who conduct them. In the present context, he thought that there was a tendency to label all anti-American groups terrorists, just as Israelis call all Palestinians "terrorists" in the aftermath of suicide bombings, acts which he viewed as more likely acts of desperation. In the end, he agreed with Winston Churchill that "jaw, jaw, jaw is better than war, war, war."

Colonel Richard Williams, Director of Western Hemisphere Policy for the Canadian Forces, spoke not on the "politics" of security, but rather on its policy trade-offs. Using a model he termed "Truman's triangle," Williams asked the audience to assume that Canadians had three objectives: to be free and sovereign, to be safe and secure, and not to be overtaxed. "Cheap" security might include the cost of trampling on civil rights and using racial profiling and other techniques of social control that conflict with concepts of equality. The only way to make good decisions, he urged, is to engage in a substantial policy debate. Captain Rollie Keith, retired after a thirty years of service in the Canadian forces, rounded out the military perspective. With his substantial "on the ground experience" in contemporary peacekeeping and peace monitoring, Keith's vision of collective security involved a social democratic kindling of ties with social movements. Keith had publicly opposed the NATO intervention in Kosovo (1999) and definitely opposed American policy on Iraq. He argued (like Noam Chomsky) that media accounts of conflict situations are often strategically manipulated, which makes it difficult (but not impossible) to stir the kind of debate called for by Colonel Williams.[10]

The final plenary was an open discussion on terror, democracy, and national identity growing out of the papers presented by Parnaby and Kealey, McBride, and Ross. Parnaby and Kealey's historical analysis led to a debate on the role of historical legacy in shaping security practices. Here, the authors regretfully concluded historical legacies live on and that the level of racial stereotyping and the broad transgression of individual rights that accompanied the September 11th security crisis was, therefore, not surprising. McBride's presentation on nationalism raised questions about globalization. Has its forward march been advanced or stalled? Could that analysis be extended beyond the thinking of business and professional political élites using a broader range of media?

Debate on Ross's presentation, well illustrated by political cartoons and other material sources that highlighted the themes of fear, panic, and alarm, led to a discussion on the American justification for, and prospects of, war with Iraq, support for and opposition to war in the United States, and a critical discourse on the appropriate courses of action for the Canadian state, politicians, and the anti-war movement in Canada. Chair Robin Mathews had the last word, offering the opinion that nationalism in Canada was not likely to go away soon, regardless of the intensification of relations with the United States or the often-rumoured demise of the Québec sovereignty project.

Summary Conclusions

The opinions expressed alike by the presenters and participants provided a glimpse of the range and diversity of Canadian reactions to the core debates of 2001–2003. In this conclusion, we briefly summarize and comment on the ways this collection of articles has furthered our understanding of the research agenda outlined above.

One important fact that emerges from these essays is that Canada's military participation in the war against terrorism has taken place within a period of continued uncertainty and conflicting demands on scant military resources. While it may seem obvious, the collection's conclusion that these uncertainties and policy conflicts will continue seems to be valid. At present, the Canadian government appears to have accepted the argument that the war against terrorism is (international) police work. The Bush Republicans, now in their second term of office, are also extending olive branches and mending diplomatic fences with allies who did not endorse or support the U.S./UK invasion of Iraq. As a result, current military issues, such as the modernization of the Canadian Forces and Ballistic Missile Defence, are discussed in a discourse separate from that of the war against terrorism — though still from the U.S. perspective of containing weapons of mass destruction.

This conference did not include any evaluation of the military aspects of the war against terrorism, nor did it explore Canada's role in the international diplomacy or participation in the various international and transnational intelligence and policing activities that have identified, checked, and destroyed terrorist networks — all matters worthy of future research. Horrific post-September 11th bombings in Bali and Madrid reinforce the strategic importance of this police campaign against terrorism.

When we contemplate going to war, it is important to identify the objectives and map out how and when it can or should end. Our contributors did not address the question of "when the war against terrorism will be over and how will we know that it is?" Instead, they indicated that it is a long-term engagement, tied at this point, at least in the minds of the current U.S. administration, to broad processes of democratization and regime change in the Middle East. The chaos that followed the invasion of Iraq and the growth of a strong urban guerrilla resistance to the U.S. occupation are among the factors that predict a long-term conflict — even with the development of a fledgling new democracy. Clearly, this area too will need further research, as will Canada's role in building a new democratic Iraq.

To what extent will the security regime developed for this war against terrorism remain embedded in the body politic? In the post-September 11th context, the contributors have pointed out that the balance between individual and collective security has swung to the latter. Many contributors look to *Charter of Rights and Freedoms* and to Parliament and public interest groups to protect the erosion of rights and personal freedom. Others point to fear of difference, poorly or ambiguously constructed legislation, the exigencies of war, and the pull of empire as forces that erode those safeguards. Some key avenues for further research flow from this collection's ambivalent conclusion on the protection of individual rights. The first wave of anti-terrorist legislation has provisions for a three-year legislative review and a five-year sunset provision. Bill C-36 is now up for review. Will it remain the same? Will immigration-related detention also be subject to legislative review? Will the Liberal minority government afford third parties, such as the NDP and the Bloc Québécois, political opportunity to take part in shaping the new national security policy?

One of the most interesting post-September 11th transitions focuses on how domestic judicial and political institutions are increasingly taking control over military detention and judicial processes. The trigger for these changes is continued international attention to sensational allegations of torture and abuse of prisoners held in Afghanistan, Cuba, and Iraq. In Canada, the inquiry into American deportation of Maher Arar to his birth country, where suspects have no effective protection against torture and abuse by security officials, is examining alleged attempts to circumvent the constitutional protections. The research in this collection has also contributed to our understanding on the effect of the war against terrorism on Canadian–U.S. relations. During the 1990s, the levels of economic integration brought into question the utility of borders — and for a brief period, Canadians debated the relative merits of maintaining the Canadian currency. September 11th both steadied and fundamentally changed the trajectory of continental integration. The new security regimes rekindled the vitality of the border as a symbol of national sovereignty. Canada's decision not to participate in the invasion of Iraq also revitalized the sense of national community.

On the question of trade integration, contributors outlined a successful marriage between security and trade objectives — though important regional and social consequences of the border security regime that have not yet been adequately studied were raised. The hypothesis that the new border regimes have made bilateral trade more vulnerable to terrorist attacks needs further research, as do their regional and social implications. On a broader historical scale, it is likely that apparent national differences have changed the dynamics of the "big idea." Current business leaders are talking of a series of policies and bilateral agreement to revamp NAFTA rather than going to the "next level."

In/Security contributors looked at Canada's role in the Middle East as a litmus test for the country to pursue an independent human security foreign policy. There could hardly have been a more difficult test — and the fact that Canada cannot viably pursue a human security strategy without commitment of resources and troops is not news. What was suggested, however, is that Canada has to follow its own foreign policy priorities to avoid being drawn under the shadow of the United States. Plainly stated, we think that there are countless opportunities and other locations where Canada can pursue an effective human security policy. We remain convinced (perhaps too optimistically) that choices exist but that the contours of constraint in the age of in/security need to be better understood. Though they have been physically erased from the North American landscape, the twin towers of the World Trade Center cast a long shadow.

Notes

1 In 2003, we posted the papers on the In/Security conference web site and authors revised them. As part of their revisions, several contributors probed the effect of September 11 on Canadian policy and discourses more broadly.

2 Huntington, S. P. (1996). *Clash of Civilizations and the Remaking of World Order.* New York, Simon & Schuster.

3 Fukuyama, F. (1992). *The End of History and the Last Man.* New York, Avon Books.

4 Gimblett, Richard (2003). *Operation Apollo: The Golden Age of the Canadian Navy in the War Against Terrorism.* Ottawa: Department of Public Works and Government Services, 2003.

5 In addition, in 2002 Canada ratified the *International Convention for the Suppression of Terrorist Bombings,* New York, 15 December 1997, and in 2004 Canada signed the *Convention on the Prohibition of the Development, Production and Stockpiling of Bacteriological (Biological) and Toxin Weapons and their Destruction,* 3 December 2004.

6 The competing political pressures that stem from the new post-9/11 realities are evident in discussions between adopting the "big idea" to restructure the terms of Canada–U.S. integration through free trade agreements such as NAFTA (1994) and the FTA (1987) or pursuing integration in incremental steps through a series of strategic agreements.

7 Giddens, A. (1991). *Modernity and Self-Identity: Self and Society in the late Modern Age*. Cambridge, UK: Polity Press.

8 For aspect of this debate see "No president's actions are beyond review: The Supreme Court ruled for the detainees," *Guardian Unlimited*, June 30, 2004 (http://www.guardian.co.uk/guantanamo/story/0,13743,1250176,00.html).

9 Brewin refers to "fault lines" in foreign policy primarily within the main political parties with regional representation from across Canada. There is no evidence whatsoever of a schism in the foreign policy of the Bloc Québécois, a party with a base only in Québec.

10 See, for example, Chomsky, Noam (2002). *Media Control: The Spectacular Achievements of Propaganda*, 2nd Edition. New York: Seven Stories Press.

PART I

Post-9/11 Perspectives on Terrorism, Defence, Security, and Insecurity

1

Canada's Asymmetrical War

Desmond Morton

One of the effects of fear, Edmund Burke warned long ago, is to paralyze the intellect and to render common sense scarcer than ever. September 11th and its aftermath will provide generations of historians with a rich supply of fresh examples. Smug and secure after centuries of immunity from external attack, after 11 September 2001 the United States displayed symptoms of a world-class neurotic. Seamless media coverage gave terrorists a triumph beyond their wildest dreams and created incentives for every psychotic exhibitionist in the universe. Remember the typhus scare—or the Maryland sniper?

North of the United States, Canadians shared the threat vicariously. Fighter aircraft scrambled to demolish errant passenger jets, sailors loaded bread and rockets to carry our "war on terror" to Afghanistan. Airport guards stood shoulder to shoulder with colleagues at Logan and O'Hare to defend against murderous toenail clippers and Swiss Army knives. Trucks bearing 83 percent of our exports, 42 percent of our GNP, piled up at border check points, pulsating proof of colonial economic dependence.

September 11th introduced us to "asymmetric" conflict, a kind of global jiu-jitsu, in which a superpower mobilizes against a mosquito in possibly the first stages of its own destruction. A conflict began, without certainty of defeat or victory, between the richest and some of the poorest people of the world. Yes, the official villain is the son of a Saudi multi-millionaire. His victims included his al-Qaida acolytes and their social counterparts, including multicultural labourers in an overweening office building, not to mention blue-collar guardians from police and fire departments. All wars are fought by the dispossessed for the powerful.

Terrorism and asymmetric conflict predated 9/11. From Northern Ireland to Indonesia, Colombo to Colombia, Chechnya to Sierra Leone, it is easier to count unaffected regions than those torn by massacres of the innocent or unsuspecting. They share frustration, fanaticism, contempt for life and super-abundant irony. Chechnya was what the former USSR hoped to avoid when it invaded Afghanistan. September 11th grew straight from U.S. policies to defeat that invasion with its money and Afghan lives. The Taliban was financed by U.S. Cold War policy, much as Osama bin Laden's family wealth is an outgrowth of American energy policy as much as his piloted missiles were American-owned civil aircraft. If Iraq has chemical, biological and other weapons of mass destruction (WMD), blame Ronald Reagan's determination to punish Iran. What goes around comes around.

Excepting Pancho Villa, the American "Zone of the Interior" or "ZI" has been immune from foreign-based enemies since 1814. After September 11th, nothing was supposed to be the same again. In fact, historical experience is intact. Experience told us how Americans under George W. Bush would react. We also mustered historical, though slightly misleading, images of impoverished but warlike Afghanis. History also gave due notice of Canada's role. We echoed, amplified, reinforced, even envied the unifying neuroses of our afflicted neighbour and frequent exemplars. Like non-family mourners at a funeral, we edged a little closer to be sure to be noticed. And we weren't. Suddenly, it was even embarrassing to have Jean Chrétien as prime minister. "If you're not with us," said Bush, "you're against us." Washington insiders knew Chrétien had preferred Clinton and Gore. Indeed, as a Canadian poll indicated just before Bush's dubious victory, so had Albertans!

What was the precedent? In August, 1940, Canada's prime minister suddenly realized that we had risen to number two in the anti-Hitler alliance. In panic, he phoned the White House. Two days later, President

Roosevelt reached Ogdensburg. Soon King felt safe. Since 1783, the United States had been our only real enemy: now it was our salvation. No one foresaw all the consequences but, in 1944, Major General Maurice Pope predicted that Washington would demand a higher standard of national security than Canada had ever needed. A great power is a target; behind two wide oceans and a polar ice cap, Canada had been the safest country in the world, 3.8 million square miles of barrier and insignificance. Now we had a neighbour to defend.

I don't believe General Pope rejoiced, but his comrades did. Since Confederation, alliance commitments have given Canada's warriors their only effective arguments for peacetime preparedness. The Cold War soon made a case for almost every admiral and general in the world. Colonel Chauvin was dead: now the brass looked to allies among allies when it came to arguments for upscaling tanks, ships, and fighter planes. By 1951, half of every federal tax dollar financed Canadian defence. The welfare state promised by Mackenzie King in 1945 was largely delayed until the successful end of the Cuban Missile Crisis gave us a new Liberal government and new priorities.

Allies kept on mattering. Admission to the G7, Trudeau learned, depended on buying German Leopard tanks. Co-existence with Ronald Reagan required closure on the CF-18 Hornet deal. An extra billion in Canadian defence spending in 2003–2004 was financed by trade-offs ranging from the television production fund to screening programs for childhood cancer. Buying the costly F-35 will be the price of partnership with George Bush's successors.

So what changed on September 11th? Do 3,000 dead change reality? Canadians have forgotten their history. Back in the 1860s, the U.S. Civil War told the Brits that defending Canada was truly hopeless. They helped organize a militia-based defence and then pulled out, leaving the task to the new Dominion. The Fathers of Confederation got smart. Staring in 1868, they saw that our security depended on making Uncle Sam feel secure on his northern frontier. A fuss-and-feathers militia was no threat to anyone and it turned into a useful framework for mobilization when the old allies that had abandoned us, Britain and France, desperately needed us in 1914 and 1939. Meanwhile, Canadians enjoyed a peace dividend big enough to build the CPR.

Remember what Dr. Bob Thompson, the old Socred federal leader, said in 1962: "Americans are our best friends, whether we like it or not." Could we be sure that no al-Qaidist had followed Achmed Ressam across the frontier? Our living conditions depend on American goodwill. In 1973, Mitchell Sharp had pleaded for a third option to economic isolationism or utter dependence on the U.S. Mel Hurtig still does. We elected politicians who felt otherwise. But frightened people lock their doors. Our danger wasn't Islamic fundamentalism but Washington. Mexicans offered little more than *schadenfreude*: we had to placate a dangerous neighbour. We mobilized grief and sent ships and aircraft wherever Secretary Rumsfeld ordered. Troops followed to Kandahar.

Canadians have been lectured by editors, the Official Opposition and the American ambassador on the woeful state of our armed forces. This should have been no surprise. Prior to September 11th, pollsters reported that Canadians want an efficient combat-capable armed force but at no added cost. The same poll found more support for an extra dollar a year to create a Canadian film industry than for military capacity.

Under Mulroney and Chrétien, Canada's forces were busier than during the Cold War, from Cambodia to Rwanda to Srebrenica. We tried out "soft power," non-intrusive interventions and other euphemisms while defence spending fell from $12 billion in 1993 to $9.25 billion by 1998. Only after a six-year pay freeze forced ill-paid service families to enter food banks was there an increase. Uniformed strength fell from 126,000 in 1970 to 86,000 in 1982 and now to about 56,000. Canada's NATO contingents, our only combat-ready land and air formations, vanished. So have the administrative and logistics troops UN peace operations depended on. For economy, we use civilianized "Alternate Service Delivery," and the UN tried to "privatize" peacekeeping by hiring civilian contractors and relying on poorly-trained, ill-equipped third-world militaries. The homeland kept the cash, the peacekeepers scrounged for food, and the tragic consequences fell on Sierra Leone, Somalia, and Bosnia.

Within NDHQ, funding and personnel cuts led to bitter struggles. In 1993, Jean Chrétien brought back General John de Chastelain, Brian Mulroney's chief of defence staff. The 1994 Liberal defence policy promised combat-ready forces able to "fight the best alongside the best." With only 60,000 members and $9 billion a year, the Canadian Forces could barely afford what Vice-Admiral Charles Thomas proposed as he retired: keep the navy and air force and forget the army. With twelve young patrol frigates and upgraded CF-18s, Canada had some up-to-date assets, though Chrétien had cancelled the EH-101 anti-submarine helicopters vital for the frigates' main role. Navy and air force units represented Canada adequately in the Gulf War, the Kossovo war, and George Bush's war on Afghanistan. But we always needed soldiers for our adventures in peacemaking, from Bosnian roadblocks to Angolan mine clearing.

Never wholly forgotten was another defence plan, associated with a Toronto-Liberal-dominated Council of 21. Their guide was Janice Stein, media-savvy future head of the U of T's Munk Centre on international relations. The Council's advice was cheap and tempting: fold the navy and air force; rework the army as a short-service peace-keeping force, recruited from young unemployed men and women willing to serve where there was no real danger. If things got rough, Canada's peacekeepers would leave.

This seems sillier now than in 1991. Cold War peacekeeping was seldom very dangerous. Modern-style "peacemaking" with F-18s and precision-guided missiles (PGMs) was seldom practised before 1989. Running away when soldiering gets dangerous made perfect sense to George Bernard Shaw, though it was not in any Hollywood script. The Council terrified the military who always mistrusted civilian illusions about peacekeeping. When Canadians came to Yugoslavia from NATO bases, they brought their full Cold War kit and armoured carriers, ready to be very robust. Later, with only Canadian-built light armoured vehicles (LAVs) and lawyer-designed Rules of Engagement (ROE), Canadians became evasive in tight spots. Shidane Arone had ruined enough careers. Soldiers from other countries might get away with murder at home or abroad; not Canadians.

After three uninterrupted terms, what you now see in Ottawa is what Jean Chrétien wants you to see. His top priority was to eliminate a Trudeau-created deficit. He did enough to be re-elected on June 2nd, 1997. He next loosened up a little, gained from prosperity, divided his opponents, and won a third majority in November, 2000. Will the next election depend on a healthy health system or an enlarged and modernized army, navy and air force? Which contributes to the asymmetric war declared by Washington on our behalf over a year ago?

Canada is a military weakling. Most of our aircraft are older than their crews. So are our tanks. We built a dozen warships but we then shut down the shipyards. We claim global reach but our transport fleet has to rent Ukrainian aircraft to deliver military vehicles. We raised military pay in 1999 but paid for it with further cuts. We bought 128 CF-18s in 1981; most will not be modernized. Many of our skilled personnel are close to retirement and we have slashed our capacity to train replacements. The state of privatized pilot training is a state secret.

Of course, that is not what you or perhaps even the Minister of National Defence hears. Compared to the 3,000 soldiers, six destroyers and biplanes of 1939, present-day Canadian Forces can even look impressive. Admiral Thomas's frigates escort U.S. carrier groups and, with a little ingenuity and borrowing, CF-18s can be interoperable with their American counterparts. The three mechanized brigades scattered at Valcartier, Petawawa, and Edmonton look fierce. Only an expert — *rara avis* in Canada — can assess obsolete training and obsolete, even defective, weapons, equipment, and vehicles. A "Clothe the Soldier" program has been the army's chief affordable reform. In Kingston, officers have their own computerized wargame, capable of wreaking "virtual" mayhem on "Aggressor" forces that look remarkably like the pre-1989 Soviet Army.

Experts would find similar weaknesses in most NATO armies and horrifying conditions in the barracks of former Warsaw Pact countries where conscripts evade service to preserve themselves from hunger, sickness, lethal bullying by senior soldiers, and corruption by senior officers. Ukrainian services are financed by "military tourism": wealthy visitors buy the pleasure of firing weapons, driving tanks and launching missiles. Conscripts practise drill. Most European countries abolished conscription and don't replace worn out equipment. We are not alone.

Like Canadians, Europeans ask where, after 1989, is the threat? Terrorism is neither new nor properly answered by soldiers, tanks, antisubmarine helicopters, or invasions of Iraq. Americans also disarmed in the 1990s but they retained by far the most powerful forces in the world, and spent more than the rest of the world combined on modernizing them. Partly this was the cost of an all-volunteer force, partly it was the cost of technological innovation. The computer age applied satellite-mounted reconnaissance, global-positioning technology and the capacity to integrate millions of bits of information in RMA—a Revolution in Military Affairs.

RMA ends a commander's guesswork. Indeed, it overwhelms a headquarters with information about the enemy. RMA is the typical American technological fix—dramatic, imperfect, over-sold but hugely powerful, even compared to the 1991 Desert War. RMA legitimates the "smart bombs" that can claim to avoid the innocent and devastate the wicked. Like any new military technology, its claims are consciously exaggerated to terrify the enemy. RMA did not prevent lots of "collateral damage" in Kossovo and friendly-fire casualties in Afghanistan. It allowed Slobodan Milosevic to bring home most of the tanks, guns, and soldiers of the Yugoslav National Army (JNA) and it could not kill Osama bin Laden or al-Qaida or even Saddam Hussein and his Baath party.

North American defence was a success until 9/11. Americans want their peace of mind restored, and Congress accepted the biggest defence budget increase since 1951 without serious challenge. Canadians—still enjoying their fragile immunity—are pressured to restore a devastated American peace of mind, kept on edge partly as a Republican Party re-election strategy in 2002 and 2004. Canada's huge economic dependence on a single customer is at stake. Indignant at our Faustian FTA bargain, our nationalists may claim that trade has nothing to do with security. They should talk to their neighbours. A trade-dependent country with only one substantial client must defend the gates of America or sit outside. Without shrewd and consistent diplomacy we might even do both.

Canadians and Americans share traditions of civil liberty and political pluralism. We both have supported "freedom-fighters" and raged at terrorists. Both countries cherish due process and judicial independence; both want the guilty punished. We both have competing security services that don't share secrets. Canada has CSIS and the RCMP; Americans have the CIA and the FBI, to name only the best-known agencies. We are both multicultural societies with large immigrant populations. Most newcomers pocket their pride, learn new ways, and prosper; most have multiple allegiances. A few exhibit the resentment and pathological behaviours the native-born would display in similar circumstances.

Canadians and Americans have much in common and no good claim to righteous superiority. We are partners in a project to make security compatible with the rights and freedoms that far outrank material affluence as our principal claim to civilization. Terrorists have been defeated by sound police methods and public awareness. International co-operation works better than unilateral vengeance. Success depends on a courageous determination to preserve values whatever the violence.

None of this related closely to Canada's armed forces. Indeed their relationship with 9/11 was almost wholly misleading. They deserve modernization with clear, rational priorities. As it happens, we currently have a Land Forces commander with a clear, contemporary vision and will. That is reason enough to give General Mike Jeffries the funds to provide a small, deployable army, in which regulars and reserves both have a role. The navy and air force need logistics ships and C-17 heavy transports to meet respond to global challenges without waiting for Ukrainian charters or the U.S. Air Force. These can be funded for $3–4 billion a year over the next ten years, a lot less than the $24 billion a year defence enthusiasts demand. This would give substance to government policy and leave plenty for Medicare, foreign aid, border security, CSIS, and whatever else the national interest and Canadians legitimately want.

Notes

1 For balance, the Council included the former Tory leader, Robert Stanfield, and a former chief of defence staff, Admiral Robert Falls.

References

Morton, Desmond. McGill Institute for the Study of Canada. (2003). *Understanding Canadian Defence*. Toronto, Penguin Canada.

——. (1999). *A Military history of Canada: From Champlain to Kosovo*. Toronto, M&S.

——. (1986). *The New Democrats, 1961–1986: the Politics of Change*. Toronto, Copp Clark Pitman.

2

Incremental Changes in Canada's Defence and Security Policy Since September 11, 2001

Houchang Hassan-Yari and Abdelkérim Ousman

Introduction

For some defence policy analysts and advisors, the Government of Canada, through the Department of National Defence (DND), has "the obligation to ensure that our defence policy is rational, constructive and respected."[1] There are those who believe that the Canadian government is not doing enough to support the American lead in the war against terrorism [see for example, Brewin and Ross in this volume. *Ed.*]. While they do not question the rationalization behind the American war on Iraq, for example, they nevertheless propose that following the Americans in the fight against terrorism is the rational choice for Canada's foreign, defence and security policy. And since they[2] believe that Western Civilization is at war against terrorists, they contend that this "warfare takes place beyond the reach of moral reason, in a realm of interest and necessity where moral argument is a pious diversion at best, at worst, a lethal distraction from the deadly serious business at hand."[3]

The above summarizes the argument of those who criticize Canadian defence and security policy-making from the perspective of rational choice theory. As many have already observed, the main thrust of the rational model to policy-making does not lie in the fact that it is a correct description of the policy-making process; rather, in reality, the policy-making process is markedly different from what is presented in the rational model. For rational choice theorists, the real issue concerns the government's inability to adopt the rational model as the proper prescriptive framework for policy planning.

This opinion is often dismissed by the Canadian Left as merely being pressure from big business and political elites. That is because the Left witnesses "on a daily basis, retired military officers, defence analysts, members of the opposition, Liberal backbenchers, and newspaper editorialists decry[ing] the alleged dilapidated state of Canada's armed forces."[4] The Left also worries that following the current U.S. administration's fight against terrorism would endanger Canada's *Charter of Rights and Freedoms*. Furthermore, it perceives military-industrial elites as manipulating the government to adopt exaggerated security threat perceptions, which in turn result in a defence budget that enhances the powers of public authorities at the expense of both the Canadian Constitution and *Charter of Rights and Freedoms*. These are legitimate concerns given Canada's close relationship with the United States, some Canadian stakeholders' pressure to increase Canadian defence budgets, and the embarrassment over the rationalization of the war on Iraq.

The rational model has little descriptive power to analyze changes in Canada's defence and security policy. It is our view that Canada's process of defence and security change exemplifies a process of incrementalism, which is more in keeping with Canada's Constitution and *Charter of Rights and Freedoms* than the rational calculation of the likely costs and benefits of policy options that are designed to please or displease current U.S. administration.

The purpose of this paper is to analyze the changes in Canadian defence and security policy since the terrorist attacks of September 11th, 2001. We contend that what is taking place, as a policy-making process, cannot be explained by rational choice theory alone. That supports the view that when it comes to assessing policy processes, options and outcomes, the wisdom of Canada's Constitution and *Charter of Rights and Freedoms* does not concern the question as to whether or not elites have made a rational decision; rather, the statutes of both the Constitution and the *Charter* provide for the protection of individual rights and freedoms over and against the excessive power of public authorities, especially during times of perceived crisis. It follows that policy processes, options and outcomes must not be dictated by visionaries or enlightened elites; rather, they should emerge incrementally through processes of learning and consensus-building, as they occur between competing concerns for defence and security, individual rights and freedoms, and economic well-being.

Incrementalism assumes that there are many individuals and conglomerates involved in the policy process, and, therefore, that there are competing preferences in policy agenda-setting. "In other words, there is a lack of consensus on identifying which issues policy should address."[5] Thus, even when the goals are identified, there are still divergent views as to how these goals should be pursued. According to Charles Lindblom, agreement upon strategy is "possible only to the extent values are agreed upon."[6] That is why, according to Frohock, policies tend to be watered down or become "modest in resources and scope."[7] This describes incrementalism in policy-making as "a process of mutual adjustment among a multiplicity of actors having different self-interests and divergent conceptions of the public interest."[8]

Like many who criticize current government defence and security measures, many regard "incrementalism as a failure of the political system to come to grips with underlying problems which put issues on the agenda."[9] But "risk-averters and some Conservatives regard incrementalism as safe, system-conserving behaviour ... [n]onetheless we must regard incrementalism as the most likely outcome of the policy formulation process."[10]

Public authorities always order the policy analysts and advisors at their service to assess the strengths, weaknesses, opportunities, and threats (SWOT) of every option they propose to the government. Thus, when dealing with public policy issues, an essential part of incremental policy-making is risk aversion. The most important aspect of risk aversion that this paper focuses on is its potential to provide for financially and legally proportioned government actions that continue to respect the wisdom of the statutes by protecting Canadians' rights and freedoms against the excessive use of power by public authorities. It is in that sense that we contend that incrementalism and proportionality are embedded in government budgetary processes and Canada's Constitution and *Charter of Rights and Freedoms*. Wayne Hayes also observes that:

> Government-induced change typically carries a price tag, but budgets are scarce and complex. Budgetary constraints prevent the initiation of new policies or the expansion of existing programs. The budget-making process is notoriously cumbersome and resistant to reform.... Finally, the legal system operates around a set of established principles which also reinforce incrementalism: Precedent, [is] especially evident in the holdings of the Supreme Court. Due process under the law, [...] provides legal standing to many interested parties and provides the opportunity to use litigation as a redress: New and bold policies get tied up in court. [...] [S]olutions offered by incrementalism are usually the most politically acceptable and generally preferred to overhaul.[11]

The analysis of these changes is based on the amendments brought to various elements of the 1994 defence *White Paper, National Defence Act*, and other bills regarding public safety, including those involving departments other than the Department of National Defence. Other items involved in this analysis are the defence and security policy options made public by means of annual reports of the Chief of Staff of Canadian Forces (CF), public domain documents published in support or criticism of the proposed policy options, and publications that are engaged in the current process of defence and security change. We believe that these changes are a response to the attempt to find the appropriate means of eradicating global terrorism, the best way of dealing with the proliferation of weapons of mass destruction (WMD), and a way to prevent the link between terrorism and the proliferation of weapons of mass destruction. Also included is the analysis of the diplomatic consequences of any considered option.

These issues pose several questions to our law and policy makers: In order to be certain that a link is not established between terrorism and weapons of mass destruction, must we change foreign regimes by means of military force? If the use of force is the option considered by the Government of Canada, what are its domestic and diplomatic consequences? What would become of our special relationship with the United States, since the latter is our ally and most important partner when it comes to our defence and economic prosperity? Must we participate in the U.S. ballistic missile defence program? What would become of NORAD if the government refuses Canada's participation in this program? What would become of the international order?

We hypothesize that these questions emanate from the issue of the "proportionality" (adequacy) between the measures that are to be taken against terrorism and asymmetric aggressions on the one hand and respect to our laws and values on the other.

There is still no agreed upon definition of the term proportionality.[12] In neo-liberal social and economic policy, it means less government; but for those concerned with protecting the citizen from the government's excessive coercive powers, it means that government actions must respect the people's rights and freedoms as granted by the Constitution, no matter what the nature of the perceived crisis or danger. Hence, bearing the latter definition in mind, the principle of proportionality means that the actions, which could be legislative provisions, measures, regulations, or authorities of the government, should not exceed what is necessary in proportion to the goals of Canadian defence and security policy, as assigned by the *National Defence Act* and other laws related to Canada's defence and public safety. Proportionality also requires that, once these laws are changed or modified, they must be both adequate to the Constitution and continue to respect our values, which are not only *Peace, Order,* and *Good Government*, but also as Kent Roach put it, "democracy, sovereignty and the protection of the individual from unnecessary harms, multiculturalism, peacekeeping, and respect for international laws and institutions."[13]

From the point of view of Canada's Constitution, as Justice L'Heureux Dubé states, "in Canada diversity is not a debate—it is a constitutionally recognized value.... Most importantly, section 15(1) guarantees equality without discrimination based on race, national or ethnic origin, colour, religion, sex, age or mental or physical disability."[14] In terms of proportionality, this means that no individual with any of these identities should have his or her freedom of action limited beyond the degree necessary for the public interest. At the same time, this principle suggests the supremacy of the individual over all decision-making authorities. It is in this sense that Canadian values must determine the proportionality of the measures to be taken for defence and security purposes. These involve almost all senior federal government departments, and also for those departments whose missions of defence and security are among their most important attributes, such as the Canadian Forces (CF).

Because Canadian defence and security policy has to be coordinated with the United States, and because it is not at all certain that Canada and the U.S. share the same values when it comes to protecting the individual's rights and freedoms, the problem of proportionality is further complicated by the bilateral requirements of military interoperability among our forces and the compatibility of our security measures. It is the adequacy of our defence and antiterrorist measures to our laws, and the compatibility of both with the bilateral requirements of interoperability and compatibility, that ultimately determine the shape of that our efforts in defence and security will take. The incremental policy-making process in the Government of Canada is not merely an attempt to hang on to the status quo. We argue that while incrementalism prevents revolutionary changes from taking place, it also allows for evolutionary changes, based on the general principles of the statutes.

In what follows, Section One describes the new security environment as perceived by Canada's policymakers, Section Two analyzes legislation change in terms of security and public safety, while Section Three analyzes the adjustment of U.S.–Canada defence relations.

The New Security Environment

Before the terrorist acts of September 11th, the United States had already developed the concept of *Homeland Security* to deal with non-traditional threats. This concept addresses a variety of situations, including attacks on the U.S. by means of weapons of mass destruction, domestic and international terrorism, attacks on computer networks, as well as problems concerning illegal drug running, immigration, and organized crime.[15] The concept of *Homeland Security* was designed to prevent, deter and defend against aggressions that aim at American territory and sovereignty, population, and infrastructures.[16]

Since 1995, the money allocated to *Homeland Security* policy has increased significantly. However, despite the fact that the American government has since then ordered at least nine studies on *Homeland Security*,[17] the hijacking of airline aircraft on American territory was not predicted.[18] From the security point of view, that terrorist act has had a profound impact not only on the United States, but also on its security partners and allies. Canada, in particular, because of its border proximity with the United States, has consequently reacted to the events of September 11th. In recognition of the changes in the international security environment, Canada initiated changes to its defence policy; it also began to witness upheavals in its relationship with the United States, as exemplified by several criticisms and verbal attacks on the Government of Canada by American officials and local critics, who contend that Canada is not doing enough to face up to the challenge of terrorism.

Nobody disputes the fact that the international security environment, within which Canadian defence and security policy is set, has evolved since September 11th. The present security environment is characterized by intense asymmetric threats against the United States in particular, but also against the North American continent in geographic and strategic terms. This sense of threat is induced by resentment over American Middle Eastern policy and the proliferation of deadly weapons technologies. No matter what the aims of the perpetrators of the September 11th terrorist acts were, the attacks led to the diminution of the American sense of geostrategic security, which in turn obliged other governments to develop new administrative and legal countermeasures.[19]

The most recent Canadian *White Paper* on defence of Canada was issued in 1994, and lists a number of concerns that constitute a threat to international security: human population growth, refugees, states in ruin, emergence of old ethnic hatreds, and the proliferation of weapons of mass destruction.[20] Terrorism was not included on this list, and consequently was not a subject of any particular concern.[21] The *White Paper*, which is still in force, defines the international environment in terms of a reconfigured relationship of forces that, arguably, occurred during the first years of the current post-Cold War era;[22] however, the *White Paper* also asserts that there are areas of disorder and instability that could threaten international security and global order. [23]

The terrorist attacks of September 11th led the United States to transform its concept of *Homeland Defence* into the concept of *Homeland Security*.[24] Instead of focusing on WMD and their means of delivery (such as ballistic missiles), the United States was obliged to acknowledge that there are threats that could emanate from conventional destructive means or from unorthodox war practices. These threats could also include nuclear, biological, chemical, and radiological weapons. The method of terrorist groups such as al-Qaida also reminds us that the enemy might not be easily identifiable.[25] Given the geographic proximity of Canada to the United States, as well as the defence agreements and military alliances that link the two countries, Canada is almost automatically involved in all antiterrorist measures taken by the U.S.

At the multilateral level, after September 11th, 2001, NATO for the first time in its history evoked Article 5 of its Charter, which holds that an attack against any one of its members is an attack against all of its members. It is for this reason that NATO deployed five early warning planes to defend Canada and the United States.[26] Immediately after the terrorist attacks, Canada recalled 3,000 men and women of the Canadian Forces to support the international coalition against terrorism.[27] The state of alert of these forces came in the form of fighter aircrafts (CF-18), which were already in a state of readiness at Canadian Forces Base (CFB) Cold Lake, Alberta and CFB Bagotville, Québec, prior to the terrorist attacks. Additional combat aircraft were deployed at Comox (British Columbia), Goose Bay (Labrador) and Trenton (Ontario).[28] At the same time, cooperation in terms of the security and management of cross-border flows of people had also been enhanced.[29]

The Canadian response to this new security environment is still in the process of being completed. Several defence and security problems regarding Canada still need to be redefined. The eventual Canadian involvement in the projected ballistic missile defence is an example. Prior to September 11th, the Government of Canada was neither engaged in formal talks with the United States over National Missile Defence, nor was it necessarily refusing to be part of this U.S.-led project, which is meant to protect the entirety of the North American continent.[30] It was predicted that a final decision on the issue would be made during the coming NORAD renewal in 2006.[31]

The new security environment has, therefore, forced the Government of Canada to reconsider its general reluctance towards ballistic missile defence. Before September 11th, the Canadian government was facing a dilemma between its commitments in terms of defence and security towards the United States (which was pushing for the abrogation of the AMB Treaty, the Cold War cornerstone of armament control) on the one hand, and its international commitment towards armament control and disarmament on the other. Since September 11th, 2001, the Canadian position regarding missile defence seems to be centred on the renewal of NORAD.[32] It is thought that NORAD could become an example of North American defence by playing an important role in terms of U.S. *Homeland Security* and continuing its aerial and aerospace surveillance, which is becoming increasingly more important for the two countries.[33] The *Northern Command* (a new important security concept for the United States) adds new security arrangements to what already exists for the protection of North America.[34]

Legislative Changes

One should ask whether the Canadian government was totally taken by surprise by the events of September 11th. Everything indicates that that was not the case. In 1999, for example, the Chief of Staff of Canadian Forces published a document entitled *Shaping the Future of the Canadian Forces: A Strategy for 2020*. In an incremental fashion, the analysis in that document served as a bridge between current and future defence and security policies.[35] Even though the document was issued prior to September 11th, its main concepts remain relevant in the new strategic environment. For example, the Chief of Staff's document states that Canadian Forces have the mission to defend Canada's territory, Canadian interests and values, but also to contribute to international peace and security.[36] While this mission statement does not specifically mention the defence of the North American continent, it is obvious that the idea of contributing to international peace and security already incorporates the idea of defending North America. The Chief of Staff also states that Canadian defence policy must adhere to five principles: (1) strategic coherence, (2) respect for our institutions, (3) partnership with our allies, (4) adequacy of legislative measures to the strategic environment, and (5) adequacy of measures to the Constitution. The elements for an evolutionary change in Canadian defence policy are present in this document, if such a change is deemed necessary. In that sense, from the administrative and policy point of view, it is difficult to maintain that Canada has been taken by surprise by the events of September 11th. This document alone sets up Canadian defence and security policy for incremental change.

Instead of formulating new laws that build on themselves, the Canadian government's response to the terrorist attacks of September 11th has rather been to choose to create new legislation and amend already existing bills in conformity with the processes of incrementalism and proportionality. For example, the *Canadian Air Transport Security Authority Act*, assented to on May 27th, 2002, established that the *Canadian Air Transport Security Authority* could carry out, among other things, the mandate of screening persons who have access to aircraft or restricted areas and security points. That "Authority is also responsible for ensuring consistency in the delivery of screening across Canada."[37] It authorizes an operator of an aerodrome or airport to deliver screening on its behalf.[38]

The most obvious changes to Canada's defence and security policy are those found in the modifications of the *National Defence Act* and creation of the *Public Safety Act* of 2002. The Government of Canada introduced the *Public Safety Act* in the House of Commons as a package of public safety initiatives in support of its antiterrorism plan. In accordance with the principle of proportionality, the new legislation is meant to:

- further define and limit the power of the Minister of National Defence to establish Controlled Access Military Zones, and of other ministers to use interim orders in emergency situations;
- provide comprehensive parameters for the new terrorist hoax offences; and
- allow for measures to ensure accountability and transparency.

By introducing this new bill, the Government of Canada responded to concerns regarding the proportionality of antiterrorism measures expressed in a similar legislation (Bill C-42) that was introduced earlier. In responding to these concerns, the Government of Canada further facilitated parliamentary evaluation and assessment of the effects of the *Public Safety Act* on Canadians. Parliamentary assessment and control is an important tool of the legislature for the assessment of the proportionality of public authorities to the needed actions of government. The legislation is meant both to enhance and to respect the rights of Canadians guaranteed by the Constitution.

One of the difficulties with regard to Bill C-42 was that the bill may have been set to build on itself and thus would justify, at the expense of the rights and freedoms of Canadians, the further expansion of the powers of public authorities. Thus, instead of modeling a law that responded to a particular sort of crime, the government was urged to create legislation on the basis of the overarching principles found in the Canadian Constitution and *Charter of Rights and Freedoms*. That is a serious concern: "Because exceptional powers tend to become normalized, one incursion on civil liberties spawns another as surely as the inevitable sequence of dramatic and violent events generates a vicious circle of ever-escalating demands for memorial-style criminal laws."[39] However, given Canadian legislative tradition and political culture, the constitutionality of Canadian laws will always be based "upon the notion that those in power should not exercise their legal powers to the fullest extent possible even in times of perceived crisis. It was fundamental to British constitutionalism that what was legal might nevertheless be improper and unconstitutional...."[40] The limitations mentioned above mean that the *Public Safety Act* qualifies as proportioned, proper, and constitutional.

It is moreover in that sense that the limitations to the powers of public authorities make the *Public Safety Act* of 2002 proportional to the Canadian government's Antiterrorist Plan. These limitations do not prevent the Government of Canada from adhering to key provisions that strengthen its capacity to prevent terrorist attacks, protect Canadians, and respond swiftly should a significant threat arise. First, it updates existing aviation security authorities to maximize the effectiveness of Canada's aviation security system when it is deemed necessary. This measure enhances the ability of the Government of Canada to provide a safe and secure environment for air travel. Second, it facilitates the sharing of law enforcement and national security information between federal departments and agencies. Third, it deters hoax terrorist scares from heightening public anxiety. Fourth, it provides for tighter controls over explosives and hazardous substances and pathogens, and over the export and transfer of dual-use technologies. Fifth, it helps the Government of Canada identify and prevent harmful unauthorized use or interference with Department of National Defence computer systems. Sixth, it deters the proliferation of biological weapons. Finally, it respects the privacy rights of Canadians.

As far as the security of the North American continent is concerned, the terrorist attacks of September 11th have clearly meant the implementation of more policing, surveillance, and control measures than of warfare measures. It is in that sense that Canada's *Public Safety Act* is more preventive than coercive, and provides for targeted measures rather than generally punitive provisions in relation to political, ethnic, or religious minorities (activists, Muslims and Arabs in Canada). That is in concordance with Canada's Constitution, the *Charter of Rights and Freedoms*, and their embedded proportionality principle. Clearly, from the legal and administrative point of view, the Government of Canada had the choice between two alternatives: "memory-like" and punitive policies and measures, such as those prevailing in the United States, or proportionally targeted proactive provisions, such as the *Public Safety Act*. The Canadian government chose the latter means to amend 20 other Acts of Parliament, among which the most important are the *Explosives Act, Export and Import Permits Act, National Energy Board Act, Proceeds of Crime (Money Laundering) and Terrorist Financing Act,* and the *Biological and Toxin Weapons Convention Implementation Act.*

Like the *Public Safety Act*, the *Antiterrorism Act*, Bill C-36, also amends 16 Acts of Parliament including the *Criminal Code*, the *Official Secrets Act*, the *Canada Evidence Act*, and the *Access to Information Act*. It received Royal Assent on December 18, 2001. Because terrorism is a political, and not a legal, concept, one of the many controversies raised over Bill C-36 was its definition of terrorism. Bill C-36 broadly defines terrorism in such a way as to create the potential to prevent political activities that may be illegal, such as a transportation blockade or a health sector strike.[41] According to Bill C-36, a terrorist act is an action that impedes the delivery of an essential service, installation, or system. The definition also targets those who have no alternative but to make use of unlawful action to seek democratic reform or resist oppressive regimes.

Since Bill C-36 was enacted, many activists continue to express their concerns about the possible use of these antiterrorist legal measures against peaceful political demonstrations. Anne Mclellan, the former

Justice Minister, replied that the measures target terrorists, and do not constitute means for repressing legitimate political demonstrations.[42] However, many still believe that the definition of the term terrorism expands Bill C-36 to cover political demonstrations. Based on this definition, the only civic protection against such antiterrorism legislation is the legality of civic actions. Therefore, the defence against such a bill is quasi-nonexistent for activists, who often commit minor infractions in their undertakings.[43]

The opposition of some politicians and militants to antiterrorist measures expresses the concerns about the proportionality of these measures to the government's task of protecting the lives of Canadians. In fact, they do not feel that government security measures are appropriate to Canadian rights as granted by Canada's *Charter of Rights and Freedoms*. If the government asserts that a bill is constitutional, according to some critics, just because it has survived *Charter* scrutiny by the Attorney General's staff, then the government is opting for a very low standard for the measurement of the constitutionality of its actions. That is because the *Charter* scrutiny of a bill says nothing about its usage by police officers, and thus entirely misses the point of the statute: that is, to protect individual Canadian rights against the potential for the excessive exercise of legal powers by public authorities.[44] These activists' worries increase when they witness several states using special measures to impose laws that allow for arbitrary detentions (at the expense of a just and equitable due process) and disproportioned measures to security requirements.[45]

From the incrementalist point of view, political activism is more constructive than rational choice theorists generally perceive it to be. For example, former Justice Minister Anne McLellan acknowledged that Bill C-36 raises many concerns and agreed to reformulate the antiterrorist legislation by imposing a five-year sunset clause to new police powers. Rather than leading the government toward hasty, ill-formed and costly decisions, incrementalism actually helped the government to strike the proper balance between individual liberties and freedoms on the one hand and security and safety on the other. That is because our system succeeded in maintaining the public interest in the defence against terrorism as an issue of the balance between Individual rights and freedoms on the one hand and public safety on the other. In the

United States and Britain, the public policy problem was framed in terms of a balance between the vague notion of "national security" and civic liberties. In Canada, by contrast, activists succeeded in preventing new legislation and amendments from fitting particular crimes or building on themselves. They forced the new measures to be based on the general principles of the Constitution and *Charter of Rights and Freedoms* and prevented hasty memorial-like new legislation and reforms from taking place.

Our advanced citizenship requires that elites should not formulate policies without engaging the citizens by means of consultation, participation, information, and education. That acknowledges that the amount of liberties that we enjoy cannot increase or decrease without affecting the quality of our freedoms, for better or worse. The question to which both the government and political activists have to answer is whether the security in this new environment must be obtained at the expense of some liberties? There is no general answer to the question of which liberty among our liberties would be sacrificed; if the majority of citizens agree that such a sacrifice is necessary, it could then result in more freedom. While it is not all clear that any sacrifice at all is necessary, the legislative amendments introduced by the government seem proportioned to the task at hand and appropriate from the point of view of the Constitution and the *Charter of Rights and Freedoms*. In that respect, the sunset clause appended to the *Antiterrorist Act* is instrumental in allowing Parliament to assess a policy's possible adverse affects on the lives of Canadians.

Adjustment of the Canadian Defence Policy

It is obvious that the legislative changes mentioned above constitute an important modification to Canadian security policy; however, other changes less known to the public have also taken place, notably those diffused in the annual reports (2000–2001, 2001–2002, 2002–2003) of Chief of Staff of Canadian Forces. The 2000–2001 and 2001–2002 reports were published respectively before September 11th, 2001, and after the terrorist attacks. Even though the 2000–2001 report[46] was a routine report, the 2001–2002 annual report was not.[47] Each report devotes a chapter to the challenges facing the Canadian Forces. The 2000–2001 report's challenges are operational support, enrolment and retention and improvement of operational capabilities. The 2001–2002 report states its challenges as follows: (1) adaptation to the new security environment after September 11th, (2) modernization of forces, (3) operational support within each of the three commands, (4) enrolment and diversity, and finally (5) a strengthened relationship between the CF and representatives of Canadian citizenry.[48] Those are also traditional concerns, which in themselves do not necessarily amount to a revolutionary change. However, the context of the new security environment within which the concerns are expressed makes them instrumental for setting Canadian defence policy on the path of evolutionary change. The Chief of Staff's emphasis on interoperability, operational support and adaptability to the new security environment builds incrementally on already existing relations and interoperability between the CF and U.S. forces.[49] While there is still room for improvement in this respect, the focus on interoperability allows our naval forces to be more interoperable with their U.S. counterparts than any other naval forces in the NATO alliance[50] and permits the Canadian Navy to operate smoothly with the U.S. Navy in the current Afghan campaign against terrorism.[51]

Interoperability is a recurrent problem since the creation of NATO and NORAD, and it often translates into a requirement for defence equipment renewal or update. In the current context of the expansion of the U.S. defence budget, efforts towards increased jointness, interoperability and ballistic missile defence, Canada is confronted with the dilemma of striking a balance between further integrating the CF to U.S. forces on the one hand and holding on to its disarmament and armament control commitments on the other. That is why some believe that Canada would gain in re-examining both its defence and foreign policies. Such a review would allow the government better to coordinate its actions in both domains, while educating the public about the military resources required in order to achieve both defence and foreign policy objectives.[52]

Given the transitory nature of the current federal cabinet, the absence of a credible opposition to the government, and the ideological nature of some policy suggestions from defence critics, the path leading to relevant and proportioned policy options is all the more obscure. In effect, Senate Committees on Defence and Foreign policy are being criticized for lacking interest, knowledge, and experience in dealing with defence and foreign policy issues.[53] Hence, one is wrongfully led to believe that the defence options to be considered by the government are solely dependent on the rational choice of the members of the Senate of Canada, with the result that any other concerns related to Canadian sovereignty or civil rights are discredited as ideologies.

It goes without saying that these criticisms are evidence of profound political divergences and debate with regard to the question of the adequacy of resources being allocated to Canada's defence and security. It also betrays a bureaucratic struggle that seems to be lost to the Canadian defence community, which until now has been proven ineffective in selling its policy options to the Canadian public. In effect, the 2000–2001 Report of the Chief of Staff of Canadian Forces recognizes that defence resources remain very limited.[54] In the 2001–2002 report, it is also clearly stated that in spite of the increase of the defence budget for the 2001–2002 fiscal year, defence resources still remain arguably below the level required by operational challenges and modernization of Canadian Forces.[55] That reflects the view that in an incremental policy-making process, modest resources always characterize government measures.

The problem is not the lack of interest in or negligence of Canada's defence by our leaders. Rather, it is the problem of resources allocation that pits defence priorities against other priorities such as health, employment and education, especially after near a decade long of Programme Review. The budget cuts that all government programs suffered during this period were understandable given the fiscal constraints of the 1990s; however, the criticisms of those who believe that Canada's defence is handicapped by "a need crisis"[56] are equally legitimate. In fact, in the current context, it has become increasingly problematic that Canada's defence budget remains at 1.2 percent of public expenditures,[57] while the public account enjoyed increasing surpluses.[58] Nonetheless, even though the fiscal capacities of the Government of Canada have been increasing considerably since 1993, politics does not allow the government to begin increasing defence budgets at the expense of social programs. That incremental policy-making budgetary process prevents the initiation of fiscally demanding new policies or the expansion of existing programs. That is why, after having resolved the legal issues in relation to the adjustment of defence and security policies, the Government of Canada still has to face the public when justifying a considerable increase in the defence budget.

The principle of *Good Government* requires that the Canadian government must continue to issue balanced budgets while continuing to maintain the well-being of Canadians. That is why a balance must be found between social programs and investments in Canadian Forces.[59] This problem is not unique to Canada. With the exception of the United States, all other NATO allies suffer from the same difficulty, and none of them have been able to meet the challenge of transforming their military forces to meet the new defence and security environment.

Facing this difficult task of transformation, the Canadian Chief of Staff suggests optimizing existing resources. In his 2002–2003 report entitled *A Time for Transformation*, the Chief of Staff maintains that "for Canada, the question is not whether to transform the Canadian Forces, [but] it is how best to achieve the required **transformation**"[60] (emphasis in original). Unlike the United States, Canada's lack of strong defence interests does not allow for a considerable increase in defence resources. However, politics asides, the two countries still have a common ground of understanding, that of *jointness* and *interoperability*, both of which are seen as acceptable modes of operation for Canadian military leaders and defence policymakers.

The link between *interoperability* and *jointness* is exemplified by the U.S. Joint Forces Command stating that:

> The Joint Interoperability and Integration (JI&I) organization will support the Joint Warfighter as the Champion of the Joint Force Integrator process. This support role will be accomplished by improving the review effort for new joint Capstone Requirements Documents and Operational Requirements Documents to ensure systems are borne jointly and by providing: Doctrine, Organization, Training, Material, Leadership, Personnel and Facilities (DOTM-LPF) synchronized solutions to select operational deficiencies (to include interoperability and integration issues) affecting the CINCs, Services, and Agencies.[61]

The Chief of Staff of Canadian Defence is inspired by these principles of Jointness and Interoperability to lead the transformation of Canadian Forces while respecting the policy of resource optimization that, according to the Chief of Staff's analysis, is required by the Revolution in Military Affairs (RMA). Like Alvin and Heidi Toffler,[62] the Chief of Defence Staff considers the RMA as a change "from an industrial hierarchical mode of thinking to a world powered by collaborative human networks.... [That is because] the application of military force and the worldwide scope of current operations will increasingly involve a multitude of military and civilian agencies at home and abroad."[63] That suggests that "as part of our transformation efforts, it is essential that we move away from a platform-centric thinking and do a better job defining the end-to-end costs involved in acquiring a capability from the equipment to the human capital and skills needed to employ it, to the development of training systems and doctrine [to] field it."[64] If the government takes this network-based Jointness and Interoperability framework seriously, then it would allow the CF far more interoperability amongst themselves and also between themselves and their American counterparts.

Adjustment of Canada–U.S. Defence Relations

After the attacks of September 11th, 2001, many agree that Canada–U.S. relations are on the verge of change.[65] One has to acknowledge that, unlike during the Cold War period, Canada is becoming increasingly less important to the defence of the United States,[66] which has led many to express the worry that Canada is running the risk of becoming irrelevant in international affairs.[67] Contrary to many analyses and concerns about the structural disjunction of the bilateral defence relations, Canada seems to have regained its military relevancy[68] to the United States, which could then result in the renewal and reinforcement of NORAD. It is highly unlikely that the Government of Canada will continue to affirm its commitment to NORAD, while decrying U.S. defence policy. Furthermore, the links between U.S. defence policy, border issues, and their economic consequences have become so intertwined that it is highly likely that the Government of Canada would reactivate a sustained level of defence cooperation with the United States.[69] It is in this sense that critics on both sides of the border recommend a new realignment of Canadian defence policy so as to serve as a better instrument in the maintenance of close relations with the United States.[70] Arguably, a well-targeted defence policy in these terms better serves Canada's foreign policy and domestic concerns, as well as their concerns for the country's economic well-being and public safety.[71]

A well-balanced approach in this regard could convince the reluctant public of the necessity of increasing defence resources. According to a public poll led by Ipsos-Reid/CTV/*Globe and Mail* on July 2001, a majority (58 percent) of Canadians agree with the government's reluctance to support the U.S. initiative of a missile defence. Only a third (33 percent) approve of the initiative. Some critics allege that the initiative violates Canadian values and approaches on multiple levels by:

- relying on pre-emption and military superiority over a rules-based international security order;
- favouring counter-proliferation over nuclear non-proliferation and disarmament;
- insisting on the weaponization of space; and
- seriously undermining a Canadian capacity for independent contributions to international peace and security through multilateral disarmament and security efforts.[72]

These are the risks most often mentioned by the Canadian Liberal Left. Thus, the government has the difficult task of convincing the Canadian public on the usefulness of a missile defence against terrorists, while facing critics who allege that Canada is running the risk of becoming militarily irrelevant, which further puts into question its security dependability to the U.S.

Recent declarations by the Ministers of Foreign Affairs and National Defence suggest that Canadians still need time fully to appreciate the usefulness of a missile defence system. On May 15, 2003, the Minister of Foreign Affairs stated that:

> The Americans have made their intentions clear. That is why this Government believes it is our responsibility to pursue talks with the United States, in order to ensure the security of Canadians and

> the future of NORAD. Of course, many questions remain about our role in this developing missile defence system, but these can only be answered by engaging our U.S. allies in formal discussions, in the interest of all Canadians. By entering into discussions, we will be able to address our concerns about the future of NORAD, about the weaponization of space, and about any associated costs.[73]

That declaration was followed by the Minister of National Defence's statement that "the Government has decided to enter into discussions with the United States on Canada's participation in ballistic missile defence.... No final decision will be taken before returning to Cabinet after these negotiations."[74]

Conclusion

Since the end of the Cold War, many concerns have been raised about changes in Canada–U.S. relations. With the modest resources at the disposal of Canadian defence, many argue that Canada is running the risk of losing its sovereignty vis-à-vis the United States. The pervasive argument among defence policy analysts and advisors is: if Canada does not care about its defence, then the Americans would, and as a result, Canadians would not be allowed to have a say in continental defence and security policy decisions. That problem is being aggravated by the ceaseless U.S. investment in new defence technologies and systems, thus widening the technological and doctrinal gap between the two countries. That gap may be further widened by the absence of Canadian consensus on the appropriate level of defence spending, which we explained by the incrementalist approach adopted in this paper.

As far as our rights and freedoms are concerned, there are no inherent problems with Canada's incremental policy-making. However, incrementalism's small-step mode of policy change could further irritate our American allies and increase the perception south of the border that Canada is becoming militarily irrelevant. That is the problem of Canada–U.S. defence relations.

However, in spite of U.S. and domestic pressures, Canada cannot afford not to seek balance between (1) civil liberties and security, (2) guns and butter, (3) economic bilateralism and multilateral diplomacy, and (4) interdependence and sovereignty. Now that the negotiations on missile defence have begun, let us hope that the Government of Canada would not sacrifice the sovereignty, liberties, and freedoms of Canadians for their safety, defence and economic well-being.

Notes

1 DND, "Department of National Defence Consultation Report. Thinking Outside the Box: The Future of Canadian Defence Policy" By Sarah Tarry and Frank Harvey, Dalhousie University Halifax, Nova Scotia, 8–9 February 2001. http://www.dnd.ca/admpol/eng/doc/532_e.htm

2 See Irwin Colter, "Does the antiterror bill go too far" *Globe and Mail*, November 20, 2001, p. A17

3 George Weigel, "Moral Clarity in a Time of War," *LeadershipU*, http://www.Leadershipu.com/humanities/moral_clarity.html, July 9, 2003, p.1.

4 "Canada's elite clamours for huge increase in military spending" World Socialist Web Site. http://www.wsws.org/articles/2002/oct2002/can-008.shtml 8 October 2002.

5 Charles E. Lindblom, "The Science of 'Muddling Through,'" in Andreas Faudi., *A Reader in Planning Theory*, Pergamon Press, 1973, p.81.

6 Ibid., p. 83.

7 F. Frohock, Public *Policy, Scope and Logic*, New Jersey: Printice-Hall, 1979, p. 55.

8 Michael T. Hayes, *Incrementalism and Public Policy*; New York: Longman, 1992, p. 13.

9 Wayne Hayes, "Incrementalism" http://www.geocities.com/~profwork/pp/formulate/inc.html

10 Ibid.

11 Ibid.

12 European Commission- Secretariat-General, *European Governance: Public Hearing. Moving Towards Better Use of Subsidiarity and Proportionality*, SdR 2001, Brussels 1 March 2001

13 Kent Roach, *September 11th: Consequences for Canada*, McGill-Queen's University Press, 2003. Cited by W. Wesley Pue "9/11: Lament for Canada. Will our Anti-Terrorism Act lead us down the road to tyranny", *Literary Review of Canada*, Vol. 11, No. 5, June 2003, p. 3.

14 Claire L'heureux Dubé, "Realizing equality in the twentieth century: the role of the Supreme Court of Canada in Comparative perspective" Article Oxford University Press and New York University School of Law 2003, I.CON, Volume 1, Number 1, 2003, p. 37.

15 Michel Fortmann et Alex Macleod, "La politique de défense future du Canada", Rapport du Forum sur la Défense: Montréal, le 8 décembre 2000, http://www.forces.gc.ca/admpol/fra/doc/534_f.htm#som

16 Michel Fortmann and David Haglund, "Canada and the Issue of Homeland Security: Does the 'Kingston Dispensation' Still Hold?" *Canadian Military Journal* 3,Spring 2002, p. 19.

17 Ibid.

18 Joseph Jockel "After the September Attacks: Four Questions about NORAD's Future." *Canadian Military Journal* 3 (Spring 2002) p. 11.

19 David L. Grange, "Asymmetric Warfare: Old Method, New Concern" *National Strategy Forum Review*, Winter 2000. Online at http://www.nationalstrategy.com/nsr /v10n2Winter00/1002002.htm

20 Government of Canada, *1994 White Paper on Defence*, http://www.dnd.ca/admpol/eng/doc/white_e.htm

21 Ibid., Chapter 2.

22 Ibid., Chapter 1.

23 Ibid.

24 Fortmann and Haglund, *op.cit.*, p. 19.

25 Ibid.

26 Joseph Jockel, *op.cit.*, p. 11.

27 *Annual Report of the Chief of Defence Staff 2001–2002*, http://www.cds.forces.gc.ca/pubs/anrpt2002/ message_f.asp, Part 1.

28 Jockel, *op.cit*, p. 13.

29 Alistair D. Edgar, "Let's Get a Continental Defence Market Treaty", *Policy Options*, avril 2002, p. 56.

30 James Ferguson, "Time for a Decision on North American Missile Defence", *Policy Options*, avril 2002, p. 32.

31 Joseph Jockel, op. cit., p. 12.

32 Ferguson, "Time for a Decision" p. 35.

33 Ibid., p. 36.

34 Please see Philippe Lagassé, "The Northern Command and the Evolution of Canada–U.S. Defence Relations," *Canadian Military Journal* vol.4, no 1, Spring 2003.

35 Chief of the Defence Staff, *Shaping the Future of the Canadian Forces: A Strategy for 2020.* http://www.cds.forces.gc.ca/pubs/strategy2k/intro_e.asp

36 Ibid., Part I.

37 *Canadian Air Transport Security Act* http://www.parl.gc.ca/37/1/parlbus/chambus/house/bills/government/C-49/C-49_4/90178bE.html#4

38 Ibid.

39 Kent Roach *September 11th: Consequences for Canada*, McGill-Queen's University Press, 2003. Cited by W. Wesley Pue "9/11: Lament for Canada. Will our Anti-Terrorism Act lead us down the road to tyranny", *Literary Review of Canada*, Vol. 11, No. 5, June 2003, p. 4.

40 Ibid.

41 Human Rights- Canada "Civil Liberties, Human Rights and Canada's New National Security Legislation" http://www.caut.ca/english/issues/hr_ can/nationalsecurity.asp

42 Noami Klein, "Hate Bill C-36? Wait until you meet its brother", 28 November 2001, http://friendsoffreedom.org/article.php?sid=106

43 Ontario NDP, "Look Out Anne: Your Antiterrorist Bill Clear-Cut Democracy," 17 October 2001. http://www.ontariondp.on.ca/issues/civil/C36_articles.htm

44 Hina Jilani (Amnesty International), "Antiterrorism Strategies and Protecting Human Rights", http://www.amnestyusa.org/amnesty now/antiterrorism.html

45 Ibid.

46 *An Honour To Serve. Annual Report of the Chief of Defence Staff*, http://www.cds.forces.ca/oonative/pdf/CDSreport_e.pdf

47 Ibid.

48 Ibid., Part 2, p. 10.

49 Ibid., Foreword, p. iii.

50 David L. King, "We Need a Romanow Commission for Defence and Foreign Policy." *Policy Options*. April 2002, p. 8.

51 Matthew Fisher, "A Real Challenge: Canada's Navy Guards the American Flank in the War Against Terrorism." *Maclean's*, February 18, 2002, p. 28.

52 David L. King, op. cit.

53 See Hugh Segal, "National Security, the Public Interest and How We Govern: A Time for Innovation." *Canadian Military Journal*, Summer 2001. p. 40.) King maintains that the lack of interest in defence issues by our elected officials may be due to the fact that they see defence as a secondary issue in relation to their function of regional representation (David L. King op. cit., p. 12).

54 *Annual Report of the Chief of Defence Staff 2000–2001*, op. cit., Part III, p. 21.

55 *Annual Report of the Chief of Defence Staff 2001–2002*, Foreword, p. ii.

56 Hugh Segal, "The Canadian-American Defence Relationship: Nostalgia Ain't What it Used to Be," *Policy Options*, April 2002. p. 24.
57 David L. King, op. cit., p. 9.
58 See David L. King, op. cit., André Corbould "The Grass is Always Greener," *Canadian Military Journal*. Winter 2001–2002. p. 61; Nelson Michaud The 1987 Defence Policy: An Analysis of a Decision-Making Process. Presented at the Canadian Political Science Association Annual Meeting, Ottawa, 1998, p. 5 and Michael Snider "Changing the Tune," *Macleans'*, February 18, 2002. p. 29.
59 Defence Highlights: Budget 2003 http://www.dnd.ca/site/reports/budget03/highlights03_e.htm
60 National Defence, *A Time for Transformation* Annual report of the Chief of Defence Staff 2002–2003, p. ii.
61 U.S. Joint Forces Command "Joint Interoperability and Integration Charter" http://www.teao.saic.com/jfcom/html/charter.html
62 Alvin Toffler and Heidi Toffler, *War and Anti-War, Survival at the Dawn of the Twenty First Century*, Boston, Little Brown, 1993.
63 *A time for transformation*, op. cit., p.ii.
64 Ibid, p. iii.
65 Fortmann and Haglund, op. cit., p. 17.
66 David L King, op. cit., p. 7.
67 David Jones "Canada–U.S. Relations After September 11: Back to Basics" *Policy Options*, March 2002. p. 26.
68 Joseph Jockel, op. cit., p. 13.
69 Ibid., p. 26.
70 David L. King, op. cit., p. 8.
71 Ibid., op. cit., p. 10.
72 Ernie Regehr "Canada and BMD," *Ploughshares Briefing* 03-5, May 2003. http://www.ploughshares.ca/
73 Dwight N. Mason "Canada Alert Canada and Missile Defense," *Hemisphere Focus*, Volume XI, Issue 22, June 6, 2003, p.1.
74 Ibid.

References

Bland, Douglas L. (Ed.) *Canada's National Defence Volume 1: Defence Policy.* Kingston: Queen's University School of Policy Studies, 1997.

Corbould, André. "The Grass is Always Greener." *Canadian Military Journal.* Winter 2001–2002. p. 61.

Edgar, Alistair D. "Let's Get a Continental Defence Market Treaty." *Policy Options.* April 2002. pp. 50–56.

Ferguson, James. "Time for a Decision on North American Missile Defence." *Policy Options.* April 2002. pp. 32–37.

Fisher, Matthew. "A Real Challenge: Canada's Navy Guards the American Flank in the War Against Terrorism." *Maclean's.* February 18, 2002. pp. 28–29.

Fortmann, Michel, and David G. Haglund. "Canada and the Issue of Homeland Security: Does the 'Kingston Dispensation' Still Hold?" *Canadian Military Journal.* Spring 2002. pp. 17–22.

Fortmann, Michel and Alex Macleod. "Future Canadian Defence Policy." Report on Defence Forum: Montréal, QC, 8 December 2000. Online at http://www.dnd.ca/admpol/org/dg_coord/d_pub/sdf/reports/mtl00_forum_e.htm

Grange, David L. "Asymmetric Warfare: Old Method, New Concern." *National Strategy Forum Review.* Winter 2000. Online at http://www.nationalstrategy.com/nsr /v10n2Winter00/1002002.htm

Jockel, Joseph T. "After the September Attacks: Four Questions About NORAD's Future." *Canadian Military Journal.* Spring 2002. pp. 11–16.

Jockel, Joseph T., and Joel J. Sokolsky. *The End of the Canada–U.S. Defence Relationship.* Occasional Paper Series, Center for International Relations, Queen's University, 1996.

Jones, David. "Canada–U.S. Relations After September 11: Back to Basics." *Policy Options.* March 2002. pp. 25–29.

King, David L. "We Need a Romanow Commission for Defence and Foreign Policy." *Policy Options.* April 2002. pp. 7–14.

Maloney, Sean M. "Canadian Values and National Security Policy: Who Decides?" *Policy Options.* December 2001. pp. 45–49.

Mansbridge, Peter. "TV News After September 11." *Policy Options.* March 2002. pp. 15–18.

Michaud, Nelson. *The 1987 Defence Policy: An Analysis of a Decision-Making Process.* Presented at the Canadian Political Science Association Annual Meeting, Ottawa, 1998.

Segal, Hugh. "The Canadian-American Defence Relationship: Nostalgia Ain't What it Used to Be." *Policy Options*. April 2002. pp. 23–26.

——. "National Security, the Public Interest and How We Govern: A Time for Innovation." *Canadian Military Journal*. Summer 2001. pp. 39–42.

Snider, Michael. "Changing the Tune." *Maclean's*. February 18, 2002. p. 29.

Other Sources

1994 White Paper on Defence. Government of Canada. Online at http://www.dnd.ca/eng/reports/ 94wpaper/ white_ paper_94.html

At a Crossroads: Annual Report of the Chief of Defence Staff 2001–2002. Ottawa: National Defence Headquarters. Online at http://www.forces.gc.ca

An Honour to Serve: Annual Report of the Chief of Defence Staff 2000–2001. Ottawa: National Defence Headquarters. Online at http://www.forces.gc.ca

Defence Strategy 2020. Government of Canada, Chief of Defence Staff Documents. Online at http://www.vcds. forces.gc.ca

Canadian Air Transport Security Authority Established. Government of Canada News Release No. H035/02. 28 March 2002. Online at http://tc.gc.ca/mediaroom/ releases/nat/2002/02_h035e.htm

International Contributions to the War Against Terrorism. Fact Sheet, Office of Public Affairs, U.S. Department of Defence, May 2002.

Public Safety Act, 2002: Improves Legislative Framework to Fight Terrorism and Protect Public Safety. Governemnt of Canada News Release No. GC001/02. 29 April 2002. Online at http://www.tc.gc.ca/mediaroom

3

Weapons of Mass Destruction, American Vulnerability, and Canadian Political Inertia

Douglas A. Ross

September 11, 2001 was an historical watershed in American foreign policy. For conservative national security planners in the U.S. their "whole world" was transformed irrevocably. The decision of the Bush Administration to launch an active, aggressive counter-proliferation campaign of indefinite duration against the "rogue state" possessors of nuclear, biological and chemical weapons (usually referred to as Weapons of Mass Destruction, hereafter as WMDs) is likely to define American grand strategy for years and possibly decades to come—as American Secretary of Defense, Donald Rumsfeld, bluntly suggested. The failure of the Democrats to challenge this approach to international security policy in the 2002 Congressional elections suggests that there is no viable liberal alternative to aggressive unilateral interventionism. The principal flaw in this grand effort to remake the Middle East and suppress extremist political Islam is that American neo-conservatives either had no coherent plan of political and economic developmental to follow up their military victories—neither in Afghanistan nor Iraq. Transformation of the Middle East and Afghanistan with equity and justice for all remains an elusive and unshaped goal for American liberals, the advice of Tony Blair to reinvent the world's political economy and impose a tolerably just peace on Israelis and Palestinians notwithstanding.

In fact, were there to be a shift in American "grand strategy" and general foreign policy orientation, it is more plausible to envisage a victory for latent isolationist sentiment. Isolationism, though still lacking any substantial support in the American political elite beyond the Patrick Buchanan fringe, may yet prevail. While the "unipolar moment" prophesied by Charles Krauthammer blossomed under Bush the Younger, its duration and record of achievements may turn out to be perilously brief. Winning quick, easy victories over the near medieval Taliban in Kabul and Kandahar, and over an Iraqi regime depleted by a decade of sanctions is hardly the stuff of military glory and honour. A continuing loss of American lives in occupied Iraq to terrorist and "resistance" attacks could trigger a geopolitical retreat to the Western Hemisphere. The perceived stakes for all Americans in the "war on terrorism" that have been the rationale of continuing intervention in the Islamic world remain high, but they may pale in comparison to the body count in coming months and years as suicide car and truck bombers carry out their missions. Radical elements across the Islamic world evidently intend to wage a protracted war of attrition aimed at American public opinion — not the U.S. military which has established itself as invincible on the battlefield. Whether the U.S. authorities can successfully "hand off" the counter-terrorist campaign to other NATO allies or to a new Iraqi government remains to be seen ("Iraqi-ization" of the civil stabilization campaign inside occupied Iraq would be the contemporary equivalent of Nixon's resort to "Vietnamization" after 1969).

By contrast, the Canadian reaction to 9/11 per Chrétien liberalism was characterized by rhetoric in support of the campaign against international terrorism but only measured, very limited actions by the federal government (modest participation in "regime removal" in Afghanistan and belated participation in running the International Stabilization Force in Kabul in 2003) with only the most modest increase in spending on defence and internal security. Prime Minister Chrétien's penchant for under-reacting produced a tepid, uninspired foreign policy apparently designed to keep most Canadians out of the line of fire while American forces fanned out to attack the rogue state threats thought to be the most menacing to American security.

Chrétien's careful under-reaction and studied avoidance of the language of crisis was part of a broader foreign policy approach that eschewed military involvement. If Canadians had to fight for reasons of "alliance solidarity" it would be on the basis of "last in and first out" — and in theatres of least risk. Accordingly under Prime Minister Chrétien's approach (often compared by critics to Mackenzie King's unenthusiastic support for collective security) the Canadian military remained a withered, still shrinking force unable to participate meaningfully in major collective security or collective defence operations. The operating and capital budgets of the Canadian Forces remained stagnant for want of political support from federal Liberals who as a group developed a party consensus to keep the Canadian role in the management of international security issues marginal, symbolic, inexpensive and low-risk.

Being highly sceptical and in many cases deeply mistrustful of the growing power of Congressional conservatives in Washington, fearing and in some cases actually despising the "moronic" American President,[1] and finally being still more suspicious of the political and strategic judgement of Bush's executive branch appointees, Chrétien's Liberal government adhered to its policy of degrading Canadian military capabilities through budgetary attrition — a publicly unacknowledged "strategy" in force since the mid-1990s — so as to inhibit any American pressure for overt support for American strategic operations. Weakness and incapacity in effect became a form of political "defence" against U.S. demands for collaborative military participation. Political inertia, fiscal myopia, ideological antipathy to "imperial America" strategists in Washington and, to be sure, anxiety about Québécois hostility to foreign military entanglement,[2] prevailed in Ottawa to the point where a sensible and prudential regard for national security became impossible — and so too any visible ability to think or plan strategically concerning the pressing international security issues of the moment.

The Legacy of the Proliferation of Weapons of Mass Destruction and Rising American Vulnerability

Foremost among these pressing issues has been the continued international proliferation of the capacity to build nuclear and biological weapons since the mid-1980s — the true WMDs of the international system (truly massive civilian casualties by terrorist attacks would be difficult to attain through the use of chemical weapons).[3] Such proliferation, especially in the Middle East, South Asia, and East Asia has created a major potential threat to all the advanced industrial states, but especially to the United States itself — hence American elite determination to pursue a policy of aggressive counter-proliferation.[4] The "horizontal" spread of nuclear weapons manufacturing capability and the evolution of "secondary markets" in key technologies has been rendered still more worrisome by the continued refusal (or political inability) of Russian authorities to close down their illegal offensive biological warfare program,[5] or to manage and secure their residual nuclear weapons stockpile.[6] The intermittent and unreliable political control of central Russian authorities has stimulated fears that much advanced WMD technology may now be for sale from rogue government bureaucrats, or from Russian "mafia" who have been able to purchase not merely technology secrets but also actual small nuclear weapons from the porous, underpaid (or unpaid), demoralized Russian military and public service.

Across the NATO policy community, only the American political elite has exercised a sustained political will to try to eliminate or contain the emergent threats of WMD proliferation before far worse attacks on "the West" than 9/11 actually occur.[7] While British Prime Minister Tony Blair provided much political support for the Bush Administration's campaign to remove Saddam Hussein's government in Iraq, his support for President Bush has left him with both a divided party and a divided country that is highly ambivalent about the military intervention in Iraq.[8]

The American government has been castigated by many commentators in countries allied with the U.S. — especially so in Canada — for behaving as a "hyperpower." Such criticism extends to charges from some that the U.S. government actually *caused* the World Trade Center and Washington, D.C. attacks by virtue of its arrogance, hubris, and greed.[9] While liberal critics of post-Cold War American foreign policy denounced sustained high levels of American military spending even before 9/11 ("Where's the post-Cold War peace dividend?"), that criticism reached a crescendo in the weeks prior to the March 2003 invasion of Iraq. American strategic unilateralism rose steadily both before and after 9/11 given the deep scepticism towards traditional American allies shown by the Bush Administration's most ardent neo-conservatives. Tony Blair, alone among Western European leaders, skilfully defended and endorsed the policies of the Bush Administration — a policy team that is apparently more disliked by Europeans and Canadians than perhaps any American administration since World War II. President Bush, like President Reagan twenty years earlier, was consistently portrayed as an ill-informed, boorish, provincial simpleton — a mere puppet in the hands of hawkish advisors. The President and his right-wing policy team were condemned as well for class avarice as manifest in tax cuts for the rich, "deregulation" for the emergent post-Cold War American corporate plutocracy, inadequate policing of Enron-style corporate thievery, and, more practically, a failure to manage the American economy effectively by driving the federal government deeply into debt — thereby setting the stage for a painful global recession.

Somewhat paradoxically, American "hyperpower" status and unquestioned global military superiority have not guaranteed security for the United States. Rarely in history has the global elite of a hegemonic state felt so exposed and vulnerable.[10] During the Cold War the thermonuclear "balance of terror," unstable and uncertain though it often was, provided a measure of consolation and reassurance to Americans. Credible threats of nuclear retaliation were thought to be adequate to ensure freedom from Communist-bloc nuclear surprise attack. September 11 convinced the American strategic policy community that deterrent threats could no longer protect the United States. Terrorist use of weapons of mass destruction, it has been assumed, would be carried out anonymously. Even if terrorist organizations like al-Qaida had base areas in countries such as Afghanistan and Sudan whose governments could be destroyed, how could retaliation be carried out against a diffuse network of agents and sympathizers much of which was already distributed in covert "sleeper cells" across Western Europe and North America?

Equally disturbing was the realization in the months after 9/11 that the U.S. and its closest allies could not mount reliable and effective defences against terrorist infiltration in the foreseeable future. Borders are too long and porous (the Canadian border with the "lower" 48 states is over 6,100 kilometres long — the Alaska portion adds another

3,000 kilometers) customs-immigration-security staff are too few and lack training in recognition of dangerous materials, concealment of biological and fissile materials is relatively easy, and the technologies of bomb- and mine-making are widely available. Access to biological, chemical, radiological and even nuclear explosive materials may be attainable for a high enough price.[11] Terrorists, for their part, have access to off-the-shelf, encrypted communications technology that can be used with impunity by telephone or Internet. Like narcotics or tobacco smugglers, terrorist cells are likely to acquire faster boats, cars, or aircraft, or newer, faster and more secure communications than those possessed by the border security personnel trying to intercept them.

American borders remain quite porous. Leading U.S. politicians have despaired publicly about how little was done in the year following September 2001 to tighten entry into the U.S. or to secure key facilities and enhance emergency response capabilities. International travel and commerce lacks adequate screening to prevent infiltration by terrorists who may have acquired WMDs. In early 2003, fewer than two percent of the 20,000 plus shipping containers that arrived daily at ports were checked in any way at all. Of that two percent only a small fraction were actually unpacked and scrutinized in detail. Both U.S. Coast Guard and customs staff will not receive training in the recognition of dangerous biological, chemical or radioactive materials for years to come. A much expanded fleet of modern Coast Guard craft remains a paper proposal only, with a sufficiently high cost that it may never be well funded. Language skills in the Coast Guard are lacking on both coasts, so that cargo ship manifests and crew lists can not be understood.[12] Computer databases and watch-lists of suspected criminals or terrorists held by the FBI, CIA, or State Department remain out of reach of Coast Guard personnel.

In an October 2002 Council on Foreign Relations report, "America Still Unprepared, America Still in Danger," former senators Gary Hart (Dem.) and Warren Rudman (Rep.) deplored the minimal or nonexistent security at seaports, nuclear and hydroelectric power plants, oil refineries, chemical plants, rail systems, and major cities. Local police and fire departments still lacked access to chemical and biological protection gear, virtually none carried portable detection equipment, nor did they have access by telephone or laptop so that they could obtain the terrorist watch-lists routinely provided by the State Department to immigration and consular officials: "The cops on the beat are effectively operating deaf, dumb, and blind. Known terrorists will be free to move about to plan and execute their attacks." This second Hart-Rudman report (their first 1998 report emphasized the same inadequacies) called for a new commitment to training an enhanced National Guard to respond to major domestic attacks. Said Hart: "The world is divided between those who believe the worst is over and those who believe the worst is yet to come. Unfortunately, I fall into the latter group."[13] In mid-2003, firefighters in U.S. cities still lacked radios, port staff remained too few and too sparsely equipped, while air marshals were removed from many domestic flights to try to save money—until media leaks embarrassed the Homeland Security officials and forced them to rescind their intended economies.[14] Almost two years after 9/11 American first responders still felt that they were woefully under-equipped to handle a major domestic terrorist attack.[15]

The Canadian military, military reserves, and customs and immigration personnel are also quite inadequately trained and equipped to be able to offer any serious threat of detection and interception of weapons of mass destruction that terrorist smugglers might wish to bring into Canada—prior to shipping them to the U.S. On a per capita basis, Canadian perimeter security efforts are far smaller than their opposite numbers in the United States. While the Office of Critical Infrastructure Preparedness has conducted comprehensive assessments of Canadian vulnerabilities, little money has in fact been provided by Ottawa to address the problems identified since 9/11. Port security remains weak and easily penetrated and immigration officials remain unable to track tens of thousands of failed refugee applicants who have simply disappeared. Border entry points are staffed often with part-time student employees and customs and immigration officials have no side arms to deal with emergencies but must rely on local law enforcement personnel who are often slow to respond.

American vulnerability to attack remains the chief concern on both sides of the border. Attacks are most likely to occur on U.S. soil, even if the planning and logistical support for the attacks were to originate in Canada. With vast sums of money being made available to the Pentagon and the new Homeland Security Agency, the Hart-Rudman report noted nevertheless, that detailed technical vulnerability assessments for the 50 largest ports remained years from completion. Major improvements would not begin until the studies were completed. Meanwhile 95 percent of trade with countries outside North America moves by sea, and the entire maritime container trade could be sabotaged and suddenly closed down with a single catastrophic (large conventional, radiological, or worst-case small atomic) explosion at one of these ports. Even the least threatening of such contingencies would be extremely costly: "If an explosive device was loaded in a container and set off in a port, it would almost automatically raise concern about the integrity of the 21,000 containers that arrive in ports each day. A three- to four-week closure of U.S. ports would bring the global container industry to its knees" — not to mention both the Canadian and American economies. If such an "event" was precipitated by a container entering the U.S. from Canada, millions of Canadians would be thrown out of work immediately for an indefinite but almost certainly very long period.

The day before the release of the Hart-Rudman report former Vice President Al Gore underlined American lack of preparedness for the "imminent threat" of biological warfare (BW) attack. In his estimate some $ 10 billion (U.S.) would be needed to upgrade a failing American public health system: "The small-scale anthrax attacks of a year ago found that our public health system is in a state of disrepair. This past summer [2002] the uncoordinated response to outbreaks of West Nile virus reminded us again how inadequate our public health system is.... Rapid communication of information about dangerous disease is an essential part of national bio-terrorism response. But many public health agencies lack equipment as basic as a fax machine or an e-mail account."[16]

For close American allies, especially for Canadians, the risk of becoming collateral damage in some future WMD terrorist campaign aimed primarily at the U.S. is also very high — although one would hardly think so based on the halting, grudging allocation of resources to internal and international security shown thus far by the Canadian government. For terrorists trying to change American behaviour (such as severing Anglo–American "Crusader" support for Israel),[17] the optimal coercive diplomatic effect of rudimentary atomic devices might best be attained from first demonstrating the destructive power of their terrorist arsenal on an adjacent ally. At least initially, American territory would be threatened only while the credibility of the terrorists' nuclear blackmail threats was being established — at Canadian, Western European, or Australian expense. This two-step process would be employed so as to minimize the risk of an irrationally vengeful American response and to maximize the prospects of a sober, chastened U.S. retreating from continued intervention in Middle Eastern countries. The most charitable thing that can be said about American allies who believe they are not at all exposed to major risks of attack is that either they are being unusually naive or that they are imprudently gambling with the lives of their own citizens. As one of Senator Colin Kenny's committee reports summed up the situation, while Canadians are not at the bull's eye of the target for international terrorism, they are certainly within the inner ring.[18]

The American Counter-proliferation Response

Given the appalling gravity of the threat posed by covertly delivered WMDs, most conservative American strategists appear to have concluded that an aggressive military outreach to all parts of the globe is essential and urgent. That campaign of counter-proliferation (the aggressive elimination of nascent WMD capabilities that is to be distinguished from the traditional non-proliferation regime of legislated mutual reassurance through international inspection and verification measures) will most likely be of indefinite duration and will be designed to seek out and destroy potential terrorist organizations, their most likely state sponsors or "silent partner" collaborators — and, most importantly, any WMD technologies to which they might have access.

The idea of a major American disengagement from global security affairs (so as to "stay out of other people's troubles" or as another commentator put it, "to stay out of the nuclear crossfire") is simply unthinkable to the current Administration. That agonizing choice for U.S. foreign policy between the poles of permanent interventionism and neo-isolationist retrenchment was forecast many years prior to 9/11 by the nuclear strategist Michael Mandelbaum.[19] His views and other similarly prescient forecasts by American security analysts were for the most part ignored by political leadership. Neither permanent aggressive "counter-proliferation" nor neo-isolationism are politically palatable options that can be acted on in any political context short of national emergency. Something like the events of September 11—or worse—had to happen to catalyze and legitimize the government's adoption of a much more radical foreign policy orientation.[20]

The diffusion of WMDs to small states hostile to "the West" has brought with it the risk that they may be further devolved into the hands of "non-deterrable" terrorist organizations.[21] The very pre-eminence of the United States in world affairs—economically, culturally, militarily—automatically engenders resentment, fear and the attribution of unconditional blame for a whole host of injustices in the international system (for example, political repression in Saudi Arabia or Pakistan, poverty across Africa via American influence within the IMF and World Bank, the economic destabilization of Southeast Asia in the late 1990s, the materialist Western/American cultural corruption of Muslim societies etc.). Whether such blame is deserved or not, as the fulcrum of the global system of political economy, American society will continue to be held responsible for the continuing misery of the wretched of the earth—even if the current crisis with "political Islam" is resolved satisfactorily (by no means a likely outcome at time of writing). The American government is likely to remain the primary target for disaffected radical terrorist groups whether they are in the Middle East, Southeast Asia, Japan,[22] or even Latin America.

The historically common tendency to scapegoat foreign powers or elites when societies enter periods of severe economic stress and cultural upheaval is likely to remain a constant feature of the international system. It is therefore a reasonable premise on which to base planning for North American security. Accordingly, until and unless American society is damaged powerfully by WMD attack and driven to retreat from world politics, or until the American elite actively chooses global disengagement from intense regional conflicts and strategically ill-advised security guarantees to allies who should now fend for themselves (perhaps as a result of accepting John Mearsheimer's "offensive realist" policy advice),[23] the U.S. is likely to remain a major target for the most disaffected and alienated elements of the international community. At the moment the war on terrorism is focussed on the members of al-Qaida. But even if they are eliminated in coming years, American strategists and national security planners fear, not unreasonably, that sooner or later others will take their place.

"Traditional" terrorism has invariably been an adjunct to other forms of warfare. It was but one instrument available to states and more commonly insurgent revolutionary movements seeking to overturn established state structures. It relied on disproportionate psychological impact on civil populations to discredit and destabilize incumbent governments, thereby degrading their ability to resist invasion from outside and subversion from within. But WMD terrorism may take the phenomenon of terrorist modalities in a fundamentally new direction. The addition of weapons of mass destruction capability transforms terrorist operations into a far more powerful form of warfare, something that is much more than a helpful harassing instrument of destabilization. Attacks with weapons of mass destruction (primarily nuclear or biological) would have two missions: the "traditional" goal of extraordinary psychological impact (to be inflicted on the civil populations of states so as to discourage their governments from intervening abroad) and an additional goal of inflicting major societal and economic damage on target countries (thus to weaken or destroy altogether their physical ability to intervene). The political will to project military force would be assaulted — as in "traditional" terrorist action — but, in addition, the physical ability to project military force or the economic foundations for military force projection would also be seriously degraded.

The Prospective Appeal of WMD Terrorism

Weapons of Mass Destruction do not have to be delivered by long-range ballistic missiles, advanced cruise missiles, supersonic bombers, or robotic aircraft — even though these are the preferred methods of professional military elites worldwide. For generals whose task is to defeat foreign armies and seize territory, remote sensors, missiles and stealthy aircraft are essential — as are the other elements of the growing panoply of intelligence, surveillance, reconnaissance, information-processing, and precision-strike technologies that together comprise the Revolution in Military Affairs (RMA). The achievement by the United States of "information dominance" or what American military analysts have termed "full spectrum battlefield dominance" in terms of conventional warfare during the 1990s to the present has, of course, helped provoke rival governments and hostile sub-national groups to become interested in other "asymmetric" means of striking at the sources of American military and economic preponderance. It was precisely their anxiety about emergent American military hegemony that apparently fuelled the declining Soviet elite to undertake three rather unusual steps. These actions, although now dated and therefore perhaps of seemingly merely academic interest should nevertheless be studied closely.

First it should be noted that during the last five years of the USSR, the Soviet nuclear security planners created what was in effect a Dr. Strangelove-like equivalent of a "Doomsday Bomb" by establishing the fully automated "Dead Hand" nuclear command and control system. According to some American researchers, the Russian leadership since 1991 apparently has retained this technical "fix" to the perceived threat of American first-strike capability to try to deter any future American flirtation with thoughts of leadership "decapitation." The substantial danger of having such technologies in place is that when the Dead Hand system is turned "on," there are unavoidable finite risks of false retaliation against North America from several possible sources: faulty information from seismic and thermal sensors in Moscow could be sent to the computers remote from the city (that are able to launch most of the Russian intercontinental arsenal without human intervention); programming errors in the autonomous launch computers are possible; third parties anxious to have Russian and the United States attack each other could penetrate the system and alter the programming; or lastly, and probably the greatest risk, terrorists (either for their own reasons or in collaboration with a government hostile to both Moscow and Washington) who have acquired a nuclear device could emplace one in Moscow and wait for an opportune moment of Russian-American tension and mistrust and then detonate their weapon in hopes that it would catalyze a Russo-American holocaust.[24]

Secondly, Soviet weapons scientists were directed between 1988 and 1992 to build a capacity to load tons of biological agents of various types on Soviet heavy ICBMs on short notice. This bizarre and historically unprecedented action again reflected growing Soviet fears of a largely successful disarming nuclear first strike against the USSR by the U.S. If because of growing American stealth, non-nuclear precision strike, and emergent missile defence capabilities, only very few Soviet retaliatory missile warheads might get through to the U.S., it may have seemed desirable to ensure that these few warheads *randomly distributed across the U.S.* could still have a high probability of killing hundreds of millions of people. Warheads filled with genetically enhanced, highly contagious, disease-causing material spread through a defenceless civilian population might provide that extra measure of confidence in their waning retaliatory credibility.

Thirdly, and for present purposes most importantly, Soviet (and after December 1991 possibly Russian) military and intelligence officials took the initial steps, and perhaps more, to place covert "suitcase" nuclear weapons in the U.S. itself near Washington and other important command and control targets. This third step certainly impressed many American political leaders after they were briefed by a GRU (Soviet military intelligence) defector on his part in the process of finding safe houses for suitcase bomb storage in northern Virginia—about a 90 minute drive from the Pentagon and Capitol Hill.

The covert nuclear attack "option" is also available to international terrorist groups—if they can purchase suitcase nuclear devices. For the former Soviet elite covert emplacement of nuclear devices was undoubtedly part of a decapitation/preventive war/preemptive strike/first-strike family of war plans relevant for the contingency of unavoidable total war with the U.S. Under most of these scenarios Washington's political and military leadership would be the primary early targets for use in a Soviet (or Russian?) effort to forestall a fully coordinated nuclear first strike by the U.S. military. For international terrorists, on the other hand, the covert introduction and anonymous detonation of nuclear devices presumably would be part of a campaign to break American political will to oppose their group's political goals and to drive American military interventionists out of their region. Decapitation of the U.S. leadership would not necessarily be the most appropriate path: any device or devices would be few, the rest of the American command system would be intact, military authorities would probably emerge to take control on an interim basis pending the recreation through elections of a new civilian government. And the interim American military authorities might be far less susceptible to public panic and demands for caving in to terrorist demands than would be elected politicians.

Thus, Washington would not necessarily be the first target of WMD terrorism — the precedent of September 11 notwithstanding. Terrorists logically would want a functioning American government to be able to order the withdrawal of U.S. forces from theatres abroad. The psychological impact of a WMD detonation on American public opinion can be obtained by attacking New York once more, or Boston, Chicago, Detroit, Dallas, or Los Angeles. If any large American city had its core destroyed during business hours by a four or five kiloton bomb, over 100,000 people might be killed (many of them slowly and painfully from radiation sickness in the days and weeks after the blast). Such a disaster, coupled with threats to detonate other weapons in other cities (spaced months apart), could produce overwhelming political pressures on American leaders to disengage immediately and completely from all foreign military involvements.

Table 1 (next page) illustrates the position that WMD terrorism may come to occupy in a pragmatic taxonomy of forms of warfare and types of war.

Given the highly permeable condition of the frontiers of all of the modern industrial states, including notably both the U.S. and Canada,[25] it is clear that it should be relatively straightforward for terrorist organizations to deliver WMD covertly — if they can obtain the necessary special nuclear or biological materials, or if they can simply purchase or otherwise acquire fully weaponized instruments from allied or sympathetic governments or black market purchasing. Unlike missile and bomber attacks, there would be no evidence to disclose the attackers' identity. WMDs — both portable atomic devices and small quantities of living (and therefore cultivatable) biological agents — can be smuggled into North America or Western Europe without great difficulty by skilled terrorists. With state support it would be easier still. Small hostile states, if they are sufficiently fearful, may choose the somewhat riskier path of delivering WMD weapons using their own agents, rather than relying on terrorist intermediaries. The potential payoff of this style of attack is considerable. WMD terrorist operations could be applied to almost all types of war, "revolutionary" war being the only exception. The use or credible threat to use such weaponry would be a potentially huge force equalizer for small or technically inferior states. The appeal of such a capability to marginalized radical elements in both developed

Table 1: The Theoretical Role of WMD Terrorism and Other Forms of Warfare in the Four Principal Types of War

	Types of War			
Forms of Warfare	**Revolutionary (Vietnam)**	**Limited (Korea)**	**General (WW II)**	**Total (heavy NW use)**
Guerrilla Warfare	Dominant early on	Supplementary	Supplementary	Likely, after NW use
Conventional Warfare (no WMDs)	Dominant in final phase	Important	Central Role	Secondary
Terrorist WMD Warfare	Least likely	Possible Supplementary	Possible Supplementary	Possible Supplementary
Tactical Nuclear Warfare	None	Unlikely	Possible	Supplementary
Strategic Nuclear Warfare	None	None	Very Rarely	Decisive

NW – Nuclear Weapon
WMD – Weapon of Mass Destruction

Source: The conceptual germ for this table was derived from Samuel P. Huntington's classification in "Guerrilla Warfare in Theory and Policy," in Franklin M. Osanka, ed., *Modern Guerrilla Warfare* (Glencoe: Free Press, 1962).

and undeveloped societies may also become high. In a world of "new" terrorism with fundamentalist, millennial, and apocalyptic ideologies in play, the will to employ WMD terrorism seems likely to occur — sooner or later.

Achieving Canadian and American Security in a Highly Proliferated World: How Feasible?

Neither Canada nor the U.S. is near to resolving the problem of armies of "disappeared" refugees in whose ranks dozens of terrorist "sleeper" agents may lurk. Over 300,000 "alien absconders" have disappeared in the U.S. and several tens of thousands of rejected refugee claimants have been "lost" in Canada. According to some estimates, as many as 140,000 rejected refugees are "off the radar screen" for Canadian immigration authorities.[26] Viewed from a national security perspective Canadian and American immigration and refugee policies are in a shambles. The would-be LAX (Los Angeles International Airport) bomber, Ahmed Ressam, and his colleagues in Canada may be just the tip of a large iceberg.

As noted earlier, the task of creating an effective screening and control regime of the global bulk transport network may prove to be both politically and ultimately even physically impossible. With some 15 million standardized cargo containers in motion on land and at sea at any given moment worldwide and 12 million entering the U.S. annually, the financial cost of establishing effective continuing surveillance over container traffic on this scale will be considerable.[27] Building cooperative, participatory security relationships with the major global corporations to create effective "pre-screening" methods will take years. Developing new, cost-effective, tamper-proof control technologies and training qualified, responsible, intelligent, knowledgeable, and well-paid personnel to run such national control systems also is likely to take many years and a huge financial commitment. Canadian and American officials are evidently very reluctant to make the kind of financial and human resource commitments needed to begin to get a handle on a threat of such daunting dimensions.

Active defence against nuclear and biological weapons smuggling *automatically and unavoidably* would mean eliminating the narcotics traffic that currently flows through the container ports in both Canada and the United States. In Canada the domestic "guerrilla warfare" that would likely be triggered by such a frontal assault on the heart of the mini-empires of the biker gangs, Asian "snakehead" human smugglers, and Russian, Latino, and Italian-American drug runners is likely to be fierce. Any such campaign would *likely require a massive buildup of local police and RCMP* and the mobilization of much of our citizenry just to protect the Canadian political and bureaucratic leadership who dare to embark on this path of confrontational reform. A protracted civil "war" over control of the dockyards is not inconceivable — on both sides of the border. Victory in this war is, nevertheless, quite conceivable, but it would be financially and politically expensive. A new paramilitary force of at least 10,000 to 20,000 would have to be created in Canada and a force of at least ten times that size to secure the ports, coasts, and airspace approaches to the United States.[28]

The crisis of North American vulnerability is already well developed — although not completely "mature." The crisis probably arrived in point of fact sometime during the decade of the 1990s,[29] but it was only broadly recognized as such by American political authorities in the aftermath of September 11, 2001. Many American citizens, like most Canadians, continue to live in a state of ignorance about these threats — of firm psychological denial. In the meantime various terrorist organizations (and states who may wish to "sponsor" and assist them) have enjoyed, and will continue to enjoy, a "window of opportunity" for the emplacement of personnel (sleeper agents), the establishment of front companies or "foundations" to facilitate weapon preparation and use, and the actual shipment of key technologies and critical materials for WMD devices to be "pre-positioned" inside the modestly tightened but still quite permeable security perimeter of an illusory "Fortress North America." For American policymakers, as noted above, the threat precedent already exists for the prepositioning of nuclear explosive devices in North America, although it has not been widely publicized.[30] Some 40 to 80 of these suitcase bombs were said to have gone missing in post-Soviet Russia according to Russian political and military authorities (including the recently deceased former Soviet General Alexander Lebed, who used a figure of 100). The sale of some of these weapons to rogue state regimes or to radical Islamic or other internationally active terrorist groups, along with the technical means to maintain and use them, is unfortunately a serious risk that American policymakers have been forced grudgingly to acknowledge. The risk of similar transactions involving weaponized smallpox, drug-resistant anthrax, or other biological agents is also real.

Because of the now intense American anxiety about the inherent unreliability of any or all "homeland defence" measures (and because of strong political resistance to changing U.S. "lifestyles" and fears of massive civil disobedience against the intrusive new internal security measures that would otherwise be necessary), American strategic planners are left with the unpalatable and politically awkward option of pursuing and destroying potential attackers at source — that is to say, "preventively." Traditional, essentially passive non-proliferation measures premised on mutual reassurance through intrusive inspection, verification, and transparency measures, are no longer seen to be adequate to the crisis at hand — still less so in the long-term. Aggressive counter-proliferation has therefore become an unavoidable imperative in American strategic policy — unless a creative multilateral "diplomacy of constraint" can summon the ingenuity to come up with a creative new mixture based on active defences and enhanced deterrence.

The Bush Administration's reluctant and ultimately unsuccessful engagement with the UN Security Council in an effort to obtain an umbrella resolution to legitimate an American campaign to remove Saddam Hussein's government was certainly preferable to a sudden entirely unilateral attack launched by the U.S. and a "coalition of the willing." But because it failed, and because the relationship between the UN and the American occupying authority remains so tenuous, Washington has found it almost impossible to persuade other governments to commit peacekeeping troops to Iraq to help reestablish civil order. As of August 2003 only 21,700 "coalition" forces were deployed alongside the 139,000 American military personnel — in a country of some 24 million people.[31]

From the perspective of international arms control analysis, the 2003 U.S. attack on Iraq was not fundamentally concerned with either saving the Iraqi people from human rights violations or securing reliable supplies of inexpensive oil — just as the Gulf War of 1990–91 was not fundamentally concerned with the liberation of Kuwait. Domestic politics required public rationales consistent with American "idealist" principles: saving Kuwaitis from aggression and saving Iraqis from Saddam's tyranny became legitimating cover stories to allow the American military to achieve its core goal — the destruction of the alleged Iraqi WMD programs and in the end the destruction of Saddam's expansionist regime. Neither conflict can be convincingly explained as instances of "blood for oil." The need to keep Saddam Hussein's oil reserves constrained (the conquest of Kuwait by Saddam would have doubled his conventional reserves) and, more importantly, the need to imprison Iraq in permanent non-nuclear and non-biologoical weapons capable status (the indirect effect of keeping his revenues limited) were far more important and basic interests of American policy than upholding international legal norms.

Michael Mandelbaum noted correctly that the first Bush Administration "could not have rallied such extensive domestic and international support exclusively to eliminate Iraq's nuclear program." "Preventive war," he went on to say, "... has neither a basis in international law nor a well-established historical precedent."[32] Saddam's blunder in timing (seizing Kuwait before he had an operational nuclear arsenal) gave the U.S. government a winning pretext for *indirect* counter-proliferation via the overthrow of Iraqi aggression against Kuwait and the follow-on de-weaponization provisions of the armistice. Al-Qaida's blunder was one of attacking the U.S. far too lightly, rather than dealing the U.S. government a truly mortal wound such as a nuclear attack on Manhattan would have delivered. Losing "only" the World Trade Center and part of the Pentagon, instead of the southern end of the island of Manhattan, merely put the U.S. on alert, triggered American determination to exterminate their attackers, and galvanized American public opinion in support of the government. The Taliban in Afghanistan has been marginalized, Saddam's regime is in its "resistance" death throes, and no country will be a haven for training, fundraising or recruiting ever again.

In 1995 Mandelbaum speculated that "the next Hiroshima could create in American public opinion a consensus in favour of preventive war to keep the bomb out of the hands of rogue states." He also thought that that there was a possibility that it could trigger a reversion to isolationism: "From the next nuclear war Americans might learn to eschew political engagement in any part of the world where nuclear weapons are located or might be used."[33] It was impossible to predict, he then thought, which way the country would swing and thus the most important and defining event of the post-Cold War era had "not yet taken place." The "learning" from the next incident of nuclear use would of course be infinitely more compelling should it occur on North American territory. What that "lesson" would be, however, remains as unclear now as it was in 1995. President Bush's March 2003 attack on Iraq was to be the first "road test" of an intermittently aggressive hegemonic leadership by the U.S. of the twenty-first century's international political order. Over the past three years, Bush, his Secretary of State Colin Powell, and his National Security Advisor Condoleeza Rice have all denied that the U.S. would ever try to play the role of "globocop." But the Bush Administration's vision of a new national security strategy clearly posits some sort of guardianship role by the U.S. with respect to a broadly defined "WMD peace." Preventive wars are endorsed — "we recognize that our best defense is a good offense". The most important targets are defined: "terrorist organizations of global reach and any terrorist or state sponsor of terrorism which attempts to gain or use weapons of mass destruction [WMD] or their precursors." And finally, there is a clearly stated goal of securing and maintaining an open-ended military hegemony over all global would-be peer competitors — "Our forces will be strong enough to dissuade potential advesaries from pursuing a military build-up in hopes of surpassing, or equaling, the power of the United States."[34] Eliminating any WMD capability or residual WMD development efforts was the core reason for the two American wars on Saddam's Iraq.[35] Richard Perle, one of the foremost "hawks" in the Bush policy process until he stepped down as chair of the Defense Policy Board in early 2003, repeatedly asserted the overriding strategic need to deal with Iraq as the most dangerous of the named state supporters of international terrorism. He and others saw Iraq's destruction as the pivotal step in winning the international war on terrorism.[36]

The world has been fortunate thus far to have been spared the experience of terrorist WMD warfare. In a world of large and growing asymmetries of power and wealth, however, the attractiveness of such methods may be growing, and certainly the temptation to use such instruments of warfare may be growing powerfully as well. The versatility of terrorist WMD warfare is clear: it is relevant for all types of war.

(1) It is a technique available to transnational organizations who may have no territorial home or base and may, in fact, be hostile to the territorial authorities where there command structure resides. (2) It is a strategic instrument available to governments as well who may be subject to coercive threats from a powerful state and who may see no other option but covert efforts to degrade severely the capabilities of their main adversary. (3) It is a strategic option for great powers (for example, both Russia and China) who may feel that they are losing ground in the conventional RMA arms race and who need an asymmetric offset to be able to deter American attack or perhaps defeat it by preemptive or preventive terrorist WMD attacks of their own.

For the most part, Canadians do not seem to understand how much the events of 9/11, "America's second Pearl Harbor," have had on the the psychology of the American political elite. Polls indicate that a large majority of Canadians believe that, at the least, U.S. actions "caused" or helped to cause the 9/11 attacks. Many may also believe that the U.S. government massively overreacted to the attacks in invading and overthrowing Saddam's regime and that Americans have failed to confront the "root causes" of the present crisis across the Muslim world. Others think the "overreaction" is part of a strategy to build a new American Empire. American analysts are no doubt annoyed and shocked by what they see as the shallow, uncooperative responses of many allied governments — Canada included. In the case of Canada they see the country's withered and still shrinking military capabilities as evidence of a fundamental lack of seriousness about international security issues — a sort of blinkered self-marginalization that is characteristic of "immature" societies. That perception does not bode well for Canadian–American security cooperation or the exercise of any sort of moderating Canadian influence over American plans and actions.

From the American perspective, the 9/11 attacks were executed by a non-nationally based terrorist network with the probable connivance and support of several state authorities.[37] There is no doubt that the 2001 and 1993 attacks were intended to cause mass civilian fatalities numbering over 100,000 in New York, and gross economic disruption in the American financial capital and across the developed world. The Washington attack in 2001 clearly aimed to destroy much of the federal government — had the attacks lived up to their maximum expectations.[38] In that respect, both the attacks of 1993 and 2001 on the World Trade Center (and despite the fact that the towers were brought down the second time) were *relative failures*—at least when judged in light of their maximum goals. The Islamic extremists who planned the first attack on the World Trade Center towers that took place on 26 February 1993 hoped to kill as many as 200,000 people—a figure commensurate with the death toll from American atomic strikes on Hiroshima and Nagasaki.[39] For many American conservatives it is now an article of faith that the Clinton Administration committed one of its worst blunders in not pursuing the network of assistance behind the 1993 attack. Evidence of facilitative support from Iraq (production of false passports for some of the principals, possible training etc.) was not acted on. And thus terrorists abroad were de facto encouraged to believe that attempted acts of terror against the U.S. would "have no costs attached to them."[40]

For American analysts, the fact that Mohamed Atta and others in his group had inquired about cropduster flight training and the spraying capacity and operational range of these aircraft is a further indication that they were exploring a range of potential mass casualty methods that included chemical and biological warfare. Evidence from al-Qaida bases in Afghanistan suggests that although the organization had not yet acquired any dangerous biological or chemical materials, its senior officers were very interested in doing so.

Terrorism in the past that has been "domestic" and "revolutionary" was for the most part undertaken for measured, political goals that sought to build political support among the affected national population. Even would-be secessionists had a perceived stake in not alienating too deeply the population from whom they sought independence. Eventually they would be neighbours and economically interdependent. Thus in the past there have been clear limits that terrorist organizations applied to their own operations out of perceived political self-interest. Public opinion in target communities was meant to be shifted incrementally into an acceptance of a changed status quo. It was not intended to be plunged into desperate fear or blind hatred; too much of an impact would cause target governments to respond fiercely and repressively. European left-wing terrorists from Ireland to Germany to Italy operated under an awareness that violence could be excessive and counter-productive. Furthermore, such organizations in the past had to be careful not to alienate their own membership — which could occur were they to consider biological weapons attacks on civilian populations. In brief, "traditional" revolutionary terrorists have wanted to overthrow and replace existing governments, not destroy the countries they wished to "liberate." Similarly, violent secessionists have usually hoped to achieve independence with only that amount of violence that will win a war of attrition against superior military capabilities.

However, the "new" international terrorism aimed at the United States and American "Jewish-Crusader" allies from the Islamic political extremists is of a very different character. After September 11, American leaders drew the reasonable conclusion that *anything* is conceivable in the way of punitive assaults on the United States — up to and including nuclear or biological attacks on American cities.[41] Claims that some self-imposed constraints on international terrorists may still be in play are no longer persuasive. Most Canadians do not seem to have understood fully these developments and their strategic and foreign policy implications.

Modern societies are extremely vulnerable to disruption and the inflicting of mass casualties. The very limited use of anthrax powder in the autumn of 2001 was apparently the work of an American citizen, possibly an employee of an American biowarfare research laboratory. The economic disruption that it achieved was massively disproportionate to the minimal effort used to carry it out. Those responsible remain at large. Furthermore, the John Allen Muhammad "D.C. sniper" case of October 2002 demonstrated graphically that an off-the-shelf rifle can be used with great effect to generate massive social dislocation and demoralization. As John McCain summed up the situation, "Even if the sniper isn't connected to al-Qaida he's showing our vulnerability."[42]

The fascination of American "hawks" with Iraq was very puzzling to many Canadian observers — especially because Iraq was thought to be some one to five years from actually possessing nuclear weapons while the "crazy state" of North Korea almost certainly already has several of them. Why the apparent double standard? Oil? Israel?

The answer is yes to the last two questions — but it is more complicated than simply trying to maintain the economic prosperity of key allies dependent on oil, or protecting the security of Americans'

Israeli allies. For the Bush policy team, of the three named "axis of evil" states, Iraq is far and away of greatest strategic concern because of Baghdad's continuing progress towards rebuilding its nuclear and biological arsenal, and the consequent menace that this creates towards the world's largest reservoirs of exportable oil. An independent Iraqi biological and nuclear weapons capability, or both, would raise the risk of an Iraqi–Israeli war in which nuclear weapons might be used with devastating human, environmental and economic consequences.[43] The developed world's economies can live without Iraqi oil, but they cannot function without access to most of the Middle East's oil. A protracted global depression would likely ensue as part of the "adjustment cost" of a massive regional nuclear war.

Even if Saddam indicated that he had no desire destroy Israel, an Iraq growing in power via conquest and technology imports would be seen to be an unacceptable risk to Israeli survival. Preventive or preemptive attacks on Iraq and its WMD sites and its suspected nuclear and biological research and production complexes might be seen as the least evil of several unattractive options, just as was the case with respect to the Osirak reactor attack by the Israelis in 1981. But in 2002 the Iraqi nuclear sites were thought to be scattered at scores of locations, many of them in populated areas. Unlike the Osirak reactor, many weapon-making complexes were thought to be buried deeply underground and are susceptible to destruction only via nuclear strikes. Thus a full-scale Israeli suppressive attack on Iraqi WMD sites might well be indistinguishable from an effort to annihilate the Iraqi civilian population. Certainly any such comprehensive attack would be perceived across the Arab world in those terms, regardless of any Israeli efforts to reduce the "collateral damage" to civilian life. Even the more limited threats of nuclear use (extensive Israeli neutron bomb attacks, for example, on potential SCUD launching zones in western Iraq)[44] said to have been articulated by Ariel Sharon in February of 2001 as he was assuming the role of Prime Minister could lead to perceptions of Israeli acts of genocide across the Middle East, if not world wide.[45]

Canadian Political Inertia and the Long-Term Outlook

Canadians are not prepared for either the "war on terrorism" or a new era of possible WMD terrorist warfare. Major new security expenditures are essential for

- improved border security and internal surveillance and security intelligence analysis,
- significantly expanded military reserves who have been trained and vaccinated appropriately so as to be able to administer medical quarantines,
- expansion of the regular Canadian Forces to at least 80,000 so that they can carry out existing tasks effectively and resume brigade level training, but also so that can carry out "force projection" operations in distant regions as part of American-led coalitions to suppress WMD development by small states and transnational terrorist organizations,
- re-equipment of the army, navy and airforce via new capital expenditure on the order of $6 billion per year (so as to be able to replace naval command ships and logistical support ships, naval helicopters, upgrade CF-18 fighter jets immediately with necessary avionics to restore full "interoperability" with U.S. units, buy or lease strategic airlift C-17s, and acquire all the new information technologies that our tactical units need to survive and win on twenty-first century battlefields),
- a dramatically expanded aid budget to assist in the rebuilding and economic and political stabilization of damaged countries in which "rogue" regimes have been deposed (Afghanistan and soon Iraq).

Are such measures likely? No, of course not. The Chrétien cuts to the military and aid budgets are unlikely to be altered much by a new Cabinet under Paul Martin. The Liberal Party continues to be dominated by those who believe that skilful "free riding" on American security expenditures makes far more sense. And it does make sense in terms of short-term party interests. Al-Qaida may well be a spent force and the next major terrorist incidents may stay at the level of "traditional" conventional explosives rather than nuclear or biological weapons attacks. In the medium to long term the future is far from bright, and a posture of permanent free riding is likely to be deeply prejudicial to Canadian national interests.

Thomas Homer-Dixon has suggested that the events of September 11 can best be seen as just the leading edge of a future wave of terror attacks from many parts of the globe against an inherently vulnerable civilization. Even if the "West" is not visited by WMD terrorist attacks, it may be hit repeatedly with paralyzing economic impact by "weapons of mass disruption." What radical political Islam might be able to accomplish, others might too. Electricity transmission lines and substations cannot be protected against determined low-tech sabotage (there are too many of them in North America's "third world energy grid") and they are presently vulnerable to cascading, system-wide disruptions from relatively small attacks. Thousands of miles of natural gas and oil pipelines are equally vulnerable and if sabotaged in large cities could cause mass casualties and major distress in winter months. Trains with toxic chemicals are easily derailed in urban as well as rural settings, and chemical plants themselves can be attacked directly. Grain terminals and train cars filled with grain in rural regions can be covertly poisoned with toxic or carcinogenic materials.[46] Homer-Dixon's central argument stresses that the long-term solution to the vulnerability inherent to excessive complexity, centralization, and urban density, is building in redundancy and rapid repair capabilities in complex transport, energy, and transmission systems. Over time economic activity and urban populations need to be much more broadly dispersed. In the short-term the sensationalizing tendencies of the media should be curbed by some form of regulatory oversight.[47]

These observations and recommendations may be very relevant for the long-term survival prospects of "lifeboat North America," but they do little to address the most acute risks of the current crisis. In the long term, Homer-Dixon is right that there is far more to worry about than the contemporary difficulties with radical political Islam and its various terrorist manifestations. In decades to come the attacks from the poor zones of the planet, the global "South," may well take the form he envisages — even if the U.S. is successful now in forcibly reversing the proliferation of WMDs. Future historians may one day look back at the

American campaign against Iraq as the first of the "North's" wars of industrial suppression of the impoversished and upstart elements in the "South." But getting to the "long term" is not going to be done easily.

Canadian–American relations are likely to be contentious and difficult for quite some time until the Canadian government can restore some degree of credibility as a significant actor with respect to international security issues. From defence spending to immigration and refugees, Washington leaders are going to want "harmonization" in policy that will surely be resisted in Ottawa — unless there is another major attack on a U.S. or Canadian city. Although many analysts of biological warfare are sceptical about the ability of terrorist organizations to handle biological agents effectively, the evidence continues to accumulate that more and more radical groups are very interested in this means of indiscriminate killing. If such groups were able to buy biological warfare agents on the black market or were able to obtain materials from some state regimes (Iraq, Iran, North Korea — each of which hired emigre Soviet biological warfare researchers), they could conceivably mount such attacks with devastating effect. The fact that since January 1, 2002, six countries have decided to follow the lead of the United States in rush orders for smallpox vaccine suggests that fears of biological warfare attack are gaining ground steadily.[48] Though the claim was later disavowed by U.S. General Tommy Franks, in late March 2002, American forces were said to have found "an al-Qaida biological weapons laboratory hidden in a mountain cave."[49] In November 2001 South Korean officials released estimates of North Korean chemical warfare and biological warfare agents as a stockpile of between 2,500 and 5,000 tons. The stockpile was said to include both smallpox and anthrax.[50] Up until two years ago, the North Korean military regularly gave all troops smallpox vaccine.

In sum, in a condition of extremely porous frontiers that will take a decade or longer to tighten effectively, with WMDs (both nuclear and biological weapons) proliferating to many rogue state regimes, and with few if any allies who can project military forces long distances, it seems highly likely that military unilateralism and aggressive counter-proliferation will characterize American policy for the next two decades. The dangers are too grave and too imminent for any U.S. administration to do much else, even if Bush were to lose the 2004 election. Even were there to be a shift in American willingness to support multilateral regimes, the diffusion of technology has gone too far to really lend itself anymore to institutional oversight and regulation. The United States and its allies may be headed for a very dark decade indeed. That is the real reason why Canadians should begin to take international security issues very seriously. While not at the bull's eye of the target for international terrorism, they are certainly in the "inner ring."

Notes

1 Francoise Ducros, Chrétien's communications director, was eventually compelled to resign for calling President Bush a moron during a private conversation with a CBC reporter that was overheard and reported by a *National Post* reporter. Chrétien initially refused to accept her resignation saying that he did not think it was "a major offence to the point that she should be fired." When the comment gained wide international publicity and further chilled the already difficult relations between Ottawa and Washington, Ducros had to step down. See Michael Friscolanti, "Iraq uses Canadian gaffe to criticize Bush, U.S. policy," *National Post,* 25 November 2002.

2 Gordon Gibson succinctly laid out the inner but publicly unstated logic of Chrétien's antagonism to any Canadian involvement in the Iraq intervention. With the Québec election to be held on 14 April 2003 (won by Charest's Liberals), it made perfect sense that a Canadian Prime Minister who had "almost lost Québec in 1995" would do almost anything to avoid giving Bernard Landry's PQ more ammunition both for the imminent election campaign and any subsequent referendum on secession. See Gibson's "Why Chrétien put us on the sidelines," *National Post,* 3 April 2003.

3 The Aum Shinri Kyo sect attempted several mass casualty attacks with nerve agents in Japan in 1994 and 1995. The largest attack on the Tokyo subway system on the morning of 20 March 1995 killed only some 12 people all told, although some 5,500 people were said to have been injured in the subway releases. See D.W. Brackett, *Holy Terror: Armageddon in Tokyo* (NY, Tokyo: Weatherhill, 1996). The sect clearly hoped to cause mass fatalities but failed badly in this respect. Had the sect's 10,000 Russian members been able to procure one of the missing Russian atomic "mines," the fatalities could have been over 100,000.

4 As the dominant state in global international security relations, the United States has inevitably become the lightning rod for those most alienated from the prevailing structures of political economy and international — mostly "Western" — culture norms. This condition is unlikely to change in the foreseeable future.

5 The CBC investigative report by the "Fifth Estate" of 30 October 2002 on the risk of bio-warfare attack highlighted continuing Russian duplicity and secrecy in developing a stockpile of many tons of offensively weaponized smallpox virus — some of which may still exist and which may also be in the hands of both North Korean and Iraqi scientists.

6 CBC Newsworld's presentation of "The Passzionate Eye" of 11 August 2003 ("Countdown to the Apocalypse") included 1997 interview footage with former Soviet (and then senior Russian) general, Alexander Lebed, in which he stated unequivocally that some 100 of 250 "suitcase" atomic bombs able to kill between 70,000 and 100,000 people in modern dense cities had disappeared. Lebed also declared that these weapons required no special arming codes or procedures to detonate them. Both a CIA analyst and a first-hand acquaintance of Osama bin Laden declared that al-Qaida had been able to acquire several of these "man portable" weapons by the late 1990s from Russian organized crime sources.

7 Seven months prior to the 9/11 attacks CIA director George Tenet outlined the risks to the U.S. arising from hard-to-monitor "secondary proliferation" of WMD technologies from Pakistan, Iran, and India in addition to the long-standing missile and nuclear technology exporting activities of China, North Korea, and Russia. See Robert Wall, "CIA Details Proliferation Concerns, Other Threats," *Aviation Week and Space Technology,* 12 February 2001.

8 The overthrow of Saddam's regime in March and April 2003 did little to heal the split within British politics over Iraqi policy, but Blair managed to survive both resignations from his Cabinet and venomous media attacks. The apparent suicide of a senior British security analyst who dissented from Blair's characterization of the Iraqi "threat" as imminent and leaked his dissent to the press added to the Prime Minister's domestic political troubles.

9 The most outspoken Canadian denunciation of American foreign policy aggression as the root cause of 9/11 was made by University of British Columbia women's studies professor Sunera Thobani who received a standing ovation from an Ottawa audience for declaring that U.S. foreign policy was "soaked in blood." Jane Taber, "500 cheer Thobani's critique," *National Post,* 2 October 2001. Almost a year later most Canadians seemed to agree with Thobani's assessment. 84 percent of respondents to a *Globe and Mail*/CTV poll said the U.S. bore some or all (69 percent some, 15 percent all) of the responsibility for the 9/11 attacks. Only 14 percent said

the U.S. had no responsibility at all. Shawn McCarthy, "Majority thinks U.S. partly to blame for Sept. 11," *Globe and Mail,* 7 September 2002. At the same time 61 percent of Canadians polled by Sun Media/Leger believe Canada will be the target of an attack, with 91 percent believing the U.S. would be struck again. Rob Granatstein, "Canada a terror target: poll," *London Free Press,* 6 September 2002. Only 39 percent of those polled felt Canadian security measures were adequate. Notwithstanding the view that the U.S. government bore some or all of the responsibility for causing 9/11, Canadians supported participation in the American led war on terrorism by a 2 to 1 ratio, while 80 percent of those polled were "very" or "somewhat" satisfied with the Canadian Forces" military performance in Afghanistan; see Rob Granatstein, "Canadian troops lauded," *London Free Press,* 7 September 2002.

10 The New York Stock Exchange announced a year after the 9/11 attacks that [it] would establish a site for a second trading floor sufficiently far from New York city so as to be able to survive a nuclear attack—at least 40 kilometres from south Manhattan. See Peter Morton, "NYSE seeks floor at safe "nuclear distance," *National Post,* 14 September, 2002. Senator Charles Schumer (Dem., NY) the same week called for an urgent billion dollar investment in nuclear detection devices for U.S. ports and border entry points: "The atomic bomb that exploded above Hiroshima was simple: two hemispheres of weapons-grade uranium were smashed together, instantly creating a critical mass that released a blast of energy comparable to ... 15,000 tons of TNT. It was such a basic device that the scientists at Alamogordo felt no need to test it. No one doubts that today's terrorist groups have the technical expertise to make such a device. Worse still, they could smuggle such a bomb into our country not by plane, or missile but, like a Trojan horse, in one of the tens of thousands of large cargo containers that enter our ports and cross our borders daily." What the terrorists need is some 110 pounds of weapons-grade uranium for each device. Charles E. Schumer, "Terror's Trojan Horse," *New York Times,* 14 September 2002.

11 Scrutiny of the al-Qaida bases in Afghanistan during early 2002 indicated the beginnings of an effort to acquire such destructive technologies. See also comments by various Russian journalists and security analysts in "Countdown to the Apocalypse" on "The Passionate Eye," CBC Newsworld, 11 August 2003.

12 Since September 2001, the U.S. Coast Guard was instructed to screen all crew of commercial ships coming to American ports. Ninety-six hours notice must now be given of arrival, not 24 and the names of all crew members must be supplied. Some 200 to 300 ships arrive per day with 20 to 30 crew each—up to 9,000 names per day are generated. The Coast Guard (CG) staff, however, frequently cannot read the languages of the

faxed forms containing the names. They have no way of verifying whether the names are valid, nor whether the passports of crew, when inspected, are authentic or forged. Coast Guard offices have no access to the databases kept by the FBI, the Customs Service, the Immigration and Naturalization Service, or the CIA. "Suspicious names" are thus merely relayed on to these organizations for comment. Comments are often received well after the ship has arrived in port. CG staff have no training or special equipment for identifying chemical, biological, nuclear or radiological weapons. Obtaining such equipment across the fleet of CG units is thought to be one to two years away. The Inter-Agency Border Inspection System database has thousands of names but poor record keeping and a huge backlog of unentered names continues to produce Justice Department criticism of the system managers. CG staff are trained to search for drugs, not terrorists or their weaponry. The CG personnel as a matter of policy rarely board container ships because of an inability to get at most of the containers that "are stacked six-deep and -wide, and so gaining access to many of them is impossible until they are unloaded, even though containers may hold terrorists or weapons of mass destruction...." See Joel Brinkley, "Coast Guard Encounters Big Hurdles In New Effort to Screen Arriving Ships," *New York Times,* 16 March 2002.

13 James Dao, "U.S. Vulnerability to Terror is Still High, Panel Concludes," *New York Times,* 26 October 2002; and James Dao, "Report Finds U.S. Unprepared for Next Terrorist Attack," *New York Times,* 25 October 2002.

14 Paul Krugman, "Thanks for the M.R.E.'s," *New York Times,* 12 August 2003. At most three percent of Canadian cargo containers are physically inspected or X-rayed and only half of those see "de-stuffing" teams actually unload and scrutinize contents. The choice of which containers to unpack is "intelligence driven." In the U.S. the average inspection ratio is close to two percent nationally with de-stuffing activity at less than half the rate in Canada. See "CSMP" Report, p. 49.

15 A majority of American police, firefighters, and school safety officers polled in June and July 2003 in 40 cities felt that measures taken since 9/11 were inadequate. Schools remained "soft targets," hazardous materials procedures and planning remained confused, hazardous materials equipment remained appropriate for industrial accidents, not chemical or bio-terror attacks. Philip Shenon, "Two Studies Cite Confusion on Terrorism," *New York Times,* 21 August 2003.

16 Robert Pear, "Gore Calls U.S. Vulnerable To More Bioterror Attacks," *New York Times,* 25 October 2002. Health officials indicated that the Bush Administration was nonetheless on track for having 160 million new doses of smallpox vaccine "by 2003."

17 That has been a recurrent theme in Osama bin Laden's various communications via Aljazeera television and elsewhere. See for example, Reuel

Marc Gerecht, "The Gospel According to Osama Bin Laden," *The Atlantic Monthly*, January 2002. Bin Laden has also emphasized American use of atomic bombs against Japan repeatedly in what seems a clear recommendation that similar retribution should be visited upon the United States itself. Other Islamic extremists involved in the 1993 first attack on the World Trade Center hoped to kill up to 200,000 also cited fatalities in Hiroshima and Nagasaki as justification. Bin Laden's communications in the late 1990s often referred to 600,000 Iraqi children allegedly killed because of Western and UN sanctions.

18 See "Defence of North America: A Canadian Responsibility" (Report of the Standing Senate Committee on National Security and Defence, Hon. Colin Kenny as Chair), First Session, Thirty-Seventh Parliament, (September 2002), p. 23. Cited hereafter as "DNACR" Report.

19 See for example Michael Mandelbaum, "Lessons of the Next Nuclear War," *Foreign Affairs*, vol. 74 no. 2 (March/April 1995), 22–37.

20 Awareness of this need for a "crisis" to create a permissive public opinion led many inclined towards conspiracy thinking to believe that there was active collaboration in the 9/11 attacks by elements within the U.S. government itself, most notably the CIA. In this view, one that is articulated fairly commonly in Canadian "grass roots" discussions, the early scattered warnings of possible hijackings of airliners received by the FBI and CIA now being investigated by American legislative bodies were not evidence of bureaucratic incompetence but rather of a strategic conspiracy that hoped to obtain a *carte blanche* permission from the American public to wage war at home and abroad on all targets of opportunity. The proposition that American officials knowingly suppressed information that would put tens of thousands of American lives at risk is simply unsupportable without "smoking gun" evidence of such conspiratorially coordinated inaction. To day such evidence is lacking.

21 Within days of the September 11 attack American analysts were asserting that terrorist mass murder was now the "weapon of choice" of groups like Osama bin Laden's al-Qaida. Senator Sam Nunn pointed out that in 1998 bin Laden had declared that acquiring weapons of mass destruction was "a religious duty." Because such groups existed without territorial homes or headquarters the threat of retaliation was impossible. See Paul Mann, "Terrorist Mass Murder: New 'Weapon of Choice,'" *Aviation Week and Space Technology*, 17 September 2001.

22 The Aum Shinri Kyo cult in Japan is said still to have several tens of thousands of Russian adherents, some of whom might be able to acquire Russian WMD "special materials" through bribery.

23 Mearsheimer's pessimism about the tragically inevitable propensity of great powers to struggle for hegemonic dominance which in turn leads to recurrent wars led to his recommendation in the autumn of 2002 that

the U.S. retrench in its security involvements around the world while at the same time recognizing that the Chinese government is in fact the only potential long-term credible peer competitor of the U.S. Accordingly it was Mearsheimer's view that Washington should do whatever was possible to retard Chinese economic and scientific development. See his views outlined on China in John J. Mearsheimer, "The Future of the American Pacifier," *Foreign Affairs*, vol. 80 n. 5 (September/October 2001). For his wider perspective on the logic of American policy as he sees it, go to his *The Tragedy of Great Power Politics* (New York, London: Norton, 2001), esp. chapter 10.

24 This fourth path for international terrorist triggering of massive nuclear use is unlikely to remain confined to the Russo-American relationship. Either the Indian or Pakistani governments (or both) might resort to building their own versions of a Dead Hand launch system, as might Chinese leaders if they fear that American missile defence capabilities may be about to threaten their own very limited retaliatory abilities.

25 In Canada the disbanding of the Ports Canada Police after 1996 allegedly has led to a proliferation of criminal elements on the docks and created a situation ripe for exploitation by terrorists. The ostensible reason for the disbandment was federal debt reduction, but "the port police service cost the federal government approximately $10 million per year, which was entirely recouped by levies against the maritime port operators." Local police forces, the RCMP and "private security companies" were to be tasked with the responsibility for overseeing ports security. But local forces lacked the personnel and training, while the RCMP was being reduced in size at approximately same time. See James Baxter, "Liberals Ignored Warnings," *National Post*, 18 March 2002. In the port of Vancouver Canada Customs officials told Senate committee investigators that "they are often subjected to intimidation as they inspect containers and reported that the Hell's Angels is the dominant criminal influence within the Port." The Port authority hires and screens only 121 of the 27,000 people working on Port property and "companies which lease Port property are free to screen or not screen their employees as they choose." In Halifax the situation is no better. RCMP Chief Superintendent Ian Atkins told the Senate committee that "container terminals are the favourite target of organized criminal activity" because Customs staff check so few of the containers. In a sample of 500 longshoremen in Halifax who were investigated by the RCMP, 39 percent had criminal records. For a sample in the Port of Charlottetown 54 percent had criminal records. According to the Committee, "through the biker gangs, organized crime had strong links to the major ports of Québec, Ontario, and British Columbia." See "Canadian Security and Military Preparedness" (Report of the Standing Senate Committee on National Security and Defence, Hon. Colin Kenny as Chair), First Session,

Thirty-Seventh Parliament, (February 2002), pp. 45–48. Cited hereafter as "CSMP " Report.

26 Critics of lax immigration procedures assert that over the past decade some 10,000 refugee claims in Canada were rejected with 2,600 "abandoned" and 2,000 voluntarily withdrawn. Immigration officials have not been able to manage to keep track of this pool of some 140,000 people. Neither have they been able to say what happened to some 20,000 self-declared refugees who never appeared for their first hearing. See Diane Francis, "Canada gets well-deserved snub," *National Post,* 22 September 2001.

27 Some 12 million maritime containers entered the U.S. in the year 2000, as did 11.5 million trucks, 2.2 million railway cars, 829,000 aircraft and 211,000 ships. A new customs/security constabulary of some 200,000 people would be needed to undertake thorough searches of such traffic volumes according to one sympathetic observer. See remarks of Robert Jackson, "Open Borders and Security," keynote address to the BCPSA meeting, 3 May 2002.

28 Robert Jackson's estimate of the number of new inspectors who would be needed to control American ports. BCPSA keynote address, May 2002.

29 One of the most succinct and accurate warnings to the American political elite was given by Richard Betts in his article "The New Threat of Mass Destruction," *Foreign Affairs,* vol. 77 no. 1 (Jan/Feb 1998), 26–41.

30 Joseph C. Anselmo, "Defector Details Plan to Plant Nukes in U.S.," *Aviation Week and Space Technology,* 17 August 1998. A former Soviet military intelligence operative who defected to the United States gave detailed testimony (under condition of anonymity and with a mask over his head) in August of 1998 to an American Congressional committee about the task he was assigned during the last years of Soviet governance (between 1988 and 1991) to identify a "safe house" for the storage of golf-bag sized nuclear devices for use in the Washington area by Soviet commandos. The former agent recounted plans to deploy "suitcase bombs" about the size of a golf bag. American Atomic Demolition Munitions typically had yields of several tens of kilotons, although according to Roger Molander American engineers tried but failed to create a 100 pound device with a 100 kiloton yield (the salience of round numbers). He claims that for this yield they never got the weight below 150 pounds. The former GRU colonel stated he did not know if weapons were ever in fact smuggled into the U.S., but he did identify a safe house in the Shenendoah region of northern Virginia, "an ideal location to stash covert weapons because of its proximity to Washington and its sparse population." Estimates of the number of missing Soviet-era suitcase bombs vary between 40 and 80. Several Russian politicians and former military personnel have attested to the "loss" of such weaponry. Any such Soviet era devices may be "only" pure fission

devices of but 5 to 15 kilotons yield. The yield of the Hiroshima bomb was some 10 to 14 kilotons.

31 Steven R. Weisman and Felicity Barringer, "U.S. Will Ask UN for Move to Widen the Force in Iraq," *New York Times,* 21 August 2003.

32 Mandelbaum, "Lessons," p. 36.

33 Ibid., p. 37.

34 See "The National Security Strategy of the United States of America," September 2002 available at the White House website: http://www.whitehouse.gov. Accessed 22 August 2003.

35 For a further elaboration of these arguments, see "National Strategy to Combat Weapons of Mass Destruction," December 2002, available at the U.S. government White House website: http://www.whitehouse.gov/news/releases/2002/12/WMDStrategy.pdf. Accessed 22 August 2003.

36 Perle declared to a Foreign Policy Research Institute dinner on 14 November 2001 that the Iraqis tried to assassinate George H.W. Bush in 1993, that they facilitated the first World Trade Center bombing attempt that same year, and that Iraqi stockpiles of anthrax could easily be disseminated to international terrorist networks for anonymous delivery in the U.S. See "Next Stop Iraq: Remarks of the Hon. Richard Perle" to the FPRI annual dinner, distributed by the FPRI on 30 November 2001 and posted thereafter on their website: http://www.fpri.org. Cited hereafter as "Next Stop Iraq."

37 See William Safire who repeatedly claimed there was clear evidence provided by the Czech intelligence service (the B.I.S.) regarding a meeting between the September 11 gang leader Mohammed Atta and Iraq's chief intelligence agent in Prague Ahmed al-Ani in April 2001. William Safire, "Protecting Saddam," *New York Times,* 18 March 2002; see also William Safire, "Tracing Saddam's links with Osama bin Laden," *New York Times,* 23 October 2001. A year later this claim was cast into doubt by Czech authorities who asserted that they could not confirm that any such meeting occurred, and that Czech intelligence officials had no definite proof of such a meeting. James Risen, "Prague discounts an Iraqi meeting," *New York Times,* 21 October 2002.

38 The hijackers of the airliner that crashed in Pennsylvania are thought to have been on a mission to bomb the Capitol itself and to kill as many American legislators as possible, thus throwing the federal government into chaos.

39 Explosives experts have estimated that if the fertilizer based materials had been stacked optimally inside the vehicle, and if the truck had been slightly better positioned in the underground parking garage of the tower, the ensuing blast would have sheared off enough of the supports on one side of the tower base to cause it to collapse and fall sideways into the other tower, bringing them both down in seconds, with no opportunity for anyone to evacuate either building. At noon — as opposed to 8:45 AM local

time — there would have been some 50,000 working in the two towers with some 50,000 visitors. The other 100,000 fatalities are the estimate of those who would have been killed in adjacent structures, people for whom there would have been no time for evacuation. Mahmoud Abouhalima, currently serving a prison sentence in California, in his effort to justify terror bombings against Americans by Islamic radicals, pointed to the atomic bombing of Japan as an example of American terrorism. His interview remarks are quoted at length by Mark Juergensmeyer, *Terror in the Mind of God* (Berkeley, L.A., London: Univ. of Calif. Press, 2000), chapter 4, "Islam's Neglected Duty," p. 63. So too did Osama bin Laden in the first video tape played by Aljazeera television. According to a Canadian diplomat, a recent poll in the U.S. found that some 70 percent of Americans cannot identify "Hiroshima" when asked to comment on its significance.

40 This argument is made regularly by Perle in public fora.

41 See for example the comments by Donald Rumsfeld and John Ashcroft in James Dao, "Defense Secretary Warns of Unconventional Attacks," *New York Times,* 1 October 2001. Henry Hyde, then chair of the House International Relations committee is quoted as saying that biological warfare agents "scare" him more than nuclear weapons because they can be smuggled "rather easily."

42 As quoted by Frank Rich, "What al-Qaida Learned in D.C.," *New York Times,* 26 October 2002.

43 Israel is typically credited with between 100 and 300 nuclear warheads, including some of advanced design and relatively low yield ("neutron bombs" or enhanced radiation weapons). For data on the Israeli capability see the website of the Federation of American Scientists at http://www.fas.org.

44 Sharon reportedly told Lt.-Gen. Shaul Mofaz, Israeli chief of staff, to prepare for pre-emptive attack on potential Iraqi missile launch sites: "Resurrecting and developing plans from the Gulf War, Sharon threatens to deploy tactical neutron bombs to "wipe out" the launch zone in the event that intelligence reports say a non-conventional weapons attack by Iraq is imminent. . . ." The presumable military value of neutron warhead detonations at altitude over a very large area is that it would generate a very powerful electromagnetic pulse able to burn out electrical circuits on an Iraqi missiles being prepared for launch. The same report also cites claims by two "former senior scientists in the Iraqi nuclear programme" and a third defector who was a former aide to Uday Hussein, that Iraq conducted two small nuclear tests in September 1989 in a cavern hollowed out beneath Lake Rezzaza. See Uzi Mahnaimi and Tom Walker, "Defectors say Iraq tested nuclear bomb," *The Sunday Times*, 25 February 2001; as at http://www.sunday-times.co.uk/news/pages/sti/2001/02/25/stifgnmido3001.html
Lt.-Gen. Mofaz was reported as saying later that Iran was in fact closer to achieving an operational nuclear capability than Iraq. See Alexander

Rose, "Chasing Nukes in the Middle East," *The National Post*, 5 March 2001; as at http://www.nationalpost.com/search/story.html?f=/stories/20010305/492027.html

45 Mahnaimi and Walker, ibid.

46 Thomas Homer-Dixon, "The Rise of Complex Terrorism," *Foreign Policy* (January/February 2002), 52–62.

47 Ibid., pp. 61–62.

48 William J. Broad and Judith Miller, "Others Follow U.S. on Smallpox Vaccine," *New York Times*, 25 April 2002. In early April the British government ordered 30 million doses of vaccine, Israel some six million, Germany six million, France three million, Ireland 600,000, Greece 150,000 and Russian authorities are now discussing nation-wide vaccination. In March of 2000 the Canadian and U.S. defence departments agreed to collaborate in developing a new generation of smallpox vaccine for military use. This same report noted a 1994 U.S. Defense Intelligence Agency report that cited a report that Russian authorities had shared smallpox technology with Iraq and North Korea. The Russians reportedly have created significant stocks of smallpox powder that is ideal for BW terrorist usage. Smallpox is but one of more than a dozen extremely virulent diseases that have been "weaponized" over the past twenty-five years. Former Soviet researchers, some of whom have found their way to Iraq, Iran, and North Korea, developed strains of anthrax and plague that were wholly resistant to any known antibiotics. Brucellosis too was weaponized, and it is known that Iraq developed its own unique contribution to the world's biological warfare stockpiles by creating aflatoxin agents that are combined with tear gas. They cause liver cancer in a high percentage of those exposed, especially in children. Iraqi efforts in building up a large stockpile of weapons grade anthrax (at least 8,000 litres) and botulinus toxin prior to the Gulf War did not diminish during the UNSCOM era; they merely went underground.

49 Michael Petrou, "US Forces find al-Qaida weapons lab," *National Post*, 23 March 2002. An unnamed British source said that the organization had acquired both a chemical and biological weapons capability. Evidence was also found of plans for using radiological weapons, prior to acquiring nuclear weapons. The highest ranking captured al-Qaida leader, Abu Zubaydah, claimed that the organization is close to building a crude atomic device and would try to smuggle it into the U.S. See Philip Shenon, "Qaeda Leader Said to Report A-Bomb Plans," *New York Times*, 23 April 2002.

50 Don Kirk," South Korea: Warning on North's Germ Supplies," *New York Times*, 21 November 2001.

References

Anselmo, J. C. (1998). Defector Details Plan to Plant Nukes in U.S. *Aviation Week and Space Technology.*

Betts, R. (1998). "The New Threat of Mass Destruction." *Foreign Affairs* 77(1): 26–41.

Homer-Dixon, T. (2002). "The Rise of Complex Terrorism." *Foreign Policy.*

Huntington, S. P. (1962). Guerrilla Warfare in Theory and Policy. *Modern Guerrilla Warfare*. F. M. Osanka. Glencoe, Free Press.

Juergensmeyer, M. (2000). *Terror in the Mind of God*. Berkeley, L.A., London, University of California Press.

Kenny, C. (2002). Report of the Standing Senate Committee on National Security and Defence: Defence of North America: A Canadian Responsibility, First Session, Thirty-Seventh Parliament.

——. (2002). Report of the Standing Senate Committee on National Security and Defence: Canadian Security and Military Preparedness, First Session, Thirty-Seventh Parliament.

Mandelbaum, M. (1995). "Lessons of the Next Nuclear War." Foreign Affairs 74(2): 22–37.

Mearsheimer, J. J. (2001). *The Tragedy of Great Power Politics*. New York, London, Norton.

United States (2002). National Strategy to Combat Weapons of Mass Destruction. Washington, White House.

——. (2002). The National Security Strategy of the United States of America, available at the White House website: http://www.whitehouse.gov/nsc/nssall.html. Accessed 22 August 2003.

4

Ontological Insecurity and the Politics of Fear

Samir Gandesha

It is hardly deniable that what has characterized the politics of so-called advanced industrialized societies since the last quarter of the twentieth century is a shattering of the consensus that was forged at the end of the Second World War (cf. Drache and Gertler 1991). Since the oil crisis and the socio-economic crises that it left in its wake, this consensus has come increasingly unraveled. In the Canadian context, the post-war consensus on the centrality of Keynesian macro-economic policies and its various social, legal and political offshoots, was not fundamentally challenged, as it was in Britain, by an established party, but by a new political party whose seeds lay deep within the alienation experienced by the western provinces. It grew under the leadership of Preston Manning as the Reform Party, which gave way to the Canadian Alliance Party and finally conquered resistance to amalgamation with the old Progressive Conservatives with the formation of the Conservative Party of Canada under Alliance leader Stephen Harper in 2004.

The Canadian New Right can be defined in terms of its economic and social agendas, which, admittedly, have not always been easily reconciled. Indeed, one could argue that the two twin aspects of its agenda are deeply contradictory, reflecting geographical as much as ideological differences (Gandesha 2000). The economic agenda is based on economic liberalism comprised of a series of measures including a reduction in personal and corporate income tax rates, the privatization of social services and deregulation. In sum, the economic agenda of the New Right involves a redoubled commodification of those services that had been provided by the welfare state within the context of a redistributive concept of "social citizenship."

The social agenda of the New Right involves a pervasive disciplining and policing of civil society with a particular emphasis on public spaces.[1] It also involves a particular targeting of lesbian and gay communities as well as, increasingly, targeting youth (Gandesha 2002) on the basis of a religiously grounded conception of morality. While in the economic realm, individuals are set loose as unrestricted consumers of products and services, in the realm of the social, they are increasingly policed by ever more pervasive forms of moral regulation. It is the social agenda of the New Right in Canada that provides particular insight into its core political philosophy, for the attacks on lesbian and gay communities, while driven in the first instance by fundamentalist Christian beliefs not unlike those motivating the White House and the U.S. Attorney General, are part of a larger agenda to rollback the history of struggles for the recognition of difference (cf. Taylor 1994; Honneth 1995; and Kymlicka 1996).[2]

As Steve Patten (1999a & b) has argued, the New Right's agenda has focused on transforming Canadian political discourse, particularly in relation to questions of citizenship and national identity, in such a way as to move away from a recognition of distinct identities, Québec, First Nations, multiculturalism, etc., in the direction of a form of unreconstructed universalism that, erected upon possessive individualism, is centred on the idea of the abstract or formal equality of persons before the law. Such a shift in Canadian political discourse is, in effect, a shift from social and cultural citizenship towards a Thatcherite notion of active citizenship; in effect, the collapsing of citizen and rate-payer.

The Canadian New Right seeks to resolve the contradiction between the economic and social axes of its agenda by virtue of a discourse of "safety" or "security" as was exemplified in Ontario by the drafting of legislation entitled the "Safe Streets Act" (Gandesha, 2002). That is to say, the various forms of insecurity—what I shall refer to provisionally as "ontological insecurity" following Giddens — economic, political, social etc., are resolved by way of a disciplinary logic, that is, as mentioned above, by a redoubled moral regulation of behaviour, in particular, regulation of those forms of heterogeneity that challenge the hegemonic, corporate normative order. Such an agenda is philosophically underwritten by the "fixing-broken-windows" approach to criminality articulated by James Q. Wilson in the 1980s (Gandesha 2002). Such a preoccupation with the insecurity unleashed by the logic of globalization has not been caused, but certainly exacerbated and deepened, by the attacks of September 11, 2001.

This chapter seeks to throw additional light on the New Right in Canada by focusing on the corresponding rise in Europe of Right Populist discourse. By casting a glance at the European example, we might hope to gain unique perspective on the Canadian context precisely because of the differences between the two experiences. In direct contrast to the Canadian context, and by extension one could argue the U.S. experience, in Europe, right populist discourse does not proceed by seeking to articulate a challenge to the politics of consensus by the assertion or reassertion of a formally universalist discourse. Rather, what this paper seeks to show is the manner in which New Right discourse in Europe, particularly in France, takes the form of what could be called a radical particularism. If the formal universalism of Canadian New Right discourse can be said to exclude by including, that is, by arguing that those who have differential claims to citizenship, as in the case of First Nations or Québécois, should, in fact, be treated the same and hence unequally, then in the European case, one could argue, right populism proceeds more directly. Indeed, as McBride shows in his contribution to this volume, Canadian elites are in the process of taking leave of nationalism. In Europe, despite or perhaps *because* of the expansion of the European Union, national, ethnic and regional identities are assuming renewed importance. In the European context, the strategy of the right is, to be blunt, to exclude by excluding, by "inventing" the national community — the "people" — in exclusionary terms.[3] What this paper seeks to suggest is that the exclusionist nature of Right populist discourse invents the "people" by transforming those who are not originally members of the national or regional community, that is to say, "strangers," into the enemies who must be expurgated.

It has become almost a cliché that globalization embodies a logic in which borders of every kind are radically called into question. As was said with rare perspicuity by the current U.S. President, after the attacks of September 11th, 2001, foreign policy has become domestic policy. In other words, by virtue of recent events, the border between the domestic and the foreign — perhaps the central binary opposition in the study of politics — has been *deconstructed*. The consequence of such a deconstruction was vividly brought home by Thomas Friedman, author of *The Lexus and the Olive Tree* (2000), who argued recently that the Bush administration ought to set aside its preoccupation with Iraq for the moment and direct more of its attention to "stop the slide of over there into over here."

Nowhere has the border between the "foreign" and the "domestic" been posed more dramatically and directly than in the recent successes of political parties and social movements of the radical right that have been sweeping through Europe in the past twenty-four months. Indeed, it seemed last spring, from my vantage point in Berlin, as if these forces, some with direct links to fascist and neo-fascist movements (which I shall call "right-populist"), were posed to alter fundamentally the ideological map of Europe.

To mention only the most notable cases: In France, Jean-Marie Le Pen not only survived challenges to his authority by his erstwhile lieutenant, Bruno Megret, who subsequently left to form the Mouvement National Republicain, but managed to win an unprecedented 17 percent of the first poll in the Presidential Election, dealing a humiliating defeat to Socialist Prime Minister Lionel Jospin. While for the French political establishment and media, Le Pen's victory was a crisis for the Fifth Republic, it served only to highlight the shift of gravity already effected by Jörg Haider's Freiheitliche Partei Österreich (FPÖ) in Austria which in 1996 won 22 percent in a general election and three years later 27 percent. In Italy, after last year's election, media mogul Silvio Berlusconi included in his Forza Italia-led government, Gianfranco Fini and Umberto Bossi, leaders of the neo-fascist National Alliance and the xenophobic, anti-southern, anti-immigrant Lega Nord respectively. In Denmark, the Danish People's Party now plays a pivotal role in the coalition Government, as does a similarly rightist party in the coalition government in Norway. After the assassination of Pim Fortuyn, his

Lisjt Fortuyn Party took nearly one fifth of the seats in the May 2002 Dutch election.

Since that time, however, there have been numerous countervailing tendencies that show that the triumph of the far-right is far from being a *fait accompli*. In Sweden, the Social Democrats have managed to hang on to power and in Britain the local elections led only to a very moderate showing for a revamped, sanitized BNP which managed to win three seats in racially-polarized Burnley. More recently, the FPÖ has entered a crisis, not unlike that of the Canadian Reform/Alliance party last summer, over the question of tax cuts in the context of an unforeseen need to increase spending because of the floods, which, in turn, has brought about a fatal crisis in the coalition government. New elections have been called for November which do not augur well for the future of the party. In October in the Netherlands, the LPF became so divided that the Christian Democratic Prime Minister, Jan Peter Balkenende, saw no alternative other than to dissolve the government less than one hundred days after the elections. Most remarkably, however, in the recent general election in Germany, voters resoundingly rejected FDP which sought to fuse an exclusionary and anti-semitic discourse with a neo-liberal agenda of dismantling the German "Sozialstaat." Combined with the success of the Greens led by Joschka Fischer, it is possible to understand the German election as a tentative step in the direction of a more liberal conception of German identity.[4]

Despite these recent setbacks, right-populism will, I think, continue to play a pivotal role, if in many cases from the periphery, in the future of European politics. It must therefore be treated with the utmost seriousness in considering the future of a united Europe, indeed, a European Union that, by 2004, will expand to 25 member states. Looming in the background, of course, is the possible membership of a Turkey in which the Islamist Justice and Development Party will more than likely play a commanding role.

The aim of this paper is to begin constructing a theoretical model within which it might be possible to engage in an analysis not only of the structure of right-populist discourse but, also, of its appeal. Accordingly, the first section of this paper defends the concept of populism, yet suggests that, unlike most other analyses, this phenomenon must be viewed in a global frame. In the second section, I clarify the concept of globalization, which I understand as the accelerated inter-penetration of the local and the global that always already underlies modern experience. In the third section of the paper, I suggest that globalization radically intensifies the problem of "ontological security" or the basic individual and social parameters of identity. Next, I suggest that capitalizing on the accumulation and intensification of the anxiety resulting from the resulting ontological *insecurity*, right-populism, with all of its internal differences, can be understood as pursuing the same strategy: the translation of pervasive yet diffuse anxiety deepened by the effects of globalization into a determinate fear of a particular object around which various economic, political, cultural, corporeal anxieties can be said to coalesce. This object is the figure of the "stranger." In the concluding section, I reflect on the challenge of right-populist discourse for liberal-democratic regimes.

Populism

While the use of the term "populism" is fairly widespread in the media (see *Die Zeit* Spring–Summer 2002 and the *New York Times* of the same period) it is necessary to provide a conceptual definition of what is one of the most used and abused concepts of politics. Populism was adopted as the name of a political party in post-Reconstruction era United States that purported to defend the interests of the farmers against those the large combines, in particular the interests of the railways (Dubiel 2002). The term also refers to the political orientations of the Russian peasants or *narodniki* in the period just prior to the Russian Revolution (Kitching 1989). Populism as an ideology was the means by which the masses were incorporated into politics in a subordinate and dependent manner in the Latin American southern cone or the semi-periphery (cf. Mouzelis 1985). The term has also been used to characterize the ideology of the Social Credit Party in Alberta in the 1930s. More recently, the term "authoritarian populism" has been used by Stuart Hall, drawing upon the work of Ernesto Laclau, to analyze the phenomenon of Thatcherism as a way of simultaneously re-inventing or re-imagining the British nation within the wider project of transforming the British state (Laclau 1977; Hall 1988; Harrison 1995; Patten 1999).

It is the latter approach that I believe to be particularly important and useful. The central reason for that is populism's formal nature. Rather than understanding populism as a specific, substantive doctrine, Hall understands it in terms of a specific ideological and political (as opposed to economic) opposition between the "people" and the "power bloc." That opposition, moreover, cannot be understood as simply reducible to any given economic contradiction, for example, between labour and capital. The formal nature of this opposition enables us to assess the relative democratic or authoritarian nature of populism. In other words, this approach, while giving a specific account of populism as a discourse can also, at the same time, account for the very amorphousness of the concept. By the same token, its explanatory power is limited in as much as, like the Gramscian theory of hegemony upon which it based, it is confined to the specific contours of nation-popular discourses that are, more or less, articulated within the framework of a single social formation. But, as we have seen, the affinities shared by the various movements and parties actually transcend the nation-state and, in many ways, are responses to the crisis of the state (Betz and Immerfall 1998).

Moreover, despite its dependence upon a certain form of psychoanalysis — Lacanian psychoanalysis to be precise — for an understanding of how discrete, seemingly contradictory ideological elements are articulated into a coherent, potentially hegemonic constellation, this approach fails to examine the subjective preconditions of the success or failure of the appeal to collective identities. It can show how identities are invented within hegemonic struggles, yet cannot account for why certain identities exert greater power over the subjects to which it appeals than others. In other words, there is not enough attention paid to the inner, psychological aspects of identity. Identity is, for the most part, understood along the lines laid down by Althusser according to which subjectivity is a function of interpellation or the manner in which subjects are "hailed" by social institutions (Althusser 1971). In this account, then, populist discourses, like all ideological discourse provide opportunities for individuals to recognize themselves in various kinds of ways. What this approach misses, however, is the *affective* dimension of identification.

It could be argued that the tremendous challenge of populist discourses is that, at both individual and collective levels, they represent the attempt to address in a decisive manner the pervasive crisis of identity lying at the heart of the modern experience — a crisis that has only been exacerbated by the dynamics arising out of the deepening interpenetration of the global and the local which I will simply refer to by the unsatisfactory term "globalization." It should also be said, however, that the specific nature of this crisis will be determined by the specific historical and social context in which it presents itself. As Betz and Immerfall have recently argued, "the success of the radical right is above all a reflection of the psychological strain associated with the uncertainties produced by large-scale economic and socio-structural change" (1998:249). Yet, the authors provide neither a convincing account of the nature of these uncertainties nor of their relation to such "psychological strain." As a way of beginning to think about how we might address the question of "psychological strain," I shall suggest that right-populism emerges as a specific response to the undermining of ontological security within the context of globalization.

Globalization

If the concept of "populism" has been highly contested, then the same holds for the concept of "globalization." It is not my intention here to add yet another voice to an already cacophonous discussion surrounding this unusually fraught concept. Nonetheless, in very general terms we can understand globalization as involving important transformations at economic, cultural, and political levels:

- *Economic Level*: The creation of a global economy that operates as a single unit on real time on a planetary scale (Castells 2000: 101). It is characterized by the specific contradiction between the "space of flows" and the "space of places" (Castells 2000: 409).
- *Cultural Level*: The homogenization of culture, predominantly through U.S. cultural industries, leads to a countervailing eruption of particularistic, exclusionary forms of culture (Barber 1996).

- *Political level*: The undermining of the sovereignty of the nation-state from above and from below. Consequently, this has brought to the fore the representational crisis of liberal democratic institutions (Loch and Heitmeyer 2001).

Globalization can be said to involve a process of simultaneous *integration* and *fragmentation*. Yet, we need to be clear that globalization does not represent an entirely novel phenomenon but, rather, intensifies crucial tensions that were always already present within modernity itself.

There are those who view the de-territorializing logic of globalization to present unique opportunities for new forms of solidarity and the creation of new emancipatory identities. For example, in *Empire*, a book that has been called the "*The Communist Manifesto* for our time" (even though it is several times as long) Hardt and Negri argue that "Far from being defeated, the revolutions of the twentieth century have each pushed forward and transformed the terms of class conflict, posing the conditions of a new political subjectivity, an insurgent multitude against imperial power" (2000:394). Yet, it is difficult not to view the processes of globalization as presenting very real problems for a new politics. While the global economy is becoming ever more closely integrated, political institutions and identities have become subjected to a progressive fragmentation. The rise of identity politics on the left is the most striking example of this process.

Already in the *Communist Manifesto* Marx had identified processes that were pointing beyond extant national economies, processes that were integrating territories via new communications and transportation technologies and creating new forms of solidarity that were now beginning to pose a spectral threat to the capitalist state:

> Modern industry has established the world-market, for which the discovery of America has paved the way. The market has given an immense development to commerce, to navigation, to communication by land. This development has, in its turn, reacted on the extension of industry; and in the same proportion the bourgeoisie developed, increased its capital and pushed into the background every class handed down from the Middle Ages (Marx and Engels 1978:337).

The logic of capitalism involved a constant revolutionizing of the means of production which, itself, played a profound role in what Weber was later to call the disenchantment (*Entzauberung*) of the world, stripping the feudal ties that bound individuals together organically by the "callous cash payment," and "drowned the most heavenly ecstasies of religious fervor, of chivalrous enthusiasm, of philistine sentimentalism, in the icy waters of egotistical calculation" (337). What was crucial about the constant revolutionizing of the means of production was that it had transformed being itself:

> All fixed, fast-frozen relationships, with their train of ancient and venerable prejudices and opinions, are swept away, all new-formed ones become antiquated before they can ossify. All that is solid melts into air, all that is holy is profaned, and man is at last compelled to face with sober senses, his real conditions of life, and his relations with his kind (338).

Yet Marx could celebrate this process in a fairly unabashed manner because he tended to view the destructive moment of modern experience as, ultimately, part and parcel of a profoundly creative dialectic. Marx believed that the process by which men and women were forced to face the "real conditions of life" would have the enlightening effect of enabling the proletariat to see more or less transparently its universal, human interest in the transcendence of the very social relations that created it. The reconciliation of creation with destruction would happen through the unfolding of history and communism would be the result. All that had melted would, so to speak, become solid once more. History was an *inherently* redemptive story.

Globalization accelerates the processes identified by Marx, yet without the reconciliation that would ultimately be achieved by the creation of a modern Prometheus no longer bound by national, religious, or ethnic identities. Indeed, the process of the fragmentation on the left is not, strictly speaking, a recent phenomenon. If the *Manifesto* was written as the founding text of the International Working Men's Association, some seventy years later, its successor organization, the Second Socialist International, would collapse as a result of the re-emergence of the very forms of particularlism, namely nationalism, that Marx had thought were a thing of the past. What was significant here is that—in the absence of a proletariat that constituted a solid majority of the population—social democracy now had to reframe its political discourse and appeal not to the "working class" as such but, rather, to the "people." The nationalism that was the undoing of the Second Socialist International with the outbreak of hostilities in 1914 became increasingly institutionalized thereafter. That is to say, after the demise of the Second Socialist International and after the long period of war stretching from 1914–1945, the non-Communist left accepted the nation-state as the fundamental unit of politics. Social democracy, in other words, was forced by purely sociological and pragmatic reasons to return to a language based on the centrality of national-popular as opposed to international proletarian solidarity (Pzeworski 1986; Esping-Andersen 1985; Laclau and Mouffe 1985).

Globalization represents an acceleration of the processes that Marx had already identified. It is to be viewed, therefore, as an intensification of the crisis in modernity: namely, a condition in which "All that is solid melts into air." While Marx believed that the nature of this crisis would resolve itself socio-economically, that is, through the contradiction between the progressive forces of production and ever antiquated relations of production, the crisis turned out to be much more extensive than he, as an Enlightenment thinker, could have ever imagined. As Horkheimer and Adorno, writing during the dark years of the Second World War, recognized, history was not to be understood as simply the passage from nature to history, from barbarism to civilization, a condition of "*bellum omnes contra omnium*" to a condition of peace, but, rather, the two conditions inter-penetrated one another. History was *inextricable* from nature, enlightenment inextricable from mythology (Horkheimer and Adorno 1972).[5] Indeed, Horkheimer and Adorno understood "enlightenment as mythological fear turned radical" (1972). Under conditions of a disenchanted and rationalized world, the primordial fear experienced by individuals—that of an overpowering nature—becomes the fear *produced* in and by a society that had congealed into a kind of "second nature"—contingent human practices that, because they appear to lie beyond the reach of human intervention, seem *as if* they were part of first nature. If mythology and enlightenment were bound up with one another, if there were no straightforward transition from nature to history, then lying just below the surface of civilization was the threat of a profound and pervasive insecurity. That is because nature can never be fully historicized and dominated; there will always remain residues of what has remained immune from instrumental reason. These residues, according to Horkheimer and Adorno, in the important "Elements of Anti-Semitism" chapter of the *Dialectic of Enlightenment,* are the objects of both utopian longing and disgust. Indeed, this provides us with our first clue as to how populist discourse can be said to operate. It constructs historical processes — i.e. migration — in terms of natural processes, indeed, as natural catastrophes.

Security

While recognizing the inherently dynamic and unstable nature of modern experience, Marx did not view this as a problem inasmuch as he saw emergent forms of solidarity, arising from within the production process itself, which would supplant fast-antiquated traditional norms. Such emergent forms of solidarity were, moreover, underwritten by a philosophy of history still deeply indebted to Hegelian theodicy. At the most immediate level, it is possible to argue that social democratic politics put into practice precisely this progressive version of history, even if it did replace Luxemburg's "revolution" with Bernstein's "reform." It did so in the form of the post-war welfare state grounded in the projection of a future based on a steady, perpetual increase in the standard of living. After the crisis of the early 1970s, such a social democratic vision becomes increasingly untenable. Is it any surprise, then, that the post-modernist skepticism towards meta-narratives takes hold in the wake of the shattering of the post-war consensus? For, at the collective level, an adherence to a progressive philosophy of history — either in liberal or Marxist form — served to provide narratives of collective and individual identity with an internal coherence. The process that Marx analyzed with such penetration, the process by which all that is solid melts into air, destabilizes and ultimately undermines the frameworks of everyday life that, as Anthony Giddens (1991) points out, serves as the basis for "ontological security." Giddens' account of ontological security is especially important for our purposes because it is premised on a dual relation between the globalizing processes, on the one hand, and personal identity on the other.

What does Giddens mean by the concept of "ontological security"? Ontological security consists of the coherence, continuity, and dependability of the relation between the self and world or "being-in-the-world." Such stability is grounded in the taken-for-granted patterns constitutive of every day life or what he calls the "natural attitude" (1991:36). The natural attitude establishes stability in our relations with others, the shared object world and, consequently, our self-identity, which is anchored in the foregoing subject-object and subject-subject relations. Giddens contends that while these patterns have a cognitive dimension, their real significance lies in the fact that, inasmuch as they progressively supplant relations between the nascent self and significant others, such patterns become deeply invested with *emotional* commitments. Indeed, socialization marks the transition from the relations of mutuality between infant and caregiver(s) constituted out of patterns that regularize the play of their presence and absence and establish temporal continuity and spatial stability. The natural attitude "brackets out" or holds in abeyance, the fundamental questions about ourselves, others and the object world that must simply be presupposed in order to "go on" (in the Wittgensteinian sense) in our everyday activities. To put it in Kuhnian terms, while the natural attitude is analogous to "normal science," the posing of fundamental questions runs parallel to "revolutionary science." Just as revolutionary science cannot sustain ongoing research projects, it is, similarly, not possible to function in everyday life when one is constantly driven to pose radical questions concerning the ontological status or the nature of the objective, inter-subjective and subjective worlds. As Giddens puts it: "To be ontologically secure is to possess at the level of the unconscious and practical consciousness, 'answers' to fundamental questions which all human life in some way addresses" (1991:47). While the *natural attitude* plays a crucial role, it is at the same time extremely fragile. Such fragility derives from the fact that, unlike *nature*, it does not possess solidity and objectivity, but, rather, is produced and reproduced through interaction with others within a shared inter-subjective world. Anxiety can erupt with the slightest rent or tear in the tissue of this world, and, when this occurs, the fundamental questions pertaining to the world can no longer be bracketed by the natural attitude (Heidegger 1962:16). These questions concern:

1. The nature of existence
2. Death and finitude
3. Relations to others
4. Self-identity

As is implicit in the foregoing, a central tension inherent in modernity is, to quote Giddens, that between "globalizing influences on the one hand and personal dispositions on the other" (1991:1). In other words, a key dimension of modernity is to be understood as a set of new mechanisms of self-identity that both *shapes* and is *shaped by* modern institutions (1991:2). The self is a reflexive phenomenon, that is to say, modern individuals not only *have* a self but also are *aware* of having a self.

But what is it, precisely, to have a self? It is to be able to organize the discreet moments of our experience into a more or less coherent biography or story that unifies past, present, and future? It is to be able to answer the fundamental questions of "Where have I come from" and "Where am I going"? The modern self is characterized fundamentally by both an increase in freedom in the sense that it understands selfhood, itself, to be a project, as something that is reflexively constructed and, that the self is constituted by an essential anxiety that arises out of its lack of solidity. Ontological security becomes a specific problem under conditions of modernity. Giddens argues that modernity must be understood in terms of a specific ensemble of institutions that (1) are dynamic and reflexive (i.e. they are able to react to changes in their immediate environments), (2) undercut traditions, customs, and habits, and (3) have a global impact, that is, do not remain tied to a specific time-space nexus. As we have already suggested, globalization with its effects at the economic, cultural, and political levels, reinforces all three aspects of modernity: it makes institutions yet more dynamic, further relativizes traditions, customs, and habits, and further severs them from a specific nexus of space and time.

All three institutional aspects of late modernity, according to Giddens, make it into what he calls a "risk culture." By this he doesn't mean that modernity is necessarily more dangerous than previous epochs. In some respects, modernity is less risky than other forms of life, for example in respect to infant mortality; in other respects, such as the threat of the nuclear annihilation of the planet, it is obviously much riskier. The idea of risk culture, rather, is that the concept of risk is inherent in the manner in which the social world is organized. Thus, the future is not simply seen as an open horizon on which progress "happens" in a unidirectional way, but rather, as a horizon of potential, precisely calculable risks. Here, again, we see an intertwining of freedom and anxiety. According to Giddens, "The risk climate of modernity is thus unsettling for everyone; no one escapes" (1991:124).

There is much to take exception with in Giddens account of "ontological security." First, like the tradition of classical sociological theory that he has done so much to introduce to the English-speaking world, Giddens assumes a binary framework consisting of the familiar oppositions between the "traditional" and the "modern," *Gemeinschaft* and *Gesellschaft*, mechanical and organic solidarity and so on. Yet as Horkheimer and Adorno have shown, there exist, in Greek mythology, aspects of the modern self—the self which takes up a prudential relation to others, the world and himself—just as the modern, Enlightenment individual exhibits certain mythological traits. That is, when confronted with external threats, the (masculine) individual either hardens himself up against them or loses himself completely. Far from being exclusively characterized by autonomy, in the Kantian sense, modernity contains within it a darker possibility. That is the possibility of "authoritarian personality" structures, characterized by utter submissiveness towards authority, on the one hand, and aggression or dominance towards members of minority groups, on the other (Adorno, Frenkel-Brunswik, et al. 1969).

Second, as a corollary of the previous point, Giddens holds that, while obviously operating within certain constraints, the "late-modern" individual is able to create the kind of self that she wants. While Giddens recognizes religious fundamentalism as a response to the unease generated by the condition of late modernity, he rationalistically suggests that such fundamentalism is, ultimately, untenable inasmuch as its adherents would be forced to recognize such a worldview as merely one choice amongst others. What this account leaves out is the possibility of a return of atavistic forms of identity that don't simply view tradition as one choice amongst others, but seek to negate the very reflexivity that constitutes the modern self. Such fundamentalism, in other words, seeks to do away with choice altogether.

Third, as alluded to above, the self is not simply a reflexive project — that is self-conscious and constantly revising its projects — but non-identical with itself. What I mean by this is simply that there are aspects of the self that resist reflexivity; such aspects of the self can never be eliminated no matter how strong what Jessica Benjamin calls the "bonds of love" established between the infant and her primary caregiver. On the contrary, as Julia Kristeva has argued, the primary caregiver (the maternal function) not only represents a source of comfort, of nourishment and protection, but also a source of anxiety that originates in the threat of being overwhelmed and the borders of the self called into question. In a patriarchal society, the "maternal function" is "abjected," that is, viewed as the negation of the self and therefore terror and disgust (Kristeva 1982).[6] Kristeva argues, moreover, that this excessive aspect of the psyche — the unconscious — isn't just repressed, as in the classical Freudian account, but *projected* onto the other (see also Horkheimer and Adorno 1972:168–208). The strangeness of the stranger is, in this sense, this overwhelming anxiety that has to do with what the self experiences as a threat to the integrity of its very boundaries. To put it another way, it is the denial of the otherness, the self (in the form of the unconscious) that transforms the other into something strange, dangerous and *potentially* fearsome.

Despite these criticisms (binary framework and the over-emphasis on reflexivity and rationality), I would suggest, nonetheless, that Giddens' concept of "ontological security" could indeed serve as the basis of an analysis of the emergence of right-populist politics. The reason for this is that Giddens ties the question of ontological security closely with the very dynamism of modernity. Thus, as we have seen, "ontological security" forms the basis by which potential threats to the self — at its incipient as well as mature stage — are warded off and kept at bay. Now, if such security is increasingly undermined by the *acceleration* of the processes inherent in modernity, itself — dynamism, the undercutting of routinized forms of action and constant tendency towards dis-embedding — then we can expect a corresponding rise of anxiety (see Putnam 2000). As Giddens puts it, "Deferment in time and remoteness in space ... reduce the disquiet that awareness of risk as risk might otherwise produce" (1991:130). If this is true, the exact obverse must also hold: the *acceleration* of time and *compression* of space can be said to increase such disquiet.

The very dynamism of modernity is embodied in the sociological type of the "stranger." Georg Simmel suggests that the stranger is not simply the absolute other; he does not come from another planet. Rather, he is the individual with whom we interact, with whom we enter into specific kinds of relations. What characterizes the stranger is a kind of distanced nearness. As Simmel puts it:

> The stranger is close to us insofar as we feel between him and ourselves similarities of nationality or social position, of occupation or of general human nature. He is far from us insofar as these similarities extend beyond him and us and connect us only because they connect a great many people (Simmel 1971:143).[7]

The stranger is strange precisely because of his *familiarity;* he participates in social interactions as a member of a given society, yet at the same time represents a normative order beyond the local contexts he inhabits. In crossing geographical borders — in moving from what Friedman refers to as the "over there" to the "over here" — the stranger takes up a more distanced, objective view of normative codes and the social identities they solidify. To put it in Giddens' terms, the stranger represents the crisis of the "natural attitude"; the very presence of the stranger serves to unsettle the taken-for-granted patterns of the everyday. Thus, the stranger represents a potential challenge to the ontological security of the self. As suggested above, anxiety and freedom need to be viewed as two sides of the same coin: anxiety arises because modern practices are radically contingent and open-ended. Otherness is the condition for the possibility of the very dynamism and freedom of the modern self (Kymlicka 1996; Parekh 2000). The image of the stranger is thus necessarily doubled: he is simultaneously an opportunity *and* a threat. While postmodern feminism and post-colonial theory and multicultural conceptions of citizenship view the relation to the other as an *opportunity* for the creation of new emancipatory, hybrid forms of subjectivity, right-populism views the stranger as a *threat*.

At this point, it is possible to identify quickly any number of ways in which ontological security has been further undermined by the processes of globalization by which the local is increasingly penetrated by the global — what happens "over here" has its roots in the "over there." At the *economic level* the remaking of the global economy in the image of the Anglo-American model, de-regulates economic life and heightens competition between firms and employees creating a pervasive climate of uncertainty. At the *geopolitical level,* the end of the Cold War has created an increasingly unstable, multi-polar order, one which, far from eliminating, has only exacerbated the nuclear threat. Such threat puts in question not simply the existence of the individual but of planetary life as a whole. At the level of *urbanization*, cities play increasingly important roles as nodes in the organization of the network society, yet given the decoupling of the "space of flows" from the "space of places" they become marked by widening socio-economic inequalities (Davis 1990). The increasingly global reach of the products of the U.S. cultural industries, aided by the emergence of new technologies, generates a perceived threat to integrity of cultural difference and the normative orders that they represent. Fundamentally, *migration* or flows of populations across is both a cause and a consequence of all of the above. Inasmuch as it leads to a further shrinkage in the distance between spaces, globalization heightens anxieties concerning *bodily integrity*, more specifically, anxieties stemming from the transmissibility of infectious diseases. At any number of levels, then, the logic of globalization dramatically underscores the increasingly fragile nature of ontological security and, thus, individual and collective identity.

Sovereignty

So far, I have suggested that globalization deepens the experience of anxiety that is a key dimension of the various geopolitical, economic, political, cultural, physical effects of globalization. I have also suggested that the figure of the stranger, as defined by Simmel as that individual who is *simultaneously* close at hand yet distant, becomes the concrete manifestation of globalization anxieties. That is to say, if "globalization," as contested and unsatisfactory the concept is, signifies the interpenetration of the global and the local in an infinite set of combinations, then the figure of the stranger can be said to embody this logic in an extremely immediate way. At all the levels that I have identified above the stranger is *potentially* implicated. The stranger is a potential source of *economic* anxiety as he represents cheaper labour-power; he is the potential source of *geopolitical* anxiety, i.e. terror; the stranger can be found concentrated in *urban* environments; the stranger is a source of *cultural* anxieties inasmuch as he is the source of norms incompatible with, even antithetical to, that of the host community; at the level of security of the body, the stranger represents the threat of transmissible disease. It is no surprise that a central axis along which globalization anxieties are organized, as alluded to above, is that of migration. Migration is, indeed, constitutive of the of the stranger's identity. As Simmel suggests, the stranger is "the man who comes today and stays tomorrow — the potential wanderer, so to speak, who although he has gone no further, has not quite got over the freedom of coming and going" (1971:143). What is especially noteworthy about this experience "of coming and going" is that it historicizes, renders contingent and ultimately disrupts the "natural attitude" (the taken for granted patterns of the everyday) and in the process represents an identity crisis at both individual and collective level; by virtue of his very difference, the stranger permits those fundamental questions — concerning existence or the nature of the good life — that are normally bracketed or held in abeyance, to be posed anew. The self's feeling of being unable to organize its experience into a coherent narrative unifying past, present, and future, correlates, according to Giddens, with the feeling of being overwhelmed. "Anxiety about obliteration, of being engulfed, crushed or overwhelmed by externally impinging events, is frequently the correlate of such feelings" (1991:53).

Yet, that is not, in and of itself, enough to suggest the connection between anxiety and the politics of right-populism. The reason for that is that anxiety remains, by definition, objectless, and politics requires specific objects. While certain processes, as I have just described them, can give rise to anxiety, it is constitutive of such anxiety that they are without determinate objects. Right-wing populism, as a political discourse, doesn't passively express shifting constellations of globalization anxieties that surround the figure of the stranger, but, rather, these movements and parties must transform a diffuse, often incoherent, unconscious *anxiety* into an articulated, determinate *fear* of a particular object.

In a path-breaking lecture entitled "Angst und Politik" (1986:261–91), Franz Neumann distinguishes between "real anxiety" of a concrete danger and "neurotic anxiety" that results from a "persecution complex." He argues that the transformation of the former into the latter is produced by way of identification with a strong leader or what he calls "Caeserism." While Neumann's strong reliance on the concept of neurosis, as well as the fact that his central frame of reference was Nazism, constitutes certain limitations in his analysis, it is nonetheless possible to use his framework to identify a crucial mechanism of right-populist discourse. That is the mechanism that transforms a real, if at the same time diffuse, anxiety into fear of the stranger. In the process, identification takes places with an emphasis not so much on the leader as with the people as a whole. By transforming diffuse and multiple forms of often scarcely articulable anxiety into the fear of the stranger, right-populist discourse accomplishes two things simultaneously: first, it transforms the social stranger from a debating partner or an economic competitor into the political "enemy"; secondly, it is able simultaneously to define the identity of the "people."

The enemy, as Carl Schmitt wrote in his influential book *The Concept of the Political*, is he who represents a danger to a collectivity's "whole way of life" (1996:27). Significantly, Schmitt argues that the political as based on the fundamental, existential opposition between "friend and enemy" can be seen as running parallel to, but irreducible to the aesthetic opposition between "the beautiful and the ugly," the moral opposition between "good and the evil," and the religious opposition of "the sacred and the profane." While irreducible to these distinctions, Schmitt suggests when some or all of these oppositions line up in a particular way, they can reinforce the basic political distinction between friend and enemy.

I would suggest that the particular force of right-populist discourse lies in the manner in which these oppositions between the beautiful and the ugly, the good and the bad, the sacred and the profane and, of course, friend and foe, are made to line up in a specific way. The mechanism through which the social stranger becomes transformed into the political enemy is what Kristeva calls "abjection." In psychoanalytic terms, abjection is the violent expulsion—as in vomiting—of that which within the body pushes against the border between "inner" and "outer." The abject, in other words, is the death that inhabits life in the form of the body's fluids and waste products. As Kristeva explains:

> These body fluids, this defilement, this shit are what life withstands, hardly and with difficulty, on the part of death. There, I am at the border of my condition as a living being. My body extricates itself, as being alive, from that border. My wastes drop so that I might live, until, from loss to loss, nothing remains in me and my entire body falls beyond the limit—*cadere*, cadaver. If dung signifies the other side of the border, the place where I am not and which permits me to be, the corpse, the most sickening of wastes is a border that has encroached upon everything (1982:3).

Ab-jection, then, is the re-establishment of borders that have somehow been threatened by the appearance of that which should have remained hidden away but now has come out into the open. Such a re-establishment of borders comes about by way of an act of repulsion and exclusion. I would suggest that contemporary right-populism can be understood in terms of an abjection, an expulsion, of the stranger precisely because of the stranger's inherent ambiguity. Thus: "It is thus not lack of cleanliness or health that causes abjection but what disturbs identity, system, order. What does not respect borders, positions, rules. The in-between, the ambiguous, the composite" (1982:4).

To summarize the argument so far, I have suggested that the economic, cultural and political processes that characterize the phenomenon of globalization should be thought of as deepening and intensifying processes that are inherent in modernity itself, namely, the dialectic through which fixed identities are unable, ultimately, to sustain themselves. The process by which "all that is solid melts into air" produces ontological insecurity or an environment of pervasive anxiety. The strategy of right-populism, despite its considerable internal differences, turns on translating such amorphous anxiety into a determinate fear of a particular object by way of a process of abjection. That object, I am suggesting, is the figure who is strange in his familiarity: the stranger.

Notes

1 For the concept of discipline, see Foucault (1977).
2 In the U.S., it takes the form, for example, of a frontal attack on Affirmative Action from an administration that emphasizes inclusiveness within the context of "compassionate conservatism."
3 That is why, for example, some version of liberal political philosophy, particularly that of someone like John Rawls, is received much more warmly by the left than has been the case in Europe. It also explains why Habermas's own emphasis on the universalist tradition of the Enlightenment has had such an impact in continental Europe rather than in North America, in which political philosophies emphasizing difference have become increasingly influential, at least within the academy.
4 However, one could also argue that it is precisely because social exclusion is explicitly articulated within the German state, in particular a conception of citizenship based on *jus sanguinis* as opposed to *jus soli*, that this by definition denies political ground to the neo-populist right.
5 The emergence of the self—its differentiation both from external nature at the phylogenic level, and from its primary caregivers, at the ontogenic level, is accompanied under conditions of modernity by the temptation to lose oneself, i.e. to regression.
6 Interestingly, Kristeva's work in the main is in agreement with Klaus Thieweleit's important analysis of the representations of women in the hyper-masculinist discourse of the proto-fascist Freikorps in the inter-war period in Germany. The recurrent theme of these discourses is the overwhelming danger posed to male identity, specifically the worker-soldier brotherhood that plays such an important role in the work of Ernst Jünger, by the feminine. And such danger is typically organized under the abject sign of the indomitable flow of bodily fluids, particularly blood (cf. Thieweleit 1987).
7 As I suggest above, it is possible to understand the stranger as the individual within our midst who not only comes from afar but, by coming from afar and remaining with us, challenges the universality and objectivity of the normative order of the community. That would explain how, not only geographical migrants, but also homeless people, youth, ravers, "squeegee kids" etc. are increasingly being targeted with aggressive policing. Such policing increasingly represents the normalization of the exception to the rule of law. If sovereign is that entity that decides on the exception, and if such suspensions occur in the name of the "people" and its "common sense," then we see the salience of the question of sovereignty in a neo-Hobbesian sense (cf. Gandesha 2002).

References

Adorno, T. W., Else Frenkel-Brunswik, et al. (1969) *The Authoritarian Personality*. New York: Norton.

Agamben, Giorgio (2000) *Means without Ends: Notes on Politics*, trans. V. Binetti and C. Casarino. Minneapolis: University of Minnesota Press.

Althusser, Louis (1971) "Ideological State Apparatuses," in *Lenin and Philosophy*, trans. Ben Brewster. London: New Left Books.

Arendt, Hannah (1973) *The Origins of Totalitarianism*. New York: Harcourt Brace.

Barber, Benjamin (1996) *Jihad vs. McWorld: How the World is Both Falling Apart and Coming Together—And What this Means for Democracy*. New York: Times Books.

Betz, H. G., and S. Immerfal (eds.) (1998) *The New Politics of the Right: Neo-Populist Parties and Movements in Established Democracies*. New York: St. Martin's Press.

Bhabha, Homi (1994) *The Location of Culture*. London: Routledge.

Butler, Judith (1993) *Bodies that Matter: On the Discursive Limits of Sex*. New York: Routledge.

Castells, Manuel (2000) *The Information Age: Economy, Society and Culture: Vol. I: The Rise of the Network Society*. Oxford: Blackwell.

Davis, Mike (1990) *City of Quartz: Excavating the Future in Los Angeles*. New York: Vintage/Random House.

Die Zeit 37, 2002

Dubiel, Helmut *Die Zeit* 37, 2002.

Esping-Andersen, G. (1985) *Politics Against Markets: The Social Democratic Road to Power*. Princeton, NJ: Princeton University Press.

Drache, Daniel, and Meric S. Gertler (1991) *The New Era of Global Competition: State Policy and Market Power*. Montréal and Kingston: McGill-Queen's University Press.

Fallaci, Oriana (2001) *The Rage and the Pride*. New York: Rizzoli.

Foster, Hal (1996) *Return of the Real: The Avant-garde at the of the Century*. Cambridge, Mass.: MIT Press.

Foucault, Michel (1977) *Discipline and Punish: The Birth of the Prison*, trans. Alan Sheridan. New York: Pantheon Books.

Friedman, Thomas (2000) *The Lexus and the Olive Tree: Understanding Globalization*. New York: Farrar, Strauss and Giroux.Gandesha, Samir (2000) "Neo-Conservatism: A Third Way for Canada?" *The European Legacy: Special Issue—Is There a Third Way?* Vol. 5, (No.6): 187-193.

Gandesha, Samir (2002) "Safe Streets" in *Crime and Ornament: The Arts and Popular Culture in the Shadow of Adolf Loos*, edited by Melony Ward and Bernie Miller. Toronto: YYZ Books.

Giddens, Anthony (1991) *Modernity and Self-Identity: Self and Society in the Late Modern Age*. Cambridge: Polity Press.

Hall, Stuart (1988) *The Hard Road to Renewal: Thatcherism and the Crisis of the Left*. London: Verso.

Hardt, M., and A. Negri (2000) *Empire*. Cambridge, Mass: Harvard University Press.

Harraway, Donna (1991) *Siminans, Cyborgs, and Women: The Reinvention of Nature*. London: Routledge.

Harrison, Trevor (1995) *Of Passionate Intensity: Right-wing Populism and the Reform Party*. Toronto: University of Toronto Press.

Heidegger, M. (1962) *Being and Time*. trans. J. Macquarrie and E. Robinson San Francisco.

Honneth, Axel (1995) *The Struggle for Recognition: The Moral Grammar of Social Conflicts*, trans. Joel Anderson. Cambridge, UK: Polity Press.

Horkheimer, M., and T. W. Adorno (1972) *Dialectic of Enlightenment*, trans. John Cumming. New York: Continuum Press.

Houellebecq, Michel (1998) *Les particules élémentaires*. Paris: J'ai lu.

Kitching, Gavin (1989) *Development and Underdevelopment in Historical Perspective*. London: Routledge.

Kristeva, Julia (1982) *Powers of Horror: An Essay on Abjection*, trans. Leon S. Roudiez. New York: Columbia University Press.

Kymlicka, Will (1996) *Multicultural Citizenship: A Liberal Theory of Minority Rights*. Oxford: OUP.

Laclau, Ernesto (1977) *Politics and Ideology in Marxist Theory*. London: Verso.

Laclau, Ernesto, and Chantal Mouffe (1985) *Hegemony and Socialist Strategy*. London: Verso.

Loch, D., and W. Heitmeyer (eds.) (2001) *Schattenseiten der Globalisierung*. Frankfurt am Main: Suhrkamp Verlag: 11-40.

Marx, Karl, and Friedrich Engels (1978) *The Manifesto of the Communist Party*, in *The Marx-Engels Reader*, ed. Robert Tucker. NY: Norton.

Menke, Christoph (2001) "Dunkelzonen der Demokratie," *Die Zeit* 15.

Mouzelis, Nicos (1985) *Politics in the Semi-Periphery*. London: Routledge.

Neumann, Franz (1986) "Angst und Politik," in *Demokratischer und autoritärer Staat*. Frankfurt am Main: Fischer: 261–91.

Parekh, Bhikhu (2000) *Rethinking Multiculturalism: Cultural Diversity and Political Theory.* Basingstoke: MacMillan Press.

Patten, Steve (1999a) "The Reform Party's Re-imagining of the Canadian Nation" *Journal of Canadian Studies* 34/1 (Spring).

——. (1999b) "Citizenship, the New Right and Social Justice: Examining the Reform Party's Discourse on Citizenship," *Socialist Studies Bulletin* 57-58 (July-Dec).

Putnam, Robert (2000) *Bowling Alone: The Collapse and Revival of American Community.* New York: Simon and Schuster.

Pzeworski, A. (1986) *Paper Stones: A History of Electoral Socialism.* Chicago: University of Chicago Press.

Schmitt, Carl (1996) *The Concept of the Political,* trans. George Schwab. Chicago: University of Chicago Press.

Simmel, Georg (1971) "The Stranger," *On Individuality and Social Forms,* ed. Donald Levine. Chicago: University of Chicago Press.

Taylor, Charles (1994) *Multiculturalism: Examining the Politics of Recognition*, Amy Gutmann (ed.). Princeton, NJ: Princeton University Press.

Theweleit, K. (1987) *Male Fantasies Vol. I: Women, Floods, Bodies, Histories,* trans. S. Conway. Minneapolis: University of Minnesota Press.

Walser, Martin (2002) *Tod eines Kritikers.* Frankfurt am Main: Suhrkamp Verlag.

PART II

Post-9/11 Responses to Terrorism, Torture, Rights, and Anti-Terrorism Acts

5

The Origins of Political Policing in Canada: Class, Law, and The Burden of Empire*

Andrew Parnaby and Gregory S. Kealey

Canada's early experience in the realm of intelligence and security matters, as in other areas of political life, was shaped decisively by its status as an outpost of the British Empire. Early experiments in this regard took place in the aftermath of the Rebellions in Upper and Lower Canada in 1837 and 1838. The authorities in Québec, drawing on the example set by colonial authorities in Ireland and Jamaica, appointed stipendiary magistrates to head up a newly created rural police force, a body charged with the responsibility of collecting political intelligence and pacifying the countryside. Decades later during the American Civil War, politicians on both sides of the Ottawa River adopted a similar, albeit much smaller version of this system to prevent military recruiters from violating Canadian neutrality. But it was in the face of other, more threatening political challenges — at once domestic and foreign, nationalist and anti-imperialist — that the Canadian government, as a colonial and later a federal body, undertook a greater, more sustained interest in political policing.[1]

In the 1860s and early 1870s, the Canadian government set its sights on Irish radicals tied to the Irish Republican Brotherhood (IRB) who were active in the United States and Canada. By the early decades of the twentieth century, its focus shifted to South Asian radicals who, like

Irish republicans before them, used North America as a staging ground for an independence struggle gathering strength on the sub-continent. The empire was striking back, globally and locally, and Canada, both as a collection of colonies and later as a nation, was caught in the crossfire. Not only was its approach to these important matters based, in part, on models of policing adopted elsewhere in the commonwealth, but the very security challenges it faced were the product of the mother country's extensive colonial reach.[2]

With an ideological pedigree that stretched back to the United Irish rebellion in the 1790s, the Irish Republican Brotherhood was founded in Dublin in 1858. It was an avowedly revolutionary organization that was committed to overthrowing British rule in Ireland and establishing an Irish republic.[3] Yet as its leaders understood well, success at home required the support of Irish immigrants abroad, most notably in the United States where tens of thousands of Irish men and women, many of whom had fled Ireland during the depths of the Famine, swelled the ranks of working-class populations in New York, Chicago, Detroit, and Cincinnati.[4] Thus, seven months after the IRB's founding, an American support group, the Fenian Brotherhood, was established. Significantly, Fenianism found a receptive audience in Canada as well. In Toronto, members of the Hibernian Benevolent Society, an Irish self-help organization founded by cooper and tavern keeper Michael Murphy, created a clandestine Fenian circle in 1859. Its members were mostly working class, and like their counterparts south of the border, they were drawn to a heady mix of camaraderie, nationalism, and collective action at a time when politics often turned on the power, privileges, and prejudices that differentiated the Orange from the Green. "It is time to cast off the habiliments of wretchedness and come forth clothed in the manly garb of equality," the Hibernian's newspaper, *Irish Canadian*, exclaimed. "[W]e Irish will yet stand erect in Canada."[5]

As the Fenian Brotherhood gathered strength, the Canadian government mobilized too. At first, the attorney general for Canada West, John A. Macdonald, was confident that local militias were capable of placing a "sufficient check" on the "mere dread of a Fenian conspiracy."

But the future prime minister's opinion of the matter changed in the fall of 1865. At that time, British officials, who were alarmed by the steady growth of the IRB and the arrival of Irish-American veterans of the U.S. Civil War, raided the organization's offices, closed its newspapers, and arrested many of its high-profile members. Closer to home, American Fenians were debating the politics of "freeing Ireland on the plains of Canada"—a contentious strategy that had split the organization into two rival factions, one in favour of a northern invasion, the other opposed. From Macdonald's perspective, that particular possibility reinvigorated concerns about the integrity of the border, and raised additional fears about the likelihood of heightened anti-Catholic agitation within the colony itself. "The Fenian action in Ireland is serious, and the Imperial government seems fully alive to it," the shrewd Kingston politician observed. "We must not be caught napping."[6]

To this end, Macdonald sought the assistance of Gilbert McMicken—a one-time customs agent, entrepreneur, member of parliament, and political ally. McMicken was also head of the Western Frontier Constabulary, the extremely modest, and largely ineffective secret police established by the Canadian government during the U.S. Civil War, in the words of one Canadian official, to "find out any attempt to disturb the public peace, the existence of any plot, conspiracy, or organization whereby peace would be endangered, the Queen's Majesty insulted, or her proclamation of neutrality infringed."[7] McMicken, who had recruited about fifteen secret agents by the end of the Civil War, increased substantially the number of men under his command. By 1870, approximately 50 agents, working both in the United States and in Canada, were attending Fenian meetings, hanging out at "Irish Saloons," and shadowing suspected "Irish Rebbles." Fragmentary evidence suggests that McMicken's recruits were usually men in their late twenties and early thirties who possessed military and police backgrounds or both; of the eighteen agents who can be positively identified, seven were Irish (six Roman Catholics), six were Scottish (one Roman Catholic), and five were English (all Protestants). Paid relatively well, many informants nonetheless took up employment in the areas under their supervision in order to allay any suspicions of how they were supporting themselves and what their real motives were. "I was impressed with the idea that he was capable and had proven his being a very intelligent Irish Roman

Catholic," McMicken wrote to Macdonald, assessing the credentials of one of his latest recruits. "[T]his, in connection with his integrity and loyalty, led me to engage his services for a time. He was to put himself in communication with the British Consul there [Buffalo] and be instructed by him and through him by me."[8]

When it came to monitoring the machinations of Fenian rebels in the United States, the Canadian government worked cheek by jowl with British consular officials in several large American cities, most notably in Buffalo, a key border crossing, and New York, a hive of Green activity. Key to this arrangement, one which both imperial and colonial authorities were anxious to piece together, was Sir Edward Mortimer Archibald, a Nova Scotia-born lawyer who served as clerk to the House of Assembly, attorney general, and Supreme Court justice in Newfoundland from 1833 to 1854 before being appointed British consul at New York in 1857. By the mid-1860s, as the Fenians gained momentum in the United States, Archibald had recruited a clutch of informers — some of whom operated in the upper echelons of the Fenian organization — and tapped his connections with local law enforcement and customs officials to keep tabs on the revolutionary outfit. Consular officials in other cities, such as H.W. Hemans in Buffalo, made similar arrangements with paid informants and, like their New York counterpart, were often in direct contact with some of McMicken's men. For his part, Archibald forwarded the information he received from this loose collection of sources to various British officials, including the colonial secretary (who, in turn, informed police forces in London and Dublin), the commander of British forces in North America, the lieutenant governor of New Brunswick, and the Governor General of Canada, Lord Monck. Drawn from inside and outside the Fenian's ranks and scattered across the north eastern corner of the U.S., it was a far-flung and eclectic battery of informants, one which pumped information through the capillaries of communication that linked governments and law enforcement agencies on both sides of the Atlantic.[9]

Through the fall of 1865, rumours of a Fenian attack continued to swirl, prompting Monck, Macdonald, and McMicken to redirect their attention to the domestic front.[10] By the end of December 1865, Patrick Nolan, one of McMicken's most reliable informants in Chicago, was recalled to Toronto where the Hibernian Benevolent Society, judging by the numerous public statements made by its leader, Michael Murphy, appeared to be on the move. Once in the city, the highly prized secret agent, who went by the name of Erastus C. Burton, submerged himself in the local Green scene, filing numerous reports between December 1865 and March 1866 that confirmed McMicken's and Macdonald's worse fears. There were approximately seventeen Fenian lodges in Canada West, nine of them in Toronto; the Hibernian Benevolent Society and the Fenians were not the same thing, but there was substantial overlap between the two organizations; and the ubiquitous Michael Murphy was indeed a Fenian and was in touch with like-minded individuals in the United States. "Capt. Prince [of the Toronto Police Department] had a lot of his men out in plain clothes some time ago watching for the Fenians. They went to the Catholic Church to look for them there," Nolan informed McMicken in late December, underscoring the friction that often emerged between regular and secret police officers. "One of them thought he had a lodge full one night on Nelson St., but it turned [out] to be an Orange Lodge. I think the Capt. got tired of them telling lies, as they are all on their beats now."[11]

McMicken and Macdonald never tired of their star informant. In March 1866, as the Toronto Hibernians geared up for their annual — and increasingly contentious — St. Patrick's Day parade, Nolan reported that Murphy and a coterie of supporters were preparing to leave the city after the celebration to assist their American comrades in a cross-border raid of some kind.[12] From his vantage point in New York, Edward Archibald reached a similar conclusion, and informed Arthur Gordon, the lieutenant governor of New Brunswick, of the possibility of a Fenian insurrection. Not only was the organization increasingly bent on an invasion of British North America, he stated, but, given the large population of Irish Catholics in Maine, the colony of New Brunswick was a likely target. Gordon received similar reports from the British colonial secretary, Edward Cardwell, and the commander of British forces in North America, Sir John Michel — a deluge of data that promoted the lieutenant governor to remark: "I know every move of the small Fenian circle in Calais and the names of all the members and have very good information at Eastport and Bangor also."[13]

In April, 1866, the Fenians launched a feeble attempt to seize Campobello Island, New Brunswick. There they were met by the combined force of six British warships and scores of U.S. troops and easily turned back. North of the border, Michael Murphy and a group of supporters, who had been under surveillance since they left Toronto, were apprehended in Cornwall, Canada West, on their way to assist their American counterparts. The arrests came at the behest of George-Étienne Cartier, attorney general for Canada East, and Alexander Galt, minister of finance, who were anxious to contain the Fenian threat before it spread to their own, largely Roman Catholic, bailiwick. Macdonald was not impressed by his colleagues' actions. Not only did Cartier and Galt not possess the necessary information to convict Murphy of treason, but the ministers' intervention scuttled his ongoing undercover operations; indeed, McMicken had no fewer than four agents keeping tabs on the prominent Irish leader at the time of his arrest. In government circles, this conflict between open prosecution and longer-range intelligence-gathering objectives later gave way to outright embarrassment as repeated spying efforts, including the use of a jail house snitch and the ransacking of Hibernian offices, failed to produce adequate evidence to prosecute. Nearly five months later, Murphy and five of his six supporters escaped from custody — they tunnelled out of the Cornwall jail, commandeered a row boat, and crossed the St. Lawrence River to Ogdensburg in upper New York state — thereby saving the future prime minister the embarrassment of going to trial. Despite the controversy surrounding the raid and Murphy's arrest, Macdonald had reason to be satisfied with his handling of the Fenian invasion. Not only had the insurrection been foiled, but the government's tough stand on the issue played a key role in boosting the idea of Confederation.[14]

The Fenians' defeat at Campobello did not, however, dampen the organization's enthusiasm for the "Canada option" or scotch rumours that an additional raid was imminent.[15] As a result, McMicken recruited additional undercover agents, many of whom were in constant contact with British Consular officials who continued to communicate with Lord Monck. "[T]hree things ... deprive the Fenian threat of their significance," Monck wrote to Macdonald on 29 April 1866. "They are, First, our power at very short notice to turn out a large body of troops and turn them on any threatened point — Second, the certainty that the Government of the United States will permit no invasion of Canada from their soils nor export munitions — Third, the inability of the Fenian leaders to get together any number of men without our knowledge."[16] But the Governor General's confidence was misplaced. Canadian authorities were indeed forewarned, but they were not, surprisingly, forearmed. Poor communication between government, secret service, and military officials, coupled with conflicting reports from some secret agents, generated a mix of confusion and complacency in official circles. So too, it appears, did a misplaced belief that U.S. law enforcement agencies would step in, as they had at Campobello. As a consequence, the Canadian government, despite its extensive preparations, was unable to prevent additional Fenian attacks in June 1866, one in Canada West (Ridgeway and Fort Erie) and another in Canada East.[17]

In the aftermath of the Fenian raids, the Canadian parliament went on the offensive. On 8 June, it amended treason legislation originally enacted in Upper Canada after the Rebellions of 1837 and 1838. Detailed in the Throne Speech and given Royal Assent on the same day, the changes permitted the government to try by military court martial any foreigner or British subject who took up arms in the province. It also suspended habeas corpus for a year, and without the burden of due process, police in both Canada East and Canada West arrested about 50 men suspected of Fenian sympathies. What was more, parliament later passed legislation "to prevent the unlawful training of persons in Military evolutions, and the use of Fire Arms, and to authorize the seizure of Fire Arms collected for purposes dangerous to the public peace" and made a huge military appropriation — $1,897,085 on a total budget of $7,003,236 — which included $100,000 for "detective and secret service work." It added an additional $50,000 and $75,000 in 1867 and 1868 respectively. Police officers and civil servants were forced to take a special loyalty oath. To the anxious provincial legislators all of these measures were both necessary and just; not only had the Fenians undertaken three separate incursions onto British territory, but in the United States, the organization's supporters, a coveted cohort for Yankee politicians charting the murky waters of Reconstruction, still numbered in the tens of thousands. "The Fenians using the politicians and the Politicians using the Fenians," McMicken wrote at the time. "It seems disgraceful, however, to see the Governor of [Illinois] … so sunk in demagogueism."[18]

In this context of public outcry, state repression, and institutional reform, Macdonald pushed ahead with significant changes in the operation and structure of the secret service. Of particular importance was the establishment of more independent and reliable sources of intelligence. The career of informant Henri LeCaron highlights this new priority well. Born in England to a modest family, LeCaron, whose real name was Thomas Beach, worked in France as a banker in the late 1850s, eventually leaving Europe for North America in 1861 to fight for the Union Army in the Civil War. Once in the U.S., Beach, who was in his early twenties, enlisted in 8th Pennsylvania Reserve as a private and adopted the name Henri LeCaron — a pseudonym that is perhaps the source of David Cornwell's *nom de plume* Le Carré. After the war, he settled in Illinois and later took a position as a medical officer at the Illinois State Penitentiary. On the basis of his military credentials and knowledge of Fenianism — he had served with Irish soldiers in the Union Army — LeCaron was recruited by British officials in the autumn of 1867 to be a paid informant. Early on, he reported directly to the British Home Office, but as he wormed his way into the Fenians' inner sanctum, he looked for a closer, more secure contact, and wrote to the Canadian government. Macdonald, apparently impressed with LeCaron's connections, authorized McMicken to hire him for $150 a month, but warned: "A man who will engage to do what he offers to do, that is, betray those with whom he acts, is not to be trusted." Macdonald's skepticism was misplaced. From the date of his recruitment, LeCaron, dubbed by one biographer "The Prince of Spies," provided the Canadian government with copious and prescient intelligence, often on a daily basis. "I succeeded in hoodwinking the poor and deluded, together with the unprincipled, blatant, professional Irish patriots," LeCaron recalled in his immensely popular autobiography. "[I was] successful in winning the confidence of almost every Fenian with whom I was brought in contact, and in obtaining the most important information and detail...."[19]

Additional changes to the secret service were spurred on by the assassination of journalist, member of parliament from Montréal, and "Father of Confederation" Thomas D'Arcy McGee on 7 April 1868. As a moderate Irish nationalist, McGee opposed republican violence and extolled the virtues of a federal union as a panacea for ethnic and racial conflict. Not surprisingly, Fenians in Montréal despised McGee and waged an ongoing battle against him in the pages of Irish newspapers, in the ranks of Irish societies, and in the streets during the summer election of 1867. Three weeks after a particularly raucous St. Patrick's Day celebration in Montréal in 1868, one that was defined by a strong anti-McGee sentiment, a suspected Fenian sympathizer shot the Irish moderate dead outside his rooming house in Ottawa. "His only crime was that he steadily and affectionately advised his countrymen in Canada to enjoy all the advantages that our equal laws and institutions gave to Irishmen and to Roman Catholics," Macdonald told a friend in England. "He sternly set his face against the introduction of Fenianism into Canada, and he was therefore a doomed man."[20]

McGee's death led to the arrests of some 70 Hibernian leaders on suspicion of Fenian sympathies. Anxious for a conviction, Macdonald dipped into the secret service fund, something he would do often during his tenure as prime minister, to help grease the wheels of partisan advantage, providing the prosecuting attorney and at least one putative eye witness with funds for room, board, and expenses. The accused, Patrick James Whelan, a former tailor and British soldier, was convicted, but the government was unable to connect him to the Fenian organization.[21] In addition to the shakedown of suspected Fenians, the assassination prompted the ruling Conservatives to create the Dominion Police in May 1868. Mandated to protect government buildings, investigate federal crimes such as mail theft, and undertake political policing, the new force provided a more permanent home for the secret service.

By the end of 1868, the Canadian government had, to some extent, carved out a more permanent role for its embryonic secret service: it boasted institutional support in the form of the newly minted Dominion Police force, possessed a stable source of funding, and, significantly, depended more and more on the expertise of its own well-paid and highly-placed agents than on the observations of well-intentioned imperial officials. Thus, when rumblings of another Fenian invasion emerged in 1869 and 1870, government officials enjoyed almost complete knowledge of Fenian planning. McMicken, for example, was so confident "with the present perfect means of gaining information at his command" that, according to the Governor General, he considered "let[ting] the raid take place so as to give the raiders a lesson which will not be easily forgotten and will probably squash the Fenian organization altogether." Whether or not this tactic carried the day is unclear. What is certain, though, is that the "raiders'" invasion plan — which included a main invasion force at Franklin, Vermont and Malone, New York and diversionary raids at Detroit, Buffalo, and Ogdensburg — was well known. LeCaron was in the thick of things, stashing guns and ammunition at key border points while simultaneously communicating the Fenians' whereabouts to McMicken. (On one occasion, two government informants reported on LeCaron's actions, unaware that the highly respected Fenian commander was himself an undercover agent.) Not surprisingly, then, when about 200 Fenian soldiers finally crossed the border from Vermont on 25 May they were met by a sizable Canadian force — one which had been called up and prepared well in advance — and were easily defeated.[22]

That the use of undercover agents had become so routine, so commonplace underscores just how *un*controversial the emergence of the secret service was amongst Canada's political classes. The only controversy about the secret service came in 1877 when Alexander Mackenzie's Liberal government investigated Macdonald's (ab)use of the secret service fund. At issue was not the legitimacy, purpose, or secrecy of the fund, but simply its misappropriation. Although the parliamentary committee that conducted the probe found the former prime minister guilty as charged, its mild reassertion of parliamentary control over the fund fell far short of equivalent standards and sentiments found in England at the same time. During his tenure as a political leader, Macdonald showed few hesitations in creating a secret police; indeed, he exerted a firm grip on his subordinates, personally controlled the secret service fund, and developed the mechanisms necessary to gather intelligence in recognition of personal, national, and imperial interests. By the time of Macdonald's death in 1891, the threat from radical Irish nationalism had waned, only to be replaced in the opening years of the next century by another anti-colonial movement that hoped, as the Fenians did, to strike a blow for independence at home by generating support in North America. This time around, however, the Canadian government possessed considerable experience in the realm of political policing, and it was all too willing to press it into service for the good of both the mother country and, in this case, the stability of British rule — the *Raj* — in India.

Between 1857 and 1914, a period bracketed by the revolt of Indian soldiers serving in the Bengal army and the onset of the Great War, British officials in London and Calcutta undertook a far-reaching inquiry into many areas of imperial policy, including the administration of land, settlement, and the military and Indian access to education, the civil service, and other political institutions. At the same time, Indians — many of whom were educated at newly created schools and universities — remained politically active. By the turn of the century, pockets of collective action, increasingly dedicated to Indian self-determination, had emerged at home and abroad. In England, France, Germany, Switzerland, and the United States, South Asian radicals mixed with left-wing and liberal intellectuals, socialists and trade unionists, and other immigrants and exiles. They rejected the moderate approach charted by the Indian National Congress, which was founded in 1885, and articulated instead a vision of independence achieved through militant tactics. Canada, like other nations where South Asian immigrants pooled, was home to vibrant radical milieu.[23]

Between 1904 and 1908, about 5,200 South Asians, most of whom were Sikhs from Punjab, immigrated to British Columbia. Drawn by the promise of work and wages in the industrializing west, they arrived at a time of intense anti-Asian agitation. Spurred on by the inflammatory rhetoric and violent demonstrations of many white British Columbians, actions that only intensified as the local economy faltered in 1907, the federal government sought to curtail Asian immigration by raising the head tax on newcomers from China and negotiating a "gentleman's agreement" with Japanese authorities. For the ruling Liberals, the outright exclusion of South Asian immigrants was somewhat more difficult to pull off, for unlike the Chinese and Japanese, they were British subjects and possessed all the rights and freedoms associated with that status. The broader connection between the plight of South Asians in Canada and the political (in)stability of the *Raj* was also a key concern. Not only would a total ban on Indian immigrants open up the Indian government to charges of hypocrisy, but it would likely fan the flames of Indian nationalism at home and abroad. As a result, the federal government endorsed an order-in-council in January 1908 that prohibited the entry of immigrants who did not travel by a "continuous journey" from the country of their birth to Canada, a voyage that was all but impossible to undertake from the Indian sub-continent. Legally dubious, yet politically sly, Ottawa's use of selective travel restrictions to curb the flow of South Asian immigrants was meant to resolve the "Hindoo crisis" in British Columbia and, significantly, minimize its empire-wide implications.[24]

The impact of the new restrictions on levels of immigration from India was decisive: between 1908 and 1915 only about 100 South Asians were admitted to Canada. As a consequence, the spirit of anti-Asian agitation — so toxic in the months and years leading up to Ottawa's intervention — was dampened temporarily.[25] On the other side of the racial divide, however, members of the South Asian community were incensed. Not only did the "continuous journey" requirements cut them off from family and friends who wished to join them in British Columbia, but they cast in bold relief the emptiness of the Crown's claim that all British subjects were equal before and under the law. That the Sikhs had remained loyal to the *Raj* during the *sepoy* revolt of 1857 and had played a key role in the Indian army in subsequent decades only added insult to injury. In this hothouse of intolerance and confrontation, nationalist, anti-British sentiments started to germinate — drawing many in the South Asian community, including a small, yet influential group of western educated students and entrepreneurs, into a political debate that was at once local and global in its consequences.

Mindful of the situation in British Columbia and the broader politics of imperial rule in India, especially at a time when unrest was rocking parts of Punjab and Bengal, the federal government was anxious to keep tabs on this pocket of agitation, both for its own benefit and the benefit of its counterparts in London and Calcutta. Its go-to man in this regard was William Charles Hopkinson. The son of a British officer in the Indian army and a Brahmin mother, Hopkinson was born in Delhi in 1880. At the age of sixteen, he joined the Indian police, working first in Punjab, then later in Calcutta from 1901 to 1907, two locales that, during this period, were seedbeds for various political movements. Fluent in English, Punjabi, Hindi, and other Indian languages, Hopkinson left the Calcutta police force sometime in 1907 and surfaced in British Columbia later that year (or early in 1908), taking up a permanent position as an interpreter with the Vancouver immigration service in February 1909.[26]

Shortly after his arrival, yet several months before officially taking up his post at immigration, the diminutive former detective had convinced local authorities to shut down a night school for South Asian workers in New Westminster and a newspaper called *Free Hindusthan*, which routinely published anti-British material. Both were run by Taraknath Das, a young activist and university graduate who at one time played a leading role in nationalist protests in Calcutta against the partition of Bengal.[27] Fragmentary evidence suggests that Hopkinson had been on the radical's trail for some time — more than likely at the behest of India's Department of Criminal Intelligence, an organization formed by the Indian government in 1907. Whatever the impetus for Hopkinson's journey to North America, the ministry of the interior, which was responsible for immigration, and the federal cabinet understood just how valuable his skills were to managing potential political unrest, both as an interpreter and later as a spy.[28]

In the fall of 1908, the federal government sought to solve the "Hindoo" problem on the west coast by removing South Asians from British Columbia to British Honduras. The scheme was first formulated by J.B. Harkin, private secretary to the minister of the interior, the summer before. "It has been pretty well established that physically and mentally the Hindoo is unfitted to compete successfully with whites or with other Orientals in a country like this," Harkin told W.D. Scott, the superintendent of immigration. "[This proposal] avoids the possibility of a precipitation of trouble in India consequent on the return of Hindoos enraged at their treatment in British territory."[29] The federal government concurred, and within weeks of receiving the Colonial Office's blessing it permitted Harkin to assemble a delegation to investigate the feasibility of the central American colony. The special group included Hopkinson, who was brought on board as a secretary and interpreter, and two representatives from the city's South Asian community, Sham Singh, a Hindu, and Hagar Singh, a Sikh. It travelled to Belize in late October. From Harkin's and Hopkinson's point of view, the trip, which lasted several weeks, was a great success. The demand for agricultural labour in British Honduras was higher than expected, and by all accounts the South Asian delegates were impressed by the working conditions there and desirous of seeing the scheme through. Or so they thought. Upon returning to Vancouver, Sham Singh and Hagar Singh rejected the relocation plan and went so far as to accuse Hopkinson of trying to bribe them into delivering a more positive assessment. Harkin, who was not in British Columbia at the time the delegates made their views public, was incensed. "[E]vidently agitators [are] at work," he informed W.W. Cory, the deputy minister of the interior, after receiving an assessment of the situation in Vancouver from Hopkinson. "[I]t is to be regretted that the efforts of the Government to better their condition and ensure their welfare in another part of the British Empire should be thus thwarted by foreign influence, over which we seem to have little control," Cory replied.[30]

The "mischievous agitator" in question was Teja Singh, an articulate, multi-lingual, and highly educated Sikh who came to Vancouver in October 1908 and quickly emerged as a local leader.[31] Shortly after the delegation's return from British Honduras, the suspected seditionist made several speeches outlining his opposition to the relocation plan, the existence of corruption in the immigration service, and, more ominously from the government's point of view, "the present unrest in India." Teja Singh's remarks, whereabouts, and personal relations were carefully tracked by Hopkinson and forwarded to local officials with the department of the interior who, in turn, kept senior bureaucrats, cabinet members, and the prime minister well informed.[32] Not surprisingly, all of this was of great concern to the Governor General, Lord Grey. Like his predecessors at Rideau Hall, he was an aristocrat, a veteran of the civil service, and the sole official link between Ottawa and London. As such, he handled the voluminous correspondence that flowed back and forth across the Atlantic and advised the Dominion government on issues of national and imperial concern. Indeed, when it came to this particular realm of political affairs, Lord Grey's opinion still carried considerable weight on Parliament Hill, despite the largely ceremonial and administrative character of his position; "[A] vigilant watch must be maintained on all events, statements, and newspaper reports which, if repeated in India, might be likely to inflame the minds of those who are tools and victims of sedition," he cautioned the prime minister in early December 1908.[33] Sound intelligence was, of course, key to this approach, and the Governor General worked hard to ensure that it found its way to the Colonial Office and India Office in London and the

Criminal Intelligence Department and Viceroy in Calcutta. (The words "Copy Sent To India" are stamped on many of these documents.)[34]

But Lord Grey was not the only imperial official to play a decisive role in the expansion of political policing in Canada. When Ottawa first proposed the idea of relocating South Asians, Colonel E.J. Swayne, governor of British Honduras and an "Old Indian officer," was in London on other business; evidently, he offered up his colony as a possible solution to Canada's "Hindoo" problem. On his way back to Belize in early December 1908, the governor travelled via Canada and met with the Governor General and prime minister, and later undertook his own investigation of "matters affecting the East Indian Community in British Columbia."[35] Less anxious than Lord Grey about the potential risks posed by the likes of Teja Singh, Swayne nevertheless possessed strong opinions on the future of South Asian immigration to Canada. It should be "controlled," he wrote forcefully, not only because it ran counter to the basic principle of "keeping the temperate zones of the Empire for the surplus white population, whilst giving full scope to our Asiatic subjects in the more tropical zones of the Empire," but because "[t]he terms of close familiarity which competition with white labour has brought about, do not make for British prestige." Swayne understood well that for a small, yet influential group of whites and South Asians, familiarity did not breed contempt; rather, on occasion, it produced solidarity.[36] "Socialists of a very undesirable type have made it their business to tamper with the East Indians in Vancouver," he wrote bluntly, referring specifically to the radical Industrial Workers of the World (IWW) and the Socialist Party of Canada (SPC).

> The return of the Sikhs to the Punjab amongst their friends, spreading as they will, new, ill-digested socialistic ideas, and the familiar knowledge of such defects amongst their white fellow labourers, such as labour rivalry would have been only too ready to pick out, cannot but tend to re-act amongst the military classes of the Punjab, to the detriment of British prestige. As — when all is said and done, looking at our position in India as a whole, it must be recognized that it is by prestige alone that India is held and not by force, the importance of a circulation of labour between Vancouver and India as affecting that prestige is such, I submit, as cannot be wisely overlooked.[37]

In that regard, he concluded, in addition to "strictly limiting" immigration from India to Canada, it was crucial that the "doings of the Brahmin section be closely watched" on an ongoing basis. "I do not think that a better man than Mr. Hopkinson of the Calcutta police could be found for this work," Swayne stated, recognizing the importance of having another old India man on the job. "I suggest Mr Hopkinson be appointed as Dominion police officer on special duty at Vancouver, for the special purpose of this enquiry, and the Government of India be asked to place him in official communication with the head of the Calcutta police in order to further this work."[38]

With the support of the department of the interior, the Governor General, and the governor of British Honduras, the federal government officially hired Hopkinson early in 1909. He was given a permanent position in the immigration department in Vancouver and was assigned to the Dominion Police, although he did not receive a formal commission in the federal force until 1911; for $100 per month, he was expected to keep tabs on the South Asian community and undertake regular duties as an interpreter. Ottawa was certainly pleased with its new agent. So, too, no doubt, were imperial officials. Just months before Hopkinson was hired, Lord Morely, the secretary of state for India, had written to Lord Minto, the Viceroy, and lamented the absence of knowledgeable undercover agents. "The whole Indian field is absolutely unfamiliar, in language, habits, and everything else," he said. "In short, both you and I can easily understand that the ordinary square-toed English constable, even in the detective branch, would be rather clumsy in tracing your wily Asiatics."[39]

Between 1909 and 1914, Hopkinson was exceptionally busy. His activities, which were initially confined to British Columbia's Lower Mainland and southern Vancouver Island, but later expanded to include Washington state, Oregon, and northern California, were many and varied: he attended suspicious meetings and rallies in order to "find out their latest move and the methods they are adopting for the bringing out of their countrymen from India," monitored the movements of community leaders and their supporters within the province and across the Canada–U.S. border, and kept tabs on foreign-language newspapers. Taraknath Das's *Free Hindusthan*, which was then based out of Seattle, but printed locally with the assistance of the Socialist Party of Canada, was of particular interest; so, too, was *Swadesh Sewak* (Servant of the Country), a Gurmukhi-language monthly published out of Vancouver by Guran Ditta Kumar, a former college instructor from Calcutta who arrived in British Columbia in 1907.[40] Kumar, a self-described "Punjabi Buddhist" and "Worker in the cause of Temperance and Vegetarianism," first came to Hopkinson's attention as a possible "agitator" nearly two years later. At that time, he was living in Victoria and running a grocery store that was set up with the assistance of his friend Taraknath Das. The link between the two men, which was common knowledge within South Asian community, prompted Hopkinson to pay a visit to Kumar's modest operation in the provincial capital in August 1909. Disguised as a lumberman looking for labourers, the rookie Dominion Police investigator discovered that Kumar not only sold *Free Hindusthan* and the radical, London-based *Indian Sociologist*, but that he was in constant contact with the ubiquitous Teja Singh and Taraknath Das, who was then living in Washington state. The following November, Kumar surfaced in Vancouver, opened the "Swadesh Sewak Home," and started publishing a newspaper by the same name early in 1910. Hopkinson kept tabs on him at all times. "The tone of this paper gradually became more and more objectionable," one government official's report concluded, based in part on his assessments. "[I]t was addressed principally to the Sikhs in the Indian Army in their own language, and was being sent out to India in considerable numbers."[41]

Hopkinson's modus operandi — the reading of seditious publications, the tracking of suspected agitators — was the stock and trade of political policing; it would have been easily recognized by the likes of Patrick Nolan or Henri LeCaron. But unlike his 19th-century counterparts, Hopkinson was not simply an undercover agent, he was an immigration inspector as well, and this dual role was fraught with both tension and danger, especially at a time when Ottawa was making use of its wide-ranging discretionary powers to curtail immigration from Asian countries.[42] Hopkinson, like other immigration inspectors, possessed the authority to admit, reject, or initiate deportation proceedings against new immigrants — powers that were eminently useful to someone concerned with both the administration of immigration policy and with limiting the development of seditious behaviour. In this important respect, not only was Hopkinson deeply lodged in the day-to-day controversies surrounding the enforcement of the landing restrictions for South Asian immigrants, but, ironically, his very actions in this regard helped to stoke the unnerving anti-British sentiment which prompted the federal government to hire him in the first place. For Hopkinson, carrying out this dual role would in the end prove deadly.[43]

From the moment that the federal government imposed the "continuous journey" restrictions in 1908, the South Asian community mounted a sustained campaign to overturn them, a development that enhanced the profile of committed radicals and brought moderates in touch with more militant ideas and tactics. One of the men who was particularly forceful in his denunciation of federal immigration policy, and Hopkinson's role in implementing it, was Chagan Kairaj Varma, a native of Porbander State in Kathiawar who came to Canada on a tourist visa in January 1910 after spending several years working in Japan and Hawaii. Known in British Columbia by the Muslim name Hussain Rahim, the middle-aged, westernized Hindu quickly assumed a leadership role in the South Asian community— an ascent that was driven, in part, by his own ongoing conflict with the immigration service.[44] Shortly after turning up in Vancouver, Rahim, who was interviewed by Hopkinson upon his arrival, established the Canada India Supply and Trust Company and applied for permission to stay in the country. Immigration officials responded to this request by arresting Rahim and initiating deportation proceedings against him. "You drive us Hindus out of Canada and we will drive every white man out of India," he snarled after being apprehended. Hopkinson, for one, took this threat seriously. Later that same day, city police located a notebook belonging to Rahim that contained information about explosives and the names of activists from other countries. In the weeks and months that followed this startling revelation, both men found themselves in court as Rahim, like other "Hindoos" before him, challenged the government's deportation order—successfully arguing that particular elements of the orders-in-council that curbed South Asian immigration exceeded the scope of authority available to the federal government under the *Immigration Act*.[45] Writing to the prime minister and imperial authorities, including Lord Crewe, secretary of state for India, in 1910, the Hindustani Association, a self-help organization that assisted in Rahim's legal defense, laid bare the wider political significance of this narrow technical argument: "[A]s British subjects, we demand our inalienable rights to reside more freely in the British Empire and request immediate redress against high-handed, impolite, and Empire-breaking actions of local authorities."[46]

For Hopkinson, Rahim's legal victory was infuriating for many reasons, not the least of which was that it heightened his prestige in the South Asian community, called into question the legitimacy and effectiveness of the immigration branch, and, by virtue of the issues at stake, provided further grist for the anti-colonial mill. "The failure ... of the Department to deport Rahim from Canada has so bolstered up his position in the Hindu community here as to make him a leader and a counsellor in respect to all matters concerning their community," he informed his Ottawa-based handler, W.W. Cory. "Canada would be well rid of Rahim and the exposure of his true character would have a very beneficial effect on [the] community."[47]

Significantly, the "true character" that Hopkinson had in mind was not simply Rahim's obvious commitment to the "liberty, equality, and fraternity of the Hindustani Nation," but his immersion in Vancouver's vibrant left-wing milieu, which was then dominated by the Socialist Party of Canada and the Industrial Workers of the World. Indeed, as the tone and content of his intelligence reports filed in the wake of the court case suggest, Hopkinson became increasingly preoccupied with this cross-fertilization of socialist and anti-colonial politics in general and Rahim in particular—eventually discovering that he joined the SPC shortly after arriving in the country, helped to form a South Asian local, and, drawing on the resources of the Canada India Supply and Trust Company, posted bail for several members of the IWW jailed during the free speech fights in 1912. "The Hindus have up to the present never identified themselves with any particular Political party and the introduction by Rahim of the socialist propaganda into this community, is, I consider a very serious matter, as the majority of these people are uneducated and ignorant and easily led like sheep by a man like Rahim," he wrote in April 1912. "The danger to the country is not here but the question is what effect will all these Socialistic and Revolutionary teachings have on the people in India on the return of these men primed with Western methods of agitation and Political and Social equality."[48]

It was, of course, a rhetorical question. Hopkinson knew well that Rahim, as important as he was in Vancouver, was but one cog in a much larger political machine: there were South Asian men "primed" with both "Western methods of agitation" and ideas of "political and social equality" operating up and down the west coast. Not surprisingly, then, Hopkinson eventually broadened his area of surveillance to include Seattle, Portland, San Francisco, and Berkeley, where Lala Har Dayal, a Delhi-born, Oxford-educated nationalist, and founder of the Ghadar (Mutiny) Party was lecturing in Indian philosophy. Hopkinson was certainly familiar with Har Dayal prior to this trip, but it was not until the British consul-general in San Francisco informed him that the university instructor was linked to both the assassination attempt on the Viceroy, Lord Hardingue, on 23 December 1912 and the Industrial Workers of the World, that he placed him under constant surveillance. By the February, 1913, the file on this suspected agitator had ballooned considerably, and Hopkinson, who was increasingly adamant that Har Dayal was one of the most dangerous men around, more dangerous than Taraknath Das, was despatched to London by the federal government to report on the current state of anti-colonial agitation on the Pacific coast.

Acting largely on the basis of his brief, British and Canadian authorities agreed that Hopkinson should be more secure, both institutionally and monetarily. As a result, in addition to his existing relationship with the Canadian government, Hopkinson was placed on the India Office's payroll — the money coming out of the Department of Criminal Intelligence's budget — and ordered to report directly to the superintendent of police for Bombay, J.A. Wallinger, who was in England at the time working in the area of intelligence and imperial defence. Canada's new Governor General, the Duke of Connaught, was not impressed with this new arrangement. "It is highly ... undesirable that this work should be dependent on the existence of a single individual," he informed the Colonial Office. "In the first place, Mr Hopkinson has to cover the entire country from San Francisco to New York and from the Canadian to the Mexican frontiers. In the second place, the entire system — if system it can be called — is dependent on one man. If any thing happens to Mr Hopkinson, the work would automatically collapse." For the Governor General, the best way to proceed was to transfer Hopkinson to the Indian government. After all, he stated, the *über*-agent's work was both costly and increasingly about imperial, not national concerns. Wallinger disagreed, and argued persuasively that "the permanent transfer of Mr Hopkinson to the Indian Government would entirely destroy Mr Hopkinson's usefulness. He is now, by very reason of his multifarious offices,... in a position to do some delicate work for us without having suspicion drawn upon himself. Once he is removed from these offices he would be a marked man."[49]

There was certainly an element of truth in Wallinger's assessment. By virtue of his "multifarious offices," Hopkinson was indeed in a position to carry out "delicate" intelligence work amongst South Asians up and down the west coast, just as he had been doing for the better part of six years. At the same time, however, the former police superintendent was dead wrong on the question of anonymity: if anything, Hopkinson's dual role as an immigration officer and undercover agent kept him in the public eye. At no time was this more obvious than during the spring and summer of 1914 when Gurdit Singh, a Sikh entrepreneur, and 376 passengers — 340 Sikhs, 24 Muslims, and 12 Hindus — challenged the federal government's ban on South Asian immigrants by sailing into the port of Vancouver on board the *Komagata Maru* on 23 May. "We are British citizens and we consider we have a right to visit any part of the Empire. We are determined to make this a test case and if we are refused entrance into your country, the matter will not end here," Gurdit Singh told the local press, shortly after dropping anchor. "What is done with this shipload of my people will determine whether we shall have peace in all parts of the British Empire."[50]

Immigration officials did with this batch of immigrants what they had done to scores of others since the federal government first introduced selective landing requirements: they refused to allow them on shore. That action, coupled with Gurdit Singh's resolve to overturn the ban, prompted a long and sometimes violent stand-off which ended on 23 July when the passengers of the *Komagata Maru*, after facing down an attempt by Canadian authorities to seize the ship by force, decided to return to India. Throughout this incident, Hopkinson handled the negotiations between those on ship and those on shore — including senior immigration officials and the immigrants' allies, the so-called "shore committee" which was led by Hussain Rahim.[51] From the perspective of many in the South Asian community, the entire *Komagata Maru* affair simply reinforced their belief that a toxic combination of fear, loathing, and racial hatred was at the core of both Canadian immigration policy and the broader white society that sanctioned it. What was more, it reaffirmed graphically the hypocrisy of the British empire. Sikhs and Hindus simply did not possess the same rights and freedoms as freeborn Englishmen — in Canada or India for that matter. And Hopkinson, by virtue of his role as an immigration officer and secret agent, was as guilty as anyone in defending this condition of inequality.

In the months that followed the *Komagata Maru*'s departure, several of Hopkinson's informants were murdered. The killings, which were carried out by militants within the South Asian community, provoked violence among Sikhs themselves. On one occasion, one of Hopkinson's supporters, Bela Singh, was attacked while praying at the Sikh temple in Vancouver. In response, he shot and killed two people, including the priest, and wounded seven others before turning himself in. On 21 October 1914, Hopkinson himself was murdered. While waiting outside a Vancouver courtroom to testify in defense of Bela Singh, he was shot and killed by Mewa Singh, a man who was apprehended during the summer standoff trying to smuggle arms into Canada, but later became an informant for Hopkinson.[52] "[He] is the last man one would have suspected of committing the deed," Malcolm Reid, Hopkinson's superior at the immigration branch, wrote to Ottawa. "[N]o doubt, however, he was influenced by the local Hindu community. The man is now perfectly cheerful in his cell and to all intents and purposes seems glad he has murdered Hopkinson."[53] Glad, perhaps, because this was not simply an act of revenge, but an act of greater political and religious significance, spurred on, in part, by the Ghadar Party's call to arms that accompanied Britain's declaration of war in August, "it was the duty of a good man to give his life for a good cause," Mewa Singh said just weeks before he was hanged for his crime. Hopkinson was given a lavish funeral by the municipal and federal government — approximately 2,000 people marched in the procession — and his widow received a lump sum payment from the Indian government. The money came from its secret service fund, for Indian, British, and Canadian authorities wanted to keep Hopkinson's activities hidden.[54]

Few institutions mirror a nation's political culture, the working logic of its government, and the preoccupations of its leaders more than its secret police — its status, its modus operandi, and its declared enemies.[55] Canada's experience in the realm of political policing was simultaneously related to its colonial legacy but also at some remove from it. If, as one prominent scholar of the history of state security has argued, England was slow to develop a political police because of its extraordinary self-confidence, even in the face of Fenian bombs, the same cannot be said of the slowly emerging new nation-state north of the United States.[56] Even at its birth, Canada's secret service went unchallenged. No political debate surrounded it; no one criticized its creation. The profound suspicion so prevalent in Victorian England of spies, spying, and secrecy found few reflections in Canada. The suspension of habeas corpus, political arrests without charges, mail seizure, secret agents, perhaps even agents provacateurs — all were present in these formatives years of the new nation-state and all went unopposed but for the victims. The immense self-confidence of Victorian liberalism that girded the powerful association of a secret police with oligarchy found little resonance in the Canadian outpost of Empire, where republicanism, bound up in broader agendas of French-Canadian and Irish nationalism, was cast as antithetical to the new nation-state. That new nation-state contained a secret service, largely imposed from above, and extended westward with a remarkable ruthlessness, from its inception.

At the same time, however, the links between Canada's colonial legacy and its foray into political policing were extensive. Throughout this period, the federal government was preoccupied with "suspected seditionists" whose real enemy was the mother country itself. While Irish and South Asian radicals possessed different histories of oppression under British colonialism, and drew on different cultural and religious resources to mount their political challenges, their activities abroad were very similar. Leavened by the freedom available to them outside their respective homelands, they dedicated considerable intellectual and financial resources to raising people's consciousness, articulating a vision of national independence, forging links between those in exile and those at home, and taking action. While the government found its embryonic secret service imminently useful in policing these pockets of anti-colonial agitation, it relied heavily on Britain's extensive diplomatic presence in the United States, as well as the imperial civil service, to get the job done. Not only were consular officials, many of whom operated their own undercover agents, important in this regard, but so too were the various Governors General who served as Canada's head of state during this time — in particular Lord Monck and Lord Grey. A position of little significance today, the governors general possessed extensive knowledge of imperial politics, served as important conduits for the copious intelligence that flowed between Ottawa and London, and were strong advocates of political policing as a means to solve both national and imperial problems. Only in the immediate post-war period, when Canada's internal security problems changed and its own capacity to monitor dissidents expanded, would the role of this imperial infrastructure diminish.

With the onset of the Great War, the question of who posed a threat to Canada's internal security and the best way to limit that potential threat would undergo a decisive shift at the highest levels of the federal government. As Hopkinson's increasing preoccupation with the influence of "socialistic ideas" suggests, signs of this transformation away from imperial concerns were already present before the outbreak of hostilities in Europe. Indeed, in the crucible of the war years, Ottawa would suspend civil liberties outright, create a new battery of repressive measures, and, under the pretext of mobilizing the nation for war, move to crush its new, more formidable opponent: labour and the left. For the better part of the twentieth century, the Canadian state was preoccupied by the "red menace."[57] With the end of the Cold War, and the events of 11 September 2001, however, its focus has shifted to new security threats: anti-globalization activists and suspected terrorists who, for extraordinarily different reasons, and in extraordinarily different ways, have mounted a challenge to the global reach of a different superpower. That Ottawa's response to these challenges has enhanced state power, eroded the balance between different branches of government, blurred the line between legitimate and illegitimate political action, and circumscribed individual and collective rights is clear. What is less appreciated is that this political solution possesses a long history in Canada, one that stretches back well over a century.[58]

Notes

* This paper has been previously published in the *Osgoode Hall Law Journal*, vol. 41; Number 2,3 (Summer/Fall 2003), 211-240. Reprinted by permission.

1 For an earlier version of this essay, which focuses solely on the Fenian threat, see Gregory S. Kealey, "The Empire Strikes Back: The Nineteenth-Century Origins of the Canadian Secret Service," *Journal of the Canadian Historical Association* 10 (1999), 3–18. The history of the Canadian secret service, from its origins to the present day, is the focus of Reginald Whitaker, Andrew Parnaby, and Gregory S. Kealey, *Secret Service: Political Policing in Canada, from the Fenians to Fortress America* (Toronto: University of Toronto Press, forthcoming).

2 For an overview of the "non-existent historiography" of political policing in Canada see, for example, Wesley K. Wark, "Security Intelligence in Canada, 1864–1945: The History of a 'National Insecurity State'," in Neilson and McKercher, eds., *Go Spy The Land: Military Intelligence in History* (Westport: Praeger, 1992), 153–178 and Larry Hannant, "Access to the Inside: An Assessment of Canada's Security Service, A History," *Intelligence and National Security* 8:3 (1993), 149–159. Greg Marquis's, "The 'Irish Model' and Nineteenth-Century Canadian Policing," *The Journal of Imperial and Commonwealth History* 25:2 (May 1997), 193–218, provides an excellent discussion of policing in British North America, including the colonies of Vancouver Island and Newfoundland. See also: Elinor Senior, *British Regulars in Montréal: An Imperial Garrison, 1832–1854* (Montréal: McGill-Queen's University Press, 1981); Allan Greer, "The Birth of the Police in Canada," in Greer and Radforth, eds., *Colonial Leviathan: State Formation in Mid-Nineteenth-Century Canada* (Toronto: University of Toronto Press, 1992), 17–49; Brian Young, "Positive Law, Positive State: Class Realignment and the Transformation of Lower Canada, 1815–1866," in *Colonial Leviathan*, 50–63; Greer, *The Patriots and the People* (Toronto: University of Toronto Press, 1993); Hereward Senior, *Constabulary: The Rise of Police Institutions in Britain, the Commonwealth, and the United States* (Toronto: Dundurn Press, 1997). The objectives of the rural police are contained in *Rule for the Government of the Rural Police: Circular Memorandum for the Information and Guidance of the Inspecting Stipendiary Magistrates, in the Montréal District* (Montréal: Montréal Police Department, 1839), 2. Britain's antipathy to political policing during the Victorian era, and the very different practices undertaken in the colonies, is taken up by Bernard Porter in his groundbreaking *The Origins of the Vigilant State: The London Metropolitan Police Special Branch Before the First World War* (London: Wakefield and Nicholson, 1987), 188 to 194.

3 The literature on the Fenians, in particular, and Irish nationalism, more generally, is massive. For the purposes of this discussion, the best place to start is with John Newsinger's slim volume *Fenianism in Mid-Victorian Britain* (London: Pluto Press, 1994); it provides a cogent account of the important debates associated with Feniansim and a thorough bibliography. W.S. Neidhardt, *Fenianism in North America* (University Park, Pennsylvania: Pennsylvania State University Press, 1975); Keith Amos, *The Fenians in Australia, 1865–1880* (Kensington: New South Wales University Press, 1988); and Brian Jenkins, *Fenians and Anglo-American Relations During Reconstruction* (Ithaca and London: Cornell University Press, 1969) are also useful. Interestingly, Fenian leader James Stephens was also a member of the International Working Man's Association, the so-called First International which included Karl Marx. See Hereward Senior, *The Fenians in Canada* (Toronto: Macmillan, 1978), 40–1. For a brief, yet informative introduction to the large literature on the Irish in urban America see Amy S. Greenberg's review essay, "Irish in the City: Recent Developments in American Urban History," *The Historical Journal* 42:2 (1999), 571–581.

4 On this last point see Jenkins, *Fenians and Anglo-American Relations During Reconstruction*; David Montgomery, *Beyond Equality: Labor and Radical Republicans, 1862–1872* (New York: Knopf, 1967), and Eric Foner, "Class, Ethnicity, and Radicalism in the Gilded Age: The Land League and Irish-America," *Marxist Perspectives* 1:2 (Summer 1978), 6–55 at 30–31. During the U.S. election of 1868, John A. Macdonald remarked: "Both Republicans and Democrats will fish for the Irish vote, and therefore wink as much as possible at any action of the Fenian body." See National Archives of Canada (NAC), John A. Macdonald Papers (JAMP), MG 26, Letterbooks, Volume XI, John A. Macdonald to Col. Ermatinger, 8 February 1868.

5 In the Canadian context, the Fenian question has been framed in many ways: as an important moment in Canadian military history; as a significant dimension of Irish immigrants' experience in the New World; and as a key variable in the debates associated with the act of Confederation in 1867. See: C.P. Stacey," A Fenian Interlude: The Story of Michael Murphy," *Canadian Historical Review* XV (1934), 133–54 and "Fenianism and the Rise of National Feeling in Canada at the Time of Confederation," *Canadian Historical Review* 3 (September 1931), 238–261. In the latter, Stacey writes: "Fenianism provided a most beneficial influence upon the immediate fortunes of the project, by creating at once a popular apprehension of danger which worked strongly against the possibility of a repudiation of parliament's decision, and by engendering eminently favourable to the success of an experiment in nation building." See also: Peter M. Toner, "The Military Organization of the 'Canadian' Fenians, 1866–1870," *Irish Sword* 10:38 (Summer 1971), 26–37; Toner and D.C. Lyne, "Fenianism in Canada," *Studia Hibernica* 12 (1972), 27–76; Toner, "The Rise of Irish Nationalism in

Canada, 1858–1884," (Ph.D. Thesis, National University of Ireland, 1974); Senior, *The Fenians in Canada*; Senior, entry for Michael Murphy in *Dictionary of Canadian Biography* Volume IX (Toronto 1976), 587–88; George Sheppard, "'God Save The Green': Fenianism and Fellowship in Victorian Ontario," *Histoire Sociale–Social History* 20:39 (May 1987), 129–44; Jeff Keshen, "Cloak and Dagger: Canada West's Secret Police, 1864–67," *Ontario History* 79 (1987), 353–77; Toner, "The Home Rule League: Fortune, Fenians, and Failure," *The Canadian Journal of Irish Studies* 15:1 (July 1989), 7–19; Oliver Rafferty, "Fenianism in North America in the 1860s: The Problems for Church and State," *History* 84 (April 1999), 257–77; Brian Clarke, *Piety and Nationalism: Lay Voluntary Organizations and the Creation of an Irish-Catholic Community in Toronto, 1850–1895* (Kingston and Montréal: McGill-Queen's University Press, 1993). The quotation from the *Irish Canadian* is taken from Clarke, p. 175.

6 NAC, JAMP, MG 26, Letterbooks, Volume VII, John A. Macdonald to Cockburn, 2 January 1865 and 7 February 1865; Volume VIII, Macdonald to Lord Monck, 18 September 1865; Macdonald to McMicken, 22 September 1865. On the counterattack undertaken by British officials in 1865 and 1866 see Newsinger, *Fenianism in Mid-Victorian Britain*, Chapter 3, "The Rising," 40–47. Stephens eventually escaped from jail with the assistance of two Fenian jailers, a development that, according to Newsinger, "highlighted the extent of the IRB's penetration of the police, the prison service, and government department generally." See p.44.

7 NAC, JAMP, MG 26, McMicken Correspondence, Gilbert McMicken, "Special Order," 31 December 1864. See also the various letters between British, Canadian, and American officials in *Correspondence Relating to the Fenian Invasion and the Rebellion of the Southern States* (Ottawa: Hunter Rose, 1869), in particular: Simon Cameron, U.S. Secretary of War, to the Right Honourable Sir Edmund Head, 24 October 1861; Lord Lyon to Lord Monck, 8 August 1864; Lord Monck to E. Cardwell, Member of Parliament, 23 September 1864; British Legation, Washington, to Seward, U.S. Secretary of State, 26 December 1864.

8 This paragraph, including the material on the social origins of the spies, is drawn from various spy reports contained in NAC, JAMP, MG 26, McMicken Correspondence, Volumes 236–240; the final quotation is taken from McMicken Correspondence, Volume 237, McMicken to Macdonald, 9 April 1866. See also Keshen, "Cloak and Dagger."

9 Archibald's time in Newfoundland corresponded with the colony's transition to responsible government; see Leslie Harris's entry for Archibald in the *DCB* Volume XI (Toronto 1982), 27–29. This paragraph is based on: Edith J. Archibald, *The Life and Letters of Sir Edward Mortimer Archibald* (Toronto: George N. Morang, 1924); William D'Arcy, *The Fenian Movement in the United States* (New York: Russell and Russell, 1947); Neidhardt,

Fenianism in North America, chapter four, "The Fenians Prepare"; Wayne A. Crockett, "The Uses and Abuses of the Secret Service Fund: The Political Dimension of Police Work in Canada, 1864–1877," (M.A. Thesis, Queen's University, 1982), 66; Leon O'Broin, *Fenian Fever: An Aglo-American Dilemma* (New York: New York University Press, 1971), 41–51; Harold A. Davis, "The Fenian Raid on New Brunswick," *Canadian Historical Review* 36:4 (December 1955), 316–334; W.L. Morton, "Lord Monck and Nationality in Ireland and Canada," *Studia Hibernica* 13 (1973), 77–100.

10 NAC, JAMP, MG 26, Governor Generals' Correspondence, Volume 93, Monck to John A Macdonald, 10 November 1865; Volume 1, D'Arcy McGee to John A. Macdonald, 2 November 1865. McGee himself was once an "Irish rebel"; see Bill Kirwin, "The Radical Youth of a Conservative: D'Arcy McGee in Young Ireland," *The Canadian Journal of Irish Studies* 10:1 (June 1984), 51–62. More on McGee and the Fenians can be found in Michael Cottrell, "Irish Catholic Leadership in Toronto, 1855–1882: A Study in Ethnic Politics," (Ph.D., University of Saskatchewan, 1988), chapter three, and in "'Grits and Fenians': The Hibernian Benevolent Society and the Politics of Nationalism, 1861–1866." The thorny relationship between Catholic religious leaders, the Hibernian Benevolent Society, and the Fenians is taken up in Clarke, *Piety and Nationalism*, chapters 7 and 8.

11 Crockett, "The Uses and Abuses of the Secret Service Fund," 40; D'Arcy, *The Fenian Movement*, 97–98.

12 Keshen, "Cloak and Dagger," 366.

13 The links between Archibald and the lieutenant governor of New Brunswick are discussed in Davis, "The Fenian Raid on New Brunswick," 316–334. See also Carl Betke and S.W. Horrall, "Canada's Security Service: An Historical Outline, 1864–1966," RCMP Historical Section, 1978, unpublished manuscript in possession of the authors, 67–70

14 Toner, "The 'Green Ghost'," 37–41; Davis, "The Fenian Raid on New Brunswick"; Newsinger, *Fenianism in Mid-Victorian Britain*, 46. The connection between the Fenian invasion and Confederation is a staple of the Canadian literature. See C.P. Stacey, "Fenianism and the Rise of the National Feeling in Canada at the Time of Confederation," and "A Fenian Interlude: The Story of Michael Murphy"; Davis, "The Fenian Raid on New Brunswick," 332–334; Senior, *The Fenians in Canada*.

15 John A. Cooper, "The Fenian Raid of 1866," *Canadian Magazine* X:1 (November 1897), 41–55.

16 Quoted in Jenkins, *Fenians and Anglo-American Relations During Reconstruction*, 140.

17 According to Keshen: "At the most crucial moment of his career as Stipendiary Magistrate for Canada West, McMicken failed miserably. His presence and that of the frontier force change nothing. The Fenian raid proceeded as planned, and the government was unprepared." See "Cloak and Dagger," 368.

18 Betke and Horrall, "Canada's Security Service," 77–79; Keshen,"Cloak and Dagger," 353–77; Philip Stenning, "Guns & the Law" in *The Beaver* (December 2000–January 2001), 6–7. The final quotation is D'Arcy, *The Fenian Movement in the United States*, 194–211.

19 Charles Curran suggests that Beach adopted this name in jest: "Le Caron is argot for 'slice of fat bacon.' Beach was lean and wiry. It has been suggested that he took the name by way of a joke." See his "The Spy behind the Speaker's Chair," *History Today* 18 (1968), 745–54. That Beach chose a French name at all was likely because of the British government's support of the South during the Civil War. See also Cole, *Prince of Spies: Henri LeCaron* (London: Faber and Faber, 1984) and Henri LeCaron, *Twenty-Five Years in the Secret Service* (London: Heinemann, 1892).

20 Hereward Senior, "Québec and the Fenians," *Canadian Historical Review* 48 (1967), 35–39; Toner, "The 'Green Ghost'," 40–44; NAC, JAMP, MG 26, Letterbooks, Volume XI, Macdonald to Anderson Hebert, 13 April 1868.

21 "In calmer times, he might well have been acquitted," Senior concluded in his "Québec and the Fenians." See p.39. Senior also provides an intriguing thumbnail sketch of James Patrick Whelan and an analysis of the trial.

22 Gilbert McMicken, "The Abortive Fenian Raid on Manitoba: Account By One Who Knew Its Secret History," The Historical and Scientific Society of Manitoba, Transaction No. 32, Season 1887–88 (Winnipeg: Manitoba Free Press Print, 1888[?]); A.H. de Trémaudan, "Louis Riel and the Fenian Raid of 1871," *Canadian Historical Review* 2 (June 1923), 132–144; J.P. Pritchett, "The Origin of the So-called Fenian Raid on Manitoba in 1871," *Canadian Historical Review* 1 (March 1929), 23–42.

23 This opening paragraph on the British in India from 1857 to 1914 is drawn from Judith M. Brown, *Modern India: The Origins of An Asian Democracy* (Oxford: Oxford University Press, 1994), 1–193. Other influential publications include C.A. Bayly, *Indian Society and the Making of the British Empire* (Cambridge: Cambridge University Press, 1988); B.S. Cohn, "Representing Authority in Victorian India," in Eric Hobsbawm and T.O. Ranger, eds., *The Invention of Tradition* (Cambridge: Cambridge University Press, 1983), 165–209. Richard J. Popplewell examines the development of political policing in India under Lord Curzon and, as the title of his book implies, its role in the defence of the empire at home and abroad. See his *Intelligence and Imperial Defence: British Intelligence and the Defence of the Indian Empire, 1904–1924* (London: Frank Cass, 1995). On the development of the Indian radical tradition abroad see Arun Coomer Bose, *Indian Revolutionaries Abroad, 1905–1922: In the Background of International Developments* (Patna: Bharati Bhawan, 1971). James Campbell Ker's *Political Trouble in India, 1907–1917* (Delhi: Oriental Publishers, 1917 [1973]) is an indispensable source. Ker was a senior officer in the Home Department of the Indian government; he also worked as personal assistant to the Direc-

tor of Criminal Intelligence. This book is a collection of the confidential documents he amassed during his tenure at the DCI. As such, it details the activities of radicals operating outside India.

24 On the emigration of South Asians to British Columbia see Hugh Johnston, *The Voyage of the Komagata Maru: The Sikh Challenge to Canada's Colour Bar* (Oxford: Oxford University Press, 1979); Norman Buchignani, Doreen M. Indra, with Ram Srivastiva, *Continuous Journey: A Social History of South Asians in Canada* (Toronto: McLelland and Stewart, 1985), 4–70; Hira Singh, "The Political Economy of Immigrant Farm Labour: A Study of East Indian Farm Workers in British Columbia," in Milton Israel, ed., *The South Asian Diaspora in Canada: Six Essays* (Toronto: Multicultural History Society of Ontario, 1987), 87; Jean Barman, *The West Beyond the West: A History of British Columbia* (Toronto: University of Toronto Press, 1991), 145–148; Richard Rajala, *The Legacy and the Challenge: A Century of Forest Industry at Cowichan Lake* (Lake Cowichan: Lake Cowichan Heritage Advisory Committee, 1993); Achana B. Verma, "Status and Migration Among the Punjabis of Paldi, BC and Paldi, Punjab" (Ph.D. thesis, Simon Fraser University, 1994); Ninette Kelley and Michael Trebilcock, *The Making of the Mosaic: A History of Canadian Immigration Policy* (Toronto: University of Toronto Press, 1998), 142–156.

On anti-Asian agitation in British Columbia see: Rennie Warburton, "Race and Class in British Columbia: A Comment," *BC Studies* 49 (Spring 1981); Patricia Roy, *A White Man's Province: British Columbia Politicians and Japanese Immigrants, 1858–1914* (Vancouver: University of British Columbia Press, 1989); W. Peter Ward, *White Canada Forever: Popular Attitudes and Public Policy Towards Orientals in British Columbia* Second Edition (Montréal: McGill-Queen's University Press, 1990); Mark Leier, *Red Flags and Red Tape: The Making of a Labour Bureaucracy* (Toronto: University of Toronto Press, 1995), 125–142; Kelley and Trebilcock, *The Making of the Mosaic*, 142–156. It is important to note that not all white British Columbians endorsed the politics of Asian exclusion; the radical labour movement and the Protestant missionaries were important voices of tolerance. On the former see Mark Leier, *Where The Fraser River Flows: The Industrial Workers of the World in British Columbia* (Vancouver: New Star Books, 1990); on the latter see Ruth Compton Brouwer, "A Disgrace to 'Christian Canada': Protestant Foreign Missionary Concerns about the Treatment of South Asian in Canada, 1907–1940," in Iacovetta, Draper, and Ventresca, eds., *A Nation of Immigrants: Women, Workers, and Communities in Canadian History, 1840s–1960s* (Toronto: University of Toronto Press, 1998), 361–383.

The prime minister's sense for the political situation in India is illustrated in India Office Library and Records (IOLR), Judicial and Public Department Proceedings (JPDP), 320/1909, Governor-General of Canada to Colonial Office, 11 December 1908. Earl Grey quotes a letter from Prime Minister Wilfrid Laurier dated 8 December 1908.

25 The immigration figures are contained in Kelley and Trebilcock, *The Making of the Mosaic*, 142–156.

26 The biographical information on Hopkinson is drawn from the following sources: Hugh Johnston, "The Surveillance of Indian Nationalists in North America, 1908–1918,"*British Columbia Studies* 78 (Summer 1988), 5 and note 4; Johnston, *The Voyage of the Komagata Maru*, 1, 7, 137 note 1, 138, note 13; Buchignani, Indra, and Srivastiva, *Continuous Journey*, 25, 30 note 42; Popplewell, *Intelligence and Imperial Defence*, 150–151, 163 note 25.

Details of Hopkinson's father's career in the army vary widely. Popplewell states that he "had been one of the military escort of Sir Louis Cavagnari massacred at Kabal in 1879," leaving Hopkinson and his mother "stranded at Lahore in the Punjab." Buchignani, Indra, and Srivastiva suggest that "Hopkinson's father was a non-commissioned officer in the British Indian army, who was reputed to have been killed by Afghan raiders when Hopkinson was young." As a result, they assert, Hopkinson was "raised in India by his Brahmin mother" and was "fiercely anti-'seditionist'." Johnston, whose work is perhaps the most comprehensive, states in *Voyage* that Hopkinson's father was "a sergeant instructor of volunteers at Allahabad."

27 The information on Taraknath Das is taken from: IOLR, JPDP, 320/1909, "(Confidential) Memorandum on Matters affecting the East Indian Community in British Columbia, by Colonel E.J.E Swayne." See also: N.N. Bhattacharya, "Indian Revolutionaries Abroad," *Journal of Indian History* 50 (1972), 415; Arun Coomer Bose, "Indian Nationalist Agitation in the U.S. and Canada until the Arrival of Har Dayal," *Journal of Indian History* 43 (1965), 227. According to Das, *Free Hindusthan* "advocates the liberal principles of man and puts forth undeniable facts and fights about the exploiting principles of the British government in Hindustan." This quotation appears in Brij Lal, "East Indians in British Columbia, 1904–1914: An Historical Study in Growth and Integration," (M.A. Thesis, University of British Columbia, 1976), 60–61. On Das see Bose, *Indian Revolutionaries Abroad*, 48–52; Ker, *Political Trouble in India*, 119–120. This source also contains translations of various articles that appeared in *Free Hindusthan*; see p. 120–122.

28 There is some disagreement amongst scholars as to whether or not Hopkinson was sent to British Columbia by Indian authorities. Popplewell argues strenuously that "the initiative in the surveillance of Indian agitators on the Pacific Coast at this time came entirely from the Canadian side and not from India, let alone from the British government in London." See p. 151 in his book. In *Voyage*, Johnston states flatly that "he had turned up in Vancouver in 1908 … an Inspector of the Calcutta Metropolitan

police ... officially on leave, but pursuing investigations for the Criminal Intelligence Department in India." These statements are not necessarily contradictory: it is possible that he was sent by the CID in India, but the proposal to place the South Asian community under constant surveillance came first from the Canadian government. On the emergence of the CID in India see Brown, *Modern India* 137–139; Popplewell, *Intelligence and Imperial Defence*, 8–164, especially 147–164.

29 IOLR, JPDP, 320/1909, J.B. Harkin to Superintendent of Immigration, 29 July 1908.

30 The rise and fall of the British Honduras scheme in chronicled in J.B. Harkin's own *The East Indians in British Columbia: A report regarding the proposal to provide work in British Honduras for the indigent unemployed among them* (Ottawa: Department of the Interior, 1908). See also: IOLR, JPDP, 320/1909, Harkin to Superintendent of Immigration, Ottawa, 29 July 1908; Harkin to Ministry of Interior, 16 October 1908 and 6 November 1908; Wilfred Collet, Officer Administering the Government, British Honduras, to Secretary of State of Canada, 19 and 26 November 1908; Collet to Colonial Office, 2 and 3 December 1908; "Certified Copy of a Report of the Committee of the Privy Council, approved by His Excellency the Governor General on 10 December 1908."

The final quotation in this paragraph is from IOLR, JPDP, 320/1909, Governor General of Canada to Colonial Office, 21 December 1908. Along with his confidential letter, Lord Grey included a detailed memorandum prepared by W.W. Cory, the deputy minister of immigration, about the relocation plan. The memo includes excerpts from the telegrams and letters exchanged between Hopkinson, Harkin, and ministry officials after the delegation returned from Belize; see Hopkinson to Harkin, 20 and 23 November 1908; Harkin to Cory, 23 November 1908. Johnston takes up the issue of Hopkinson's alleged corruption in "The Surveillance of Indian Nationalists," 6, note 11. "Hopkinson was loyal to British India and Anglo Canada and behaved accordingly," he concludes. "One does not need evidence of personal corruption to explain the part he played."

31 This brief biography of Teja Singh is based on: IOLR, JPDP, 320/1909, "(Confidential) Memorandum on Matters affecting the East Indian Community in British Columbia, by Colonel E.J.E. Swayne; Information as to Hindu Agitators in Vancouver"; Buchignani, Indra, and Srivastiva, *Continuous Journey*, 26–27; Johnston, *Voyage*, 12; Bose, *Indian Revolutionaries Abroad*, 52–55. Harkin certainly did not think much of Teja Singh either, referring to him as the "absolute dictator of the community." See his *East Indians in British Columbia*, 4.

32 IOLR, JPDP, 320/1909, Governor General of Canada to Colonial Office, 21 December 1908. Lord Grey's letter included a memorandum prepared by W.W. Cory, the deputy minister of immigration, which included ex-

cerpts from correspondence exchanged between Hopkinson, Harkin, and ministry officials. On this issue see: Hopkinson to Harkin, 20 November 1908; Cory to Harkin, 4 December 1908; Vancouver *Province*, 23 November 1908.

33 On the role of the Governor General during this period see Robert Bothwell, Ian Drummond, and John English's *Canada: 1900–1945* (Toronto: University of Toronto Press, 1987), 111–118; IOLR, JPDP, 320/1909, Governor General of Canada, Lord Grey, to Prime Minister Wilfrid Laurier, 3 December 1908.

34 IOLR, JPDP, 320/1909, Governor General of Canada to Colonial Office, 9, 10, 11 and 21 December 1908; Secretary of State for the Colonies to Governor General of Canada, 23 December 1908; Colonial Office to India Office, 30 December 1908. See also Johnston, "The Surveillance of Indian Nationalists," 9.

35 IOLR, JPDP, 320/1909, Colonel Swayne to Governor-General of Canada (Confidential), 30 December 1908. The "old Indian officer" quotation is from Colonel Swayne to Officer Administering Government, British Honduras, 20 December 1908. The most important document in this regard is Swayne's report: "(Confidential) Memorandum on Matters affecting the East Indian Community in British Columbia, by Colonel E.J.E Swayne; Information as to Hindu Agitators in Vancouver."

36 On the links between the IWW, SPC, and East Indian community in British Columbia see IOLR, JPDP, 1309/1909, Hopkinson to J.B. Harkin, 19 December 1908. Prime Minister Laurier was particularly enchanted with Colonel Swayne, remarking in a letter to the Governor General after meeting the governor, "[he is] the very embodiment of that most valuable class of officers developed by Indian service, trained for war and civil service, honest and true as the sun's light, modest and firm, devoted to the Empire and equally devoted to the those over whom they are appointed to rule. Happy the country served by such men, and no country but England ever produced such men." See: IOLR, JPDP, 320/1909, Laurier to Lord Grey, 8 December 1908.

37 IOLR, JPDP, 320/1909, "(Confidential) Memorandum on Matters affecting the East Indian Community in British Columbia, by Colonel E.J. E Swayne; Information as to Hindu Agitators in Vancouver."

38 Ibid. As a servant of the empire, Swayne was aware of wider, global patterns of political violence linked to radicalism and nationalism, including the Fenian bombing campaigns that took place in Britain in 1881 and 1884, the wave of anarchist bombings that rocked western Europe and North America in the 1890s, and the nationalist agitation that had been destabilizing parts of India on and off for decades.

39 Quoted in Popplewell, *Intelligence and Imperial Defense*, 129. It is important not to overstate the novelty of this manoeuvre; this was not the first time

that Ottawa had been caught between the rock of national politics and the hard place of imperial concerns and used secret agents to help solve the conundrum. That Hopkinson was hired into the ranks of the Dominion Police with little difficulty or debate underscores just how commonplace this practice had become. At the same time, however, that the British and Indian governments were relying on a Dominion Police officer to track "wily Asiatics," instead of fielding their own agents in North America, suggests that intelligence gathering at the imperial level was still a somewhat ad-hoc affair.

40 This brief section on the general nature of Hopkinson's duties is based on the following: IOLR, JPDP, 1309/1909, Hopkinson to Cory, 10 September 1908; 19 December 1908; Hopkinson to Cory, 4, 18 January 1909; 15 April 1909; 18 May 1909; Hopkinson to Cory, 14 January 1910; 6/1604, Hopkinson to Cory, 10, 23, and 29 March 1911; Hopkinson to Cory, 7 June 1911; 4 August 1911; Hopkinson to Cory, 7 and 8 December 1911.

41 This section on Kumar is based on: IOLR, JPDP, 1309/1909, Hopkinson to Cory, 12 August 1909; Hopkinson to Cory, 12 August 1909; 6/1064, Hopkinson to Cory 8 May 1911; 13 May 1911; 4917/1911, Secretary to the Government of India to Sir Richmond Ritchie, His Majesty's Under Secretary of State for India, 25 November 1911. The final quotation in this paragraph is taken from a report entitled "History Sheet of G.D. Kumar" attached to the secretary's letter of 25 November 1911. The reference to Kumar being a "Punjabi Buddhist" is taken from Johnston, "The Surveillance of Indian Nationalists," 9.

42 On this changing nature of Canadian immigration policy at this time see Kelley and Trebilcock, *The Making of the Mosaic*, chapter four, "Industrialization, Immigration, and the Foundation of Twentieth-Century Immigration Policy, 1896–1914," 111–163; Barbara Roberts, *Whence They Came: Deportation from Canada, 1900–1935* (Ottawa: University of Ottawa Press, 1988), 1–70. The 1910 revisions to the *Immigration Act* sought further to insulate boards of inquiry created under the auspices of the immigration branch from judicial scrutiny; section 23 of the revised Act stated that "no court or judge could interfere with a decision of a "Board of Inquiry." See Johnston, *Voyage*, 18.

43 IOLR, JPDP, 1309/1909, Hopkinson to Cory, 20 September 1909; Harkin to Cory, 22 September 1909; 6/1064, Hopkinson to Cory, 14 October 1910; Hopkinson to Cory, 17, 19 and 28 November 1910; Hopkinson to Cory, 16 March 1912; 6/1064, Hopkinson to Cory, 28 June 1912.

44 This brief biography of Rahim is culled from IOLR, JPDP, 6/1064, Hopkinson to Cory, 26 March 1912; 1 April 1912; Buchignani, Indra, and Srivastiva, *Continuous Journey*, 36–47; Johnston, *Voyage*, 9–12; Peter Campbell, "East Meets Left: South Asian Militants and the Socialist Party of Canada in British Columbia, 1904–1914," *International Journal of Canadian Studies*

20 (Fall 1999), 35–65. Johnston is dismissive of Rahim's left-wing politics, writing that he "assimilat[ed], in a half-digested way, the language of class warfare." For a more sympathetic reading see Campbell's "East Meets Left" and *Canadian Marxists and the Search for the Third Way* (Montréal and Kingston: McGill-Queen's University Press, 1999), 10–11, 18, 74, 247 note 2, and 248 note 25.

45 IOLR, JPDP, 6/1064, J.H. MacGill, Immigration Agent, to Cory, 28 October 1910; Hopkinson to Cory, 3 November 1910; Hopkinson to Cory 17 February 1911.

46 Quoted in Lal, "East Indians in British Columbia," 65–66. G.D. Kumar was the organization's secretary treasurer.

47 IOLR, JPDP, 6/1064, Hopkinson to Cory, 26 March 1912.

48 IOLR, JPDP, 6/1064, Hopkinson to Cory, 22 February 1912; Hopkinson to Cory, 1 April 1912; Hopkinson to Cory, 9 May 1912. Rahim's involvement in the SPC is detailed in Campbell, "East Meet Left," 46–50. More on the IWW can be found in Mark Leier, "Solidarity on Occasion: The Vancouver Free Speech Fights of 1909 and 1912," *Labour/Le Travail* 23 (Spring 1989), 39–66; *Where the Fraser River Flows*; *Rebel Life: The Life and Times of Robert Gosden, Revolutionary, Mystic, and Labour Spy* (Vancouver: New Star Books, 1999).

49 Quoted in Popplewell, *Intelligence and Imperial Defence*, 158.

50 See Johnston, *Voyage* and Popplewell, *Intelligence and Imperial Defence*, 159–161. The quotation is from Johnston, 37–38.

51 By all accounts, he carried out his duties well and was largely responsible for keeping a tight leash on the more belligerent and pugnacious elements within government ranks.

52 See Johnston, *Voyage*, chapter 12, "Assassination," 125–136.

53 IOLR, JPDP, 6/1341, Reid to Scott, 22 October 1914.

54 Johnston, "The Surveillance of Indian Nationalists," 22–27.

55 On this thought, see David Vital, "Not single spies, but in battalions: Espionage uncovered in France, Russia, Britain, and the US," *Times Literary Supplement* (December 2000), 4–6: "As more than one old intelligence hand has been moved to observe, few institutions reflect national character and the operative norms of government so closely as a state's intelligence arm, the status granted it, the modus operandi to which it is habituated and the confidence with which it proceed to its targets in a foreign environment."

56 For example, Porter writes of Britain's lack of "political police" that "nearly everyone in Britain regarded this as a matter for national self-congratulation: one proof, among others, of Britain's superiority over all other societies everywhere." See *Origins of the Vigilant State*, 2.

57 See the following articles by Gregory S. Kealey, "State Repression of Labour and the Left in Canada, 1914–1920: The impact of the First World War,"

Canadian Historical Review LXXIII:3 (1992), 281–315; "The Surveillance State: The Origins of Domestic Intelligence and Counter-Subversion in Canada, 1914–21," *Intelligence and National Security* 7:3 (1992), 179–210; "The Early Years of State Surveillance of Labour and the Left in Canada: The Institutional Framework of the Royal Canadian Mounted Police Security and Intelligence Apparatus, 1918–26," *Intelligence and National Security* 8: 3 (July 1993), 129–148. *The RCMP Security Bulletins* 8 Volumes (St. John's: Canadian Committee on Labour History, 1989–1997) edited by Kealey and Reginald Whitaker document the extensive surveillance undertaken by the Mounties during this period.

58 On the federal government's response see Ronald J. Daniels, Patrick Macklem, and Kent Roach, eds., *The Security of Freedom: Essays on Canada's Anti-Terrorism Bill* (Toronto: University of Toronto Press, 2001).

References

Amos, Keith. *The Fenians in Australia, 1865–1880*. Kensington: New South Wales University Press, 1988.

Archibald, Edith J. *The Life and Letters of Sir Edward Mortimer Archibald*. Toronto: George N. Morang, 1924.

Barman, Jean. *The West Beyond the West: A History of British Columbia*. Toronto: University of Toronto Press, 1991.

Bayly, C.A. *Indian Society and the Making of the British Empire*. Cambridge: Cambridge University Press, 1988.

Bose, Arun Coomer. *Indian Revolutionaries Abroad, 1905–1922: In the Background of International Developments*. Patna: Bharati Bhawan, 1971.

Brown, Judith M. *Modern India: The Origins of An Asian Democracy*. Oxford: Oxford University Press, 1994.

Buchignani, Norman, Doreen M. Indra, with Ram Srivastiva, *Continuous Journey: A Social History of South Asians in Canada*. Toronto: McLelland and Stewart, 1985.

Clarke, Brian. *Piety and Nationalism: Lay Voluntary Organizations and the Creation of an Irish-Catholic Community in Toronto, 1850–1895*. Kingston and Montréal: McGill-Queen's University Press, 1993.

Cole, J.A. *Prince of Spies: Henri LeCaron* . London: Faber and Faber, 1984.

Daniels, Ronald J., Patrick Macklem, and Kent Roach, eds., *The Security of Freedom: Essays on Canada's Anti-Terrorism Bill.* Toronto: University of Toronto Press, 2001.

D'Arcy, William. *The Fenian Movement in the United States.* New York: Russell and Russell, 1947.

Greer, Allan. *The Patriots and the People.* Toronto: University of Toronto Press, 1993.

Harkin, J.B. *The East Indians in British Columbia: A report regarding the proposal to provide work in British Honduras for the indigent unemployed among them.* Ottawa: Department of the Interior, 1908.

Israel, Milton, ed. *The South Asian Diaspora in Canada: Six Essays.* Toronto: Multicultural History Society of Ontario, 1987.

Jenkins, Brian. *Fenians and Anglo-American Relations During Reconstruction.* Ithaca and London: Cornell University Press, 1969.

Johnston, Hugh. *The Voyage of the Komagata Maru: The Sikh Challenge to Canada's Colour Bar.* Oxford: Oxford University Press, 1979.

Kealey, Gregory S. and Reg Whitaker, eds., *The RCMP Security Bulletins.* 8 Volumes. St. John's: Canadian Committee on Labour History, 1989–1997.

Kelley, Ninette, and Michael Trebilcock. *The Making of the Mosaic: A History of Canadian Immigration Policy.* Toronto: University of Toronto Press, 1998.

Ker, James Campbell. *Political Trouble in India, 1907–1917.* Delhi: Oriental Publishers, 1917 [1973].

LeCaron, Henri. *Twenty-Five Years in the Secret Service.* London: Heinemann, 1892.

Leier, Mark. *Rebel Life: The Life and Times of Robert Gosden, Revolutionary, Mystic, and Labour Spy.* Vancouver: New Star Books, 1999.

——. *Red Flags and Red Tape: The Making of a Labour Bureaucracy.* Toronto: University of Toronto Press, 1995.

——. *Where The Fraser River Flows: The Industrial Workers of the World in British Columbia.* Vancouver: New Star Books, 1990.

Montgomery, David. *Beyond Equality: Labor and Radical Republicans, 1862–1872.* New York: Knopf, 1967.

Newsinger, John. *Fenianism in Mid-Victorian Britain.* London: Pluto Press, 1994.

Neidhardt, W.S. *Fenianism in North America.* University Park, Pennsylvania: Pennsylvania State University Press, 1975.

O'Broin, Leon. *Fenian Fever: An Anglo-American Dilemma*. New York: New York University Press, 1971.

Popplewell, Richard J. *Intelligence and Imperial Defence: British Intelligence and the Defence of the Indian Empire, 1904–1924*. London: Frank Cass, 1995.

Porter, Bernard. *The Origins of the Vigilant State: The London Metropolitan Police Special Branch Before the First World War.* London: Wakefield and Nicholson, 1987.

Rajala, Richard. *The Legacy and the Challenge: A Century of Forest Industry at Cowichan Lake*. Lake Cowichan: Lake Cowichan Heritage Advisory Committee, 1993.

Roberts, Barbara. *Whence They Came: Deportation from Canada, 1900–1935* . Ottawa: University of Ottawa Press, 1988.

Roy, Patricia. *A White Man's Province: British Columbia Politicians and Japanese Immigrants, 1858–1914*. Vancouver: University of British Columbia Press, 1989.

Senior, Hereward. *Constabulary: The Rise of Police Institutions in Britain, the Commonwealth, and the United States* . Toronto: Dundurn Press, 1997.

——. *The Fenians in Canada*. Toronto: Macmillan, 1978.

Senior, Elinor. *British Regulars in Montréal: An Imperial Garrison, 1832–1854*. Montréal: McGill-Queen's University Press, 1981.

Ward, W. Peter. *White Canada Forever: Popular Attitudes and Public Policy Towards Orientals in British Columbia*. Second Edition. Montréal: McGill-Queen's University Press, 1990.

Whitaker, Reginald, Andrew Parnaby, and Gregory S. Kealey, *Secret Service: Political Policing in Canada, from the Fenians to Fortress America*. Toronto: University of Toronto Press, forthcoming.

Articles

Brouwer, Ruth Compton. "A Disgrace to 'Christian Canada': Protestant Foreign Missionary Concerns about the Treatment of South Asian in Canada, 1907–1940," in Iacovetta, Draper, and Ventresca, eds., *A Nation of Immigrants: Women, Workers, and Communities in Canadian History, 1840s–1960s*. Toronto: University of Toronto Press, 1998, 361–383.

Campbell, Peter. "East Meets Left: South Asian Militants and the Socialist Party of Canada in British Columbia, 1904–1914," *International Journal of Canadian Studies* 20 (Fall 1999), 35–65.

Cooper, John A. "The Fenian Raid of 1866," *Canadian Magazine* 1 (November 1897), 41–55.

Cohn, B.S. "Representing Authority in Victorian India," in Eric Hobsbawm and T.O. Ranger, eds., *The Invention of Tradition*. Cambridge: Cambridge University Press, 1983, 165–209.

Curran, Charles. "The Spy behind the Speaker's Chair," *History Today* 18 (1968), 745–54.

Davis, Harold A. "The Fenian Raid on New Brunswick," *Canadian Historical Review* 36:4 (December 1955), 316–334.

Foner, Eric. "Class, Ethnicity, and Radicalism in the Gilded Age: The Land League and Irish-America," *Marxist Perspectives* 1:2 (Summer 1978), 6–55.

Greenberg, Amy S. "Irish in the City: Recent Developments in American Urban History," *The Historical Journal* 42:2 (1999), 571–581.

Greer, Allan. "The Birth of the Police in Canada," in Greer and Radforth, eds., *Colonial Leviathan: State Formation in Mid-Nineteenth-Century Canada*. Toronto: University of Toronto Press, (1992), 17–49.

Hannant, Larry. "Access to the Inside: An Assessment of Canada's Security Service, A History," *Intelligence and National Security* 8:3 (1993), 149–159.

Harris, Leslie. "Edward Mortimer Archibald" in *DCB* Volume XI (Toronto 1982), 27–29.

Johnston, Hugh. "The Surveillance of Indian Nationalists in North America, 1908–1918,"*BC Studies* 78 (Summer 1988), 3–27.

Kealey, Gregory S. "The Empire Strikes Back: The Nineteenth-Century Origins of the Canadian Secret Service," *Journal of the Canadian Historical Association* 10 (1999), 3–18.

——. "The Early Years of State Surveillance of Labour and the Left in Canada: The Institutional Framework of the Royal Canadian Mounted Police Security and Intelligence Apparatus, 1918–26," *Intelligence and National Security* 8:3 (July 1993), 129–148.

——. "State Repression of Labour and the Left in Canada, 1914–1920: The Impact of the First World War," *Canadian Historical Review* LXXIII:3 (1992), 281–315.

——. "The Surveillance State: The Origins of Domestic Intelligence and Counter-Subversion in Canada, 1914–21," *Intelligence and National Security* 7:3 (1992), 179–210.

Keshen, Jeff. "Cloak and Dagger: Canada West's Secret Police, 1864–67," *Ontario History* 79 (1987), 353–77.

Kirwin, Bill. "The Radical Youth of a Conservative: D'Arcy McGee in Young Ireland," *The Canadian Journal of Irish Studies* 10:1 (June 1984), 51–62.

Leier, Mark. "Solidarity on Occasion: The Vancouver Free Speech Fights of 1909 and 1912," *Labour/Le Travail* 23 (Spring 1989), 39–66.

Marquis, Greg. "The 'Irish Model' and Nineteenth-Century Canadian Policing," *The Journal of Imperial and Commonwealth History* 25:2 (May 1997), 193–218.

McMicken, Gilbert. "The Abortive Fenian Raid on Manitoba: Account By One Who Knew Its Secret History," The Historical and Scientific Society of Manitoba, Transaction No. 32, Season 1887–88 (Winnipeg: Manitoba Free Press Print, 1888[?]).

Morton, W.L. "Lord Monck and Nationality in Ireland and Canada," *Studia Hibernica* 13 (1973), 77–100.

Pritchett, J.P. "The Origin of the So-called Fenian Raid on Manitoba in 1871," *Canadian Historical Review* 1 (March 1929), 23–42.

Rafferty, Oliver. "Fenianism in North America in the 1860s: The Problems for Church and State," *History* 84 (April 1999), 257–277.

Senior, Hereward. "Michael Murphy," in *Dictionary of Canadian Biography* Volume IX (Toronto 1976), 587–88.

——. "Québec and the Fenians," *Canadian Historical Review* 48 (1967), 35–39.

Sheppard, George. "'God Save The Green': Fenianism and Fellowship in Victorian Ontario," *Histoire Sociale–Social History* 20:39 (May 1987), 129–144.

Stacey, C.P. "A Fenian Interlude: The Story of Michael Murphy," *Canadian Historical Review* XV (1934), 133–54.

——. "Fenianism and the Rise of National Feeling in Canada at the Time of Confederation," *Canadian Historical Review* 3 (September 1931), 238–261.

Toner, Peter M. "The Home Rule League: Fortune, Fenians, and Failure," *The Canadian Journal of Irish Studies* 15:1 (July 1989), 7–19.

——. "The Military Organization of the 'Canadian' Fenians, 1866–1870," *Irish Sword* 10:38 (Summer 1971), 26–37.

——. and D.C. Lyne, "Fenianism in Canada," *Studia Hibernica* 12 (1972), 27–76.

Trémaudan, A.H. "Louis Riel and the Fenian Raid of 1871," *Canadian Historical Review* 2 (June 1923), 132–144.

Vital, David. "Not single spies, but in battalions: Espionage uncovered in France, Russia, Britain, and the US," *Times Literary Supplement* (December 2000), 4–6.

Wark, Wesley K. "Security Intelligence in Canada, 1864–1945: The History of a 'National Insecurity State'," in Neilson and McKercher, eds., *Go Spy The Land: Military Intelligence in History.* Westport: Praeger, 1992, 153–178.

Unpublished Manuscripts

Betke, Carl, and S.W. Horrall, "Canada's Security Service: An Historical Outline, 1864–1966," RCMP Historical Section, 1978.

Cottrell, Michael. "Irish Catholic Leadership in Toronto, 1855–1882: A Study in Ethnic Politics." Ph.D. Thesis, University of Saskatchewan, 1988.

Crockett, Wayne A. "The Uses and Abuses of the Secret Service Fund: The Political Dimension of Police Work in Canada, 1864–1877." M.A. Thesis, Queen's University, 1982.

Lal, Brij. "East Indians in British Columbia, 1904–1914: An Historical Study in Growth and Integration." M.A. Thesis, University of British Columbia, 1976.

Toner, Peter M. "The Rise of Irish Nationalism in Canada, 1858–1884." Ph.D. Thesis, National University of Ireland, 1974.

Verma, Achana B. "Status and Migration Among the Punjabis of Paldi, BC and Paldi, Punjab." Ph.D. thesis, Simon Fraser University, 1994.

Other Sources

National Archives of Canada, John A. Macdonald Papers.

India Office Library and Records, Judicial and Public Department Proceedings.

Rule for the Government of the Rural Police: Circular Memorandum for the Information and Guidance of the Inspecting Stipendiary Magistrates, in the Montréal District (Montréal: Montréal Police Department, 1839).

Correspondence Relating to the Fenian Invasion and the Rebellion of the Southern States (Ottawa: Hunter Rose, 1869).

6

Anti-Terrorism and Rights in Canada: Policy Discourse on the "Delicate Balance"

Patrick J. Smith

A delicate balance was the title of the November, 1983 Special Senate Committee (Pitfield) Report on Security Intelligence in Canada. According to committee chair, Michael Pitfield and colleagues: "the need to balance collective security — the safety of the state and its institutions from threats of espionage, terrorism and subversion — with individual rights to privacy, to dissent, to be politically active and to hold and express unpopular or radical opinions is a challenge to be faced (and) perhaps the most important ... matter ... to be considered when dealing with ... the establishment of a security intelligence system."

Many critics at the time concluded that the legislative compromise of Bill C-9 which created the Canadian Security Intelligence Service (CSIS) in 1984 had not met all the tests of balance which the Pitfield Committee had recommended. The Senate Committee concluded the following:

> There is a very basic tension between the concepts of collective and individual security, and it must be addressed at virtually every stage in the formation and operation of a security intelligence agency. To a significant degree, ... individual rights depend upon maintenance of collective security. Both ends are desireable, but they also make

> competing demands on the institutions of a democratic state. Either end, by itself, could be easily attained, but at great expense to the other. The crucial task is to arrive at an appropriate balance of the two. The raison d'être of a security intelligence agency is the preservation of a free and democratic state in which individual liberty can be maintained. Thus, the degree to which such an agency impinges unjustifiably on freedom is a measure of its failure.

The Canadian compromise of the 1980s was to allow for an "efficient" security intelligence service but to balance this with clear mechanisms for accountability. And in some ways, the creation of both an Inspector General (the Minister's "eyes and ears" in CSIS), and the Security Intelligence Review Committee (SIRC—a post-audit oversight committee made up of five governmental and opposition recommended appointees which could instigate investigations on their own or based on complaints, including queries from the public), became Canadian contributions to the world of security intelligence and its governance.

Despite some early tensions and initial operational concerns critiqued by the Security Intelligence Review Committee (SIRC), by the "five-year" official review, Parliament concluded that CSIS was "In Flux, But Not In Crisis" and the Government (in response), simply that the agency was "On Course." Those conclusions set the tone for the rest of the 1980s and throughout the 1990s.

Then came September 11, 2001. The aftermath of those acts of terrorism on the United States has had a profound and unsettling effect on the so-called balance of rights and security in countries such as Canada in the months which immediately followed.

As with the original (C-157 and C-9) bills to create CSIS, the post-September 11, 2001 legislative efforts on anti-terrorism in Canada faced the same dilemma—rights vs. security. Most indications from the policy discourse around anti-terrorism efforts—including continuing efforts to amend relevant legislation—whether by civil libertarians, the Canadian Bar Association, the federal privacy commissioner, media or NGOs such as Amnesty International—are that the delicate balance has not been maintained: in September 11th's aftermath, security has won out over rights in Canada.

This article seeks to do two things: (1) Trace the debates around rights vs. security in the early 1980s creation of CSIS; and (2) Look at this same debate around anti-terrorism and public order and safety post-September 11 in Canada.

Finding the Balance: CSIS and Policy Discourse on Security and Rights in the 1980s

At the centre of earlier debates about how Canada ought to deal with issues of security and intelligence and the maintenance of basic human rights were two fundamental issues — accountability and efficiency. Peter Self has argued that the central question in public administration is how to find the appropriate balance between these two values.[1] In the case of a governmental structure such as CSIS, with its potentially intrusive investigatory capacity, the issue is even more fundamental. Finding the appropriate balance between accountability and efficiency for a spy agency in a democracy is no easy task. It is also one that engaged a wide variety of Canadian citizens and organizations.

The policy discussions on security and rights during the late 1960s, 1970s and early 1980s focussed on *six central questions*. These were:

1. Necessity;
2. The security of the collectivity and individual rights;
3. Mandate and functions;
4. Powers (plus immunities and protections);
5. Structure and location (including management and control);
6. Accountability: maintenance and review.

Trying to find appropriate public policy responses to these questions has been problematic — in Canada and other jurisdictions. Each is briefly looked at separately.

Necessity

The premise of a perceived need for "a distinctive security intelligence capacity" is twofold: (1) that there are threats to Canadian security and (2) that the Canadian state has the duty to protect itself from these threats.

Threats to Canadian Security

Both the 1968 Mackenzie *Royal Commission on Security* and the 1981 McDonald *Commission of Inquiry Concerning Certain Activities of the RCMP* concluded that there were threats to the security of Canada. McDonald summarized three types of threats:

1. *Activities of foreign intelligence agencies*: This threat required that information was necessary on terrorist techniques, recruitment methods of foreign agents[2] and world conditions.[3]
2. *Terrorism*: This threat required intelligence and security services for special events such as Olympic Games, World Expositions, G-7 Meetings, Summit Meetings, etc. or crises such as hijackings, kidnappings, bombings, "Squamish 5," etc.
3. *Domestic Subversion*: Routine monitoring to provide advance warnings of threats to Canadian security such as by the FLQ, etc.

The response of the Trudeau government to Justice McDonald's report was Bill C-157 — a new proposed law on security and intelligence. C-157 garnered considerable opposition from groups as varied as civil liberties associations, ethnic groups, and the Canadian Bar Association. Within months, the government established a Senate Committee on Security and Intelligence which held hearings in late 1983. The Committee was chaired by Senator Michael Pitfield, former senior bureaucrat and Clerk to the Privy Council. Seventy-six individuals and organizations — former Solicitors General, provincial governments, Canadian Police associations, Civil Liberties organizations, Bar Associations, and ethnic organizations — appeared before the Committee. As well, 25 additional briefs were submitted to the Standing Committee of the Canadian Senate on the Canadian Security and Intelligence Service. These came from the Canadian Labour Congress, the Canadian Union of Public Employees, Human Rights organizations, other provincial governments, and other associations and individuals. All participants recognized some necessity for a security and intelligence capacity.

Not all participants accepted *all* the conditions as supporting the *necessity* argument, however. Civil Liberties groups were prepared to accept the necessity of securing Canadian interests from foreign agents and terrorism, but had difficulty with how to find an appropriate balance between security and intelligence needs and democratic rights when it came to the problem of domestic subversion.

In a May, 1984 brief to the Pitfield Committee, the B.C. Civil Liberties Association felt that such matters could be left under "normal policing," with some special unit of the police to deal with foreign agents and terrorism. Also in the brief was a concern with the desirability of premising a Security Service on domestic subversion threats. The McDonald *Commission of Inquiry Concerning Certain Activities of The RCMP* whose investigation had precipitated this particular discussion of a discrete security and intelligence agency pointed out advantages of a separate Security Service, yet argued that the "need for security has to be balanced against other values" and that such a service has to be justified to the public: if there is to be a Security Service, especially one with intrusive investigative powers, both the government and the public must have a clear understanding of the need for it."[4] The B.C. Civil Liberties Association argued there was no need to determine the answer by a cost-benefit analysis: the need for a Security Service "must be demonstrable."[5]

The Canadian State's Duty to Protect Itself from Threats

This duty was not new in the 1980s. In the 1960s the *Royal Commission on Security* chaired by Max Mackenzie, had concluded that Canada has a duty "to protect its secrets from espionage, its information from unauthorized disclosure, its institutions from subversion, and its policies from clandestine influence." Mackenzie recommended a separate Security Service, but that was not proceeded with at that time. Security and Intelligence remained a part of the RCMP—at least until RCMP "wrongdoings" precipitated the McDonald Report recommendations that a new civilian service be established at the start of the 1980s.

The result of this initial Canadian discussion was that on May 18, 1983, a bill to establish a Canadian Security and Intelligence Service, C-157, was introduced. This came about because of the "encouraged overzealousness" of the Security Branch responding to the duty to protect Canada from subversion—particularly as a result of the FLQ crisis in Québec, and the October Crisis in 1970, which resulted in the implementation of the *War Measures Act*.[6] It was supported by contentions that the RCMP Security Service failure resulted in the need for a *War Measures Act* "overkill." This overzealousness involved members of the Security Branch in "wrongdoings." The disclosure that the Security Branch was involved in breaking and entering, illegal mail openings and wiretap, as well as barn burnings, etc. forced the Government to respond.

First it established the McDonald *Commission of Inquiry Concerning Certain Activities of The RCMP*. McDonald reported, in 1981, with recommendations to change substantially the nature of security and intelligence operations in Canada. McDonald discovered that the RCMP had infiltrated the Parti Québécois and New Democratic Party's "Waffle movement," and that it had been engaged in other illegal activities. Civil liberty associations' submissions to McDonald concluded that "there were pressures on the police to ignore the niceties of lawful behaviour, ... to regard police illegalities as merely 'technically illegal'."[7] They also noted that the RCMP internal disciplinary action might result from failure to obey an order and that the RCMP paid the fines and salaries of convicted members while suspended or imprisoned, thereby tolerating illegal behaviour. That was all because of an "overemphasis on national security" versus "the protection of democratic values." While Security Services may have — as Mackenzie noted — special skills in ferreting out information, they were not similarly adept in evaluating its significance — particularly where it develops a "world view in the organization which may give too much weight to perceived threats." The tendency to overuse the *Official Secrets Act* and other emergency powers was also problematic; illegal activity often resulted.

The Security of the Collectivity and Individual Rights

The (1982) Canadian Charter of Rights and Freedoms — itself a product of constitutional discourse on rights and other issues in the early 1980s[8] — reminded Canadians that rights and freedoms were not absolute: Section 1 stated that the *Charter* "guarantees the rights and freedoms set out in it subject only to such reasonable limits prescribed by law, as can be demonstrably justified in a free and democratic society."

The 1983 Pitfield *Senate Committee on Security and Intelligence* summed the policy dilemma around creating CSIS most clearly: "The need to balance collective security — safety of the state and its institutions from threats of espionage, terrorism, and subversion — with individual rights to privacy, to dissent, to be politically active, and to hold and express unpopular or radical opinions is a challenge" regarding a security service. This tension "must be addressed at virtually every stage of the formation and operation of a security intelligence agency."[9]

The Pitfield Committee's conclusion was that "the raison d'être of a security intelligence agency is the preservation of a free and democratic state in which individual liberty can be maintained."[10] In that, the Committee was supported by the McDonald Commission: "Canada must both meet the requirements of security and the requirements of democracy: we must never forget that the fundamental purpose of the former is to secure the latter." Much of the policy discourse on creating CSIS was less certain. In pointing out the disadvantages, the B.C. Civil Liberties Association, for example, noted that "there is no reason to think that the history of other security services will not be substantially repeated here, and this must give us pause in two particulars: (1) the tendency of such agencies to exaggerate threats; and (2) the fact that personnel of dubious virtue and judgment often find homes — sometimes in high places — there."[11] The result was often spectacularly bad advice and flagrant violations of civil liberties. John Sawatsky noted that subversion combined with espionage and terrorism in the security branch of the RCMP proved the point.

The key policy dilemma remained how to find the "appropriate balance" between these two needs. Regarding the establishment of a separate security service, the issue dilemma was heightened as it involved such dimensions as "intrusive investigatory powers." The question, as posed by civil libertarians, is "are the risks worth the benefits?" In Canada, Mackenzie, McDonald, Pitfield and the Liberal Government of Pierre Trudeau believed they were.[12]

As a result of "events," such as those uncovered by McDonald, the Canadian Government concluded that it needed to restructure security intelligence activity in Canada, partly because the current arrangement (involving the RCMP) brought "normal" policing and the administration of justice into *general* disrepute. Its May 18, 1983 introduction of Bill C-157 raised a variety of other policy concerns — particularly with regard to mandate, powers, structure and accountability. Bill C-157 received strong opposition from a variety of interested groups and individuals, which resulted in Senate hearings — the Special Committee of the Senate on Canadian Security Intelligence — which began on June 30, 1982. This Pitfield Committee held hearings until October 13, 1983. On November 3, 1983, it issued its report *A Delicate Balance: A Security Intelligence Service in a Democratic Society*. on January 18, 1984, the Government introduced a new bill, Bill C-9 — a revised version of this bill became law in Spring, 1984 creating the Canadian Security Intelligence Service (CSIS).

As an example of public policy making, the period from the introduction of *Bill* C-157 to the Pitfield Committee hearings and report to Bill C-9 took only eight months — clearly an issue on the governmental agenda. The differences between the two bills and the commentary are very illustrative of the debate over trying to find that balance on each of the four remaining central issues: mandate, power, structure and authority.

Mandate/Functions

As envisaged by Bill C-157, the primary mandate was contained in Section 14 (1) — the collection, analysis and retention functions. Section 14 (1) stated that:

> The Service shall collect, by investigation or otherwise, and analyze and retain information and intelligence respecting activities that may on reasonable grounds be suspected of constituting threats to the security of Canada and, in relation thereto, shall report to and advise, the Government of Canada.

As the Pitfield Committee concluded, on the face of it, this subsection "is unobjectionable." Yet it raised a very important question: What constitutes the "threats to the security of Canada"? Section 2 of Bill C-157 set out the meaning of such "threats":

a) Espionage or sabotage against Canada or any state allied or associated with Canada, or supporting activities;

b) Foreign influenced activities within/relative to Canada that are detrimental to Canada's interests (or any ally/associate), that are clandestine or deceptive or involve a threat to any person;
c) Activities within/relative to Canada directed toward or in support of the threat or use of acts of violence against persons or property for the purpose of achieving a political objective;
d) Acts directed toward undermining by covert unlawful acts, or directed toward or intended ultimately to lead to the destruction or overthrow of the constitutionally established system of government in Canada.

Immediately, these sections raised issues over how the agency's mandate was to be defined — broadly or narrowly. Section 14 (2) of Bill C-157 implied broadly: "Nothing in this Act restricts the service from remaining informed about the political, economic and social environment within Canada, and matters affecting that environment."

McDonald had recommended (prior to Bill C-157) that the mandate include a restriction on agency work — that it "should be limited to what is strictly necessary for the purpose of protecting the security of Canada." Pitfield's Committee heard this critique and responded — partially. Bill C-9 maintained the definitions of "threats" included in Bill C-157, but added that these did "not include lawful advocacy, protest or dissent, unless carried on in conjunction with any of these activities referred to in paragraph …" (see a–d above). The section of Bill C-9 (12:1) on Duties and Functions allowed CSIS to collect, analyze and retain, but only "to the extent that is strictly necessary." Section 12 (2) also restricted CSIS from "remaining informed except through public sources of information." Civil libertarians found these changes represented "improvements" but concluded that the definitions were "fearfully broad and open, and textured in a number of ways."[13] For example, Section 2 of Bill C-9 set out espionage but nowhere was this term defined in the CSIS Act.[14] In the end it could be broadly interpreted — as in *Webster's Dictionary* — as "any close watching, observing secretly spying." This meant that in terms of the issue of finding balance, it could be abused. McDonald had been in favour of incorporating the definition from Section 46 2(b) and Section 52 of the Criminal Code or Section 3 of the *Official Secrets Act.*

The B.C. Civil Liberties Association also concluded that additions to the end of these definitions of threats did "nothing to narrow the mandate," unless the legislation ended the sentence with dissent.[15] In the end, the B.C.CLA was "prepared to acknowledge that it was impossible to frame legislation to service the objectives of a Security Service which will not be open to serious abuse." The question therefore was whether changing these definitions was worth the potential abuses, which brought the questions back to "Is it worth it?" and "How do you find the right balance?"

Powers (and Immunities)

Section 22 of the original Bill C-157 set out the powers of CSIS: with a warrant, it allowed CSIS to:

> ... intercept any communication, or obtain any information, record, document or thing and for that purpose, authorizes those (CSIS) persons: (a) to enter any place or open or obtain access to any thing; (b) to search for, remove or return, or otherwise take, extract from or record in any other manner, the information, record or document or thing or (c) to install, maintain, or remove any thing.

Civil libertarians noted the judicial check and the necessity for the warrant to specify the type of communication to be intercepted; to identify the person (if known) whose communication was to be intercepted; the period of time the warrant would be in force; and any other judicial conditions. As Pitfield acknowledged, these intrusive investigative techniques allowed electronic surveillance, wiretapping, surreptitious entry, and mail opening, plus access to personal information in the government's possession, with the authority of a warrant.

Civil libertarians were against such broad powers. While the Pitfield Committee was in favour of broad powers, it was against Bill C-157 warrant safeguards — as having "unreasonably low standards"; warrants could be issued "too easily." It preferred the Criminal Code Part IV (1) provisions regarding electronic surveillance — i.e., try other investigative procedures first and if unsuccessful and urgency exists and there was "a grave threat to national security" then there was the possibility of warrants with fixed limits rather than leaving it solely up to judges.

They also favoured use of the Federal Court to prevent "judge shopping," and the requirement that every warrant application include details of previous applications on the same subject.

The Government's new Bill C-9 responded—though again, only partially: under Part II, Judicial Control, for example, Section 21 (5) limited warrants to one year. Opponents of this provision noted that Part IV (1) of the Criminal Code was superseded regarding interception of a communication (if warranted). Section 21 of Bill C-157 also said that regarding the protection of CSIS employees, the Director and CSIS employees "are justified in taking such reasonable actions as are reasonably necessary to enable them to perform the duties and functions of CSIS."

Bill C-9, amended via the Pitfield Committee recommendations, changed this so that the Director and his employees "have in the performance of their duties and functions the same protections under the law as peace officers have in performing their duties and functions as peace officers." Bill C-9 stated that "Where unlawful conduct is apparent, the Director must report this to the Minister" (as in Bill C-157).

Location and Structure

In 1968, Mackenzie noted the "fundamental differences between security and law enforcement." He concluded a separation of structure was therefore necessary. In 1981, McDonald did likewise. Here perhaps two issues stood out in the policy discussions: location and structural form.

Location

The location issue became known as the "civilianization debate." Many in the civil liberties community were in favour of leaving the security function with the "police." All but one of the Senate Committee supported the Bill C-157 conclusion that it should be a civilian agency. The Committee felt that security "training" was very different from training for policing and that it was also necessary to keep the police autonomous for political control; yet autonomy was against the need for a strict process of control or review of any security agency.

Pitfield concluded "that civilianization will not be a panacea" and that there would be problems of transition—yet on "balance" it was preferred, and the RCMP would keep a small branch for security liaison. (Early Security Intelligence Review Committee (SIRC) reports suggested that this RCMP-CSIS liaison was often problematic, especially in the early years of CSIS;[16] the 2002 discussions on FBI-CIA liaison in the United States in the period leading up to the events of September 11, 2001, suggest that this is not an uncommon organizational issue.) The emphasis in Pitfield's Report was that the problems of the RCMP Security Service were not of personnel in the RCMP but of "an unsatisfactory institutional framework," and "an undesirable mixture of police and security functions."[17]

The structure intended by Bill C-157 and the implementation with Bill C-9 was for the establishment of the Civilian Canadian Security Intelligence Service consisting of a Director and Employees with the principal office in the National Capital Region and with Minister-appointed offices elsewhere in Canada. The Director was to be appointed by the Government in Council (cabinet) for five years during good behaviour and allowed for reappointment, with no Director to serve more than ten years. The salary of the Director and travel and living expenses for duties were to be set by the Governor-in-Council.

Structural Form

With regard to the management of CSIS, in Bill C-157, the Minister was not empowered to override the Director regarding information gathering and disclosure—or with regard to what was to be given to the Government. In Bill C-9, the Minister could issue directives, provided that a copy of these directives was provided to the Security Intelligence Review Committee (SIRC). That provision was contained in Section 8 (4): the Governor-in-Council may make regulations (a) governing the exercise of powers and the performance of duties and functions of the Director (b) in relation to employees, governing their conduct and discipline (plus grievances). The Director and employees were required to swear oaths of allegiance and secrecy.

The changes in structure between Bill C-157 and Bill C-9 related most to the relationship between the Director and the Minister. Pitfield agreed that Bill C-157 "would give too much unchecked power to the Director with dismissal as the only sanction." Furthermore, it would remove the Minister from CSIS operations. It was felt necessary to have a Ministerial override. The B.C. Civil Liberties Association noted that Bill C-157 "arguably eliminated Ministerial responsibility for the actions of the Director of CSIS." Bill C-9 put the ultimate responsibility in the hands of the Solicitor General, which was an improvement.

Accountability

Pitfield concluded that monitoring and reviewing was of "great importance" — vital to monitoring both the effectiveness and the propriety of agency activities. Bill C-9 was a slight improvement over Bill C-157 regarding such review; even civil libertarian groups, in general, found the changes reasonable. Problem number one remained, however: the mandate of CSIS was simply too broad.

Bill C-157 broke new ground in oversight of a security intelligence agency. The Bill established two review institutions: an Inspector General's Office (IGO): and a Security Intelligence Review Committee (SIRC). Both were new ideas for security organizations generally. Pitfield wholeheartedly agreed with the accountability concepts: he called these innovations "among the most positive aspects of the proposed legislation." Indeed these lay at the heart of the Committee's efforts to achieve *balance.*

Inspector General

This officer was to be appointed by cabinet, responsible to the Deputy Minister. The duties of this position were:

- To monitor compliance of CSIS with its operational policies:
- To review operational activities of CSIS;
- To submit certificates (twelve month reports of the Director) to the Review Committee, to insure that the Inspector General was "satisfied" with the report and that no unreasonable or unnecessary exercise of power was undertaken. The Inspector General was to be "the Minister's 'eyes and ears' in the Service"

not a functionary of CSIS, and to maintain an appropriate degree of ministerial responsibility.

The Security Intelligence Review Committee (SIRC)

Pitfield concluded that "SIRC would be the final element in the balance between mandate and powers on the one hand and the control and review on the other." SIRC was seen as having a crucial review function regarding the *Act* — in a variety of forms — e.g. regarding warrants and judges, operations and Inspector General Certificates, Ministerial directives, and a post audit on CSIS.

Under Bill C-157 SIRC was to be made up of three members appointed by Cabinet from the Canadian Privy Council (in general former Cabinet members) after consultation with Opposition and any other other Official Party (any party over twelve sitting Members of Parliament) leaders. Members of SIRC are to be appointed for a five year term and receive per diem pay (set by the Cabinet) and such staff as it required (with Treasury Board approval). All members of the SIRC were required to take an oath of secrecy. As Privy Councillors, they already had "agreed" to such conditions.

SIRC functions included a broad review capacity.

SIRC Functions

1. To ***review generally the performance by CSIS*** of its duties and functions, and specifically to:

   - Review the Reports of the Director and Certificates of the Inspector General;
   - Review the directives of the Minister;
   - Review CSIS operations regarding information gathering and monitoring;
   - Review any report, comment or complaint to SIRC;
   - Monitor any request to CSIS;
   - Review regulations;
   - Compile statistics on the operations of CSIS.

2. To ***arrange for reviews and conduct investigations*** regarding:

- Complaints;
- Reports under the Citizenship and Immigration Acts;
- Matters brought to SIRC under the *Canadian Human Rights Act*.

The procedures for SIRC were to be determined by SIRC. Bill C-9 allowed for a membership of five: all had to be Privy Councillors. Other party leaders were to be consulted, so that initial and recent membership has included Conservatives, Liberals, New Democrats, and others. SIRC has access to CSIS information or information held by the Inspector General; no information may be withheld. Anyone can complain to the SIRC (if he or she has not already done so with the Director), and if the SIRC is satisfied the complaint is not "trivial, frivolous, vexatious or made in bad faith," it will be investigated. Any SIRC member can act alone regarding complaints or investigations.

Lessons on the 1980s Policy Discourse

The annual reports of SIRC underscored a number of issues in the early operations on CSIS which reflected the policy disagreements at its inception. Many of these related to efficiency; some focussed on accountability. On the former, relations between the RCMP and CSIS were problematic for a number of years. There were also clear administrative problems, for example, between headquarters and regional offices. That was apparent in early Air India bombing investigations and led to the resignation of the first Director of CSIS. As required in the Bill C-9 legislation, there was a Parliamentary review of the Act, and of CSIS and SIRC, after its first five years. The five year Parliamentary Review Committee concluded that the spy agency was still *In Flux, But Not in Crisis,* the title of its report. As noted in the introduction, the Mulroney Conservative Government, after considering the Parliamentary review, responded with its own conclusion, also summed up by the title of the Solicitor General's report: its conclusion was that the agency was *On Course.*

Both reports, and the early SIRC annual reviews, remain useful reading for anyone wishing to understand the policy discourse—and lessons — on the basic issues set out in Pitfield and the creation of CSIS. The core dilemma of both policy and administration — *balancing the competing needs of collective vs. individual protections and rights* — was central in the 1960s, 1970s, and early 1980s. That issue would reappear after September 11th, 2001.

Off-Balance? Security, Anti-Terrorism, Public Safety, and Rights in Canada after 9/11

On October 15, 2001, just thirty-four days after the September 11, 2001, terrorist attacks in the United States, the Government of Canada introduced Bill C-36 — *An Act to amend the Criminal Code, the Official Secrets Act, the Canada Evidence Act, the Proceeds of Crime (Money Laundering) Act and other Acts, and to enact measures respecting the registration of charities, in order to combat terrorism* — aka *The Anti-Terrorism Act.*

There were *four central objectives of* Bill C-36:

- Stop terrorists from getting into Canada and protect Canadians from terrorist acts;
- Bring forward tools to identify, prosecute, convict and punish terrorists;
- Prevent the Canada–U.S. border from being held hostage by terrorists and impacting on the Canadian economy; and
- Work with the international community to bring terrorists to justice and address the root causes of such hatred.[18]

Safety and security, rather than the more careful concerns of a balance between security and rights evident in the early 1980s, was the order of the day. As noted by Ministers, the bill:

> will give law enforcement and national security agencies new investigative tools to gather knowledge about and prosecute terrorists and terrorist groups, as well as protect Canadians from terrorist attacks, including:

- Making it easier to use electronic surveillance against terrorist groups;
- Creating new offences targeting unlawful disclosure of certain information of national interest;
- Amending the *Canada Evidence Act* to guard certain information of national interest from disclosure during courtroom or other judicial proceedings;
- Amending the *National Defence Act* to continue and clarify the mandate of the Communications Security Establishment (CSE) to collect foreign communications;
- Within carefully defined limits, allowing the arrest, detention and imposition of conditions of release of suspected terrorists to prevent terrorist acts and save lives;
- Requiring individuals who have information related to a terrorist group or offence to appear before a judge to provide that information; and
- Extending the DNA warrant scheme and data bank to include terrorist crimes.[19]

Despite assurances from the Minister of Justice — that "the measures we are introducing strike the right balance between civil liberties and national security, and signal our resolve to ensure Canadians will not be paralyzed by acts of terrorism" — Canada's new *Anti-Terrorism Act* clearly tipped the delicate balance between rights and security toward security. Despite the assurances that "the proposed *Anti-Terrorism Act* includes rigorous checks and balances in order to uphold the rights and freedoms of Canadians," the only recognition on the rights side were to amend the Criminal Code to add "on-line hate" and "mischief against places of religious worship/religious property" and to amend the *Canadian Human Rights Act* to prohibit "spreading repeated hate messages" by any communications technology. To counter anticipated criticisms "the scope of the Criminal Code provisions (were) clearly defined to ensure they only apply to terrorists and terrorist groups."[20] A "three year Parliamentary review" of the legislation was added as well.[21]

Even before the introduction of Bill C-36 — and related legislative efforts C-35 and C-42 — civil libertarians anticipated a "trampling of civil rights" in the post September 11 "war on terrorism." B.C. Civil Liberties Association President John Dixon, for example, reminded Canadians of the McCarthy era attack on "civil rights — presumptions of innocence, privacy, and freedoms of conscience, association and speech." For Dixon, there was the likelihood that intelligence gathering through the overriding of privacy rights would alter "the balance to be struck between principle and need.... That depends both upon the importance of the principle and the likelihood that some sacrifice of it will yield significant results." His conclusion: "trampling on civil rights will not lead to a genuine victory against terrorism."[22] Editorial writers came to the same conclusion; the *Vancouver Sun's* David Beers, for example, bemoaned attacks on free speech following 9/11, arguing that the "you're either with us or you're against us" strategy made one wonder "whether any of it served to bring us closer to defeating the enemy out there, or whether it really was about manufacturing an enemy within."[23]

That rights-centred concern continued following introduction of Bill C-36: within days, there were widespread calls for amendments to the speedily drafted legislation. One of the biggest issues was the definition of terrorism which seemed to include both illegal strikes and civil disobedience, ("an act or omission … intended to endanger a person's life …[and] to cause serious interference with or serious disruption of an essential service" and an unlawful act committed for "ideological purpose" that causes "serious disruption of an essential service, facility or system").[24] That was far more than the U.S. definition of terrorism: "premeditated, politically motivated violence perpetrated against non-combatant targets by subnational groups or clandestine agents."

Beyond this, critics objected to others powers and controls:

- The power of detention — to allow holding a suspect without charge, with judicial approval, for 72 hours;
- The power to detain, without charge, with judicial approval, for up to one year, if the person does not agree to reasonable restrictions on his or her behaviour as a condition of release;
- The possibility of up to ten years imprisonment for "legally" "participating or contributing" to activities of a known terrorist group;

- The requirement to testify at "investigative hearings";
- Allowing the Solicitor General the power to create a "List of Terrorists" on "reasonable grounds" only—and then not require the government even to notify individuals or groups that they are on the list.

As one editorial noted, "... balancing freedom and security is always complex.... We've seen legitimate dissent suppressed in the name of public safety.... Some revision [to C-36] is needed before the law is passed. It's a free and democratic society we seek to protect and those values aren't adequately served by this draft of the law."[25]

After much pressure, the Government agreed to consider amendments in early November 2001. The discourse during this period was in both directions—though mostly the calls were for major changes to rebalance the rights side of the equation: the Canadian Police Association called for even greater investigative tools to wiretap, guard the borders and catch people with fake ID, and rejected a call for a five year sunset clause, claiming that sensitive work on ongoing terrorist investigations could be "put on hold in the months leading up to a vote on the sunset clause"; while civil rights groups charged the bill gave far to much power to authorities and threatened basic rights and freedoms.[26]

A positive Governmental response on some of the rights concerns was largely predicated on the recommendation of Canada's Senate that a five year sunset clause be included. In a unanimous Senate bipartisan committee report, the senators noted that "Bill C-36 gives powers that, if abused by the executive or security establishments of this country, could have severe implications for democracy in Canada." As a result, the Senate committee recommended that "new police powers of detention, investigation and surveillance be rescinded in five years unless specifically extended by Parliament."[27] This view was supported by civil libertarians and groups like the Canadian Bar Association.[28]

Confronting dissent from the senate and even within his own Cabinet, as well as a "national backlash" Prime Minister Jean Chrétien indicated he was "flexible" in terms of considering several amendments to the "hastily-conceived and ill-defined act," C-36.[29] One B.C. lawyer, constitutional law expert James Aldridge, in appearing before the House justice committee, argued that people and groups could have all their assets stripped away without there even having been a charge, a trial or a finding of guilt." For him, Bill C-36 was simply "a law that strips away basic legal protections" because of fear, and "as surely as night followed day, will be misused."[30] Amnesty International Canada stated that it "recognizes the right, indeed the obligation, of governments to provide to their citizens meaningful protection in the face of potential human rights abuses, including attacks of the nature of those that took place on September 11th" but that,

> … peaceful forms of dissent, widely recognized as legitimate and supported and defended by groups such as Amnesty International, could conceivably fall under the unacceptably broad definition of "terrorism" found in Bill C-36.
>
> The proposed legislation applies not only to acts motivated by political belief, ideology or religion that cause or lead to deaths or serious threats to public safety — human rights abuses that clearly must be addressed with utmost seriousness — but also to acts motivated by political belief, ideology or religion that disrupt an essential service, facility or system whether or not this disruption is intended or is likely to endanger lives and public safety.[31]

For Amnesty International Canada, "the only protection that the Bill provides for peaceful protest is that it excludes 'lawful' acts of dissent that don't endanger lives or cause a serious risk to public health or safety." Yet, "even 'unlawful' forms of dissent should not be characterized as 'terrorism' unless they endanger lives or public safety. The line between 'lawful' and 'unlawful' is too fine and often too arbitrary to say that one is acceptable, perhaps even commendable, and the other is 'terrorism,'" said Alex Neve, Secretary General of the English speaking branch of Amnesty International Canada.

> Protesters often stray beyond the bounds of what is strictly lawful through acts of trespass or civil disobedience. Should Canada respond to such acts as 'terrorism'? Absolutely not…. By asserting that acts of political protest can be considered 'terrorist' acts, even when lives and public safety are not endangered, the Canadian government plays into the hands of governments that ruthlessly suppress human

> rights.... Not only does Bill C-36 have the potential to stigmatize legitimate human rights defenders in other countries, it could create a chill on Canadian organizations trying to assist these defenders when they most need our help.[32]

In their brief to the Commons committee, Amnesty International Canada presented five case histories of human rights defenders abroad who could conceivably be considered terrorists under Bill C-36 because they led disruptive strikes, anti-logging blockages and civil disobedience campaigns declared to be unlawful by their respective governments. These activists included recipients of international human rights prizes and prisoners of conscience currently being defended by Amnesty International. Amnesty International Canada's recommendation to the government was that "Bill C-36 be amended to cover only acts that result in or are likely to lead to deaths, serious bodily harm or grave threats to public health and safety."[33]

The human rights organization also noted some positive elements in Bill C-36 such as "the commitment to launch judicial proceedings against individuals accused of serious human rights abuses such as attacks on civilians" and "the provisions ... which would strengthen Canada's laws dealing with hate crimes and propaganda."[34]

Bill C-36 was amended and passed by the House of Commons on November 28, 2001; Justice Minister Anne McLellan's Edmonton constituency office was the subject of a protesting sit-in during parliamentary consideration of C-36.[35] The *Anti-Terrorism Act* was passed by Senate and received Royal Assent on December 18, 2001. The key amendments introduced on November 20, 2001, included the following "responses" to rights criticisms:

- *A sunset clause*—in addition to a three-year Parliamentary review, the government agreed to add a sunset provision to both preventive arrest and investigative hearing provisions. These would expire after 5 years unless renewed by Parliament;
- *An Annual Report to Parliament*—a new provision which would require the federal Attorney- and Solicitor-General, and their provincial equivalents, to report annually to Parliament

on any use of either preventive arrest or investigative hearings;

- *A New Definition of Terrorist Activity* — "to ensure that protest activity, whether lawful or unlawful, would not be considered a terrorist activity unless it was intended to cause death, serious bodily harm, endangerment of life or serious risk to public health or safety"; a separate interpretive clause was added for greater clarity regarding the protection of political, religious or ideological beliefs and expression;
- *A Review Mechanism for A.G. Certificates* — rather than being issued "at any time," these could be issued only after an order by the Federal Court in a proceeding; they were to be published in the *Canadian Gazette* and could last for no more than 15 years. FOI provisions were to be the rule rather than the exception;
- *A Re-definition of Facilitation* — offences related to facilitating terrorism were to be clarified by an interpretive section on such activity;
- *Technical Amendments* — to clarify the intent of the Act and some technical changes.[36]

Bill C-36 had garnered substantial criticism from trade unions such as: the Canadian Labour Congress (CLC) and the Canadian Auto Workers (CAW); civil liberties organizations such as the Canadian Human Rights Commission; Amnesty International and the B.C. Civil Liberties Association; ethnic organizations such as the Canadian Arab Federation; the National Association of Japanese Canadians; and the Canadian Race Relations Foundation; privacy advocates and freedom of information officials from federal and provincial jurisdictions; religious groups such as the Mennonite Central Committee; university associations such as the Canadian Association of University Teachers; peace activists; environmentalists; anti globalization entities; pro-choice advocates; and Canadian nationalists.[37] All commented on the incorrectness of the Government's tilt away from a balance between rights protection on the one hand and perceived security needs after September 11 on the other. The only real shift from the early 1980s debate was that the later focus was no longer on necessity. Despite the fact that the 1980s debate had simply been on the creation of a civilian security and intelligence agency, all other areas of the '80s policy discourse continued in 2001-2002 (1) on security of the collectivity versus individual rights, (2) mandate and functions for various authorities, (3) powers, (4) structure and location of this emergency authority, and (5) centrally, accountability. All the concerns of the early 1980s had reappeared. The only difference was that the new anti-terrorism plan's legislative framework in the twenty-first century was spread across most departments and a broad cross-section of amended legislation.

Overlapping the initial Canadian anti-terrorism legislation, C-36, was another important piece of the Government's Anti-Terrorism *Plan*: Bill C-42 — the *Public Security Act*. If the Chrétien Government tipped its original C-36 legislative proposals too far in the direction of security over rights, then C-42 represented a complete unbalancing. Bill C-42, the second Anti-Terrorism Bill, was introduced in November, 2001 — before final approval of C-36. From the Government's perspective, this second Bill, the *Public Security Act*, was "an appropriate continuation of the legislative amendments tabled in Bill C-36 and introduces new amendments to the *National Defence Act* (NDA), etc. Some of the highlights of the Bill are:

> Measures to ensure the Canadian Forces have the authority to protect their computer systems networks and the information they contain from attack or manipulation. The unique role of the Canadian Forces and their ability to operate with their allies requires that they have the authority to protect their networks. Modernization of the definition of "emergency" to reflect the new security environment that would include clear reference to circumstances of armed conflict short of formally declared war. A number of important powers under the National Defence Act, such as the authority to generate forces to deal with terrorist threats, are tied to the existence of an emergency. The authority to establish temporary "military security zones" to protect Canadian Forces and visiting forces personnel and equipment that are located off Defence establishments. Military security zones may also be established to protect property, places and things that the Canadian Forces have been directed to protect.
>
> The establishment of a panel of military reserve judges to increase the flexibility of the Military Justice System to respond to increased

> demands for judicial services flowing from sudden changes in the operational tempo of the CF.
>
> The Bill includes job protection measures for reservists in the event that they must be called out compulsorily by the Government in an emergency such as armed conflict or war. At the conclusion of a period of compulsory call out, employers would be required to reinstate reservists in equivalent employment. This amendment ensures that reservists do not have to choose between possibly losing their livelihoods and breaking the law that requires them to serve when called. The new legislation will also amend the procedures that are followed when Provinces request military assistance and align it with existing mechanisms that permit the Canadian Forces to provide assistance to civilian law enforcement, which involve Federal Government input. Requests for aid of the civil power will continue to be made directly to the Chief of Defence Staff (CDS). However, the NDA amendments would allow the Minister of National Defence to provide direction to the CDS to ensure that the Government of Canada is able to manage simultaneous or multiple requests for assistance during an emergency.[38]

According to the Minister of National Defence,

> … proper security measures are necessary to safeguard our freedom and democracy. This legislation is an appropriate response to the security threat facing Canada. The Bill introduces legislation that will help the Government of Canada, the Department of National Defence and the Canadian Forces improve their ability to protect Canadians from terrorism and its effect.[39]

If Bill C-36 garnered criticism for the range of its provisions, C-42 was seen as insupportable on narrower grounds — though one seen as just as fundamental re: rights vs. security. Backbench governmental criticisms, opposition questioning and the same array of rights-centred entities all suggested that one of its central intents was to allow the Minister of National Defence to declare the June 2002, G8 summit site at Kananaskis, Alberta as "a military zone" to prevent protests. That, despite the fact that C-42 involved amendments to the following Acts:

> *Aeronautics Act; Canadian Environmental Protection Act, 1999; Criminal Code; Department of Health Act; Explosives Act; Export and Import Permits Act; Food and Drugs Act; Hazardous Products Act; Immigration Act; National Defence Act; National Energy Board Act; Navigable Waters Protection Act; Office of The Superintendent of Financial Institutions Act; Pest Control Products Act; Proceeds of Crime (Money Laundering) Act; Quarantine Act; Radiation Emitting Devices Act; Canada Shipping Acts; Biological and Toxin Weapons Convention; and The Proceeds of Crime (Money Laundering) Act.*[40]

Because of internal dissent and extensive external criticism, Bill C-42, intended to deal with the "emergency" situation perceived after the events of September, 2001 was allowed to languish in Parliamentary limbo. On April 24, 2002, it was formally withdrawn. Within a week a replacement bill—Bill C-55—the *Public Safety Act* was put before Parliament by the Government. As one media columnist noted "Bill C-42 replacement is less offensive than original," but also noted that C-42 was most likely "yanked due to concerns about its capacity to withstand a legal challenge":

> Don't for a moment believe federal government claims that the decision to dilute blatantly anti-democratic security legislation is the result of a deliberative consultation.... Much to the embarrassment of the ruling Liberals, Bill C-42 was yanked last week and replaced yesterday with a modest sibling for the more pressing reason that it was, and may still prove to be, lousy legislation. In its political wisdom, the government reached the inescapable conclusion that the original bill would fail the first, inevitable, legal challenge. So Liberals today are deep in damage control.... Bill C-42 was bad law and the Liberals knew it was bad law. They were told that by a Who's Who of non-partisan critics whose concerns ranged across the original bill's four main provisions before settling on egregious, potentially dangerous infringements of personal privacy and plans to give cabinet ministers extraordinary, unnecessary, powers. Some of those concerns were sidelined when the government split and amended legislation primarily dealing with air safety. Still, the queue

> of critics remained long and impressive ... (for) a bill that had already raised the hackles of lawyers, academics and activists.
>
> C-42 badly failed critical tests. If that legislation became law, Canadian ministers would have gained powers that would raise eyebrows and howls of protest in places with a more suspect grasp of democratic principles. Grabbing powers that more properly belong to Parliament and the people, the legislation would have given some ministers unprecedented authority to impose interim orders in secret. Loaded with the baggage of martial law and free of the necessary constraints imposed on the similar but more open Emergencies Act, the orders could have only required only cabinet approval within 90 days of being imposed. More remarkable than the powers themselves is the singular absence of any justification. No minister or government background papers ever convincingly explained why such obvious infringements of the federal Charter of Rights and Freedoms were necessary or how the legislation would make Canadians safer. Still, the government hoped to slide this law past a public grown unwary in the aftermath of other security legislation hurriedly amended with sunset clauses.
>
> That intention is now the most worrisome aspect of this sorry adventure in law making. It is reassuring the original bill is dead. What isn't comforting is that this government would once have willingly given it life.[41]

Bill C-55: The Public Safety Act

On April 29, 2002, five days after the withdrawal of Bill C-42, the Chrétien Government introduced what they termed "an improved package of public safety initiatives in support of its Anti-Terrorism Plan." This single, integrated Bill (Bill C-55 amended 21 Acts of Canada) kept key elements of the tarnished C-42. For Minister of Transportation, David Collenette, "this legislation ... responds to the need for enhanced security while respecting the rights of Canadians."[42] Not all agreed. The new C-55 legislation responded to some of the concerns raised with respect to Bill C-42, by, for example:

- further defining and circumscribing the power of the Minister of National Defence to establish Controlled Access Military Zones, and of other ministers to use interim orders in emergency situations;
- providing comprehensive parameters for the new terrorist hoax offences; and,
- providing strong measures to ensure accountability and transparency.

The *Public Safety Act*, 2002 still contains key measures that will increase the Government of Canada's capacity to prevent terrorist attacks, protect Canadians, and respond swiftly should a significant threat arise. Notably, it will:

- clarify and update existing aviation security authorities to maximize the effectiveness of Canada's aviation security system and enhance the ability of the Government of Canada to provide a safe and secure environment for air travel;
- facilitate the sharing of law enforcement and national security information between federal departments and agencies;
- deter hoaxes that endanger the public or heighten public anxiety;
- establish tighter controls over explosives and hazardous substances, activities related to other dangerous substances such as pathogens, and the export and transfer of technology;
- help identify and prevent harmful unauthorized use or interference with Department of National Defence computer systems;
- deter the proliferation of biological weapons; and,
- respect the privacy rights of Canadians.

In addition, the legislation includes new provisions to:

- improve the capacity of federal departments and agencies involved in anti-terrorism and national security activities to share critical information and coordinate their work;

- provide for the smooth flow of information between Canada and its partners internationally, particularly the United States, in order to prevent terrorist activity and protect public safety; and,
- provide a mechanism by which the Government of Canada can provide financial assistance, where necessary, to enhance marine security.

Despite the change, the new bill continued to garner mostly negative response. The *Public Safety Act*, C-55, was seen *by the Government* as the next step in its broad-based anti-terrorism plan which began with the *Anti-Terrorism Act* (Bill C-36) and was bolstered by a $7.7 billion investment in Budget 2001.[43] "Where the *Anti-Terrorism Act* focused mainly on the criminal law aspects of combating terrorism, C-55 addressed gaps in the federal legislative framework for public safety and protection."[44]

One of the measures that continued to cause concern was the powers given to the new Canadian Air Transport Security Authority, funded with $2.2 billion for air security in the December, 2001 federal Budget, and responsible for aviation security services in Canada, including:

- Pre-board screening of passengers and their belongings;
- certification of screening officers;
- Purchase, deployment, maintenance and operation of explosives detection systems;
- Federal contributions toward airport policing related to civil aviation security; and
- Contracting with the RCMP for armed officers on board aircraft.[45]

Under C-55, changes to the *Aeronautics Act* allow officials the use of passenger data in the interest of transportation security:

> The amendments would enable the Government of Canada to require air carriers and operators of aviation reservation systems (systems that provide the capability to make air reservations or issue tickets for air services) to provide information on passengers while balanc-

> ing the privacy rights of passengers. Specifically, the new provisions would require that an air carrier must, upon request, provide a designated RCMP or CSIS officer with passenger information for the Air Carrier Protective Program (RCMP officers on board aircraft), for reasons related to: immediate threats to life, health, safety or transportation security; execution of warrants for serious offences, such as murder or kidnapping, as well as warrants under the *Immigration Act*; compliance with subpoenas or court orders; and counter-terrorism investigations by CSIS. The proposed scheme would include strict controls on access, use, and disclosure, and strong privacy safeguards. Another section of the *Aeronautics Act* is being amended to clarify that air carriers may only provide information to a foreign country on passengers on board an aircraft departing from Canada, or on a Canadian airlines aircraft departing from somewhere else, if that flight is scheduled to land in that country.[46]

Canada's Privacy Commissioner, amongst others considered this an unnecessary intrusion on the privacy rights of Canadians. George Radwanski expressed "serious concerns" about C-55, noting it "raised very, very serious privacy issues."[47] He was supported by Privacy Commissioners in several provinces. These concerns were expressed even within the Liberal caucus — Montréal MP Irwin Cotler criticized C-55;[48] and Amnesty International also raised concerns about the capacity of Ministers to designate "controlled military zones" in ways which would infringe on free speech and assembly rights. Here the June, 2002 Kananaskis, Alberta G8 Summit was front and centre.[49]

These concerns were reflected in editorials and columns across the country. The *Ottawa Citizen*, for example, asked "why should police be allowed to see the private data Canadians give airlines? It's not enough to cite, as Solicitor General Lawrence McCauley did last week, the 'changed security environment'.... It (the Government) should amend the bill (C-55) to remove this unwarranted intrusion into our privacy."[50] Federal Privacy Commissioner George Radwanski called C-55 provisions simply "a power grab by the police."[51]

With the September, 2002 Throne Speech and a new session of Parliament, C-55 died on the old Order Paper. Its successor — Bill C-17, the *Public Safety Act* — seems to have learned few lessons from the protests around its intrusiveness and impingement on rights of Canadians. The Government sought to continue surfing airline manifests for information on travelers. Some small concessions appear likely here but the thrust of the most recent Canadian responses to post 9/11 appears significantly dictated by our closest North American neighbour.[52]

Even here that does not appear "enough": American responses such as racial profiling led to an October, 2002 Canadian Government travel advisory to Canadians of Arab origin.[53] Even when Canadian pressure and possible constitutional challenges produced an alteration to this U.S. policy, photographing and fingerprinting will only "no longer be automatic by place of birth"—but will continue as deemed useful by INS officials.[54]

Conclusions

The policy discourse of 2001/2002 around anti-terrorism (C-36) and public safety (C-42 and C-55—and its autumn 2002 successor) turns out not to be dramatically different than that posed in the early 1980s debates over (C-157 and C-9) the creation of the Canadian Security Intelligence Service (CSIS).

The governmental side in both eras tended to exaggerate threats and over-emphasize security needs. In both cases, the critics were able to force withdrawal of legislation (C-157 and C-42 or to wring small concessions from the new *Public Safety Act*), but, that success aside, lost ground on the rights vs. security balance. More importantly, the contents of the criticisms were remarkably similar and forced each Government of the day to recognize a need to move toward a closer balance between security needs and rights protections.

The fact that C-55 was not passed before the summer, 2002 recess of the Canadian Parliament[55] and died on the order paper until reintroduced as C-17 in late October 2002 after a new Throne Speech does not diminish the fact that the current legislative proposals continue to generate vigorous opposition based on the same rights-concerns as in the early 1980s. The main difference between the policy discourse of the two eras may be that the Canadian Government of today is able to generate more concerns on the security side of the equation to bolster their fundamental re-balancing of security over rights.[56] In response to the new Public Safety legislation, Canada's Privacy Commissioner George Radwanski suggested it "effectively expanded police powers in the guise of fighting terrorism; and "raises the spectre of a "police state."[57] As the Privacy Commissioner has stated:

> In Canada, it is well established that we are not required to identify ourselves to police unless we are being arrested or we are carrying out a licensed activity such as driving. The right to anonymity with regard to the state is a crucial privacy right. Since we are required to identify ourselves to airlines as a condition of air travel and since section 4.82 would give the RCMP unrestricted access to the passenger information obtained by airlines, this would set the extraordinarily privacy-invasive precedent of effectively requiring compulsory self-identification to the police.
>
> I am prepared, with some reluctance, to accept this as an exceptional measure that can be justified, in the wake of September 11, for the limited and specific purposes of aviation security and national security against terrorism. But I can find no reason why the use of this de facto self-identification to the police should be extended to searching for individuals who are of interest to the state because they are the subject of warrants for Criminal Code offences unrelated to terrorism. That has the same effect as requiring us to notify the police every time we travel, so that they can check whether we are wanted for something.
>
> If the police were able to carry out their regular Criminal Code law enforcement duties without this new power before September 11, they should likewise be able to do so now. The events of September 11 were a great tragedy and a great crime; they should not be manipulated into becoming an opportunity—an opportunity to expand privacy-invasive police powers for purposes that have nothing to do with anti-terrorism....
>
> The place to draw the line in protecting the fundamental human right of privacy is at the very outset, at the first unjustifiable intrusion. In this instance, that means amending the bill to remove all reference to warrants and thus limit the police to matching passenger information against anti-terrorism and national security databases.

> The concerns that I have raised in this matter since last spring have been publicly endorsed by the Information and Privacy Commissioner of British Columbia and the Information and Privacy Commissioner of Ontario; by members of every party in the House of Commons, notably including a member of the government's own Liberal caucus who is an internationally recognized expert on human rights, Irwin Cotler; and by editorials in newspapers including the *Toronto Star*, the *Globe and Mail*, the *Vancouver Sun*, the *Vancouver Province*, the *Calgary Herald* and the *Edmonton Journal*.
>
> These concerns have now been ignored by the Government.
>
> The changes that have been made in this provision in the new bill do nothing to address the fundamental issues of principle that are at stake.
>
> The Government now proposes to have regulations limiting the *Criminal Code* offence warrants for which the RCMP will be searching. But this does nothing to address the fundamental point of principle that the police have no business using this extraordinary access to personal information to search for people wanted on warrants for any offences unrelated to terrorism.... [58]

In Canada — as in the United States with its *Patriot Act*, and elsewhere — September 11, 2001 did alter the "delicate balance" between security and rights; and despite "watchdogs" in and out of government, a real re-balancing may be some time in coming.

Notes

* I am grateful for research assistance from Wendi Postnikoff and Liam Smith on this issue of anti-terrorism and rights.

1 Peter Self, *Administrative Theories and Politics*, London: Allen and Unwin, 1977, pp. 277–78.

2 See, for example, The *Globe and Mail*, March 21, 1995 on Indian Government infiltration of Sikh Youth Movement information on bombings.

3 For example, the CIA ensure academic analysis on European Union foreign policy capacity as it relates to U.S. capacity in dealing with foreign affairs.

4 The McDonald Commission, 413–14.

5 Ibid.

6 The strategic planning discussion in the October, 1970 crisis was premised on a notion of concentric circles regarding the perceived internal threat — an "apprehended insurrection." See earlier discussion on this in Chapter 7, this text.

7 B.C. Civil Liberties Association, January, 1979.

8 See, for example, Lenard Cohen. Patrick Smith and Paul Warwick, *The Vision and the Game: Making the Canadian Constitution*, (Calgary: Detselig, 1987).

9 Efficiency vs. accountability concerns regarding a security service.

10 B.C. Civil Liberties Association, Brief on C-157, p. 9.

11 Op. cit., p. 2.

12 At the same time, the French Government was rejecting such balance concerns in its dealings with Greenpeace and its ship the *Rainbow Warrior*, which French security forces sank; balancing concern about fundamental civil liberties where these contradicted perceived national interests did not seem a significant consideration.

13 B.C.CLA, Brief, op. cit., May, 1984.

14 It was elsewhere, for example in the Criminal Code, or *Official Secrets Act* or the *War Measures Act*.

15 B.C.CLA, op. cit., May, 1984 p.8.

16 Kim Bolan, "Erased tapes violate rights of Air India accused: court — Documents show rift between CSIS, RCMP," The *Vancouver Sun*, June 8, 2002, pp. A1-2.

17 Ibid., p. 8.

18 http://canada.justice.gc.ca/en/news/nr/2001/doc_27785html (Date accessed, February 3, 2002)

19 Ibid.

20 Ibid.

21 Ibid., "News release: Government of Canada Introduces *Anti-Terrorism Act*," 2001-10-15.

22 John Dixon, B.C. Civil Liberties Association, "Repeat of McCarthy Era Would Imperil Democracy," The *Vancouver Sun*, September 27, 2001, p. A15

23 David Beers, Commentary, "The New McCarthyism," The *Vancouver Sun*, October 6, 2001, p. A6.

24 *Anti-Terrorism Act*, Bill C-36.

25 Editorial, "Revision needed, now, to terrorist legislation: Adequate safeguards must control potential for abuse," The *Vancouver Sun*, October 17, 2001, p. A20; see also Daniel LeBlanc, "Senators Unite Against Anti-terror Bill," The *Globe and Mail*, November 2, 2001, p. A10..

26 See, for example, Janice Tibbetts, "Major changes to anti-terrorism legislation hinted at by Ottawa: The justice minister says "we are listening to people's concerns," The *Vancouver Sun*, November 2, 2001, p. A9.

27 See, for example, Daniel LeBlanc, "Senators Unite Against Anti-terror Bill," The *Globe and Mail*, November 2, 2001, p. A10.

28 See, for example, Editorial, "Sunset's Good Sense," The *Globe and Mail*, November 2, 2001, A14. As noted in this editorial, "... there are provisions in this bill (C-36) that should be accepted only in the context of an emergency.... Those who value the liberties enshrined in the *Charter* and championed in earlier laws are unwilling to see their curtailment become the status quo, an accepted part of the legislative scenery."

29 See, for example, Jim McNulty, "Liberals to amend bungled anti-terrorism act," The *Province*, November 14, 2001, p. A23

30 Ibid.

31 In a brief presented to the House of Commons committee reviewing Bill C-36, Amnesty International Canada, November 6, 2001, Press release.

32 Ibid.

33 Ibid.

34 Ibid.

35 Canadian Press, "Festive mood at anti-terrorism-bill sit-in," The *Province*, December 9, 2001, p. A25.

36 Department of Justice, Canada "Royal Assent To Bill C-36" December 18, 2001, http://canada.justice.gc.ca/en/news/nr2001/doc_28217.html [date accessed January 7, 2002.]

37 On these see, for example, http://www.caw.ca/visual+printlibrary/speeches+briefs/110901.asp; http://www.crr.ca/en/MediaCentre/NewsReleases/eMedCen_ NewsRel20011119.htm; http://www.prochoice connection.com/pro-can/0102win.html#terrorism; http://www.rsf.org/rsf/uk/html/ameriques/cplp01/lp01/121201.html; http://www.wsws.org/articles/2001/nov2001/can-n20.shtml; http://www.arena.org.nz/canbil.htm; http://www.chrc-ccdp. ca/ar-ra/_AR2001RA/AR01RA/annualReport_1_rapportAnnuel.asp; http://www.canadianliberty.bc.ca/liberty-vs-security/ http://www.privcom.gc.ca/media/nr-c/02_05_b_011130_e.asp;http://www.

policyalternatives.ca; http://www.geocities. com/ericsquire/articles/np042502.htm; http://perc.ca/PEN/2002-02/s-johnson2.html; www.canadianactionparty.ca

38 http://www.dnd.ca/eng/archive/2001/nov01/22NDA_b_e.htm [Date accessed. May 20/02.]

39 Transport Canada: http://www.tc.gc.ca; date accessed April 12, 2002.

40 http://www.parl.gc.ca/37/1/parlbus/chambus/house/bills/government/C-42/
C-42_1/C-42TOCE.html

41 James Travers, "Bill C-42 replacement is less offensive than original," Torstar News Service, http://www.hamiltonspectator.com/travers/562775.html

42 David Collenette, Ministerial Statement on Bill C-55, April 29, House of Commons.

43 Attached backgrounders and information are available online at http://www.canada.gc.ca.

44 Ibid.

45 http://www.tc.gc.ca/mediaroom/terrorism/faq.htm — date accessed= May 4/02.

46 http://canada.gc.ca/wire/2002/04/300402_e.html — accessed 2002-04-30.

47 See, for example, Jim Bronskill, "New anti-terrorism bill worries privacy chief: Provisions would allow police to check air travellers," The *Vancouver Sun*, May 8, 2002, p. A8, on Radwanski's letter to Minister of Transport David Collenette.

48 Ibid.

49 Ibid.

50 Editorial, Ottawa Citizen, May 23, 2002.

51 Jim Bronskill, "Passenger List Bill Draws Fire from Watchdog," The *Vancouver Sun*, May 16, 2002, p. A8.

52 See Jim Bronskill, "Security bill watered down: RCMP would have had increased powers," *Vancouver Sun*, November 1, 2002, p. A6. The changes accepted by the government will prevent the RCMP from combing airline passenger manifests according to changes tables on October 31, 2002. but could screen passenger lists for transportation security; CSIS could do likewise for transportation or national security. The revised *Public Safety Act* would also provide some limits on designating security zones — now limited to established military areas — or "on a case-by-case" basis. (In Ibid.)

53 See, for example, *Canadian Press*, "Canadians of Arab origin advised not to visit the US," *Vancouver Sun*, October 31, 2002, p. A9.

54 See Mike Trickey, "US to ease entry rules for us: Place of birth no longer an automatic trigger for rigour, Cellucci tells Graham," *Vancouver Sun*, November 1, 2002, p. A6.

55 Up to the summer 2002 recess, Bill C-55 was in Second Reading in the House of Commons — with Committee stage next. Information provided by Minister of Transportation's office, June 12, 2002. See also www.parl.gc.ca/bills. [Accessed June 12, 2002.]

56 There has been a broad discourse initially around terrorism generally, which supported governmental action on C-36 (Anti-Terrorism); then in 2002, much of this shifted to broader public safety issues, (Bills C-42 and C-55) such as bio-terrorism and cyber-terrorism. See, for example, Jeff Lee, "Reno fears a cyber Pearl Harbor: Former U.S. attorney-general is not optimistic that nations are ready for a sustained attack on support systems like food and transportation," The *Vancouver Sun*, May 1, 2002, p. A9; Kathryn May and Jim Bronskill, "Canada looking for a few good e-spies: CSIS (and CSE) launches major recruitment drive," The *Vancouver Sun*, May 13, 2002, p. A1; Joseph Brean, "Glory, fighting draw recruits to join Forces: There's no doubt that sending troops to Afghanistan was very popular," *National Post*, May 4, 2002, p. A10; and Bill Miller and Guy Gugliotta, "Dirty" Bomb meant to cause panic: U.S. authorities foil al-Qaida operative's plan to detonate a crude radiological weapon," The *Vancouver Sun*, June 11, 2002, pp. A1, A5.

57 See Jim Bronskill, "Privacy watchdog still opposes anti-terror bill: George Radwanski says the latest changes don't allay his fears of a "police state," *Vancouver Sun*, November 2, 2002, p. A6.

58 Ibid.

59 See http://www.privcom.gc.ca/media/nr-c/02_05_b_021101_e.asp for Nov 1, 2002 news release. Accessed November 3, 2002.

7

Should Canada Allow Torture Warrants for the Interrogation of Alleged Terrorists?

David MacAlister

Introduction

Debate surrounds the issue of whether a scheme should be developed whereby police may apply to a judge for a warrant authorizing the use of torture on terrorist suspects if the torture is expected to save a large number of lives. This issue is addressed from the Canadian perspective, particularly looking at the utilitarian philosophy that has typically been called upon to support such a scheme. The relevance of international and constitutional law arising in this context is also entertained, as is the applicability of the necessity defence to justify the use of torture without a warrant. Torture warrants in Canada are contrary to international and constitutional law, yet police officers employing torture tactics may be able to avail themselves of the defence of necessity on a case-by-case basis. Such warrants would permit the police to use illegal interrogation tactics in order to extract information believed to be in the possession of individuals with ties to terrorist organizations. In the post September 11th environment, it is foreseeable that police or other security agents could find themselves in a position where they would perceive a need to extract information from a person linked to terrorism in order to save the lives of innocents.

Following the events of September 11th, 2001, Harvard Law Professor Alan Dershowitz appeared on the television news program "*60 Minutes*," advancing an argument outlined in his recent writings, that Americans should develop a scheme whereby police and security forces would be able to apply to a judge for a warrant permitting them to torture alleged terrorists in certain circumstances (CBS News 2002). In recent months he has published two books, each of which elaborates his argument (Dershowitz 2002a; 2002b). In his public statements on the matter, he has issued a call for open debate on the issue. In an era when other commentators are calling to repress torture by the police (Babovic 2000) Professor Dershowitz has taken a bold step by advocating the regulated use of torture by state authorities. However, citizens of western nations should be careful about making expedient concessions to law and order. Many civil liberty concerns surface in regard to governmental response in the post-September 11th environment (Heymann 2002). One such concern is the control of police wrongdoing in the hunt for terrorists (Stuntz 2002; Uildricks and van Reenen 2001). Torturing terrorist suspects is, therefore, an area of grave civil libertarian concern.

Should the state condemn acts of torture by government agents in all circumstances? Should it be tolerated on an ad hoc basis, and if so, how do we determine when it should be tolerated? Should torture activity be structured and regulated, and if so, what form should this structure and regulation take? An argument will be presented that the state should not establish a scheme for torture warrants, but that torture should be dealt with on a case-by-case basis, as situations arise.

Terrorism transcends national boundaries, and it is foreseeable that Canada could be the target of foreign terrorist activity. Circumstances may arise where Canadian security authorities bring into custody a suspected terrorist that the police believe is holding information pertaining to the imminent loss of innocent life. It is also at least foreseeable that terrorists seeking to enter the United States to commit terrorist acts could be intercepted by Canadian authorities, and Canadian police have been grappling also with how to respond to potential terrorist attacks in the future (Hamilton 2001).

Most discussions of the use of torture entail hypothetical or "hard case" scenarios, generally involving a variation on the "ticking bomb" scenarios that have entertained legal philosophers at least since the time of Jeremy Bentham. The scenarios typically involve the police bringing into custody a person who seems to have information of a heinous deed, such as people being currently harmed, or people in a position of facing imminent harm, perhaps involving a nuclear bomb exploding in an urban area. Of course, the prisoner refuses to reveal the location, and the police contemplate torture to obtain information. Professor Dershowitz presents the following scenario, partly true and partly fantasy:

> Several weeks before September 11, 2001, the Immigration and Naturalization Service detained Zacarias Moussaoui after flight instructors reported suspicious statements he had made while taking flying lessons and paying for them with large amounts of cash. The government decided not to seek a warrant to search his computer. Now imagine that they had, and that they discovered he was part of a plan to destroy large occupied buildings, but without any further details. They interrogated him, gave him immunity from prosecution, and offered him large cash rewards and a new identity. He refused to talk. They then threatened him, tried to trick him, and employed every lawful technique available. He still refused. They even injected him with sodium pentothal and other truth serums, but to no avail. The attack now appeared to be imminent, but the FBI still had no idea what the target was or what means would be used to attack it. We could not simply evacuate all buildings indefinitely. An FBI agent proposes the use of nonlethal torture—say, a sterilized needle inserted under the fingernails to produce unbearable pain without any threat to health or life, or the method used in the film Marathon Man, a dental drill through an unanesthetized tooth (Dershowitz 2002b:143–144).

Professor Dershowitz asserts that the simple cost-benefit analysis for employing such nonlethal torture is overwhelming. He goes on to assert that virtually all members of the public support the use of nonlethal torture in "ticking bomb" cases. Even those who do not support such tactics, he claims, believe torture would happen regardless (Dershowitz 2002b:150). Given that it will happen anyway, he goes on to claim, in a democracy it is important that state agents operate above board and be accountable. He tacks on a requirement that, before they torture, they should first obtain judicial authorization in the form of a warrant.

Utilitarian Justification for Torture

Christopher Tindale identifies five justifications that have been advanced in support of the use of torture:

1. it is part of some popular tradition or established precedent;
2. it is, or is equivalent to, legitimate wartime behaviour;
3. it is justified by the need for information;
4. it is required for state security; and
5. it is justified by some compelling social good (Tindale 1996).

The first justification is no longer valid since torture is not a popular or established practice in western countries, and has not been for quite some time. The latter four justifications, however, have been advanced to justify torture in more recent years. The second justification advances the notion that war brings with it a collection of mitigating circumstances that legitimizes acts which otherwise would not be considered tolerable. However, modern warfare has outlawed torture. The Americans, however, have denied the status of Prisoners of War to supporters of al-Qaida captured in Afghanistan, referring to them as "unlawful combatants." Furthermore, war envisages a fight between opposing sides, both of which are armed and constitute a threat to their opposition. Accordingly, "just-combat killing" entails killing an opponent who is still a threat at the time he or she is killed (Shue 1978). That scenario does not apply to the tortured terrorist scenario. Tindale's third justification may be set aside for the moment and dealt with in conjunction with the fifth. The fourth justification, advanced by Tindale, is rationalized as a deterrent effect that torture may have if potential enemies know of the possibility of being subjected to torture when caught. There is no informational purpose to this form of torture, and it has typically been encountered in jurisdictions where dictators have attempted to control opposition through such tactics of intimidation. It is not relevant to the current discussion.

Professor Dershowitz justifies the use of torture on what are essentially utilitarian grounds, incorporating Professor Tindale's third and fifth justifications. Under his approach, in times of national emergency, civil liberties are suspended for the better good:

> The simple cost-benefit analysis for employing ... nonlethal torture seems overwhelming: it is surely better to inflict nonlethal pain on one guilty terrorist who is illegally withholding information needed to prevent an act of terrorism than to permit a large number of innocent victims to die (Dershowitz 2002b:144).

Cesare Beccaria, the classical utilitarian criminologist of the sixteenth century, clearly denounced the use of torture in his 1764 *Essay on Crimes and Punishment* (1963); however, his tract addressed the use of torture to generate incriminating evidence for use at trial. He did not address the use of torture in non-testimonial context. Jeremy Bentham responded to Beccaria's attack on the use of torture in the years following (Twining and Twining 1973). Bentham constructed a utilitarian justification for torture, composed of five major points:

1. Torture should not be applied unless there is good proof that the prisoner possesses the information being sought.
2. Torture should be confined to cases where time is of the essence. Harm must be a highly probable consequence of not acting with great urgency.
3. The harm that will be averted must be great, and the use of torture must be proportionate to the harm being prevented.
4. The use of torture should be regulated and limited by law.
5. The pain inflicted should be sufficiently acute to achieve its purpose but be capable of being turned off quickly (Twining and Twining 1973:313–315).

Professor Dershowitz appears to accept Bentham's utilitarian justification for the use of torture (2002b:142–143). Indeed, Bentham's hypothetical situation of a person being detained by the police with apparent knowledge of the whereabouts of 100 innocent persons being subjected to the infliction of pain, sounds very much like the kind of hypothetical scenario in which Professor Dershowitz calls for the use of judicial torture warrants. Professor Dershowitz refers to Bentham's hypothetical as a "compelling" one in support of the utilitarian justification for torture (2002b:142).

Bentham calls for careful scrutiny of proposed torture, such that the investigator is as certain as he can be that the prisoner possesses the desired knowledge. He indicates that he should be satisfied to a level akin to the burden at trial applying to a serious offence. Professor Dershowitz would use a judge, an individual perhaps better suited for the weighing of evidence than the investigator in the field. However, there will rarely be time for a judge to weigh the evidence and make a decision. That sentiment is echoed by Professor Morgan:

> ... today, if not in Bentham's day, an examination the equivalent of a full trial of the facts where guilt is contested is scarcely consistent with the urgent circumstances which Bentham stipulates must prevail for torture to be justified — the ticking bomb, the imminent massacre of the innocents. Any urgent examination would literally have to be conducted in crisis circumstances where judgements would scarcely be unclouded and judgements calmly arrived at. The examination would have to be cursory, the evidence untested, the protective safeguards of representation and independent examination lacking (Morgan 2000:188).

At one point, Professor Dershowitz appears to confine his case for torture warrants to those individuals already convicted of terrorist offences. He seeks to fend off the argument that opening up the door to torture will start us down a slippery slope in which torturing to the point of death or threatening to torture innocent family members of a terrorist would be justified under a utilitarian calculus if the greater number were preserved by so doing (2002b:146–147). To defend himself, he proposes what he calls a "principled break," a sharp line beyond which torture would not be tolerated:

> For example, if nonlethal torture were legally limited to convicted terrorists who had knowledge of future massive terrorist acts, and were given immunity, but refused to provide the information, there might still be objections to the use of torture, however they would have to go beyond the slippery slope argument (2002b:147).

Until the publication of Professor Dershowitz's position, it seems that arguing against the practice of torture was unnecessary since it could be assumed that no one would seriously argue in favour of the use of torture, much less the systematized and state regulated use of torture. All of that has now changed. Arguments against the use of torture warrants may be divided into five areas. First, there are philosophical problems with the utilitarian justification for torture. Second, there are practical problems with implementing a scheme to warrant torture. Third, the practice is contrary to international law. Fourth, it is in violation of guaranteed constitutional law. Firth, the use of torture undermines the legitimacy of the state.

Criticism of the Utilitarian Position

The limits imposed on the use of torture by Professor Dershowitz would result in torture not being available in his most carefully constructed hypothetical scenario. Zacarias Moussaoui has not been convicted of any terrorist offence. He presently faces several charges arising out of his involvement in the preparation for the September 11th attack, but his trial has faced several delays.

Indeed, in virtually every conceivable real world scenario, the police would not be encountering a convicted terrorist in a "ticking bomb" scenario. In hindsight, investigators are now fairly sure that Moussaoui was connected to the September 11th events, but are still not certain of that. He still awaits trial. With hindsight, it is easy for the authorities to demonize such an individual and allow themselves to consider torture, but in the real world, a circumstance is unlikely to arise where we have the benefit of the hindsight provided by almost two years worth of FBI investigation.

In his review of Professor Dershowitz's recent book on civil liberties (2002a), Professor Jeremy Waldron of Columbia University criticizes Professor Dershowitz's willingness to allow torture of terrorists by showing that Dershowitz claims that rights do not come from God or any other source of "natural law," but rather, they arise out of experiences of atrocity and injustice (Waldron 2002). In other words, "rights come from wrongs" (Dershowitz 2002a). Professor Waldron says that if we take this view and try to ascertain what rights come from our experiences of injustice in recent months, we are not particularly helped. We have recently experienced the "injustice of terrorist outrage" arising out of the plane attacks, and we have the experience of hideous acts of torture committed by state agents around the world. Professor Waldron goes on to ask: "Which should inform our thinking about torture in the wake of September 11?" If it is both, then we are involved in a balancing act, and have embarked on a road of moral compromise, which, "in the case of torture, has always been the beginning of great evil and has always been prohibited in the human rights tradition" (Waldron 2002).

To authorize torture is to permit the state to punish presumptively innocent people. Every one is presumed innocent until proven guilty. Of course, we tolerate interference with our liberty as a person accused of a serious crime may be remanded into custody, and denied bail, if the risk of harm to others appears to be too great. But that is to be the exceptional case. We usually presume that pretrial release will be granted unless the state presents a compelling case to the contrary. That is as it should be. All accused persons detained by the state are to be presumed innocent until their trial has been completed and a verdict rendered. Similarly, we tolerate interference with our privacy interests prior to being adjudicated guilty, but again, that is typically only permissible where the state has made a compelling argument to a judicial officer that such a privacy invasion is necessary for the collective good. While these incursions into our rights and liberties exist, we should not forget that they are, nonetheless incursions into the rights of presumptively innocent people. We should be reluctant to expand the categories of state interference with the rights of people who are, in the eyes of the law, innocent of any alleged crime. Professor Dershowitz claims to be advocating the use of torture against terrorists. However, we will rarely know that we are actually dealing with a terrorist. Under our system of law, we are all presumed to be innocent until proven guilty. To argue in favour of torturing suspects in police custody is to advocate the use of torture against legally innocent people. To paraphrase Ed Greenspan, until they are found guilty, there are no other kinds of people (Greenspan and Jonas 1987).

Professor Dershowitz uses the medium of a warrant to attempt to minimize the problem that typically will arise in real world scenarios. We will rarely know for certain that the captured individual is in fact a terrorist. It will be even more rare that we know what the suspect and his or her accomplices intend. Furthermore, it will be still more rare that the authorities know that the suspect has the information they are seeking. In answering the "how do we know that he knows" question, Bentham sidesteps the issue by saying "perfect certainty ... is an advantage scarce permitted to human kind" (Twining and Twining 1973:317). Accordingly, he claims we can leave it to the court to make a "good enough" determination. Professor Dershowitz's approach is similar, leaving it to a judge to issue a torture warrant upon being satisfied to an acceptable level that the police have got it right. But what would the standard be? Probable cause to believe, or the Canadian standard of reasonable grounds to believe the accused is a terrorist and has the required information? Would we require the higher standard, as Bentham did, of requiring proof analogous to that at a criminal trial: proof beyond a reasonable doubt. Our sense of justice propels us toward the latter standard; however, there will rarely be sufficient time in a "ticking bomb" scenario for a full trial of the facts. As Professor Morgan notes, in such circumstances the examination of the facts would, of necessity, have to be "cursory, the evidence untested, the protective safeguards of representation and independent examination lacking" (Morgan 2000:188). Christopher Hitchens has noted that "if you hire torturers then you hire torturers, whose whole outlook is based on stupidity and coercion, and you can bet that even with a ticking bomb nearby they would be busily gang-raping the wrong guy" (Hitchens 2002).

Practical Problems with Torture Warrants

The police in Canada have shown a willingness to "construct" cases to fit their view of reality (Williams 2000). This has resulted in numerous high profile cases of wrongful conviction. In their zeal to "make a case," the police have been known to adopt "tunnel vision" (Kaufman 1998) or "missile lock," ignoring evidence that may exculpate an accused and interpreting available evidence in a manner that reifies their suspicions about a suspect. Police conducting interrogations tend to operate under a presumption of guilt (Williams 2000; Ericson 1994) that leads to a narrowing of the field of investigation, foreclosing on alternative suspects and a channelling of police beliefs that "they have the right man" (McConville and Baldwin 1982) or that their suspect holds the information being sought. Judicial oversight of police investigative practice would not provide an acceptable solution to the problem of vesting investigators with unbridled discretion in interrogation practices (Epp 1997), in part, because police are wont to "construct a case" (McConville, Sanders, and Leng 1991). Constructing a case involves investigators selecting portions of the available evidence and presenting it to the judiciary in a warrant application, as the only available credible evidence (McConville et al. 1991).

While the foreclosure of investigation leads to obvious injustices that may or may not be undone at trial, the suspect who is tortured during interrogation does not receive the benefit of having his or her rights verified at a subsequent trial. The harm is already done, and the clock cannot be turned back to undo the harm caused by the infliction of pain during torture.

If the judiciary were to issue warrants to authorize torture, how could this be effected in such emergent circumstances? Before the state can seek the authority to inflict serious pain on a presumptively innocent person, a judge would no doubt expect to hear a well articulated, and elaborate justification, for the issuance of the warrant. Surely, there would not be sufficient time to prepare such an application for judicial authorization. Applications for warrants take time to prepare. Warrants with such a profound impact, as a torture warrant, would likely be carefully scrutinized by senior investigators in most cases. Are we to expect lesser standards of preparation in applications for torture warrants than we have come to expect in regard to search warrants? In the urgent cases, the victims will likely be dead before a warrant is obtained. The ticking bombs will have gone off; the soon to be hijacked planes will already be under the control of terrorists.

In Canada, a provision exists for obtaining warrants to conduct searches over the telephone. These telewarrants arguably allow the police to obtain a warrant in crisis circumstances, particularly where they fear the loss of evidence or other reasonable grounds exist to act swiftly. Presumably, Professor Dershowitz would envisage the use of such a process to deal with the rapidly emerging situation likely to be encountered in a "ticking bomb" scenario.

In the early 1980s, the Law Reform Commission of Canada conducted a survey of search warrant procedures and concluded that almost 60 percent of the warrants they sampled were invalidly issued as they stood (Law Reform Commission of Canada 1983:83). In 1999, a panel composed of a judge of the Ontario Superior Court of Justice, a Crown Attorney, and a defence lawyer reviewed a sample of 100 consecutive warrant applications in Toronto (Hill, Hutchison, and Pringle 2000). They found that 69 percent of their sample of search warrants exhibited a degree of invalidity, with 43 percent of the sample displaying more than one substantive defect in either the application or the warrant itself (2000:91).

Hill, Hutchison, and Pringle found that 21 percent of the search warrants they examined were telewarrants. While all but three applications examined in the sample revealed that the requested telewarrant was issued, their examination of the documents revealed that only ⅓ of them should have been issued. In other words, ⅔ of the telewarrants were invalid as issued. In addition, the authors noted that in the first year and a half of Ontario's centralized telewarrant operation, warrants were refused in 47 percent of the applications coming to the centre. Our expectation that investigative authorities applying for warrants will not routinely err is not borne out by the research findings. Trusting the decision to torture presumptively innocent suspects to the telewarrant system, or even the regular warrant system does not inspire confidence given the rate of factual invalidity found in this recent research.

Torture does not generally work, and is perhaps least likely to work with terrorist extremists. If a terrorist is willing to give up his or her life in a towering inferno, it is difficult to envisage that Professor Dershowitz's sterilized needles will loosen their tongues if caught. A fanatic committed to a cause is of the one class of persons who would rather die under torture than provide information contrary to the cause.

Torture is Prohibited by International Law

In recent years, it has been argued that the prohibition on torture is approaching, or has attained the status of a peremptory norm in international law. A peremptory norm is a norm that is recognized by the international community of nations as a norm from which no derogation is permitted, and which prevails over all other treaties. It may only be modified by a subsequent norm of general international law possessing a similar character. In *R. v. Bow Street Metropolitan Stipendiary Magistrate et al., Ex parte Pinoche Ugarte (No. 3)* (1999), Lord Browne-Wilkinson in the English House of Lords noted that the parties before him had accepted that the prohibition on torture had reached this stature. In *Suresh v. Canada* (2002), the Supreme Court of Canada indicated that the prohibition on torture is approaching the status of a peremptory norm in international law.

In *Suresh*, the Supreme Court of Canada noted that there are three compelling indices that the prohibition on torture has achieved the status of a peremptory norm. First, there are a significant number of multilateral instruments raising torture to the status of a universally proscribed act. A significant number of multilateral treaties prohibit torture. Key among these are the following:

1. *Convention Against Torture and Other Cruel, Inhuman or Degrading Treatment or Punishment*, Can. T.S. 1987 No. 36 (CAT).
2. Article 3 of the *Geneva Convention Relative to the Treatment of Prisoners of War*, Can. T.S. 1965 No. 20.
3. Article 3 of the *Universal Declaration of Human Rights*, G.A. Res. 217A (III), UN Doc A/810 (1948).
4. Article 5 of the *Declaration on the Protection of All Persons from Being Subjected to Torture and Other Cruel, Inhuman or Degrading Treatment or Punishment*, G.A. Res. 3452 (XXX), UN Doc. A/10034 (1975).
5. *International Covenant on Civil and Political Rights*, Can. T.S. 1976 No. 47 (ICCPR).
6. Article 7 of the *European Convention for the Protection of Human Rights and Fundamental Freedoms.*, 213 U.N.T.S. 221 (1950).

The argument that the prohibition on torture is approaching the status of a peremptory norm is bolstered by the fact that most, if not all, states officially prohibit the use of torture as part of their regular administrative practices. Additionally, a number of international law authorities assert that the prohibition on torture has become an established peremptory norm. In *Suresh*, the court looked at the status of the prohibition on torture in international law, and accepted "the fact that such a principle is included in numerous multilateral instruments, that it does not form part of any known domestic administrative practice, and that it is considered by many academics to be an emerging, if not established peremptory norm, suggests that it cannot be easily derogated from" (2002:para. 65). The court went on to hold that deportation to face torture is contrary to international law.

In Canada, torture is a crime. The *Criminal Code* offence was created in the late 1980s to implement the United Nations *Convention Against Torture and Other Cruel, Inhuman or Degrading Treatment or Punishment* (CAT). This convention was adopted by the UN General Assembly on December 10th, 1984, ratified by Canada on June 24th, 1987, and came into force on June 26th, 1987. The offence is outlined in s. 269.1 of the *Criminal Code*:

> 269.1(1) Every official or every person acting at the instigation of or with the consent or acquiescence of an official, who inflicts torture on any other person is guilty of an indictable offence and liable to imprisonment for a term not exceeding fourteen years.
>
> (2) For the purposes of this section, "official" means
> (a) a peace officer,
> (b) a public officer,
> (c) a member of the Canadian Forces, or
> (d) any person who may exercise powers, pursuant to a law in force in a foreign state, that would, in Canada, be exercised by a person referred to in paragraph (a), (b), or (c),
>
> whether the person exercises powers in Canada or outside Canada; "torture" means any act or omission by which severe pain or suffering, whether physical or mental, is intentionally inflicted on a person
>
> (a) for a purpose including

(i) obtaining from the person or from a third person information or a statement,

(ii) punishing the person for an act that the person or a third person has committed or is suspected of having committed, and

(iii) intimidating or coercing the person or a third person, or

(b) for any reason based on discrimination of any kind, but does not include any act or omission arising only from, inherent in or incidental to lawful sanctions.

(3) It is no defence to a charge under this section that the accused was ordered by a superior or a public authority to perform the act or omission that forms the subject-matter of the charge or that the act or omission is alleged to have been justified by exceptional circumstances, including a state of war, a threat of war, internal political instability or any other public emergency.

(4) In any proceedings over which Parliament has jurisdiction, any statement obtained as a result of the commission of an offence under this section is inadmissible in evidence, except as evidence that the statement was so obtained.

This provision implements CAT, creating it an offence for state agents to act in contravention of its provisions. Canada is bound by its multilateral obligations to maintain as an offence acts of this nature.

Constitutional Prohibition on Torture

While there is no case law directly on point, in Canada, torture is very likely to be considered constitutionally prohibited. Torture may be viewed as a "cruel and unusual treatment or punishment" in contravention of s. 12 of the *Canadian Charter of Rights and Freedoms*. In the alternative, it may be asserted that the general right in section 7 that protects everyone from being deprived of "life liberty and security of the person" except in accordance with the "principles of fundamental justice" bans the use of torture.

In the pre-*Charter* era, Justice Lamer (as he then was) of the Supreme Court of Canada noted that the police must be given some leeway in the investigative process. However, they are not without limits. In *R. v. Rothman* (1981), a case dealing with the admissibility of a statement given by an accused, he noted:

> It must be borne in mind that the investigation of crime and the detection of criminals is not a game to be governed by the Marquess of Queensbury rules. The authorities, in dealing with shrewd and often sophisticated criminals, must sometimes of necessity resort to tricks or other forms of deceit and should not through the [confession] rule be hampered in their work. What should be repressed vigorously is conduct on their part that shocks the community (1981:697).

This statement has come to be regarded as the origin of the "community shock test" in Canada. This test was incorporated into much of our jurisprudence dealing with the exclusion of evidence under the *Charter* in its early years. It is instructive in terms of showing the need to balance police investigative powers against the rights of the suspect in a criminal investigation.

The community shock analysis made its way into other *Charter* analysis relevant to the discussion at hand. In *Kindler v. Canada* (1991), and its companion case *Reference Re Ng Extradition (Can.)* (1991), the Supreme Court of Canada ruled that the prisoners, alleged murderers who were the subject of extradition requests by the United States, could be extradited to those jurisdictions, even though the Canadian Minister of Justice had not sought assurances that the death penalty would not be imposed. The decision as to whether to seek assurances that the death penalty would not be imposed was within his discretion under the terms of the extradition treaty between the United States and Canada. In one of the majority judgments in the *Kindler* case, Justice La Forest stated that extradition must be refused if surrender of the fugitive would "shock the conscience." La Forest reached this conclusion after analyzing the process of extradition in the context of the loss of "life liberty and security of the person" and the "principles of fundamental justice" found in s. 7 of the *Charter*, as contextualized by the prohibition on cruel and unusual treatment or punishment found in s. 12 of the *Charter*. He went on to state: "There are, of course, situations where the punishment imposed following surrender—torture, for example—would be so outrageous to the values of the Canadian community that the surrender would be unacceptable" (1991:832). That approach mirrors an earlier judgment in *Canada v. Schmidt* (1987), where La Forest stated that to surrender a prisoner to a requesting state that would inflict torture on the individual would run afoul of the principles of fundamental justice.

In *United States v. Burns* (2001), the Supreme Court of Canada revisited the issue of extradition to face the death penalty. While Kindler had lost his fight against extradition to face the death penalty, his case involved returning to his home country to face a homicide allegation. *Burns* involved a fight against extradition by two young Canadian men alleged to have committed murder in Washington State. The top court unanimously decided that extradition to face the death penalty could no longer be tolerated, particularly in light of recent concerns over potential miscarriages of justice resulting in the execution of innocent individuals. While the approach of the court in *Kindler* and *Ng* was approved, a unanimous court in *Burns* cautioned that the "shocks the conscience" test does not devolve the court's analysis into one of assessing public opinions on acceptable punishment practices. The court is to remain the "guardian of the constitution" (para. 35) and "guardian of the justice system" (para. 70), performing the appropriate balancing exercise to determine whether extradition conforms to the principles of fundamental justice.

In *Suresh v. Canada* (2002), the Supreme Court of Canada recently addressed the issue of balancing the need to fight terrorism against the right to be free from torture, but not in a "ticking bomb" scenario. The case involved an appeal by a refugee claimant who was fighting deportation by the Canadian government. Suresh was alleged by the Canadian Security Intelligence Service to be a member and fundraiser for the Tamil Tigers, a group alleged to be engaged in terrorist activity in Sri Lanka. Members of this organization have reportedly been subjected to torture in Sri Lanka. The Supreme Court overturned lower court rulings and ordered a new hearing for the appellant. In doing so, the unanimous court issued a strong statement condemning torture as contrary to the principles embodied in the *Charter*:

> When Canada adopted the Charter in 1982, it affirmed the opposition of the Canadian people to government-sanctioned torture by proscribing cruel and unusual treatment or punishment in s. 12. A punishment is cruel and unusual if it "is so excessive as to outrage standards of decency.... It must be so inherently repugnant that it could never be an appropriate punishment, however egregious the offence. Torture falls into this category. The prospect of torture induces fear and its consequences may be devastating, irreversible, indeed, fatal. Torture may be meted out indiscriminately or arbitrarily for no particular offence. Torture has as its end the denial of a person's humanity; this end is outside the legitimate domain of a criminal justice system.... Torture is an instrument of terror and not of justice. As Justice Lamer stated "... some punishments or treatments will always be grossly disproportionate and will always outrage our standards of decency: for example, the infliction of corporal punishment." As such, torture is seen in Canada as fundamentally unjust (para. 51).

The principles of fundamental justice prohibit the imposition of torture by state agents. That is a substantive restriction on the state's crime control agenda. As an aspect of the principles of fundamental justice, the prohibition on cruel and unusual treatment or punishment bolsters the conclusion that the state is constitutionally barred from torturing suspects.

Torture Undermines the Legitimacy of the State

Police conduct amounting to torture implicates the abuse of process doctrine. Clearly, that type of illegal police conduct results in an abuse of the court's process and would operate as a bar to conviction of the person being investigated (Brauti and Welsch 1999). The abuse of process doctrine has been incorporated into the body of rights protected by Canada's *Charter* (MacAlister 2000). A police officer committing an act of torture would be subject to the possibility of criminal prosecution, and with good cause.

Instituting a regime of torture would turn back the clock on efforts to eradicate the world of this insidious practice. Once torture is deemed to be legitimate in western democracies, a message will be sent to nations less respectful of civil liberties that torture is an acceptable practice. That should not be a message that we are willing to send. Professor Dershowitz claims that that is the strongest argument against any resort to torture (2002b:145). However, he attempts to sidestep the argument by converting it into a slippery slope argument. Once torture is institutionalized in a restricted form, other situations will no doubt arise that call out for the use of torture. These may not meet the stringent criteria that have been set. In such instances, he notes, a "case utilitarian" would up the ante and impose torture in an ever-expanding series of circumstances as long as the particular facts of the case appear to justify the use of torture. Accordingly, he moves on in search of limiting principles, which he frames as a "principled break" to place a hard and fast cap on permissible torture scenarios. As noted above, once he does that, he concocts scenarios so far fetched as to be unlikely to occur in the real world. Additionally, he fails to show how that alters the impression created by a western state putting torture back on the books. That would send a message to every third rate dictator around the world that torture *per se* is tolerable in whatever guise. It would also send a message to the citizenry of our country, as capital punishment sends a message to Americans, that the state does not really value the sanctity of human life to an absolute standard.

Defence of Necessity

Numerous commentators have argued that leaving the police in a situation where torture is not permissible, yet tolerated when it is carried out "below the radar screen," as Professor Dershowitz puts it, is not an acceptable approach. The "necessity approach" to torture would generally prohibit torture conduct, leaving such acts a criminal offence as they are currently. However, in those rare cases where it is employed from the necessitous circumstances that present themselves, the state agent carrying out the torture may be able to raise a defence of necessity to the charge of torture.

According to Professor Dershowitz (1989), necessity is one the most "lawless of legal doctrines" that can be used as an emergency measure. Professor Dershowitz argues that it is not well suited for situations that are likely to recur over a long period of time. It is meant to cover those emergency situations where there is a need for leniency in the law. In particular, it should not be used to benefit a state agent. Yet, the very cases that arise in the hypothetical scenarios involving torture are not likely to recur. They are rare, and emergency cases. Indeed, some might argue that the "ticking bomb" scenarios are so fanciful that they will never arise in real life situations.

Professor Dershowitz claims it would not be fair to the police to be judged after the fact through the application of the defence of necessity. They would not necessarily know if the circumstances were sufficiently necessitous to justify the court allowing the use of the necessity defence. If an adverse judgment arises, the police officer would be punished. If the court agreed with the police or other state agent invoking torture, they would be exempted from criminal culpability. That uncertainty offends Professor Dershowitz, yet it applies to all of us who seek to avail ourselves of any criminal defence at trial. The uncertainty should result in state agents questioning themselves very carefully before embarking on a course of torture. Only in the clearest of cases, should they actually go forward and utilize torture techniques. The uncertainty is no greater when a police officer who uses deadly force on a suspect relies on the defence of self defence, or other defences based upon the reasonable use of force. The police should fear being put in jeopardy when they contemplate employing torture.

A cursory review of Canada's torture offence provision may result in the conclusion that the defence of necessity is not available. Subsection 269.1(3) of the *Criminal Code* removes the defence of "superior orders" from those alleged of torture. The subsection also appears to remove any other "justification" based on exceptional circumstances such as war or public emergency. However, in Canada, the defence of necessity has been structured by the courts as an "excuse" rather than as a "justification." At first glance, that appears to be one of those distinctions that only a lawyer could love — or even appreciate. Yet, the distinction is an important one:

> Claims of justification concede that the definition of the offence is satisfied, but challenge whether the act is wrongful; claims of excuse concede that the act is wrongful, but seek to avoid the attribution of the act to the actor. A justification speaks to the rightness of the

> act; an excuse, to whether the actor is accountable for a concededly wrongful act (Fletcher 1978:759).

A justification negates the wrongfulness of the conduct. In contrast, an excuse accepts the wrongfulness of the conduct, but negates only the culpability of the actor for his or her wrongful conduct. Excuses, such as necessity in Canada, do not express "policy goals" but rather simply reflect compassion and justice in the individual case (Fletcher 1974: 1308–1309). Recent calls for the abolition of the distinction between justifications and excuses in criminal codes have gone unheeded in this country (Gur-Arye 1992).

In *R. v. Perka* (1984), the Supreme Court of Canada declared that the defence of necessity is best characterized as an "excuse" rather than a "justification." The criterion for its application is the moral involuntariness of the accused's actions. In essence, the accused is morally compelled to act in the circumstances. Inaction would be morally unthinkable. The criterion of "moral involuntariness" has recently been held by the top court to be a constitutional imperative.

In *R. v. Ruzic* (2001), the Supreme Court of Canada ruled that "moral involuntariness" is a principle of fundamental justice protected by s. 7 of the *Charter*: "It is a principle of fundamental justice that only voluntary conduct — behaviour that is the product of a free will and controlled body, unhindered by external constraints — should attract the penalty and stigma of criminal culpability" (para. 47). The deprivation of liberty and the stigma of criminal conviction would violate the principles of fundamental justice if the accused did not have a rational choice other than to commit the offence.

The characterization of necessity as an excuse was affirmed in *obiter* in *Ruzic*. As an excuse, it does not negate the *mens rea* or the *actus reus* of the offence, but rather accepts that the crime occurred and excuses the accused from culpability because of the circumstances of the offence. It relieves him of the penal consequences and the stigma associated with a criminal conviction. In circumstances where the accused is deprived of a realistic choice whether to break the law, he or she is acting in a morally involuntary fashion. That concedes the "wrongfulness" of the act but withholds the imposition of culpability because of the "dire circumstances" under which the offence was committed (para. 29).

Since necessity is characterized as an excuse rather than a justification, it is arguable that it is still available as a defence to a charge under s. 269.1 of the *Criminal Code*. Only circumstances of justification are negated by the provision in s. 269.1(3). The *Criminal Code* preserves both justifications and excuses arising at common law:

> s. 8(3) Every rule and principle of the common law that renders any circumstance a justification or excuse for an act or a defence to a charge continues in force and applies in respect of proceedings for an offence under this Act or any other Act of Parliament except in so far as they are altered by or are inconsistent with this Act or any other Act of Parliament.

Even if s. 269.1(3) is interpreted as taking away the defence of necessity, the provision would have to be declared of no force or effect, since the availability of a defence to the person who acts in a morally involuntary manner is constitutionally mandated as a principle of fundamental justice under s. 7 of the *Charter*: *R. v. Ruzic* (2001).

In Israel, the Landau Commission (1987) justified the use of "moderate physical force" by the General Security Service (GSS) as an act of necessity. A subsequent decision of the Supreme Court of Israel sitting as the High Court of Justice in 1999, in *Judgment Concerning the Interrogation Methods Implied by the GSS*, barred the use of torture and other forms of physical pressure in the interrogation of terrorist suspects, indicating that the necessity defence, as found in the Penal Law, could not be used systematically to authorize the use of physical pressure. However, the judgement did go on to indicate that the defence of necessity is potentially available on a case-by-case basis. Additionally, the presence of necessity was found to be a legitimate factor for the Attorney General to take into account in determining whether to go forward with charges against an interrogator. Despite this finding, the possibility of routinized or administratively sanctioned torture practices by the Israeli security forces appears to be something that is confined to the past (Uildriks 2000), although the Israeli government continues to toy with the idea of authorizing the use of "special measures" for terrorist interrogation (Gross 2001).

Conclusion

This paper seeks to add to the debate presented by Professor Dershowitz, by systematically contributing a contrary view to his. It is hoped that this will promote further critical thought on the issue of governmental torture both here and abroad.

Nations in the western world, like Canada or the United States, that entertain the implementation of torture tactics, even if constrained by the need for a prior warrant, will send a message to the rest of the world that we do not take human rights seriously. An editorial in *The Lancet* (2001) asks how we can call dictators to account when they use torture if we have resorted to the same tactics ourselves. Such concerns echo Michael Ignatieff's plea that "the era of human rights has come and gone" (2002:A25). To permit torture warrants would be to accept a "culture of security" that undermines basic human rights (Toope 2002). The events of September 11th have caused many western nations to seek out "the enemy within." Such searches have resulted in reliance on judicial torture warrants in the distant past (Thurston 2000; Russell 2001). However, in the contemporary era, reliance on such warrants, cannot be accepted.

The paramilitary, authoritarian and hierarchical composition of most police forces in Canada and the United States has been linked to unacceptable police violence (Hodgson 2001). At a time when policing is being pushed to reorganize along less violent lines, law authorities should not be encouraged to find new means to impose torture on presumptively innocent suspects. However, in rapidly emerging circumstances in which the decision of whether to torture or not is effectively no decision at all, the defence of necessity may avail itself on a case-by-case basis.

Policing terrorism will possibly place the police, or other state agents, in situations where good ends can be achieved through dirty means (Sartre 1989; Walzer 1972). When the ends that are to be achieved are "urgent and unquestionably good" the state agent is placed in a genuine moral dilemma of "dirty hands" (Klockars 1980:33). In such a dilemma, the actor cannot emerge innocent, no matter what course of action is chosen. Carl Klockars referred to these as "Dirty Harry" problems; so named after the dilemma Inspector Harry Callahan found himself in the film *Dirty Harry.* In such situations, the danger is not that the actor will make a decision that is wrong; that is inevitable given the circumstances. The danger lies in thinking that one has found a way to escape the dilemma that is inescapable. What is most troubling about Professor Dershowitz's thesis is that he appears to be convinced that he has found a solution to the dirty hands dilemma. From this conclusion, negative consequences flow. If his recommendations are adopted, we will begin to lose our sense of morality, we will fail to care and become cynical, or allow our passion to override our sense of morality, leading to the employment of dirty means too readily, and in ever increasing increments of severity. The best means to ensure that does not occur is, perhaps, to maintain the criminalization of torture and ensure state agents violating the torture prohibition are brought to trial. At trial, they will have to take their chances with a jury and the defence of necessity.

While Professor Dershowitz claims everyone would support the use of torture to prevent another tragedy like the September 11th events, that surely cannot be true. A CNN/USA Today poll conducted in the fall of 2001 found only 45 percent of the Americans surveyed supported torture to prevent terrorist attacks (Morse 2001). The level of support for such tactics in Canada is unknown at present. Knowledge of the level of support for torture by state authorities would provide valuable insight into whether the use of torture would shock the conscience of Canadians, as the Supreme Court of Canada asserts it would.

The prevailing attitudes of police investigators toward moral dilemmas such as the "ticking bomb" scenario would also provide us with useful knowledge. How the police would deal with the hypothetical scenarios, advanced by Professor Dershowitz and others, would provide valuable insight into the need for policy development in this area. Police attitudes towards the legitimacy of torture warrants would also further our knowledge on these matters. Research on these issues would help to inform ongoing debate regarding the torture of alleged terrorists in western democracies.

References

Babovic, B. (2000) "Police brutality or police torture." *Policing: An International Journal of Police Strategies & Management* 23:374.

Beccaria, C. (1963) Essay on Crimes and Punishment. (Henry Paolucci, Trans.) Indianapolis, IN: Bobbs-Merrill.

Brauti, P.M., and C. Welsch (1999) Illegal police conduct in the course of a bona fide investigation. *Criminal Law Quarterly* 43:64.

CBS News (2002) "Legal torture?" Posted online. Retrieved October 30, 2002 at: http://www.cbsnews.com/stories/2002/01/17/60minutes/printable324751.shtml

Dershowitz, A.M. (2002a) *Shouting Fire: Civil Liberties: Past, Present and Future*. Boston: Little, Brown.

——. (2002b) *Why Terrorism Works: Understanding the Threat, Responding to the Challenge*. New Haven, CT: Yale University Press.

——. (1989) "Is it necessary to apply 'physical pressure' to terrorists — and to lie about it?" *Israel Law Review* 24:192.

Epp, J.A. (1997) Penetrating police investigative practice post-*Morin*. *University of British Columbia Law Review* 31:95.

Ericson, R.V. (1994) "The decline of innocence." *University of British Columbia Law Review* 28:367.

Fletcher, G.P. (1978) *Rethinking Criminal Law*. Boston: Little, Brown.

——. (1974) The individualization of excusing conditions. *Southern California Law Review* 47:1269.

Greenspan, E.L., and G. Jonas (1987) *Greenspan: The Case for the Defence*. Toronto: Macmillan.

Gross, M.L. (2001) "Just and Jewish warfare." *Tikkun* 16:31.

Gur-Arye, M. (1992) "Should a criminal code distinguish between justification and excuse?" *Canadian Journal of Law and Jurisprudence* 5:215.

Hamilton, H. (2001) RCMP analysts discuss how September 11 changed the game. *RCMP Gazette* 63:9.

Heymann, P.B. (2002) "Civil liberties and human rights in the aftermath of September 11." *Harvard Journal of Law and Public Policy* 25:441.

Hill, C., S. Hutchison, and L. Pringle (2000) "Search warrants: protection or illusion?" *Criminal Reports* (5th) 28:89.

Hitchens, C. (2002) "In case anyone's forgotten: torture doesn't work" *The Guardian*. Retrieved January 21, 2002, online: http://www.guardian.co.uk/Print/0,3858,4298448,00.html.

Hodgson, J.F. (2001) "Police violence in Canada and the USA: analysis and management." *Policing: An International Journal of Police Strategies and Management* 24:520.

Ignatieff, M. (2002) "Is the human rights era ending?" *The New York Times*. February 5:A25.

Kaufman, F. (1998) The Commission on Proceedings Involving Guy Paul Morin, Vol. 2. Toronto: Ontario Ministry of the Attorney General.

Klockars, C.B. (1980) "The Dirty Harry Problem." *The Annals of the American Academy of Political and Social Science* 452:33.

Landau Commission (1987) Report of the Commission of Inquiry into the Methods of Investigation of the General Security Service Regarding Hostile Terrorist Activity. (Official English Translation).

Law Reform Commission of Canada (1983) Police Powers – Search and Seizure in Criminal Law Enforcement. Working Paper No. 30. Ottawa: Supply and Services Canada.

MacAlister, D. (2000) "Does the abuse of process doctrine still exist?" *Criminal Reports* (5th) 28:72.

McConville. M., and J. Baldwin (1982) "The role of interrogation in crime discovery and conviction." *British Journal of Criminology* 22:165.

McConville, M., A. Sanders, and R. Leng (1991) *The Case for the Prosecution*. London, UK: Routledge.

Morgan, R. (2000) "The utilitarian justification of torture: denial, desert and disinformation." *Punishment and Society* 2:181.

Morse, J. (2001) "How do we Make Him Talk? Would Torture be Justified in Trying to Squeeze Information From Captured al-Qaeda COO Abu Zubaydah?" Retrieved November 7, 2002, online: http://www.time.com/time/nation/printout/0,8816,227493,000.html.

Russell, S. (2001) "Witchcraft, Genealogy, Foucault." *British Journal of Sociology* 52:121.

Sartre, J.P. (1989) *Dirty Hands in J.P. Sartre, No Exit and Three Other Plays*. S. Gilbert, Trans. New York: Vintage International.

Shue, H. (1978) "Torture." *Philosophy & Public Affairs* 7:124.

Stuntz, W.J. (2002) "Terrorism, federalism, and police misconduct." *Harvard Journal of Law and Public Policy* 25:665.

Thurston, R.W. (2000) "The rise and fall of judicial torture: why it was used in early modern Europe and the Soviet Union." *Human Rights Review* 1:26.

Tindale, C.W. (1996) "The logic of torture: a critical examination." *Social Theory and Practice* 22:349

Toope, S.J. (2002) "Fallout from '9-11': will a security culture undermine human rights?" *Saskatchewan Law Review* 65:281.

Twining, W.L., and P.E. Twining (1973) "Bentham on torture." *Northern Ireland Legal Quarterly* 24:307.

Uildriks, N. (2000) "Torture in Israel." *Human Rights Review* 1:85.

Uildriks, N., and P. van Reenen, (2001) "Human rights violations by the police." *Human Rights Review* January-March:64.

Waldron, J. (2002) "Alan Dershowiz's 'Shouting Fire': The Great Defender." *The New York Times – Book Review.* Retrieved November 2, 2002 online: http://www.johnlaxmi.com/WWHow/DershowitzBook.htm.

Walzer, M. (1972) "Political action: the problem of dirty hands." *Philosophy and Public Affairs* 2:160.

Williams, J.W. (2000) "Interrogating justice: a critical analysis of the police interrogation and its role in the criminal process." *Canadian Journal of Criminology* 42:209.

Cases Cited

Canada v. Schmidt, [1987] 1 S.C.R. 500.

Judgment Concerning the Interrogation Methods Implied by the GSS. (September 6, 1999) Electronic version, online: http://62.90.71.124/mishpat/html/en/system/index.html.

Kindler v. Canada (Minister of Justice), [1991] 2 S.C.R. 779.

R. v. Bow Street Metropolitan Stipendiary Magistrate et al., Ex Parte Pinoche Ugarte No. 3), [1999] 2 W.L.R. 827 (H.L.)

R. v. Perka, [1984] 2 S.C.R. 232.

R. v. Rothman, [1981] 1 S.C.R. 640.

R. v. Ruzic, [2001] 1 S.C.R. 687.

Reference Re Ng Extradition (Can.), [1991] 2 S.C.R. 858.

Suresh v. Canada (Minister of Citizenship and Immigration), [2002] 1 S.C.R. 3.

United States v. Burns, [2001] 1 S.C.R. 283.

Statutes Cited

Criminal Code, R.S.C. 1985, c. C-46

Canadian Charter of Rights and Freedoms, Part I of the *Constitution Act, 1982*, being Schedule B to the *Canada Act 1982*, c. 11.

8

Why We Would be Better Off Without an Anti-Terrorism Act

Avery Plaw

> Terrorist acts like those that occurred on September 11 constitute a substantial threat to domestic and international stability. The challenge of eradicating terrorism requires cooperation among the community of nations and a strengthening of our capacity to suppress, investigate, and incapacitate terrorist activities. To achieve this we know that Canada must work with other nations to combat terrorism. Furthermore, we believe that Parliament must act to combat terrorism while continuing to respect and promote the values reflected in and the rights and freedom guaranteed by the *Charter of Rights and Freedoms*. Finally, we believe that legislation is one part of a comprehensive government response against terrorism.
>
> These are the considerations that motivate our legislation and they are reflected in its preamble and its contents.[1]
>
> *Anne MacLellan, October 15, 2001*

On October 15, 2001, Canadian Federal Justice Minister Anne MacLellan introduced Bill C-36, Canada's *Anti-Terrorism Act*. The omnibus 186 page Act was formulated in the aftermath of the September 11th attacks in the United States, just over a month before, and followed the general lines of legislation that had already been enacted in the United States (*USA Patriot Act*, 2001) and the United Kingdom (the *Terror Act*, 2000). The proposed Act, designed to enhance the federal government's capacity to protect Canadian citizens from attacks like that of September 11th, sought at once to amend ten distinct Canadian statutes as well as to ratify two United Nations Conventions — for the Suppression of the Financing of Terrorism and for the Suppression of Terrorist Bombings. Most importantly, it introduced and defined, for the first time in Canadian law, the idea of a "terrorist activity."[2] As Ms. MacLellan emphasized, the new Act offered a strong and symbolic commitment to the "War on Terrorism." It thus served at least two important political purposes: first, it offered reassurance about their safety to Canadians badly shaken by the September 11th attack, and, second, it helped the government to appear firm and focused in the face of the real threat to Canadian security. No doubt, the Act was good politics. But the Act went far beyond a mere political gesture. It also represented a major project of law. It, therefore, raised the question not only of whether it was good politics, but also, as Kent Roach reminds us, of whether it was "good law."[3] Was it, for example, clear? Did it cohere well with our moral intuitions? And most importantly, did it protect Canadians from terrorism, as the Supreme Court's Proportionality Principle requires, in the way that least impairs their "rights and freedom"?[4]

From the moment of its introduction Bill C-36 attracted criticism as law, particularly in terms of the potent threat it was often seen to pose to the rights and liberties of Canadian citizens. In response, the government, despite initial reluctance, eventually accepted a number of important revisions of the Act, including, perhaps most importantly, a full review of the Act by parliament within three years and a five year sunset clause on certain key provisions dealing with "preventive arrest and investigative hearing powers."[5] On the 18th of December, 2001, the revised Bill C-36 received royal assent, and on the 24th of that month, the *Anti-Terrorism Act* came fully into force.

There can be little doubt that the revisions introduced to the *Anti-Terrorism Act*, particularly the provision for a review of the whole package within three years and the introduction of a five year sunset clause on key provisions, did mitigate some of the most troubling elements of the new legislation.[6] Even the government which formulated the legislation seems disinclined to dispute that point now. However, the government's grudging admission of the need for serious reflection on, and review of, the bill as a whole invites the question of whether its goals might be equally well served by more prosaic means, such as the strengthening, or even the execution, of previously existing Canadian law.

The very magnitude of the Act prevents any comprehensive treatment here. I, therefore, propose to cut directly to what I think is the most important question raised by the new legislation — that is, do we really need or want an *Anti-Terrorism Act* at all?

I think the best arguments for an emphatic "yes" to this question have already been well articulated by the Justice Minister and her colleagues in government; although the Minister allowed that "Our current laws [i.e., before the *Anti-Terrorism Act*] allow us to investigate terrorism and prosecute those who have engaged in various specific activities generally associated with terrorism, including hijacking, murder and sabotage,"[7] she nonetheless concluded that "these and other laws are not sufficient." She argued that Canadians expect the government to do "everything it can" to ensure its capacity "to suppress, investigate, and incapacitate terrorist activities." Moreover, she insisted that this objective of thoroughly suppressing and incapacitating terrorist activities required a comprehensive, integrated program, and the *Anti-Terrorism Act* was, in effect, "the only game in town." If it is seen by some as an intrusive intervention into Canadian law and practice, then that is the price to be paid for peace, order and good government.

I will proceed then by formulating and assessing the comparative strength of the opposing position that we really would be better off without this general *Anti-Terrorism Act*. The implication of this argument is, at the very least, that when the new legislation comes up for review in three years, parliament and the Canadian people should reconsider the main provisions of the new legislation — in particular, the introduction of the legal concept of terrorism into domestic law. Canadians should ask whether the Act's goals might be equally well served by more prosaic means, such as the strengthening, or in some cases simply executing, existing Canadian law.[8] After all, the Front de Libération du Québec (FLQ) was successfully prosecuted as an "unlawful organization" in the 1970s without any special terrorist legislation.[9] On the other hand, as Kent Roach observes, a year after its introduction, there is no report of the new legislation's more controversial powers (notably preventive arrest and investigative hearing) being used.[10]

Certainly the threat posed by terrorism takes on a vastly increased urgency in the face of the events of September 11th, 2001, but it remains implausible, at least logically, to demand that government "do everything it can" to prevent future acts of terror — say, by interrogating everyone. We would do better to pursue a proportional, balanced response. The goal must be to ensure security in ways that, as Clive Walker puts it, "derogate as little as possible from 'normal measures.'"[11] We should therefore begin now to consider ways of enhancing the security of Canadians both through the adjustment of the criminal code and the organization, operation, and regulation of relevant state agencies and government policies, so that Bill C-36 is no longer "the only game in town" when the parliamentary review of the legislation occurs.

The first point that needs to be made is simply this: the terrorist acts of September 11th to which the Act responds, and others like them, are already covered in the Criminal Code, from hijacking (ss.76-8) to kidnapping (ss.279) and murder (s.230), to causing bodily harm (ss.222, 269), sabotage (s.56), offences relating to explosives, nuclear materials and poisons (ss.7, 81–2, 245), uttering threats (s.264) and intimidation of legislatures or peoples (ss.51, 423). Moreover, conspiracy to commit these crimes, which is a major target of the new legislation, is also already a crime, prosecutable under the law (s.465). Indeed, as Errol Mendes and Stan Cohen stress, police already have the "preexisting power ... to arrest without warrant where they believe that the commission of a crime is immanent."[12] Finally, as Don Stuart emphasizes, "We already had likely the widest electronic surveillance powers in the Western World."[13] In short, terrorist crimes were already prohibited in Canadian law before the *Anti-Terrorism Act,* and Canadian authorities already possessed an extensive array of powers both to prevent and punish terrorist acts.[14] If we are (understandably) concerned that the threat associated with these crimes has risen sharply with changes in Canada's international environment, then it makes sense to modify the definitions of these crimes and the penalties associated with them. It may also be prudent, particularly in view of the scale of the potential threat, to pursue prevention by increasing our commitment to policing and to intelligence gathering through CSIS, the RCMP, and local law enforcement, and to encourage the cooperation of the these agencies. Certainly it seems pressing, particularly in view of recent revelations aired on the TV program *60 Minutes* regarding terrorist activity in Canada, to revisit our policies on immigration and refugees.[15]

None of these reforms, however, requires the introduction of terrorism as a legal concept, or the adopting of a general Act introducing sweeping extraordinary government powers to redress the threat; indeed, I will argue that doing so may entail some serious difficulties, and may even be counterproductive. On the other hand, the Criminal Code R.S.C. 1985 c.C-34 s.467 already criminalizes participating in the activities of a criminal organization, knowing that any members of the organization engaged or have engaged in indictable offences, and being a party to the commission of an indictable offence for the benefit or at the direction of a criminal organization.

I want to suggest that this category of criminal organization can provide a basis for addressing the threat posed by "terrorist organizations," while remaining within the traditional framework of criminal justice. In short, as Kent Roach has recently stated in relation to the *Anti-Terrorism Act*, "Many of these provisions are unnecessary because the issues they confront are already addressed in existing laws."[16] These existing laws, however, focus on the crimes that terrorists may commit, not their general motivation in committing the crimes. The core of this paper is the suggestion that the efficacy of such traditional laws should be examined, and the instrumentalities of enforcing such laws enhanced, before accepting whole new and problematic categories of crime into Canadian law. There is, to date, no clear and direct evidence that the Canadian legal structure as it existed before the *Anti-Terrorism Act*, let alone as it might today be reformed and strengthened, is inadequate to protect Canadians from the threat of terror. The *Anti-Terrorism Act* is thus at least seriously premature, if not wholly ill-conceived.

It probably is important to strengthen the instruments of the detection and investigation of criminal organizations — indeed, not only in relation to terrorist organizations if the government's Anti-Gang legislation is taken as evidence. The designation of such organizations should, however, follow the traditional precedent of proof before a court rather than, as for terrorist organizations, the standard of reasonable grounds in the eyes of the Solicitor General (in the light, in part, of their alleged political, religious, or ideological goals). This alternative strategy, I suggest, would be preferable to adopting a general Anti-Terrorist Act that is bound to be "bad" law.

But why is the *Anti-Terrorism Act* bound to be "bad" law? Beyond the central issue of its general redundancy, I will argue that six key points deserve attention. In the first place, terrorism is a particularly difficult term to define; David Dyzenhaus thinks it "undefinable."[17] As Oren Gross, Antonio Cassese and others have recently argued to effect, "The very attempt to define terrorism is problematic. Attempts to arrive at an agreed upon definition of 'terrorism' on the international level have failed consistently."[18] As Geoffrey Levitt has it, "the search for a definition of terrorism ... resembles the quest for the Holy Grail."[19] The Supreme Court of Canada came to a similar conclusion in 2002; it held that: "There is no single definition [of terrorism] that is accepted internationally. The absence of an authoritative definition means that, at least at the margins, the term is open to politicized manipulation, conjecture and polemical interpretation."[20] As Kent Roach observes, "Because of the difficulties of defining terrorism, it is not included in the mandate of the new International Criminal Court."[21] The attempt to define terrorism is likely therefore to be ultimately futile, and the attempt to introduce it into our legal code positively dangerous. As the Canadian Bar Association (CBA) argued in its submission on the *Anti-Terrorism Act*:

> Defining terrorism is not a simple task. While the September 11th attacks were incontrovertibly terrorist, other examples may not be so clear. Perhaps recognizing that acts constituting terrorism can depend on (among other things) social context, historical perspective and racial, religious or other group identity, our courts have consistently refused to define the concept.[22]

The argument is, in short, that the courts had good reason for their reluctance to define terrorism.

The second argument begins from what may be part of the reason for the difficulty in defining terror — that is, the central distinguishing feature of terrorist acts, at least in Bill C-36, turns on what is often a particularly elusive question of general motivation. This question of motivation is a much deeper and more complex issue than the question of simple intentionality or volition with which the courts struggle today.[23] In essence, the *Anti-Terrorism Act* asks the courts to delve more deeply into the psyche of the accused than the Canadian courts have traditionally been willing to go. As Kent Roach says, a "striking feature of the definition of terrorist activities in Bill C-36 is its requirement for proof of political or religious motives.... The criminal law has traditionally been based on the proposition that it is not necessary for the Crown to establish motive as an element of the offence."

As recently as 1997, the Supreme Court of Canada reaffirmed its commitment to avoid questions of general motivation in the following terms: "It does not matter to society, in its efforts to secure social peace and order, what an accused's motive was, but only what the accused intended to do."[24] In short, it is true that courts are concerned with issues of intent — with the question of whether there is a guilty mind, either through commission or omission. But the question of purposes is much deeper and more problematic than the question of willing intent. You do not have to say just whether an accused was in some sense a participant, but also why the accused was a participant. What were the accused's purposes? In some cases, it may become obvious that the perpetrator's motives fit neatly into one of the general categories specified in the Act. In the vast majority of cases, however, this determination must be a highly interpretive venture. The incorporation of a motivational component into the legal concept of terrorist activity then signals a new type of law or at least a law that implicates a whole new subject. The question then arises whether we need to burden the legal systems and the courts with problematic new categories of law, or whether we might not be better off more proactively applying existing laws based traditionally on criminal action (or conspiracy) and intent.

The third point is that, given the difficulty of defining terrorism and the problematic interpretive demands such category of law introduces, it seems likely that any such definition will end up covering some activities that would not normally be considered as terrorist, and excluding some that would. Don Stuart offers a useful example of an exclusion under the Anti-Terrorist Law which links with the difficulty of interpreting motives: "For years criminal law has sought to avoid proof of a bad motive as a requirement for criminal responsibility. It is too hard to prove and may, as here, lead to curious results. Why should a violent terrorist with unfathomable motives not be included?"[25] So the terrorist with incomprehensible or incoherent motives seems to escape the C-36 definition. On the other hand, Henry Thoreau's famous act of civil disobedience of refusing to pay the poll tax as a protest against the war with Mexico (and slavery) looks like it might very well qualify. It meets what we will shortly see are the requirements of the definition of "terrorist activity." Clearly Thoreau's act was undertaken with a well-defined "political, religious, or ideological motive." Clearly it was directed to pressure "a person, a government or a domestic or an international organization to do or refrain from doing an [any] act." Clearly non-payment of taxes, especially if carried out in coordination with others (as Thoreau exhorts), threatens "serious interference with or serious disruption of an essential public service." Indeed, as Thoreau's critics were quick to observe, his action, if imitated, posed "a serious risk to the health or safety of the public or a segment of the public" — most notably to American forces engaged in the Mexican war. No doubt advocates of the Anti-Terror legislation would want to argue that, all things considered, an action like Thoreau's, even if it had been widely imitated, would be likely be exempted under the *Anti-Terrorism Act*. That answer, however, only reinforces other problems, beginning with the next point.

The fourth point is that once general motivations are introduced into the law, we are faced with two equally unattractive choices as to how to deal with them. On one hand, we may treat them as a simple, undifferentiated category — if you have a "political, religious, or ideological" motivation, you qualify under the provision. That seems to be the government's intent in drafting the legislation. As the Minister herself stressed, the key definitional category of "political, religious, and ideological" motives is meant to be applied without discrimination. If that is the case, then we are bound to punish actions taken for political, religious, or ideological motives that we approve of — say, protesting war or freeing slaves — just as harshly as ones we deplore — say, slaughtering the heretics. The other option of course is that we do, in practice, discriminate between different types of good and bad motives. If this is the case, however, then we are asking the courts to make moral judgments on behalf of the nation about peoples' general moral views and purposes. Apart from moving well beyond the traditional purview of the courts and raising the issue of inequality before the law, that is at least going to make those who embrace "bad" moral views very unhappy even if their convictions are, at the moment, a purely a private affair. It is perhaps this unwelcome dilemma that has motivated the courts to avoid incorporating questions of general motivation into Canadian law to date.

In the fifth place, in legally recognizing acts under the Law's definition as terrorist, we thematize their wider political, religious, or ideological motivation, and reinforce the terrorist's self-portrayal as a martyr for a larger cause. In so doing, we do the terrorist's work of disseminating a political message for him or her. In these ways, we encourage the political efficacy of such acts — which are finally (according to the government) to send a message about an underlying political, religious, or ideological struggle. In these ways, it would be better simply to prosecute terrorists as criminals and not worry about their elusive underlying motivations.

Finally, in the sixth place, I will also argue that the law lines up poorly with our moral intuitions — indeed in an important way inverts them — because it seeks to treat people who act out of principle (however misconceived) more harshly than people who commit similar crimes out of simple self-interest or general cruelty.

Today we have in a sense the worst of all worlds. In response to what the Justice Minister compellingly described as a long-term threat to the security of Canadians, we have a temporary, ad hoc Act of "bad" law. Indeed, one of the reasons that the Act was only acceptable with the addition of review and sunset clauses was because of its many (albeit perhaps unavoidably) ambiguous, morally problematic, and impractical features. The good news, however, is that the insertion of a revision clause ensures the future opportunity eventually to reconsider the Act. Nonetheless, if we are to escape the C-36 worst-of-all-worlds, particularly once it has developed institutional inertia, we will need to have a more considered and promising long-term alternative available. It is as a first step towards that goal that the following critique is offered.

A Closer Look at Canada's Anti-Terrorism Act

To make this paper's six main arguments against an *Anti-Terrorism Act* clear and perspicuous, it will be helpful to turn to a closer analysis of the details of the Canadian legislation, and in particular to the definition of terrorism outlined in Section 83.01. As Kent Roach has argued, this section is really the heart of the new legislation, "because all of the new investigative powers, enhanced sanctions, and the definition of terrorist groups are predicated upon it."[26] This examination will raise some difficulties with the drafting of the legislation which, when examined, will lead to the deep problems underlying not only the legislation itself, but any such legislation, and thus back to the main lines of general argumentation against an *Anti-Terrorism Act*.

Section 83.01 is divided into two main parts, the first part addressing the matter of what qualifies as a terrorist activity, and the second what qualifies as a terrorist organization. I propose to leave aside the second part and to concentrate on the first. As the organization of the section indicates, the second definition rides on the first, and so problems with the definition of terrorist activity will be reproduced in the definition of terrorist organizations.

The first part of the Section 1 dealing with terrorist activities is itself sub-divided into two sections, 'a' and 'b'. The relation between these Subsections can be described by an 'or' conjunction. Any act meeting the stipulations of either Subsection 'a' or 'b' of part 1 of the Section is sufficient to identify a terrorist activity.

The first Subsection 'a' simply lists a series of international conventions and protocols, i. through x., for the suppression of various "unlawful acts," including things like hijacking, piracy, "terrorist bombing," and "terrorist financing." Committing any of the specific acts identified in these conventions and protocols will now qualify in Canadian law as a terrorist act. In short, rather than outlining a general category of terrorist activity, the first Subsection simply enumerates, via the conventions it endorses, a list of specific activities which will qualify under this category. All that I wish to say about this first section is that all of the things listed under this Subsection are already crimes under International and Canadian law. Beyond the matter of adopting two additional UN conventions, which could be done without drafting a general Act against terrorism, it can be usefully asked what this new legislation contributes.

Subsection 'b' of the first part of 83.01 outlines a general category or terrorist activity.

A terrorist activity is...

(b.) an act or omission, in or outside Canada,

(i.) that is committed

(A.) in whole or in part for a political, religious, or ideological purpose, objective or cause, and

(B.) in whole or in part with the intention of intimidating the public, or a segment of the public, with regard to its security, including its economic security, or compelling a person, a government or a domestic or an international organization to do or refrain from doing any act, whether the person, government or organization is inside or outside Canada, and

(ii.) that intentionally

(A.) causes death or serious bodily harm to a person by the use of violence,

(B.) endangers a person's life,

(C.) causes a serious risk to the health or safety of the public or any segment of the public,

(D.) causes substantial property damage, whether to public or private property, if causing such damage is likely to result in the conduct or harm referred to in any of the clauses (A.) to (C.) and (E.), or

(E.) causes serious interference with or serious disruption of an essential service, facility or system, whether public or private, other than as a result of advocacy, protest or dissent or stoppage of work that is not intended to result in the conduct or harm referred to in any of the clauses (A.) to (C.)

To qualify as terrorist then, under this section of the act, an activity must meet the standards implied in both biA and biB, and at least one of the clauses from biiA-E. In general terms, any person or organization suspected of direct or indirect involvement in activities as described above will be subject to augmented state powers of surveillance, detention, interrogation, financial regulation, and in the case of immigrants and refugees, deportation. Persons convicted of crimes which also qualify under the definition of terrorist activities can face additional sentences of either ten or fourteen years to be served consecutively with other sentences. Indeed, Section 83.27 (1) provides that: "Notwithstanding anything in this Act, a person convicted of an indictable offence ... where the act or omission constituting the offence also constitutes a terrorist activity, is liable to imprisonment for life." The definition of terrorism then is an extremely serious matter, for any crime that qualifies under the definition can carry a sentence of life in prison.

What I will do, then, in the next few pages is to consider briefly the required clauses iA and iB, and then the alternative clauses iiA through E, and finally the overall significance of the definitional requirements of Section 83.01 and the *Anti-Terrorism Act* as a whole. At this point I will return to what I take to be the main objections both to the *Anti-Terrorism Act* in particular, and to the need for any such Act in general.

Clause biA requires that "terrorist acts" be committed "in whole or in part for a political, religious, or ideological purpose, objective or cause." In brief, it seems to me that the biggest problems with provision biA can be summarized as follows: (1) its terms are highly general, vague and contestable (and seem to include things that we wouldn't want to include, and to exclude some things that we would); and (2) it involves an interpretation of deep motive (as opposed to simple intention) which takes a big step beyond the normal scope of judicial interpretation and, thus, delegates extraordinary responsibility to the courts.

To begin with, despite following closely the wording of the UK *Terror Act* (2000), biA seems troublesomely vague. What could qualify as a "political, religious, or ideological purpose"? Perhaps the better question is "what would not qualify?" All three terms are vague to the point of indistinctness, especially when taken as a group. In particular, the term "ideological" seems dangerously unclear. Ideology in its most basic sense simply refers to the framework of fundamental social and ethical ideas through which we interpret our normal experience. In this sense, ideological purpose would seem to refer to any goal connected with our basic social, moral, and political ideas or values. On the other hand, it might be objected at this point that the legislation probably employs the term in a more limited sense, as referring to specifically political ideologies, such as nationalism or socialism. However, even a more limited sense of ideology, such as political ideology, remains extremely vague, and could encompass a very wide range of purposes, from democratic to environmental to liberal or humanistic or pluralistic. Moreover, the wording of the legislation suggests something beyond simply political ideologies, for political purposes in general were already covered in the first adjective "political." Ideology then points to a further but effectively undefined range of potential purposes.

In short, people have diverse religious, political, and particularly ideological commitments. The degree that related purposes influence our daily action is a difficult question at virtually any time. Probably most of what most people do on most days can be seen as at least partially directed towards some political, religious, or ideological purpose.

What kinds of motives are then excluded by the range of the political, religious, or ideological? The most obvious candidate for exclusion seems to be material self-interest. Material self-interest, although presumably a relevant motive in most crimes, seems deliberately absent from the list of eligible motives under biA.[27] Economic self-interest, then, is not considered a sufficient motive for terrorism. In effect, the best defence when charged under biA is to claim to have been wholly motivated by self-interest.

If, however, material self-interest provides a limiting case, and thus helps us to see that at least some things will not fit under the requirements of the biA clause, it still does little to clarify what should fit under the "political, religious, or ideological purpose" requirement. It does, however, raise two further serious concerns: first, why do actions motivated by material self-interest warrant less heavy punishment than those motivated by more general "political, religious, and ideological purposes?" I will return to this question below. Second, if "political, religious and ideological" purposes are essential to characterizing terrorist activities, how is the difficult determination of underlying motivation, particularly in view of the ambiguity of the three categories, to be accurately made?

The two main criticisms of biA can be summarized as follows: the provision relies on a wholly vague criterion of purpose which it seeks to apply through a highly problematic judicial interpretation that criminal justices have understandably tried for years to avoid. Now there is much more to say about the difficulties entailed by section biA, but the points will be clearer once the remaining provisions are on the table.

Subsection biB is similar to biA in the sense of being required for the identification of a terrorist activity, and it is obviously intended to help to focus the very general requirements biA. However, while biB certainly does go some distance towards narrowing the definition of terrorist activities by connecting them with interference with public or private interests, the language is again surprisingly broad — in important respects even broader than the corresponding British and American legislation.

Subsection b1B distinguishes two main categories of terrorist activities: first, it refers to activities undertaken "in whole or in part with the intention of intimidating the public, or a segment of the public, with regard to its security, including its economic security"; second, it refers alternately to any activity which compels "a person, a government or a domestic or an international organization to do or refrain from doing any act." The first category extends beyond comparable legislation by combining the "intimidation of any segment of the public" with the specific inclusion of their economic security. The second category exceeds comparable legislation in stressing not only the disruption of the essential functions of government, but in compelling any person, government or international organization "to do or refrain from doing any act."

Subsection biB, then, does not effectively narrow the ambit of Subsection biA as much as one might hope. Indeed, it seems to encompass a whole range of activities that we would not normally regard as terrorist at all. On one side, it seems to encompass a whole range of crimes which, while certainly warranting punishment, do not seem terrorist. On the other side, it fails to clarify biA so as to prevent it from excluding some activities that we would normally want to include as terrorist.

It may be helpful at this point to raise briefly a couple of examples of activities which would seem to qualify under the definition. Imagine, for example, that a radical environmentalist group interferes with the operation of a multinational company by throwing themselves in front of bulldozers or trucks, or, more radically, kidnapping the CEO, and demands that the company agree to stop some practice that they see as harmful — say, for example, marketing certain genetically engineered foods, employing sweatshop labour, selling weapons or enabling technology to some country actively suppressing domestic minorities, or killing off some endangered species. I choose these examples because

I think that they very obviously will qualify under biB (as well as biA and the bii provisions). Evidently, the kidnappers want to intimidate a certain segment of the public (particularly in regard of their economic security), and they undeniably are trying to get a person or international organization to do or refrain from doing something. Either way they qualify under biB. It is also evident that they are acting in pursuit of political, religious, or ideological purposes, and that they are threatening someone's health and safety. In fairness, it must be acknowledged that such activities are later included in an exemption that was added in the legislation under biiE, but that exemption relates only to that one provision, and as we will see, that provision is unlikely to be definitive. Both cases of blocking bulldozers and trucks and kidnapping the CEO qualify independently under biiB and C — endangering someone's life, and causing a risk to the health or safety of a member of the public. So these kidnappers would qualify under all the demands of the definition of terrorist activity, and yet my strong intuition is that we would not want to treat these protesters as terrorists, but simply as in violation of the highway code, or as kidnappers, and punish them accordingly. Once the law is on the books, however, it becomes difficult to explain "consistently" why we would not prosecute them as terrorists. Now, what I want to suggest is that many less fanciful cases of protest qualify under the legislation, although it is by no means clear that we would want to treat them as terrorist activities.

Turning, then, more specifically to section bii, iiA-C, which seem[s] at any rate much clearer and more specific than the somewhat vague and over-generalized language of bi: they are concerned with violent harm, endangerment, and the health and safety of any segment of the public. What these provisions seem to overlook completely is the possibility that the terrorists, or in the current example, protesters, might be endangering their own lives, subjecting themselves to the possibility of violent harm, and risking their own health and safety. Under a literal reading of the act, protesters putting themselves in danger can be a sufficient reason for regarding their actions as terrorist. The fact is that a certain amount of physical danger is part and parcel of engaging in a protest. That is part of why we usually think of it as a noble activity. Ironically, the danger to protesters is more often than not caused by the representatives of the state, and that raises the important question of whether the state can engage in terrorist activities, say in dispersing a widespread demonstration, and thus endangering a segment of the population (the protesters), especially if the dispersal results in injuries (as at the APEC summit), and even death. Indeed, is it legally possible for the state to be engaged in terrorist activities at all? The answer seems to be that while nothing in the definition of terrorist activity precludes the possibility of the government being engaged in terrorist activity, neither is there any mechanism in the legislation by which the state can be held accountable, or, in the extreme, be designated a terrorist organization, unless it is by the Governor in Council at the behest of the Solicitor General. The absence of any acknowledgement of the possibility of state terrorism, however, renders the bill open to a charge of contradiction: in seeking to combat terrorism, the Act grants extraordinary powers with little oversight to what is potentially the most powerful and threatening terrorist organization of all.

Subsection biiD extends legislative protection to public and private property in a more explicit way than the comparable UK and U.S. legislation, providing that the damage described is that named in A-C or E. But all of these linked provisions are already listed, so that D must provide additional protection for property, both public and private. It might be objected here that damage to property is better understood as vandalism than as terrorism. A defender of the legislation, however, might respond by stressing that the Act does not make property damage itself terrorist (even if it has some larger political purpose), but only property damage that causes the harm or endangerment outlined in A-C (and is politically motivated to pressure someone into doing something). It is worth noting here that E is also a sufficient condition for the operation of D, but does not directly entail any harm to actual persons, but only to an "essential service, facility or system." Still, it is easy enough to imagine how in the course of demonstration and police control, property could be damaged and someone's health or safety could be threatened.

Subsection biiE allows activities to be designated as terrorist if they "seriously interfere" with or "seriously disrupt" an "essential service, facility or system" (whether public or private). The legislation provides no information on what exactly is to be regarded as an essential system, but it could be reasonably inferred to include things like the power system, water systems, road systems, hospitals, telecommunications, computer networks, and the like. If E is interpreted expansively, to include all roads and power lines, then D could be a very strong protection for property. However, whether biiE is interpreted narrowly or expansively, essential services may certainly be "seriously interfered" with or "disrupted" in the course of public protests (and strikes, especially in the public sector). It is no doubt for this reason that a specific exemption was added to the clause: "other than as a result of advocacy, protest or dissent or stoppage of work that is not intended to result in the conduct or harm referred to in any of the clauses (A.) to (C.)." So, in essence, advocacy, protest and work stoppage are given special protection in relation to clause E of Subsection bii.

This special exemption clause, however, raises a number of questions. In the first place, if advocacy, protest, and work stoppages are not considered terrorist acts in relation to essential public and private services, facilities and systems, as other terrorist acts are, why are they not exempted in terms of other bii clauses? Why, for example, if they are protected here in terms of an "essential service, facility or system," are they not protected under the general property clause D? The basic point here is that it does not seem either meaningful or sensible to provide an exemption under biiE that is not extended to other bii clauses. We must either accept a principled exclusion for forms of protest, advocacy and work stoppage which applies to the whole range of possibilities or give up the notion of a meaningful exemption altogether. The need for consistency here is particularly strong because, as noted, protests and demonstrations frequently involve risks to health and safety, and often result in bodily harm and sometimes even serious injuries.

A Fundamental Contradiction? Lawful Protest as Terrorism

Beyond the issue of consistency, however, clause biiE raises the spectre of something approaching a contradiction, which, I think, reflects deep tension running through the definition. In short, clause E asserts that protest, advocacy or strikes shall not be treated as terrorist activities even when they meet the other requirements (i.e., biA and biB). They represent a special case. However, the first clause, biA required that all terrorist activities must be directed towards some specific "political, religious, or ideological purpose." Yet, if all terrorist activities by definition pursue political, religious, or ideological purposes, then they are by definition forms of advocacy or protest. To pursue a goal through public action, particularly action in defiance of the law, is manifestly advocacy of, and characteristically protest in support of, the goal or principle in question. Yet if terrorist activity is always by definition advocacy or protest, then it is always exempted under biiE—in other words, the whole clause is rendered moot. So the contradiction consists in saying that activities are terrorist in view of pursuing larger political, religious, or ideological goals, except in certain cases where they involve the pursuit of wider political, religious, or ideological goals. The point is that in incorporating the exception clause, the government effectively allowed that in trying to define terrorism expansively enough to go beyond the existing criminal legislation, it winds up potentially encompassing a range of legitimate activities which it has to then go back and exempt. That, then, provides the reason for the question posed earlier: why is the exemption clause applied, seemingly arbitrarily, to biiE? Because if it were applied more consistently to each of the bii clauses, A to E, then it would render the whole section moot, and leave us with legislation that pronounces any political, religious, or ideologically motivated action, which encourages anyone to do anything, as terrorism.

In the original text of the legislation, the exempted activities were distinguished as "lawful." Under this wording, there is a clear contrastive force between the general pursuit of political, religious and ideological goals and the specific sub-class of lawful public protest activities. The difference was that in the latter case all illegal advocacy, protests, demonstration and work stoppages were excluded, whereas in the former case they were all included. On this initial formulation of the Act, at least some of the cases which qualified under the biA clause would not qualify for the exemption under the biiE clause (i.e., any of those activities for the advancement of political, religious, and ideological purposes that were illegal in nature). What fits under the biA definition but not under the biiE exemption then is any illegal protest.

The problem with the original formulation of the bill including the qualifier "legal" in biiE was, as many critics pointed out, that some perfectly legitimate forms of protest, advocacy, and work stoppage are illegal, and the enactment of the biiE exception would allow the state enormous regulatory power over what did and did not qualify as legitimate dissent, and what was in danger of being identified as terrorism.

The government did eventually agree to the removal of the "legal" qualifier to the biiE exemption, but with this went the contrastive force with the provision of biA. Since all terrorist acts are by their nature acts of protest (motivated by political, religious, or ideological agendas), biiE effectively exempts terrorist acts, as long as they are directed only at "an essential service or facility or system." Indeed, in order to avoid a blanket exemption of all terrorist activities from the *Anti-Terrorism Act*, the government is compelled to include an exemption to the exemption: the exception for protest activities does not extend to those intended to result in the harms referred to in clauses A to C. So illegal protests may be permitted, but only providing that they are "intended" to risk nobody's life, health, or safety. This convoluted definition, however, is hardly more satisfactory than the original. Under the new definition, for example, it looks as if blowing up Parliament (off-session) as an act of illegal protest could be exempted provided there is no "intention" to harm anyone, but lying down in front of a logging truck to make an environmental point would be terrorism. What this shows is that once the government tries to press the definition of terrorism beyond what is already manifestly criminal, they encounter ineradicable difficulties of specification. In essence, the legislation is either largely redundant or dangerously unclear. I think the difficulty can be illustrated by considering some real cases.

Consider the Oka crisis of 1990 as an example. Here a protest erupted among mainly Aboriginal Canadians over the municipality of Oka's claim to, and plans for, a parcel of land claimed by the natives. The protest led to the barricading of essential access roads to Montréal, and ultimately to an armed showdown between Native Warriors and first the Sûreté du Québec and later the Canadian Army. The lengthy confrontation involved a number of violent encounters, including the fatal shooting of a young Sûreté officer, Corporal Marcel Lemay.

The point is that the protest activities at Oka seem clearly to qualify as political, religious, or ideological in purpose. They also fit the biB criteria of compelling a government to do or refrain from doing any act. It also clearly meets the bii clause not only in terms of endangering life (causing a death) but in fact under every point of Subsection ii (risking the health and safety of segments of the public, causing property damage, and disrupting an essential facility or system). Nonetheless, I do not think that we would want to characterize the protest as a terrorist activity.

Now, it may be objected that the Oka case is a particularly difficult and troubling one, and that these ambiguous cases are rare and can still be decided by the courts (albeit with difficulty). What I want to suggest to the contrary is that the Oka case is exemplary of a whole range of cases which could qualify under the 83.01 definition. Think, for example, about recent protests at the G7 and APEC summits, or even the recent protests at my own university, Concordia, on the ninth of September, 2002, to pick a few obvious cases. In each case there were injuries, there were disruptions of public services, and there were attempts to influence and even intimidate public institutions and international organizations from "doing or refraining from doing any act." Indeed, these criteria are bound to be met any time a protester chains himself to a tree or stands in front of bulldozers or takes to a boat to defend his or her fisheries, or when people link arms to obstruct access to an abortion clinic. Still, none of these cases, I think, are among those that we would want to designate as terrorist activities and subject to augmented surveillance, detention, interrogation, and punishment. All of these examples, then, help to illustrate the overreaching character of the *Anti-Terrorism Act* and the definition of "terrorist activities" in particular.

On the other hand, the point can also be made in the other direction. As overreaching as the Act may be, it also fails to capture some activities that we might well want to designate as terrorist acts. As we have seen, for example, the crucial biiA clause requires a clear "religious, political or ideological" motive for a terrorist act. As Don Stuart points out, a terrorist whose motives are "unfathomable" or obscure must be excluded under the law. If the Unabomber (Ted Kaczynski), for example, had not conveniently provided a manifesto shortly before he was caught, it might be very difficult to have prosecuted him successfully under this type of law. Kaczynski's motives, as represented in his manifesto, were both highly elaborate and idiosyncratic, and by consequence would have been extremely difficult to discern and prove without his helpful guidance. Some motives, by their nature, do not lend themselves to either comprehension or effective prosecution.

Moreover, even if terrorists' motives are in themselves comprehensible, they may nonetheless be deliberately hidden or obscured. In some cases, this sort of deception may fit in well with terrorists' objectives — to panic and terrorize an enemy population. Eruptions of violence may be all the more terrifying if they have no identifiable purpose. Indeed, they may do more to discredit Western liberal government if they appear to arise as a natural by-product of this form of life rather than as an assault on it from the outside. A terrorist may then have ideological as well as pragmatic purposes (i.e., avoiding the additional punishments outlined in the anti-terror legislation), to hide his or her motives. So terrorists may not only have obscure motives which escape legislative regulation, they may also deliberately hide their motives to escape legislative sanctions.

Finally, the Act seems to ignore entirely the category of state terrorism, either domestically or internationally; indeed, one of the points of the act is to protect the freedom of the Canadian state "or a domestic or an international organization" by allowing the designation of any violent or disruptive protest against the government, or international organization, as acts of terrorism. That seems like a particularly odd omission because state terrorism has been a major theme of the ongoing war on terrorism in which Canada has been participating — whether in Afghanistan under the Taliban, or in Iraq under Saddam Hussein. Moreover, the issue of state terrorism has been a central news item for months, whether in reference for example to Sharon's Israel or Arafat's quasi-state of Palestine.

Now, an objection is likely to be raised at this point that the Canadian or even the American government is far less threatening in this respect than the former Iraqi or Afghani governments. That is no doubt true. Nonetheless, there are historical incidents which might certainly come close to what we would be likely to identify as state terrorism elsewhere and which seem to meet the essential qualifications laid out in the new legislation. Consider, for example, the internment of Japanese Canadians (and Japanese Americans) during the Second World War. If Iraq or Israel forced entire segments of their population into internment camps on the basis of their ethnic backgrounds in a fashion similar to Canadian treatment of citizens of Japanese extraction, that would likely be widely recognized as a form of state terrorism. Certainly such a policy would be directed towards "political, religious, or ideological purposes," and would qualify under biB as "intimidating ... a segment of the public, with regard to its security, including its economic security ... or compelling a person ... to do or refrain from doing any act." It would also meet the stipulation of biiC by causing "a serious risk to the health or safety of ... a segment of the public." Yet, short of the government choosing to prosecute itself, or designate itself as a "terrorist organization," the Act provides no means for identifying such policy as a terrorist activity. In that way, the *Anti-Terrorism Act*, as over-inclusive as it may be, still leaves out acts which we, or at least some, would normally want to characterize as terrorist.

As the examples I have cited indicate, the act is at once too inclusive, and not inclusive enough. This charge, however, seems to leave open the possibility of making amendments to the definition of terrorism that might bring it more consistently in line with our impression of what terrorism is. However, the deeper point towards which I am gesturing is that there is no such definition of terrorism towards which to turn. Canadians, like much of the rest of the world, are deeply divided about exactly what is, and what is not, terrorism. Svend Robinson [former MP from Burnaby BC, who was stopped by Israeli authorities in an attempt to visit Yasser Arafat in early 2003], for example, wants to side with the Palestinian people because he believes that they are being terrorized by the Israeli state, and many Canadians agree with this basic assessment. Indeed, a resolution by the United Nations Commission on Human Rights passed last year, during a high point in the suicide bombings, endorsed Palestinian resistance to Israeli occupation "by any means necessary."[28] That resolution was widely taken as, and indeed seems clearly to suggest, a recognition on the part of the Human Rights Commission of a right to inflict civilian casualties in response to an extended foreign occupation. Many Canadians will also accept that perspective, and therefore argue that suicide bombs cannot be terrorism because they represent the exercise of a legitimate right of resistance. On the other hand, Mr. Bush came to the conclusion this past summer that the Palestinian leadership was "compromised by terror" and had placed itself, therefore, beyond the boundaries of civilized discourse and had to be replaced before any substantial steps towards a lasting peace could be made in the region. Indeed, Mr. Bush has repeatedly driven the point home that suicide bombings are a terrorist activity and has even recently taken to calling them "homicide bombings" in order to reflect better their terrorist character. Many Canadians will also likely agree with Mr. Bush.

My essential point here is that Canadians are conflicted over the meaning of terrorism. No doubt, there are at least some extreme cases on which most everyone can agree — such as the September 11th attack, or perhaps even the FLQ kidnappings of James Cross and Pierre Laporte. That, however, shows only that terrorism has something of the elusive quality of the legal concept of pornography — we may sometimes know it when we see it, but that does not make us any more capable of framing a clear and comprehensive definition. This point brings us back around to the first argument with which this discussion began — the difficulty of defining terrorism.

Conclusions

At this point I will draw the lines of the specific examination and discussion of the definition of terrorist activity in the Canadian *Anti-Terrorism Act* back into the six main lines of argument laid out at the beginning. In the first place, Canadians' conflicting opinions, and indeed the anomalies and even contradictions revealed in the examination of the definition in Canadian law, attest to the difficulty of defining terrorism, and thus to the first main reason to be sceptical of the need for an *Anti-Terrorism Act* and a legal concept of terrorism. The suspicion here is that terrorism defies clear definition, or, to state the charge in a weaker form, that it can be made really clear and sharp only by narrowing it to the point of redundancy with existing offences, so that we would be better off not introducing it as a separate legal concept, but rather focusing on the actual crimes that terrorist commit.

One of the main reasons for this difficulty in defining terrorism is, as claimed in the second line of argument, that the concept of terrorism relies, at least when we get past the easiest cases, on the elusive question of general motivation — a question that for sound reasons the courts have understandably avoided to this point: for example, such decisions must, by their nature be, in most cases, deeply speculative, and therefore cannot play an important role in proving a person's innocence or guilt. In many cases courts cannot make such assessments beyond a reasonable doubt. One important consequence of this feature of the Canadian legal tradition is that it has developed no instruments through which such assessments can even begin plausibly to be made. The concept of terrorism, then, introduces an element of interpretation which threatens the judicial system's crucial appearance (and reality) of fair and disinterested objectivity.

Perhaps the difficulty can be illustrated by asking the question "is Charles Manson is a terrorist?" He certainly claimed that he acted with "a political, religious, or ideological purpose, objective or cause," he is certainly guilty of "compelling a person ... to do or refrain from doing any act," and his intent and effect was (A.) to cause death or serious bodily harm to a person by the use of violence, (B.) to endanger a person's life, (C.) to cause a serious risk to the health or safety of a segment of the public, and (D.) to cause substantial property damage. Moreover, he intended and succeeded in terrorising a community. He certainly meets all the criteria for "terrorist activity" set out in 83.01. A judgment on the question would have to be based on an understanding of his general motivation, and that is something that a judge or a jury might understandably be reluctant to furnish. Moreover, it is entirely unclear how reliable a guide we could expect them to be. The "Washington Sniper," John Allen Muhammad, and his young accomplice, John Lee Malvo, are being prosecuted as terrorists under the new American legislation. If they had committed their crimes in Canada, would they be prosecuted as terrorists under the Canadian law? Finally, a case with at least a Canadian component would be that of James Charles Kopps who is charged with shooting a doctor who performed abortions — Dr. Garcon Moralis, in 1994. Mr. Kopps is currently on trial in the U.S. for the murder in October 1998 of another doctor who performed abortions. Recently, Dr. Moralis was again assaulted and stabbed in the lobby of his clinic in West Vancouver: so perhaps Canadian courts soon will be asked to decide under the law whether his assailant, likely an anti-abortion activist, is a terrorist. The result of the elusiveness and injusticiability of the concept of terrorism means that when we try to force a legal definition, as in Section 83.01 of Canada's *Anti-Terrorism Act*, we wind up both including and excluding too much. The definition seems to cover some cases, like Oka, the APEC protests, and the September 9th

episode at Concordia, which most people would be loathe to term terrorism, but also excluded cases that most people would want to include, like forms of state terrorism, or terrorists with unfathomable motives.

The fourth line of argument suggested that adopting a legal concept of terrorism also places us in an awkward dilemma. We must either apply the categories of the definition, and particularly the very broad criterion of "political, religious, or ideological" motives consistently across the board, or open the judicial system to charges of discrimination. If, however, we elect to apply the categories rigidly, we lose the capacity to distinguish legally between acts whose "political, religious, or ideological" motives we admire (as, I hope, with Thoreau and my imaginary eco-terrorists), even if we may sometimes disapprove of their methods, and acts of cruelty and hatred that are truly repugnant, like the persons who carried out the events of September 11th.

My fifth line of argument is simply that prosecuting terrorists under Subsection biiA of Section 83.01 would draw unnecessary attention to the underlying purposes, objectives or goals of terrorist activities and their motivating ideology, and hence would serve the terrorists' interests in disseminating their "political, religious, or ideological" cause. It would serve, moreover, to reinforce terrorists' self-portrayal as martyrs in a greater cause. A prosecution for terrorist activity under Subsection b of 83.01 would then articulate the two main components of terrorists' positive messages—what it is that they stand for, and their commitment to this purpose, not only to the point that they will risk their own freedom to advance it, but that they are willing to risk their own lives, and in some cases even kill those who do not support them. In other words, the *Anti-Terrorism Act* insists on breaking with the traditions of Canadian law, to treat terrorists instead in light of their own self-image as fighters and even martyrs in a political, religious, or ideological cause. Prosecution under this legislation then serves the terrorists' practical purpose and perpetuates the image of terrorists as courageous fighters in a greater cause. That image is further reinforced to the degree that the Act actually lines up protesters of various kinds who qualify under the 83.01 definition of terrorists.

It may be objected at this point that although prosecution under the *Anti-Terrorism Act* would contribute to distilling and disseminating terrorist purposes, it might still deter terrorists because it escalates the punishments that terrorists face. Martha Schaffer makes the point, however, that the terrorists who C-36 is most specifically directed to deter — those who are willing to sacrifice themselves and others in their cause — are unlikely to be deterred by even a significant increase in the potential penalties, should they get caught.[29] They are, after all, in many cases planning to give their lives. The consequence is that the defenders of the legislation are forced to fall back on the elements of the Act which contribute to detection and prevention. These elements, however, we can reinforce without adopting a general *Anti-Terrorism Act.* All in all, then, I think that it can be argued forcefully that the *Anti-Terrorism Act* does less to deter and more to encourage terrorist activities. That counter-productive outcome could, however, be avoided simply by treating the activities as criminal, considering only whether the accused intended an act proscribed in the Criminal code, and thus avoiding the problematic analysis of the deeper "political, religious, or ideological" motivations of intending such an act.

The last main argument I want to make is that even if the court is able in some way to determine the underlying motive of an accused terrorist and his or her accomplices, the intent of the law to augment the sentence for specifically "terrorist" crimes actually inverts our normal moral reasoning. The point here is that the state undertakes to show something that we would normally see as a kind of mitigation — that the crime was not committed out of self-interest, but was in fact motivated by some larger purpose or principle that the accused terrorists felt bound them to commit the act. If someone did something bad, but we can clearly see that they did it in pursuit of what they believed to be a good cause, while it would not eliminate the crime, it would nonetheless be a mitigating factor. Thus, to take up the most clichéd of examples, if someone steals a crust of bread to feed his starving family, while the sincere motive does not dissolve the crime, it does provide an important extenuating circumstance which suggests a degree of mitigation in sentencing. That is part of the reason that we are not too disturbed about the fact that though Robin Hood is a bandit, he can remain a heroic figure for us: he is clearly (at least as we imagine him) engaged in a philanthropic project of redistributing income to those who need it most. Normally, then, we are inclined to see the criminal who is purely self-interested as worse than the criminal who is sincerely motivated by what he or she sees as a higher purpose. The new Anti-Terrorism legislation, however, insists that terrorist activities are motivated by general "political, religious, and ideological" purposes rather than simply self-interested ones, and then uses this distinction as a basis to impose harsher punishments on the terrorist than on the self-interested criminal. It thus fails to cohere with out basic moral intuitions.

The *Anti-Terrorism Act*, in short, is irredeemably "bad" law, and should be repealed. It is, at its definitional core, a futile endeavour. It imposes the onerous and likely unmanageable burden of assessing general motivation on the judicial system. It leaves us with an unclear and ambiguous concept of terrorism which both includes and excludes too much. It traps us in an unenviable dilemma of either adopting an undiscriminating moral equivalence to all "political, religious and ideological," or opens us to charges of structural discrimination in the judicial system itself. It forces us to do terrorists' work for them by formally affirming their claims to a form of martyrdom to a cause, and by disseminating their message. In this way, it is in an important sense practically counterproductive in relation to its own defined purpose—that is, to deter terrorism.

As a result of these and other deficiencies and dangers, The Anti-Terrorism law has proved only acceptable as a temporary expedient, requiring reconsideration in three years, and carrying a five year sunset clause on certain key provisions. In the meantime, we find ourselves in the worst of all worlds: in the face of what the Minister has rightly pointed out is likely to be a serious enduring threat to Canadians, we have responded with temporary, ad hoc, bad legislation. Nonetheless, the only condition under which the Act is likely to be repealed is if a set of better and more consistent adjustments to the law are available or already in place. We must, therefore, begin the process of deciding how to deal with the problems implied by the rise of terror and other threats to Canadian security in the long term, in a manner consistent with our own tradition of criminal law and justice.

Notes

1 Anne MacLellan, "New Powers to Fight Terrorism," in *Canadian Speeches*, Volume 15, Issue 4 (September – October, 2001), p. 30 (2).

2 Ronald J. Daniels, "Introduction," in Ronald J. Daniels, Patrick Macklem, and Kent Roach (ed.s), *The Security of Freedom: Essays on Canada's Anti-Terrorism Bill* (Toronto: University of Toronto Press, 2001), p. 4.

3 Kent Roach, "Dangers of a Charter-Proof and Crime-Based Response to Terror," in *The Security of Freedom*, p. 132; also see Ziyaade Mia, "Terrorizing the Rule of Law: Implications of Anti-Terrorism," in *National Journal of Constitutional Law*, 14 (1) (2002), p. 144.

4 This last point invokes what has come to be known as "the Proportionality Principle." The content of the principle is clearly outlined by the Canadian Supreme Court in *R. v. Oakes* [1986] 1 S.C.R. 103, 1986 Carswell Ont 95, 1986 Carswell Ont. 1001 (S.C.C.): "First, the measures adopted must be carefully designed to achieve the objective in question. They must not be arbitrary, unfair, or based on irrational considerations. In short, they must be rationally connected to the objective. Second, the means, even if rationally connected to the objective in this first sense, should impair as little as possible the right or freedom in question. Third, there must be a proportionality between the effects of the measures which are responsible for limiting the *Charter* right or freedom, and the objective which has been identified as of 'sufficient importance.'"

5 For resistance, see Anne MacLellan quoted in the *Globe and Mail*, October 25, 2001, p. A18.

6 Although, as Irwin Cotler points out, the clauses inserted into the legislation are not full sunset clauses, in that they do not cause the provisions to lapse automatically, and "No Parliamentary re-enactment is necessary." The provisions can be reaffirmed "by way of a simple resolution." Irwin Cotler, "Terrorism, Security and Rights," in *National Journal of Constitutional Law*, Volume 14, p. 41.

7 See "Notes for the Minister of Justice: Appearance before the House of Commons Standing Committee on Justice and Human Rights — Bill C-36" at http://canada.justice.gc.ca/en/news/sp/2001/doc_27900.html

8 Suspects linked to the September 11th events and other planned terrorist activities who have been arrested crossing the border from Canada to the United States, like Nabil Al-Marabh and Ahmed Ressam, were refused refugee status in Canada and ordered deported, but the sentences were not carried out: See John Berlau, "Canada turns into a Terrorist Haven," in *Insight on the News*, Volume 18, Issue 23 (June 24, 2002), p. 15–8. The potential of existing laws to redress the threat is also argued forcefully in Kent Roach, *September 11th: Consequences for Canada* (Montréal: McGill-Queen's University Press, 2003), pp. 81–82.

9 For a useful overview, see Kent Roach, *September 11th: Consequences for Canada* (Montréal: McGill-Queen's University Press, 2003), p. 29. [However, it should be noted that the primary tool used against FLQ militants was simply prosecution under the Criminal Code. *Ed.*]

10 Kent Roach, *September 11th: Consequences for Canada* (Montréal: McGill-Queen's University Press, 2003), p. 51.

11 Clive Walker, "Anti-Terrorism Laws for the Future," in *New Law Journal*, Volume 146 (1996), pp. 586–587.

12 Errol Mendes, "Editor in Chief's Introduction," in *National Journal of Constitutional Law*, 14 (1) (2002), p. 7; also see Stanley Cohen, "Safeguards in and Justification for Canada's New *Anti-Terrorism Act*," in *National Journal of Constitutional Law*," 14 (1) (2002), p. 71–98. As Irwin Cotler stresses, however, that "the [Anti-Terrorism] Act would allow warrantless detention on a mere suspicion that a terrorist activity is planned, without the need for a reasonable belief that the activity is in any way immanent." See Irwin Cotler, "Terrorism, Security and Rights," p. 43.

13 Don Stuart, "The Anti-Terrorism Bill C-36: An Unnecessary Law and Order Quick Fix that Permanently Stains the Canadian Criminal Justice System," in *National Journal of Constitutional Law*, 14 (1) (2002), p. 159.

14 For an extensive list, see Canadian Bar Association, *Submission on* Bill C-36 *Anti-Terrorism Act*, October 2001, pp. 10–11.

15 For details see, for example, Kevin Michael Grace, "Who's Terrorizing Who?" in *The Report* Magazine, November 19, 2001; also, John Berlau, "Canada Turns into a Terrorist Haven," in *Insight on the News*, June 24, 2002, pp. 15–18; and especially Stewart Bell, *Cold Terror: How Canada Nurtures and Exports Terrorism Around the World* (Toronto: John Wiley & Sons Canada, 2004).

16 Gary T. Trotter, "The Anti-Terrorism Bill and Preventative Restraints on Liberty," in *The Security of Freedom*, p. 247.

17 David Dyzenhaus, "The Permanence of the Temporary: Can Emergency Powers be Normalized," in *The Security of Freedom*, p. 28.

18 Oren Gross, "Cutting Down Trees: Law-Making Under the Shadow of Great Calamities," in *The Security of Freedom*, p. 46; also see Antonio Cassese, *Terrorism, Politics, and Law* (New York: Blackwell, 1983).

19 Geoffrey Levitt, "Is Terrorism Worth Defining?" in *Ohio Northern University Law Review* 13 (1986), p. 97.

20 *Suresh v. Canada* (2002), 208 DLR (4th) I at paragraph 94 (SCC).

21 Kent Roach, *September 11th: Consequences for Canada* (Montréal: McGill-Queen's University Press, 2003), p. 29.

22 Canadian Bar Association, no. 10 at 17.

23 See, for example, Ruzic (2001) 41 C.R. (5th) 1 (S.C.C.).

24 *United States v. Dvnar* 2 S.C.R. 462, 1997, Carswell Ont. 1981, 1997 Caswell Ont. 1982 (S.C.C.).

25 Don Stuart, "The Dangers of Quick Fix Legislation in the Criminal Law," in *The Security of Freedom*, p. 208.

26 The quotation is Ronald J. Daniels' summary of Kent Roach's argument in Kent Roach, "The New Terrorist Offenses and the Criminal Law," in *The Security of Freedom*, pp. 153–156.

27 Although it may certainly be argued that self-interest too is, or can be, a kind of ideology.

28 See United Nations Economic and Social Council, E/Cn.4/2002/L.16, at http://193.194.138.190/Huridocda/Huridoca.nsf/(Symbol)/E.CN.4.2002.L.16.En?Opendocument; for commentary see Aronold Beichman, "UN Lynching Prelude," in *Washington Post*, May 2, 2002; Tom Carter, "UN Commissions Backs Palestinian 'Armed Struggle'," in *Washington Times*, April 18, 2002.

29 Martha Schaffer, "Effectiveness of Anti-Terrorism Legislation: Does Bill C-36 Give Us What We Need?" in *The Security of Freedom*, p. 195.

References

Beichman, Aronold. "UN Lynching Prelude," in *Washington Post*, May 2, 2002.

Bell, Stewart. *Cold Terror: How Canada Nurtures and Exports Terrorism to the World*. Toronto: John Wiley & Sons, 2004.

Berlau, John. "Canada turns into a Terrorist Haven," in *Insight on the News*, Volume 18, Issue 23, June 24 2002.

Canadian Bar Association. *Submission on* Bill C-36 *Anti-Terrorism Act*, October 2001.

Carter, Tom. "UN Commissions Backs Palestinian 'Armed Struggle,'" in *Washington Times*, April 18, 2002.

Cassese, Antonio. *Terrorism, Politics and Law*. New York: Blackwell, 1983.

Cohen, Stanley. "Safeguards in and Justification for Canada's New Anti-terrorism Act," in *National Journal of Constitutional Law* Volume 14, Number 1, 2002.

Cotler, Irwin. "Terrorism, Security and Rights," in *National Journal of Constitutional Law*, Volume 13.

Daniels, Ronald J., Patrick Macklem, and Kent Roach, (eds.). *The Security of Freedom: Essays on Canada's Anti-Terrorism Bill*. Toronto: University of Toronto Press, 2001.

Grace, Kevin Michael. "Who's Terrorizing Who?" in *The Report* Magazine, November 19, 2001.

Levitt, Geoffrey. "Is Terrorism Worth Defining?" in *Ohio Northern University Law Review* 13, 1986.

MacLellan, Anne. "New Powers to Fight Terrorism," in *Canadian Speeches* Volume 15, Issue 4, September–October, 2001.

Mendes, Errol. "Editor in Chief's Introduction," in *National Journal of Constitutional Law* Volume 14, Number 1, 2002.

"Notes for the Minister of Justice: Appearance before the House of Commons Standing Committee on Justice and Human Rights" Bill C-36 at http://canada.justice.gc.ca/en/news/sp/2001/doc_27900.html

Roach, Kent. *September 11th: Consequences for Canada.* Montréal: McGill-Queens University Press, 2003.

Ruzic (2001) 41 C.R. (5th) 1 (S.C.C.).

R. v. Oakes [1986] 1 S.C.R. 103, 1986 Carswell Ont. 95, 1986 Carswell Ont. 1001 (S.C.C).

Stuart, Don. "The Anti-Terrorism Bill C-36: An Unnecessary Law and Order Quick Fix that Permanently Stains the Canadian Criminal Justice System," *in National Journal of Constitutional Law*, Volume 14, Number 1, 2002.

Suresh v. Canada (2002), 208 DLR (4th) I at paragraph 94 (SCC).

United Nations Economic and Social Council. *E/Cn.4/2002/L.16*, at http://193.194.138.190/Huridocda/Huridoca.nsf/(Symbol)/E.CN.4.2002.L.16.En?Opendocument

United States v. Dvnar 2 S.C.R. 462, 1997, Caswell Ont. 1981, 1997 Caswell Ont. 1982 (S.C.C.).

Walker, Clive. "Anti-Terrorism Laws for the Future," in *New Law Journal* Volume 146, 1996.

Ziyaade, Mia. "Terrorizing the Rule of Law: Implications of Anti-Terrorism," in *National Journal of Constitutional Law* 14 (1), 2002.

Related Material

Alexander, Yonah (ed). *Combating Terrorism: Strategies of Ten Countries.* Ann Arbor, MI: University of Michigan Press, 2002.

Chomsky, Noam. *9-11.* New York: Seven Stories Press, 2001.

Daubney, David. Te*rrorism, Law and Democracy: How is Canada Changing Following September 11th?* Montréal: Éditions Thémis, 2002.

Dershowitz, Alan M. *Why Terrorism Works: Understanding the Threat, Responding to the Challenge.* New Haven: Yale University Press, 2002.

Hafner, Gerhard. "Certain Issues of the Work of the Sixth Committee at the Fifty-Sixth General Assembly" in The *American Journal of International Law*, Vol. 97, No. 1, January 2003: pp. 147-162.

Kushner, Harvey W. (ed). *Essential Readings on Political Terrorism: Analyses of Problems and Prospects for the 21st Century*. New York: Gordian Knot Books, 2002.

Lennon, Alexander T. J. (ed). *The Battle for Heart and Minds: Using Soft Power to Undermine Terrorist Networks*. Cambridge, Mass.: MIT Press, 2003.

United Nations Publication: *International instruments related to the prevention and suppression of international terrorism*. New York: United Nations, 2001.

Unger, Rhoda. *Terrorism and its Consequences*. Malden, MA: Blackwell Pub., 2002.

PART III

Post-9/11 Examinations of Trade Security, Border Security, and Privatized Security

9

*Trade Concentration and "Homeland Security" on the Canada–United States Border**

Matthew S. Mingus

Introduction

Peace, trade, and culture are the three pillars of Canadian foreign policy, yet the *Canada–U.S. Smart Border Declaration* and 30-point *Action Plan for Creating a Secure and Smart Border* demonstrate that trade is clearly first among equals. The events of September 11, 2001, have increased the political and administrative spotlight on border security with the prevailing rhetoric that an "efficient flow" of routine trade and traffic will allow border officials to focus on "higher risk" individuals and freight. However, the maintenance of a dangerous concentration of trade through a limited number of border crossings is an unintended consequence of this approach. That concentration poses its own threat to binational economic security and will likely be worsened because the 30-point *Action Plan* has five points that facilitate increased concentration at the border and entirely lacks a focus on deconcentrating the flow of goods. The article concludes with a few speculative policy ideas for long-term deconcentration.

In his 1961 address to the Parliament of Canada, President John F. Kennedy said, "Geography has made us neighbours, history has made us friends, economics has made us partners, necessity has made us allies." In the intervening 40 years, Canada and the United States have remained strong allies in the international arena. The horrific events of

September 11, 2001 reinvigorated this alliance and created an additional stress for the world's largest trading partnership. The Federal Aviation Administration started to divert 224 inbound flights with more than 33,000 passengers to Canada even before American Airlines Flight 77 hit the Pentagon, providing clear evidence of a highly functional, cooperative relationship. Additionally, nearly 3,000 Canadian troops, including the Princess Patricia's Canadian Light Infantry Battle Group — representing the largest deployment of Canadian Armed Forces outside of Europe since the Korean War — have served in the Afghanistan region as part of the U.S. military presence.

These examples of strength in the bilateral relationship cannot hide one serious stress: Canada–U.S. border security, which has received considerable political attention lately. One reason the border has received increased attention is that shortly after September 11th it was widely misreported that some of the 15 hijackers entered the United States from Canada (Russo 2001; Laucius and Wake 2001). While the White House eventually announced that none of the hijackers entered the U.S. via Canada (O'Neill 2001), the inaccurate reports and a few prior incidents, such as when Ahmed Ressam was caught by U.S. Customs trying to enter the U.S. from Canada with a car full of explosives, helped make border security an extremely hot topic. In response, on December 12, 2001, Canada and the United States signed the *Canada–U.S. Smart Border Declaration* and agreed on a 30-point *Action Plan for Creating a Secure and Smart Border.* Canada "saved face" for something that had not happened,[1] and the Bush administration demonstrated its resolve to secure the homeland along the 5,500-mile "world's longest undefended border." In an ironic twist, that eventually involved the use of thousands of National Guard troops at the busiest border crossings.

While this long-overdue attention may lead to numerous positive changes, some decisions have been made that may create a more dangerous and insecure border because of a failure to look twenty or more years down the road. The purpose of this paper is (1) to explain that most of the 30-point *Action Plan* items are not new and are about fast trade rather than a secure border; (2) to demonstrate that the intense concentration of U.S.–Canada trade through six or eight border crossings presents a prime opportunity for terrorists, who could immediately endanger binational economic security; (3) to show how the 30-point

Action Plan supports a continued or increased level of concentration as an unintended side effect of the capitalistic desire to make the border more efficient; and finally (4) to suggest that if border security is the real objective, then creative, long-term ideas for deconcentrating the flow of trade between Canada and the United States must be part of the mix.

Deconcentrating trade, while it may make sense from a security perspective, will prove to be an exceptional challenge, given that Canada and the U.S. are each market-driven capitalist democracies. An exhaustive literature search did not uncover any research articles on trade concentration as a border security concern, perhaps because it is generally perceived to be the job of governments in the global capitalist economy to facilitate trade wherever and whenever the market determines trade should flow.

30-Point Action Plan Focused on Trade Efficiency

The political crisis following the destruction of the World Trade Center and the attack on the Pentagon spelled "administrative opportunity" for customs, immigration, and transportation officials. Four points in the action plan focus on airline preclearance, joint review of passenger lists, and the like — items that are directly related to the modus operandi of the 9/11 terror attacks — while the other 26 points cover the whole gamut of border, immigration, and customs issues. A comparison of the 30-point *Action Plan* to previous U.S.–Canada agreements reveals that most of the 30 points represent projects that had been under discussion and development for many years, including nine action-plan items that represent deals to implement policies from binational agreements that had already been negotiated and signed. In addition, ten action plan points were contained in the February 1995 *Canada/United States of America Accord on Our Shared Border* and ten points were in the December 2000 Canada–U.S. Partnership (CUSP) forum report, *Building a Border for the 21st Century*. That indicates that the 9/11 crisis moved items from the discussion phase to the implementation phase because both nations signed the action plan and provided resources for implementation. A renewed sense of political support for implementing old ideas may be the lasting impact.

The four key *Action Plan* themes are facilitating the movement of low-risk people and goods, jointly identifying threats before they enter North America, protecting and enhancing the border infrastructure, and strengthening intelligence sharing and coordination among enforcement agencies. Physical security and economic security are intertwined, and so the American concept of "homeland defense" must and does include Canada, and vice versa. Canadian Deputy Prime Minister (formerly Foreign Affairs Minister) John Manley was designated as Governor Tom Ridge's counterpart for homeland security. What seems clear on both sides of the border is that our efforts to protect ourselves must not obstruct the economic relationships that make us each other's biggest trading partner. That is in keeping with research on the U.S.–Mexico border in which Peter Andreas demonstrated that U.S. policymakers' promotion of "borderless economies based on free market principles in many ways contradicts and undermines" their pursuit of other policy goals regarding drugs and illegal immigration (1996:51). Andreas (1996, 1998, 2000) identified numerous symbolic border actions designed to reinforce a sense of territorial integrity amidst a continued and dominant policy preference for increasing economic and social integration. Andreas even referred to the symbolic actions as "image management" rather than coherent policy designed to achieve the identified objectives.

Likewise, on the Northern border this has not been a time for political or administrative risk taking. For example, the idea of perimeter security,[2] promoted a few years ago by the U.S. Ambassador to Canada at a border security conference (Giffin 2000) and in the CUSP report (Department of Foreign Affairs and International Trade (DFAIT) 2000), did not make the 30-point plan. Also, the overall philosophy of expediting low-risk travelers and goods to free up resources to focus on higher risk people and goods has remained intact (DFAIT 2000:4, 2001; Embassy of the United States of America [Canada] 1995). Writing in *Foreign Affairs*, Stephen Flynn identified the external pressure that drives these policies: "officials are finding themselves under mounting pressure to improve the 'facilitation' of transborder flows. After all, a just-in-time delivery system works only if the goods actually do arrive just in time.... Advocates of better-policed borders are battling against rising volume and mounting pressure for expedited customs clearance" (2000:61).

Bilateral Trade Flows are Intensely Concentrated

George Costaris from the Canadian Consulate General in Detroit makes the trade ramifications of disrupting specific crossings along the Canada–U.S. border abundantly clear. He stressed that a full 43 percent of the $1.4 billion per day of trade between these two nations flows through just three Michigan-Ontario border crossings (Mingus 2002:5). Nevertheless, the data on this topic are muddled, leaving Costaris with one view, Industry Canada and Transport Canada with another, and so on. One reason the data are muddled is that Statistics Canada maintains data by Port of Clearance (not synonymous with specific border crossings) whereas Transport Canada maintains the data by border crossing but does not capture the value of the goods or all transportation modalities. Several Canadian Ministers were contacted in September 2002 and each referenced Transport Canada as the source for statements in their press releases and on their websites. The reason is quite simple: Transport Canada knows how many trucks travel across each border crossing with a high degree of accuracy, and its reports are readily available electronically. They are not, however, an acceptable proxy for import and export data because they do not indicate the value of the goods. When thinking of economic security, the value of disrupted goods is more critical than the number of disrupted trucks.

Statistics Canada maintains detailed import and export information by Port of Clearance, but the information is less accessible and less user friendly than the Transport Canada data. Most tables and figures in this article are based on original analysis of an extensive data set (474,620 records) purchased from Statistics Canada. Table 1 presents Canadian imports and exports by mode of transportation for the entire world and for the United States in particular. Canada runs a substantial trade surplus in its roughly $400 billion annual trade flow. While 87 percent of Canadian exports are bound for the U.S., only 64 percent of the imports are from the U.S. Furthermore, the U.S. runs a large trade deficit with Canada. It is noteworthy that 76 percent of exports to the U.S. are by rail and road as are 87 percent of imports from the U.S. The reason for the difference in value by mode of transportation is primarily attributable to Canada's energy exports to the U.S. via pipelines and power lines.

Table 1: Canadian International Trade by Mode of Transportation

	Total Imports		Imports from USA	
Mode	Value	%	Value	%
Air	48,479,828,927	14.1%	21,121,701,854	9.7%
Other	5,608,159,230	1.6%	3,556,175,482	1.6%
Rail	24,455,328,338	7.1%	19,606,322,848	9.0%
Road	210,672,372,753	61.4%	170,502,462,652	78.1%
Water	53,777,503,728	15.7%	3,535,788,639	1.6%
TOTAL	$342,993,192,976	100.0%	$218,322,451,475	100.0%

	Total Exports		Exports to USA	
Mode	Value	%	Value	%
Air	34,443,452,355	8.6%	21,875,022,607	6.2%
Other	51,550,096,307	12.8%	51,549,906,375	14.7%
Rail	76,119,960,300	18.9%	75,268,400,229	21.5%
Road	195,803,660,077	48.7%	192,449,700,919	54.9%
Water	44,548,345,618	11.1%	9,591,970,389	2.7%
TOTAL	$402,465,514,657	100.0%	$350,735,000,519	100.0%

Note: Trade data is for 2001 and is in Canadian dollars.
Source: Original analysis of Statistics Canada database.

In focusing on the question at hand, trade concentration at U.S.–Canada border crossings is shown in Figures 1 and 2. (Table 3 and Table 4 in Appendix A provide some of the aggregate data used to develop these figures.) This data was developed by excluding trade that is transported by water or air and by excluding all trade that is not directly between Canada and the U.S. The analysis is complicated by two factors: (1) knowing the exact Port of Clearance does not ensure that the goods crossed at a specific border crossing; and (2) the Ports of Clearance for imports and for exports are not identical. In fact, there are more than twice as many Ports of Clearance for rail and road imports as for rail and road exports. Fortunately for the purpose at hand, the extent of concentration is evident and unavoidable in spite of these potential limitations and would likely be even more concentrated if the exact border crossing was available. The reason for that is that goods cleared through some Ports of Clearance away from the border are also likely to cross through the busiest land crossings while goods cleared at a Port of Clearance near a border crossing are unlikely to turn around and cross the border elsewhere.

Figure 1: Canada's Busiest Land Export Border Crossings (to the USA)

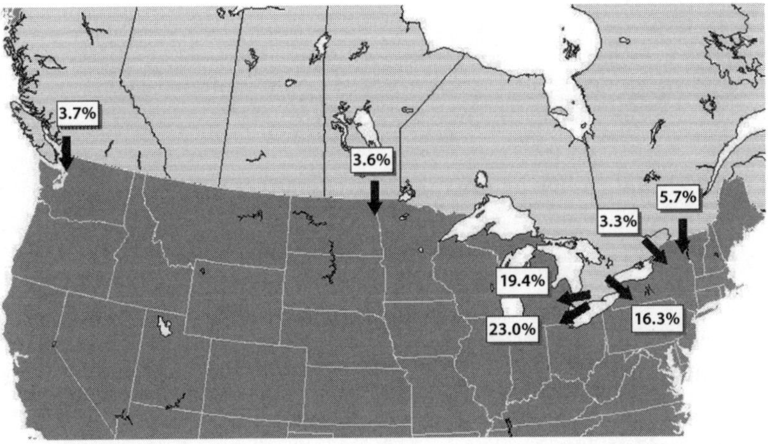

The bottom line is that the Windsor-Detroit and Sarnia-Port Huron crossings account for 42.4 percent of Canada's land exports to and 47.2 percent of Canada's land imports from the U.S. Add the Fort Erie-Niagara Falls-Buffalo crossings and another 16.3 percent of these exports and 14.2 percent of these imports are accounted for. At this point we are talking about 60 percent of land trade between Canada and the U.S. crossing five vulnerable bridges and tunnels. In all, 81 percent of land exports and 76 percent of land imports are cleared through the ten busiest Ports of Clearance with 95 percent of land exports and 89 percent of land imports being cleared through the top twenty (see Appendix A). The geography of the Great Lakes truly makes these two nations

Figure 2: Canada's Busiest Land Import Border Crossings (from USA)

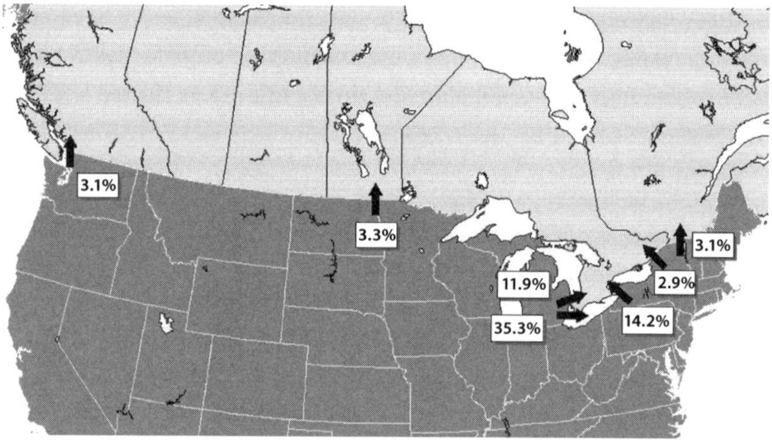

extremely vulnerable to potential terrorist attacks on the trans-border infrastructure. Add a few natural gas pipelines and hydroelectric cables to the list of targets and the picture is bleaker.

The reader may ask, "Why are these likely targets?" These are targets for the same reason terrorists would attack the symbolic centre of the capitalist world by attacking the World Trade Center in New York. The trading relationship between Canada and the United States is the largest in the world and the goal of modern terrorists is to "create a climate of extreme fear. It is directed at a wider audience or target than the immediate victims of the violence. And it inherently involves attacks on random and symbolic targets" (Wilkinson 1996:12).

To add global perspective, trade between the U.S. and the Province of Ontario exceeds U.S. trade with all European nations combined. Ontario-Michigan trade alone exceeds all U.S. trade with Japan. For those who may believe that this trade is all automotive related, take note that in 2001, 44 different Harmonized System 02 categories exceeded $1 billion in total imports whereas 45 different categories exceeded $1 billion in total exports. Canada–U.S. trade is therefore much more diversified in terms of content than one might expect, further exacerbating the potential economic impact of border disruptions, which need only occur at a few border crossings to have substantial impact because of the hazardous level of trade concentration.

Post 9/11 Actions Likely to Increase Concentration

One aspect of the New Public Management (Peters and Pierre 1998; Box et al. 1999) and Reinventing Government (Osborne and Gaebler 1992; Toonen 1998) movements in public administration is an increased focus on responding to the needs of the customer (client, consumer, taxpayer, end user, etc). This philosophy sways modern public administration to a great extent, including moving politicians and administrators away from a broader conception of serving the "public interest." When discussing border crossings and customs issues, the largest customer group is the businesses that ship goods back and forth and the second largest customer group is the border town residents ("locals") who regularly cross the border for work, education, pleasure, shopping, etc. In addition there is the tourist, who is the single largest source of income for many modern communities. Tourists are less relevant to border administrators because their ability to impact the policy process is minimized by their lack of a visible, organized presence. Business groups in tourist-economy towns, however, may help offset this dynamic. An examination of participation in the recent CUSP process indicates these "clients" clearly enough.

At an abstract level these customer groups all desire a safe border; however, at a concrete level they are more concerned with speed and efficiency at the border. Delays are expensive. Unpredictability is costly. Closing the border for security reasons has an almost immediate impact on people who may never have crossed the border. For example, when the borders were closed on September 11, 2001 and slowed dramatically in the following days, the *Toronto Star* reported on September 13th that "Honda, Ford, General Motors, and DaimlerChrysler plants in the province [Ontario] cancelled some shifts on Tuesday, yesterday, and today because of delays in delivery of auto parts from the United States" (Theobald 2001). By September 15th Ford had shut down plants on both sides of the border, including plants as far away as Atlanta, Georgia (CP 2001). Reportedly some just-in-time contracts between Michigan and Ontario businesses require delivery of parts from suppliers in Ontario to plants in Michigan in as little as six hours from signing the contract (Flynn 2000:59).

Imagine the impact of a terrorist attack that removes even one of these critical bridges or tunnels, or a more comprehensive attack on five or six key crossings. Border security officials should be imagining such a possibility and planning to minimize its impact. Table 2 lists five points adopted in the *Action Plan* that seem likely to increase the concentration of trade at critical crossings. The main reason is that these items seek to make the border even more efficient for shippers — a laudable goal — by allowing goods to clear at customs centres away from the border, improving the on-the-ground infrastructure to allow more vehicles across these key bridges, and so forth. What is of even more concern is that no item in the *Action Plan* seeks to reduce the concentration of trade through these critical bottlenecks rather than facilitating additional trade.

Table 2: Probable Increase in Concentration at Border Crossings

Five (5) Key Items in 30-Point Action Plan Increase Concentration of Trade Flows

3. *Single Alternative Inspection System* — Resume NEXUS pilot project, with appropriate security measures, for two-way movement of pre-approved travelers at Sarnia-Port Huron, complete pilot project evaluation and expand a single program to other areas along the land border. Discuss expansion to air travel.

15. *Clearance away from the Border* — Develop an integrated approach to improve security and facilitate trade through away-from-the-border processing for truck/rail cargo (and crews), including inland pre-clearance/post-clearance, international zones and pre-processing centres at the border, and maritime port intransit pre-clearance.

18. *Intransit Container Targeting at Seaports* — Jointly target marine intransit containers arriving in Canada/U.S. by exchanging information and analysts. Work in partnership with the industry to develop advance electronic commercial manifest data for marine containers arriving from overseas.

19. *Infrastructure Improvements* — Work to secure resources for joint and coordinated physical and technological improvements to key border points and trade corridors aimed at overcoming traffic management and growth challenges, including dedicated lanes and border modeling exercises.

20. *Intelligent Transportation Systems* — Deploy interoperable technologies in support of other initiatives to facilitate the secure movement of goods and people, such as transponder applications and electronic container seals.

As explained earlier, the overall philosophy driving recent U.S.–Canada border policy facilitates concentration of trade by expediting low-risk travelers and goods, ostensibly to free up resources to focus on higher risk people and goods. Although individually they each sound like good ideas, the five points listed in Table 2 will clearly increase the flow of people and goods through an overly burdened and easily targeted border infrastructure. In point of fact, the twentry-first item in the Action Plan is the only item that recognizes this danger. It reads, "Critical Infrastructure Protection. Conduct binational threat assessments on trans-border infrastructure and identify necessary additional protection measures, and initiate assessments for transportation networks and other critical infrastructure" (DFAIT 2001). The fact that this point focuses on "assessment" rather than action is of significant concern. The author visited five of these critical border crossings in 2002, including walking around them to observe the structural design, and did not detect active attempts to protect the structures or to keep individuals away from critical design elements.

Ideas for Long-Term Deconcentration of Trade

Perhaps policymakers in North America need reminding of Eric Hoffer's words in *The True Believer* (1951:73): "A pleasant existence blinds us to the possibilities of drastic change. We cling to what we call our common sense, our practical point of view. Actually, these are but names for an all-absorbing familiarity with things as they are. The tangibility of a pleasant and secure existence is such that it makes other realities, however imminent, seem vague and visionary. Thus it happens that when the times become unhinged, it is the practical people who are caught unaware." The argument, in other words, is that in spite of the traumatic attacks on September 11th, everything is basically business as usual in North America. Americans have largely recovered from the horrific shock. While citizens and businesses have increased the political pressure to implement much of what was in the border policy pipeline well before the attacks, the policymaker's mind frame still dwells in the "house of common sense" in spite of the all-too-uncommon enemy. Trade magazines are still able to boldly declare, "The Canada–U.S. Border is Always Open for Business" (McElrea 2002:7).

In terms of trade concentration, border officials and policymakers need to consider some vibrantly non-linear proposals if for no other reason than to recognize actively the quandary these two nations find themselves stuck in so that when opportunities arise they may take incremental steps toward a more secure future. This section presents some ideas for change, unconventional as they may seem to common sense.

If one concludes that economic security is a critical element of North American border security and homeland security, then more questions must be asked. Key among these questions is "Can economic security exist so long as current forces are aligned to maintain the concentrated flow of trade through so few tunnels and bridges?" One might ask, "Of what good is a 5,500 mile long undefended border when so little of it is actively used for commercial purposes?" Intensive physical security is required at these concentrated border crossings, perhaps even by the military, as well as discussions on a long-term plan to deconcentrate the flow of trade. Six ideas designed primarily to start this discussion follow.

1. *Reconsider free trade in North America* — U.S.–Canada trade has more than doubled since implementation of the FTA in 1989, and cross-border truck traffic is expected to continue rising at 10 percent per year. That has helped make Canada the strongest economy in the world and has dramatically increased the commercial traffic across key bridges and tunnels. Much of this trade is repeated at each step in the manufacturing process. For example, (a) Canadian mineral ores and hydroelectric power head to an American steel mill, (b) steel heads back to numerous Canadian parts manufacturers, (c) engine parts made in Canada travel to a U.S. plant that builds engines and (d) sends them back to Canada to be put into vehicles that are (e) sent to automobile dealers back in the U.S. This obviously simplified example suggests picture perfect market integration if you are an economist, but in total the dynamic creates a precarious situation for an opportunistic terrorist group seeking visible economic damage. Such trade might be less economically desirable if those who move the goods back and forth across the border incurred the cost of maintaining the border infrastructure, including border security.

2. Balance out cross-border trade over time by charging crossing fees that decrease as the goods are moved through less busy and less risky crossings. No fee would be charged at dry land border crossings. In effect, the fee might start to balance out the increased transportation costs of taking other routes and other modes or both to get goods to market. The goal here would be to make using the more concentrated crossings a more expensive alternative. (An alternative approach would be significant tax credits for moving goods through a specified list of less concentrated and less risky border crossings. Credits would apply even if the mode of transportation were switched to rail, thereby providing a potential subsidy to struggling rail lines, which could become a key part of the solution. The goal would be to make using less concentrated crossings less costly and therefore more appealing.)

3. Invest in turning the Trans-Canada Highway into an efficient four-lane highway above Lake Superior and invest in interstate highways that allow truck traffic to connect efficiently from the Trans-Canada in a Southwesterly direction to I-90 and I-80. That might provide a competitive alternative route that could help billions of dollars of goods flowing from Ontario to the West avoid the existing concentrated crossings. Specifically, over $4 billion in exports move from Ontario to North Dakota, South Dakota, Montana, Idaho, Oregon, and Washington each year, with an additional $21 billion moving from Ontario to California, Nevada, and Utah. The current focus on trade corridors lacks a focus on developing new alternative corridors to diversify Canada–U.S. trade movement. While some might argue that this may lack a significant return on investment, such an argument would be missing the point that the existing interstate highway system (that feeds the concentrated border crossings) was not developed on a cost-benefit rationale.

4. Calculate the public investment per "truck mile" traveled on highways in highly concentrated trade corridors; then offer similar funding for corporations and transportation companies or both that make long-term commitments to move goods through less concentrated crossings. For example, CN Rail could plan on such funding in

developing infrastructure if they could attract enough business to support their strategic approach.

5. End tax subsidies and abatements that encourage continued development in North America's industrial core. If the proximity of, and compactness of, industries in this area really creates an economic symbiosis, then let those economic advantages speak for themselves. Even though transportation and communications costs have dropped dramatically since the 1950s (Boeckelman 1996:2), a less concentrated economic system has been stifled in the United States, in part because of the development of active state and local tax weapons to attract and retain manufacturers in the industrial core.

6. Ask other people who are willing to voice "uncommon sense" to give this issue some serious thought and add their best discussion points to this conversation. A new forum is needed that will be different from the useful consumer-driven CUSP process because that process made it difficult for even standard public investment allocation pricing to be utilized in policy making.

These six points are intended to spur discussion and, it is hoped, move thought among border officials and policymakers out of its current rut. The detailed arguments are omitted to focus attention on the core ideas. Little such dialogue appears to be occurring among the customs, immigration, and border security community and their political leaders in Canada and the U.S. Perhaps these officials are simply realists because they see an array of forces aligned against an ambitious economic security agenda. Those factors would likely include the Canadian Trucking Alliance, Detroit Chamber of Commerce, Canadian Manufacturers & Exporters, Canadian/American Border Trade Alliance, and countless other advocacy groups on both sides of the border. Nevertheless, those who might oppose meaningful change in the short-term may be the same people who have much to lose if border officials fail to address the hazard to economic security that is posed by trade concentration along the Northern border of the United States.

Matthew S. Mingus

The author thanks the Association for Canadian Studies in Montréal, Québec, for support to present a draft of this research at the April 2003 Canadian American Research Seminar in Niagara Falls, Ontario, acknowledges financial support for this research from his home institution (Arts and Sciences Teaching and Research Award and the School of Public Affairs and Administration), and thanks Christina Barker for assistance in map preparation.

Appendix A — Canadian Land Imports and Exports

Table 3: Concentration of Canadian Land Exports to USA

Port of Clearance	Value	Percent	Cumulative
Windsor - Ambassador Br.	73,064,979,697	22.89%	22.89%
Sarnia	61,850,345,169	19.37%	42.26%
Fort Erie	49,326,690,907	15.45%	57.71%
Lacolle	18,281,520,358	5.73%	63.43%
Pacific Highway	11,698,179,557	3.66%	67.10%
Emerson	11,394,416,978	3.57%	70.67%
Lansdowne	10,643,347,596	3.33%	74.00%
Coutts	9,527,932,813	2.98%	76.98%
Fort Frances	6,934,367,780	2.17%	79.16%
North Portal	6,721,843,848	2.11%	81.26%
Huntington	6,449,186,553	2.02%	83.28%
Kingsgate	6,384,141,991	2.00%	85.28%
Philipsburg	6,312,754,262	1.98%	87.26%
Monchy	4,558,339,024	1.43%	88.69%
Regway	4,188,698,200	1.31%	90.00%
St. Stephen	3,873,976,330	1.21%	91.21%
Gretna	3,359,954,742	1.05%	92.26%
Niagara Falls	2,854,740,647	0.89%	93.16%
Prescott	2,831,304,855	0.89%	94.05%
Rock Island	2,594,650,557	0.81%	94.86%
Woodstock	2,243,675,965	0.70%	95.56%
Carway	2,230,305,902	0.70%	96.26%
Sault Ste. Marie	2,208,978,273	0.69%	96.95%
Trout River	1,811,856,620	0.57%	97.52%
Sidney	939,015,363	0.29%	97.81%
Next 75 Ports of Clearance	6,982,457,035	2.19%	100.00%
TOTAL	319,267,661,022	100.00%	

Note: Trade data is for 2001 and is in Canadian dollars.
Source: Original analysis of Statistics Canada database.

Table 4: Concentration of Canadian Land Imports from USA.

Port of Clearance	Value	Percent	Cumulative
Windsor - Ambassador Br.	61,834,032,901	31.93%	31.93%
Sarnia	23,000,151,862	11.88%	43.81%
Fort Erie	17,837,333,555	9.21%	53.02%
Niagara Falls	9,644,436,145	4.98%	58.00%
Emerson	6,433,450,915	3.32%	61.32%
Pacific Highway	6,078,648,380	3.14%	64.46%
Lacolle	6,056,576,9 39	3.13%	67.59%
Windsor - Main Long Room	5,816,578,197	3.00%	70.59%
Lansdowne	5,684,248,511	2.94%	73.52%
Ontario	4,720,061,656	2.44%	75.96%
Coutts	4,378,878,602	2.26%	78.22%
Toronto - Main Long Room	3,855,423,251	1.99%	80.21%
North Portal	3,674,663,669	1.90%	82.11%
Montréal - Main Long Room	2,356,635,151	1.22%	83.33%
Calgary	2,217,481,198	1.15%	84.47%
Philipsburg	2,172,293,293	1.12%	85.60%
Oshawa	1,760,230,523	0.91%	86.50%
Toronto - Pearson Int. Airport	1,712,421,533	0.88%	87.39%
Vancouver - Main Long Room	1,552,051,868	0.80%	88.19%
Edmonton	1,436,667,709	0.74%	88.93%
British Columbia and Yukon	1,404,340,007	0.73%	89.66%
Montréal - C.D.L. Intrm. Term	1,401,979,064	0.72%	90.38%
Toronto - Dixie I. Suff. Wh.	1,000,555,083	0.52%	90.90%
Winnipeg	934,189,275	0.48%	91.38%
Sault Ste. Marie	933,339,070	0.48%	91.86%
Next 219 Ports of Clearance	15,759,622,877	8.14%	100.00%
TOTAL	193,656,291,234	100.00%	

Note: Trade data is for 2001 and is in Canadian dollars.
Source: Original analysis of Statistics Canada database.

Notes

* A later version of this paper appeared as "'Economic Security is Not So Cheap as the December 2001 Canada-U.S. Smart Border Declaration Would Imply: Suggestions for Moving Beyond the Post-9-11 Rhetoric on Borders" in the *Journal of Borderlands Studies*, vol 17, issue 2, Fall 2003.

1 While the Standing Committee on Citizenship and Immigration (Parliament of Canada 2001) was insistent in its recommendation that Citizenship and Immigration Canada "make an effort to educate the public" to refute "unsubstantiated and unwarranted" concerns about Canada's border security, expert public relations will hardly erase reporting such as this excerpt from Canada's own *Ottawa Citizen*: "'There's no question that groups affiliated with political violence consider Canada a safe haven,' Vincent Cannistraro, a former director of counterterrorism for the CIA, told the *Los Angeles Times*. 'It has been that way for a long time due to a benign environment'" (Laucius and Wake 2001). None of the fifteen hijackers involved in the events of September 11, 2001, arrived in the United States via Canada, but that does not mean that Canada is not still a significant concern because of past events.

2 Movement toward the concept of a common North American perimeter might make Canada a more desirable target for terrorists if such movement means that Canada would adopt immigration, refugee, and customs policies similar to U.S. policies. The "perimeter" idea is focused on harmonizing entry policies to Canada and the United States so that controls on the common border could be reduced or eliminated. Mexico is sometimes included in this concept as well.

References

Andreas, Peter R. 1996. "US–Mexico: Open Markets, Closed Border." *Foreign Policy* 103:51–69.

——. 1998. *The Paradox of Integration: Liberalizing and Criminalizing Flows Across the US–Mexican Border.* University Park, PA: Pennsylvania State University Press.

——. 2000. *Border Games: Policing the US–Mexican Divide.* Ithaca, NY: Cornell University Press.

Boeckelman, Keith. 1996. "Federal Systems in the Global Economy: Research Issues." *Publius: The Journal of Federalism* 26 (1):1–10.

Box, Richard C., Gary S. Marshall, B.J. Reed, and Christine M. Reed. 1999. "New Public Management, Faux Democracy, and the Challenge to Democratic Governance." Paper presented at Public Administration Theory Network Annual Conference, 4–5 March, Portland, Oregon.

CP. 2001. "Lack of Parts Cause Ford Plants Shutdowns." *Cambridge Reporter* (September 15):B9.

Department of Foreign Affairs and International Trade. 2000. "Building a Border for the 21st Century." CUSP Forum Report, December 2000. Ottawa.

——. 2001. "Action Plan for Creating a Secure and Smart Border" (cited October 15, 2002), www.dfait-maeci.gc.ca.

Embassy of the United States of America (Canada). 1995. "A Canada/United States of America Accord on Our Shared Border" (cited October 15, 2002), www.usembassycanada.gov.

Flynn, Stephen E. 2000. "Beyond Border Control." *Foreign Affairs* 79 (6):57–68.

Giffin, Ambassador Gordon D. 2000. "Rethinking The Line: the US/Canada Border. Introductory Remarks." Transcript of speech at Canadian Policy Research Conference, 23 October, Vancouver, British Columbia.

Hoffer, Eric. 1951. *The True Believer. Thoughts on the Nature of Mass Movements*. New York: Perennial Classics (2002 Ed.).

Laucius, Joanne, and Bev Wake. 2001. "Terrorists' Haven Canada the Destination for Criminals" *Ottawa Citizen* (September 13):B4.

McElrea, Rick. 2002. "The Canada–U.S. Border Is Always Open for Business" *Site Selection* 47 (3):supplement 7.

Mingus, Matthew S. 2002. "Strong Foundations Equal Strong Future. Canada–U.S. Relations in the post-September 11 Era." PA Times 25 (2):5.

O'Neill, Juliet. 2001. "Sept. 11: U.S. Admits No Attackers Came from Canada: Two Countries Announce Plan to Tighten Borders." *Vancouver Sun* (December 4):A1.

Osborne, David, and Ted Gaebler. 1992. *Reinventing Government: How the Entrepreneurial Spirit is Transforming the Public Sector.* New York: Penguin Books.

Peters, B. Guy, and John Pierre. 1998. "Governance without Government? Rethinking Public Administration." *Journal of Public Administration Research and Theory* 8 (2):223–243.

Russo, Robert. 2001. "Hijackers May Have Entered the U.S. through Canada, Triggering Echoes of Ressam" *Canadian Press* Newswire (September 13).

Theobald, Steven. 2001. "Economy Gears Down; Grounded Planes, Lineups." *Toronto Star* (September 13):D1.

Toonen, Theo A.J. 1998. "Networks, Management and Institutions: Public Administration as 'Normal Science.'" *Public Administration* 76 (Summer):229–252.

Wilkinson, Paul. 1996. "How to Combat the Reign of Terror." *New Statesman* (August 2):12–13.

10

Smart Borders and Safe Borders: Is there a Distinction?

Darren Prokop

Introduction

Both John Manley, Deputy Prime Minister of Canada, and Tom Ridge, United States Secretary of Homeland Security, have gone on record promoting a "Smart Border for the 21st Century" — a border that is "open for business but closed to terrorists." U.S. Customs Commissioner, Robert Bonner was quoted as saying: "[U.S.] Customs is mindful of the need to heighten security without choking off the flow of trade that is so important to the U.S. economy. If business takes steps to secure its cargo against terrorism, we will give it the 'fast lane' through the border."[1]

This paper examines the trade-off implied by securing a border while promoting efficient trade and supply chain management. Both governments can promote a more secure set of supply chains that cross the Canada–U.S. border by either setting up incentives for firms to bring about that security, or simply require them by regulation. The former is a market-based mechanism while the latter is a political-based one. The currently-evolving border initiatives appear to be seeded with both types of mechanism. This structure will be appraised in terms of the security-efficiency trade-off.

Transportation and the Canada–U.S. Border

The Canada–U.S. border, at 4,000 miles, is the world's longest unguarded border. Both countries are each other's number one trade partner in terms of value and volume. No two countries trade more goods and services than Canada and the United States.

Canada–U.S. trade in goods in 2001 totaled U.S. $345 billion, about 68% of which was moved by truck. About 13.2 million trucks crossed the Canada–U.S. border that year, or about 25 trucks per minute. Rail accounts for 17% of Canada–U.S. trade by value, followed by air (6%) and marine (2%).

The Canada–U.S. border makes up 40% of the U.S. ports of entry. These ports are staffed with only 14% of the U.S. Customs Service's inspectors, and they handle about one-third of its total workload (Coalition for Secure and Trade Efficient Borders 2001:6). Thus, the border is understaffed given that Canada–U.S. merchandise trade has more than doubled over the 1990s while the number of U.S. inspectors has remained basically unchanged.

At the same time shippers are becoming more cautious about how, and who, is providing their transportation. For many years, shippers have been asking carriers to show them their insurance certification documents. In the wake of the September 11, 2001 tragedy (hereafter 9-11) the U.S. Federal Aviation Administration (FAA)[2] has, since October 8, 2002, enforced the "known-shipper" rule which prohibits an air cargo carrier and/or freight forwarder from accepting a shipment from an "infrequent user" unless the carrier takes the time to visit/inspect the shipper's premises to determine the legitimacy of his operation. The frequency criteria for the carrier/forwarder are: (1) at least 24 shipments since September 1, 1999; and (2) a record of doing business with the shipper *before* September 1, 1999.

Efficiency and Safety

Each day along the Canada–U.S. border people of all sorts pass: business people, students, and tourists. Goods of all sorts pass in trailers on motor carriers, boxcars attached to locomotives, and in containers[3] transported on the road, by sea, by rail, and in the air. Is it possible for the efficient flow of Canada–U.S. trade to be maintained, or even enhanced, while providing for a reasonable level of security? Or is it an unavoidable trade-off?

In terms of this trade flow, are just-in-time (JIT) and lean-manufacturing models still workable?[4] Will the result of security compliance be an increase in safety stocks across the supply chain in order to compensate for a slowing in border clearance of goods?

In December of 2001, the Canada–U.S. "Smart Border" initiative was announced. The intent is to manage the trade-off implied by securing the Canada–U.S. border and yet promote trade flows. Using a system known as "free and secure trade" (FAST), low-risk freight and vehicle operators are to be expeditiously granted access across the border while tougher scrutiny is reserved for the remaining cargoes.[5] In other words, the trade-off is to be managed by dividing shippers and carriers into two distinct categories.

In December of 2002, six of the 82 Canada–U.S. road-based border crossing points implemented FAST. Motor carrier traffic figures for these points are listed in Table 1 (next page). It should be noted that these six points represent the busiest border crossing points for motor carriers and account for almost 75 percent of motor carrier-based cross-border traffic. Dedicated lanes are to be used by trucks that have pre-cleared the customs process. Canada Customs and Revenue Agency and the U.S. Customs Service will pre-screen the freight before it has arrived at the border. Thus, shippers that use a JIT system of cross-border trade or simply make frequent border crossings have an incentive to integrate customs pre-screening into their supply chains. Regular and respectable shippers (e.g., the "Big 3" automakers) will be separated out from the shippers and carriers deserving of tougher scrutiny — those using rental vehicles and those hauling unmarked trailers or containers.

In terms of rail crossings through the border, both the Canadian Pacific Railway and Canadian National Railway have been electronically submitting manifests to U.S. Customs since 2000. By foregoing paper manifests delivered at the border, U.S. Customs' Automated Manifest System (AMS) has allowed train crossing times to be reduced from several hours to about ten minutes. U.S. railroads — Burlington Northern Santa Fe, Union Pacific, and Wisconsin Central (a subsidiary of Canadian National) — have all been using AMS on their import runs

Table 1: The Top Six Motor Carrier Based Canada–U.S. Border Crossing Points

Canada–U.S. Border Crossing	Number of Motor Carrier Crossings (2001)	Mean Growth Rate of Crossings (%) (1996–02)	Share of Canadian-Registered Motor Carriers (%)
Ambassador Bridge (Windsor–Detroit)	3,274,754	1.5	55.8
Blue Water Bridge (ON 402 – U.S. I-94)	1,467,580	1.9	74.6
Peace Bridge (ON QEW – U.S. I-190)	1,351,672	0.7	80.1
Lewiston-Queenston Bridge (ON 405 – U.S. I-190)	1,004,178	1.1	67.8
Douglas-Blaine (BC 99 – U.S. I-5)	788,076	-0.1	74.5
Lacolle-Champlain (QB 15 – U.S. I-87)	762,512	1.4	83.1

Source: Nix (2002) p. 20

out of Canada. AMS was introduced along the U.S.–Mexico border in 2001.

As a bi-national initiative, FAST will blend Canada's Customs Self Assessment (CSA) program with the U.S.'s Customs-Trade Partnership Against Terrorism (C-TPAT) program. In both cases, shippers who *volunteer* to join these programs and are deemed to be "low-risk" will accumulate data regarding their shipping transactions and report and pay any applicable customs duties on a monthly basis. Information on each shipment in transit, however, will have to be sent electronically to customs officials at the border in advance of the truck arriving at the primary inspection lane (PIL). Bar-codes will be presented to the customs official by the driver showing that he, the carrier he works for, the shipper(s) of record, and the shipment(s) have all been pre-approved. After the bar codes are scanned, the vehicle is simply waved through without the usual questions about the shipping manifest, the vendor, the consignee, and the contents of the vehicle. The actual proof of the transaction will be sent to customs officials as part of the monthly data reports.[6]

As FAST develops, it appears that the United States will be requiring more information for pre-clearance than will Canada. Canada will carry on with three CSA identifiers: shipper of record (the importer or exporter), the carrier, and the driver. The United States will require further elements: the goods' vendor (if different from the shipper of record), a description of the goods, and the route to be traveled. In any case, the Canadian and U.S. customs services will be integrating their computer systems into one harmonized database and clearance system.[7]

Two impediments remain: (1) infrastructure and manpower at several border crossings are not ready to handle the volume of vehicles expected to be expedited so quickly; and (2) the majority of trucks crossing the border are less-than-truckload (LTL) and haul freight consolidated from among several shippers. All that is needed is for one of the shippers not to be in the low-risk category for the truck to face tougher inspection. Or if a carrier subcontracts the shipment to one of the thousands of owner-operators that are not part of FAST, a compliant shipper's position within FAST is in effect voided. It would seem likely that shippers would require contracts that guard against these possibilities from their carriers. In the interim, FAST will by no means completely eliminate congestion at border crossings.

Beyond FAST is the issue of shipments not credited as low-risk. International couriers are worried that serving shippers that are not within the FAST framework will cut into their ability to provide 10 a.m.–noon, next-day service.[8] In Canada, shipments not eligible for CSA will be relegated, as of December 2002, to a customs program called Advance Commercial Information (ACI). While the details are not yet worked out — and the courier companies are discussing possible exemptions — Canada Customs and Revenue Agency will require full and complete manifest data to be sent electronically and at least 12 hours in advance of arrival at a customs area (either the Canada–U.S. border itself or the customs clearance area of the courier's sorting warehouse at the shipment's destination).

In the United States the timing of electronic manifest submissions is broader, though even less clear, than in Canada. An omnibus trade bill (the *Trade Act of 2002*) was passed by the U.S. Congress in January, 2003. There is nothing in the bill that specifies the time frame for electronic submission to the U.S. Customs Service; however, the discretion will rest with Customs in that it must (1) take into account the differences among transport modes in terms of speed, technology, etc. and (2) limit data requirements to those which are "reasonably necessary to ensure transportation safety and security" (Edmonson 2002:24). At this point, only the timing for ocean vessel containers has been made clear (q.v., *supra*-note 3).

Container Security

In January 2002, U.S. Customs Service implemented the Container Security Initiative (CSI). The first step is to set up CSI at the top 20 *foreign* ocean vessel ports (which account for about 68 percent of the 5.7 million foreign containers entering the United States each year). Currently, U.S. Customs physically inspects about two percent of containers entering the 301 ports of entry to the United States. All countries that are ports-of-origin for the containers will be required to sign a bilateral agreement with the United States so that U.S. Customs inspectors might pre-clear these containers at the foreign ports themselves.

As of February 1, 2003, detailed vessel cargo manifests related to the containers and their contents have to be submitted electronically by carriers or forwarders to U.S. Customs at least 24 hours before the vessel leaves any non-U.S. port. Under the *Trade Act* (2002) U.S. Customs will be required to devise similar submission time requirements for air, rail and motor carriers by October 1, 2003. The "straw man" proposals that U.S. Customs put out for industry discussion were eight hours for couriered air cargo, 12 hours for all other types of air cargo, eight hours for rail freight, four hours for motor carrier freight, and 24 hours for exports via all modes. The import information is relayed to U.S. Customs through AMS; and the export information reaches U.S. Customs (in its role as monitor of exports sales that might be counter to national security) through the Automated Export System (AES).[9] Oddly, cargo transported by the U.S. Postal Service received a blanket exemption from any advance manifest submission.

With respect to ocean carriers fourteen points must be specified on the electronic manifest as indicated in the customs regulations (paragraph 4.7a; Title 19 Code of Federal Regulations). These are as follows:

1. Foreign Port of Departure
2. Standard Carrier Alpha Code (SCAC)
3. Voyage Number of the Vessel
4. Date of Scheduled Arrival in the First U.S. Port
5. Number and Quantity of Packages based on the Bill of Lading (i.e., the contract between the shipper and the carrier or forwarder)
6. First Port of Receipt by the Carrier
7. Cargo Description: Detailed Shipper Description or a six-digit Harmonized Tariff Schedule Number; and the Cargo's Weight
8. Shipper(s) Name(s) and Address(es) or I.D. Numbers Assigned by U.S. Customs
9. Consignee(s) Names(s) and Address(es) or I.D. Numbers Assigned by U.S. Customs (i.e., these are the party or parties that will accept delivery of the cargo in the United States. The shipper is the consignor)
10. Name of the Vessel, National Flag, and Vessel Number
11. Names of Foreign Ports Visited Beyond (6)

12. International Hazardous Goods Code if Applicable to the Cargo
13. Container Number
14. Numbers on all Seals Affixed to the Container

Vague descriptions such as "freight all kinds" (FAK), "said to contain …" (STC), "chemicals" and "foodstuffs" are no longer acceptable. Electronically, submission may be handled through U.S. Customs' Automated Manifest System (AMS). Of course, those carriers and forwarders (i.e., non-vessel operating common carriers, NVOCCs) that are not hooked into AMS will have longer waits before Customs receives the documentation. Of course, carriers and NVOCCs will have to impose their own discretionary deadlines on shippers over and above the 24-hour cut-off so that they may collect, process, and transmit the data to U.S. Customs on time. Unfortunately, electronic or not, that means that a container will be sitting idle at a port for at least one extra day beyond the average two to three day wait. Also, perishables such as food are often at the farm-gate 24 hours prior to being loaded into a container and put on a ship — the quick turnover from farm to vessel being done to ensure freshness. Containerized cargo that is simply passing through the United States (i.e., foreign "freight remaining on board" [FROB] also falls under the 24-hour rule). For example, a Canadian vessel with only some U.S.-bound containers on board would have to provide manifests for *all* containers on board if vessel entry to a U.S. port is to be granted. Note that bulk shipments (e.g., coal, grain, oil, lumber, steel beams, etc.) and palletized shipments are exempt from the 24-hour rule because these are not containerized. However, manifests must reach U.S. Customs 24 hours before the ship reaches a U.S. port. Even empty containers being hauled as part of repositioning plans may require notice to U.S. Customs 48 hours prior to arrival. On June 2, 2003, U.S. Customs and selected carriers will embark on a pilot project to test the efficacy of that proposal. According to U.S. Customs about 600,000 empty containers entered the United States in 2001.

To date the 21 ports that have agreed to accept U.S. Customs inspectors as part of CSI are Vancouver, Montréal, and Halifax, in Canada; Algeciras, Antwerp, Bremerhaven, Felixstowe, Genoa, Hamburg, La Spezia, Le Havre, and Rotterdam, in Europe; Hong Kong, Kobe, Nagoya, Pusan, Shanghai, Tokyo, Yantian, Yokohama and Singapore, in Asia. It should be noted that the European Commission is taking legal action against the European Union (EU) countries that signed the bilateral CSI agreement with the United States because, as with bilateral air agreements, the Commission feels that only a multilateral approach is legal within the EU. Currently, U.S. Customs inspectors are on-site at seven of the 18 ports: all three Canadian ports, Le Havre, Rotterdam, Antwerp, and Singapore.

In the spirit of reciprocity, Canada Customs inspectors are now being stationed at the U.S. ports of Seattle, Tacoma, and Newark. However, there is a question as to whether U.S. Customs is physically able to process and screen the flood of information that CSI is requiring. Their estimation is that the pre-screening through AMS will flag five to ten percent of inbound containers that will need to be inspected physically on arrival. Unlike FAST (q.v., *supra*-note 5) which separates shippers and carriers into cohorts, CSI requires *all* manifests to be expeditiously delivered to AMS. It is also curious that a straight 24-hour rule has been established across all commodity types irrespective of their different logistical requirements.

What is clear is that the choke points will be at the foreign ports. What is also clear is that shippers, carriers and NVOCCs all have incentives to acquire or maintain electronic submission capabilities and be certain that their data is accurate. Certainly, shippers may wish to jump-start the process by electronically submitting the cargo data to the carrier or NVOCC for processing *before* the container is actually filled and transferred to the carrier or NVOCC. Indeed, those NVOCCs which are not electronically hooked into AMS—and needing to expedite their forwarding activities—will have to provide the manifests directly to the carriers. That reveals their shipper-customers to the carriers and creates opportunities for them to "back-sell" directly to the shipper. Before October 2002 NVOCCs did not have access to AMS, and their manifests passed along by the carriers to U.S. Customs on their behalf did not have to reveal the name of the originating shipper. But carriers too face problems: loading a container before the documents arrive (and facing a customs fine) or holding the container over until the next vessel (and facing a port storage charge). In any case, such charges are likely to be passed back to the shipper.

A North American Transportation Network?

It is not often understood that neither the Canada–U.S. Trade Agreement (CUSTA) nor the North American Free Trade Agreement (NAFTA) addressed the transportation sector explicitly. Despite the spirit of free trade that permeates these agreements, and the lowering of tariff barriers among Canada, the United States and Mexico, cross-border transportation remains a significant non-tariff barrier to trade.

The best example of transportation as a non-tariff barrier comes in the form of *cabotage* regulations.[10] Examples of these include restricting commercial ocean vessel travel along U.S. coasts to only U.S.-flagged, U.S.-built vessels, and no point-to-point domestic haulage of U.S. (Canadian) freight by a Canadian (U.S.) driver and vehicle.

The effects of *cabotage* regulations within the Canada–U.S. transportation network are a prevalence of excess capacity on backhauls, a limiting of foreign competition, and higher freight rates for both fronthaul and backhaul shippers (Prokop 1997). While deregulation of transportation has been occurring domestically in both Canada and the United States, continental regulations remain largely unchanged.

The North American free trade area has fallen behind the European Union on the issue of building a truly continental transportation network and fleet. And it is certainly the case that U.S. security concerns will slow this process down significantly.[11] Given a truly North American fleet, customs and immigration services on both sides of the border could concentrate on the shipment itself and not be burdened with enforcing regulations on foreign conveyances and operators in the areas of driver and vehicle origin and destination, vehicle routing, and value and volume of "allowable" *cabotage* freight, etc.

Economic Analysis of U.S. Security Policy

What FAST, Nexus and CSI have in common is that the point of compliance is moved away from U.S. territory. Where the difference lies is in terms of where the bottlenecks may occur. FAST (Nexus) merely fast-tracks cargo (people) through the border, provided that the shipper's outbound logistics are compliant. If it is not, a simple delay at the U.S. border is possible. CSI results in the bottleneck occurring at the foreign port if the shipper's outbound logistics are not compliant. Of course, the ocean carrier is also the repository of all the compliance information. Non-compliance results in fines and the possibility that the containerized-shipment, and indeed the entire ocean vessel, will be denied entry. Finally, CSI is a compulsory program, whereas FAST and Nexus are optional.

As far as U.S. Customs is concerned, a shipper's outbound logistics require both the shipper and the carrier to be compliant. Do both the shipper and the carrier enjoy the same compliance incentives? This section will examine that question using a game-theoretic model.

Table 2: Security Compliance as a "Game of Chicken"

		Carrier: T	Carrier: W
Shipper	T	(3, 3) (c, c)	(2, 3.5) (p, f)
Shipper	W	(3.5, 2) (f, p)	(1, 1) (u, u)

Payoffs: (Shipper, Carrier)

Payoff Types: $f>c>p>u$ and $2c > f + p$

The game matrix in Table 2 shows a shipper and a for-hire carrier that both independently choose one of two levels of security compliance: tough (T) and weak (W). Security compliance takes the form of allocating money toward the technology and protocols necessary to satisfy U.S. Customs. This allocation leads to payoffs, as shown in the table (both in numeric and symbolic terms). The numeric values are not important, just their relative values are. It is also important to note that when the shipper uses the carrier for its outbound logistics, the total level of security compliance provided becomes a two-party public good. Both parties want a level of security even if they paid for it alone. The danger in this arrangement is that if one chooses to be compliance-tough, the other could simply free-ride on that decision by choosing to be compliance-weak.

The payoff types may be defined as: c=coordinated security; f=free-rider security; p=paternalistic security; and u=uncoordinated security. The other point is that the summed payoffs of coordinated security (2c) outweigh the summed payoffs when a free rider is present. Thus, the shipper-carrier supply chain is more secure when each player coordinates than when one chooses to free-ride.

The provision of a public good is characterized as a "game of chicken" (Mueller 1989:15–17). There are two Nash equilibria, given by the shaded cells, whereby one player chooses W and the other chooses T. That means that in the short run there is no incentive for one player to change his mind so long as the other one does not change his mind either. There is also a first-mover advantage in that the choice of W necessarily means that the other player must choose T in order to provide Pareto-improving security.

With CSI, the shipper actually makes the first move (i.e., sending a container and contents to the ocean carrier's port). Since the onus of compliance related to AMS rests with the carrier, it has little choice but to be compliance-tough; therefore, the shipper has an incentive to be compliance-weak. The shipper's pre-commitment strategy is to choose W knowing that it will not be dealing directly with U.S. Customs. With the specifics outlined in U.S. Customs' 24-hour rule, its protocols must be treated as a state of nature in this game.[12] FAST, by contrast, does not have an explicit rule for compliance, nor does the onus rest with the shipper or carrier exclusively. The program is voluntary and the incentive structure facing the shipper and carrier need not be symmetric as it was presented in Table 2. FAST is being used for the most part by shippers operating in a JIT environment. Operating within FAST means, by necessity, choosing T because U.S. Customs directly interfaces with both the shipper and the carrier. There is no first-mover advantage; both the shipper and the carrier are regulated so that both choose T and the game above converges to the T,T cell. Any other combination would not be workable under FAST, and it is, therefore, the case that only FAST-compliant carriers would be used to handle the outbound logistics of FAST-compliant shippers. It should also be noted that CSI could, in the long run, promote a T,T result, so long as the shipper and carrier deal with each other long enough to form a cooperative relationship. The carrier could devise "punishments" to make the shipper adopt T over time; e.g., passing demurrage charges back to the shipper when containers do not arrive on time for the contracted vessel.

Now consider an LTL-trucker that is FAST-compliant but simultaneously handles the freight of shippers that are FAST-compliant along with those that are not. That is presumably done as a means to fill excess capacity. Effectively, the carrier is making a pre-commitment to W to the extent that some freight on board is not eligible for FAST. The FAST-compliant shipper faces a potential trade-off: higher TL freight rates for exclusive carriage in order to guarantee a FAST clearance versus lower LTL freight rates along with the possibility of a delay at the U.S. border, even when the carrier itself is part of the FAST program. Of course, if the shipper persuades the LTL carrier to provide JIT-style service, the LTL carrier has less of an incentive to haul freight that might jeopardize speedy border clearance.

Conclusions

In June, 2002 the U.S. Administration proposed creating a *bona fide* Department of Homeland Security which would bring together border security and inspection functions that were spread over 80 federal agencies (e.g., Customs, Immigration and Naturalization, the Border Patrol, the Coast Guard, the Transportation Security Administration, the Federal Emergency Management Agency, the Secret Service, etc.). Congress passed the legislation in November, 2002, and in March, 2003 the new Department opened for business with a workforce of about 180,000 personnel. U.S. Customs is now called the Bureau of Customs and Border Protection.

At the Canada–U.S. border there is no agency better equipped to handle trade related security issues than the U.S. Customs Service. Of course, that service used to be under the U.S. Department of the Treasury because of its role in trade compliance and revenue gathering.

Now, because of its security role, the U.S. Customs Service has been put under the Department of Homeland Security. Given this dual role, will shippers be subject to two rather than one set of regulations and inspection procedures? In any case, how will the roles of security and trade-compliance stay balanced as a matter of government policy? There is a danger that this new Department of Homeland security — top-heavy in security functions — could, by synergy, tip the Customs' balance even further toward security at the expense of trade-compliance.

The effects of tightening times for electronic submission of manifests and for enhancing security at ports of entry (or pre-screening at foreign ports of exit) are that the burden will be shifted back to the shipper. The sooner that customs officials require information before actual transit takes place, the likelier it is that manufacturers will not be able to ship the last day's production. Inventory carrying costs will therefore be higher if they cannot meet the time frame. That will be a problem for JIT shippers and shippers with freight subject to spoilage.

It is useful to note, however, that FAST is designed to look at cargo on a shipper-by-shipper basis as opposed to a cargo-by-cargo basis. Once a shipper has been deemed to be low-risk, customs officials can focus their energies elsewhere. But this paper has noted that customs compliance procedures are in a state of flux, and focus is less than clear because in some cases the procedures are evolving transport mode-by-transport mode and in others they are evolving shipper-by-shipper.

Customs services are merely the enforcers of security measures. True security comes from securing the entire cross-border supply chain. That further encompasses shippers and carriers at all stages of production, warehouse operators, and intermediaries such as freight forwarders and customs brokers.

The role of technology cannot be overstated. Despite current discussions that lead in this direction, manual inspection of every vehicle and every container is impossible if trade flows are to remain at anything better than a standstill. The cost in terms of inventory buildup and productivity loss is too large to contemplate; therefore, new technologies such as "scanning in motion," "weighing in motion," and electronic documentation must be more rapidly deployed. Radio tags attached to containers, trailers and boxcars at the point of shipping can essentially make these conveyances "smart" by having wireless readers deployed at strategic points along the supply chain to feed real-time information on the status and location into a database that may be used for "track-and-trace" and for security as well. Microchips with fibre optic cables can be placed by the locks on conveyance doors. The microchip creates a magnetic field around the lock that can detect tampering and transmit such outcomes in real time to the carrier.

There is no doubt that the cost of all such technologies will be passed along to the consumer. That is to be expected since security compliance is a costly issue. However, securing the supply chain is a collaborative effort as noted in this paper, and it is through that effort that costs will be minimized and a reasonable mix of efficient and safe trade between Canada and the United States can be maintained.

Notes

1 Quoted in Harrington (2002; p. 66).

2 The newly created U.S. Transportation Security Administration (TSA) has since taken over the FAA's jurisdiction over security matters. The TSA was created through the *Aviation and Transportation Security Act* (Nov. 19, 2001). Currently, U.S. passenger airlines have been restricted to carrying pieces of mail weighing no more than one pound. The resulting drop in cargo volumes has had a negative effect of passenger airline revenues. Heavier packages have been relegated to air cargo freighters operated by the commercial airlines. About 10–25% of their revenue flows derive from cargo transport. Needless to say, the main beneficiaries have been Federal Express and United Parcel Service. On November 19, 2002 all security screeners at airports became federal employees; and on December 31, 2002 all U.S. airports were required to have explosive detection systems installed in order to examine all luggage/parcels. It should be noted that the TSA has been mandated to handle security issues over all modes of transportation into the United States.

3 The security issues surrounding containers on ocean vessels have been developing relatively quickly. These will be explored ahead in a separate section.

4 In the wake of 9/11, DaimlerChrysler, General Motors, Ford, Toyota, and Honda shut down U.S. plants for a time because they did not maintain enough safety stock to wait out the shutdown of U.S. and Canadian airspaces nor the bottleneck of trucks at the Canada–U.S. border. Manufactured vehicles represent the largest share of export and import trade by value carried by road and rail along the Canada–U.S. border. The figures are:

Table 3: Canada's Merchandise Trade with the United States (1996) (millions of current U.S. dollars)

	Mode of *Vehicles-Only* Merchandise Exports*		
Total Exports to the U.S.	Road	Rail	Total
163,682	22,969	17,778	40,747 (25%)

	Mode of *Vehicles-Only* Merchandise Imports*		
Total Imports from the U.S.	Road	Rail	Total
115,188	20,034	5,700	25,734 (22%)

* Road and rail only. Parentheses indicate vehicle-trade's share of total export or import trade where appropriate.

Source: *North American Transportation in Figures* (2000); tabs. 6-1a, 6-1b & 6-6b.

As can be seen, Canada ran a large merchandise trade surplus with the U.S. both overall and on a vehicle trade basis.

5 FAST is preceded by a program used to expedite tourist passage through the Canada–U.S. border. The NEXUS system is currently in use at the Blue Water Bridge and Douglas-Blaine border crossings. The goal of both governments is to implement NEXUS at all major border crossings.

6 Needless to say, shippers and carriers using FAST must have electronic goods-tracking, accounting and reporting systems in place that are connected to customs officials. DaimlerChrysler, for example, is well-positioned to take advantage of FAST. It sends about 1,500 truck loads per day through the Windsor-Detroit border crossing (with about a 50/50 split of northbound and southbound traffic). Currently, about 50% of its northbound traffic is cleared into Canada through the CSA (Tower 2002:

22). Other automakers using CSA are Ford, General Motors, and CAMI Automotive (the Canada-based, GM-Suzuki assembly partnership).

7 At the Group of Eight (G8) meetings in Kananaskis, Alberta (June 25–26, 2002) it was decided that the Brussels-based World Customs Organization (WCO) would be charged with developing a Customs Data Model which would allow a shipper to submit required electronic information to the applicable customs service in the G8. The information would subsequently be shared in customs-to-customs exchanges among the G8. A preliminary assessment of the WCO's model is expected by June, 2003.

8 Canada–U.S. courier service is dominated by Federal Express (with 10 Canada–U.S. flights/day) and United Parcel Service (with 16 Canada–U.S. flights/day).

9 In response to the concerns of industry resulting from the "straw man" proposals, U.S. Customs formed the Commercial Operations Advisory Committee (COAC). The latest recommendations for e-manifests, issued March 14, 2002, are air cargo no later than one hour prior to arrival, motor carrier cargo (under FAST) no later than 30 (15) minutes prior to arrival at the U.S.–Canada/Mexico borders, and rail cargo no later than four hours prior to arrival at the U.S.–Canada/Mexico borders. It is proposed as well that Canada receive an exemption to the 24-hour rule for ocean containers such that containers inbound from Canadian ports must have the e-manifests submitted four hours before arrival at a U.S. port. No revision has been suggested for exports except for a one-hour notice for outbound rail cargo. In any case, rules that are arrival-based make more sense than rules that are departure-based given in-transit contingencies.

10 For an overview of *cabotage* regulations across several modes, see: Prokop (1999); and Prokop and Dean (1999).

11 However, there has been one exception to date. In June of 2002, the U.S. Administration ceased blockage of a NAFTA requirement that Mexican motor carriers be allowed full export-import access to U.S. territory. While this provision was to be implemented by 2000, the previous Administration followed a line of argument promoted by the Teamsters Union that Mexican trucks are unfit and unsafe for U.S. highways. Through June 2002, Mexican trucks could proceed only within 20 miles north of the U.S.–Mexico border and would have to interline its freight with a U.S. motor carrier. The Executive Order lifting of the ban is now before a U.S. federal court pending a study of the environmental impact of an influx of Mexican motor carriers.

12 The National Customs Brokers and Forwarders Association of America (NCBFAA) deals electronically with U.S. Customs through the Automatic Broker Interface (ABI). In the same month that the 24-hour rule began to be enforced, the NCBFAA proposed to U.S. Customs that it amend the rule's AMS-filing requirement for carriers to include an ABI-filing

requirement by the customs broker (Edmonson 2003). The incentive for this in the eyes of NVOCCs is that cargo manifests would not have to be given directly to the carrier and thus breach customer confidentiality. The NCBFAA method would be that the U.S. importer passes to his customs broker data on the containerized cargo received from his overseas supplier. The broker files a record to U.S. Customs through ABI which the latter may use to match components of the record filed by the carrier through AMS. U.S. Customs can then rule whether or not the container should be shipped. In terms of the shipper-carrier "game of chicken" nothing has changed — the carrier must still comply with CSI and the new player, the broker, merely is a conduit to U.S. Customs of information that would have been routed through the carrier. There is still no incentive for the shipper to be compliance-tough.

References

Coalition for Secure and Trade Efficient Borders. (2001). *Rethinking our Borders: A Plan for Action*. Position Paper.

Edmonson, R. (2003). "A 24-Hour Alternative." *JoC Week*. Mar. 17–23. p. 22.

——. (2002). "What's in the Box?" *JoC Week*. Aug. 5–11. pp. 23–24.

Harrington, L. (2002). "Sourcing Globally now that the Rules have Changed." *Inbound Logistics*. October. pp. 62–69.

Mueller, D. (1989). *Public Choice II*. Cambridge: Cambridge University Press.

Nix, F. (2002). "Making the Best of It." *Motor Truck*. April. pp. 18–20.

North American Transportation in Figures. (2000). Washington: Bureau of Transportation Statistics.

Prokop, D. (1997). "The Welfare Gain from Trucking Deregulation: Transborder Trucking and Cabotage." *Canadian Transportation Research Forum*. Proceedings of the 32nd Annual Conference. pp. 555–573.

——. (1999). "In 1988 We Freed Trade. Now Let's Free Transport." *Policy Options*. June. vol. 20. no. 5. pp. 37–40.

Prokop, D., and J. Dean (1999). "The Goods and Services Tax and the U.S. Federal Excise Tax: Barriers to Trucking Cabotage Reform in Canada." *Canadian Tax Journal*. vol. 47. no. 5. pp. 1180–1193.

11

The Privatization of Security in Canada, Post-9/11: An Assessment of Continuing Trends and Issues to Manage

Christopher Spearin[1]

At first glance, "the state" seemed to obtain a renewed sense of purpose and utility in the wake of the al-Qaida attacks of September 11, 2001. After approximately two decades of downsizing, downloading, and outsourcing brought about by the embrace of neo-liberal economic thinking the world over, governments generated and applied substantial state assets and resources in order to reassure their populaces and to deter other potential terrorist activity. That was certainly the case with Canada. As outlined in the December 2001 "Security Budget," Ottawa assumed a larger role in airport security, it implemented new border controls, and it substantially increased spending on certain security sector actors. In total, the federal government directed some C$7.7 billion in funding towards countering potential terrorist threats and expanding state capabilities.

Generally, in light of this vigorous activity, one might think that there was a reverse shift favouring governmental activism at the expense of private, non-state initiative and resourcefulness. Specifically, as the provision of security is thought to be the raison d'être of the state, post-9/11 state activity in Canada and elsewhere seemed to substantiate the state's niche role in political life. The public/private status quo in place since the 1980s appeared to be coming to an end; it was not to be business as usual after the terrorist attacks.

Upon closer examination, however, the state has clearly not reacquired its overall dominance, even in the realm of security. Private actors, either on the behalf of the state or independent from it, are still involved in ensuring that Canadians are made secure. That applies both to domestic policing and to the activities at home and abroad of the Canadian Forces (CF), and that suggests that factors other than just neo-liberal economic thinking promote the private presence in the provision of security.

The threefold objective of this chapter, therefore, is to make plain the full extent of this private presence, to reveal the importance of this presence in countering the terrorist threat posed to Canada, and to consider what needs to be improved, given this importance. This chapter concentrates upon the economic, political, legal, and sociological aspects that together with neo-liberal economic thinking make real the private presence. It also contends that even though state activism in Canada has been renewed, little governmental attention, despite the need, has been directed towards managing the public-private relationship pertaining to security. This chapter seeks to reverse this neglect by suggesting ways in which government might act and also by recognizing the challenges that will make coordination and implementation in the Canadian state difficult. Identification of all the potential and pitfalls is necessary in order to promote awareness of how greatly the government of Canada and Canadians rely upon private actors for protection against terrorism.

The Privatization of Security in Canada

Private Security

The rise in numbers and importance of private policing actors has been defined by some as a "quiet revolution," by others as nothing less than a "profound development in the securing of society."[2] Whatever the descriptive tone, it is clear that this change is occurring in policing in Canada.[3] Estimates place the ratio of those employed in private security to those employed in public security at between 2:1 and 4:1.[4] Another estimation is that the private security industry in Canada grew ten times in size between 1988 and 1995.[5] In contrast, Statistics Canada reported in 1998 that the ratio of police officers to population stood at its lowest levels since 1970.[6] Today, one can find private security deployed anywhere from shopping malls to office buildings to factories to universities to power plants to ports to housing communities. In some cases, the private security personnel are "in-house" and in other instances they are contracted out to firms.

In terms of catalytic ingredients, this development in policing does involve to a certain degree the direct embrace of neo-liberal thinking. Public police forces across the country have introduced economic models so that they will spend money "smartly" and to greater effect in the future. Part of this shift sees the "civilianization of policing." This shift is characterized by the employment of civilians to conduct tasks once performed by police officers: radio dispatch, prisoner transport, administration, fleet maintenance, parking, and even station security. The objective of this civilianization is not only to reduce the cost of public policing, but also to maximize cost effectiveness and provide a higher standard of public service through treating and deploying highly trained (and paid and unionized) police officers as specialists.[7]

This explanation, however, is not complete and cannot account for such a significant increase in the activities of private security. One must also consider other substantial social and economic trends and changes in Canadian society that are either the indirect effects of neo-liberal policies or that have their own unique elements:

Expectation Gap: Canadian police forces are being asked to do more (e.g., community-based policing and anti-drug programs) despite the fact that their budgets have mostly remained fixed since the early 1990s.[8] Additionally, police are faced with an expanding and complex variety of potential criminal activities. The end result, according to George Rigakos, is that private security serves to fill an "expectation gap." Public perception expands this gap, giving rise to the sociological development of the "risk society" in which unease exists regardless of the level of crime or danger.[9]

"Responsibilization": With neo-liberal downsizing in other areas of government, "responsibilization" entails that individuals feel that they increasingly must take charge of their own affairs, including their personal security.[10]

Rise of Mass Private Property: Many areas and buildings that are essentially "private" in terms of ownership are nevertheless open to substantial public access (e.g., shopping malls, universities, retail parks, factories, and business offices). For Clifford Shearing and Philip Stenning, "[b]ecause more and more public places are now located on private property, the protection of property ... has increasingly come to include the maintenance of public order, a matter which was, hitherto, regarded as the more or less exclusive prerogative of the public police."[11] Unless special arrangements are made, public police forces are legally limited to the degree that they can claim regular access to private property.[12] Private security is needed in these places to reduce vulnerability, damage, and theft, in addition to issues related to liability.

On the basis of these developments, it is clear that private security personnel are not always *replacing* the public police as the direct result of neo-liberal thinking. The rise of private security cannot be simply deemed a zero-sum game.

Military Contractors

Private actors are also playing a prominent role in the activities of the armed forces, the military component of Canada's security sector. Private contractors are present in a range of military activities deemed to be "tail" or non-core, non-war fighting, and non-"tooth" activities, ones like airlift, logistics supply, base maintenance, satellite communications, weapons support, and construction engineering.[13]

Once again, a complex mix of factors, some with roots in neo-liberal thinking, brought about this presence. First, a desire to cut costs, save money, and conduct business more efficiently and effectively are prominent features in Canadian defence policy, seen particularly in the 1994 White Paper.[14] If a private firm can do a certain task for less, the task is likely to be tendered to the private sector. To facilitate this approach, DND initiated, in July 1995, its policy of Alternative Service Delivery (ASD) in order to realize potential savings and efficiencies. Since then, the department's Defence Management Committee has identified over 75 ASD projects. Additional supporting measures have complemented the ASD program, such as the Task Force National Support Element (NSE), a contract held by ATCO-FRONTEC Logistics Corporation. Under the NSE, the private contractor replaced half of the combat support and combat service support personnel in Canada's contribution to NATO's Stabilization Force (SFOR) in Bosnia. Other endeavours include the Canadian Contractor Augmentation Program (CANCAP), designed to serve as a "logistics force multiplier" at home and abroad.[15] On its face, this collection of activities is simply intended to achieve savings that are then to go towards reinvestment in combat capabilities and, like the police, to turn military personnel into specialists.[16]

These developments are also a response to, and part of, the sharp decline in defence spending over the 1990s. As the defence budget forms the largest part of the national government's discretionary budget envelope, it was particularly targeted in order to tackle the federal deficit and improve Canada's global economic standing. That was done to the degree that Canada saw the largest post-Cold War defence budget reduction of any NATO country.[17] The present budgeted sum for defence, approximately $12 billion, is 40 percent less than the amount in 1985.[18] Ongoing contracting by Ottawa, then, is meant to ensure the continued efficient use of limited resources.

As well, the presence of contractors exists because of the limited numbers of personnel now available to the military. Whereas the number of authorized military personnel has fallen by 25,000 from the 1988 levels of 85,000, the number of actual employees is even less. The Auditor General reported in 2002 that staffing of the Canadian Forces stood at 57,600 in September 2001 and that the "effective" number of those ready for duty with the appropriate training stood at only 52,300.[19] Two general matters have led to this decline:

> **Doing More With Less:** As of October 1999, Canada had 4,500 military personnel stationed worldwide—its largest deployment since the Korean War. Moreover, Canada had contributed to a variety of operations over the course of the 1990s. The increased operational tempo along with substantial and numerous periods away from home, when combined with a decreased number of troops and reduced budgets, caused quality of life issues and helped create burnout and retention problems. These factors are documented in surveys com-

pleted by departing military personnel and have been recognized by the Chief of Defence Staff (CDS), General Raymond Henault.[20]

Reduced Recruitment: From 1994 to 2000, the Canadian military recruited less than half the number of personnel it lost.[21] Though part of this development is an effect of downsizing, it also indicates that young Canadians do not wish to enter the services in the first place. For instance, the military in 2001 undershot its desired annual recruitment levels by approximately 1,200 personnel. One reason for that may be the increased opportunities for skill development and economic reward in areas other than the military. As noted by the Centre for Military and Strategic Studies, "[t]he basic cause of the recruitment and retention crisis is that the increasing need for technically capable and well-educated young men and women to meet the demands of the modern military places the CF in direct competition with major sectors of the economy."[22] In that regard, the image of poorly paid soldiers operating antiquated equipment does not serve well the cause for enlistment. Another reason may be the decline of a sense of nationalism that fuelled the supply of personnel in earlier times. In a similar vein, base closures, the declining number of military personnel, and the fading memory of Canada's military exploits earlier in the twentieth century have all limited the exposure of young Canadians to the armed forces.[23]

The resulting demographic troughs created by these two broad points cannot be easily overcome in the military as the structure allows only for personnel to be brought in at the entry level.[24]

Moreover, it is clear that the level of enlistment is not to increase in the near future. Even with newly devised recruitment and retention plans initiated in the face of massive baby boomer retirement, the CDS projects that effective force levels in the future will rise to only 55,000.[25] Hence, contracting out is driven by two, perhaps conflicting, agendas: the desire to cut costs and the need to maintain capacity. Even the CDS has made plain these dual matters. General Henault writes that CANCAP, for instance, is designed to provide capabilities that may be missing or insufficient such that "[i]t may not produce financial savings but I anticipate benefits in operational flexibility and on relieving pressures."[26] Regardless of the tension between these two catalysts, the demand for accrued savings and acquiring needed capacity, their mutual effect is clear in current conditions: not only is the reliance on contractors by the Canadian military a current necessity, but the presence of contractors will likely increase well into the future.

Assessment

Even if neo-liberal thinking was somehow to be completely abandoned by the state, private actors would not disappear in the provision of security. A complex set of relationships exists involving both private and public actors that blurs what exactly constitutes the list of core duties and attributes the state is traditionally thought to possess. In terms of policing, even if substantial funding was put into Canadian public policing, the presence of private security would not end. Though the security Canadians receive may come through diversified providers, individual initiative and the legal distinctions with respect to private property remain. As for the Canadian Forces, different organizations and governmental bodies have called for increased funding to the military so that it can reach manpower levels of between 75,000 to 85,000.[27] But even if the Department of National Defence received a large budgetary boost, military manpower would likely not rise, and capabilities would not vastly improve, because of significant factors affecting recruitment noted earlier and the entry-level approach of the military.[28] Therefore, private actors and market dynamics, equally, cannot be easily wished away in Canadian policing and military endeavours. Instead, the key matters for assessment pertain to the new issues and challenges private actors bring, how the public-private network is managed, and to what effect.

Contemporary Terrorism and the Privatization of Canadian Security

It is clear that the presence of private security and private contractors is intimately involved in countering the contemporary terrorist threat. That is partially because of the sheer number of private actors. Indeed, the average Canadian is now more likely to encounter private security than he or she would the public police in day-to-day living.[29]

But private actors are also involved because of the nature of the threat itself and how it pertains to security measures both within and beyond Canadian borders.

Contemporary terrorism has been described as both "postmodern" and "complex." For Walter Laqueur, the postmodern label applies because unlike the terrorist activities of earlier times, the guiding motivations and strategies of today's terrorists are different.[30] In particular, there has been a shift away from the earlier thinking that, "[t]errorists want a lot of people watching, not a lot of people dead."[31] The latter no longer holds. In terms of complexity, the fear is that industrialized societies are increasingly vulnerable to deadly attacks because of their organizational and technological configurations. For Thomas Homer-Dixon, though an economic and infrastructure system of intricate networks and geographic concentrations, largely in the developed world, has led to unparalleled prosperity, it has also heightened the potential devastation that resourceful terrorists might release through a targeted attack.[32] Hence, this terrorism is "complex" both in terms of the nature of the systems that might be targeted and the ingenuity and technological prowess of the terrorists who would do the deed.

Therefore, with respect to internal matters, private security can now be perceived not simply as contributing to law enforcement, but, given the nature of the terrorist threat, as contributing to national security as well. Although Canada may not leave as significant a geopolitical footprint as the United States, it is, nevertheless, still a "complex" Western society in its own regard and one with substantial economic and infrastructure links with its neighbour to the south. Thus, in many ways, private security forms the front-line against terrorism within Canada, whether it is in terms of prevention or immediate response. If a terrorist objective was to attack critical infrastructure (CI) in Canada, such as water, sewage, communications, food supply, power production, transportation, and/or financial services, it is important to note that in many instances the responsibility for their physical protection rests in the hands of in-house or contracted out security. If a terrorist objective was to attack symbols of Western economic and industrial strength, one should recall that dozens of high profile "brand name" branch plants exist in Canada that are crucial to the country's economic well-being and are protected by private security. If a terrorist objective was to inflict massive casualties, it is of key importance to be aware that private property which has considerable public access, whether it be office buildings or shopping malls, is generally guarded by a private presence. Given that the "War On Terrorism" is thought to be an on-going concern well into the future, that speaks to the need to recognize that continued domestic vigilance involves privately owned assets and the accompanying private security.[33]

In the domestic realm, the terrorist threat also draws in the public-private relationship between the military and private contractors. From one standpoint, the Canadian Forces would have to rely upon a vast array of private contractor relationships, due to their involvement in day-to-day operations, maintenance, and upkeep, should it have to respond to a terrorist incident in Canada and/or the implementation of the 1988 *Emergencies Act*. From another standpoint, additional special arrangements might also have to be made to backstop the in-house domestic capabilities of the CF. That was required for Operation ABACUS, the Y2K plan for military assistance to civilian authorities should elements of Canada's CI have failed. As noted by Macarena Barker and Pam Hatton, "[t]he potential Y2K catastrophe during a Canadian winter required maximum availability of troops without committing them to tasks that could be performed by others."[34] Thus, with the War on Terrorism potentially coming to Canada, generally benign contractor relationships in Canada take on a new and substantially different significance.

Contractor support would also likely be needed in the on-going prosecution of the war against terror, given that the CF's expeditionary capabilities in all its facets would have to be utilized: traditional peacekeeping, peace enforcement, intervention and war fighting, and peacebuilding. As Canada does not possess substantial long-haul airlift or sealift capacity to bring personnel in and out of areas of operations in far away places, contractors become involved.[35] Contractors would also likely become involved in response to the need for operational logistics and maintenance, something made plain in the CF's ongoing reliance on CANCAP.

Issues of Concern

Private Security

Because private security plays a substantial role in ensuring the well-being of Canadians, both in terms of the number of personnel and the critical nature of what they protect as highlighted by the terrorist threat, some worrisome issues arise. At present, the regulation of private security (i.e., the setting of employment standards, oversight, and training) is part of the constitutional responsibility of the provinces and territories in governing policing and property rights. True, because this responsibility is held by 13 different units, one might expect a lack of uniformity, but the situation borders on the lackadaisical. Only two provinces, British Columbia and Newfoundland, require private security employees to meet minimum training standards. Other provinces and the territories target only certain sectors of the private security industry and, even then, consider licensing criteria only for the employers and their employees.[36] Nowhere are provisions stipulated for mandatory training upgrades. Also, in all cases, the minimal guidelines that do exist apply only to contract employees; in-house security for shopping malls, office blocks, companies and the like, are exempt.[37]

As for accountability mechanisms, they are different from those applicable to the public police and are not as substantial. On the one hand, it perhaps is to be expected that the complex array of police boards and public complaints commissions is commensurate with the fact that public policing is a manifestation of the state — personnel have extensive powers to deny liberty, and technically these personnel are to serve the public good. In contrast, private security is accountable to its clients rather than to political and administrative bodies. In that regard, provincial and territorial regulatory acts do not establish independent oversight mechanisms.[38] Instead, private security is subject to market mechanisms whereby clients can "walk away" or make firings if they dislike the quality or nature of the service provided. Those who feel they have been abused by private security personnel have recourse to civil litigation. On the other hand, given the high volume of people in private places, the critical nature for Canadian society of many of the things protected privately and the costliness and difficulties of civil prosecutions, the nature of this accountability would seem to be less than required. At present, then, provincial and territorial guidelines lag behind what is in the general public interest given the prominent place of private security.[39]

Potential problems associated with the lack of quality guarantees and consistent and effective oversight and training have been made plain in the threat posed by terrorism. As asserted by Charles Sennewald, "[i]t goes without saying that the process of risk identification, evaluation, and control in any dynamic organization, public or private, requires constant attention by professionals who possess the necessary knowledge and tools to accomplish the task."[40] Yet in the highly competitive private security marketplace, not only are salaries often kept low, but training, for the sake of reducing overhead, is also frequently limited, if it occurs at all. The result is a high rate of turnover in the business coupled with a lack of know-how — two matters that affect the quality and diligence of private security activities as they relate to the design and administration of the necessary procedures and capabilities.

All that, in turn, exacerbates vulnerabilities in three areas:

First Responder: The literature often notes the need for first responders to a chemical or biological terrorist attack, deemed to be the public police, fire, and ambulance services, to have adequate training and resources in order to assess the situation, respond appropriately, and provide an initial diagnosis for their superiors and government.[41] However, despite the fact that private security personnel may be the first on the scene, given their numbers and their presence in sensitive areas, little uniform attention alike by industry and government is directed at the issues of training, equipment, and standards.[42]

Training of Others: Private security personnel are often responsible for raising the security consciousness of others, such as management and other employees. They serve as trainers and educators. The process of training and educating must be on-going given changes in the types of threat and personnel turnover in other fields. [43] However, if private security personnel themselves do not appreciate the significance of their position and do not have the appropriate expertise, it is unlikely that they will somehow improve the security consciousness of others.

Civil Liberties: Though much attention was directed towards the increased powers of the police and toward potential civil liberties implications generated by the federal government's anti-terrorism legislation Bill C-36, it is equally important to note the possible negative effects with respect to private security. From one standpoint, earlier surveys have found that private security personnel do not have adequate knowledge of the limits of their legal authority.[44] From another standpoint, the judiciary is about two decades behind in dealing with the role of private security in contemporary Canadian society.[45] The result, as Rigakos and David Greener note, is that the private security employee is not "held to the same degree of constitutional standards as a peace officer in relation to arbitrary detention, security of the person, right to counsel, and search."[46] Similarly, he or she can conduct surveillance activities and compile information databases in ways the public police cannot.[47] Hence, there is a dual fear with respect to private security. On the one hand, the diligence of private security personnel may not be enough. On the other hand, excessive, uninformed diligence may lead to breaches in *Charter* rights.

Obviously, the potentially negative implications of these matters became even more acute in the wake of the 9/11 attacks when companies and institutions bulked up their private security presence for the sake of protecting their employees, clients, and visitors. A greater number of possibly poorly trained personnel would have entered the private security marketplace to respond to the increased need.

Military Contractors

The presence of private contractors in the Canadian Forces' operations does also pose a number of interesting and difficult issues related to the effectiveness of the public-private network. They concern the potential loss of capability that is made more problematic by the nature of the terrorist threat.

Harm's Way: It is Canadian policy not to introduce intentionally military contractors into unstable environments overseas. This policy, however, has received some criticism, given the dynamic and often dangerous nature of even long-standing overseas deployments.[48] Note, for instance, that a contractor support unit accompanied the 2003 Canadian peacekeeping contingent in Kabul—hardly a very secure place. One of the primary concerns, then, driving such criticism is that contracted personnel, instead of being directed by an oath, as are soldiers, are directed by contractual obligations—ones that can be unilaterally terminated should danger, such as a chemical or biological attack, arise.[49] Such a departure would precipitate an immediate loss of capacity, and delays would be incurred as the military's replacements arrived, assuming that they were even available.

Potentially more detrimental would be the availability of "non-core" contractor support should the Canadian Forces have to respond to a terrorist incident within Canada. Even if the CF took extra precautions such as outfitting contracted personnel with the appropriate equipment or providing them with vaccinations, there is no guarantee that they would respond. Though the contracted firm would have to contemplate seriously the likely future loss of business with the CF, even then the firm, should it choose to act, is largely limited to the threat of firing individual employees who fail to respond.

Loss of Control: By entering into contractor relationships, the Canadian Forces open themselves to the vagaries and incentives of the global marketplace. In particular, in order to obtain the necessary resources and to achieve savings, contractors will often sub-contract their requirements to other providers. The Canadian Forces, however, are potentially exposed to issues related to different nationalities and to purely private disputes with an impact, nevertheless, on the military. For example, in August 2000, CF personnel had to board and take-over a cargo ship in international waters, the GTS *Katie*, which was holding "hostage" 10 percent of Canada's armored equipment and three CF members.[50] The owner of the vessel, Third Ocean Marine Navigation Company of Annapolis, Maryland, was the sub-contractor for the Canadian firm SDV Logistics, which was sub-contracted by Andromeda Navigation Company of Montréal, the company initially tasked by DND to return to Canada the $223 million worth of equipment deployed for KFOR. The American company was withholding the CF's equipment because of a dispute over lack of payment with the Canadian contractor. Defence officials, for their part, were initially unaware that the job had been subcontracted.[51] Ottawa eventually ordered CF personnel to take hold of the vessel in order to continue to fulfill other national security tasks at home and abroad, but in doing so, had to consult not only the United States, but also the ship's flag-holder, St. Vincent and the Grenadines. While this situation was successfully resolved, at least from DND's standpoint, it highlighted how Canada might be held "hostage" both to commercial interests and to the interests of other states. Whereas nationality and loyalty are longstanding components of operational success, the introduction of contractors upsets this calculation.[52]

Availability: In addition to a standing private contractor presence, the Canadian Forces can also interact with contractors on an ad hoc and contingency basis. But, the issue of being put in harm's way aside, the nature of globalized industry is such that resources may not be easily or readily brought to bear when called upon. As Rhys Dogan and Michael Pugh contend, "[w]ell managed firms simply do not have fleets of contractually uncommitted aircraft, motor vehicles and highly trained personnel hanging about, unpaid."[53] Whereas the military traditionally follows a just-in-case posture, manifest in such activities as mothballing and stockpiling, reliance on private contractors introduces a just-in-time posture.[54] Such a shift in thinking poses obvious potential difficulties for the timely arrival and effective operations of the CF at home and abroad.

In sum, though the CF's reliance on contracting may be intended to enhance its readiness and sustainability, the risk also exists that private contractors operating in a global market and a dangerous world may, in fact, detract from that readiness and sustainability. From one angle, searching out comparative advantages via reliance on the global marketplace through outsourcing and privatization should, in theory, expose DND to high quality services and products in order to fulfil the CF's needs. From another angle, such an approach also exposes DND to the commercial marketing considerations and internal policies firms need to follow in order to survive, to compete, and to accrue profit in the global marketplace. The negative effects of such exposure highlight the lack of sufficient redundancy, or even capability, in the CF, matters of importance in prosecuting the War on Terrorism.

Changes and Challenges

Private Security

Implementing the changes in the Canadian federation for the needed regulatory oversight will be a complex task because controversial and problematic issues are at play. While the federal government might be able to set a higher and nationally consistent level of regulatory scrutiny and demand the acceptance of a comprehensive training, the fear of the overbearing "Big Brother" looms with such a unilateral imposition. That is because of the pervasive presence of private security from one standpoint and the pervasive nature of the terrorist threat from another. Provincial governments might resist a dictatorial intrusion into their constitutionally designated responsibilities because they might perceive it as a precedent setting act, one that leads to potentially more federal intrusions into the provincial sphere. "Private" interests—private security firms and those that hire them—might also resent unilateral acts made by government. Additionally, there is the delicate issue of costs. What body would bear the costs for licensing, training, and the on-going monitoring of standards? What body would implement these tasks? Too great a responsibility taken by government, federal or provincial, might greatly overtax the public purse, while too much burden placed upon private actors might affect their commercial viability.

Since the presence of private security is so great, the areas it protects are so critical, and the potential consequences should a terrorist incident occur are so tragic, the need to think of the provision of security in a more holistic fashion is clear. While it is beyond the scope of this chapter to conduct the substantial task of indicating each necessary ingredient of an improved and all encompassing regulatory regimen, it is important, in order to realize holistic regulation, to identify possible paths to follow, and issues that might be encountered. First, at the national level, the federal government could lead by example. Present policy indicates that to ensure a higher level of quality, private security personnel employed by the federal government are to be trained to the standards laid out by the Canadian General Standards Board. The very development of these standards, in fact, speaks to the necessary coordination required as it involved government, business, and consumers. But while these standards might help ensure that personnel receive higher pay and a better level of training, the federal government does not have a mechanism to guarantee that those standards have actually been met and maintained. Thus, as part of ensuring higher and consistent standards across the country, greater diligence in monitoring existing standards at this level is needed. That is required for the federal government to show that it takes them seriously in order to make better the case to the provinces and the private sector.

Second, nascent mechanisms exist through which the federal component of the partnership for private security regulation could be nurtured. In February 2001, the federal government created within DND the Office of Critical Infrastructure Protection and Emergency Preparedness (OCIPEP), the successor to Emergency Preparedness Canada. This office possesses attributes which might allow it to take a substantial role in ensuring effective private security operations:

1. It is a body designed to form partnerships and to facilitate cooperation between the federal and provincial governments and with the private sector;
2. Security concerns pertaining to critical infrastructure do not always pertain solely to cyber issues;
3. Private security deals with both the physical protection of CI and responsibilities that affect large numbers of Canadians on a daily basis; and
4. OCIPEP provides annual training to nearly 2,000 individuals alike from government and business at the Canadian Emergency College in Arnprior, Ontario. The OCIPEP has the obvious potential to grow and deal with important issues as they relate to private security, regulation, and terrorism and to serve as the focal point for federal leadership on these matters.

At the provincial and territorial level, greater legislative attention and scrutiny towards private security than has been exhibited in the past will be required. For provincial and territorial governments, that means a shift away from their general hands-off approach towards private security and a rethinking of the roles they play, and that means a recasting of priorities in preparing to counter terrorist incidents. Whereas provincial and territorial officials demanded more money and direction from the federal government in the wake of 9/11 to pay for enhanced security measures (a point which itself speaks to a space that might be allowed to the federal government in provincial affairs), their priorities were largely centred on improving public attributes.[55] In the case of Ontario, for instance, upgrades in funding and expertise were predominantly directed at what are perceived to be the primary responders to and protectors from a terrorist incident: public fire departments, police organizations, and ambulance services. While these public actors are obviously not unimportant, enhancing the quality of their efforts should be coupled with improving those of private ones.

Indeed, there is some initial base upon which to expand. In the Ontario example again, the *Emergency Readiness Act* has a provision for the provincial government to develop emergency plans with the owners and operators of large buildings. Similarly, it contains directives that could potentially reinvigorate the province's responsibility regarding private security: "The new legislation would also require that ... every minister of the Crown, who has been assigned an area of responsibility, and every designated agency, board, commission and other branch of government develop and implement emergency management programs and exercises, public education and any other element prescribed by regulation."[56] Acting upon such directives could be expansive and apply to contracted and in-house security equally.

Finally, perhaps the most substantial challenge to consider rests with the industry itself. From one viewpoint, it is plain that the industry— both privately contacted firms and in-house security—will not rise uniformly to regulate its own activities. Indeed, it is fairly certain that even in the wake of the attacks, universal industry-imposed regulation is unlikely because competitive impulses, the pursuit of profit, and divisions between the different types of private security providers have historically diluted any zeal for the self-implementation and enforcement of standards.[57] From another viewpoint, it is also difficult for the industry to speak with a united voice regarding the creation of government regulations and the proportion of the expenses the private sector will incur. No national professional body exists that can speak for the industry as a whole. Therefore, impetus rests with smaller provincial bodies, unions, and hundreds of individual firms and consumers to devise somehow a coherent stance towards regulation. These factors, then, speak to the even greater need for governments, federal, provincial, and territorial, to be a necessary catalyst for successful regulation to come about.

Military Contractors

For the military, more rigorous governmental attention is also required, but here too, there are limits to the degree that problematic issues can be resolved. In expansion, greater attention must be directed at the considered development and diligent monitoring of contractual arrangements to ensure that the Canadian Forces are provided with the maximum amount of flexibility and surge capacity. On one front, that entails that DND stay abreast of subcontracting endeavours. As well, contracts should stipulate that subcontracting should not occur, or alternatively, if it did, that a Canadian company be selected. Perhaps only Canadian firms should be contracted in the first instance. The tradeoffs, however, go beyond upsetting international trade agreements. While mitigating some negative consequences, actions such as these might reduce the commercial desirability of a contract, or they might face barriers in that there may not be an adequate all-Canadian capacity to respond.

On another front, contracts should be devised to ensure that the contractor response is effective when and where it is needed. Problems have been found in earlier contracting efforts. For example, DND had to make 33 amendments to the contract governing the large-scale privatization of operations at Canadian Forces Base Goose Bay.[58] In addition, a recent audit of DND contracting practices found that regulations were often breached and that oversight and management suffered to the degree that it was impossible to determine, globally, the number of contractors the department employs and how long these arrangements have been in existence.[59] Even military officials have recognized the problem. In response to frictions that exist between CF and ATCO-FRONTEC Logistics Corporation personnel, one officer contended that "[w]e need a better vision on how Frontec is supposed to operate, the contract needs to be more flexible, human resources selection needs to improve, and the civilian employees need more training before working in theatre.... Our long-term needs have to be addressed on the contracts. We are now in the window to take the next step, to make it better."[60] In the end, the words of Kim Nelson ring true in the Canadian context: "[t]he art and science of writing contracts will become extremely critical to ensuring flexibility, sustainability, and survivability."[61]

While more precise contracting arrangements might mitigate some problems, others, because of the differences between public and private approaches and responsibilities, will undoubtedly remain. Again, a contractor presence cannot be guaranteed. In the case of ATCO-FRONTEC in Bosnia, the attrition rate of civilian workers was 68 percent in 2001, and that was for reasons related more towards the terms of the contract and the conditions of employment than it was to any life-threatening dangers.[62] The loss rate was so high that the CF were forced to make last minute postings, thus further contributing to, rather than relieving, over-stretch. Should Ottawa attempt to counter these problems simply through the commandeering of private resources, it would likely come across three problems: (1) a difficulty in controlling non-Canadian owned assets, (2) a reduced amount of resources should it only be able to control Canadian assets, and (3) a limited ability to bring those Canadian resources to bear given the global, just-in-time structures characteristic to many firms. Inescapable, then, are factors concerning contractor obligations, Canada's own limited resource base, and the global market policies of firms.

As a result of these findings, before contractual obligations are even considered, thinking must be directed not just towards what can be privatized, but rather towards what should be privatized given the potentially negative effects of contracting. In making this statement, it is recognized that, because of limited manpower, the CF have been forced to accept a substantial amount of risk by turning to contractors. Therefore, in light of the importance of the contractor presence and the nature of the terrorist threat at home and abroad, determining what should or should not be privatized, core and non-core distinctions are problematic. Instead, a reasoned assessment must be made of what fields or regarding what resources the Canadian Forces are willing to accept the most risk. That looks at the significance of each potential contractor presence and, in a related manner, the ready availability of other resources, both in-house and private. Such an approach would take into account existing assets and manpower base and be based not upon what the military simply needs, but rather upon what it can ill afford not to have under its control, and would affect future capital acquisition and targeted recruiting endeavours. In the Canadian case, military contractors cannot and will not be wished away, but steps might be taken to better manage the effectiveness of the public-private network for the sake of the security of Canadians.

Conclusion

It is evident that, for reasons related to, but also distinct from, neo-liberal thinking, the distinction between "public" and "private" is not easy to make in the Canadian security milieu. This point is made particularly plain in the aftermath of the 9/11 attacks. Privately owned and directed personnel working on private property, such as certain types of critical infrastructure or "private" gathering spaces, serve a goal that is in the public's interest. Also, private assets and personnel are employed by public security sector elements to carry on with their tasks. In fact, because of the prominent place private actors now hold in terms of their numbers and their responsibilities, they must be viewed alongside the publicly owned and funded security sector instruments as key elements in the provision of security for Canadians.

At the same time, however, such an introduction of private actors with their own unique operating dynamics, structures, and pressures, requires a rethinking, not only of who provides security for Canadians, but also of how they are organized, directed, and to what effect. At present, legal structures and legislative guidelines lag behind actual practice. What is more, government needs to come to terms with the fact that, in some cases, even more diligent and precise regulatory and contractual scrutiny will not overcome fundamental differences between contractually employed personnel and those that have taken an oath of service. Instead, the issue is one of thought directed at lessening exposure to risk. Additional efforts will have to be made, and limitations will have to be contended with, in order to come to terms with how Canadians are now made secure.

As Canadian governments and the private sector continue to revamp their stances, two particular matters should lead to fruitful and beneficial analysis. First, in a comparative fashion, one might examine how other countries with a substantial private actor presence have restructured relationships and responsibilities in the post-9/11 environment. In the United States, for instance, the *Patriot Act*, a collection of emergency measures passed in the fall of 2001, included a portion on improving the standards of private security. Has this development been a success, in what ways, and is it applicable to the Canadian case? Second, one should look into how outside pressures might influence the degree, nature, and speediness of the recasting of public-private relations in Canada. From one standpoint, existing tensions in the Canadian-American relationship are such that a rethinking in Canada of the public-private network might help prove to its southern neighbour that it is a reliable and serious-minded partner in the War on Terrorism. Certainly, such tensions complement the longstanding trend of American concern regarding threats posed by instability in its northern neighbour.[63] From another standpoint, foreign pressures, from the United States, NATO, and others, have been directed at expanding the Canadian Forces' stature and resources, thus leading to more substantial international commitments. Similarly, such pressure reinforces Canadian reasoning. Many Canadian analysts have determined that such a shift has its own independent merits, for it would help to promote Canada's geopolitical stature and Canadian normative ideas.[64] As the CF, at present and likely into the future, do not have the appropriate level of capacity, the coming to terms with the benefits and limitations of military contractor relationships is therefore necessary. That is necessary to ensure that when contractors offset the lack of Canadian attributes, they do so in such a way that Canada's international presence is the most prominent and effective it can be. Because Canada is not alone in the privatization of security, and it must contend with the influences of the outside world, there are further avenues to explore for the sake of continued learning and investigation.

Notes

1 The views expressed in this chapter are those of the author alone and do not necessarily reflect those of the Canadian Department of National Defence or the Government of Canada.

2 Nigel South, "Private Security, The Division of Policing Labor and the Commercial Compromise of the State," *Research in Law, Deviance, and Social Control* 6 (1984), p. 190.

3 For this study, policing refers to a social function rather than to a government-funded organization — "the police." As defined by Trevor Jones and Tim Newburn, policing is "organised forms of order maintenance, peacekeeping, crime investigation and prevention and other forms of investigation — which may invoke a conscious exercise of power." Trevor Jones and Tim Newburn, *Private Security and Public Policing* (Oxford: Clarendon Press, 1998), p. 18.

4 For analyses employing different ratios, see Robert J. Gerden, *Private Security: A Canadian Perspective* (Scarborough: Prentice-Hall Canada Inc., 1998) and George S. Rigakos, "Hyperpanoptics as Commodity: The Case of the Parapolice," *Canadian Journal of Sociology* 24, no. 3 (Summer 1999), pp. 381–409. More liberal counts include a wider range of professions including "in-house" security officers, vault manufacturers, alarm specialists, and locksmiths.

5 "Is the public interest served when potentially criminal matters are settled privately? — Excerpts from a debate," in Jane Richardson, ed., *Police and Private Security: What the Future Holds* (Ottawa: Canadian Association of Chiefs of Police, 2000), p. 148.

6 Dale Kinnear, "Privatization — a threat to public police and the public good," in *Police and Private Security*, p. 109.

7 Jaap De Waard, "The Private Security Industry In International Perspective," *European Journal on Criminal Policy and Research* 7, no. 2 (1999), pp. 170–171.

8 George S. Rigakos, "In Search of Security: The Roles of Public Police and Private Agencies," Law Commission of Canada Discussion Paper, 2002, p. 19.

9 Ibid., pp. 3–4, p. 19.

10 That issue is explored in David Garland, "The Limits of the Sovereign State: Strategies of Crime Control in Contemporary Society," *British Journal of Criminology* 36, no. 4 (1994), pp. 445–471.

11 Clifford Shearing and Philip Stenning, "Private security: Implications for Social Control," *Social Problems* 30, no. 5 (1983), p. 229.

12 South, "Private Security," p. 179.

13 Another matter of importance with respect to contracting is that technology has frequently advanced far beyond a military's ability to train support

personnel. At present, that is a far more prominent issue for armed forces such as those of the United States, but could very well become a significant issue for the Canadian military in the future.

14 Canada, Department of National Defence, *1994 White Paper on Defence* (Ottawa: Minister of Supply and Services Canada, 1994), chapter 7.

15 Macarena Barker and Pam Hatton, "Contractors in Support of Operations: A Canadian Perspective," *PASOLS Log* no. 20 (August 2000), (www.pasols.org/log20contents.htm), p. 2.

16 There are contentions, however, that while savings may be achieved, they are not being reinvested in the military, let alone in the designated areas. See, for instance, Doug Bland, "Funding Canada's Defence Policy," Research Paper, Council for Canadian Security in the 21st Century, (www.ccs21.org). There is also some concern that the fiscal returns are not as great as expected. See, for instance, Canada, Office of the Auditor General of Canada, *1999 Report of the Auditor General of Canada to the House of Commons* (Ottawa: Minister of Public Works and Government Services Canada, 1999), chapter 27.

17 Ray Dick, "Featherweight Procurement," *Legion Magazine* (January/February 2002), (www.legionmagazine.com/features/militarymatters/02-01.asp), p. 3.

18 Brian Finlay and Michael O'Hanlon, "NATO's Underachieving Middle Powers: From Burdenshedding to Burdensharing," in Adekeye Adebajo and Chandra Lekha Sriram, eds., *Managing Armed Conflicts in the 21st Century* (London: Frank Cass Publishers, 2001), p. 146.

19 Canada, Office of the Auditor General of Canada, *2002 Report of the Auditor General of Canada to the House of Commons* (Ottawa: Minister of Public Works and Government Services Canada, 2002), p. 3.

20 David Pugliese, "Bitter troops give up on Forces brass," *Ottawa Citizen*, 12 April 2002, (www.canada.com); Canada, Department of National Defence, *At A Crossroads: Annual Report of the Chief of Defence Staff 2001–2002* (Ottawa: Department of National Defence, 2002), pp. 19–23.

21 Office of the Auditor General of Canada, *2002 Report*, p. 3.

22 Centre for Military and Strategic Studies, "To Secure a Nation: The Case for a New Defence White Paper," Council for Canadian Security in the 21st Century, November 2001, p. 23.

23 Office of the Auditor General of Canada, *2002 Report*, p. 9. This trend is obviously not unique to Canada. See, for instance, Christopher Coker, "Outsourcing War," *Cambridge Review of International Affairs* 13, no. 1 (Autumn/Winter 1999), pp. 95–113.

24 Office of the Auditor General of Canada, *2002 Report*, p. 3, p. 12.

25 Sharon Hobson, "Canada faces some tough choices in budget crunch," *Jane's Defence Weekly*, 8 July 2002, p. 8.

26 Canada, Department of National Defence, "Framework for the Development of the Canadian Contractor Augmentation Program," Letter signed and released on 7 July 2000, (www.forces.gc.ca/j4log/index_e.htm).

27 Granatstein, "A Friendly Agreement in Advance"; Conference of Defence Associations, "Caught in the Middle: An Assessment of the Operational Readiness of the Canadian Forces," September 2001; Canada, Parliament of Canada, Standing Committee on National Defence and Veterans Affairs, *Facing Our Responsibilities: The State of Readiness of the Canadian Forces*, Report No. 4 of the Standing Committee on National Defence and Veterans Affairs (May 2002), (www.parl.gc.ca/InfoComDoc/37/1/NDVA/Studies/Reports/ndvarp04-e.htm).

28 In recognition of the difficulties posed by this approach, the CF now distributes bonuses for recruits with already existing skill sets.

29 Dennis Forcese, *Policing Canadian Society*, Second Edition (Scarborough: Prentice-Hall Canada, Inc., 1999), p. 249.

30 Walter Laqueur, "Postmodern terrorism," *Foreign Affairs* 75, no. 5 (September/October 1996), p. 25. Laqueur also notes that more traditional forms of terrorism do still exist.

31 Citation taken from Brian M. Jenkins, "Will Terrorists Go Nuclear?" *Orbis* 29, no. 3 (Autumn 1985), pp. 507-516.

32 Thomas Homer-Dixon, "The Rise of Complex Terrorism," *Foreign Policy* no. 128 (January/February 2002), (www.foreignpolicy.com/issue_jan-feb_2002/homer-dixon.html).

33 Janice Gross Stein, for instance, suggests that the War on Terrorism may take at least a generation. Janice Gross Stein, *The Cult of Efficiency* (Toronto: House of Anansi Press, 2001), p. 233.

34 Barker and Hatton, "Contractors in Support of Operations," p. 1. ATCO-FRONTEC Logistics Corporation was called upon to establish a contingency logistics contractor capability involving the provision of troop transportation, catering, water and electricity, laundry, showers, cleaning, building maintenance, and refueling services.

35 Note, for instance, that in addition to relying upon American aircraft to facilitate Operation APOLLO, Air Malaysia was chartered to bring Canadian troops back home from Diego Garcia via Guam to Edmonton.

36 This covers the moral character, the financial position, and any recent criminal records of employers and employees. Karen Hughson and Michael J. Connolly, "A review of two-tiered policing — a New Brunswick government perspective," in *Police and Private Security*, p. 95.

37 Operators of in-house security often suggest that their services are of a higher quality than contracted, third party private security because of better working conditions, benefits, training, employee selection, and supervision. Studies, however, have found that in many cases in-house security personnel did not have adequate training, were not subjected to

background checks, and did not operate under appropriate supervision. See, for example, British Columbia, Ministry of the Attorney General, *Commission of Inquiry into Policing in British Columbia: Final Report* (Victoria: Ministry of the Attorney General, 1994), p. F15.

38 Rigakos, "In Search of Security," p. 30.

39 Yes, there are avenues other than the strict categories of governmental regulation and marketplace pressures to ensure better quality, but they also have their limitations. No national professional association exists to self-regulate the industry and create national standards; only province-based bodies exist.

40 Charles A. Sennewald, *Effective Security Management*, Third Edition (Boston, MA: Butterworth-Heinemann, 1998), p. 197.

41 See, for instance, Christopher F. Chyba, "Biological Terrorism and Public Health," *Survival* 43, no. 1 (Spring 2001), pp. 93-106.

42 See Stuart Deans, "The perspective of the private security practitioner," in *Police and Private Security*, p. 84.

43 See Sennewald, *Effective Security Management*, especially Chapter 22.

44 See, for instance, Ministry of the Attorney General, *Commission of Inquiry*, p. H60.

45 George S. Rigakos, and David R. Greener, "Bubbles of Governance: Private Policing and the Law in Canada," *Canadian Journal of Law and Society* 15, no. 1 (2000), p. 184.

46 Ibid., p. 151. Canada's *Charter of Rights and Freedoms* does not apply to interactions between two private individuals.

47 Greg Marquis, "Social contract/private contract: the evolution of policing and private security," in *Police and Private Security*, p. 30; Don Morrison, "The legal status of police and private security," in *Police and Private Security*, p. 51.

48 See, for instance, James Cudmore, "Support Services Contracted out by the Military," *National Post*, 9 June 2000, (www.nationalpost.com).

49 In the American context, a Pentagon report issued in the mid-1980s estimated that should contractors be subject to a biological or chemical attack while on duty, there would be a resulting 30 percent drop in worker availability and effectiveness. That number was calculated on the basis that the contractors had the appropriate equipment and training to return to the contaminated areas. Noted in Kim M. Nelson, "Contractors on the Battlefield: Force Multipliers or Force Dividers?" Air Command and Staff College, Air University, Maxwell Air Force Base, Alabama, April 2000, p. 13.

50 *ARA Free Press*, 13 August 2000, (home.earthlink.net/~araplans/08132000.html).

51 Murray Brewster, "Leasing new supply-transport ships one option for Canadian navy says report," *Canadian Press*, 29 September 2002, (www.cp.org).

52 The issues of nationality and loyalty are noted in Rhys Dogan and Michael Pugh, "From Military to Market Imperatives: Peacekeeping and the New Public Policy," Plymouth International Papers No. 8, International Studies Centre, University of Plymouth, July 1997, pp. 24–25.

53 Ibid., p. 21. The authors point out that even seasonal variation comes into play. Many aircraft, for instance, are chartered to facilitate the delivery of Christmas gifts, thus placing the squeeze on those who require the aircraft for other purposes. Note 57, p. 21.

54 Ibid., p. 21. The difference in postures is noted in David M. Moore and Peter D. Antill, "British Army Logistics and Contractors on the Battlefield," *Royal United Services Institute Journal* 145, no. 5 (October 2000), p. 46.

55 See, for instance, the demands placed upon the federal government in Ontario, Office of the Solicitor General, "Ontario's counter-terrorism summit a success," Press Release, 19 February 2002, (www.newswire.ca/government/ontario/english/releases/February2002/19/c3374.html).

56 Ontario, Ministry of Public Safety and Security, "Report Card: Ontario's Response to September 11, 2001," (www.solicitorgeneral.msg.gov.on.ca/english/public/reportcard.htm); Ontario, Office of the Attorney General, "Ontario legislation will improve emergency response," Press Release, 6 December 2001, (www.newswire.ca/government/ontario/english/releases/December2001/06/c4494.html).

57 For analysis of this lack of enthusiasm, see Steve Hess, "Standards in policing and private security," in *Police and Private Security*, pp. 124–25.

58 Public Service Alliance of Canada, "Supply Chain Project: Our Challenge—Fighting for a Better Future!" (www.psac.com/organize/supplychain/Bulletin3-e.htm).

59 Jim Bronskill, "DND broke contracting rules: audit," *Ottawa Citizen*, 8 June 2002, (www.canada.com).

60 Howard Michitsch, "Armed Forces' civilian program hits snags," *Ottawa Citizen*, 25 August 2001, (www.canada.com).

61 Nelson, "Contractors on the Battlefield," p. 26.

62 Michitsch, "Armed Forces' civilian program hits snags."

63 That is a theme in Desmond Morton, *A Military History of Canada: From Champlain to Kosovo*, Fourth Edition (Toronto: McClelland and Stewart, Inc., 1999).

64 Fen Osler Hampson and Dean F. Oliver, "Pulpit Diplomacy: A critical assessment of the Axworthy doctrine," *International Journal* 53, no. 3 (Summer 1998), pp. 379–406; Louis F. Nastro and Kim Richard Nossal, "The commitment-capability gap: implications for Canadian foreign policy in the post-Cold War era," *Canadian Defence Quarterly* 27, no. 1 (Autumn 1997), pp. 19–22; Allen Sens, "From Peacekeeping to Intervention: Expeditionary Capabilities and the Canadian Force Structure Debate," Research Paper, Council for Canadian Security in the 21st Century, (www.ccs21.org).

References

ARA Free Press, 13 August 2000, (home.earthlink.net/~araplans/08132000.html).

Barker, Macarena, and Pam Hatton. "Contractors in Support of Operations: A Canadian Perspective," PASOLS Log no. 20 (August 2000), (www.pasols.org/log20contents.htm).

Bland, Doug. "Funding Canada's Defence Policy," Research Paper, Council for Canadian Security in the 21st Century, (www.ccs21.org).

Brewster, Murray. "Leasing new supply-transport ships one option for Canadian navy says report," *Canadian Press*, 29 September 2002, (www.cp.org).

British Columbia. Ministry of the Attorney General. *Commission of Inquiry into Policing in British Columbia: Final Report*. Victoria: Ministry of the Attorney General, 1994.

Bronskill, Jim. "DND broke contracting rules: audit," *Ottawa Citizen*, 8 June 2002, (www.canada.com).

Canada. Department of National Defence. *At A Crossroads: Annual Report of the Chief of Defence Staff 2001–2002*. Ottawa: Department of National Defence, 2002.

Canada. Department of National Defence. "Framework for the Development of the Canadian Contractor Augmentation Program." Letter signed and released on 7 July 2000, (www.forces.gc.ca/j4log/index_e.htm).

Canada. Department of National Defence. *1994 White Paper on Defence*. Ottawa: Minister of Supply and Services Canada, 1994.

Canada. Office of the Auditor General of Canada. *1999 Report of the Auditor General of Canada to the House of Commons*. Ottawa: Minister of Public Works and Government Services Canada, 1999.

Canada. Office of the Auditor General of Canada. *2002 Report of the Auditor General of Canada to the House of Commons*. Ottawa: Minister of Public Works and Government Services Canada, 2002.

Canada. Parliament of Canada. Standing Committee on National Defence and Veterans Affairs. *Facing Our Responsibilities: The State of Readiness of the Canadian Forces*. Report No. 4 of the Standing Committee on National Defence and Veterans Affairs (May 2002), (www.parl.gc.ca/InfoComDoc/37/1/NDVA/Studies/Reports/ndvarp04-e.htm).

Centre for Military and Strategic Studies. "To Secure a Nation: The Case for a New Defence White Paper." Council for Canadian Security in the 21st Century, November 2001.

Chyba, Christopher F. "Biological Terrorism and Public Health," *Survival* 43, no. 1 (Spring 2001), pp. 93–106.

Coker, Christopher. "Outsourcing War," *Cambridge Review of International Affairs* 13, no. 1 (Autumn/Winter 1999), pp. 95–113.

Conference of Defence Associations. "Caught in the Middle: An Assessment of the Operational Readiness of the Canadian Forces." September 2001.

Cudmore, James. "Support Services Contracted out by the Military," *National Post*, 9 June 2000, (www.nationalpost.com).

Deans, Stuart. "The perspective of the private security practitioner." In Jane Richardson, ed., *Police and Private Security: What the Future Holds*. Ottawa: Canadian Association of Chiefs of Police, 2000, pp. 83–85.

De Waard, Jaap. "The Private Security Industry In International Perspective," *European Journal on Criminal Policy and Research* 7, no. 2 (1999), pp. 143–174.

Dick, Ray. "Featherweight Procurement," *Legion Magazine* (January/February 2002), (www.legionmagazine.com/features/militarymatters/02-01.asp).

Dogan, Rhys, and Michael Pugh. "From Military to Market Imperatives: Peacekeeping and the New Public Policy." Plymouth International Papers No. 8, International Studies Centre, University of Plymouth, July 1997.

Finlay, Brian, and Michael O'Hanlon. "NATO's Underachieving Middle Powers: From Burdenshedding to Burdensharing." In Adekeye Adebajo and Chandra Lekha Sriram, eds., *Managing Armed Conflicts in the 21st Century*. London: Frank Cass Publishers, 2001, pp. 145–160.

Forcese, Dennis. *Policing Canadian Society*. Second Edition. Scarborough: Prentice-Hall Canada, Inc., 1999.

Garland, David. "The Limits of the Sovereign State: Strategies of Crime Control in Contemporary Society," *British Journal of Criminology* 36, no. 4 (1994), pp. 445–471.

Gerden, Robert J. *Private Security: A Canadian Perspective*. Scarborough: Prentice-Hall Canada Inc., 1998.

Granatstein, J. L. *A Friendly Agreement in Advance: Canada-US Defense Relations Past, Present, and Future*. C.D. Howe Institute Commentary (No. 166, June 2002).

Hampson, Fen Osler, and Dean F. Oliver, "Pulpit Diplomacy: A critical assessment of the Axworthy doctrine," *International Journal* 53, no. 3 (Summer 1998), pp. 379–406.

Hess, Steve. "Standards in policing and private security." In Jane Richardson, ed., *Police and Private Security: What the Future Holds*. Ottawa: Canadian Association of Chiefs of Police, 2000, pp. 122–125.

Hobson, Sharon. "Canada faces some tough choices in budget crunch," *Jane's Defence Weekly*, 8 July 2002, p. 8.

Homer-Dixon, Thomas. "The Rise of Complex Terrorism," *Foreign Policy* no. 128 (January/February 2002), (www.foreignpolicy.com/issue_janfeb_2002/homer-dixon.html).

Hughson, Karen, and Michael J. Connolly. "A review of two-tiered policing — a New Brunswick government perspective." In Jane Richardson ed., *Police and Private Security: What the Future Holds*. Ottawa: Canadian Association of Chiefs of Police, 2000, pp. 89–102.

"Is the public interest served when potentially criminal matters are settled privately? — Excerpts from a debate." In Jane Richardson, ed., *Police and Private Security: What the Future Holds*. Ottawa: Canadian Association of Chiefs of Police, 2000, pp. 144–155.

Jenkins, Brian M. "Will Terrorists Go Nuclear?" *Orbis* 29, no. 3 (Autumn 1985), pp. 507–516.

Jones, Trevor, and Tim Newburn. *Private Security and Public Policing*. Oxford: Clarendon Press, 1998.

Kinnear, Dale. "Privatization — a threat to public police and the public good." In Jane Richardson, ed., *Police and Private Security: What the Future Holds*. Ottawa: Canadian Association of Chiefs of Police, 2000, pp. 108–116.

Laqueur, Walter. "Postmodern terrorism," *Foreign Affairs* 75, no. 5 (September/October 1996), pp. 24–36.

Marquis, Greg. "Social contract/private contract: the evolution of policing and private security." In Jane Richardson, ed. *Police and Private Security: What the Future Holds*. Ottawa: Canadian Association of Chiefs of Police, 2000, pp. 16–34.

Michitsch, Howard. "Armed Forces' civilian program hits snags," *Ottawa Citizen*, 25 August 2001, (www.canada.com).

Moore, David M., and Peter D. Antill. "British Army Logistics and Contractors on the Battlefield," *Royal United Services Institute Journal* 145, no. 5 (October 2000), p. 46–52.

Morrison, Don. "The legal status of police and private security." In Jane Richardson, ed., *Police and Private Security: What the Future Holds*. Ottawa: Canadian Association of Chiefs of Police, 2000, pp. 45–60.

Morton, Desmond. *A Military History of Canada: From Champlain to Kosovo*. Fourth Edition. Toronto: McClelland and Stewart, Inc., 1999.

Nastro, Louis F., and Kim Richard Nossal. "The commitment-capability gap: implications for Canadian foreign policy in the post-Cold War era," Canadian Defence Quarterly 27, no. 1 (Autumn 1997), pp. 19–22.

Nelson, Kim M. "Contractors on the Battlefield: Force Multipliers or Force Dividers?" Air Command and Staff College, Air University, Maxwell Air Force Base, Alabama, April 2000.

Ontario. Office of the Attorney General. "Ontario legislation will improve emergency response." Press Release, 6 December 2001, (www.newswire.ca/government/ontario/english/releases/December2001/06/c4494.html).

Ontario. Ministry of Public Safety and Security. "Report Card: Ontario's Response to September 11, 2001," (www.solicitorgeneral.msg.gov.on.ca/english/public/reportcard.htm).

Ontario. Office of the Solicitor General. "Ontario's counter-terrorism summit a success." Press Release, 19 February 2002, (www.newswire.ca/government/ontario/english/releasesFebruary2002/19/c3374.html).

Public Service Alliance of Canada. "Supply Chain Project: Our Challenge — Fighting for a Better Future!" (www.psac.com/organize/supplychain/Bulletin3-e.htm).

Pugliese, David. "Bitter troops give up on Forces brass," *Ottawa Citizen*, 12 April 2002, (www.canada.com).

Rigakos, George S. "Hyperpanoptics as Commodity: The Case of the Parapolice," *Canadian Journal of Sociology* 24, no. 3 (Summer 1999), pp. 381–409.

——. "In Search of Security: The Roles of Public Police and Private Agencies," Law Commission of Canada Discussion Paper, 2002.

Rigakos, George S., and David R. Greener. "Bubbles of Governance: Private Policing and the Law in Canada," *Canadian Journal of Law and Society* 15, no. 1 (2000), pp. 145–185.

Sennewald, Charles A. *Effective Security Management.* Third Edition. Boston, MA: Butterworth-Heinemann, 1998.

Sens, Allen. "From Peacekeeping to Intervention: Expeditionary Capabilities and the Canadian Force Structure Debate." Research Paper, Council for Canadian Security in the 21st Century, (www.ccs21.org).

Shearing, Clifford, and Philip Stenning. "Private security: Implications for Social Control," *Social Problems* 30, no. 5 (1983), pp. 498–505.

South, Nigel. "Private Security, The Division of Policing Labor and the Commercial Compromise of the State," *Research in Law, Deviance and Social Control* 6 (1984), pp. 171–198.

Stein, Janice Gross. *The Cult of Efficiency.* Toronto: House of Anansi Press, 2001.

PART IV

Post-9/11 Reviews of Middle East Policy and Human Security

12

A Critical Review of Canada's Policy Rationales for the Middle East: The Twentieth Century

H. Ayla Kiliç

The triumph of neo-liberal globalization following the end of the Cold War has not only reshaped the classic security paradigm but traditional foreign policy rationales as well. New, more multi-layered security concerns comprising domestic, global, socio-economic, political, religious and cultural issues diminished the separation between national and international security and changed the raison d'être of foreign policy. The endeavor of readjustment has faced a serious challenge since September 11, 2001. The Middle East, which has always been an important region in world politics, or is at the centre, once more, of a game of global politics of security and diplomacy in which Canada has long been problematically involved

Canada's policy rationales for the Middle East are now more important than ever, not only because Canada is an active player in international politics, but also because of the changing demographics of Canadian society which bring the regional issues of the Middle East closer to home. More importantly, Canada's relationship with its closest ally the United States has been going through one of the tensest periods in its history because of Canada's "assumed" reluctance to adjust its foreign policies in accordance with American security and national interests. Here, the key question is whether Canada's Middle Eastern policy in this new era will be an authentic expression of what is vitally important to Canadians, and will it reflect Canada's long-term interests under the new circumstances.

In order to answer these questions, it is imperative to establish the historical background for the evolving principles of Canada's Middle East policy and show the continuities and changes in the policy rationales for the region with reference to socio-political, economic, domestic, regional, international and transnational dynamics. For this purpose, first a brief presentation of various interpretations of Canada's Middle Eastern policies will be given. In the second section, the relevance of these explanations will be tested within specific periods of Canadian history: the pre-Cold War period, the Cold War Era, and the post-Cold War Era until September 11, 2001. In each period, the main interpretations of Canada's foreign policy rationales will be analyzed within a complex combination of the interplay of the individual, group, state and international levels of influence on policy making.[1]

Interpretations of Canada's Middle East Policies

The "Ready Aye Ready" Approach

Ivan L. Head once quoted a leading Canadian newspaper which, over a hundred years ago, wrote: "We could not be freer than we are now, for we have no foreign policy to complicate things, and no army to provide" (1972:237). Head's interpretation of this editorial is that, although Canada had relations with other countries, its foreign policy rationales had always been constrained by the influence of two states with which Canada had been most "intimately" related throughout its history, the United Kingdom and the United States. It is, indeed, within these perimeters that Canada has tried to pursue a course to forward its interests in the international arena. Although Canadian foreign policy rationales have periodically been reviewed to reflect the changes in Canadian society and in the world system, it has never been able totally to break away from this constraint. The final policy action has always been attuned to accommodate the policy objectives of its country of "special relationship" — the "Ready Aye Ready" reflex born of the imperial past and present.

Canada's Middle East policy is a palpable reflection of this dilemma. Although during the last sixty years the intensity and priority of Middle East related issues in Canada's agenda have changed in relation to external and internal developments, such as changing demographics dynamics within in the country, the country or countries of special relations have always defined the framework of Canada's Middle East policy. As it will be explained later in this article, this unwritten rule of Canadian foreign policy has also failed to satisfy both domestic and international actors involved in the Middle East conflict.

The Helpful-fixer Approach

Multilateralism, of course, has always been the main tenet of Canada's modern foreign policy. While promoting the idea of the responsible commitment of world nations to multilateralism under the auspices of international institutions, Canada has created a niche for itself as a "helpful-fixer" trying to find a middle ground between foes, to ease the obstacles for its country of "special relations" and to lower the level of tension in the international arena in order to maintain global stability and security. As a "middle-power," Canada was promoting liberal-internationalism in the world arena to pursue its foreign policy objectives during the Cold War Era (Nossal 1997; Munton and Kirton 1992). Under the neo-liberal globalism of the post-Cold War Era, Canada's foreign policy agenda has become more sensitive towards global, regional and domestic developments and economic and social issues pursued by various transnational, international and domestic actors through multiple channels.

When Canada's involvement in the Middle East is analyzed from this perspective, it can be argued that Canada's primary policy objective is maintaining harmony among its allies while responding to the developments in the region. Canada's involvement in the Suez Crises in 1956, for example, aimed to bail out the British and French, bring them back into realignment with the United States and thus prevent a rift within the Euro-Atlantic alliance (Ismael 1994). By the same token, the Canadian Compromise of February 2003 to set a deadline for Iraqi disarmament aimed at bridging the gap between the permanent members of the United Nations, namely the United States and Britain on the one hand, and Russia and France on the other.

The Economy First Approach: No Policy!

A third approach identifies Canada's national interest in economic terms and considers international stability as the key element in the achievement of Canada's economic as well as political goals. It is argued that as a market-oriented country relying on international trade for its growth and security, Canada does not have a foreign policy but a trade policy (Scott 1932; Lipsey 1985; Cohen 1995). According to this view, the Euro-Atlantic region, which constitutes almost 95 percent of its trade relations, has always been the focus of Canada's national interest defined in economic terms. Liberal Defence minister Arthur Eggleton acknowledged this reality in his speech at the 37th Munich Conference on Security Policy in March 2001 stating: "Through two world wars, throughout the Cold War, … Our policy is simple: the stability of Europe is a central concern for Canada."

The Middle East with its miniscule share in Canada's foreign trade — 0.3 percent of Canada's foreign trade — (Statistics Canada 2001) is not significant in terms of indirect economic relations. The oil-rich region, however, is crucial for the stability of the industrialized economies of the Euro-Atlantic community. Borrowing Janice Stein's (1977) observation that Canada has a policy *on* the Middle East but not *in* the Middle East, it can be argued that to maintain the uninterrupted supply of oil for its trade partners which heavily depend on Middle Eastern oil is one of the cornerstones of Canada's policy objectives *on* the Middle East. A cheap and secure supply of Middle East oil was typically vital to the reconstruction of Europe as a Canadian trade partner after World War II. Euro-Atlantic trade, totalling 80 percent of Canada's exports, was a significant contribution to Canada's economic boom during the Cold War era. By the same token, the 1973 and 1979 "oil shocks" produced global cycles of recession that had profound impacts on international trade, threatening Canada's growth and security, despite the undeniable benefits accruing to investors in Canada's energy futures at that time (Statistics Canada: various sources).

At present, Canada's major trade partners heavily depend on Middle Eastern oil as a major energy source. According to the Japan Information Network, eighty-seven percent of that country's oil is imported from the Middle East. As of 2001, thirty-five percent of Europe's oil was imported from the Middle East. When Libya and Algeria are included, this figure rises to sixty-five percent (International Energy Agency). Canada's major trade partner, the United States, consuming 28 percent of the world's oil, received over 37 percent of that from the Persian Gulf states, not including Iran (American Petroleum Institute). Canada's national security — defined in terms of economic securities of its trade partners — places the Middle East among the priorities of its foreign policy objectives.

The Honest Broker Approach

Rather than setting proactive policy rationales, Canada has improvised its niche as an "honest broker" within the policy framework drawn by its country of "special relations." Mixing its role as helpful-fixer with the promotion of Canadian values abroad, Canada has developed an official line of policy, the "honest broker with an even-handed approach," trying, without taking sides, to help the parties involved to solve their differences through negotiations (Special Representative 1980). Although "honest-brokerage" has manifestly failed to convince interested parties both in the region and at home, it has still been promoted by the government as the best approach towards the Middle East. Then, foreign minister Bill Graham, during a television interview with the CBC's Brian Steward on November 3, 2002, interpreted the merit of this approach by saying that "if we are disliked by all sides, then it may mean we are doing the right thing."

Scholars of Canadian foreign policy, however, have interpreted it differently. While the pro-Arab argument pointed to the dilemma of acting even-handedly while expressing Canada's admiration, friendship, support, and commitment to Israel, the pro-Israeli side has emphasized the moral responsibility of Canada towards Israel and criticized the even-handed policy as being anti-Israeli in essence (Ismael 1976; Burton 1991). Depending on the ethno-religious and ideological frame of reference of the critic, Canada's Middle East policy is thus labeled pro-Israeli, pro-Arab, anti-Semitic or anti-Islam. The widening gap between the supporters of these opposing arguments has become crucial in balancing Canada's foreign policy objectives with the interests of domestic groups.

Domestic Stability Approach

Canada, like other multi-cultural, multi-ethnic societies has to recognize and find a way to reconcile, or at least manage, the diverse interests of domestic groups in its foreign policy making process. Saideman (2002) argues that smaller but unified ethnic groups can play a significant role in influencing a country's foreign policy on their plights and the plights of their kin elsewhere. When a highly politicized ethnic group encounters competition from other groups equally committed to swaying policy outcomes towards their own plights, government's ability to balance these interests to maintain domestic stability may be severely restricted.

Although surveys suggest that over 60 percent of Canadians claim "indifference" or non-partisanship towards the Middle East and its regional problems (The Gallup Poll 2002), the ethno-religious groups representing the major divides of the region play significant roles in shaping Canada's public opinion and put pressure on the foreign policy making process by pursuing every possible venue to achieve their objectives. An influential Jewish community has been actively trying to influence Canada's foreign policy in the direction of Israel's interest during the last 60 or more years. Both the long-divided Arab and Muslim communities started to overcome their differences and unite around common issues, such as the realization of a Palestinian state and ending the sanctions on Iraq. The expanding Muslim community in Canada, whose population is estimated around 700,000 (The Jannah Organization),[2] makes it harder for policy makers to ignore Muslim demands. Increasing tension, occasionally leading to violent clashes between the pro-Jewish and Israeli and pro-Muslim and Arab groups creates a potentially serious domestic security threat in Canada requiring a multi-dimensional response from the government and a major revision of Canada's foreign policy rationales for the Middle East.

A Concise History of Canada-Middle East Relations in the Twentieth Century

The relative weight of the Middle East in Canada's agenda has increased and become more complicated over the years because of changing domestic and global circumstances. This section will glance at the characteristics of Canada's policy rationales for the Middle East from an historical perspective and assess the priorities of Canada's foreign policy, as explained above, in relation to the Middle East in three different periods: before the Cold War, during the Cold War, and after the Cold War.

Before the Cold War

At the turn of the twentieth century, Canada had no direct interest in, or contact with, the Middle East. Albeit a member of the British Empire, the foreign policy rationale of the Dominion of Canada was to stay out of "minor" imperial skirmishes (Department of Foreign Affairs and International Trade History, DFAIT). In that period, true to Ivan Head's interpretation, Canada had always tried to harmonize its interests with those of Britain's imperialist interests. Commencing its duty as the helpful-fixer, Canada worked on improving relations with the Americans, not only for fostering Canadian economic interests, but for abetting the British interests in North America as well. Maintaining domestic stability at home was a major concern for politicians. Risking Canadian lives in British wars involving Muslim movements or states had been avoided in order to prevent a fracas between French and British Canadians. During the Sudanese uprising in 1885, for example, Canada did not offer troops but only volunteers who had to be paid by the British government. In 1922 Canada failed to make any commitment to British interests in Greece or Turkey during the highly controversial "Chanak Incident."

During the inter-war era, Canada intensified its efforts to acquire a place for itself in the international arena as an independent actor. Ironically, it was again in this period that Canada acknowledged that it had little choice but to follow the great powers. Loring Christie, an official in the Department of Foreign Affairs, said that "if the great powers start you start, if they don't you don't; where they go, you go.... The theory of our having a voice and control is eyewash" (Nossal 1997:53). Indeed, the equal member status at the League of Nations, the international organization of the inter-war era, did not bestow upon Canada any influence in the organization.

Canada's limited contact with the Middle East endured during the inter-war era. Unless certain developments inspired a public outcry, political and economic efforts were focused on the improvement and maintenance of Canadian-British and Canadian-American relations. The public sentiment and moral reaction to the situation of the Armenians in the Ottoman Empire at the end of WWI, for example, led the Canadian Government to request that the British Colonial Office not let the Turks get away with what they had done to Armenians (Department of External Affairs 1967). In this period, Canada's economic involvement with the Middle East was extremely limited. There was only one trade Commissioner Office located in Egypt to deal with the whole area, including Turkey. It was in only the mid-1950s that Canada opened its first embassies in the region (in Cairo, Tel Aviv, and Beirut).

During the Cold War

Canada's economic, political, and cultural ties with Britain and America were the main determinants of its foreign policy rationales in this period. During the early years of the Cold War, Canada tried to inject an activist "internationalism" into the bipolar power structure of the post-World War II world system. That first appeared as the policy preference of individual leaders such as Louis St. Laurent and Lester B. Pearson, who guided the Department of External Affairs during the pivotal years 1945 through 1957, but was later elaborated into a set of principles that defined Canada's foreign policy rationales as including active participation in world politics, management of conflicts through containment, commitment to international organizations, collective security, and responsibility towards its allies within a multilateral framework (Nossal 1997:155–158). During this period, Canada's core national interest was articulated in spatial terms as in the intertwined economic and geographical sphere of the Euro-Atlantic region. Increased economic ties with the European states put the stability of Europe in the forefront of Canada's foreign policy, and that required an intense effort to ease the tension between the rival superpowers (the Americans and the Soviets) and to keep international trade routes open.

Meanwhile, the Middle East had gone through dramatic changes, including the end of British and French mandate rule and the emergence of independent states such as Jordan, Iraq, Syria, and Lebanon. The birth of the state of Israel, the increasing importance of oil in world trade and security, and super power political activity to gain spheres of influence in the region, pushed Canada to take an active stand on regional issues. Even though the Middle East was not vital for Canada's immediate security, the region's importance in the achievement of Canada's overall foreign policy rationales had been acknowledged. The unfettered access to cheap oil (approximately $1.50 U.S. per barrel up until the 1970s) was crucial for the economic development and restructuring of the Euro-Atlantic region and the collective security of the "free world."

The most overwhelming regional issue of the first part of the Cold War era was the Arab-Israeli conflict which reflected the complex interplay of contrasting interests at societal, national, and international levels. In the domestic arena, the Jewish community (some 180,000 at that time) increased its lobbying activities at the governmental level to secure Canada's support for a Jewish homeland in Palestine. Canadian Arabs on the other hand, with a sparse population of less than 12,000, had few eminent figures or political contacts to promote the Arab cause and to fight against the negative image of the Arabs as "lazy people who had dried up Palestine into a desert" (Tauber 2002). Post-war political leaders in Canada were generally eager to erase the country's own legacy of anti-Semitism — Diefenbaker, with his expressed sensitivity to the needs of the Jewish people, and Pearson with his occasional references to himself as "Rabbi Pearson" because of his emotional closeness to the Jewish cause (ibid.). Although an elite cadre in the foreign service included Middle East expert Elizabeth MacCallum, who believed that the foundation of the Israeli state would not be in the best interest of Britain (Canada's country of special relations) and advised the government accordingly (Bercuson 1985:35–40), these voices were not loudly heard. It was the cultural, religious and personal values of political leaders, worked within the constraints of radically altered relations within the "North Atlantic Triangle" (Canada, the UK, and USA) that defined the final policy outcome: important diplomatic support for the

United Nations' Palestine Partition Resolution and the foundation of a Jewish state.

Canada's role as a helpful fixer reached its peak in this period. While trying to maintain strategic and business interests with its country of "special relations," which had shifted towards the United States, and keeping the harmony and peace among its Western allies, Canada was also struggling to ease the tension between the rival blocks of the Cold War Era. During the UN discussions over the partition of Palestine, Pearson described his, and connectedly Canada's, position in the following terms: "here I am in the middle ... between an obstinate Russian [a] not too skillful American and ... a completely detached [British delegate] exhausted by the obvious failure of imperial policy in Palestine" (Department of External Affairs, 5475-CD-2-40).

A similar helpful-fixer approach was taken during the 1956 Suez crises. A joint French, British, and Israeli attack on Egypt following Egypt's nationalization of the Suez Canal in July 1956 created a major rift within NATO and the British Commonwealth and cooled the relationship between the British and the Americans. Canada, being true to its role, responded to the situation to prevent its allies from further embarrassment and to bridge the gap within the Western alliance (Ismael 1994:16–18). Regional developments starting from the mid-1960s increased American involvement and leadership in the Middle East. At the same time, a gradual increase in America's share in Canada's trade vis-à-vis Britain and Canada's dependency on America for its security, both through NATO and NORAD, limited Canada's ability to develop independent policies regarding the Middle East. Canadian officials avoided complicating matters for the U.S. in the region and harming American-Canadian relations. The main determinant of Canada's Middle Eastern policy became supporting America's positions and America's broader interests in the region. Canadian ambassadors at the United Nations were told that Canada's votes on the resolutions should be, "as much as possible with the U.S. on the Middle East issues and that, in any case, Canada's vote on these matters should never be one step removed from that of the U.S." (Noble 1981).

Under the circumstances, conceding its middle-power status Canada tried to find its niche in the field of conflict management as a peacekeeper. Within the policy framework drawn by the United States and under the auspices of the United Nations, "Canada the Peacekeeper" played its role as helpful-fixer to prevent the Middle Eastern conflict from turning into an international one with direct involvement of the super powers, while at the same time asserting Canadian values overseas and developing an image for itself as an "honest broker." However, analysis of the important Middle Eastern developments of the period indicates that the protection of the interests of its Western allies in the region was more imperative than the promotion of Canadian values. Canada's support of the British-led embargo on Iranian oil following the 1954 nationalization of oil in Iran, and voting against Algerian independence from France at the United Nations before the formal treaty that ended the Algerian war in 1962, were not directed towards the promotion of Canadian values but of Canadian interests defined in economic and strategic terms which were closely connected with the interests of its trade allies.

Canada's explicit support of Western interests in international forums created doubts about its assumed role as an honest broker. Canada had constantly been warned by Arab leaders to be "neutral" in the Arab-Israeli dispute. Canada's role was by no means trusted throughout the Arab world. Abdul Nasser, the president of Egypt from 1952 to 1972, opposed Canada's participation in the peacekeeping mission of the United Nations Emergency Force (UNEF) in Gaza after the 1956 Suez War, arguing that Canada was too closely identified and allied with the British and represented the American and connectedly Israeli interest (Delvoie 1997:5). Nasser agreed to Canada's participation in the UNEF only after a personal call from the UN Secretary-General and on the condition that Canada would deploy logistics support troops rather than combat troops (ibid.).

The lack of trust in Canada's impartiality was revealed as well after the October 1973 War (the Yom Kippur War) when Canada's participation in the UNEF II peacekeeping force was resisted by Egypt and other Arab countries on the basis that Canada was strongly pro-Israeli and an extension of the United States (Ismael 1994:27). Once again, Canadian participation went only after the personal involvement of the UN Secretary-General, which resulted in the inclusion of then Soviet-aligned Poland in the peacekeeping force (ibid.). Personal preferences of political leaders continued to play a role in the direction of Canada's foreign policy. Then minister of External Affairs, Don Jamieson (1976–1979), for example, claimed to be even-handed on Middle East issues but interpreted them with a pro-Israeli emphasis which, according to him, was good for domestic politics, the Arab vote being not considered significant to the Liberal Party of the 1970s (*Toronto Star*, 12 October 1976).

Détente

Canada's foreign policy rationales went through significant changes in the 1970s. Among various contributing factors, the shift in balance of power politics from a tight bipolar to a loose bipolar system, under which the two superpowers were contained by several middle powers, gave countries like Canada a leverage and relative independence in international relations. Temporarily fading super power tension in the mid-1970s also provided Canada an opportunity to distance itself from the United States and to take a more independent stand in international issues. Improved economies of middle powers like Canada, and the opening of inter-block trade between the West and the East, as well as with the third world countries, also helped to reduce their reliance on the superpowers for economic and national security. Pierre Trudeau, seizing the opportunity, tried to reformulate Canada's foreign policy rationales around six major themes, the most important one being "Fostering Economic Growth" by embracing a wide range of economic, commercial, and financial objectives in the foreign field (*Foreign Policy for Canadians* 1970).

The 1970s were also an era of change for the Middle East. The spillover effect of the newfound wealth of certain Arab states after the 1973 oil-shock created an overall improvement in the Middle East and opened new venues for trade and development. Putting economic interests at the centre of his foreign policy, Pierre Trudeau tried to improve Canada's relations with the Arab countries of the Middle East through trade. Under Trudeau's version of the "economy first" doctrine, Canadian businessmen increased their efforts to get a bigger share from the Middle East pie and became more sensitive towards Middle East issues. The belated response of the Trudeau government in acting against the 1973 Arab boycott of Israel (a pressure tactic of Arab governments who tried to force foreign companies to choose between commercial links with Israel and the Arab world) raised criticism at home by pro-Israeli groups.

A changing international climate and new foreign policy objectives were reflected in Canada's immigration policy as well. The gradual removal of ethnic and racial preferences after 1950, and especially after 1967, increased immigration from Muslim countries of the Middle East and Asia. The increased Muslim population, over 98,000 by the year 1981 (Statistics Canada) started to change domestic balances and invoked new pressures in the domestic arena. Politicians who had so far dealt with only the pro-Israeli lobby, started to feel the pressure from the Arab and Muslim communities as well. While pro-Israeli groups were, as we have seen, always vigilant, pro-Arab groups accused Canadian officials of being biased against the Arab cause, turning Middle East related issues into a "hot potato" for politicians. Trudeau was arguably the only high-level politician who was immune to pressure from "narrow" groups, typically drawing a line between the communal demands of an ethnic or religious group, and lobbying on behalf of a foreign country. Although his constant refusal to meet with the Canadian Israeli Committee, known for its financial support towards Israel, in favour of the Canadian Jewish Congress, typically caused a tempest, he was protected by his political popularity and well-known respect for the Jewish community at large (Taras 1989). Other political leaders were not able to benefit from Trudeau's "charisma" and found themselves caught in the crossfire. The most famous example was provided by Joe Clark, who made an impetuous decision to move the Canadian embassy from Tel Aviv to Jerusalem during his short tenure as prime minister in 1979, and was seared by negative reaction from Arab-Muslim Canadians, as well as by more general criticism of his diplomatic style. His own speech at the Canadian Israeli Committee, criticizing the Israeli invasion of Lebanon (1982) on the other hand, predictably angered that particular audience and its supporters. A subsequent consensus among leading Canadian politicians (Clark included) was to stay out of the domestic debate between the two groups.

Canada's shifting policy towards the acknowledgment of Palestinian rights of self-determination, or a two-state solution to the conflict, reflects the transformation of Canada both domestically and internationally. In the 1950s, following the Anglo-American lead on the issue, Canada had recognized the Palestinians, not as a nation, but as a group of refugees. In the 1960s, again in accordance with the Anglo-American view, the Palestinians existence was acknowledged as a distinct group within the greater Arab nation. During the Trudeau era the Palestinian Liberation Organization (PLO) was granted limited recognition as the representative of the Palestinian people, but it was only larger international events in the 1990s, most specifically an American imprimatur to the idea, that led to Ottawa's acknowledgement the possibility of the establishment of an independent Palestinian state. By the same token, Canada avoided taking a strong or "too strong" a stand against Israel at the United Nations on controversial issues such as withdrawal from its occupied territories. Following the Camp David Accords of 1978 between Israel and Egypt, Canadian officials were warned not to support any approach that would undermine American diplomacy and certainly did not do so.

In sum, the long Cold War produced social, cultural, and geopolitical transformations that had their affects on Canadian Middle East policy While in the west the "baby boomers," with their more egalitarian values and humanitarian worldviews, were acquiring political power, in the third world, more and more countries were gaining their independence. The economic developments of European countries, Japan, and Canada weakened the control of the two super powers over world affairs and provided the middle-power countries a more independent and flexible policy platform. In Canada, these changes were best reflected in the personality of Prime Minister Pierre Trudeau who took advantage of Détente to pursue a foreign policy more reflective of Canada's new domestic and social balances and broader economic interests. Although Canada's role as a helpful-fixer for its country of "special relations" had been lessened, the traditional constraints on Canada's foreign policy did not disappear. Regarding Middle East issues, Canada still had to attune its policy towards the United States, a pressure that would soon increase.

Toward the End of the Cold War Era

When Brian Mulroney became Canada's prime minister in 1984, Canada's two "special relations" countries were ruled by strong-willed adherents of neo-conservatism advocating free markets with minimal state interference and a powerful military presence: the United States under the leadership of Ronald Reagan, and Britain with its "Iron Lady" Margaret Thatcher who fully shared Reagan's beliefs regarding the need finally to vanquish the threat of (failing) Soviet communism. One other thing they had in common was their dislike of Trudeau's signature "peace initiative" of 1983, which they believed was thoroughly compromising of broader Western interests. They, therefore, welcomed the new conservative leadership of Mulroney as a shift towards the revitalization of the traditional Canadian role as junior partner in the Anglo-American alliance (Bothwell 1998:99–101).

The Mulroney era (1984–1993) witnessed, indeed, radical changes in the international arena, while Mulroney's most strategic decision was moving Canada firmly back into the continental orbit. Although Mulroney tried to balance his personal views with shrewd appointments of political moderates (Joe Clark at the newly-renamed Department of Foreign Affairs, and Stephen Lewis, as Ambassador to the UN), his pro-American emphasis was obvious. As he once stated, his primary aim was to establish "good relations, super relations" with the United States (Granatstein and Hilmer 1999). Mulroney defended the American cause at international platforms, followed the American lead on Communism and terrorism, which, fairly or not, earned him the title of "Canada's Minister of American Relations" (Canada and the World Backgrounder 1999). At the United Nations, Canada faithfully supported core American political and security interests. Acting as a part of the traditional trivet of the United States, Britain, and Canada, the Mulroney government staunchly supported American actions directed towards certain Arab states, such as the American air strike on Libya in 1986. In cases where Israel was involved Canada generally followed the American lead, the voting record being second only to the USA in support for Israel among major participants in the debates (Kirton and Lyon 1989).

At the domestic level, however, Mulroney tried to keep the appearance of an even-handed approach regarding the Palestinian-Israeli issue. On certain occasions he either took or had to take a critical stand against Israeli policies in order to avoid a domestic backlash, not only from the pro-Arab groups but from human rights groups and business circles as well. The tensest moments came over the Israeli response to the Intifadah (Palestinian uprising in the occupied territories). The first

Intifadah started in December 1987, triggering a severe response from the Israeli government, television coverage of Isreali soldiers breaking the arm of a teenage rioter being typical of disturbing images of the revolt that slipped into North American living rooms. Israel's "iron fist" policy caused a strong reaction and criticism against it from every segment of Canadian society, including some Jewish organizations allied with the Canadian left or American Reform Judaism (Goldberg and Taras 1989:209). Mulroney's own allegedly pro-Israeli remarks on the issue significantly created rifts between the prime minister and other cabinet members, as well as unelected mandarins at Foreign Affairs.

The most crucial Middle East development during the Mulroney era, however, was the Iraqi invasion of Kuwait in August 1990 — the first test of the "New World Order" ushered in by the collapse of the Soviet Union between 1989 and 1991. The 1991 Gulf War had obviously far reaching consequences, not only for the Middle East but for the global politics as well. Though practically confined to relatively minor action by the navy and air force, Canada's involvement in the war precipitated passionate debate over such oppositional slogans as "No Blood for Oil" and the role of the Parliament in the decision-making process. The majority of Canadians were against Canada's direct involvement in the conflict, while opposition parties insisted that the decision to participate should have been made by the House of Commons. (The basic consensus favoured the continuation of economic sanctions against Iraq under the mandate of the United Nations.) The government's declaration of its readiness to join the war and its determination to use force to drive the Iraqis out of Kuwait "even without the United Nations approval" was considered a significant divergence from the Pearsonian internationalism of the Cold War Era (*House of Commons Debates* 1991), though this question never actually came to the fore, as Mulroney, Clark and others contributed their measure of influence to gaining UN approval of military action in the Persian Gulf. All that said, Canada's participation in the first Gulf War can be regarded as a milestone in Canada's role in international arena, conjoining a "helpful-fixer" role with a more robust involvement in "peacemaking" overseas. The realities of the "New World Order," however, proved rather less certain than any development since the end of the Second World War.

After the Cold War

The emergence of neo-liberalism as the world's dominant economic model after the collapse of the Soviet system led to the institutionalization of the transnational structures of finance and production by large oligopolistic companies and major capitalist states under the rules and regulations of international organizations such as the World Trade Organization (Gill 2000). Increased competition between states made them more sensitive towards the demands of the forces of global markets (Cox 2000). Meanwhile, the implementation of neo-liberal economic policies on developing countries increased poverty in the third world and widened the gap between the rich and the poor within and between countries. The impacts of these developments on Canada's post-Cold War policy rationales were deeper than those of other Western countries because of the asymmetric interdependence of Canada–U.S. relations. The North American Free Trade Agreement (NAFTA) increased Canada's dependence on the United States, turning the American factor into the single most influential determinant in defining Canada's policy rationales.

The end of the Cold War also dissolved the traditional structure of super power control of client states, creating, in all too many cases, a truly morbid picture of disarray and new security challenges for the world. The proliferation of failing or failed states triggered intra-state conflicts, increased immigration and the transnational flow of refugees, boosted transnational terrorism, underground economies, and black markets, and turned them into global insecurities. The changing nature of conflicts required a new notion of multi-dimensional involvement in intra- and inter-state conflicts under the auspices of multilateral institutions. Under the new "cooperative security" approach which superseded the sovereignty rights of states in order to achieve greater security for the people, Canada revised its international role from peacekeeper to peacemaker and peace builder. Although Canadian peacemaking was justified as part and parcel of a "war of values" (Rigby 2001:50), the underlying concern for the government in participating in peacemaking operations was to keep the Canadian voice heard in global issues and to secure a place on the table during the post-conflict negotiations. As Trudeau's Liberal successor, Jean Chrétien, expressed the point, Canada could never be a "bystander" in world affairs (*House of Commons Debates* 1998). As always, it was also believed that, by the virtue of being in a coalition, Canada would be able to influence the outcome of the conflict and have more opportunities on restraining the Americans in taking independent action.

Canada and the Middle East in the Post-Cold War Era

There were three major issue-areas in the Middle East during the immediate post-Cold War period: the Palestinian problem, continuing economic sanctions against Iraq, and Islamist radicalization. The expulsion of almost 1.5 million Yemeni, Egyptian, and Palestinian workers from the oil exporting countries for political reasons during the Gulf War caused unsettling economic and social consequences in the region and well beyond (Abi-Aad and Grenon 1997:171–174). Their homecoming caused a significant loss in revenues for the poorer Arab states and triggered unemployment rates of over 50 percent in countries like Jordan. The oil-rich countries were not better off either; their financial obligations to the United States and other countries that supported the war being a staggering 60 billion dollars in U.S. currency. Instead of addressing the social and economic problems they were facing, such as public debt averaging 40 percent of Gross Domestic Product (GDP) and unemployment averaging 20 percent, the Gulf states increased their military expenditures up to 15 percent of GDP. The failure of Arab leaders to satisfy the needs of their people, over half of whom were under the age of 21, triggered social unrest, buttressed the support for Islamic radicalism, and turned these countries into recruitment grounds for radical organizations. Globalization, with the advanced structures of knowledge and technology, helped to export the regional problems all over the world, both virtually and tangibly, and turned them into global issues.

The Gulf War nonetheless confirmed America's dominance in the Middle East. After the war, partly to ease the critique of the Arab masses on America's double standard in its dealings with the Israelis and the Arabs, and partly to relieve the pressure that friendly Arab leaders were feeling from their public for their support of the United States, President George Bush Senior initiated an international Middle East peace process. The succeeding president Bill Clinton took over the mission of finding a permanent solution to the ongoing Palestinian-Israeli problem which was defined by America's global interests, domestic concerns and historical ties between the Democrats and the American Jewish community. Canada, as usual, had to work around American interests in order to be able to achieve some of its policy objectives on the Middle East.

During the Clinton era, Canada was able to play a relatively constructive role in certain regional issues such as the Middle East Peace Process (MEPP) within the boundaries defined by the United States. When the multilateral working groups were launched in the second phase of the MEPP in 1992, Canada was included the Arms Control and Regional Security Working Group and was chosen as the "gavel holder"[2] of the Refugee Working Group (RWG) by the United States. It has been argued that Canada was pushed into this post by the United States because Canada was considered more likely to be acceptable to Israel, which opposed to the establishment of the refugee group (Sigler 1995–96). Acting within the framework drawn by the United States, Canada was to act as a peace builder to maintain long-term human security in the region. Canada's contributions to the Peace Process were a combination of its traditional functions as a "helpful-fixer," trying to help its country of special relations to achieve its promise of the "New World Order" in the Middle East, and mitigating the opposition from the Arab countries to American policies, an "honest-broker" with an assumed even-handed approach assisting the parties to solve their problems through multilateral negotiations and an internationalist promoting Canadian values of humanitarian aid and moral justification while acting within the limits set by its country of special relations.

Throughout the 1990s, Canada continued to support American views and actions in Middle East related issues at international forums. In the United Nations, Canada strictly followed its "not more than one step apart" rule in casting its vote in issues related to the Middle East in general and Israel in particular, as in April 1997, when Canada abstained on the UN General Assembly resolution calling on Israel to suspend constructions in the settlements in the occupied territories, while the U.S., Israel and Micronesia were the only countries that voted against it. The official explanation for the vote was that the resolution was not "helpful at that time" (Sigler 1997–98). When a serious rift occurred among Canada's special relations countries and the rest of the European allies over the economic sanctions on Iraq, which were imposed by the UN in 1990, Canada tried to find a middle way by submitting a proposal at the UN Security Council urging them to replace the economic sanctions with "smart" ones that would punish the right people and ease the impact that had been borne by civilians. The failure of Foreign Affairs Minister Lloyd Axworthy's April 17, 2000 proposal because of the Anglo-American veto is also significant in showing the actual limits of Canada as a "helpful-fixer" acting within the boundaries set by its country or countries of special relations.

Even-handedness continued to be the main policy rationale. When responding to the Israeli security forces' use of excessive violence and urging Israeli authorities to demonstrate maximum restraint, Palestinians were asked to refrain from increasing the tension. On the issue of the Jewish settlements, Canada's rejection of permanent Israeli control over "occupied territories" was balanced with its silence on the "natural expansion" of the existing settlements. Each vote in the United Nations condemning Israel's use of violence in its dealings with Palestinians was followed by an official statement clarifying that the vote did not mean a change in Canada's position in Israel's right to exist. Canada's insistence on playing the role of the "honest broker with an even-handed approach" in the Palestinian-Israeli issue kept failing to satisfy interested parties both at home and in the region. Following the American lead, Canada's official position was adjusted to the achievement of a political settlement based on Israel's right to exist as a legitimate and independent state within secure borders while recognizing the need for a Palestinian state in "occupied territories."[3]

On issues related to the American-British actions in Iraq, such as the frequent bombings of Iraqi targets, Canada almost always sided with its two "special relations" countries. While France, Russia, and China, along with other Western countries, regularly condemned the bombings, Canada supported the so-called "routine response" actions. In 1998 when the American and British forces launched "Operation Desert Fox" against Iraq, Canada was the only Western country that supported the American position. In spite of the opposition from its own party, as well as from the Bloc Québécois and the New Democratic Party, the Liberal government decided to send HMS *Toronto* to the Persian Gulf.

During the House of Common Debates, Chrétien defended his decision with an argument that Canada could not stand on the sidelines in such a moment when Canada's closest allies, the Americans and the British, had asked Canada support the mission (1998). Again, in February 2000 when the Americans and the British bombed Iraq, Canada was the only western country defending the action. The Prime Minister evaluated the attacks as necessary and said that it was their (the Americans' and British) duty to make sure that Iraq respected the no-flight zone (*CBC News World*, February 17, 2000).

Under the "economy first" approach, the Middle East continued to be a grey area in Canada's foreign policy objectives. Prime Minister Jean Chrétien and Foreign Minister André Ouellet (1993–1996) focused on trade and worked to create new partnerships in Asia, Latin America, and the Eastern Europe. The Middle East, with less than a one percent share in Canada's foreign trade, continued to be economically insignificant for Canada. Canadian Foreign Direct Investment (FDI) in the Middle East remained between 0.2 percent and 0.4 percent throughout the 1990s, whereas the FDI in Latin America jumped up from 10 percent in 1991 to 20.4 percent in 1999 (Statistics Canada). When a choice had to be made between economic interests and human security interests, like the activities of Talisman (a Canadian oil company) in Sudan, human security had been sacrificed in favour of corporate economic interests.

Canada's domestic balances became an important determinant in Canada's policy rationales for the Middle East in the post-Cold War era. In the 1990s, flight from failed or failing states transformed the country's demographics significantly. The most dramatic change was seen in the composition of the Muslim and Jewish communities. According to Citizenship and Immigration Canada, throughout the 1990s, more than half of the refugee claimants (15,000 of 29,291 in 1996) were from Muslim countries. By the end of the decade, the Muslim population in Canada was estimated around 700,000, which made them a "had to be recognized" group in the political arena.

Meanwhile, the Jewish population, reaching 350,000 showed a dramatic change in its background composition. According to the World Jewish Organization, 25 percent of Jews who immigrated to Canada in the 1990s were born in the former Soviet Union while an additional 20 percent were born in Israel. Although there has not been detailed research on the impact of the country of origin of Jewish immigrants on their behavioural patterns, it can be assumed that the new group of Jewish immigrants who were from countries with equally abrasive "protest culture" as their Arab-Muslim counterparts might also have played a role in the radicalization of the inter-communal relations in Canada.

Table 1: Muslim and Jewish Population Growth in Canada: 1981–2000

	Muslim Population	Increase (%)	Jewish Population	Increase (%)
1981	98,165	n/a*	296,425	0.93
1991	253,260	40	318,065	0.93
2000**	700,000	36	350,000	0.91

* The Muslim population was statistically insignificant and included within the "others" category.

** Religious affiliation was not asked after the 1991 census. Figures are estimates gathered from the Jinnah Organization and the World Jewish Congress websites.

The pro-Israeli and pro-Arab groups, both actively trying to create a public opinion favourable for their interpretations of the regional developments, increased the tension in the country and constrained the policy options of elected leaders. Each political statement and decision triggered objection and accusation of bias from either one of the sides. The pro-Arab Middle East Discussion Group criticized Canada's Middle East policy as unhelpfully "tilted towards Israel" and urged the Chrétien government to move closer to the European position on balance and fairness, while Norman Spector, the former Canadian ambassador to Israel, accused the Middle East section of Foreign Affairs of being dominated by a group of "Arabists" who misled the government with false information (Sigler 1996–97). Those supporting ostensibly left-wing ideologies were placed in the anti-Israeli camp, on the assumption that anti-Americanism tainted or coloured their views on the Middle East. Some on the Arab/Muslim side, on the other hand, accused "corporate Canada" of being part of a vast American-Israeli conspiracy and criticized the Canadian media for their alleged control by "Zionist interests." Alert to the importation of ethnic conflicts to the country, Canada, thus, found itself facing a new challenge: finding a balance between the two ethno-religious communities in order to prevent the Arab-Israeli dispute from fragmenting and polarizing Canadian society.

Meanwhile, within the vacuum created at the crossroad of post-Cold War developments, ethnically or religiously motivated underground activities were nourished and turned into global threats. During the 1990s, the Canadian government in cooperation with several other countries increased its efforts to create an international network with a new set of rules to sever the financial and logistic support of global terrorism in Canada and other countries. The Canadian Security Intelligence Service (CSIS), in its counter-terrorism program, identified over 50 organizational targets in Canada that sprang predominantly from the Muslim countries and included groups such as Hezbollah and Hamas (CSIS 2000, 2000–04). Canadian connections of Ramzi Yousef, who was considered the ringleader of the 1993 World Trade Center attack, and Ahmad Ressam, the millennium bomber who was arrested in December 1999 attempting to enter the U.S. from Canada with a carload of explosives, intensified the negotiations between the American and Canadian governments regarding border security. Post-Cold War developments took an abrupt turn on September 11, 2001 changing the rules of global game of politics drastically and leading Canada to reshape its foreign policy rationales for the region once more.

Conclusion

Throughout its existence as an independent state, Canada has set its foreign policy priorities according to its limitations and relied on international organizations to secure a place for itself in the global game of politics. For a long time, the Middle East was not a priority within Canada's foreign policy. It was rather a nuisance to be dealt with in order to keep the harmony among its partners and allies. Although the relative weight of the Middle East in Canada's agenda has increased and become more complicated over the years because of changing domestic and global circumstances, Canada's policy rationales for the region have remained more or less the same.

During the Cold War Era, Canada tried to develop a niche for itself on Middle East related issues within the framework drawn by its country of special relation by adopting the role of "helpful-fixer" and acting under the banner of an honest broker. According to Sigler (1997–98) it was a tit-for-tat strategy in Canada's relationship with the United States. Rather than rebutting American leadership on issues which are important for Americans but relatively marginal for Canadian interests, such as Middle East related issues, Canada provided the U.S. the support it needed in these issues and later used that support as bonus points on issues which directly affect Canadian interests (ibid.).

Global developments and the changing demographics of the country since the end of the Cold War have pushed Canada towards a more active role in the region, which Canada has always insisted on handling with a presumed evenhandedness. Soon Canada's ability to fulfill its role as "helpful-fixer" became harder to achieve because of the failure of American initiatives to bring peace to the Middle East. Canada's image of an "honest broker" with an "even-handed" approach has started to sound more and more unconvincing both at home and in the region. On the domestic front the main issues were balancing the demands of the Arab/Muslim and the Jewish/Israeli groups, which have become more vocal and less compromising, and finding a middle-way between economic and empathic interest groups in defining policy priorities. At the international level, trying to accommodate American interests while promoting Canadian values and building a bridge between its traditional allies were two main challenges.

Post-September 11 developments created a new set of rules in world politics. Canada, like the rest of the world, is faced with new challenges and needs to redefine its policy rationales for the Middle East. Although Canada's role in regional as well as international developments in the coming era is still unknown, there are indications that changing domestic and global realities are pushing for a comprehensive review of Canada's policy rationales for the Middle East. Whether Canada's Middle Eastern policy in this new era will be an authentic expression of what is vitally important to Canadians and reflect Canada's long-term interests under the new circumstances is yet to be seen.

Notes

1 In international relations, a state's foreign policy behaviour is explained by four separate, yet connected, levels of analysis: the systemic level contends that the realities of the international system define the state's foreign policy behaviour. State level analysis relies on the unique societal, governmental, and ideological characteristics of nations as the main determinants of foreign policy. Group level analysis concentrates on the role of certain governmental agencies, such as foreign policy bureaucracy, ethnic or economic interest groups and nongovernmental groups of empathetic nature; the unique skills, beliefs, personalities, and cognitions of leaders come into play at the individual level of analysis.

2 According to Statistics Canada 2001 census, 579,600 identified themselves as Muslim.

3 The complex diplomatic arrangements acknowledged the leadership of America and Russia in the MEPP, entrusting them as the co-chairs of the Steering Group, as well as two of the five working groups. Middle Powers like Canada, the European Union, and Japan were assigned as the "gavel holders" in the remaining three working groups (DFAIT, The Middle East Peace Process 1998).

4 The final draft of UN Resolution 242 omitted "the" from the occupied territories, which provided Israel a legal basis to refuse to withdraw from all the territories it had taken during the 1967 war. Currently only Canada, the United States and Israel refer to the land described in resolution 242 as "occupied territory" rather than "the occupied territory," thereby recognizing Israel's right to keep part of the land.

References

Abi-Aad, Naji and M. Grenon. 1997. *Instability and Conflict in the Middle East: People, Petroleum and Security Threats*. New York: St. Martin's Press.

American Petroleum Institute. *Fact sheets: oil imports*. http://www.apiinformation.org/ fact_sheets/ oil_imports.html (7 March 8, 2003).

Bercuson, David J. 1985. *Canada and the Birth of Israel: A Study in the Canadian Foreign Policy*. Toronto: University of Toronto Press.

Bothwell, Robert. 1998. *The Big Chill: Canada and the Cold War.* Concord, ON: Irwin Publishing.

Burton, B. E.1991. "Of Mice and Monsignors: The Press and Canadian Policy towards the Middle East," *Canadian Journal of Communications* 16(3/40) http://www.wlu.ca/~wwwpress/jrls/cjc/backissues/16.3/burton.html (13 November, 2001).

Canada and the World Backgrounder. 1999. *The Helpful Fixer.* 65(1). Retrieved November 2, 2002 from Academic Search Elite database (item 2647493). Available from the University of Winnipeg Library Website http://www.cybrary.uwinnipeg.ca/resources/db/index.cfm.

Debates of the House of Commons of Canada (Hansard). January 1991. 17027-17562.

Canadian Peacebuilding Construction Committee (CPCC). 1997. *Peacebuilding Census.* http://www.cpcc.Ottawa.on.ca> (October 12, 2002).

Clark, Joe. 1997. "Why we must not abandon Canada's activist foreign policy." *Canadian Speeches.* 11(4).p 12–16.

Cohen, Andrew. 1995. "Canada in the world: the return of the national interest." *Behind the Headlines* 52:4. Cited in *The Politics of Canadian Foreign Policy,* Kim Richard Nossal. 1997. Scarborough, Ontario: Prentice-Hall Canada.

Canadian Security Intelligent Service (CSIS). 2000. *International Terrorism: The Threat to Canada.* Perspectives, Report #2000/04.

Center for Defence Information. *Terrorism Project.* http://www.cdi.org/terrorism.network.cfm (14 April 2003).

Cox, Robert W. 2000. "Political Economy and World Order: Problems of Power and Knowledge at the Turn of the Millennium." In *Political Economy and the Changing Global Order,* eds. Richard Stubbs and Geoffrey R. D. Underhill. Don Mills, Ontario: Oxford University Press.

Delvoie, Louis A. 1997. *Canada and Egypt: From Antagonism to Partnership.* Occasional Paper Series, Centre For International Relations: Queen's University.

Department of External Affairs, Canada. *DEA 5475-CD-2-40C, Pearson to St Laurent, 1692,* 17 November 1947. Cited in *The Domestic Battleground: Canada and the Arab-Israeli Conflict,* eds. David Taras and David H. Goldberg. 1989. Montreal: McGill-Queen's University Press.

——. Canada .1967. *Documents on Canada's External Relations,* Vol.1:1909-1918. Ottawa, Queen's Printer.

Department of Foreign Affairs and International Trade (DFAIT). 2003. *A Dialogue on Foreign Policy*. http://www.foreign-policy-dialogue.ca (2 February, 2003).

——. 2002. *History*, http://www.dfait-maeci.gc.ca (17 October, 2002).

——. 1998. *The Middle East Peace Process: Canadian Policy*. http://www.dfait-maeci.gc.ca (March 9, 2002)

——.1995. *Canada in the World*. Ottawa: Canada Communications Group.

Foreign Policy for Canadians. 1970. 6 vols. Ottawa: Department of Supply and Services.

The Gallup Poll of Canada, *The Gallup Report*. Released on September 7, 1957; December 22, 1973; February 22, 1988. Toronto: Gallup Canada, Inc.

Gill, Stephen. 2000."Knowledge, Politics, and Neo-Liberal Political Economy." In *Political Economy and the Changing Global Order*, eds. Richard Stubbs and Geoffrey R. D. Underhill. Don Mills, Ontario: Oxford University Press.

Goldberg, David H., and D. Taras. 1989. "Collision Course: Joe Clark, Canadian Jews and the Palestinian Uprising." In *The Domestic Battleground: Canada and the Arab-Israeli Conflict*, eds. David Taras and David H. Goldberg. Montreal: McGill-Queen's University Press.

Granatstein, J. L., and N. Hillmer. 1999. *Prime Ministers: Ranking Canada's Leaders*. Toronto, Harper Collins Publishers.

Head, Ivan L. 1972."The Foreign Policy of the New Canada," *Foreign Affairs* 50(2):237–252.

Hoff, Joan. 2001. "How the U.S. Sold Its Soul to Win the Cold War?" *International Journal*. 56(3):373–390.

International Energy Agency. http://www.iea.org (7 March 8, 2003).

Ismael, Tareq Y. 1976. "Canada and the Middle East." In *Canada and the Third World*, eds. Peyton Lyon and Tareq Ismael, Toronto:Macmillian.

——. 1994. *Canada and the Middle East: the Foreign Policy of a Client State*. Calgary, Alberta: Detselig Enterprises.

Jannah Organization. Can*adian Muslim Population Statistics*. http://www.jannah.org/popstatistics/canadamuslims.html (9 May, 2002).

Japan Information Network. *Energy fact book*. http://www.jinjapan.org (7 March, 2003).

Kirton, John, and P. Lyon. 1989. "Perceptions of the Middle East in the Department of External Affairs and Mulroney's Policy 1984-1988." In *The Domestic Battleground: Canada and the Arab-Israeli Conflict*, eds.

David Taras and David H. Goldberg. 1989. Montreal: McGill-Queen's University Press.

Lipsey, Richard G. 1985. "Canada and the United States: the Economic Dimension." In *Canada and the United States: Enduring Friendship, Persistent Stress*. Eds. Charles F. Doran and John H. Sigler. Englewood Cliffs, NJ: Prentice-Hall. Cited in *The Politics of Canadian Foreign Policy*, Kim Richard Nossal. 1997. Scarborough, Ontario: Prentice-Hall Canada.

Munich Conference on Security Policy. 2001. http://www.securityconference.de (30 August, 2002).

Munton, Don, and John Kirton. 1992. *Canadian Foreign Policy: Selected Cases*. Scarborough, Ontario: Prentice-Hall Canada.

Noble, P. 1981. "Where Angels Fear to Tread: Canada and the Status of Palestinians 1967–1981." Cited in Jack A. Zubrzycki. 1986. *Canadian Public Opinion and Government Policy Toward the Middle East*, Toronto: NECEF Publications.

Nossal, Kim R. 1997. *The Politics of Canadian Foreign Policy*, Scarborough, Ontario: Prentice-Hall Canada.

——. 1998. "Foreign policy for Wimps," *Ottawa Citizen*, 23 April, A19.

Nye, Joseph, Jr. 1990. *Bound to Lead: The Changing Nature of American Power*. New York: Basic Books.

Rigby, Vincent. 2001. "The Canadian Forces and Human Security: A Redundant or Relevant Military." In *Canada Among Nations 2001: The Axworthy Legacy*. Don Mills, Ontario: Oxford University Press.

Saideman, Stephen M. 2002. "The Power of the Small: The Impact of Ethnic Minorities on Foreign Policy." *SAIS Review*, 22(2):93–105.

Scott, F. R. 1932. "The Permanent Bases of Canadian Foreign Policy." *Foreign Affairs* 10:627. Cited in *The Politics of Canadian Foreign Policy*, Kim Richard Nossal. 1997. Scarborough, Ontario: Prentice-Hall Canada.

Sigler, John H. 1995–96; 1996–97; 1997–98. *Conflict in the Middle East: Canada and the Middle East*. http://www.ulaval.ca/iqhei/circa/cm95-96/C_Sigler_f.html (12 October, 2002).

Special Representative of the Government of Canada and Ambassador-at-Large. 1980. *Final Report of the Special Representative of the Government of Canada Respecting the Middle East and North Africa*. Ottawa.

Statistics Canada. 2001. *Canadian Economic Observer*. http://www.statcan.ca (15 November 2001).

——. *Population by Religion: 1981 and 1991 Censuses*. http://www.statcan.ca (15 November 2001).

——. *Historical Statistics of Canada, 11-516-XIE.* http://www.statcan.ca (15 November 2001).

Stein, Janice G. 1977. "Canadian Foreign Policy in the Middle East after the October War." *Social Praxis* 4(3–4):272. Cited in *The Domestic Battleground: Canada and the Arab-Israeli Conflict*, eds. David Taras and David H. Goldberg. 1989. Montreal: McGill-Queen's University Press.

Taras, David. 1989. "From Passivity to Politics: Canada's Jewish Community and Political Support for Israel" in *The Domestic Battleground: Canada and the Arab-Israeli Conflict*, eds. David Taras and David H. Goldberg. 1989. Montreal: McGill-Queen's University Press.

Tauber, Eliezer. 2002. *Personal Policy Making: Canada's Role in the Adoption of the Palestine Partition Resolution*. Westport, Connecticut: Greenwood Press.

Terrorism Research Center. 2003. *International Terrorist Organizations.* http://www.terrorism.com (9 January, 2003).

World Jewish Congress. http://www.wjc.org.il (9 May, 2002).

External Affairs and International Trade. 1991. *Foreign Policy Themes and Priorities: 1991–92 Update*. GC Catalogue Number: E2-130/1992E.

13

Ottawa, the Ottawa Convention, and the War on Terrorism

Lisa L. Ferrari

After becoming Minister of Foreign Affairs in 1996, Lloyd Axworthy sought to redefine Canada's security concerns, arguing that the conflation of "security" and "threat to the state" encouraged governments to ignore real obstacles to worldwide peace and stability. Axworthy instead emphasized that security should be measured by what it could provide day-to-day for individual persons. That is, a secure society would not only be free from military threat, but could also protect its citizens from a myriad of other threats (disease, instability, physical harm, poverty, the effects of environmental degradation, etc.), which Axworthy described as matters of "human security" (Axworthy 1997). This concept of human security takes "the human being as the referent object for defining security" ("Human Security Paradigm Shift" 1999:1; see also Irwin 2001:5). As part of this focus on human security, Axworthy committed Canada as a major player in creating the 1997 *Convention on the Prohibition of the Use, Stockpiling, Production and Transfer of Anti-Personnel Mines and on their Destruction*, now commonly known as the Ottawa Convention.

Canada has been a major proponent of international mine action since then, even without being the largest financial donor to the cause. In 1997, Prime Minister Jean Chrétien established the Canadian Landmine Fund (CLF), funded with $100 million in federal monies over five years. The CLF is jointly governed by the Department of Foreign Affairs and International Trade (DFAIT), Canadian International Development Agency (CIDA), Department of National Defence (DND), and Industry Canada. The involvement of these several agencies reflects the federal government's broad-ranging interest in the land mine issue. In addition, "to coordinate this effort, and to signal the priority it places on these efforts," the federal government created a special ambassadorship concerned exclusively with "all matters pertaining to the implementation of the [Ottawa] Convention" ("Canada's Mine Action Policies" 2002).

The Ottawa Convention has been only one manifestation of Canada's commitment to human security. Through DFAIT, the federal government sponsors programs addressing the concerns of internally displaced persons, children in wartime, and the physical protection of civilians during wartime. Canada supports the Rome Statute and the creation of the International Criminal Court. DFAIT sponsors and funds policy research on a variety of human security issues, including conflict prevention, trafficking in firearms and drugs, and violent conflict fueled by diamonds. Through its Corporate Social Responsibility program, DFAIT works with businesses to create non-binding standards for promoting and respecting human rights in the workplace. Many of Canada's human security programs are joint initiatives under the auspices of the United Nations, and Canada sponsors many UN resolutions on human security and human rights issues.[1] However, there is evidence that the federal government is now backing away from its financial commitment to human security programs (Mack and Rohlfs 2003; Axworthy 2003).

Recent world events suggest that Canada's concern with human security is timely and appropriate. The September 11, 2001 terrorist attacks on the United States validate Axworthy's vision of changing global security. The events of September 11 were not primarily the result of military insecurity on the part of either the U.S. or al-Qaida, although Osama bin Laden has long criticized U.S. military presence in Saudi Arabia. Rather, the attacks seem to have been prompted by threats to human security: ongoing sanctions against Iraq, incursions on traditional culture in other Muslim societies, gross, and apparently exploitative, economic disparities between Western and Muslim societies, and other offenses against Muslims as a group. For example, in a videotaped message broadcast on October 7, 2001 by the Qatari television network Aljazeera, bin Laden refers to America and its allies as "infidels" in the "land of Mohammad," and as "the modern world's symbol of paganism." He also mentions the effects of economic sanctions against Iraq and of violence against Palestinians, Afghanistan, and Iraq as evidence of American evil ("Bin Laden's Statement" 2001). If we take bin Laden's statement at face value, the September 11 attacks were motivated in large part by anger over Western (primarily American) threats against the religious and bodily integrity of persons in the Islamic world. Furthermore, poverty and oppression made young men from the Arab world willing recruits to al-Qaida (Sachs 2001; Friedman 2001).

The threat of terrorism is also clearly a measure of Americans' human security.[2] Subsequent attacks, such as the October 2002, bombing of a Bali nightclub popular with Australian tourists, suggest that Americans are not the only group whose security in day-to-day activities is at significant risk. While the United States is clearly the focal point of al-Qaida's hostility, other Westerners are not immune from attack.[3] Thus, Axworthy correctly identified the potential for human insecurity to disrupt international stability.

As Kresl has argued in this volume, while U.S. policy always has an impact on Canada, that effect is greater after September 11 than ever before (see also Hart and Tomlin 2002:59). Ironically, the events that most spectacularly confirm the importance of human security to global security appear to have sapped resources formerly devoted to human security programs and may undermine one of Axworthy's highest-profile human security campaigns, the eradication of anti-personnel land mines. Although there has been no official change in Canadian policy on land mines since September 11, Canada's new commitment to the war on terrorism has had a clear impact on Canada's security priorities and thus on the depth and credibility of Canada's commitment to human security, including the land mine ban. This impact has taken two forms. First, the new foreign policy demands of the post-September 11 world have meant a re-allotment by the federal government of finite material resources, including the military, human, financial, and other tangible factors necessary to undertake foreign security policy. Second, support for the war on terrorism has affected Canada's allocation of conceptual resources, including all of the legal, ideological, normative, and other intangible factors that can be brought to bear on a security policy initiative. Specifically, Canada has begun to defend the letter rather than the spirit of the Ottawa Convention. This trend inhibits the development of customary international law in accordance with Convention provisions, and thus limits the Convention as a tool for promoting human security. This analysis will address the two types of resources in turn, with particular emphasis on conceptual resources.

Material Resources

Unquestionably, the September 11 attacks have diverted significant Canadian resources to combating terrorism. From the morning of September 11, 2001, Canadian citizens poured out material and moral support for their neighbours to the South. The federal government quickly followed suit, pledging many forms of assistance, including military, for an attack on al-Qaida and the Taliban in Afghanistan. Canada also revamped substantial areas of its policies and practices in international trade, border control, and domestic civil liberties. Mingus, Prokop, Smith, and Plaw have treated a number of those issues elsewhere in this volume. Most recently, while it refused to participate in the 2003 attack on Iraq and clearly distressed the Bush Administration with this lack of support, Canada did not fully disengage its material resources from the Iraq war, leaving a handful of support personnel and equipment in place.

The Canadian Forces commitment to the war in Afghanistan, Operation APOLLO, was the fourth largest in the world. At its height, the Canadian military contribution included nearly 3,000 personnel, including a headquarters at MacDill Air Force Base in Tampa, a Naval Task group (six warships carrying Sea King helicopters), a Battle Group of about 800 persons working in the Kandahar region of Afghanistan, a Tactical Airlift Detachment to move cargo and persons, and "special operations support" as part of Joint Task Force Two (JTF 2) (Department of National Defence 2002). While the Canadian presence is no longer at its height, as of this writing Canada still has nearly 1,000 personnel in Afghanistan, naval vessels in the Arabian Gulf region, and significant forces devoted to surveillance and transport (Department of National Defence 2003).

In order to support Operation APOLLO and the security infrastructure necessary to prevent terrorism, the 2001 federal budget allotted DND "an additional $1.2 billion through to fiscal year 2006–07" (Department of National Defence 2002). However, provisions for human security programs are notably absent from the 2001 and 2003 budgets. Although Foreign Minister Graham (2002) told representatives of the Human Security Network that "Canada's commitment to a people-centred approach to security policy not only survives but becomes stronger with time," the term "human security" is neither prominently mentioned in the budget nor mentioned at all in the summary documents made available by the federal government. That is particularly striking in the 2001 budget, which has been characterized as "predominantly a security budget" (Boag 2001).[4]

To the consternation of the Bush Administration, Canada declined to participate in hostilities against Iraq in Spring 2003, arguing that weapons inspections were succeeding and should be given more time. While the U.S. government officially announced its "disappointment" with this choice, Canada did not fully disengage from the Iraqi enterprise, allowing the few Canadian Forces personnel serving with U.S. or British forces to maintain their positions throughout the Iraq war (Brown 2003).

Operation APOLLO, increased border and trade security, and even the minimal involvement in Iraq came at a price. Even though Canada has recently experience a federal budget surplus, budget allotments are best understood as a zero-sum game because a government's financial resources are finite. The likelihood of one budget line being increased without a corresponding decrease somewhere else is very low. The increase in funding for fighting terrorism means losses elsewhere in the budget, even within DND. Although mine action enjoyed a significant funding increase in the 2001–2002 budget, that increase evaporated in the subsequent allocation of funds.

Canada's 1997 financial commitment of $100 million to CLF over five years ran out in 2002. Activists inside and outside Canada advocated continued federal funding at least at existing levels ("Report Shows" 2002). In the 2003 federal budged, although it set the overall International Assistance Envelope to grow by 8 percent annually, Ottawa allotted only $72 million over the next five years to fund CLF, a decrease of nearly 30 percent from the previous allocation (Department of Finance 2002).[5] It is nearly unthinkable that Canada would cut support altogether for the promotion of a treaty so closely associated with Ottawa, but future funding certainly is at risk. There is no evidence that land mine action has been specifically targeted for unique budget cuts. More likely, its losses are the effects of a budget-wide constriction of resources available to agencies and programs not directly active in executing the war on terrorism. Nonetheless, the 2003 budget cuts and priorities suggest to Axworthy and others that "Canada's commitment to human security [has been] downgraded" substantially (Axworthy 2003; see also Mack and Rohlfs 2003). That approach to human security may actually feed the conditions that inspire terror and unrest, and thus run counter to the goals of the war on terrorism (Axworthy 2002).

Conceptual Resources

In addition, Canada's position regarding U.S. policy and practice may entail significant costs in conceptual resources for the campaign to eradicate land mines globally. Canadian commitments of capital, personnel, and materiel are not the only measures of Canada's support for the Ottawa Convention and the war on terrorism. In promoting each of these policy programs, Canada's input is arguably more valuable for its symbolic and rhetorical, rather than its material, contributions to the conduct of international relations. For example, while it is not the largest material supporter of worldwide mine action, Canada's leadership role lent prominence and credibility to the campaign to ban anti-personnel land mines. The relevance of the war on terrorism to Canada's promotion of global human security can be understood by answering two related questions. First, is "hot" war itself incompatible in principle with the promotion of human security? Second, according to what rationale will Canada frame its support both of the land mine ban and of the war on terrorism? This section will consider how Canada has brought its conceptual resources to bear on the war on terrorism.

War and Human Security

Fighting a war involves material resources, but the rationale for entering and continuing the war is built from conceptual resources. While some observers have questioned whether the tactics inherent to *any* military action could be consistent with a policy emphasis on human security, others have found the two forms of security interest to be compatible in principle. If the former set of observers is to be believed, then Canada's participation in the war on terrorism is clearly a betrayal of its commitment to promoting human security. Even if the latter observers are correct, however, we must still ask whether this *particular* use of military force (i.e., in Afghanistan, with the specific tactics employed) compromises Canada's commitment to human security in any way.

In an essay published just before the first anniversary of the September 11 attacks, Lloyd Axworthy (2002) writes,

> Military responses feed the anger, poverty, rhetoric—the climate of grievance—which create and sustain terrorist intentions.... I see the need to depart from conventional wisdoms and seek out new navigational guides to aid in the search for security. Not to replace the template of basic protection of national security, but to layer onto it new responses to global threats and risks which don't lend themselves to flexing biceps and going it alone.

Axworthy argues that the military response to terrorism "is leading inexorably into further crisis, expanding the orbit of danger and accelerating the cycles of violence" (Axworthy 2002). That is, terrorism is a product of human insecurity, and military action does nothing to ameliorate that insecurity. Even worse, by using a military response to terrorism, the U.S. and its allies exacerbate the very problem they seek to eradicate.

However, not all observers agree with Axworthy's assessment. Notably, Foreign Minister Bill Graham has clearly rejected the claim that the war on terrorism has shaken Canada's commitment to promoting human security. As he observes, the "attacks demonstrated in the most graphic and devastating way that armies alone cannot defend us against new threats nor provide us with complete security" (Graham 2002).

Armies alone may be insufficient, Graham says, but that need not mean armies are irrelevant or counterproductive to the promotion of human security. Graham continues, "There is no contradiction between the promotion of human security and the maintenance of national security. It is a common misconception that greater security can be ensured by compromising our respect for human rights.... [I]n combination with military, intelligence and law enforcement efforts, the human security agenda is a crucial dimension of the broader response to terrorism." Thus, Graham is arguing that military action is a credible tool for promoting human security. From that perspective, Canada is not *prima facie* compromising its human security commitment by using its military as an instrument of foreign policy. It remains only to determine whether this particular use of military force is consistent with human security goals. To that end, it is valuable to consider Canada's stated goals in joining the war on terrorism, especially as contrasted with U.S. goals.

Goals of the War on Terrorism

United States

The U.S. responded to the September 11 attacks with moral outrage. From the very first, the U.S. government described the situation as an apocalyptic struggle of morality against immorality. In his September 11, 2001 address to the nation, President George W. Bush said that "today our nation saw evil" and repeatedly referred to the attacks and their perpetrators as evil (Bumiller and Sanger 2001:A4). He also quoted from the Bible.[6] Furthermore, the President said that the U.S. response to the attacks would be a "crusade," though the administration quickly stopped using this term because of its offensiveness to Muslims (Apple 2001a). The call for a war on terrorism arose from a mood of righteous anger, including a particularly American brand of "frontier justice."[7]

In terms of foreign policy, the U.S. articulated very broad goals in conducting a "war on terrorism." Three days after the attacks, Secretary of State Colin Powell remarked that after assembling a case against Osama bin Laden and al-Qaida as the September 11 culprits, "we will go after that group, that network, and those who have harbored, supported and aided that network, to rip the network up.... When we're through with that network, we will continue with a global assault against terrorism in general" (as quoted in Apple 2001b). American security, whether understood in human or national terms, had been grievously compromised, and the U.S. government claimed for itself nearly unrestricted leeway in reestablishing that security.

The U.S. rationale for attacking Iraq was equally broad ranging. Citing its fear of Iraqi cooperation with al-Qaida, especially regarding weapons of mass destruction, the Bush Administration demanded stricter accounting by the United Nations of Iraq's compliance with post-Gulf War disarmament resolutions. While some of its members, notably France and Russia, were hesitant about U.S. allegations, the Security Council passed Resolution 1441 on November 8, 2002, warning that Iraq "will face serious consequences as a result of its continued violations of its obligations" under previous Resolutions (UN Security Council 2002:5). At various times in the run-up to the hostilities, the U.S. cited Resolution 1441, Iraqi cooperation with al-Qaida, and humanitarian regime change as grounds for attacking Iraq. Shortly after the war began, John D. Negroponte, U.S. Ambassador to the UN, articulated five goals for the invasion. "Eliminat[ing] Iraq's terrorist infrastructure" was third on the list (Negroponte 2003).[8] In all of its arguments, the Bush Administration repeatedly fell back on the moralistic rhetoric and reasoning it had used to justify attacking Afghanistan. Notably, President Bush quoted Elie Wiesel, a holocaust survivor and Nobel laureate, "We have a moral obligation to intervene where evil is in control. Today, that place is Iraq" (Bush 2003).

While the U.S. rhetoric has often mentioned "justice," the context emphasizes justice's role in meting out punishment rather than in establishing order. For example, the Department of State defines U.S. counterterrorism policy as comprising four goals:

1. Make no concessions to terrorists and strike no deals.
2. Bring terrorists to justice for their crimes.
3. Isolate and apply pressure on countries that sponsor terrorism to force them to change their behaviour.
4. Bolster the counterterrorism capabilities of those countries that work with the U.S. and require assistance (Department of State 2002).

Examining American rhetoric, it is difficult to identify the distinction between rule of law and rule of will. In the Iraqi case, the Bush Administration claimed to be upholding UN Security Council Resolution 1441; but the level of Security Council resistance to the U.S.'s interpretation of 1441 suggests that Washington was using its own standards, not internationally agreed upon ones, to determine the appropriateness of military intervention. In fact, non-Americans questioned the legality of the war and feared U.S. behaviour would undermine the UN system (e.g. "Former UN Head" 2003; "Unsanctioned War" 2003; Graham 2003). Furthermore, given the Bush Administration's dismissal of millions-strong worldwide antiwar protests on February 15, 2003, it is all the more plausible that the U.S.'s claims to seek multilateral support and consensus were insincere (see Shribman 2003, "Trouble at home" 2003, "What now?" 2003). In formulating its war on terrorism, the U.S. has placed great emphasis on finding its enemies and pressuring them to behave as the U.S. considers civilized, but has offered few standards, besides its own judgment, for assessing the appropriateness of this response.

Canada

On October 8, 2001, Chrétien announced that Canadian Forces would support U.S.-led hostilities against Afghanistan. Shortly thereafter, he became the first Prime Minister in fifty years to send Canadian ground troops into combat. Canada stated its goals for the campaign in a much less flamboyant, moralistic rhetoric than had the U.S. Repeatedly, the Canadian government characterized its involvement as intended to promote security, protect Canadian values, and bolster rule of law (e.g. Department of National Defence 2002). For example, one Canadian newspaper editorial expressed frustration with Prime Minister Chrétien's lack of vigour in supporting the campaign, especially in contrast to the rhetorical stances of British Prime Minister Tony Blair, then Mayor of New York Rudy Giuliani, and President Bush ("We're Right" 2001). The point here is not that Chrétien annoys some Canadians, but that Canada's explanation of its wartime goals is notably different from that of the U.S. and its chief ally in Afghanistan and Iraq, Britain.

While Canada's goals are nonetheless compatible with the U.S.'s, the difference in rhetoric is telling. The Canadian rhetoric indicates a confidence in international agreements and institutions to mitigate rogues' potential to harm the international system. Various government press releases emphasize the importance of UN oversight and NATO authorization for the mission to Afghanistan, in addition to solidarity with the U.S. In a March 2002, CBC interview, the Prime Minister noted that Canada's minimum commitment to the campaign in Afghanistan would be to restore a stable government to that country (Chrétien 2002).

For similar reasons, Canada declined to participate in the 2003 war in Iraq. The Chrétien government emphasized the successes of UN weapons inspection teams, and the likelihood of ongoing success ("Chrétien restates" 2003). On March 17, Chrétien announced that Canada would not be part of the war effort unless the conflict was specifically authorized by a UN resolution (Brown 2003). Perhaps to mollify the Bush Administration, Canada did not withdraw troops or materiel that were already integrated into U.S. military operations in the Persian Gulf region. Thus, 31 Canadian Forces personnel, three transport aircraft, and three Canadian ships remained in the region and continued their missions (Brown 2003; Bailey 2003; "Canadians could serve" 2003). Although Chrétien publicly called on Canadians to "respect the decision of the Americans," Washington clearly regarded Canadian policy as a betrayal and snubbed Canada a few months later when Bush cancelled a planned visit to Ottawa, citing war-related duties at home (Brown 2003; "Bush Postpones" 2003).

Canada's emphasis on establishment of order, promotion of rule of law, and heeding international institutions illuminates a Canadian vision of the international system promoted by human security policy, and especially through legal instruments such as the Ottawa Convention. It also reflects existing goals and interests of Canadian foreign policy (Beal 2002). That is, Canada's stated goals in participating in the war on terrorism appear entirely consonant with Canada's overall human security approach.

If fighting is potentially compatible with Canada's human security agenda, and given Canada's refusal to participate in the 2003 war on Iraq regardless of that potential compatibility, why might the war on terrorism threaten Canada's promotion of the Ottawa Convention? The problem lies in the genesis of international law.

Ramifications for International Law

The Relationship between Treaty and Custom

Canada's conduct in the war on terrorism and its response to others' conduct may have ramifications for international law associated with the Ottawa Convention. Scholars have often assumed that treaty and custom are discrete categories among the sources of international law.[9] However, that is not necessarily the case. States may recognize differing sources of obligation for the same point of law. That is, a particular rule of international law may ultimately be binding through treaty for some states and through custom for others. In fact, some treaty law contradicts custom, and often has the unstated purpose of generating custom, even among non-signatory states (Gamble 1998:79, 81–82). Scholars report that an international customary norm against use of anti-personnel land mines is emerging since the Ottawa Convention opened for signature in 1997 (e.g. Rutherford 2001; Benesch et al. 1999). Thus, Nelson (2003) comments that use of antipersonnel land mines by either the U.S. or Iraq, both of which remain outside the Ottawa Convention, would be of "questionable legal status." Even without universal consent of states, international custom would have the force of law, and would define the international community's expectations for state behaviour.

Such a customary norm would be entirely in keeping with Canada's goals in promoting the land mine ban. Canada's rationale for promoting the ban has been that antipersonnel land mines are inhumane, target civilians, remain dangerous even after hostilities have ceased, and interfere with normal human activities such as farming, building basic infrastructure, and traveling (e.g. *Reaffirming the Commitment* 2001). That is, Canada promoted the ban to change policy and behaviour, not merely to collect signatures on a document. Presumably, Canada would like states to become parties to the Ottawa Convention as an indication of their willingness to alter policy. If, however, the motivation for the ban were truly a commitment to human security, then ultimately Canada would be most interested in having states recognize the ban as legally binding, regardless of whether the obligation arises from custom or treaty. As Member of Parliament Bill Blaikie observed, "if one thinks something is wrong enough to have a treaty about it, one should think it is wrong when it is used" (House of Commons 2003b). In that case, an important purpose of the treaty is to promote compatible custom.

The Canadian government has clearly stated its desire to "establish a new international norm against [anti-personnel land mines]" (Charles 1997). Yet, According to Defence Minister Art Eggleton, should American troops have begun to deploy land mines in Afghanistan, Canadian troops could have worked alongside them provided the Canadians were not "involved in putting [the mines] in place" (House of Commons 2002). That hardly seems the sort of behaviour to encourage the growth of customary law banning land mine use. Instead, it suggests that parties to the treaty must behave one way, but are mistaken to expect non-parties to follow suit. That is, the Canadian government's position ignores and even discredits the very process by which customary international law emerges.

Since joining the war on terrorism, the Canadian government has taken positions on U.S. military action, even when Canada has refused to join that action, which seem inconsistent with the norms emerging from the Ottawa Convention. Especially in its reactions to U.S. tactics, Canada has reinforced a dichotomy between treaty and custom regarding the land mine ban. It is yet unclear whether the U.S. deployed antipersonnel land mines in Afghanistan or Iraq. At the outbreak of hostilities there, Afghanistan was one of the most heavily mined countries in the world. Thus, while a number of mine-related injuries were reported from Afghanistan, that is not, in itself, evidence of U.S. mine use. In the case of Iraq, even the U.S. military command has admitted uncertainty as to whether antipersonnel land mines were used by U.S. troops. When asked in a press conference whether U.S. forces were using such mines, Brigadier General Vincent Brooks, Deputy Director of Operations for the U.S. Central Command, replied:

> I don't know specifically what's happening down inside of tactical units. We do have some land mines that are available to us, like the Claymore antipersonnel mine, that's a put-in-place-and-remove type of mine. We take it with us, and we use it for protection.

> So, yes, we do have them. But in terms of specific tactical actions, I don't know where they're being used and where they're not (Brooks 2003).

In other words, the U.S. cannot or will not deny using land mines in Iraq. While the Canadian government has not responded specifically to potential U.S. land mine use in Iraq, the Prime Minister has stated that it would not be illegal for the U.S. forces to deploy land mines in Afghanistan because, "the Americans did not sign that treaty" (House of Commons 2001c). Presumably, that rationale holds for U.S. action in Iraq, as well. Thus, Canada has clearly excused U.S. action contradictory to the customary law that signatories might reasonably expect to develop around the Ottawa Convention.

While there is some ambiguity about whether antipersonnel land mines were even used by U.S. forces, there is no question as to whether those forces deployed cluster bombs, a related type of weapon, in Afghanistan and Iraq. Canada's handling of this fact highlights the impediments inherent to current Canadian rhetoric and practice for the development of customary international law. Insofar as it reinforces that dichotomy between treaty and custom regarding issues related to the Ottawa Convention, Canada undermines the Convention's human security goals.

The Problem of Cluster Bombs

The use of cluster bombs is one of the critical issues inhibiting the development of customary law surrounding the Ottawa Convention. Although there has been no clear evidence of U.S. anti-personnel land mine use during the wars in Afghanistan and Iraq, American forces have unquestionably deployed cluster munitions. These munitions are fragmentation bombs, usually delivered by air and designed to explode upon impact with the ground. A relatively high failure rate has meant that many bombs remain unexploded until triggered by direct human contact, causing the bombs to function like land mines (Jenkins 2001). In many cases, only a light touch is necessary for detonation. The explosive force of a cluster bomb greatly exceeds that of an anti-personnel land mine.[10]

Land mine activists are divided as to whether cluster bombs should be considered as a separate category of weapon from anti-personnel mines. The most obvious distinction between the two weapons is that land mines are designed to lie in wait and explode upon human contact, whereas cluster bombs function that way only when they do not operate properly. That is, cluster bombs behave like land mines only when the bombs fail to operate as designed. Regardless of how easily mines and cluster bombs can be equated, however, an important similarity remains. That is, the harm done by land mines comes about because they are unexploded ordnance, not because they were *designed* to be unexploded ordnance. Their function, rather than the intention of their creators, is the source of their undesirable traits. The same is true of cluster bombs. Both munitions have a significant likelihood of creating the human security threats that led Canada to seek a land mine ban in the first place. In fact, Canada sought to include cluster bombs in the Ottawa Convention, but was outvoted (House of Commons 2003a; 2003b). Thus, the Canadian government's current emphasis on the differences between the two weapons seems contradictory to Canada's stated foreign policy priorities.

U.S. forces clearly deployed cluster munitions in both Afghanistan and Iraq (Leahy 2003; Human Rights Watch 2003). However, the Prime Minister and his Cabinet vigorously defended the use of cluster munitions in both Afghanistan and Iraq, using three major lines of argumentation. First, the government argued that Americans, not Canadians, would actually be deploying the bombs. For example, Defence Minister Art Eggleton responded thus to a question in the House of Commons:

> **Ms. Francine Lalonde (Mercier, BQ)**: But giving one's support [to America and the international coalition against terrorism] does not mean giving a blank cheque. It means taking part in the debate and expressing one's views, one's way of seeing the situation. Unfortunately, this is not what the Prime Minister is doing.
>
> Does the Prime Minister not realize that he is caving in, that he is letting them use cluster bombs, that he is abdicating his responsibility as a head of state?

> **Hon. Art Eggleton (Minister of National Defence, Lib.)**: Mr. Speaker, with respect to allowing the use of cluster bombs, Canada is not using cluster bombs. We are not involved in the bombing of Afghanistan (House of Commons 2001c).

Earlier, Eggleton had defended the U.S.'s tactics and goals, and commented that "[The U.S.] will continue to use whatever weapons they feel are necessary to bring about [the destruction of al-Qaida and the Taliban]" (House of Commons 2001b).

Second, the government argued that use of cluster bombs had not been banned under treaty law. In continuing the remarks quoted above, Minister Eggleton said, "The United States is using [cluster bombs], but they are lawful to use. They are not banned in the same way that anti-personnel land mines are banned" (House of Commons 2001c). One week earlier, the Prime Minister had stated, "There is a war on right now, and these bombs are not illegal under international treaties. That is why we have no reason and no way to protest at this time, because this is part of the arsenal of war" (House of Commons 2001a).

Third, the government tried to point out technological differences between cluster bombs and land mines that would render the comparison moot. While there are plausible arguments along these lines, the government did a poor job of presenting them. Primarily, Eggleton and the Prime Minister repeated that the main evil of anti-personnel land mines is their persistent threat to civilians, even decades after a war is over (House of Commons 2001a; 2001c). In fact, that is a similarity, rather than a distinction, between cluster bombs and land mines.

Some Members of Parliament recognize that this rationale for government support of U.S. operations, to the extent that such operations involve cluster bombs or anti-personnel land mines, threaten the goals of the Ottawa Convention. In effect, the government relied on the letter of the law, rather than its underlying intention, to justify U.S. action and Canadian support for the same. Americans, not Canadians, were deploying the suspect weapons. No existing treaty law specifically banned cluster bombs. The U.S., as a non-signatory of the Ottawa Convention, was free to deploy land mines if it so chose.

These arguments re-emerged as Chrétien's government discouraged Canadian criticism of the U.S. war in Iraq (Brown 2003). While a handful of Canadian forces personnel were involved in the Iraqi conflict, Chrétien again claimed that Americans were legally free to do as they chose regarding wartime tactics, and that Canadians were following the letter of the law in not directly deploying the banned weapons (House of Commons 2003a). On a number of levels, that is an ethically simplified and problematic view of the situation. Notably, the Canadian government ignores the fact that Canadian personnel engaged in logistical support may well set the stage for Americans to engage in suspect tactics. While such indirect involvement in allies' actions may simply be the nature of political and military relations, it lessens Canada's credibility as a voice for ethically based change in foreign policy.

Canada's justification for U.S. policy highlights a main problem with the war on terrorism for the land mine ban. The U.S. is perhaps the most prominent non-signatory of the Ottawa Convention. Canada, the bellwether state of the ban, has now explicitly excused the U.S. for acting out of accord with norms surrounding the treaty.[11] As one MP pointedly asked, "Does the Prime Minister not realize that by not condemning the use of cluster bombs, he is not only denying the spirit of his anti-personnel land mines treaty, but he is also jeopardizing Canada's reputation?" (House of Commons 2001c).

The reputation in question here has two dimensions. The first is whether Canada is rightly understood as a transformational leader. According to James MacGregor Burns (1978), such leaders seek to restructure existing conditions in the service of ethically uplifting goals such as justice or equality. Transformational leaders guide their followers to new conceptualizations that allow politics better to serve (the leader's) ethical goals. Many scholars have noted that Canada's means of promoting its foreign policy agenda is generally through "soft power" (i.e., influence through persuasion, role modeling, provision of reliable information, etc.) (e.g. Knight 2001; Doern 2001:6; Saywell 1999:Ch. 12).[12] Canada's human security rhetoric, and its stated motivations for promoting the Ottawa Convention, suggest that Canada was deliberately positioning itself as a transformational leader on the land mine issue.

The second dimension of Canada's reputation is its standing as an honest and fair champion of human rights. Especially for a middle power, that reputation is invaluable. Since it often lacks the resources to enforce its policy preferences single-handedly, Canada relies on negotiation and coalition building to promote its political agenda. The importance of reputation to cooperation is well documented (Axelrod and Keohane 1986). Should Canada's promotion of the Ottawa Convention and acceptance of U.S. deployment of cluster bombs, land mines, or both, in fighting terrorism appear hypocritical to other states, Canada's ability to achieve its own international goals would be compromised. The critical factor in this case will likely be other states' perception of Canada's overall political integrity. As one scholar notes:

> A reputation for integrity, absent skill or ungirded by some larger principled commitment, can be easily destroyed amid the inevitable maneuvers, bargains, and discarded promises of politics. Deviations and compromises are forgivable, even acceptable, however, where the compromiser is visibly, ably and consistently committed to particular goals and principles. Tactical retreats and digressions are legitimate if they are clearly for the sake of such larger ends (Kane 2001:21).

If it wants to maintain its reputation for fairness and consistency, Canada must continue to ensure that its accommodation of U.S. preferences is seen globally in the context of a larger commitment to human security.

Beyond that, by unquestioningly tolerating the U.S.'s choice of weapons, Canada may be discouraging a critical holdout state from having to accept the legal commitment of the Ottawa Convention and the custom that develops around it. Although the Clinton administration promised the U.S. would sign the Convention by 2006, President Bush subsequently repudiated that claim. Having the world's largest military power refuse to sign a major disarmament treaty is a major setback for promoters of the treaty. The practices of holdout states undercut the effectiveness of a treaty, and in this case the problem is compounded by the prominence of the U.S. in the international system (Human Rights Watch 2002).

In part, the holdouts are problematic because of their relationship to emerging norms of customary international law. Benesch and her colleagues (1999) argue that since the creation of the Ottawa Convention there has been rapid and significant movement by states to establish such norms. Even non-signatory states have indicated support for a ban on anti-personnel land mines. For example, the U.S. was initially open to the idea of a mine treaty and until recently planned eventually to become a party to the Ottawa Convention. Since June 2001, the Bush Administration has been undertaking a comprehensive review of U.S. land mine policy. It is telling that the U.S. Department of Defense's recommendation to abandon the idea of becoming a party to the Ottawa Convention came in November 2001, only a month after the hostilities against Afghanistan began (Human Rights Watch 2001b). U.S. anti-terrorism policy seems to have triggered a reversal on the tentative plan to join the land mine ban. Thus, Canada may be jeopardizing the nascent customary norms banning anti-personnel land mines by its defense of Canadian and U.S. policies in Afghanistan. If Canada's criterion for regarding a state as bound by the land mine ban is solely whether that state is a party to the Ottawa Convention, what does this say about the commitment to human security that supposedly underlies the ban?

Conclusion

In material terms, Canada has been a major supporter of the war on terrorism. Canada has revamped its border control and immigration practices, and passed significant anti-terrorism legislation domestically. While there was no direct Canadian participation in the war on Iraq, Canada's military commitment in Afghanistan was substantial. However, that support may come at a high cost for other of Canada's foreign policy priorities. So far, both U.S. and Canadian war conduct challenge the good that the Ottawa Convention can do in the name of human security. As it has defended U.S. tactics in Afghanistan and Iraq, the Canadian government has made arguments that undercut the rationale for the land mine ban. Canada has argued that anti-personnel land mines should be banned because they jeopardize the human security of innocent civilians, even over the course of multiple generations, wherever such weapons are used. The danger from anti-personnel land mines is not lessened because states promise to stop deploying mines; it is lessened when states actually cease deployment and support demining efforts.[13] That is, the treaty exists to change behaviour, not merely to extract promises. If the Ottawa Convention is intended to stop an inhumane use of force, the defense of such behaviour solely on the basis of a state's status vis-à-vis the treaty is nonsensical, if not hypocritical.

Furthermore, treaty law can help generate international custom such that the goals of the treaty will be met even in the absence of universal signature. Given that, promoting customary international norms is as important to the goals of the Ottawa Convention as is persuading states to become parties. By justifying U.S. actions as permissible because they are either outside the letter of the law or arise from treaties to which the U.S. is not party, Canada impedes the progress in human security that can result from the Ottawa Convention and the international regime it engenders. Clearly, the entire international regime is not immediately at risk because of Canadian actions in this case; but given that the U.S. will likely continue to prosecute a military war on terrorism and that tactical disagreements may arise in the future, Canada needs to be especially careful of precedent in this case.

In terms of its own reputation, Canada probably risks little in the short run. No one really expects Chrétien's government to be able to talk the Bush Administration out of its war plans. In the longer term, though, Canada needs to be attentive to a larger problem. There is no reason to believe the Bush Administration regards the war on terrorism as complete with the military operations in Afghanistan and Iraq. If it continues to make excuses for the U.S. and to undertake joint operations while the U.S. uses tactics that are illegal for Canadian forces, Canada risks undercutting the generation of customary international law crucial to universal acceptance of an anti-personnel land mine ban.

Notes

1 For an overview of DFAIT's human security programs, see their website at http://www.humansecurity.gc.ca.

2 Interestingly, the U.S. rejected a UN "human rights-based 'unifying strategy'" as suitable for addressing counterterrorism but not terrorism itself. See Moley 2002.

3 Of course, people of many nationalities lost their lives during the September 11 attacks. However, the clear material and rhetorical target in that case was the USA.

4 The major security allotments were \$6.5 billion for the Department of National Defence, with \$2.5 billion specifically earmarked for U.S.–Canada border security, \$2.2 billion for air security, and substantial amounts specified for "emergency preparedness and military deployment" especially as they relate to weapons of mass destruction. See Boag 2001.

5 Even this decreased amount was enough to rank Canada among the top six donor governments to global mine action. See Mines Action Canada 2002.

6 Bush referred to a portion of Psalm 23, "I will fear no evil, for You are with me."

7 Notably, on 17 September 2001, President Bush announced that Osama bin Laden was "Wanted: Dead or Alive," echoing Old West notices offering rewards for the capture of outlaws. See, for example, Woodward 2001, A1.

8 The five goals were liberation of the Iraqi people, disarmament of weapons of mass destruction and their delivery systems, elimination of terrorist infrastructure, preservation of Iraq's territorial integrity, and reconstruction of Iraq's economic and political systems.

9 Indeed, the standard citation, *I.C.J. Statute,* Art. 38, lists custom and treaty separately when enumerating sources of international law.

10 This is especially true of the CBU-87 bombs used by the U.S. in Afghanistan in October, 2001. See Human Rights Watch 2001a.

11 In fact, Chrétien may have been promising the U.S. future absolution for potential transgressions since the U.S. has not publicly acknowledged deploying land mines during its Afghan campaign.

12 In 1996, Raymond Chan, then secretary of state (Asia-Pacific) recognized Canada's international comparative advantage as being in the areas of agriculture, transportation, and telecommunications, none of which are critical power resources in the traditional, *realpolitik* sense. See Smith 2001, 81.

13 A parallel argument about human rights can be found in Shue 1996, Ch. 1. This is relevant because Canada's promotion of global human security is often linked to its stance on human rights.

References

Apple, R.W., Jr. (2001). "A Clear Message, 'I Will Not Relent'," *New York Times*, 21 September, A1.

——. (2001). "No Middle Ground," *New York Times* (National Edition), 14 September, A1, A4.

Axelrod, Robert, and Robert O. Keohane. (1986). "Achieving Cooperation Under Anarchy," in Kenneth Oye (ed.) *Cooperation Under Anarchy* (Princeton, NJ: Princeton University Press), 226–260.

Axworthy, Lloyd. (1997). "Canada and Human Security: The Need for Leadership," *International Journal*, vol. 52, Spring, 183–196.

——. (2002). "The Human Security Solution to Terrorism," *Winnipeg Free Press*, 5 September.

——. (2003). Letter to Minister of Foreign Affairs Bill Graham, 26 March, available at http://www.humansecuritybulletin.info/news_1.html.

Bailey, Lt(N) Morgan. (2003). "Realignment of Op APOLLO's Assets," 3 July, available at http://www.forces.gc.ca/site/Feature_Story/2003/jul03/02_f_e.asp.

Beal, David. (2002). "Civil Society Input in the 2002 Foreign and Defence Policy Reviews," report of a Canadian Peacebuilding Coordinating Committee Workshop, Ottawa, 14 June.

Benesch, Susan, Glenn McGrory, Cristina Rodriguez, and Robert Sloane. (1999) "International Customary Law and Antipersonnel Landmines: Emergence of a New Customary Norm," *Landmine Monitor Report 1999*, Appendix.

(2001). "Bin Laden's Statement: 'The Sword Fell'," *New York Times* (National Edition), 8 October, B7.

Boag, Keith. (2001). "Federal Budget 2001 (Analysis)," CBC-TV, available at http://www.cbc.ca/news/indepth/budget2001/ analysis.html.

Brown, DeNeen L. (2003). "Chrétien Tells Canadians To Respect U.S. Decision," *Washington Post*, 21 March, A29.

Bumiller, Elisabeth, and David E. Sanger. (2001). "A Somber Bush Says Terrorism Cannot Prevail," *New York Times* (National Edition), 12 September, A1, A4.

Burns, James MacGregor. (1978). *Leadership*, New York: Harper Colophon.

(2003). "Canadians Could Serve in an Iraq War: Ottawa," CBC News Online, 14 March.

(2002) "Canada's Mine Action Policies and Programs," DFAIT mine action website, available at http://www.mines.gc.ca/IV-en.asp.

Bush, George W. (2003). Radio address, 15 March 2003. available at http://www.whitehouse.gov/news/releases/2003/03/print/20030315.html.

(2003). "Bush Postpones Ottawa Visit," CBC News Online, 12 April.

Charles, Anne. (1997). Notes for an address by the High Commissioner of Canada, 4th NGO Conference on Anti-Personnel Landmines, Maputo, Mozambique, 25 February.

Chrétien, Jean. (2002). Interview with Peter Mansbridge on the National, CBC-TV, 18 March.

(2003). "Chrétien Restates Opposition to Iraq War," CBC News Online, 18 March.

Department of National Defence (Canada). (2002). "The Department of National Defence and Canadian Forces Response to September 11, 2001," DND Press Release BG-02.030, 4 September.

——. (2003). "The Canadian Forces' Contribution to the International Campaign Against Terrorism," DND Press Release BG-02.001I, 26 June.

Department of State (U.S.). (2002). Counterterrorism policy, available at http://www.state.gov/r/pa/ei/rls/5968.htm.

Friedman, Thomas. (2001). "Spiritual Missile Defense," *New York Times*, 16 December, D13.

(2003). "Former UN Head Calls Iraq War 'Illegal'," CBC News Online, 19 March.

Gamble, John King, Jr. (1998). "The Treaty/Custom Dichotomy," in Charlotte Ku and Paul F. Diehl (eds.), *International Law: Classic and Contemporary Readings*, Boulder, CO: Lynne Rienner, 75–90.

Graham, Bill. (2002). Notes for an address by the Minister of Foreign Affairs, to the ambassadors of the Human Security Network, Ottawa, 7 June.

——. (2003). Letter to Hon. Lloyd Axworthy, Chair, National Advisory Board for the Canadian Consortium on Human Security, 10 April, available at http://www.humansecuritybulletin.info/news_1.html.

——. (2003). Notes for an address by the Minister of Foreign Affairs, on the occasion of the House of Commons Take-Note Debate on Iraq, Ottawa, 29 January.

Hart, Michael and Brian Tomlin. (2002). "Inside the Perimeter: The U.S. Policy Agenda and Its Implications for Canada," in G. Bruce Doern (ed.) *How Ottawa Spends 2002–2003* (Don Mills: Oxford University Press), 48–68.

House of Commons (Canada). (2001). *House of Commons Debates: electronic Hansard* (Ottawa: House of Commons) Number 106, 31 October.

——. (2001). *House of Commons Debates: electronic Hansard* (Ottawa: House of Commons) Number 109, 5 November.

——. (2001). *House of Commons Debates: electronic Hansard* (Ottawa: House of Commons) Number 111, 7 November.

——. (2002). *House of Commons Debates: electronic Hansard* (Ottawa: House of Commons) Number 135, 30 January.

——. (2003). *House of Commons Debates: electronic Hansard* (Ottawa: House of Commons) Number 83, 2 April.

——. (2003). *House of Commons Debates: electronic Hansard* (Ottawa: House of Commons) Number 84, 3 April.

Human Rights Watch. (2001). *Cluster Bombs in Afghanistan Backgrounder*, October.

——. (2002). "Holdout States Undercut Landmine Treaty," press release, 13 September.

——. (2001). "US: Pentagon Mine Policy Rollback," press release, 21 November.

——. (2003). "US Misleading on Cluster Munitions," press release, 25 April.

(1999). *The Human Security Paradigm Shift: A New Lens on Canadian Foreign Policy*, report of the UBC Symposium on Human Security, 18 June.

Irwin, Rosalind. (2001). "Linking Ethics and Security in Canadian Foreign Policy," in Rosalind Irwin (ed.) *Ethics and Security in Canadian Foreign Policy* (Vancouver: UBC Press), 3–13.

Jenkins, Simon. (2001). "Cluster Bombs: These are Landmines by Any Other Name," *The Times* (London), 26 October.

Kane, John. (2001). *The Politics of Moral Capital*, New York: Cambridge University Press.

Knight, W. Andy. (2001). "Soft Power, Moral Suasion, and Establishing the International Criminal Court: Canadian Contributions," in Rosalind Irwin (ed.) *Ethics and Security in Canadian Foreign Policy* (Vancouver: UBC Press), 113–137.

Landmine Survivors Network. (2002). "US Soldier Killed by Landmine in Afghanistan," press release, 28 March.

Latham, Andrew A. (2001). "Theorizing the Landmine Campaign: Ethics, Global Cultural Scripts, and the Laws of War," in Rosalind Irwin (ed.) *Ethics and Security in Canadian Foreign Policy* (Vancouver: UBC Press), 160–180.

Leahy, Patrick. (2003). "On the Use of Cluster Bombs and Landmines in Iraq," statement, 10 April.

Mack, Andrew, and Oliver Rohlfs. (2003). "The Great Canadian Divide," *Globe and Mail*, 28 March.

Moley, Kevin E. (2002). Statement of the Head of the U.S. Observer Delegation, 58th Session of the United Nations Commission on Human Rights, Geneva, 20 March.

(2001). *Reaffirming the Commitment: Canadian Landmine Fund Report 2000–2001*, (Ottawa: DFAIT).

(2002). "Report Shows Landmine Convention is Working," CBC Ottawa, 13 September.

Negroponte, John D. (2003). Statement before the United Nations Security Council, 27 March.

Nelson, Krista. (2003). "Iraq: Questions Regarding the Laws of War," Center for Defense Information, 18 March.

Rutherford, Ken. (2001). "State Legal Obligations to Landmine Victim Assistance," *University of California, Davis Journal of International Law and Policy*, vol. 7, no. 1, Winter, 42–55.

——. (2000). "The Evolving Arms Control Agenda: Implications of the Role of NGOs in Banning Antipersonnel Landmines," *World Politics*, vol. 53, no. 1, October, 74–114.

Sachs, Susan. (2001). "North Africans in Europe said to Preach War, Enlisting Young Immigrants," *New York Times*, 11 December, B2.

Saywell, John. (1999). *Canada: Pathways to the Present* revised edition (Toronto: Stoddart).

Shribman, David M. (2003). "Ignoring the Noisy Street," *Maclean's*, 3 March, 19–20.

Shue, Henry. (1996). *Basic Rights* 2nd ed. Princeton, NJ: Princeton University Press.

Smith, Heather. (2001). "Niche Diplomacy in Canadian Human Rights Policy: Ethics or Economics?" in Rosalind Irwin (ed.) *Ethics and Security in Canadian Foreign Policy* (Vancouver: UBC Press), 77–94.

(2002). Statement by Ambassador Kevin E. Moley, Head of the U.S. Observer Delegation to the 58th Session of the United Nations Commission on Human Rights, Geneva, 20 March.

(2003). "Trouble at Home," *Economist*, 27 February, 1.

United Nations Security Council. (2002). *Resolution 1441*, 8 November.

(2003). "Unsanctioned War in Iraq Could Lead to End of UN: Former Official," CBC News Online, 30 January.

(2001). "We're Right and They're Wrong," *Toronto Sun*, 3 October, 14.

(2003). "What Now?" *Economist*, 17 February, 1.

Woodward, Bob. (2001). "CIA Told to Do 'Whatever Necessary' to Kill Bin Laden," *Washington Post*, 21 October, A1.

14

Canada in the Middle East: The Problems of Human Security and Institutionalism

Shaun Narine

Introduction

The Arab–Israeli conflict remains one of the most volatile and politically difficult issues in international politics. Within Canadian domestic politics, the issue evokes powerful feelings and considerable controversy (Gatehouse 2002:20–25). Historically, Canada's foreign policy and political disposition have been strongly biased in favour of Israel against the Arab world. In recent years, Canada has tried to adopt a more balanced approach to the conflict. Nonetheless, the question of how to approach the conflict poses significant problems for the operation of Canadian foreign policy. In the post-Cold War environment, Canada has tried to make the concept of "human security" one of the keystones of its foreign policy. However, applying human security in the context of the Middle East has proven to be quite difficult.

Traditionally, Canadian foreign policy has been highly deferential to the United States. However, Canada has also promoted international law and multilateralism as the foundations of the international system (Keating 2002). In the aftermath of the September 11th, 2001 terrorist attacks on the United States, the U.S. began pursuing a foreign policy that has damaged some of the basic structures of international order and threatens to divide the world into confrontational "civilizational" blocs, with the United States arrayed against the Islamic world and pulling the rest of the Western world into the conflict. Under these circumstances, how Canada approaches the Arab–Israeli dispute has a significance that extends far beyond the conflict itself. The American assault on international institutions also compromises Canada's ability to pursue its "human security" agenda. In the post-September 11th world, Canada faces the increasingly difficult task of balancing its need to accommodate American interests with its own distinct interests in fostering international institutional development.

The primary question for this paper is what are the implications of the Arab–Israeli conflict for Canadian foreign policy? How does the conflict affect Canada's pursuit of human security and how does it influence Canada's larger approach to the Islamic world? Those issues are connected; the ability to pursue credibly human security initiatives is affected by the Arab–Israeli dispute which is taking on even greater symbolic value in the Islamic world as the U.S. "war on terrorism" unfolds. The basic argument of this paper is that Canada's commitment to human security is undermined by the conflict. Canada's ability to follow human security principles is also compromised by the weakening of international institutions. As the international system unravels, human security approaches to dealing with the world's problems become more essential but also more difficult to implement.

This paper is divided into four sections. The first section explains the concept of "human security" and the core principles underpinning Canada's abiding commitments to international law and multilateralism. Section two discusses Canada's history in the Middle East and evaluates the evolution of Canadian policy towards the different actors in the Arab–Israeli conflict. Section three is an examination of how the terrorist attacks of September 11, 2001 on the United States, and the American response have affected the political landscape in the Middle East and, accordingly, the environment to which Canada must respond. Finally, section four draws these factors together and argues that there are tensions between politics and principles in the case of human security and the Arab–Israeli conflict. Nonetheless, the pursuit of human security principles may grow in importance as the multilateral international system falls into crisis.

Shaun Narine

Canadian Foreign Policy: Human Security, International Law, and Multilateralism

Scholars have defined Canada as a "middle power" in the international system. The concept of middle power is contested; various analysts ascribe geographical or normative characteristics to middle power states. Cooper, et al., reject these approaches and argue that "middle powers are defined primarily by their behaviour: their tendency to pursue multilateral solutions to international problems, their tendency to embrace compromise solutions in international disputes, and their tendency to embrace notions of 'good international citizenship' to guide their diplomacy" (Cooper et al. 1993:18).[1]

Canada has defined its role in the international community as one of helping to build and support international institutions and international law. This disposition is a realistic reflection of Canada's national interest. Canadian policy-makers have long recognized that, for smaller states, a world governed by law and structured by institutions is necessary to create an orderly and productive international system. Multilateral institutions and international law provide predictability to the conduct of international relations. Multilateral institutions act as constraints on the actions of larger powers and, at the same time, allow smaller states to exercise greater influence than would otherwise be the case. Within such institutions, resources other than raw military and economic power are meaningful. For Canada, its diplomatic and political resources allow it to exercise an influence beyond what more traditional measures of power would indicate. Canada's commitment to multilateralism and international law, however, must always be balanced by the imperatives of its relationship to the United States. These demands are sometimes in conflict, and Canada is then faced with difficult choices (Keating 2002).

In recent years, Canada's commitment to multilateralism and international law has been joined by "human security" as a primary focus of Canadian foreign policy. That idea has been called the "Axworthy Doctrine," named after former Canadian Foreign Affairs Minister Lloyd Axworthy. The Axworthy Doctrine is a Canadian interpretation of the human security concept that was originally introduced in a United Nations Development Program (UNDP) report in 1994. That report outlined seven areas of human security: economic, food, health, environmental, personal, community and political. The Canadian approach to human security focuses upon preventing individuals from being caught in violent conflict and, if that is impossible, alleviating the ramifications of such conflict.

"Human security," in all its variations, "brings to the fore the safety and dignity of the individual human person, as opposed to the power and authority of the state or the regime" (Acharya and Acharya 2000:1). Human security emphasizes human rights and focuses on justice and emancipation for human beings. These emphases distinguish it from other, more state-centred concepts of international security. Other notions of security, such as the Asian idea of "comprehensive security," may mention human rights but clearly give priority to the state, not the individual. In human security, the dignity of the individual human is an end in itself, rather than the by-product of state survival or legitimation (ibid.).

The human security agenda emerged in the aftermath of the Cold War. To Canada, the post-Cold War environment presented problems and opportunities. It required a move away from more traditional Canadian efforts to support and enhance multilateral institutions. The Axworthy Doctrine proceeded from the observation that the end of the Cold War led to an increase in security for states, but that did not mean an increase in security for the world's peoples. The post-Cold War period has seen a global increase in intra-state violence. A new foreign policy approach was needed, one which could incorporate a definition of security more in line with the realities of the post-Cold War era. That led to the focus on human security. According to Axworthy, human security:

> is much more than the absence of military threat. It includes the security against economic privation, an acceptable quality of life, and a guarantee of fundamental human rights. [Security] requires that basic needs are met … [and] acknowledges that sustained economic development, human rights, and fundamental freedoms, the rule of law, good governance, sustainable development, and social equity are as important to global peace as arms control and disarmament (Axworthy cited in Sharma 2002:75–76).

International stability will be possible only once the demands of human security are properly met.

Canada pursues human security through "promoting safety for people from threats of violence" (DFAIT 2001). The five priority areas emphasized by the Canadian approach are:

1. The protection of civilians;
2. Peace support operations;
3. Conflict prevention;
4. Accountability; and
5. Public safety.

Canada draws on the UN Charter, the Universal Declaration of Human Rights and the Geneva Conventions as the foundations of its approach to human security. While Canada acknowledges the 1994 UNDP Human Development Report as the source of the term "human security," the Department of Foreign Affairs and International Trade (DFAIT) criticizes the report for focusing too much attention on threats related to underdevelopment and paying less attention to the problems caused by violent conflict. Canadian support for the international efforts to ban land mines and create an International Criminal Court (ICC) are cited by DFAIT as examples of the human security agenda.

The Axworthy Doctrine asserts that Canada has both the capacity and credibility to play a leadership role in promoting human security on the international stage. Canada is already deeply engaged in advancing human security through its extensive participation in peacekeeping, peace-building, disarmament, protecting the rights of children, and promoting rules-based trade which furthers economic development. Axworthy also argues that Canada is among a select group of countries that enjoys a certain kind of "soft power." Axworthy defines "soft power" as: "the art of disseminating information in such a way that desirable outcomes are achieved through persuasion rather than coercion.... [soft power] blurs, even counters, the perception of traditional power assets, such as military force, economic might, resources, and population. Power in this context is obtained from networking and coalition building" (Axworthy cited in Sharma 2002:75).

Soft power is also affected by the international image of the country wielding it. Canada has "an attractive set of values and an image as a trustworthy partner" in the international system, as well as a positive image as a wealthy, tolerant society (ibid.). Soft power, therefore, is the ability of a state to influence the normative environment of the international system through its own normative stature.

Axworthy has been roundly criticized by Canadian scholars for various aspects of the Axworthy Doctrine. "Soft power," for example, was a concept developed by Joseph Nye to describe aspects of American power. In Nye's conception, however, the United States had the advantage of a global culture, the ability to set the international agenda, and the recourse to "hard power" (military and economic resources) as a necessary complement to its soft power. The appeal of American ideas is the one aspect of soft power, mentioned by Nye, that Axworthy adapts to the Canadian context. Nonetheless, however appealing Canada's ideas may be, it has a limited ability to export norms to other parts of the world (Nossal 1998–1999).

Scholars have also criticized and analyzed the relationship between the human security agenda and the fiscal constraints imposed on Canadian foreign policy by a cost-cutting federal government. The Axworthy Doctrine was advanced as Canada was reducing its foreign aid contributions and allowing its military to stagnate. Under these conditions, a foreign policy that relies upon promoting selected norms and ideas is relatively low-cost. That approach can easily backfire. The human security agenda requires that Canada be prepared to commit its resources to advancing human security. However, continuing military stagnation is affecting Canada's ability to meet its peacekeeping obligations.[2] As a result Canada may become incapable of meaningfully contributing to human security initiatives, or at least be very limited in what it can contribute. If other states perceive Canada as needing to depend on them to advance Canadian initiatives, Canada's credibility will be severely compromised (Nossal 1998–1999). As it stands at present, the moralistic tone of Canadian diplomacy ("pulpit diplomacy") is irritating to other states; their disposition towards Canadian initiatives is likely to worsen if Canada is unable to support its rhetoric with a strong commitment of resources (Hampson and Oliver 1998). Finally, many scholars have criticized the Canadian concept of human security as being too broad to be a useful analytical category, though that may be more of a concern to academics than to policy-makers, who appreciate the term's flexibility (Dalby 2000).

Despite these criticisms, it is important to note that the Canadian agenda is, in part, derived from other initiatives at the United Nations. Beyond the influence of the UNDP report, noted above, the Axworthy Doctrine also mirrors important aspects of former UN Secretary-General Boutros-Ghali's *Agenda for Peace*. Present Secretary-General Kofi Annan has also called for international intervention in the affairs of sovereign states when the international community knows that those states are committing egregious human rights abuses. Canada argues that its approach to human security is part of a larger shift towards new norms of international relations, though there are still aspects of the Axworthy Doctrine that make it distinct from other approaches. Canada, along with other countries, is part of a larger movement to redefine the nature of international relations (Bain 1999).

When Axworthy retired from politics, many observers inside and outside DFAIT expressed the concern that the human security agenda would go with him. However, Foreign Minister Bill Graham has explicitly stated that Axworthy's legacy is the continuing Canadian commitment to human security. Graham argues that human security is actually an extension of, and complement to, Canada's traditional concerns:

> For some time now questions have been raised about the future of human security within Canada and internationally. In Canada, the question has been raised about whether human security was simply the agenda of former Foreign Affairs Minister Lloyd Axworthy. Yet for those familiar with the fundamentals of Canadian foreign policy, promoting human security was more the drawing together of long-standing priorities, including human rights, peacekeeping, humanitarianism, and disarmament, than a fundamentally new departure.... Canada's commitment to a peoples-centred approach to security policy not only survives but also becomes stronger with time (Graham 2002a).

Thus, Canada's commitment to human security—at least rhetorically—remains firm. Canada's enduring commitments to multilateralism and international law remain intact (Graham 2002b). Yet Canada's ability to pursue these priorities — particularly its efforts to utilize its "soft power" in support of Canadian initiatives — is complicated by Canada's application of human security to the Arab–Israeli conflict. The events of September 11th, the American "war on terrorism," and its subsequent effects on the Middle East conflict, have only exacerbated these tensions and compromised Canada's ability to pursue its foreign policy interests.

Canada's Involvement in the Middle East: An Historical Review

Canada has a long history of involvement in the Middle East, starting with the creation of Israel. Canadian Supreme Court Justice Ivan Rand was the most prominent member of the UN Special Committee on Palestine(UNSCOP), the UN Commission that recommended the partition of Palestine into Jewish and Arab states. Canadian diplomat Lester Pearson was a key figure in elaborating the plan of partition and in negotiating a compromise between the U.S. and USSR regarding the termination of the Palestine mandate. Pearson's influence may have been "decisive" in getting the partition plan accepted by the UN. For his efforts, Pearson was called the "Balfour of Canada" by Canadian Zionists.[3] Pearson later, and most notably, won the Nobel Peace Prize for proposing the idea of a United Nations peacekeeping force to separate the warring parties in the aftermath of the 1956 Suez Canal Crisis. Throughout this early history, Canada and its leaders were clearly and strongly supportive of Israel. In that sense, Canada was not much different from the rest of the Western world. Until 1967, Canada largely viewed the Arab–Israeli conflict in terms of the refugee crisis it created, but the notion that Palestinians were a people with distinct rights — let alone the idea that they may have been unjustly displaced from their homeland — was not of particular importance (Ismael 1985:9–13; Hillmer 1989:125–143).[4]

After the 1967 Arab–Israeli war and over the next three decades, Canada — again, as with much of the world — gradually became more sensitive to the plight of the Palestinians. In 1975, Canada distinguished itself on the issue by forcing the cancellation of a United Nations Crime Conference, scheduled to take place in Toronto, because of political and popular opposition to the prospect of Palestine Liberation Organization (PLO) observers participating in the meeting (Ismael 1993:29). Nonetheless, Canada's support for the UN meant that Canada allowed the PLO into the country for a UN conference the next year and resisted domestic political pressure not to do so (Ismael 1993:44). Canada adopted a contradictory attitude towards Palestinian rights, supporting the notion of Palestinians' participation in negotiating their own future, while frequently voting against UN resolutions that would, seemingly, advance this goal. Canada also officially opposed recognizing the PLO as the voice of the Palestinians while realistically recognizing the political importance of the PLO (Ismael 1993:44–45).

Various events over the next few decades, however, promoted a shift in Canadian policy towards the Middle East. Israel's invasion of Lebanon in 1982 and the associated loss of life, including the massacres of Palestinian refugees in the Sabra and Chatila refugee camps by allied Lebanese forces, shook the Canadian public's positive view of Israel and made the Palestinian side of the conflict better known within Canada. The first Palestinian intifada in the late 1980s, and Israel's efforts to put it down, further damaged Israel's image in Canada and led to a confrontation between Joe Clark, Minister of External Affairs in the Mulroney government, and the Canada–Israel Committee (CIC) (Ismael 1993:51; Lyon 1992–93:20). This public argument was particularly remarkable given that Prime Minister Brian Mulroney was strongly pro-Israel in his personal and political leanings (Kirton and Lyon 1989:201–203; Dirlik 1991:37). Even so, Canada still refused to recognize the PLO as the legitimate representative of the Palestinian people, and Barbara McDougall, a staunchly pro-Israel politician, eventually replaced Clark as Minister of External Affairs (Lyon 1992–93:14, 18).[5]

Within the wider world community, Canada was viewed as "biased" in favour of Israel. That perception, particularly in the Arab world, was formed as early as the 1960s and was caused by Canada's determination to align itself with the U.S. and Britain, Israel's strongest supporters, in its foreign policy. Immediately before the 1967 Arab–Israeli war, President Nasser of Egypt ordered the Canadian UN peacekeeping contingent to leave Egypt, claiming that the Canadian government had a "biased stand in favour of Israel" (Ismael 1985:21; see also Kiliç, Chapter 12 in this text). After the 1973 Arab–Israeli war, Canada had to exert considerable pressure on the UN to be accepted as part of the UN peacekeeping force. Egypt did not want Canada's participation because it saw the country as an extension of the U.S. Only a phone-call from the UN Secretary General to Egyptian President Anwar Sadat saved Canada's international reputation as a peacekeeper. Finally, Canada was surprised to find itself one of the targets of the Arab oil boycott in 1973. Canadian political figures argued that Canada had always been neutral on the Arab–Israeli conflict and, therefore, should not be penalized. The Canadians failed to appreciate the Arab point-of-view on the conflict or how Canada's actions and attitudes were understood in the rest of the world (Ismael 1985:21).

Whether or not Canadian policy is actually tilted towards Israel, or simply reflects particular Canadian interests or sensibilities is a controversial subject. David Dewitt has argued that Canadian UN voting behaviour in the late 1970s was ambivalent:

> During the five years following the passage of Security Council Resolution 242 in 1967, Canada's General Assembly votes on Mideast matters coincided with those of the United States about 80 percent of the time, and with those of Canada's European Community allies just over 40 percent of the time. However, 1974 to 1977 brought a dramatic reversal, with Canada's agreement with the United States ... plummeting to under 40 percent and Canada's agreement with the European Community skyrocketing to almost 90 percent. On the narrower but more fundamental question of the Arab–Israeli conflict Canada's votes from 1975 through 1979 placed it midway between the European Community and the United States, with a shift back towards the latter in 1978 after Don Jamieson had fully assumed the reins as Secretary of State for External Affairs (Dewitt and Kirton 1984:20).

Dewitt notes other shifts in Canadian policy at the UN around this time, including a willingness to condemn Israeli actions in Gaza and the extension of Israeli law to the Golan.

Between 1988 and 2002, Canada's voting patterns in the UN indicate that Canada voted with the UN majority most of the time on resolutions dealing specifically with Israel. During this period, Canada participated in 121 UN Security Council and General Assembly votes regarding Israel. In 68 percent of the cases, Canada voted with the majority against the Israeli position; in five percent, Canada voted with Israel, and in 27 percent of the votes, Canada abstained (UNbisnet.org). Canada has supported the application of the Geneva Conventions to the Occupied Territories, affirmed the illegality of Jewish settlements on occupied land (including Jerusalem), and condemned Israeli practices affecting the human rights of Palestinians. When Canada was a member of the Security Council during the 1998–99 session, it voted against Israel's position fifteen times, and abstained five times (UN and Israel 1999). These votes do not tell the whole story, however. Some of Canada's positions are reversals of earlier positions, and Canada has often abstained on supporting, or adopted initial positions that are hostile to, the aspirations of the Palestinians. For example, between 1987 and 1992, Canada abstained on the call for the return of refugees displaced since 1967, then in 1993 voted in favour of the motion. In 1988 and 1990, Canada voted against a motion calling Israel's occupation of the Golan and Palestinian territory "illegal," then switched to abstention in later years, before supporting the motion in 1997. Between 1987 and 1995, Canada abstained on resolutions supporting the "inalienable rights of the Palestinian people." There are many other examples of Canada shifting its vote from abstention to support.

Today, Canada's voting patterns at the UN generally reflect Canada's stated policy on the region (explained below). However, the circuitous route that Canada has followed to this point has reinforced the impression in the international community that Canada is a strong supporter of Israel, or at least has not offered much support to the Palestinians (Lyon 1992–93:17; Kirton and Lyon 1989:198; Dirlik 1991:37). This impression has been shaped by Canada's stand on some fundamental symbolic issues. In 1987, Canada found itself isolated on the issue of recognizing Palestinians' right to self-determination at the meeting of La Francophonie. During that period, Canada maintained cordial but low-level relations with the PLO at the UN, a fact noted and resented by the Arab states. In the end, Canada allowed full diplomatic contact with the PLO only in 1995, after the United States. By contrast, Canada has extended what appears to be preferential treatment to Israel. In 1997, the Canada–Israel Free Trade Agreement (CIFTA) came into effect. At the time, that was the only FTA that Canada has with a country outside the Western hemisphere. Moreover, Canada has shown a marked reluctance openly to criticize Israeli policies.

In recent years, Canada's human security agenda has complicated its Middle East policy. Sean McMahon traces the politics surrounding Canada's support for Security Council Resolution 1322 (passed October 7, 2000) and its rejection of draft SC Resolution 1171 on December 18 2000. SCR 1322 condemned Israeli conduct at al-Haram al-Sharif (the Temple Mount) in Jerusalem and, *inter alia*, called on Israel to abide by international law. Draft SCR 1171 expressed the UN's determination to dispatch a force of observers to the Occupied Territories, with the goal of contributing to the implementation of agreements and protecting the security of Palestinian civilians. Canada supported SCR 1322, and defended its support using the language and philosophy of human security. Canada later justified its rejection of draft SCR 1171, however, by arguing that Israel had not accepted the idea of observers. As McMahon points out, that position places considerations of state sovereignty above human security, a notion explicitly rejected by Canada's Ambassador to the UN Paul Heinbecker only a few days earlier when he articulated the principles of human security in a speech at the UN. Moreover, the argument is misplaced: the international community does not recognize Israel's sovereignty over the Occupied Territories. As McMahon says, requiring Israeli consent before deploying observers "would have been like securing Iraqi acceptance before deploying a UN force to Kuwait" (McMahon 2001:9). Canada also made no effort to reach a compromise over draft SCR 1171, despite many opportunities to do so. McMahon attributes Canada's waffling on this issue to American pressure. Whatever the explanation, it appears that Canada's promotion of its human security agenda at the UN runs the risk of foundering on the politics of the Arab–Israeli dispute.

How Canada formulates its Middle Eastern policies is a controversial question. Lyon has argued that the Canada–Israel Committee (CIC), an umbrella group consisting of the Canadian Jewish Congress, the Canadian Zionist Organization and the B'nai B'rith, is unusually effective and influential in shaping Canadian policy towards Israel and the Palestinians. Certainly, that was the perception in DFAIT where past surveys of Foreign Affairs officials indicated that they judged the Canadian Jewish community as being the single most decisive influence on Canadian Middle Eastern policy, even ahead of themselves (Lyon 1992–93:6; Kirton and Lyon 1989:195). Some commentators argue that the CIC has no more influence or access to government policy-makers than any other group (Dewitt and Kirton 1984; Lyon 1992–93:16). Nonetheless, it is clear that Canada's policy towards the Middle East is an unusually sensitive issue. Throughout the 1980s, any amendments to Canada's UN positions on the Arab–Israeli conflict required Cabinet approval, "the only UN issue to be handled with such care" (Lyon 1992–93:16). Lyon argues that the CIC has been more of a brake on Canadian policy towards the Middle East as opposed to a permanent obstruction. If not for its influence, Canada would have been voting along European lines and formulating policies more closely aligned with the "Western mainstream" much sooner than it has.

Currently, Canada's stated policy on the Middle East Peace Process is as follows: Canada supports the security of Israel; it supports a comprehensive peace plan, including the Oslo process, and based on UN Security Council Resolutions 242 and 338; it calls for Israeli withdrawal from all occupied territories; it does not recognize Israeli claims over the Occupied Territories, and opposes the creation of Jewish settlements and the annexation of East Jerusalem, considering these actions to be contrary to international law and unproductive for the peace process. Canada recognizes the rights of the Palestinian people to self-determination "to be exercised through peace negotiations"; Canada recognizes the PLO as the principal representative of the Palestinian people and Yasser Arafat as its Chairman; Canada supports the right of the Palestinians to a state, but believes that goal is best served through peaceful means. Canada supports various UN resolutions on the Mideast conflict, except for UN General Assembly Resolution 3379, which equates Zionism with racism. Canada supports a just resolution of the Palestinian refugee problem, and believes it must be resolved through bilateral negotiations. Canada condemns all acts of terrorism and "respects Israel's right to a proportionate response against attacks, including terrorism. However, Canada believes that force in the absence of political engagement will not result in a solution to the underlying security problem" (DFAIT 2002). These positions accord with the international consensus.

Despite its official position, Canada is still hesitant openly or directly to criticize Israel, and considerable evidence suggests that Ottawa remains inordinately sensitive to Israel's Canadian supporters. In March, 2002, newly-appointed Foreign Affairs Minister Bill Graham made his first major foreign policy address, which was to the CIC. Despite offering the mildest criticisms of Israeli policies, Graham received a frosty and almost hostile reception from his audience. More telling is that Graham decided not to deliver his prepared speech, choosing to edit many of his criticisms of Israeli policy. Among his deleted comments were the statements that "[t]he demolition of civilian housing by armed forces impoverishes vulnerable families and instills a sense of bitterness," and "incursions into refugee camps only seem to exacerbate the situation and continuing settlement activity [undermines Palestinian hopes]" (Sallott 2002a). Later, when asked explicitly by the press if the deleted statements were true, Graham answered: "in some circumstances, yes."

The possible political costs of adopting a more critical approach to Israel are also indicated by the strength of Israel's supporters in the news media. The late Israel Asper, the majority owner of Southam News and Canwest Global (the largest Canadian media conglomerate) claimed that most international news agencies are grossly biased against Israel (ABC Online:2002).[6] Asper corrected this bias in his own news outlets by censoring columnists and news stories critical of Israel and requiring all of Southam's newspapers to run national editorials (which cannot subsequently be contradicted by local editorial boards) solidly supportive of Israeli policies (Newworldpeace.com 2002). These general policies have not changed with the death of Mr. Asper. The *Globe and Mail*, owned by Thomson Corporation, also has a strong pro-Israel tilt. Although the *Globe's* editorial page policy on the Middle East conflict is relatively sensitive to both sides of the conflict, most of the *Globe's* regular columnists who write on the Middle East, are strongly supportive of Israel.[7]

The refusal of Canadian politicians to adopt a strong position on the Arab–Israeli dispute seems to be the politically prudent course of action. The Canadian political establishment, in this case, is well attuned to the Canadian public. According to an April, 2002 Ipsos-Reid poll, 80 percent of Canadians do not believe the country should take a side in the Arab–Israeli conflict. A majority of Canadians think that the Israelis have used excessive force against the Palestinians (54 percent), while the distribution of blame is almost evenly divided between those Canadians who feel both sides are equally to blame for the conflict (28 percent), those who blamed the Palestinians (25 percent) and those who blame the Israelis (23 percent) (Ipsos-Reid 2002).

In the end, Canada still "tilts" towards Israel in the Arab–Israeli conflict, but only in a very subtle way. As the Muslim population in Canada grows and becomes more politically organized, the Canadian stand towards the Middle East may reflect these new political realities, though other important factors will continue to influence Canadian policy (Kilic 2004). In recent years at the UN, Canada has voted in support of international law and human security when dealing with Israel, and that has meant consistently taking positions against Israel. However, in some instances, Canada remains willing to compromise on its human security principles when dealing with Israel. Canada makes every effort to limit its overt criticism of Israel. Canada takes a stand, but tries to avoid drawing attention to that stand. Over time, this may make it difficult for Canada to promote human security. At the same time, it may be a prudent way of balancing the competing political demands around this controversial issue.

The Aftermath of September 11: New Developments in the Middle East

The September 11, 2001 terrorist attacks on the United States significantly affected the American approach to the Middle East and, indeed, its broader international relations. The overall effect was to exacerbate the tendency towards unilateralism in the Bush Administration. The U.S. has formulated policies that — in general — are undermining the multilateral institutions of the international system. In the Israeli–Palestinian conflict, the U.S. has adopted such a strong pro-Israel position that it has lost most of its credibility in the Arab world — and beyond — as an "honest broker" in the conflict. The current American occupation of Iraq is also adding to tensions between the U.S. and the Islamic world. For Canada, these developments have potentially profound implications. Canada has always favoured international institutions as necessary for maintenance of order and stability in the international system. These institutions now appear to be in crisis, and their decline means the decline of Canada's ability to pursue human security. At the same time, Muslims perceive the "war against terror" as a war against Islam, and that complicates Canada's foreign and domestic policies.

Immediately after September 11, the U.S. followed policies that created some hope, among international observers, for the rejuvenation of multilateral institutions. The U.S. orchestrated its war on Afghanistan and the al-Qaida terrorist network through the United Nations and with the support of an international coalition. Optimists hoped that the narrow unilateralism of the second Bush Administration, typified in its rejection of the Kyoto Accord on Global Warming, would give way to multilateralism, particularly as a multilateral approach would be required to combat terrorism effectively. However, buoyed by its easy victory in Afghanistan, the Bush administration soon reverted to unilateralism. The U.S. abrogated the Anti-Ballistic Missile (ABM) Treaty in December, 2001 in order to pursue research into Nuclear Missile Defence (NMD). The U.S. vetoed efforts to add an inspection regime to the Biological and Chemical Weapons accord, apparently because the U.S. itself is engaged in developing weapons that might violate the agreement (Borger 2002:1). The U.S. also set out on a crusade to have its citizens and soldiers exempted from the jurisdiction of the new International Criminal Court (ICC) — an institution to which Canada is particularly committed. The U.S. has been largely successful in its efforts to undermine the court (Economist 2002b; Ibbitson 2002; Axworthy 2002). It is in its war against Iraq, however, that the U.S. has posed its most serious challenge to the structures of multilateralism.

On March 19, 2003, the U.S. and Britain (and a few minor allies) attacked Iraq. The first stage of the war lasted only three weeks and ended in the U.S. and UK deposing Saddam Hussein and occupying Iraq. The war was conducted without the sanction of the UN, in probable violation of international law, and against the wishes of most of the world's public. (Only in the United States and Israel were public majorities in support of the war.)[8] Canada decided not to support the American war effort — a stand that enjoyed majority public support but also alienated the United States and resulted in veiled threats against Canada by the American Ambassador, Paul Cellucci (Cellucci 2003; Simpson 2003).

In the aftermath of the war, the situation in Iraq has become complex. The U.S. and UK justified their war with the argument that Saddam Hussein possessed, or was in the process of developing, weapons of mass destruction which he might use, or provide to terrorists to use, against U.S. and UK interests. However, no weapons of mass destruction have been found in Iraq. Subsequent investigations and revelations from an embarrassed intelligence community have revealed that intelligence was misused or distorted by the political leaders in the U.S. and the UK to convince their publics of the need for war.[9]

As the original justification for the war has become problematic, the Americans have emphasized the argument that the war was fought as the first step in remaking the Middle East into a democratic region (Milbank and Allan, August 1, 2003:A14). According to this argument, Middle East autocracies create populations that are inherently anti-American; creating a "democratic" Iraq in the heart of the Arab world will demonstrate that democracies can be established in the region and will force regional despots to reform. Thus, long-term American security interests will be served by placing the U.S. on the side of democracy and freedom, undermining the regional anti-Americanism. Unfortunately, the U.S. has little credibility among Arabs when it presents itself as a champion of democracy (Klein 2002; Perlez 2002; Biedermann 2002; Shehata 2002).

In this context of changing U.S.–Arab relations, the Arab–Israeli conflict takes on even more important symbolic and political value. Even if the rebuilding process in Iraq goes exactly as the U.S. hopes, the Israeli–Palestinian dispute remains a major stumbling block that must be addressed if American plans for the Arab world are to have any chance of success. Writing before the war, Michael Ignatieff makes this point:

> Unseating an Arab government in Iraq while leaving the Palestinians to face Israeli tanks and helicopter gunships is a virtual guarantee of unending Islamic wrath against the United States. The chief danger in the whole Iraqi gamble lies here — in supposing that victory over Saddam, in the absence of a Palestinian–Israeli settlement, would leave the United States with a stable hegemony over the Middle East. Absent a Middle East peace, victory in Iraq would still leave

> the Palestinians face to face with Israelis in a conflict in which they would destroy not only each other but American authority in the Islamic world as well.... [W]ith every day that American power appears complicit in Israeli attacks that kill civilians in the West Bank and in Gaza, and with the Arab nations giving their tacit support to Palestinian suicide bombers, the imperial guarantor finds itself dragged into a regional conflict that is one long hemorrhage of its diplomatic and military authority.... Properly understood, then, the operation in Iraq entails a commitment ... to enforce a viable peace on the Palestinians and Israelis. Such a peace must, at minimum, give the Palestinians a viable, contiguous state capable of providing land and employment for three million people. It must include a commitment to rebuild their shattered government infrastructure.... This is an awesomely tall order, but if America cannot find the will to enforce this minimum of justice, neither it nor Israel will have any safety from terror.... A successful American political strategy against terror depends on providing enough peace for both Israelis and Palestinians that extremists on either side begin to lose the support that keeps violence alive (Ignatieff 2003:5).

From the outset, the Bush Administration has supported Israel to an unprecedented degree, even for an American administration. September 11th exacerbated this tendency, as Bush adopted the "with us or against us" approach to terrorism. In this world view, the political context in which terrorism occurs does not matter. It was difficult for Bush to insist that Israel show restraint in dealing with Palestinian terrorism when the U.S. had insisted on its right to deal with terrorism without restraint. At the same time, however, the Bush Administration recognized, and was constantly receiving the message from its Arab and Western allies, that an attack against Iraq would be politically unacceptable if there was not, first, a serious attempt to resolve the Israeli–Palestinian conflict (*The Economist* 2002:51–52; Malone 2002; Said 2003).

In response, Bush laid out his plan for the Middle East on June 24, 2002. He specified that there should be an interim Palestinian state established within three years, but set onerous conditions on the Palestinians (Kessler, June 25, 2002). Bush called for the removal of Yasser Arafat as the leader of the Palestinian Authority and his replacement with leaders who are "untainted" by association with terrorism, as well as the restructuring of Palestinian governmental institutions (Kamiya 2002b; Bush 2002; Biedermann 2002b; Sudarsky 2002; Benn 2002; Salutin 2002:A17; Schweid 2002; Khatib 2002:A13; Falk 2002). Currently, efforts to reach a Mideast peace revolve around implementing the "Road Map" to peace, based on Bush's June 24 speech. The Road Map is sponsored by the Quartet (the United States, the European Union, Russia, and the United Nations) and represents the lowest common denominator position among the diverse parties. Still, it is the only "consensual peace plan on the table that has broad international backing" (Bar-Yaacov 2003:74). The parties are to implement the Road Map in three stages: the first stage calls on the Palestinians to end terrorism and reform their institutions; at the same time, Israel must freeze settlement construction and gradually withdraw from Palestinian areas; the second phase envisages a Palestinian state within interim borders; the third phase envisages negotiations leading to a final Palestinian state in 2005 (Bar-Yaacov 2003; Benn 2003). What all observers agree on is that any hope of a Mideast peace depends upon the U.S. being deeply engaged in the process and willing to use its considerable leverage with Israel to push for a just settlement to the dispute (Pressman 2003; Allin and Simon 2003; Bar-Yaacov 2003).

Both sides quickly sabotaged the Road Map. Yasser Arafat, the Palestinian President, undermined Mahmoud Abbas, the new Palestinian Prime Minister. Arafat refused to give up his power over various security forces and refused to be sidelined by the U.S. and Israel. Abbas refused to attack directly the Palestinian militant groups conducting terrorism against Israel, fearing a Palestinian civil war. Instead, he tried to negotiate ceasefires with the most active militant groups. Israel would not accept that, fearing that militants would use a ceasefire to rearm. Israel continued its own military policies against the militants, thereby helping to keep the regional cycle of violence going. Israel also continued its settlement activities. In the end, Abbas resigned from his post, undermined by both Arafat and Israel. Ahmad Quereia replaced him. Escalating violence on both sides has left the plan unworkable.

A new problem has also arisen: Israel is in the process of building a "security fence" to separate itself from the Palestinians.[10] Meant to keep suicide bombers out of Israel, the security fence is approximately 700 km long. The fence does not stay on Israel's internationally-recognized border but is designed to wind its way through the Occupied Territories, encompassing Jewish settlements and making life much more difficult for Palestinians as it cuts them off from their land, their livelihoods, and each other. The barrier's current course will restrict Palestinians to about 42 percent of the West Bank. To critics, the fence is an Israeli effort to make the eventual return of Palestinian land much more difficult, to remove the political imperative to reach a negotiated settlement, and to create a de facto border (Bronner 2003; Bar-Yaacov 2003:72, 78). The Israelis argue that what is built can eventually be taken down, once a negotiated settlement is finalized. At present, two court cases have challenged the fence. One case was brought before Israel's Supreme Court by an Israeli human rights organization which questions the legality of building on occupied land and emphasizes the hardship caused to the Palestinians. The other case was referred to the International Court of Justice in the Hague by the UN General Assembly.[11] The ICJ's decisions are not binding, and many states — including Canada — have argued that the ICJ should not hear the case and that the issue should be decided through political negotiations.

The construction of the security fence has been accompanied by a startling new development: Prime Minister Ariel Sharon's stated decision to evacuate Jewish settlements in the Gaza Strip and some remote settlements in the West Bank. Despite considerable opposition from within his own Cabinet and party, Sharon has pushed ahead with unilateral plans to move Jewish settlers out of Gaza and — more ominously — relocate them in the West Bank. His decision to abandon Gaza was probably based on the realization that within the next ten years, at current relative rates of population growth, there will be more Arabs living under Israeli control than Jews.[12] Palestinians have noticed that, and many had begun to argue that if Israel is reluctant to permit the creation of a Palestinian state, then Palestinians should simply demand that Israel annex the Occupied Territories and give its inhabitants full Israeli citizenship. By leaving Gaza, Sharon has dropped a million Palestinians out of the potential Israeli population and, at least, delayed the day of reckoning. Even so, a nightmare scenario for Israel would be a situation where Israel controlled a majority Arab population and denied them citizenship rights. Such a situation would force Israel to choose between being a democracy or a Jewish state. Sharon is looking for support for the withdrawal from Gaza from the U.S., and has agreed to put the plan to a referendum within his own political party on April 29, 2004. Sharon has also indicated that his Gaza plan is part of a unilateral disengagement by Israel from the Palestinians. While the Palestinians approve of Israel's pullout from Gaza, they want Israel to withdraw from the West Bank too, and they argue that the fundamental questions of dispute between the two sides must be resolved through negotiation, not imposition.

The decision to leave Gaza provoked a massive escalation of violence on both sides, as Hamas and other militant groups increased their attacks on Israeli soldiers and settlers, hoping to be able to claim that they drove Israel out of Gaza when the withdrawal comes. Israel increased its own attacks in Gaza specifically to avoid the impression that terrorism had forced it out of the territory. Israel stepped up its campaign of targeted assassinations of Hamas leaders, and finally succeeded in killing Sheik Yassin, the spiritual leader of Hamas. That event was roundly condemned by the international community as certain to provoke even further violence, and there are early signs that Yassin's death has led to a greater level of cooperation between Hamas and other militant groups, including Lebanon's Hezbollah.

The White House has traditionally condemned Israel's settlement expansion and has argued against building the security fence. Some American officials have suggested that the U.S. might withhold the costs of the fence from its loans to Israel. However, these costs are relatively minor and neo-conservative American officials have dismissed the idea of withholding funds from Israel as an idea from the State Department, not the White House (Dowd 2003). The Bush Administration is politically vulnerable, attacked for its handling of Iraq and its mishandling of the U.S. economy. Heading into a new election campaign in 2004, it seemed very unlikely that Bush would take the domestic political risk of putting pressure on Israel (Benn 2003; Allin and Simon 2003:136–139; Bar-Yaacov 2003; Pressman 2003). [At a meeting held in Washington on April 14, 2004, Bush gave tacit approval for the unilateral withdrawal from Gaza in return for recognition of some settlements on the West Bank. Bush explicitly foreclosed the Palestinian "right of return" as a point for future negotiations. *Ed.*]

Analysis: Canada and the Middle East–Adapting to Changing Circumstances

In trying to be "even-handed" on the Arab–Israeli conflict, Canada has tried to appear neutral (Sallott 2002:A4). However, while the effort to appear neutral may be politically prudent, it does complicate Canadian efforts to adhere to human security principles. As Richard Falk points out:

> It is important to appreciate that on virtually every issue in contention, the Palestinians have international law on their side, including the Israeli duty to withdraw from land taken during a war, the illegality of settlements under Article 49(6) of the Fourth Geneva Convention, the right of refugees to a safe return to the country that wrongly expelled them and the generalized support for a Jerusalem that belongs to everyone and no one (Falk 2002:3).

Insofar as human security supports international law, these arguments are difficult to ignore. Beyond these issues, Israel has violated international law and international consensus in numerous other ways. Israel's use of collective punishment in response to terrorist activity and its destruction of family homes are violations of international law. According to Amnesty International, many Israeli military actions during the IDF assault on Jenin and Nablus in early 2002 constituted war crimes. An Amnesty report on the subject noted many instances of the IDF blocking ambulances from reaching the wounded, the use of civilians as human shields, the destruction of homes with the residents inside (killing the residents), and the mass destructions of homes using tank fire, air-to-ground missiles, and bulldozers, "in most cases without any military justification and after the fighting had ended" (*Ha'aretz*, Nov. 4, 2002).[13]

The Palestinians, of course, are hardly blameless. The use of terrorism, particularly suicide bombings by Palestinian militant groups, has generally targeted Israeli civilians and has exacted a considerable toll in life and injury. Canada consistently recognizes Israel's right to protect and defend itself against terrorism. In this respect, it is being consistent with human security's focus on the protection of civilians in time of war. Indeed, the deliberate targeting of civilians is exactly the kind of violent activity that human security specifically opposes.

Nonetheless, Israel is more often in violation of international law than the Palestinian side in this conflict. There are numerous reasons for that. Israel is the state in this conflict, and so the laws of war and other international obligations apply more readily to its actions. It is also, by far, the more powerful of the two parties and, therefore, has greater opportunity to break international law. The UN Special Rapporteur of the Commission on Human Rights, John Dugard, spells the out the extent of the problem:

> Many of the rights contained in the International Covenant on Civil and Political Rights and the International Covenant on Economic, Social and Cultural Rights have been violated by the Israel Defence Forces (IDF) in their actions against the Palestinian people. Many of the obligations of international humanitarian law have likewise been violated. These violations are, however, justified by Israel as action taken in self-defence and legitimate anti-terrorism action. That Israel has legitimate security concerns cannot be denied. That it is entitled to take strong action to prevent suicide bombings and other acts of terror is not disputed. On the other hand, there must be some limit to the extent to which human rights may be violated in the name of counter-terrorism … a balance must be struck between respect for basic human rights and the interests of security. Here the principle of proportionality recognized by international humanitarian law has a key role to play. It is not possible to adopt an armchair attitude in assessing Israel's response to suicide bombings and Palestinian violence. Israel is entitled to a wide margin of appreciation in its response. But, even allowing for this … Israel's response to terror is disproportionate. On occasion, Israel's action in the OPT (Occupied Palestinian Territories) is so remote from the interests of security that it assumes the character of punishment, humiliation. and conquest (Dugard 2003:6).

The situation is complicated by the fact that many of Israel's military actions are taken in support of Israeli settlements in the Occupied

Territories. Thus, illegal acts are often being done in support of illegal settlements.

Insofar as Canada's approach to human security is rooted in the UN Charter, the UN Declaration of Human Rights, the Geneva Conventions, and the other instruments of international law, the Arab–Israeli situation creates significant problems. Canada's ability to exercise "soft power" — to draw upon its international reputation as a principled and tolerant state to push for normative change — depends upon Canadian credibility. Canada will lack the capacity to speak with authority on issues of human rights, international law, and international normative change if it seems unwilling to apply these principles to Israel. For Canada, which sees itself as a Middle Power and wishes to exercise international influence through the human security initiative, silence on this issue simply draws attention to the inconsistency when Canada does choose to speak out on other issues. More significantly, the instruments and organizations of international law are now under considerable stress within international society. The harmful effects on international legal structures of American unilateralism and defiance of international law should not be underestimated. For states that value multilateralism and international law, reinforcing these principles has never been more important.

Nonetheless, it is also clear that a blind adherence to international law may not be politically advantageous in all situations, and the application of human security may need to take this into account. Canada defended its decision to oppose the UN reference to the ICJ on the Israeli security barrier by arguing that the request for an advisory opinion may not be a "useful step at this time, in this highly charged environment" (Swords 2004). Canada argued that the issues surrounding the barrier and the conflict in general needed to be "addressed in a broader negotiation context rather than within the procedural limitations of a judicial hearing" (ibid.). That position was mirrored by numerous other Western states, including the European Union.

The overall claim that the legal process will muddy the political negotiations is valid and underlines the differences between the international and domestic realms. However, it also highlights the limitations inherent in the application of human security. If legal instruments are subject to political considerations, then what will be the basis for deciding which issues remain in the political realm and which are subject to international law? International law has always been subject to political considerations, but if Canada is serious about constructing meaningful human rights regimes within the international system, then part of its effort must be in moving away from the politicization of the application of law. Canada's failure to do this — not just on this issue, but also in other applications of human security — raises legitimate questions about the role of human security principles in Canadian policy-making.[14] It may be that Canada may need to make a choice about its commitment to human security vs. its political interests. Certainly, many critics of human security have argued that the policy is wildly unrealistic and subject to too many inconsistencies. Yet, at the same time, the "war on terrorism" may actually be best prosecuted from a human security perspective. Given its surreptitious nature, terrorism can be fought effectively only through multilateral means. In addition, the human security agenda explicitly recognizes the need to address the economic, social, and political disparities and injustices that feed support for terrorism.[15] That implies that the surest route to a more just and ordered and effective international system is through multilateralism and the rule of law.

At the political level, Canada's approach to the Arab–Israeli conflict is relatively balanced. Canada tries to adhere quietly to its principles while recognizing the mutual tragedy of what the Palestinians and Israelis are doing to each other. The Canadian position also reflects the political realities of Canadian society. Some observers have suggested that the United States might take offence if Canada followed a distinctive approach to the Middle East (McMahon 2001:15, 18). However, Canada has differed from the U.S. on issues of international relations in the past — sometimes in very significant and provocative ways, such as Canada's continuing relationship with Cuba or its early recognition of Communist China — without damaging Canadian–American relations. Lyon's past studies of Canadian foreign affairs professionals have indicated that these experts generally did not regard U.S. policy on the Arab–Israeli conflict as being a decisive influence on Canadian policy (Kirton and Lyon 1989:195).

Finally, we cannot overlook the political symbolism of the Arab–Israeli conflict. If the United States is serious about promoting democracy and human rights in the Arab world, a just resolution of the

Arab–Israeli conflict is essential. As Ignatieff argues, the longer this conflict remains unresolved, the greater will grow the barriers between the democratic and human rights claims of the Western world and the reality on the ground.

Conclusion

Canada's efforts to incorporate human security into its foreign policy are challenged by the realities of the Arab–Israeli conflict. Political imperatives—including the divisive nature of this dispute within Canadian society and the role of the United States in the conflict—all require that Canada approach this issue with a great deal of care. At the same time, however, human security's focus on the importance of international law presents a conundrum for Canada in that the weight of international law favours one side in the dispute. Canada's claims to promoting international institutions and trying to build effective human rights regimes on the international level are potentially compromised by its political inability to follow the logic of human security through to its conclusion in this particular case.

The political symbolism of the Arab–Israeli conflict is becoming even more pronounced because of the growing American presence in the Arab world. At the same time, the United States's undermining of international institutions requires that other states compensate for the damage to multilateralism caused by American unilateralism. In that context, the human security approach, even with all of its flaws, may be even more imperative now than in the past. Terrorism can be effectively resisted only through multilateral means; the Western world's need to show that it is willing to abide by the principles it espouses is more important than ever.

Notes

1 For more on Canada as a middle power, see: Chapnick 2000:6–24.
2 For a discussion of evolving Canadian military policy, see: Dewitt 2000.
3 Israel named Pearson an honorary fellow of the Weizemann Institute for Science in 1968, and in 1969 the Zionist Organization of America awarded him the Theodore Herzl Award for his "commitment to Jewish freedom and Israel." These personal accolades probably affected the perception of the Arab world that Canada was and is biased towards Israel (Ismael 1985:10).
4 A significant exception here is Elizabeth MacCallum, the External Affairs Arab expert at the time of Israel's creation. MacCallum had counselled Lester Pearson to push for greater regard for Arab rights and further negotiations before agreeing to the creation of Israel. Her advice was ignored, and she correctly forecast the political and social consequences of creating Israel at the expense of the Palestinians (Kirton and Lyon 1989:193).
5 Lyon suggests that the fact McDougall represented the heavily Jewish-Canadian constituency of St. Paul's-Toronto "seems to have been one of the reasons why Prime Minister Mulroney chose her for External Affairs" (Lyon 1992–93:14). Mulroney was trying to mend fences with the Jewish-Canadian community after it had come to "view Clark as disturbingly pro-Palestinian" (ibid.).
6 This includes the *New York Times*, the Canadian Broadcasting Corporation (CBC) (In his comments, Asper specifically singled out CBC journalist Neil McDonald for criticism), Cable News Network (CNN), the British Broadcasting Corporation (BBC), and the *Guardian*. For the CBC's response, see Burman 2002.
7 These include Margaret Wente, Marcus Gee (the *Globe's* international relations columnist), William Johnston, and Norman Spector. Not coincidentally, these voices are all on the political right. Rick Salutin is the paper's only regular voice that is strongly supportive of the Palestinians. Naomi Klein's occasional columns are also more sensitive to the Palestinian side of the dispute. Other commentators, such as Jeffrey Simpson and Paul Knox, make efforts to take a "balanced" approach.
8 Most experts agree that the U.S.–UK war was illegal, though the U.S. argues that it was implementing UN Security Council Resolution 1441 when it attacked Iraq. For the legal debate see: Brunnee 2002; Wingfield 2002.
9 Note that the fact that there was never any convincing evidence that Saddam had WMD capability, particularly nuclear weapon capability, was well-known outside the U.S. in the run-up to the war. See: Kamiya 2002c; Goldberg 2002a.
10 The fence was originally suggested by the centre-left Labour Party and was meant to follow the "Green Line," Israel's 1967 borders. The idea of the

fence was appropriated by Likud, however, and is now snaking through the Occupied Territories.

11 Ninety UN members supported the resolution submitting the referencing to the ICJ. Eight were opposed and 74 countries, including Canada, abstained (*BBC News* 2004).

12 Sharon's political problems may also have contributed to the timing of the decision. At the time, the Israeli attorney general was being faced with a decision on whether or not to proceed with a further investigation into allegations that Sharon and his son had been bribed by an Israeli developer a few years earlier, and Sharon may have made the announcement both to distract public attention from his problems and impress upon the Attorney General that indicting the PM could have major consequences for the country.

13 Amnesty International accepts that Israel has a right to defend itself from terrorist attacks but argues that Israeli actions were far in excess of what was justifiable. In the past, Amnesty has condemned Palestinian suicide bombers as having committed "crimes against humanity." Note that Human Rights Watch has also condemned Palestinian suicide bombers in the same terms (Associated Press 2002).

14 As an example, as Foreign Minister, Lloyd Axworthy argued that human security should be subject to Canada's economic interests. Later, he failed to convince the Canadian Cabinet to impose sanctions against Talisman Oil of Calgary for its involvement in the Sudanese civil war.

15 Note that I am not arguing that terrorism can be stopped simply by addressing its "root causes." As Denis Stairs points out, some of these root causes may well be beyond political resolution (Stairs 2002). However, many people in the world, while not terrorists, are sympathetic to terrorist actions because of injustices that could be alleviated through political and economic actions.

References

ABC Online (2002) "Canadian publisher slams media on Middle East coverage," Friday, November 1: http://abc.net.au/cgi-bin/.

Acharya, Amitav and Arabinda Acharya (2000). "Human Security in Asia Pacific: Puzzle, Panacea or Peril?," *Cancaps Bulletin* no. 27, November: 1-5.

Algazy, Joseph (2002). "Peres plays down Amnesty report accusing Israel of war crimes," *Ha'aretz*, November 4: http://www.haaretzdaily.com/hasen/objects/pages/

Allin, Dana H., and Steven Simon (2003) "The Moral Psychology of U.S. Support for Israel," *Survival* 45(3) Autumn:123-144.

Aruri, Naseer (1998) "Oslo's Muddled Peace," *Current History*, January:7–12.

Associated Press (2003) "Defying peace plan, Israel approves new Gaza construction," Globeandmail.com, July 31: http://www.theglobeandmail.com/servlet/story/RTGAM.20030731.wsett0731/

——. (2002) "Human Rights Watch Condemns Palestinian suicide attacks," *The Jerusalem Post*, November 1: http:/www.jpost.com/

Axworthy, Lloyd (2002) "Stop the U.S. foul play," The *Globe and Mail*, July 17:A13.

Bain, William.(1999) "Against Crusading: The Ethic of Human Security and Canadian Foreign Policy," *Canadian Foreign Policy*, 6(3):85–98.

Bar-Yaacov, Nomi (2003) "New Imperatives for Israeli-Palestinian Peace," *Survival* 45(2) Summer:72-90.

BBC News (2003) "US warns Israel on settlements," BBC News Online, July 31: http://news.bbc.co.uk/2/middle_east/3115325.stm

BBC News (2004) "Q and A: What is the West Bank barrier?", BBC News Online, accessed April 11, 2004: http://newsvote.bbc.co.uk/mpapps/pagetools/print/news.bbc.co.uk/2/hi/middle_east/3111159.stm.

Benn, Aluf (2003) "Bush's Mideast Test," Salon.com, May 15: http://www.archive.salon.com/news/feature/2003/05/15/peace/.

——. (2002) "The calm before the storm," Salon.com, July 12: http://www.salon.com/news/feature/2002/07/12/calm/

Bennett, James (2003) "Palestinian Leader Orders the Arrest of Islamic Militants," The *New York Times*, August 20: http://www.nytimes.com/2003/08/20/international/middleeast.20CND-MIDEAST.html.

Biedermann, Ferry (2002a) "Damned if we do, damned if we don't…", Salon.com,, September 13: http://www.salon.com/news/feature/2002/09/13/egypt/

——. (2002b) "Hopeless in Hebron," Salon.com, July 3: http://www.salon.com/news/feature/2002/07/03/hebron/

Borger, Julian. (2002) "US 'has secret bio-weapons programme'." The *Guardian Weekly*, 167(19), Thursday October 31-Wednesday November 6:1.

Bronner, Ethan (2003) "An Israeli Barrier That Could Have Reduced Conflict Is Increasing It," The *New York Times*, August 8: http://www.commondreams.org/views03/0808-13.htm.

Brunnee, Jutta (2003) "The Use of Force Against Iraq: A Legal Assessment," *Behind the Headlines*, 59 (4) Summer:1–9.

Burman, Tony (2002) "Asper should cover Israel, not lecture," The *Globe and Mail*, November 9: http://www.workopolis.com/servlet/Content/qprinter/20021109/COBURMAN.

Bush, George W. (2002) "An opportunity and a test," Salon.com, June 25: http://www.salon.com/news/feature/2002/06/25/bush_speech/

Cellucci, Paul (2003) "Cellucci's Statements — Speech by U.S. Ambassador to Canada A. Paul Cellucci to the Economic Club of Toronto," March 25: www.cbc.ca/news/national/news/iraq/cellucci/

Chapnick, Adam (2000). "The Canadian middle power myth," *International Journal*, 55 (2) Spring:6-24

Cooper, Andrew, Richard Higgott and Kim Richard Nossal (1993). "Can Canada's Foreign Policy be Best Understood by the Concept of 'Middle Power'? in *Relocating Middle Powers: Australia and Canada in a Changing World Order*, Vancouver, University of British Columbia Press:16-32.

Dalby, Simon (2000). Geopolitical Change and Contemporary Security Studies: Contextualizing the Human Security Agenda, Institute of International Relations Working Paper no.30, Vancouver, Institute of International Relations, University of British Columbia.

Dao, James (2002) "US May Abandon Support of U.N. Population Accord," The *New York Times*, November 2:http:nytimes.com/2002/11/02/international /asia

Department of Foreign Affairs and International Trade (2001). Human Security Program: http://www.dfait-maeci.gc.ca/foreignp/humansecurity/HS_program-e.asp

——. (2002) The Middle East Peace Process: Canadian Policy: http://www.dfait-maeci.gc.ca/peaceprocess/keyqu-en.asp

Dewitt, David B., and John J. Kirton. (1984) "Canada and Mideast realities," *International Perspectives*, February:19–23.

Dewitt, David (2000) "Directions in Canada's international security policy," *International Journal*, 55(2) Spring:167-187.

Dewitt, David B. (1989) "Intifada and Canadian Foreign Policy: Pressures and Constraints for Policy Adjustment," *Middle East Focus*, Winter:21-24.

Dirlik, John. (1991-1992) "Canada-Israel Committee Calls Bush 'Idiot', Baker 'Pompous Jackass'," The *Washington Report on Middle East Affairs*, December-January:30.

——. (1991) "Mulroney's Pro-Israel Bias Forces Canada to Speak with Two Tongues," The *Washington Report on Middle East Affairs*, April:37.

Donnelly, John and Anthony Shadid (2002) "Where hawks dare," The *Edmonton Journal*, September 15:D3.

Dowd, Maureen (2003) "Neocon Coup at the Department d'Etat," The *New York Times*, August 6.

Dugard, John (2003) Question of the Violation of Human Rights in the Occupied Arab Territories, Including Palestine. United Nations Commission on Human Rights, September 8.

Economist (2002a). "Listen George," July 6:51–52.

——. (2002b). "Right to the brink," July 6:29.

Engel, Matthew (2002) "Meet the new Zionists," The *Guardian*, Monday October 28: http://www.guardian.co.uk/g2/story0,3604,820465,00.html

Falk, Richard (2002) "Ending the Death Dance," *The Nation*, April 29: http://www.thenation.com/doc.mhtml?I=20020429&s=falk

Gatehouse, Jonathan (2002) "The New Solitudes," *Maclean's Magazine*, 115 (21) May 27:20-25.

Guardian, (2003) "Iraq exposes divided alliance," Friday, February 7: http://www.guardian.co.uk/

Goldberg, Michelle (2002a) "'Regime change'—and then what?," Salon.com, October 10: http://www.salon.com/politics/feature/2002/10/10/regime/

——. (2002b) "Why American Jewish groups support war with Iraq," Salon.com, September 14: http://www.salon.com/news/feature/2002/09/14/jews_iraq/

Graham, Bill (2002a) Notes for an address by the Honourable Bill Graham, Minister of Foreign Affairs, to the Ambassadors of the Human Security Network on Canadian Perspectives on the Human Security Network and its Activities, June 7: http://webapps.dfait-maeci.gc.ca/minpub/

——. (2002b) Notes for an address by the Honourable Bill Graham, Minister of Foreign Affairs, to the Canadian Institute of International Affairs "Affirming Canadian Sovereignty in an Interdependent World." April 4: http://webapps.dfait-maeci.gc.ca/minpub/

——. (2002c) Notes for an address by the Honourable Bill Graham, Minister of Foreign Affairs, to the 17th Policy Conference of the Canada-Israel Committee, March 6: http://webapps.dfait-maeci.gc.ca/minpub

Hale, Ellen (2002) "Global warmth for the U.S. turns to frost," *USA Today*, August 14: http//www.usatoday.com

Hampson, Fen Osler, and Dean F. Oliver (1998) "Pulpit Diplomacy," *International Journal*, 53 (2), Summer:379–406.

Hillmer, Anne Trowell (1989) "'Here I am in the Middle':Lester Pearson and the Origins of Canada's Diplomatic Involvement in the Middle East," in David Taras and David H. Goldberg (ed) *The Domestic Battleground: Canada and the Arab-Israeli Conflict*, Montreal: McGill-Queen's University Press:125–143.

Ibbitson, John (2002) "Canada condemns world court compromise," The *Globe and Mail*, July 13: http://www.globeandmail.co/

Ignatieff, Michael (2003) "The Burden," *New York Times* Magazine, January 5: http://www.nytimes.com/2003/01/05/magazine/05EMPIRE.html/

Ipsos-Reid (2002)"Eight in Ten (79%) Canadians Believe We Should Not Take Either Side in Israeli-Palestinian Conflict," Ipsos-Reid-*Globe and Mail*-CTV Poll. Released Friday, April 12, 2002: http://www.ipsos-reid.com

Ismael, Tareq Y. (1985) "Canada and the Arab World: A Diplomatic History," in Tareq Y. Ismael, ed., *Canadian Arab Relations*, Jerusalem: Jerusalem International Publishing House:7–36.

——. (1993) *Canada and the Middle East: The Foreign Policy of a Client State*. Calgary: Detselig Enterprises Ltd.

Kaiser, Robert G. (2003) "Bush and Sharon Nearly Identical On Mideast Policy," The *Washington Post*, February 9:A01.

Kamiya, Gary (2003) "A faint sliver of Mideast hope," Salon.com, June 5: http://www.salon.com/opinion/feature/2003/06/05/peace_plan/

——. (2002a) "Bush's frightening Middle East appointment," Salon.com, Decmber 10: http://www.salon.com/news/feature/2002/12/10/abrams/

——. (2002b) "Fiddling while the Middle East burns," Salon.com, June 25: http://www.salon.com/news/feature/2002/06/25/israel/

——. (2002c) "President Bush's distorted case for war," Salon.com, October 10: http://www.salon.com/politics/feature/2002/10/10/intelligence/

Keating, Tom (2002) *Canada and World Order*, Second Edition. New York: Oxford University Press.

Kessler, Glenn (2003) "Bush Sticks to the Broad Strokes," The *Washington Post*, June 3:A01.

Khatib, Ghassan (2002) "Recognition is a two-way street," The *Globe and Mail*, July 10:A13.

Kilic, H. Ayla (2004) "A Critical Review of Canada's Policy Rationales for the Middle East: The Twentieth Century."

Kirton, John, and Peyton Lyon (1989). "Perceptions of the Middle East in the Department of External Affairs and Mulroney's Policy," in David Taras and David H. Goldberg (ed) *The Domestic Battleground: Canada and the Arab-Israeli Conflict*, Montreal: McGill-Queen's University Press:186–206.

Klein, Naomi (2002) "America is not a hamburger," The *Guardian*, March 14: http://www.guardian.co.uk/bush/story/0,7369,666880,00.html

Lind, Michael (2003) "How neoconservatives conquered Washington – and launched a war," Salon.com, April 9: http://www.salon.com/opinion/feature/2003/04/09/neocons/

Lobe, Jim (2003) "Of Intimidation and Israel," *Asia Times*, February 1: http://www.atimes.com

Lyon, Peyton (1985) "Canada's Middle East Tilt," in Tareq Y. Ismael, ed., *Canadian Arab Relations, Jerusalem*: Jerusalem International Publishing House:37–74.

Lyon, Peyton (1992-1993) "The Canada Israel Committee and Canada's Middle East Policy," *Journal of Canadian Studies*, 27(4):5–25.

Malone, David (2002) "The dial's stuck on crisis control," The *Globe and Mail*, May 10:A15.

Milbank, Dana, and Mike Allen (2003) "US Shifts Rhetoric On Its Goals In Iraq," The *Washington Post*, August 1:A14.

McMahon, Sean (2001) Canada–U.S. Relations and the Al-Asqa Intifada, Unpublished paper.

Mousseau, Michael, Havard Hegre and John R. O'Neal (2003) "How the Wealth of Nations Conditions the Liberal Peace," *The European Journal of International Relations*, 9(2):277–314.

New Worldpeace (2002) "Journalists enraged at 'censorship' by pro-Israel owners," May 6: http://newworldpeace.com/human20b.html

Nossal, Kim Richard (1998-1999). "Pinchpenny Diplomacy," *International Journal*, Winter:88–105.

Perlez, Jane (2002) "Anger at U.S. Said to Be at New High," The *New York Times*, September 11: http://www.nytimes.com/2002/09/11/international/middleast.11ARAB.html

Pressman, Jeremy (2003) "The Primary Role of the United States in Israeli-Palestinian Relations," *International Studies Perspectives*, 4(2) May: 191–194.

Roberts, Adam (1990) "Prolonged Military Occupation: The Israeli-Occupied Territories Since 1967," *American Journal of International Law*, 84:44–103.

Russo, Robert (2002) "Sympathy turns to scorn," The *Edmonton Journal*, December 29:D5.

Sagay, I. (1972) "International Law Relating to Occupied Territory: Can Territory Be Acquired by Military Conquest Under Modern International Law?," *International Law Journal*, 4(1):56–64.

Said, Abdel Monem (2003) "For Arabs, the problem is America," *International Herald Tribune*, January 31: http://www.iht.com/

Sallot, Jeff (2002a) "Graham's Mideast speech met with hisses," The *Globe and Mail*, Thursday, March 7: http://www.globeandmail.com/

——. (2002b) "Is Canada's Middle East policy evenhanded or biased?," The *Globe and Mail*, Friday, April 5:A4.

Salutin, Rick (2002) "World events around the water cooler," The *Globe and Mail*, June 28:A17.

Sanger, David E., and James Dao (2003) "US is Completing Plan to Promote a Democratic Iraq," The *New York Times*, January 6: http://www.nytimes.com/2003/01/06/international/middleast/

Schneider, William (2002) "Bush's European Problem," The *Atlantic Monthly*, September 4: http://www.theatlantic.com/politics/nj/scheider2002-09-04.htm

Schweid, Barry (2002) "Powell tries to exclude Arafat from peace process," Salon.com, June 28: http://www.salon.com/news/wire/2002/06/28/powell_arafat/

Sharma, Serena (2001) "Identity Searching in the International Arena," Partager: The *UBC Journal of International Affairs*, 17, Spring:75–83.

Shehata, Samer (2002) "Why Bush's Middle East propoganda campaign won't work," July 12: http://www.salon.com/news/feature/2002/07/12/propaganda/

Simpson, Jeffrey (2003) "Open letter to Paul Cellucci," The *Globe and Mail*, April 5: www.theglobeandmail.com/servlet/story/RTGAM.20030405.ibsimp0405/

Sontag, Deborah (2001) "Quest for Mideast Peace: How and Why It Failed," The *New York Times*, July 26:A1.

Stairs, Denis (2002) "9/11 'Terrorism', 'Root Causes' and All That: Policy Implications of the Socio-Cultural Argument," *Policy Options*, September:6–10.

Sudarsky, Noah (2002) "Sharon's master plan: Endless war, endless occupation," Salon.com, July 25: http://www.salon.com/news/feature/2002/07/25/sharon/

Swords, Colleen (2004) "Written Statement of the Government of Canada to the International Court of Justice," *Canada and the Middle East Peace Process*, January 29: http://www.dfait-maeci.gc.ca/Peaceprocess/canadian_ICJ_Submission_29jan04-en.asp

The Responsibility to Protect: Report of the International Commission on Intervention and State Sovereignty (2001). International Development Research Centre, Ottawa.

Wingfield, David R. (2003) "Why the Invasion of Iraq was Lawful," *Behind the Headlines*, 59(4) Summer:10–16.

United Nations and Israel, "Voting Record of the Security Council, 1998–99": http://www.cdn-friends-icej.ca/un/record9899.html

UNBisnet-UN Bibliographic Information System: http://unbisnet.un.org/

Zacher, Mark (2001) "The Territorial Integrity Norm: International Boundaries and the Use of Force," *International Organization*, 55, 2 (Spring):215–250.

PART V

Post-9/11 Evaluations of Foreign Policy, Canadian Response, Economic Union, and Elite Nationalism

15

The Impacts of the September 11 Events on Canada's Foreign Policy

Peter Karl Kresl

On September 10, 2001, the Bush administration was only slightly concerned with foreign policy. It had expressed its distaste with anything that smacked of the approach of the Clinton government. There was no place now for nation building, "foreign entanglements" were to be eschewed, the seductions of internationalism and collective security were to be rejected in favour of the narrow interest of the U.S. and if not isolationism then at least unilateralism. The primary policy concerns were domestic: getting a tax cut adopted that would bring short-run political gain while postponing the negative economic and social impacts until later in the decade, reducing the role of government in American life, and substantially increasing defense expenditures. In short, a rerun of the policies of the first years of the Reagan government. The president could still go to sleep at 9:30 in the evening and spend an hour or two in the gym every morning. The next day, of course, everything changed. Even while the president was being shunted from secret location to secret location and while Mayor Giuliani served as, in Frank Rich's words, "the nation's paterfamilias,"[1] an almost total reshaping of the interests and objectives of the U.S. government was taking place. Foreign policy was positioned front and centre, domestic policy was dropped from the "inside the Beltway" discourse, and a no-nonsense, single-minded focus on terrorism emerged, shortly to be replaced by another foreign policy issue — Iraq and Saddam Hussein — that promised a quicker and more decisive result. That latter policy issue will be excluded from this discussion.

For most countries in the world that was something that was worthy of note; for Canada, given the almost exclusive concentration on the U.S. in its external economic relations, this was a shift of tectonic proportions. No longer would Canada have to concern itself with getting attention from the White House on something other than softwood lumber; it would now find itself and its policies subjected to intense scrutiny with the prospect of significant negative consequences should it and they be found wanting. As stated in the information describing this conference, the three pillars of Canada's foreign policy are: peace, trade, and culture. In general, one could argue that peace is being supplanted as an objective by a desire for order, free trade is giving way to managed trade, and the idea of distinctive national cultures is being challenged by an increased perception of a need to promote a single voice concerning basic values of what passes for "the West." The challenges to these pillars are being mounted externally, and what is intriguing is the impact they will have on internal policy formation.

The *first* transition is being driven by a need to contain and, if possible, to eradicate forces that could possibly generate new September 11-type events. The noble aim of peace and the adoption by all countries of the values many argue are its requirement, democracy and markets, is being replaced by a need to enlist any government with any values in the cause of event containment. Control of activities and maintenance of an order with desired characteristics is now primary value.

The *second* transition to management of trade relations is a consequence of the need to control instability in the flows of goods, services and capital. The recent crises of Argentina, Asia, and Russia all suggest that free and unmanaged flows can lead to unpredictable and unacceptable inconvenience and loss of output for the developed, G7/G8, nations. Mounting a sustained effort of global security requires financial resources that simply cannot be put in jeopardy by recession and the need to divert funds to income maintenance and stimulatory tax reductions.

The *third* transition is motivated by a patriotic need to buttress the populations of various homelands behind the cause of response to terrorism. That requires the expenditure of tax revenues and of human lives for which the enhancement of Benedict Andersen's notion of the nation as an "imagined political community" requires a heightened sense of loyalty and willingness to accept sacrifice. Under these altered conditions, the community in question is under pressure of being expanded conceptually from the individual nation to the "western alliance."

While much has been made of the United States willingness to proceed with its post-September 11 initiatives, it is nonetheless pressing its allies most forcefully to comply with its agenda. In my presentation I will examine the pressures this imposes on Canada and how Canada has responded to these pressures.

The Impacts of the Events of September 11 on the Pillars of Canadian Foreign Policy

The phrase "a shift of tectonic proportions" (used above) is a very powerful image—the ground literally shifting, structures collapsing, and confusion everywhere. A bit dramatic to be sure, yet there is something of the current reality that is captured by this image. The existing architecture of Canada's relationship with the U.S. is indeed being reconsidered in fundamental ways, and the future of that relationship is one that is marked by deep confusion. Both of these points can best be illustrated through examination of each of the three pillars of Canadian foreign policy. First we will examine the nature of these challenges, and in the following section of the paper we will consider the specific consequences for Canadian policy.

Peace

The *Oxford Concise Dictionary* defines peace as "freedom from or cessation of war" and "freedom from civil disorder." It also means "quiet; tranquility." The most relevant definition of order is "a state of peaceful harmony under a constituted authority," and "the condition in which every part, unit, etc. is in its right place; tidiness." Peace, thus, stresses the absence of conflict and aggression. That can be the result of an acceptance by relevant individuals or throughout communities of a common vision of society, or of intense bonds of affinity that preclude conflict. Order stresses authority and everything being in its place, by whatever means. During the post-World War II period both of these approaches have been pursued: the former by Canada and the latter by the U.S. Canada has generally been an advocate of peacekeeping as an agent of the United Nations in various wartorn parts of the world.[2] The objective of these initiatives has been the cessation of aggression while diplomats have tried to bring the principals to some accommodation that would cause the bloodletting to cease. Essential to this approach is the attempt to resolve the underlying conflict and to put in place a lasting peace between the antagonists.

The U.S., on the other hand, has sought to use force to cause a belligerent state or non-state entity to accept defeat or to realize that the cost of further conflict would be outweighed by its costs. Resolution of the underlying conflict has been less important that simply getting the "enemy" to give up the struggle and to have the favoured participant installed as the legitimate government. That was clearly the case in Viet Nam as it was in a series of less cataclysmic confrontations, and we see it today in Iraq. The U.S. has usually been willing to support a strongman who has little regard for the democracy and the market economy it publicly endorses — "he is a thug, but he is *our* thug." While seeking to establish peace involves a long-term view, order is more instrumental and short-run — keep a lid on things until the next period.

At first, September 11 tilted the balance in favour of multilateral peacekeeping. The opponent was clearly identified, although it was not the traditional nation state. This was perceived to be a struggle that would probably take years to resolve. Allegiances were sought by the U.S. in the Arab world, in Western Europe, in Asia — indeed in all parts of the globe — for the threat was one which could seek out targets anywhere. Then the Bush administration lowered the emphasis on terrorism and turned to Saddam Hussein and Iraq as the primary enemy. The emphasis, it was felt, must be placed on reduction of the short-term threat; the long-term will take care of itself. Multilateral institutions such as the United Nations are fine if they are in service of that objective, but can be scuttled if they get in the way. The same is true for more narrowly defined alliances such as NATO, or bilateral partnerships such as that with Canada. The media and scholarly publications are replete with discussions as to whether this approach is viable, but it is clear that the Bush administration is committed to it. The likelihood that success in the short term with regard to Iraq may result in failure in the longer term initiative against the terrorism of September 11 has not been publicly discussed or analyzed; however, recently that has been the case by some op-ed page writers.

Canada and other allies of the U.S. have been asked to accept positions as sherpas for the U.S. expedition to Iraq. However, most of them continue to be more disposed to accept the legitimacy of the concern about terrorism than to see Iraq as a threat that is "imminent, overwhelming and not susceptible to resolution by means other than military force." The result is a fundamental schism between the U.S. and most of its major allies.

Trade

Since the Roosevelt administration's *Reciprocal Trade Agreements Act* of 1934, from the establishment of the *General Agreement on Tariffs and Trade*, in 1948, to the World Trade Organization, successive governments in most of the western, developed world have pursued the objective of trade liberalization. That is, freer trade. The ultimate goal has been a world economy in which there were no tariffs and no non-tariff barriers, but there are effective dispute resolution mechanisms. Most governments have had their periods of less than enthusiastic attachment to this objective: often domestic political pressures have militated against free trade, and occasionally a government was elected that was philosophically opposed to trade liberalization.

Although the free trade initiative among Canada, the United States and the United Kingdom was ultimately not supported by Canadian Prime Minister Mackenzie King in 1948, Canada began a serious fascination with free trade with its increasingly dominant trading partner to the south with the report of the Gordon Commission (the Royal Commission on Canada's Economic Future) in 1956. The first product of this interest was the Canada–U.S. Auto Pact of 1965. The work of Ron and Paul Wonnacott in the mid-1960s on Canada–U.S. free trade caused many economists in both Canada and the U.S. to do research on aspects of this policy proposition and to stimulate formation of a lobby of sorts that pressed for negotiation of such an agreement. The

Canada–U.S. Free Trade Agreement (1986) was quickly followed by the North American Free Trade Agreement (1992). In all of these initiatives the U.S. has been a willing and encouraging partner. Sometimes the administration was philosophically committed to trade liberalization, but at other times it was responding primarily to pressure from a specific industry, such as the automobile industry in the midi-1960s, or to industry in general, as was the case twenty years later.

Today the situation is quite different, although the causation is open to debate. On the one hand, one could argue that the Bush administration is willing to give protection to any industry that can promise two congressional districts in the congressional or presidential elections. Hence the hard position of Canadian softwood lumber, the 30 percent tariff on steel imports and the reluctance to make concessions on imports of clothing and textiles, even to Pakistan, one of our strongest allies in the post September 11 period. On the other hand, one could be more charitable and argue that it is the attacks on September 11 that have put freer trade on the back burner. Since all governments are to some degree responsive to pressure from their major political supporters, it makes more sense to focus our attention on the events of September 11 as the cause of the transition from free trade to managed trade.

The term managed trade refers to trade relations and initiatives being motivated, not by a philosophic commitment to economic efficiency through specialization and exchange, but rather by geopolitical, strategic, or macro-economic considerations. A phenomenon such as September 11 is the sort of thing that can bring the latter factors to the fore. Even Adam Smith argued that protectionist measures were sometimes necessary since the first obligation of any state is to ensure its own survival, and that that far outweighs the efficiency gains of free trade. That is the realization that is embedded in the legacy of September 11, and the one that governs Canada's trade relations.

Other events have affected the international acceptance of free trade. Latin America is most potentially relevant to Canada; so the discussion here will be limited to that region. Several countries in South America have adopted the market-oriented reforms that were being promoted by international lending agencies and by governments such as those of the U.S. and Canada. Only Chile seems to have had success with these policies, and many of the rest, Argentina, Colombia, Venezuela, and

Brazil for example, have experienced economic decline, currency collapse, and increased popular support for governments that promised to slow down or greatly modify the reform agenda. The global skepticism about globalization in general has been powerfully felt throughout Latin America. As a result of that, the enthusiasm for the Free Trade Area of the Americas — taken by many economists to be the natural next step after NAFTA — has waned dramatically during the past three or four years. It may be a decade or more before this proposal can be seriously discussed by the relevant governments, in spite of FTAA talks having just begun in Quito, Ecuador.

Another consequence of September 11 is the diminishing prospect for another round of WTO trade liberalization anytime in the near future.[3] Just about the only trade initiatives being discussed anywhere in the Americas today are the efforts of the European Union to establish bilateral agreement with Central American economies or MERCOSUR (Brazil, Argentina, Paraguay, and Uruguay). The EU has accepted that Mexico and Canada are fully within the U.S. orbit, although many in each of these countries would vehemently resist this characterization — at least in the longer run. Hence, on all fronts grand global efforts and trade liberalization have given way to managed bilateral relationships, with their objectives being a mixture of economics, domestic politics, global strategy, and cultural affinity. Sidney Weintraub has warned: "We are buying an unstable situation that will create problems and need correction over time.... (F)or now, the issue is to benefit U.S. exporters.... It is not clear that we are taming this monster by leaping head first ourselves into serial FTAs of our own, particularly bilateral or plurilateral FTAs, as opposed to regional (the Western Hemisphere) or global trade liberalization."[4]

The importance of September 11 for trade relations is largely based on the impact it is having on the pressure the U.S. has been exerting on the rest of the world to adopt free trade. It is obvious that the attention of the Bush administration understandably has been diverted from trade policy to more pressing things. But beyond that, however, is the reality that circles of security and of friends are being formed — circles are being drawn in the sand, so to speak. The only two major governments to have supported the U.S. on its Iraq initiative are the UK and Italy; even Jean Chrétien has taken a position that is contrary to what

President Bush would find to be congenial. It may well be that Tony Blair and Sylvio Berlusconi will be the only leaders to have ready access to the front door of the White House. For freer trade relations with the U.S. to be developed, the partner country or countries may have to adopt security measures, police scrutiny and so forth as a condition of entry, not because of any particular eagerness to do so. We have seen the sorts for pressures for security harmonization that the U.S. has raised in its relationship with Canada. That should also reduce the impetus for free trade, and privilege more structured, managed trade relationships.

Culture

Culture policy and culture relations have been one of the most contentious aspects of international relations during the past quarter century. Following the Second World War, the cultural contrast was part of the contrast between the Soviet system and that of the West. That was portrayed in the West as a conflict between the mindless subservience to a totalitarian system of the Soviet bloc and the liberation of the human spirit as self-described by the West.[5] The U.S. was the prime promoter of the cultural values of the West, and the Soviet Union was chief spokesman of its alternative; each approach or system gained its adherents. During the Vietnam War U.S. culture came to be perceived in many, if not most, countries as overbearing, imperialistic, and militaristic. The U.S. argument that free markets and democracy were universal values that could only lead to the liberation and betterment of individuals everywhere seemed in this environment to be instrumental and self-serving, as well as being promoted only when convenient. The instruments of U.S. cultural exports — films in particular — appeared to critics to be Trojan horses that would lead to the absorption of the political processes and economy of the host nation into a structure that was dominated by the Western super power. In many countries there was a counter reaffirmation of the value of the national culture; that has been the case most notably in France and in Canada.

Those who wanted to celebrate their own national culture were tolerated as long as they focused on those cultural values as constituents of a western culture that had universalist components. Conflicts between these two notions of culture were met with antagonism and with derision. That was dramatically the case when proponents of a national culture sought to implement cultural protectionism measures, such as quotas on imports of films or television programming, or taxes on foreign cultural goods.

The European Union was in the unenviable position of trying to protect something that no one was certain actually existed. "European culture" could not be identified as what was common to the member states of the EU, since that membership periodically expanded, with the next step being the inclusion of ten countries from the Baltic states to the Visegrad Four (Poland, Hungary, the Czech Republic, and Slovenia), Malta, Cyprus, and the Slovak Republic. How could one fashion a cultural unity out of such a disparate collection of national cultures — the six, the nine, the ten, the twelve, the fifteen, or the twenty-five? It is no wonder that Americans saw EU cultural policy as little more than a protectionism that was no more legitimate for film than it was for shoes. The way out for the EU was to celebrate not "European culture," but rather the cultures of its member states and their regions.[6]

France soldiered on articulating a distinctive national culture that was the result of centuries of literary, artistic, and diplomatic achievement, and recognition of the integrity and value of local accomplishments of "*la France profonde*" in food, music, and material craft. The former was engrained in French society certainly since the initiative of *les maisons de la culture* of Léon Blum in the 1920s, and the latter has always had its impact on high and low culture in France.[7] The battles of Jack Lang in the government of François Mitterand, while gaining much in publicity, do not stand out as unique in the history of twentieth-century France. It is also of interest that at the recent meeting in Beirut of La Francophonie, Québec Premier Bernard Landry called for an exemption for cultural goods from world trade rules.[8]

Canada has been in the front lines of the cultural battles because of its proximity to the primary source of cultural exports, the U.S., and to the facts of history, language and economics that make it so vulnerable to the alleged negative impacts of cultural homogenization. Active policy in the area of cultural exchange is a child of the 1970s. The Canada–U.S. Auto Pact (1965) was seen by many as the first step on a slippery slope that would lead inexorably to a free trade, if not to a customs union, and ultimately to the absorption of the smaller nation into the larger. Thus for Canada the resistance to free importation of U.S. cultural goods was partly due to a desire to give breathing room for the domestic product and partly due to an aversion to the perceived longer term consequences of their being given free access to the Canadian market.

The events of September 11 are having the effect in the U.S. cultural policy community of drawing the wagons closer together and of solidifying the notion that "either you are with us or you are against us," or as Washington analyst Toby T. Gati puts it, "What's good for America is good for the world."[9] The U.S. has long argued that its values are dominated by democracy, free markets, the individual, Christianity, and human freedom. To argue a position in opposition to the spread and free circulation of cultural goods that articulate and express U.S. cultural values is perceived by many in Washington to be an act that questions those values themselves. The issue is made far more complex by the fact that the cultural goods in question are often the products of corporations that stand to make or lose millions or billions of dollars on the question of their free circulation — Disney and Time-Warner-AOL are not likely to evoke much sympathy from those who are neither employees nor shareholders.

The bottom line with regard to the environment within which Canada tries to articulate cultural policies that defend or promote its distinctive national culture is that the country that is so dominant in its world is likely to be less tolerant of the notion of cultural diversity. Departures from the desired cultural homogenization approach will probably be met with little sympathy and with raised eyebrows and the question — are you with us or not?

The Canadian Response

Some of the impacts elabourated in the previous section are being realized already and are affecting Canadian policy; others are still only potential impacts that may have noticeable consequences in the near future. In this section of the paper I will review actual Canadian responses to these impacts and will suggest some other responses that may be anticipated. Due to the nature of the limited time that has transpired since September 11 and of the time involved in formulation of policy responses to specific events, some of what follows will by necessity be of a speculative rather than an objective nature. After examining the general response, I will consider individually each of the three pillars of Canadian foreign policy.

General

The single theme that runs through the many documents detailing the Canadian response to September 11 is that both countries should continue to facilitate the easy flow of low-risk goods and people across the Canada–U.S. border and that more resources should be devoted to dealing with high risk flows. With trade with the U.S. accounting for about 36 percent of Canadian GDP one can easily understand this desire. There was, however, a concern that the U.S. would insist on a security circle that would create a "fortress North America" and on "establishing a common security perimeter to protect both Canada and the United States."[10]

There were some early potential portents of things to come that turned out to be rather less. Part time Canadian students were to be denied freedom to cross the border for classes in educational institutions in the U.S. That was later resolved for Canadians, but Mexican students will be required to apply for visas. Apparently, Canada at this point was deemed to be inside the security circle, but fellow NAFTA member Mexico was not. More earthshaking in its implications was the decision that Canadian retirees were not going to be able to spend their winters in the U.S. Sunbelt, at least not beyond the time permitted for short-term visitors. That too has been resolved. Then there was the short-term determination that some General Motors workers in London, Ontario, were sent home on the grounds that they were security risks because of dual citizenship — in many cases British. That may have been caused by a misinterpretation by the company of U.S. law. Most recently, in late October (2002), the U.S. made it mandatory that visitors from certain countries (primarily from the Middle East) be fingerprinted, photographed and interrogated on suspicion that they may be members of terrorist organizations. The Canadian response has been to advise travelers from those countries not to continue through Canada to U.S. destinations and to argue that this policy entails unacceptable racial or ethnic profiling. This issue, too, has been resolved by the U.S. clarifying that those traveling on Canadian passports will not be so scrutinized. The concern remains that other, less easily resolved issues may arise as the Bush administration seeks both an effective border security policy and successes in congressional and presidential elections.

Canadian Ambassador to the U.S. Michael Kergin responded a year after September 11 that discussions that would limit Canadian sovereignty in this way had yet to be proposed. His comment in conclusion is as follows: "We don't need closer integration with the United States to reinforce our common security. For example, we can still have our own legislation and regulations relating to immigration, and the Americans can have their own legislation and regulations.... What we need here is not so much a 'perimeter of security' as a 'zone of confidence' around North America."[11] Ambassador Kergin was asserting that Canadians would not have to accept U.S. policies on asylum seekers, police scrutiny of immigrants, work visas, residency requirements, and so forth. Stephen Clarkson concurs that Canada's immigration, border security and anti-terrorism procedures have been in fact better thought-out and implemented than have their U.S. counterparts, and that "Ottawa could continue managing its crucial bilateral relationship on a pragmatic, case by case basis."[12] The Coalition for Secure and Trade-Efficient Borders stated that the "zone of confidence" should be thought of as "a collabourative and integrated approach that better coordinates and manages existing practices, and establishes new steps that will ensure the protection of all North American citizens by focussing security resources on higher-risk areas through three integrated lines of security."[13] Be that as it may, Canadian policies and actions will nonetheless have to be such as to give the U.S. a feeling of "confidence" that the desired results can be achieved in a less intrusive manner than full policy and procedure harmonization of Canada with the U.S. It is likely that Canada will have to continue to define its national interest and to resist being drawn into policies, procedures and institutions that are designed to serve the U.S. interest.

Peace

The general thrust of U.S. foreign policy is that of reducing the importance of multilateral efforts and of relying increasingly on unilateral

U.S. initiatives. Canada's primary focus in its defense/security approach has been keyed to the multilateral approach. The demands placed on Canada's military for United Nations peacekeeping activities were rather limited — a few ground troops and a small number of ships and aircraft. NATO membership consisted of the U.S., with its superpower arsenal of weapons, and Western European nations that, in Robert Kagan's analysis, were beyond using force, albeit because of their current weakness.[14] Thus, here too it was possible for Canada to justify limiting its expenditure on defense and military goods. Total active duty personnel now number about 50,000, hardly enough for participation in anything but joint efforts with other nations. Western Europe has shown its inability to act as a significant entity through its inability of develop a common position in ex-Yugoslavia. The result of that is to leave Canada few options other than to participate as a junior partner in ventures undertaken by the U.S. or the NATO forces in Afghanistan, as part of the forces' Operation Apollo in the period after September 11.

This integration of the Canadian into the American military forces is known as "interoperability." That can be evaluated in two distinct ways. On the one hand, it can be seen as the inevitable consequence of the emergence of international terrorism as a dominant reality of international relations. As David Grondin wrote, "September 11, 2001, has mandated what one must call the continentalization of Canadian security."[15] On the other hand, Dean Oliver offers the possibility that September 11 "may in the end, prove an illusory threat, blown out of proportion globally by the tactical but spectacular success of the bin Laden terrorist group on a single unfortunate day."[16] In the latter case, interoperability need not be all inclusive for Canadian defense forces except for specific aspects of Canada's security needs.

September 11 has concentrated the efforts of Canada's dominant partner on establishing a predictable, low-uncertainty environment, going so far as to state explicitly its willingness to use "the option of preemptive actions to counter a sufficient threat to our national security."[17] That policy has been used several times in the past, but making it an integral component of the official strategy of the government legitimizes this action for other states that would like to tidy up some unpleasant situation. But more importantly for Canada, it also informs close allies, including Canada, that the U.S. will go ahead with such actions if and when it chooses to do so and that truly close allies will approve and support these decisions and participate in the actions they generate. Peacekeeping is fine, but when push comes to shove, a stable and controlled order is what is now needed.

In clear contrast, Canada has emphasized the importance of multinational organizations in the battle against terrorism. In several presentations, Canadian government officials and agencies have stressed the need to work in collabouration with the North Atlantic Treaty Organization, the Organization for American States, the Asia Pacific Economic Cooperation forum, the Commonwealth, *La Francophonie* and the UN.[18] In one publication the continuing work that was being done on the International Criminal Court was touted as representing "an extremely significant step in the ongoing struggle to eliminate impunity for the worst crimes known to humankind."[19] What clearer conflict with the Bush administration in fundamental policy could there be than this position on the International Criminal Court?

Trade

Canada is in the unfortunate position of having 80 percent of its trade with one partner and trade amounting to over 40 percent of its GDP, while the comparable figures for that partner are 25 and 10 percent. Thus the bilateral trade flows account for 35 percent of Canadian GDP but only about 2.5 percent of that of the U.S. This imbalance means that Canada will always be the *demandeur* in trade discussions, that the attention that the U.S. will devote to this issue will always be very limited, and that Canada has little clout in the relationship. While the largest trade gains were to be had from a deal with the U.S., both academic economists and government trade specialists have always argued that Canada must seek these gains in the context that puts them as an integral component of multinational trade negotiations, first through the GATT and now through the WTO.

The U.S. response to September 11 has to a considerable degree been, so to speak, that of taking multilateral trade liberalization off the front burner. Hence the U.S. trade position has shifted to negotiation of a series of bilateral trade agreements with Jordan, Chile, Singapore, China, and the Central American Common Market. One could argue that that is merely an effort to keep trade liberalization on the global agenda until the next WTO round. However, given the low probability that Doha will be followed by another round, one has to accept that managed, bilateral trade arrangements will be the approach taken for the foreseeable future. The prototypes of this less-than-global approach were, of course, the agreements with Canada and with Canada and Mexico. While U.S. Trade Representative Robert Zoellnick continues to be a persistent global free trade enthusiast, the terrorism-related exigencies that weigh so heavily on the rest of the Bush administration have increased the benefits of managed relationships regarding industries and to trading partners, and have brought this policy approach to the fore. Since the U.S. has been the primary force pressing for freer trade on a global basis, much of the impetus for WTO-based trade liberalization has become weakened.

For Americans, CUFTA and NAFTA took care of trade relations with Canada. In effect, the feeling is "we have signed the free trade agreement with Canada and with Mexico, so let's move on to other issues." The only things that remain are specific disputes over lumber, fish, motion pictures, and so forth. In other words, while it is routine to note the enormous flows of goods and services that cross the border in both directions, at the margin, Canada is in the U.S. trade policy arena primarily a source of irritation. An independent position on the other issues treated in this paper, peace and culture, will put Canada only in a more difficult negotiating situation on trade matters.

Canada's options in trade are extremely limited. Thirty years ago Mitchell Sharp presented the image of "the Third Option" in which the preferred situation for Canada was neither autarky nor a closer trading relationship with the U.S., but a contractual trade expanding arrangement with the EU and increased trade with Asia. However, since the decade of the 1970s, the U.S. share of Canada's exports in 2001 has increased from 67.7 to 85 percent, while the EU share has declined from 11.5 to 5.3 percent, that of Japan from 5.8 to 2.3 percent, and the rest of the world from 14.9 to 7.4 percent.[20] Given the robust growth of the U.S. economy during the 1990s and the enormity of its trade deficit, the U.S. has become the major and growing market for many of its trading partners. That suggests the increasing relevance of the model of the U.S. as the hub and other partners as spokes, which makes very difficult anything approaching a bargaining relationship of equality between the U.S. and Canada and its other trading partners. Nonetheless, there are many issues, such as cultural goods and services, energy, raw materials, intervention by Congress on behalf of well-funded constituents, and so forth, on which Canada and other trading partners of the U.S. could find common ground and present a common position in trade negotiations. In accord with that, Joseph Nye has written that "some allies may follow the American bandwagon on the largess security issues but form coalitions to balance American behavior in other areas such as trade or the environment."[21]

Culture

In recent years Canada has moved away from the policies of the Trudeau government—policies that seemed to be designed to elicit a negative response from the U.S. Intervention on the side of Canadians' demand for U.S. cultural goods appeared, from south of the 49th parallel, to be blatant protectionism. These demand-side interventions were followed by policies that were perhaps a bit more accommodating to U.S. producers of cultural goods but, more importantly, they also had their primary impact on the supply side of the Canadian cultural goods industry.[22] While a U.S. producer can legitimately complain about being deprived access to the Canadian market, there is no legitimate complaint if a foreign country's policy simply adds to consumer choice. So in recent years, culture policy relations have been far less incendiary than they were in the 1970s. Nonetheless, the line taken is still not as straight as one would hope.

On the one hand, in a document detailing the negotiating strategy Canada would pursue in the negotiations for the Free Trade Agreement of the Americas, the Department of Foreign Affairs begins by stating the "Canada will seek a cultural exemption." It then goes on to state that the language Canada would propose for the preamble of the FTAA would stress the importance of "cultural diversity" as articulated in the report of SAGIT (the Cultural Industries Sectoral Advisory Group on International Trade). On the other hand, SAGIT states in its 1999 report *New Strategies for Culture and Canadian Culture in a Global World* that there is a conflict between the two approaches, with the cultural trade exemption being the policy of the past and that "negotiation of a new international instrument that would specifically address cultural diversity and acknowledge the legitimate role of domestic cultural polices in ensuring cultural diversity" constitutes a "new strategy."[23]

The U.S. has never been happy with the policy of cultural exemption because it has never recognized a distinction between cultural goods and services and other goods and services. All goods and services are produced by individuals who earn a living doing that activity, and they are purchased by consumers who choose among all goods and services of all categories when spending their income. For the U.S., protectionism is protectionism, and the national culture is expected to take care of itself. Cultural diversity is fine and satisfying when it takes the form of a diversity which is subordinate to the overriding national culture. In times of high stress, such as we have following September 11, national cultural divergence from what the Council of Canadians refers to as the "Washington Consensus,"[24] is considered to be diversionary and contrarian and to weaken the common "values front" against the common enemy. If the world is viewed from the vantage point of Samuel Huntington's *Clash of Civilizations*,[25] and if the opposing civilization is perceived to be a solid front, then anything that causes fissures in the solid façade of Western Civilization is not to be tolerated. And the supreme hegemon in the West will determine of what that façade will be composed. That suggests that Canada's efforts to ensure that the articulation and expression of its distinctive national culture will be given a jaundiced eye by the Bush administration.

In this situation Canada has two choices. First, the government can stall like the good soldier Schwejk and wait until the period of high stress passes—that could take a considerable period of time and could subject Canada's cultural industries and its policy agencies to a great deal of probing and thrusting by the U.S. in search for weakness. Most importantly, that would leave unchallenged the U.S.'s notion that all cultural goods and services are completely commercial in nature. Second, the government could continue to embed its resistance to quasi-wartime conformity through joint efforts within the structure of multinational institutions and in alliances with entities, such as the European Union, that share Canada's preference for cultural diversity. That is, Canadians can get behind the approach of SAGIT and press for a "new international instrument" that would recognize the importance of cultural diversity, acknowledge the distinction between cultural and other goods and services, and put in place an accepted set of policies and rules in conformity with these two notions.[26] This second approach would seem to be the one that is best suited for these times.[27]

Some Final Thoughts

As has already been noted, many of the U.S. reactions to September 11 are still in the process of being developed, although the general outline of the approach being taken is fairly clear. The Canadian response to this developing body of policy is equally in flux. Hence, some of what has been argued in this paper is necessarily speculative. Nonetheless the governments of both the U.S. and Canada have issued a sufficient number of policy statements and documentation to provide a fairly firm ground for this speculation.

The September 11-induced transformations of the three pillars of Canadian foreign policy — from free to managed trade, from peace to order, and from national distinctiveness to international conformity in culture — are having significant impacts on policy and on practice. They are also having an impact on the nature of the Canada–U.S. relationship. In recent decades, Canada has had to take the U.S. into account in virtually all of its foreign policy decisions. September 11 has upped the ante, so to speak, by making the U.S. less tolerant of dissention within the ranks and less willing to make accommodations to national distinctiveness. As Joseph Nye has noted "many of America's European friends continue to worry about recent American behavior. The specter of U.S. isolationism that haunted Europe during the Cold War has been replaced by the specter of U.S. 'unilateralism' and that the U.S. has become 'arrogantly unilateral.'"[28] In this context, Canada may choose to pursue peacekeeping, cultural diversity, and diversity in its trading partners to some extent, but it is most likely to be the case that the cost of doing so will be greater during the first decade of the twenty-first century that it was during the last decade of the twentieth century.

Notes

1 Frank Rich, "The De Facto Capital," *The New York Times Magazine*, October 6, 2002, p. 66.
2 This commitment was continued in the 1994 White Paper on Defence and in the most recent document, Strategy 2020 — Canadian Defence into the 21st Century. See: http://www.dnd.ca/eng/min/reports/94wpaper/ and http://www.vcds.forces.gc.ca/cds/strategy2K.
3 Daniel Drache and Sylvia Ostry, "From Doha to Kananaskis: The Future of he World Trading System and the Crisis of Governance," *Trade Policy Research: 2002*, Ottawa: Government of Canada, Department of Foreign Affairs and International Trade, p. 30.
4 Sidney Weintraub, "History Repeats itself in Trade Policy," *Issues in International Political Economy* (Center for Strategic and International Studies,) October 2002, No. 34 http://www.csis.org/simonchair/issues200210.pdf.
5 Frances Stonor Saunders, *The Cultural Cold War*, New York: The New Press, 1999; and Richard Pells, *Not Like Us*, New York: Basic Books, 1997.
6 "A fresh boost for culture in the European Community," *Bulletin of the European Communities*, Supplement, 4/87, Brussels: Commission of the European Communities, 1987, p. 6.
7 David Wachtel, *Cultural Policy in Socialist France*, New York: Greenwood Publishing Group, 1987.
8 David Buchan, "Québec PM in opt-out call over culture," *The Financial Times*, 22 October 2002, p. 2:1.
9 Quoted in Serge Schmemann, "Controlling Iraq's Oil Wouldn't Be Simple," the *New York Times*, November 3, 2002, Section 4, p. 14.
10 "Fortress North America: How our world will change," *Maclean's*, October 15, 2001, p. 23.
11 Michael Kergin, "Interview," *Canada World View*, Ottawa: Government of Canada, Department of Foreign Affairs and International trade, Issue 14, Winter 2002, pp. 12–13.
12 Stephen Clarkson, "Uncle Sam and Us One Year Later: The Geopolitical Consequences for Canada of September 11th," *Canadian issues: Thèmes Canadiens*, September 2002, p. 18.
13 Quoted in *Towards a Secure and Trade-Efficient Border* (Report of the Subcommittee on International Trade, Trade disputes and Investment), Ottawa: Government of Canada, House of Commons, November, 2001.
14 Robert Kagan, "Power and Weakness," *Policy Review*, No. 113, June 2002.
15 David Grondin, "Le Canada à la croisée des chemins: l'apres-11 septembre comme présage d'une intégration militaire Nord-americaine," *Canadian issues:Thèmes Canadiens*, September 2002, p. 14.
16 Dean Oliver, "Going Global? Exporting Security Post-9-11," *Canadian issues:Thèmes Canadiens*, September 2002, p. 63.

17 *The National Security Strategy of the United States of America*, Washington: The White House, September 17, 2002, p. 10 of 22.
18 "Canada's Point Man: Interview with Foreign Affairs Minister John Manley," and "From Ground Zero to coalition building Canada's diplomats gear up," *Canada World View*, Ottawa: Government of Canada: Department of Foreign Affairs and International trade, Issue 14, Winter 2002, pp. 5 and 16, respectively.
19 "From Ground Zero to coalition building Canada's diplomats gear up," p. 16.
20 *Third Annual Report on Canada's State of Trade*, Ottawa: Government of Canada, Department of Foreign Affairs and International Trade, May 2002, p. 9.
21 Joseph S. Nye, Jr., *The Paradox of American Power*, New York: Oxford University Press, 2002, pp. 16 and 17.
22 I have argued this in Peter Karl Kresl, "The Political Economy of Canada's Culture Policy: The 1990s," in André Lapierre, Patricia Smart, and Pierre Savard Language, *Culture and Values in Canada at the Dawn of the 21st Century*, Ottawa: Carleton University Press and The International Council for Canadian Studies, 1996.
23 Quoted in Bruce Jamieson, "Trade Liberalization: Culture, Identity and Social Cohesion," *Trade Policy Research: 2001*, Ottawa: Government of Canada, Department of Foreign Affairs and International Trade, p. 126
24 *Zip Locking North America*, Ottawa: the Council of Canadians, 2002, p. 17 of 37.
25 Samuel P. Huntington, *The Clash of Civilizations and the Remaking of the World Order*, New York: Simon and Schuster, 1997.
26 Bruce Jamieson, p. 127.
27 That is also the opinion given in Keith Acheson and Christopher Maule, *Much Ado about Culture: North American Trade Disputes*, Ann Arbor: The University of Michigan Press, 1999, ch. 18.
28 Joseph S. Nye, pp. 35 and 156.

References

Acheson, Keith, and Christopher Maule. *Much Ado about Culture: North American Trade Disputes*. Ann Arbor: The University of Michigan Press, 1999.

Buchan, David. "Québec PM in opt-out call over culture." *The Financial Times*, 22 October 2002.

Bulletin of the European Communities, Supplement, 4/87. Brussels: Commission of the European Communities, 1987.

Canada World View. Ottawa: Government of Canada: Department of Foreign Affairs and International trade, Issue 14, Winter 20.

Clarkson,Stephen. "Uncle Sam and Us One Year Later: The Geopolitical Consequences for Canada of September 11th." *Canadian issues: Thèmes Canadiens*, September 2002.

Drache, Daniel, and Sylvia Ostry. "From Doha to Kananaskis: The Future of he World Trading System and the Crisis of Governance." *Trade Policy Research: 2002*. Ottawa: Government of Canada, Department of Foreign Affairs and International Trade.

Government of Canada. *Strategy 2020 – Canadian Defence into the 21st Century*, http://www.vcds.forces.gc.ca/cds/strategy2K.

Government of Canada. *White Paper on Defence*, 1994, http://www.dnd.ca/eng/min/reports/ 94wpaper/.

Grondin, David. "Le Canada à la croisée des chemins: l'apres-11 septembre comme présage d'une intégration militaire Nord-americaine." *Canadian issues: Thèmes Canadiens*, September 2002.

Huntington, Samuel P. *The Clash of Civilizations and the Remaking of the World Order*. New York: Simon and Schuster, 1997.

Jamieson, Bruce. "Trade Liberalization: Culture, Identity and Social Cohesion." *Trade Policy Research: 2001*. Ottawa: Government of Canada, Department of Foreign Affairs and International Trade.

Kagan, Robert. "Power and Weakness." *Policy Review*, No. 113, June 2002.

Kergin, Michael. "Interview," *Canada World View*. Ottawa: Government of Canada, Department of Foreign Affairs and International trade, Issue 14, Winter 2002.

Kresl, Peter Karl. "The Political Economy of Canada's Culture Policy: The 1990s." In André Lapierre, Patricia Smart, and Pierre Savard Language. *Culture and Values in Canada at the Dawn of the 21st Century*. Ottawa: Carleton University Press and The International Council for Canadian Studies, 1996.

Maclean's, October 15, 2001.

Nye, Joseph S. Jr. *The Paradox of American Power*. New York: Oxford University Press, 2002.

Oliver, Dean. "Going Global? Exporting Security Post-9-11." *Canadian issues: Thèmes Canadiens*, September 2002.

Rich, Frank. "The De Facto Capital." *The New York Times Magazine*, October 6, 2002.

Saunders, Frances Stonor. *The Cultural Cold War*. New York: The New Press, 1999; and Richard Pells. *Not Like Us*. New York: Basic Books, 1997.

Schmemann, Serge. "Controlling Iraq's Oil Wouldn't Be Simple." *The New York Times*, November 3, 2002.

The National Security Strategy of the United States of America. Washington: The White House, September 17, 2002.

Third Annual Report on Canada's State of Trade. Ottawa: Government of Canada, Department of Foreign Affairs and International Trade, May 2002.

Towards a Secure and Trade-Efficient Border (Report of the Sub-committee on International Trade, Trade disputes and Investment). Ottawa: Government of Canada, House of Commons, November, 2001.

Wachtel, David, *Cultural Policy in Socialist France*. New York: Greenwood Publishing Group, 1987.

Weintraub, Sidney. "History Repeats itself in Trade Policy." *Issues in International Political Economy* (Center for Strategic and International Studies), October 2002, No. 34, http://www.csis.org/simonchair/issues200210.pdf.

Zip Locking North America. Ottawa: the Council of Canadians, 2002.

16

A Model of the Canadian Response to the Events of September 11

Louis-Blaise Dumais-Lévesque
and
Anne-Marie Durocher[1]

Introduction

In the wake of last year's terrorist attacks in the United States, Canada took a series of measures aimed at protecting the country from potential attacks and at maintaining good relations with the United States. The tightening of immigration laws, improved border security, and an increased cooperation with the U.S. military and intelligence agencies — these constitute measures taken by the government of Canada that are usually referred to as the "North American security perimeter." The puzzle we want to address is: (1) why the Canadian government decided to take the measures it took, apparently without being directly under threat from al-Qaida, and (2) why these measures ended up taking the form they took. Is it possible to connect the two questions into a coherent framework? After all, it is relatively easy to figure out an answer to each of the two questions, but it is less obvious to integrate them into one model.

We want to show how the Canadian government tried to satisfy the requirements of U.S. security and Canadian prosperity on the one hand, and the requirement of sovereignty on the other, when these competing requirements clashed after September 11. Our hypothesis is that U.S.

pressure led to the establishment of the security perimeter through the intervening variable of Canada's domestic structures.

We do not pretend to bring any new empirical facts to the debate; what we want to do is simply to formalize what many understand intuitively. We believe that the puzzle can be addressed from a theoretical angle, and that doing so will serve two purposes. First, it will contribute to a better understanding of Canada's relationship with the United States. Second, and from a more academic point of view, drawing on the theoretical literature in political science to understand Canadian foreign policy can have many advantages, of which the "cumulation" of knowledge and an opening to approaches other than historical perspectives may be the most important.

The Theory

In a nutshell, we argue that U.S. pressure toward the creation of a security perimeter was filtered through Canadian domestic institutions, and that led to the current security arrangements. Canada had no choice but to establish a security perimeter, but doing so entailed significant costs in terms of sovereignty. Thus, the key elements of the security perimeter content may have been imposed by Washington, but the specific form of the security perimeter is definitely Canadian.

Power-centred theories are fairly clear as to what should be the observed pattern in U.S.–Canada relations. Canada is so much weaker than the United States, and its economic dependence on them is such that the United States should usually be able to impose its will on Canada. While that is consistent with a realist understanding of sovereignty,[2] according to which severe constraints on behaviour does not represent a decrease in sovereignty, it clearly clashes with what most people think about when they think of the idea of sovereignty. For most people, sovereignty is a normative goal that should be pursued by their state, often because they see sovereignty as symbol and protector of their national identity. Sovereignty *is* freedom of action, a freedom to pursue one's definition of the good life. That a state could impose its will on another state is inconsistent with this conception. Stephen Krasner has argued that this popular understanding of sovereignty is not empirically accurate: in fact, it has never existed.[3] Different entities can possess different attributes of sovereignty, and to different degrees. Of key importance to us is that a state's sovereignty is often a function of its environment. By that, we do not mean only international recognition, but also its interactions with its neighbours. For example, Eastern European states during the Cold War were not sovereign in the same way that the United Kingdom was, and that difference stems from the fact that the former were under the influence of the Soviet Union which severely restricted their freedom of action in choosing their domestic institutions. As Krasner puts it, "the international system is not a game of chess. Constitutive rules never exclude alternatives."[4] In other words, sovereignty may be a norm shared by the actors of the international system and their populations, but it is always possible for states to break the rules when they need to.

Sovereignty is also part of a state's international identity.[5] An international identity is not only intersubjectively grounded, but it is also a function of the particular institutions of the different states. By that, we simply mean that a state will act on the international stage according to a certain pattern which is determined by how values held by the population and the elite manifest themselves through state institutions. In the case of Canada, a large proportion of the Canadian electorate have nationalist feelings. Since Canada is a functioning democracy, these preferences are represented in Parliament. If the ruling party's constituency is strongly nationalist, we can expect that the foreign policy of the government will be more nationalist. It will be more independent from the United States, and concerns with preserving sovereignty will be central. Nationalist feelings are unequally distributed in the different regions of Canada. Therefore, Canadian identity as it manifests itself on the international stage is also a function of the country's electoral system because the electoral system in the last few years has been producing only one national party and a relatively strong regional concentration of the various parties, including the national party. That leads to the conclusion that Canadian identity is not constant; it may be more important for certain political parties to appear to be upholding sovereignty than it is for others.

Legally speaking, Canada is a sovereign country. It also includes a large percentage of the population that highly values having a Canadian sovereign state. But because of the nature of its relations with the United

States, it may not be possible for Canada to be fully sovereign in the popular sense of the term. Because of its unique geographical position, Canada has to produce a certain good — security — in order to satisfy its powerful neighbour,[6] which in turn will allow the Canadian state to produce a second good, prosperity. Nothing made the tensions between sovereignty and the production of these goods clearer than September 11. How can one reconcile the foreign-imposed requirement of producing the good of security and the normative requirement of safeguarding one's sovereignty? Simple: you produce the goods while pretending this is not affecting your sovereignty. A manifestation of this "organized hypocrisy"[7] is the way the North American security perimeter was established: what the Canadian government did was to create this security perimeter, which was the good the United States wanted Canada to produce, but it labelled it otherwise and did not sign any all-encompassing treaty, choosing instead to sign administrative agreements and introduce bills in Parliament, and that allowed it to keep on pretending that Canadian sovereignty had been protected.

Nils Brunsson, in a book titled *The Organization of Hypocrisy*, noted that often organizations do not evolve in synchronicity with the norms of their environment. The organization is efficiently producing a range of goods, but how it goes about doing so does not necessarily accord with the prevailing norms of its environment anymore. When that happens, "two sets of organizational processes arise: one generates action; the other does not, but is kept for purposes of demonstration or display to the outside world. These second processes can be defined as rituals. Companies follow all the rules of joint consultation, for example, but this does not necessarily have any effect on subsequent decisions or actions...."[8] Replace the expression "joint consultation" with the word "sovereignty" and you have a description of the Canadian government's behaviour following the events of September 11.

The Canadian state is an organization that produces a wide range of goods, from security to prosperity. It must do so efficiently in a context of multiple constraints. One major set of constraints is the values and norms of the society in which the state is operating and which it serves. Another major set of constraints originates from Canada's proximity to the United States and its economic dependence on them: Canada simply cannot afford to ignore its powerful neighbour's concerns, and it must act accordingly. When these two sets of constraints clash, the Canadian government must find a way to satisfy them both; if it cannot reconcile the values with the production of the goods, it has to "coat" its external relations with talks of protecting Canadian sovereignty and respecting and protecting other Canadian values. The option of neglecting one set in order to meet the requirements of the other is not a viable solution, especially in the context of Canada's relationship with the United States. Canadian domestic structures are such that *openly* compromising on sovereignty to satisfy the United States is not possible whenever the ruling party has a strong nationalist base. Whenever the ruling party does not have to adhere closely to the demands of the protection of Canadian sovereignty, it is possible to satisfy openly the United States. When a Canadian government must satisfy the United States is an empirical question that should be answered on a case by case basis. However, it is safe to assume that whenever core U.S. interests are at stake, the U.S. will do what they can, and Canada will do what it must.

Canada–U.S. Relations

Several empirical elements following the attacks of September 11 appear to support the model. First, vital American interests were at stake, and they were related to Canadian policies in some way. Second, the United States exerted pressure on Canada. Third, the Canadian government took a series of measures that restricted its freedom of action. Fourth, these policies were *not* part of an overall treaty implementing a security perimeter, but they were rather decided upon and implemented separately through regulations and agreements that are sector specific. The model also predicted that the government would insist on the idea that sovereignty had not been altered following these measures, a pattern that was indeed present throughout the period under study (from September 11, 2001 to October 26, 2002).

September 11 was the first attack on American soil since Pearl Harbor. It took almost everyone by surprise and undoubtedly demonstrated that American vital interests were threatened by terrorism. The U.S. government felt compelled to take several initiatives in order to improve the security of its population and infrastructures. To do that, the U.S. government had to determine what the United States' potential vulnerabilities were. Unfortunately for Canada, the "longest undefended border in the world" became one very important focus of the U.S. leadership.

The U.S.–Canadian border is more than 6,000 km long and could never be completely sealed. It is important to note that a number of U.S. border personnel had been removed from the northern border following the ratifying of NAFTA and placed along the Mexican border. Even though the level of personnel gradually returned to pre-NAFTA levels, it was not raised proportionally to the increase in traffic since 1993.[9] Even with more people guarding the border, it still is impossible to control migration. Border agents from either side generally agree on the impossibility of effectively keeping the "unwanted" from entering their country.[10]

Even though the September 11 terrorists did not enter the U.S. through Canada, American authorities still believe, based on previous experience, that future terrorists could use Canada as a transit to the U.S. The most famous case of an attempted attack coming from Canada is, of course, the Ahmed Ressam case. However, he was not the only one caught at the border. In 1988, members of a Syrian terrorist group tried to enter the U.S. with a large amount of explosives. In 1993, some of the perpetrators of the first World Trade Center attack had entered the U.S. through Canada. Even more recently, in 1996, a member of Abu Nidal's terrorist group attempted to enter the U.S.[11] Logically, if the border is so difficult to guard, it means that many more terrorists could possibly have entered the U.S. from Canada or could do so in the future. It follows that a better strategy for the United States is to check people in international airports and in ports, before they enter Canada. That is the idea of the Security Perimeter: keeping the border inside open while reinforcing the border around the two countries.

U.S. vital interests affecting Canada thus involve immigration and domestic security policies. More specifically, questions of information sharing between intelligence agencies and refugee policies were the main objects of U.S. requests and pressure on Canada. Those are also areas of jurisdiction that are directly affecting the sovereignty of a state, the control over a state's population being part of most definitions of sovereignty. If a state imposes its standards on another, it follows from the popular understanding of the term that sovereignty is weakened. Canada made most of its policy changes in these areas since September 11.

In order to show that the changes were provoked by U.S. pressure, one has to show that these pressures actually occurred. Even though most of the pressure must have been applied behind closed doors, it is still clear that this pressure existed. As soon as September 12th, the American Ambassador to Canada Paul Cellucci declared that both countries' immigration policies should converge and become more and more similar.[12] At the end of October, he reiterated his position more firmly: "Everyone has to have a sense of urgency about this.... We shouldn't be talking years here. We should be talking, for some things, months and for other things, a year or two."[13] He was insisting on the need for harmonization and not solely on the addition of new technologies to improve the security at the border (which was the main focus of the Chrétien government).[14] In fact, Mr. Cellucci had been an advocate of the Security Perimeter since his appointment to Ottawa in April 2001, but the events of September 11 added weight to his proposals. Many of the policies adopted were already planned before the attacks, but their adoption or implementation was substantially accelerated because of these events.

As we stated earlier, the Canadian government after September 11 had to provide three goods: security for the Americans, prosperity for Canadians and a preservation of sovereignty for the nationalists. Mr. David O'Brien, president of the Canadian Pacific, representated the position of the business circles when he argued on September 14th in favour of the creation of a security perimeter, saying that Canadians would lose sovereignty but that in the end they had no other choice. He said: "The truth is we have a limited ability to create our own foreign policy today, let's not kid ourselves. We have some room to maneuver, but only within a limited framework which is pretty well pre-set. We can't be taking positions on a whole range of issues that are diametrically opposed to the U.S."[15] The business circles have also formed the *Coalition for Secure and Trade-Efficient Borders*, which made three recommendations to the government: to take measures "(1) to facilitate the passage of low-risk goods and people across Canada's borders, (2) to strengthen Canadian security, immigration and border management, (3) to increase cooperation between Canada and the U.S. and other allies to prevent entry of terrorists, illegal immigrants, contraband and illegal goods into our country."[16] Members of the government were also aware of this crucial problem as exemplified by the remarks of Mr. Manley almost one year after the attacks: "It was the first time that the security of Americans in the United States was at stake. We had to demonstrate that we were on their side, and show solidarity. Our principal client is the United States. Their main preoccupation is security. If I want to sell 87 percent of my goods to my client, I need to understand his preoccupations."[17] In other words, Canada had to follow Washington's guidelines in order to keep the border open. And thus, the goods of security and prosperity were efficiently produced.

Pressure from the United States led the government to adopt a series of measures that, in all, consists of a security perimeter. We will focus mainly on the new immigration policies that were adopted this summer. The Safe Third Country Agreement was signed by both countries on August 30, 2002. The gist of this agreement is that Canada recognizes that the United States complies with article 33 of the Refugee Convention and article 3 of the Convention against Torture. Therefore, Canada recognizes that a refugee will receive fair treatment by the United States. Because of that, it seems logical to ask refugees to make only one demand in either country but not in both: thus, Canada will refuse claims to refugee status to individuals coming from the United States. This agreement is reciprocal, but since almost 60 percent of the refugees arriving in Canada come from the United States (the reverse is not true), it means that many people who wanted to claim refugee status in Canada will not be able to ask for this status anymore. In essence, the government of Canada has agreed to let the United States decide who will be eligible for refugee status in cases where Canada would previously have had to take this decision by itself.

Admittedly there are exceptions to this rule: most notably the new regulation does not apply to people who may face the death penalty in the United States or elsewhere, and to people who already have family members who are Canadian citizens or permanent residents. Also, minor refugees who could face detention in the United States could also be exempted from this regulation.[18] However, even with these exceptions, this treaty is a sharp departure from the traditional Canadian values concerning refugees.[19] It is also an agreement in which the

Canadian government voluntarily limits its own power to decide who will be allocated a refugee status. It is not simply important to note that the arrangement limits Canadian sovereignty—in the popular meaning of the term—but also that it was one of many "little" steps to reinforce the security perimeter. Instead of a general all encompassing treaty, the demands of the United States were met through this sort of agreement. Other examples include the Declaration on the Intelligent Border of December 12, 2001, the negotiations to achieve a "Troop deal" that would allow American troops to operate inside Canada in case of an attack,[20] the budget of December 11, 2001 which saw a huge increase in funding for domestic security ($1.2 billion just for border security and a total of $7.7 billion on security), bills *C-55* (*Public Safety Act*) and *C-36* (*Anti-Terrorism Act*), and various agreements have been adopted concerning information sharing.[21]

As soon as the suggestion to harmonize immigration policies came up, the issue of sovereignty was raised and the government felt uneasy about a closer collabouration with the U.S. On September 13, the Prime Minister declared that no change had been made concerning immigration. He replied to those critiquing Canadian immigration policies by saying that no state could guarantee that no terrorist would enter its territory. He also avoided specific questions about harmonization by saying that terrorism was a global problem needing international cooperation.[22] Mr. Chrétien reiterated his position on the 19th of September by saying that "The laws of Canada will be adopted by the House of Commons."[23] At that point it seemed that some of the ministers agreed with the demands of Mr. Cellucci. The Prime minister's firm position at the time was meant to reduce the impression of dissention within the cabinet. Mr. Martin Cauchon, minister of Canada Customs and Revenue Agency said that both the United States and Canada should work to find ways to attain, each in its own way, the same security objectives. He added that that did not mean that Canada had to harmonize its laws with those of the United States or that Canada should give up parts of its sovereignty.[24] It is also interesting to note that the word perimeter was and still is controversial among cabinet members. They have banned the use of the word for fear of a backlash from nationalists. As the *National Post* points out, "The Prime Minister and Mr. Manley worry that a common perimeter implies a loss of sovereignty because security decisions would have to be made jointly with a partner ten times bigger and more powerful than Canada."[25] Other ministers also refuse to use the label "perimeter"; for example, Mr. Cauchon prefers to talk about a "shared border." Clearly the concept of perimeter makes the political leadership uncomfortable.

The American ambassador also played this language game, but still with a clear message from Washington. He said on December 10th, 2001:

> Some have cast this as a choice between security and prosperity. There is no choice. We can not have one without the other. Security is the necessary foundation on which we build our prosperity. No one's asking Canada to give up any sovereignty. We expect Canada will still make its own decisions about immigration, how many immigrants will be welcome, where they will come from. All we're saying is that as you welcome immigrants and refugees, make sure we have some common security standards in place.[26]

Notice how the last sentence contrasts with the idea of a sovereign state deciding on its own its immigration policy, and notice also the veiled threat that directly links the behaviour of Canada to its access to the American market.

Conclusion

A few days after September 11, the pattern we are describing in this paper already had emerged. The Canadian government had recognized that U.S. vital interests were at stake, that Canadian vital interests — mainly economic — were also at stake, and that it had to work to "satisfy" the U.S. without acknowledging the impact on sovereignty.

The closure of the border is an excellent case of how the U.S. did what it could to protect itself from a perceived threat and of what Canada had to do in order to keep on producing prosperity. That is, Canada had to comply with U.S. demands for the establishment of a security perimeter in order to get the flow of goods across the border going. Since the establishment of a security perimeter according to U.S. guidelines clashed with the norms and values upheld by the Canadian state, the government had to find a way to escape the dilemma. It did so by producing the good, that is, creating a security perimeter, while pretending it did not, by banning the term security perimeter and giving the perimeter a shape that allowed the government to claim it had successfully protected Canadian sovereignty. That is truly organized hypocrisy as described by Brunsson and Krasner: you do something that contradicts certain values and pretend these values have been upheld in order to maintain the appearance of consistency. Brunsson sums it up quite well: "In other words hypocrisy is a fundamental type of behaviour in the political organization: to talk in a way that satisfies one demand, to decide in a way that satisfies another, and to supply the products in a way that satisfies a third."

Notes

1 We would like to thank the organizers of the conference, the Research Group in International Security at McGill University and Université de Montréal, and especially Professor Mark Brawley from McGill University, Professor Stéphane Roussel from the Canada Research Chair in Canadian Foreign and Defence Policy at UQAM, and Professor Michael Brecher from McGill University and Heather Komenda and Alden Skidd from McGill University, for their helpful comments.

2 Kenneth Waltz, *Theory of International Politics* (New York: McGraw-Hill, 1979), 95–96.

3 Stephen Krasner, *Sovereignty: Organized Hypocrisy* (Princeton: Princeton University Press, 1999).

4 Ibid., 237.

5 This passage is inspired from the second causal pathway in Peter J. Katzenstein, ed., *The Culture of National Security* (New York, Columbia University Press, 1996), 58–60. See also Andrew Moravcsik, "Taking Preferences Seriously," *International Organization* vol. 51 no.4 (Autumn 1997), 513–53. Whether our interpretation is more constructivist or liberalist is a debate that is outside of the scope of this presentation.

6 This is the expression used by John Manley, then Minister of Foreign Affairs, in the week following the attacks to explain what Canada had to do; but he added that satisfying the United States did not necessarily

imply having to harmonize the laws of the two countries. "Immigration: le Canada défend sa souveraineté," *Le Devoir*, September 20, 2002, p. A4.

7 The expression "organized hypocrisy" originally comes from Nils Brunsson, *The Organization of Hypocrisy* (Chichester and New York, John Wiley & Sons, 1989).

8 See Brunsson, ibid., 7.

9 Sands, Christopher, "Canada and the War on Terrorism: The U.S. Challenge on the North American Front," *Canada Focus* 2, 3 (October 2001) http://www.csis.org/americas/canada/focus/Focus0110.htm

10 Sergeant Jean-Pierre Girard from the RCMP echoes many of his colleagues by saying that it is physically impossible to seal the border. Thibodeau, Marc, "La frontière oubliée," *La Presse*, Samedi 27 Octobre 2001, p. A1.

11 Sands, Christopher, op cit.

12 Cornellier, Manon, "Cellucci plaide pour une politique d'immigration harmonisée," *La Presse*, jeudi 13 septembre 2001, p.A4.

13 Albert, Sheldon, "Border deal imminent: U.S. envoy: Joint perimeter security: Sense of urgency over new immigration control, screening of potential terrorists." *National Post* November 1, 2001, A06.

14 Toupin, Gilles, "Création d'un périmètre de sécurité," *La Presse* samedi 3 novembre 2001, A-11.

15 Stevenson, James, "EDS : Moves General and Business." *The Canadian Press* Friday, September 14, 2001.

16 Coalition for Secure and Trade-Efficient Borders, *Rethinking our Borders: A Plan of Action*, December 3, 2001, ii. http://www.cme-mec.ca/coalition/english/reports.html

17 Bellavance, Joël-Denis, "L'appui aux Américains sert les intérêts économiques du Canada, soutient Manley." *La Presse* 9 septembre 2002.

18 See the Regulation amending the immigration and refugee protection regulation in the *Canada Gazette* vol. 136, no. 43 (Ottawa: Commons) Saturday, October 26, 2002, p. 44. This regulation has not yet been accepted formally, but the agreement with the United States has been signed. The text can be found at http://www.cic.gc.ca/francais/politiques/pays-surs.html. The principle of a safe third country is already in the new immigration law that came into effect on June 28, 2002. The designation of another country as a safe third country is done, according to the paragraph 101(1)(e) of the *Immigration and Refugee Protection Act*, through regulation.

19 According to a public officer, the problem of harmonization is not the right one. She argues that, in fact, Canada and the United States have already very similar regulations. The only difference is that the United States has more money to detain people, which makes it a more widespread policy. In Canada each case is looked at individually, and detention is used only when a refugee is likely to have committed criminal acts. This policy is unlikely to change since the costs of detentions are very high.

20 Daniel Leblanc, "Canada, U.S. near troop deal," *Globe and Mail,* August 28. See also www.cbc.ca "Canada, U.S. military work on emergency plans," September 17, 2002.

21 The budget can be found at http://www.fin.gc.ca/news01/0(1)118f.html, Daly, Brian, "Le FBI souhaite être plus present au Canada," *La Presse* December 17, 2001, A4.

22 Cornellier, Manon, "Immigration : pas question de changer la loi à la hâte, dit Chrétien." *Le Devoir,* vendredi September 14, 2001, p. A2.

23 Cornellier, Manon, "Immigration : le Canada défend sa souveraineté." *Le Devoir,* September 20, 2001, p. A4.

24 Idem.

25 Robert Fife and Paul Wells, "'Perimeter' has Liberals drawing battle lines: Semantics split Cabinet," *National Post,* November 1, 2001, A01. See also, Bellavance, Joël-Denis, "Plaidoyer pour un périmètre de sécurité nord-américain," *La Presse,* November 2, 2001, A9.

26 Macafee, Michelle, "Border backlog could ease in weeks with cooperation, technology : Celluci." The *Canadian Press* Monday December 10, 2001.

References

Brunsson, Nils. 1989. *The Organization of Hypocrisy.* Chichester and New York: John Wiley & Sons.

Hall, Rodney Bruce. 1999. *National Collective Identity: Social Constructs and International Systems.* New York: Columbia University Press.

Katzenstein, Peter J., ed. 1996. *The Culture of National Security.* New York: Columbia University Press.

Krasner, Stephen. 1999. *Sovereignty: Organized Hypocrisy.* Princeton: Princeton University Press.

Michaud, Nelson. 2002. "Souveraineté et sécurité: Le dilemme de la politique étrangère canadienne dans 'l'après 11 septembre'," *Études Internationales* vol.33 no.4 (December), 647–666.

Moravcsik, Andrew. 1997. "Taking Preferences Seriously," *International Organization* vol.51 no.4 (Autumn), 513–553.

Roussel, Stéphane. 2002. "Pearl Harbor et le World Trade Center: le Canada face aux États-Unis en période de crise," *Études Internationales* vol.33 no.4 (December), 667–696.

——. 2002. "Le Canada et le périmètre de sécurité nord-américain : Sécurité, souveraineté ou prospérité?" Policy Options vol.23 no.3 (April), 15–22.

17

Securing Access: Discussing Monetary and Customs Union for North America

Denis Michaud

Introduction

In the months that preceded the events of September 11, 2001, many were already discussing various ways of reaching increased integration between Canada and the United States. From a military perspective, they were considering the possibility of creating a North American security perimeter and a continental missile defence system (see the chapter by Matthew Mingus, *this volume*). On the economic front, a growing number of observers were offering positive appraisals of the free trade agreements signed by Canada, the United States and Mexico and were suggesting that full considerations be given to further continental integration by way of structural changes to the countries' monetary and industrial policies.

Among the various proposals was that of Canada's replacing its floating exchange rate with a fixed exchange rate system whereby its currency's value would be tied to the U.S. dollar. Also discussed was the idea of a North American Monetary Union (NAMU), either by creation of a new continental currency or by Canada's (and possibly Mexico's) adopting the U.S. dollar as legal tender. This chapter examines the context that brought the rise of such proposals as they were put forward by Canadian economists, mainly between the summer of 1999 and the spring of 2002. We argue that, ultimately, the proposals for a customs union will prove to have greater political appeal than those for a fixed exchange rate or a NAMU and will stop short of describing in details the microeconomic characteristics of the various forms of monetary union that were offered as possibilities. However, we will broadly underline the global and domestic dynamics prevalent when these proposals were put forward.

The discussions between economists and other members or groups of the Canadian business community over a NAMU take renewed importance when one considers that, after being under intense pressure for pondering the benefits of further economic integration with the United States in the fall of 2001 and in the winter of 2002, many holding important positions within the federal government have publicly talked about the merits of a Canada–U.S. customs union. This last project has been defined in its more general variant as one where the participating countries agree to put in place "a common tariff against imports from the rest of the world [and allow] for the free circulation of goods within their common area" (Goldfarb 2003:1).

After reviewing the political reaction to the proposals for monetary integration as delivered by Prime Minister Jean Chrétien, Finance Minister Paul Martin, and Governors of the Bank of Canada Gordon Thiessen and David Dodge, we explain why the aforementioned political elite and others decided to move the discussion toward the project of a Canada–U.S. customs union. We argue that, whereas it did not appear to this political elite that, on political grounds, the American government and Canadian civil society would be ready to consider a NAMU, they gave a larger chance of success to the idea of a customs union, mainly because, just as was the case with the project of Canada–U.S. free trade agreement in the early 1980s, room to manoeuvre is available in defining what such a project would include and exclude. Such was not the case with a NAMU. In fact, it became clear to the key decision-makers at the federal government that a NAMU, in fact, would mean the adoption by Canada of the U.S. dollar as its legal currency (also referred to as "dollarization") and that even simple considerations for this would prove to be highly unpopular with the general electorate.

That did not prevent them, however, from remaining convinced that the government of Canada should look for ways to enhance the country's commercial relationship with the United States. The difficulties seen at the Canada–U.S. border in the weeks that followed the events of September 11, 2001, gave powerful weight to the arguments of those who were saying that the Canadian government has to find ways to provide predictable and fluid access to U.S. markets for its business community, as well as the elimination of the remaining trade and investments barriers between the two countries. After surveying the reaction of the political elite to the discussions over a NAMU, this chapter shows that this same group is now actively positioning itself on the debate over a form of continental integration that could take the shape of a customs union and is now receiving proposals for this idea with much more interest. Although the discussions on these two subjects have been extended to many more participants in the civil society, in the federal government, and in opposition parties, we limit our presentation to the debate between economists and to the reaction of a few decision-makers at the executive branch of the federal government and of the Bank of Canada. From an economic perspective, the Canadian security in the period following the autumn of 2001 could then take the form of the construction of a Canada–U.S. customs union.

Contextualizing the Debate: The Origins of the Proposals for a Monetary Union

In the summer of 1999, the discussions among Canadian economists over the idea of a NAMU and a monetary policy operated by a supranational central bank (see, for example, Courchene and Harris 1999; Grubel 1999a) took a renewed importance as the national media presented further North American integration as "inevitable" (Scoffield 1999). Listing their arguments in favour of such economic integration, economists repeatedly mentioned that a common currency would eliminate the transaction costs tied to cross-border trade and would facilitate the movement of goods and capitals on the continent. Additionally, getting rid of the floating exchange rate regime would eliminate the volatility of the Canadian nominal exchange rate and could lead to an increase in international investments. Overall, they link the process of North American integration to a promise for a higher standard of living for Canadians (Fortin 1999).

The development that generated this extensive discussion (referred to as a "media frenzy" by Watson 1999) over the future of the country's monetary policy was the downfall of the value of the Canadian dollar as compared to its American counterpart. Its value went from $0.7101 U.S. in March 1998 to $0.6202 U.S. in January 2002, before climbing back to a value of $0.7491 U.S. in June 2003. After offering stability in its value from 1995 to 1997, the Canadian dollar then suffered from the 1997–1998 financial crisis in East Asia, a context that brought a downfall in the prices of raw materials and a movement away from investors' seeking refuge in the dependable American dollar. This last phenomenon contributed to an overvalued U.S. dollar, a situation that would persist until the spring of 2003 (International Monetary Fund 2001:54).

From the summer of 1999 to the winter of 2002, a reference to the value of the currency became an easy synonym of the growing disparity between the performances of the American and Canadian economies. As noticed by Don Drummond and Marc Lévesque (2001), both of the Toronto Dominion (TD) Bank Financial Group, the decline in the value of the currency, and the idea of abandoning the Canadian dollar altogether as a solution to this "problem," caught the attention of the general public. Numerous polls were also conducted where the respondents were asked whether it would be a good thing for Canada to have a common currency with the United States (Wallace 1999; Léger 2002). Some economists then proceeded to suggest that larger integration of the Canadian monetary policy to the American Federal Reserve's would provide solutions to Canada's economic woes (Chwialkowska 2001) and ways to reverse the widening gap in labour productivity between Canada and the United States, a phenomenon mostly noticeable from 1996 to 2000 (Fortin 2002; see also Dupuis and Tessier 2000).

For others, it was time to realize that an international redefinition of the monetary order was under way and that we are now heading toward a world where only a handful of currencies will be used (Beddoes 1999; Hausmann 1999). They predicted that the Canadian dollar would not be part of that select group and that North America will most likely use the American dollar or a new regional currency. Seeing that as inevitable, they recommended discussing this issue immediately so that it could be possible for Canada to negotiate the best deal for itself. In a study prepared for the C.D. Howe Institute, Thomas Courchene and Richard Harris (1999:24) have written that "if ... dollarization proceed[s] apace in the rest of the Americas without Canadian influence, Canada's negotiating stance will be permanently weakened.... If a pan-American currency area were to develop without Canada's participation, the United States would derive fewer marginal benefits from adding Canada to the arrangement and be less inclined to trade influence (or seigniorage) in exchange for Canada's later accession." In that regard, it is important to note that a bill entitled the *International Monetary Stability Act* was introduced in the American Congress in November 1999 and aims at drawing a set of guidelines for countries (primarily in South America) who would adopt the U.S. dollar as legal tender. Such a move has recently been made by countries like Ecuador, El Salvador and Guatemala.

A third argument is that free trade is fundamentally incompatible with a floating exchange rate and that Canada will truly reap the benefits of NAFTA only when its monetary policy is aligned to that of the American Federal Reserve (Mundell 2001). Following this logic, the growing disparity observed in the last decade between the economic performances in the United States and in Canada was not coincidental. That fundamental inconsistency can be fixed, proponents of this argument believe, only by an irreversible alignment of the monetary policy of both countries (and of Mexico's). Such a change would also provide considerable restrictions over the capacity of the Canadian government to intervene in the economy since, in a monetary union, "ideology or politicians will no longer drive monetary policy adventures in Canada. [The new North American central bank] will only maintain price stability, without pursuing full employment or any other objective" (Grubel 1999b:C7).

Finally, some saw the perpetually low value of the dollar as a national embarrassment and suggested that something drastic needed to be done before the value of the dollar went below $0.60 U.S., an eventuality they saw as inevitable. While Sherry Cooper (2001) of BMO Financial Group was arguing that in an integrated market, the Canadian dollar simply can not match the performance of the dominant American dollar, Jeffrey Rubin of CIBC World Markets was questioning the rationality of a floating exchange rate. In an article written for the *Globe and Mail*, he was of the opinion that "while the [Canadian monetary] policy is called a floating exchange rate, the reality is a sinking exchange rate. Within that monetary regime, the only determinant of how low the dollar will go is time" (Rubin 2001:B8).

There was, therefore, no consensus among the economists as to what would motivate a structural change in the monetary policy, but all those cited above agreed that further continental integration was to be expected (and, for some, aggressively sought after). Their proposals for change varied as they were oscillating between different forms of a fixed exchange rate, a currency board, the creation of a new North American currency, and the adoption by Canada of the U.S. dollar as legal tender. The details of their proposals will not be described here, as the attention will be shifted rather to the reaction of the political elite to this extensive discussion over a NAMU.

However, suffice it to say that other economists replied to the suggestions of their colleagues, questioning the validity of some of their premises. Whereas David Laidler and Shay Aba (2002) of the C.D. Howe Institute emphasized the benefits of a floating exchange rate for Canada, Mario Seccareccia (2002) reiterated that the Canada–U.S. markets do not represent an optimal currency area and should therefore keep distinct monetary policies. That allows each country to answer on its own to internal and external shocks that may or may not be experienced by its neighbour. For their part, William Robson and David Laidler of the C.D. Howe Institute questioned the presumption of the inevitability of deeper integration, so predominant in the argumentation of some proponents of a NAMU, and underlined the fact that microeconomic variables alone are not sufficient for a final evaluation of the proposals. Examining the various suggestions put forward, they wrote that the "systems that are more economically desirable seem to be less politically feasible: their creation would require difficult political decisions from Canada, as well as cooperation from the United States in matters where Americans have little to gain and have shown little interest" (Robson and Laidler 2002:27). Finally, John Murray and James Powell (2002:1) of the Bank of Canada used empirical evidence to demonstrate that "by many measures, Canada is less dollarized now than it was twenty years ago," thereby undermining the argument of those who ask the government to act before *de facto* dollarization has taken over the country.

The Reaction from the Political Elite of the Federal Government

From 1998 to the summer of 2001, the strategy of the members of the executive branch of the federal government of Canada who were asked to comment on the concerns and proposals of the economists introduced above could be summarized as dismissal of the calls of those who were defeatists over the long term prospects of the Canadian dollar. Ducking questions about monetary integration, they sent the message that those who were asking for changes were simply trying to duplicate the type of integration that was being implemented in Western Europe. In January of 1999, Governor Thiessen (1998–1999:123) stated that "the political objectives that motivated monetary union in Europe do not have a parallel in North America." Prime Minister Chrétien also rejected the idea of a North American currency by talking about Europe's unique situation. In August 2000, he said that "we have the United States, which is enormous, and two countries that are much smaller on either side. [I don't think] we can apply European rules [and have a monetary union]" (cited in Scoffield 2000:B1).

As the value of the Canadian dollar kept falling, Minister of Finance Paul Martin was pressed to take a stand on the issue and explained that: "the Canadian government's position is unequivocal. We are going to stay with the Canadian dollar. It is by far the best course of action for us economically and in terms of our sovereignty" (cited in Toulin 2001: A1). For his part, Governor Dodge justified the need for the status quo by pointing out the importance of the structural differences in the nature of the Canadian and American economies. In linking the structures of the economies to nation-states, he suggested that, at least for the time being, the advantages for Canada of using a distinct currency [and a floating exchange rate] were greater than the detriments (Toulin 2001: 1). He also expressed serious doubts about the inevitability of further monetary integration on the continent by saying that "we are not drifting towards dollarization. If we go down that road, it will be a deliberate choice" (cited in la *Presse Canadienne* 2002:C2).

In the winter of 2002, the intensified discussions over deeper cooperation at the border and a more integrated system of continental defence coincided with the Canadian dollar trading at an all-time low value of $0.6202 U.S. That context provided for aggressive actions from key players at the federal government aimed at countering the message of the economists who were proposing the most radical of all changes to the monetary policy, the adoption by Canada of the U.S. dollar as legal tender.

The first part of the political offensive can by summed up by saying that members of the political elite tried to bring about a rise in the value of the Canadian dollar. Some of the highest-ranking officials of the federal government made major political interventions over the Canadian dollar, and one is usually led to believe that they were offering a reply to the economists who were asking for structural changes because of the low value of the currency in relation to the U.S. dollar. As observed by Aron Gampel of the Bank of Nova Scotia, "it's viewed as a fundamental shift in policy [for the Bank of Canada] to become more vocal in the dollar's defence" (cited in Toulin 2002:A8).

These interventions came to a head at the end of January 2002. The Minister of Finance then suggested that the value of the dollar was not reflecting the sound fundamentals of the Canadian economy, and he predicted that a rise in the value of the dollar was to be expected as soon as the international markets became better informed of the economic and fiscal performances delivered by Canada over the last few years (McCarty and Stinson 2002). He concluded by saying that "no one is happy with what has been happening with the Canadian dollar — certainly not the government of Canada" (cited in McCarty and Stinson 2002:A1).

After delivering this message, the Prime Minister, the Minister of Finance and the Governor of the Bank of Canada left for New York where they spoke before a group of Wall Street investors and bankers. That trip received a lot of attention in the Canadian media (see, for example, Whittington 2002:A1) and was complemented with ads placed in the January 30 and February 1 editions of the *Wall Street Journal*. That campaign seemed to be at least somewhat successful, for the Canadian dollar was traded at a value of $0.6545 U.S. on May 31, 2002.

The second series of actions were initiated on January 9, 2002, when Prime Minister Chrétien asked the House of Commons' Standing Committee on Foreign Affairs and International Trade to "review everything from adopting the U.S. dollar to a unified customs regime" (Jack 2002:A1). The Committee's report, made available in December 2002 and titled *Partners in North America: Advancing Canada's Relations with the United States and Mexico,* rejects any consideration of monetary union in the near future. On page 205, it reads "as of yet, there is no common market or free movement of labour in North American [*sic*] to support a currency union." In a final recommendation on the subject, the members add on page 209 that: "given that certain vital preconditions to North American monetary integration (e.g. similarity in the economic structures of NAFTA participants, existence of labour mobility across borders, availability of a fiscal transfer system) are not presently met, the Government of Canada should oppose any current calls to abandon its existing flexible exchange-rate system."

It then appears that the members of the Committee, for the time being, are convinced of the need to offer strong resistance to monetary union and have concerns about a continental economic integration that would go too far. (It has to be kept in mind, though, that the Committee's report is supplemented with dissenting opinions addressing these last two points and coming from representatives of the New Democratic Party, the Canadian Alliance, and the Bloc Québécois. The last two parties are promoting deeper North American integration and are asking for immediate actions from the government on this front.) It is important to note, however, that the members have taken this position while specifying that their recommendation was based on the fact that Canada has yet to reach an adequate level of integration for the project of a common currency to be considered. Some doubts are offered on the merits of the idea, but it is immediately explained that it is first and foremost the timing that is problematic and that a preferential course of action would be to come back to the question at a later time. By mentioning that it is premature to have a monetary union because we have yet to reach the steps found in a customs union, the members of the Committee, in fact, open the door to this last project.

On page 194 of the report, the authors strongly solicit further discussions on the idea of a continental customs union: "While the Committee has taken no position on the merits of a North American customs union, we believe it would be useful for the Government concurrently to initiate a detailed review of the advantages and disadvantages of the concept in the North American context. The review could include an assessment of the use of the integrated North American steel industry, among others, as a prototype for a broader customs union of some kind."

Some key players of the political elite in the federal government have already positioned themselves in the group of those who would favour serious considerations for a type of customs union. Speaking before the House of Commons Finance Committee on October 23, 2002 and on April 29, 2003, Governor Dodge argued that Canada needed to seek a continental arrangement that would ultimately allow for the free mobility of labour, capital, goods and services on the continent. That position is broadly similar to the ones expressed by two ministers of the federal government, namely John Manley and Pierre Pettigrew (Dawson 2002: A1; Chase and Keenan 2003:B2) as well as by the chairman of the House of Commons Finance Committee, Maurizio Bevilacqua, who argued that the federal government needed to aid North America in becoming "a powerful, integrated economic unit where people benefit from economies of scale, productivity, efficiency and specialization" (cited in Chwialkowska 2001:A1). These interventions all came while some economists were discussing the perspective of a generalized or sectoral common external tariff for North America as part of a revamped macroeconomic arrangement among the NAFTA countries (Dobson 2002; Hufbauer and Vega 2002). An extensive study of the topic was also authored by Danielle Goldfarb who suggested that the American government might be ready to listen to proposals in that area. She writes that "a customs union might be more interesting to the U.S. as part of a larger package of security and economic initiatives.... A larger package could provide momentum for sectoral tariff harmonization or a basic customs union project that would otherwise be likely to get lost in the diffuse U.S. political system" (Goldfarb 2003:27). Such interest should be well-received by the Canadian political elite who will see that some are ready to put their weight into the preparation of new continental project.

Conclusion

When considering the proposals put forward by economists, one needs to understand the distinction between their evaluation of the merits of a floating exchange rate for a country like Canada and their observations on the trend taken by the value of the currency. On this last point, it was generally agreed that, during the 1998–2002 period, the Canadian dollar was undervalued. That, however, did not translate into a consensus among economists as to what type of changes would be needed in Canada's monetary policy to strengthen the dollar. Some even asked for the creation of a royal commission on the topic of exchange rate systems (Watson 1999:C7; Crane 2001:B6).

As mentioned by Courchene and Harris (1999:22), in the range of possibilities covered by the different types of monetary unions, the most attractive option for Canada was the creation of a NAMU. It soon became clear, however, that the American government would not contemplate any form of integration that would force it to abandon the U.S. dollar, thereby making dollarization the only available option when political factors were taken into account. That point was made by Jack Carr and Bernard Wolfe in a testimony before the Senate Committee on Banking, Trade and Commerce on March 25, 1999 (Carr, et. al. 1999:10–13) and was hinted at by American Ambassador to Canada Paul Cellucci in June of 2001 (Fife and Toulin 2001:A1). That reality left very little manoeuvring room for the Canadian political elite to design a project based on the idea of a NAMU.

It has been generally accepted that we have to recognize a certain degree of a *de facto* dollarization of the Canadian economy with about 18 percent of the firms interviewed by Murray and Powell (2002:11) preparing their financial statements solely in U.S. dollars or using a combination of the Canadian and U.S. dollars. Although *official* dollarization was favoured by some members of Québec's political elite like Richard Marceau (1999), Jacques Parizeau (see Giroux 2000), and Bernard Landry (see Breton 2002), the idea proved much more difficult to sell in the rest of the country's political community. However, that was not to say that members of the executive branch of the federal government were not prepared to contemplate proposing a scheme that would bring the continent to a higher level of economic integration. After signing the *Smart Border Accord* in December 2001, the federal government has now produced a document titled *Securing Growth: Beyond the Border Accord*. It has also been said that the Department of Foreign Affairs and International Trade and the government's policy arm, the Policy Research Initiative, are actively studying the various implications of an eventual Canada–U.S. customs union (Goldfarb 2003:28).

After keeping a near constant silence for almost three years over the implications associated with the decline in the value of the Canadian dollar, some key players of the political elite in the federal government have now favourably presented a project that might prove to have greater political appeal than a continental monetary union and seem to be ready to engage their American counterparts on a proposal for a customs union. Were this project to become the topic of high-level discussions between the Canadian and American governments (with the possibility of including the Mexican government), one would have to go back to a description of the economic and political contexts that were prevalent in the months that followed the events of September 11, 2001, in order to provide an understanding of why the federal government's political elite chose aggressively to seek structural changes to the continental economic arrangement that came about with the 1989 and 1994 Free Trade agreements. It would then appear that, despite intense pressure coming from the country's economic circles, the political elite managed to keep a good level of control over the macroeconomic agenda of Canada–U.S. relations. While not changing its direction, incremental, rather than radical changes were favoured and seem to be under preparation.

References

Beddoes, Zanny Minton, "From EMU to AMU? The Case for Regional Currencies," in *Foreign Affairs*, July-August 1999, pp. 8–13.

Breton, Pascale, "Dollar américain: Landry invite Ottawa à réfléchir," in *La Presse*, March 7, 2002, p. A8.

Carr, Jack, Courchene, Thomas, Crow, John W. Grubel, Herbert G., and Bernard Wolf, "Round Table on a North American Currency," in *Canadian Parliamentary Review*, Summer 1999, pp. 5–13.

Chase, Steven, and Greg Keenan, "Canada, U.S. consider one steel market," in the *Globe and Mail*, February 1, 2003, p. B2.

Chwialkowska, Luiza, "Our Future is Continental: Key MP," in *National Post*, August 2, 2001, p. A1.

Cooper, Sherry, "Time for U.S. loonie: Like it or not, the U.S. dollar is simply too strong for us," in the *Financial Post*, November 9, 2001, p. FP13.

Courchene, Thomas J. and Richard G. Harris, *From Fixing to Monetary Union: Options for North American Currency Integration*, Toronto, C.D. Howe Institute, June 1999.

Crane, David, "Near silence on integration issue," in the *Toronto Star*, June 10, 2001, p. B6.

Dawson, Anne, "Pettigrew confirms push to add labour to NAFTA," in the *National Post*, October 26, 2002, p. A1.

Dobson, Wendy, *Shaping the Future of the North American Economic Space: A Framework for Action*, Toronto, C.D. Howe Institute, April 2002.

Drummond, Don, and Marc Lévesque, "Plus ça change.... Pressure is building to swap the loonie for the greenback," in the *Globe and Mail*, December 12, 2001, p. A13.

Dupuis, David, and David Tessier, *Une analyse empirique du lien entre la productivité et le taux de change réel Canada–É.U.*, Ottawa, Bank of Canada, working document 2000–22, 2000.

Fife, Robert and Alan Toulin, "US Aims to Dismantle Borders," in the *National Post*, June 30, 2001, p. A1.

Fortin, Pierre, "Imiter l'Europe ... de la bonne manière," in *L'Actualité*, March 15, 1999.

——. "La productivité canadienne: À quand le rattrapage?" in *ISUMA, Canadian Journal of Policy Research*, Spring 2002, pp. 43–47.

Giroux, Raymond, "Déçu par le PQ; 'Les souverainistes ont le dos au mur,' constate Parizeau," in *Le Soleil*, January 30, 2000, p. A1.

Goldfarb, Danielle, *The Road to a Canada–U.S. Customs Union: Step-by-Step or in a Single Bound?*, Toronto, C.D. Howe Institute, June 2003.

Grubel, Herbert G., *The Case for the Amero: The Economics and Politics of a North American Monetary Union*, Toronto, The Fraser Institute, September 1999a.

——. "Life with the Amero," in the *Financial Post*, April 14, 1999b, p. C7.

Hufbauer, Gary Clyde, and Gustavo Vega-Cánovas, "Whither NAFTA: A Common Frontier?" in Peter Andreas and Thomas J. Biersteker, eds., *The Rebordering of North America*, New York, Routledge, 2003.

Hausmann, Ricardo, "Should There Be Five Currencies or One Hundred and Five?" in *Foreign Policy*, Fall 1999, pp. 65–79.

International Monetary Fund, *World Economic Outlook, May 2001: Fiscal Policy and Macroeconomic Stability*, Washington, World Economic and Financial Surveys, 2001.

Jack, Ian, "MPs forcing PM's hand on dollar: Committee to solicit views on economic integration with US," in the *National Post*, January 10, 2002, p. A1.

Laidler, David, and Shay Aba, *Productivity and the Dollar: Commodities and the Exchange Rate Connection*, Toronto, C.D. Howe Institute, February 2002.

Léger, Marie-France, "Les Canadiens contre la devise commune avec les États-Unis," in *La Presse*, September 7, 2002, p. E1.

McCarthy, Shawn, and Marion Stinson, "Dollar hits new low as Martin laments," in the *Globe and Mail*, January 22, 2002, p. A1.

Marceau, Richard, "Pour la création d'une union monétaire panaméricaine," in *Revue parlementaire canadienne*, Summer 1999, pp. 2–4.

Mundell, Robert, "One World, One Money?" in *Policy Options*, May 2001, pp. 10–30.

Murray, John, and James Powell, *Dollarization in Canada (The Buck Stops Here)*, Ottawa, Bank of Canada, April 2002.

Presse canadienne, "L'adoption du dollar américain n'est pas pour demain," in *La Presse*, October 6, 2002, p. C2.

Robson, William, and David Laidler, *No Small Change: The Awkward Economics and Politics of North American Monetary Integration*, Toronto, C.D. Howe Institute, July 2002.

Rubin, Jeffrey, "Hands-off approach punishing the loonie," in the *Globe and Mail*, August 9, 2001, p. B8.

Scoffield, Heather, "Canada pushed on several fronts toward integration with US," in the *Globe and Mail*, June 4, 1999.

——. "Move toward common currency speeds up," in the *Globe and Mail*, April 22, 2000, p. B1.

Seccareccia, Mario, *North American Monetary Integration: Should Canada Join the Dollarization Bandwagon?*, unpublished document, February 2002.

Standing Committee on Foreign Affairs and International Trade, *Partners in North America: Advancing Canada's Relations with the United States and Mexico*, Ottawa, Public Works and Government Services Canada, December 2002.

Thiessen, Gordon, "The euro: Its economic implications and its lessons for Canada," in *Bank of Canada Review*, Winter 1998–1999, pp. 117–123.

Toulin, Alan, "Rift Opens Over Dollar's Future," in the *National Post*, May 3, 2001, p. A1.

——. "PM joins pro-dollar bandwagon," in the *National Post*, January 24, 2002, p. A8.

Wallace, Bruce, "What Makes a Canadian?," in *Maclean's*, December 20, 1999, p. 36.

Watson, William, "Keep studying the currency union," in the *Financial Post*, June 30, 1999, p. C7.

Whittington, Les, "Wall Street to hear loonie pep talk," in the *Toronto Star*, January 31, 2002, p. A1.

18

The Long Goodbye: Elite Nationalism in The Era of Globalization

The Significance of September 11

Stephen McBride

Often depicted as "changing everything" in Canada's relationship with the U.S., the events of September 11, 2001 may have changed very little, except to bring into stark relief the degree to which the Canadian elites' perspective on the world is now fully conditioned by its relationship with the United States. September 11 can thus be considered as a seminal event, reaction to which revealed far more of the real world assumptions and opinions of Canada's elite than was previously apparent.

The paper actually grew out of analysis of another, though less dramatic event — the death of Pierre Trudeau in October 2000. His death and funeral provided an opportunity for "life and times" reflections fitting a major figure whose career spanned a period of crisis, change, and transition. One of the themes which emerged in the various commentaries was nostalgia for a period in which Canada appeared to have greater autonomy vis à vis the United States than was apparent in the post-Free Trade Agreement (FTA) era. In the Trudeau era, Canada had been redefined as a bilingual, multicultural middle power, tied to the U.S. through NATO and NORAD certainly, but nonetheless attempting to play a genuine middle power role as peacekeeper and honest broker in world affairs. The country had promoted a mild form of nationalism through foreign investment review, cultural protectionism, and an attempt to use energy as the basis for an industrial strategy in the National Energy Program.

In retrospect, it might be argued that Trudeau's career spanned the period when the Canadian economic and political elite finally gave up on nationalism, at least to the extent that nationalism involved viewing Canada as a distinct society with separate and sometimes conflicting interests to those of the U.S. By the mid-1980s the economic, and much of the political, elite had come to accept the logic of continentalism.

The roots of continentalism run deep. Economically, the United States gradually displaced Britain as Canada's chief market and source of investment in the early part of the last century. The Second World War had led to ever-increasing defence co-operation and consultation with the United States. In 1940, the agreement between President Roosevelt and Prime Minister Mackenzie King at Ogdensburg established a Permanent Joint Board on Defence. Joint policy declarations, notably the Hyde Park declaration in 1941, left no doubt that complete integration of North American resources and facilities was the common aim. To a large extent North America became the arsenal of the Allied forces. With the onset of the Cold War it became clear, in Desmond Morton's words, that "Washington would be the sole judge of N. America's security; Canadians could play their assigned role or Americans would do it for them" (Morton 1988:580). Canada supported the NATO alliance, contributed troops to the Korean War, joined NORAD, a bilateral air defence agreement with the United States, and stationed armed forces in Europe. On the 1957 NORAD agreement, Morton commented that it made sense militarily but politically "gave Washington effective control over Canada's right to make war or peace" (Morton 1988:591).

During Trudeau's tenure there was some, though limited, substance to Canadian efforts to maintain a sense of distance from the United States, expressed through initiatives like the Foreign Investment Review Agency, the Third Option, and the National Energy Program. Perhaps, as Clarkson and McCall put it, these efforts "were too cursory and too cynically cosmetic to satisfy most ardent nationalists. But they alienated big businessmen further from a government that seemed to them decidedly out of touch with the private sector's desire to accelerate, not reverse, Canada's integration into the U.S. economy" (1994:111). With the election of Mulroney, the economic elite found political leadership more suited to its ambitions.

However, the scale of the attitudinal shift amongst Canada's economic and political elite was obscured until 2001 by a number of factors. The older nationalism persisted among, and was aired by, other elites — cultural, academic, labour, social movements, and some media. And entirely symbolic representations of nationalism continued: examples might include Team Canada export missions, expressions that Canada is a "winner" and "international competitor" which periodically "kicks ass," flag-waving, and even television commercials of the "I am Canadian" type. Further, efforts to fabricate a middle power role for Canada through "niche diplomacy" and "soft power" attracted more attention than the dull facts of Canada's real foreign policy — its promotion of economic integration with the United States and the correlations of that position in being a good ally of the superpower. A whole industry arose dedicated to identifying and articulating this Canadian role.

For example, the Canada 21 Council (1994:12) concluded that Canada must rely on its social, human, and intellectual capital to carve out an influential role for itself in the international arena. Cooper, Higgott, and Nossal (1993:13) considered that waning American hegemony (*sic*) had given way to alternative forms of leadership whereby "games of skill" have increasingly replaced "tests of will." Emphasis on technical and entrepreneurial leadership refers to what Foreign Minister Lloyd Axworthy has termed "soft power," a concept which he argues must be cultivated and wielded by Canada if it is to emerge as an important and influential actor in the twenty-first century (Axworthy 1997:192). Reduced Cold War tensions should have expanded the terrain in which "middle powers" could operate. But for Canada the end of the Cold War seemed to increase the contradictory nature of its foreign policy.

By participating in peace-building and the campaigning to outlaw anti-personnel land mines, promoting the concept of human security, advocating a UN-sponsored international criminal court, Canadian foreign policy demonstrated its aspirations to a middle power role. In this view, the growth of multilateralism and international institutions since 1990 broadened the scope for action of middle powers. Such factors as the reform and enlargement of NATO, membership in the OAS, and the increased incidence of peacekeeping represented new opportunities for countries such as Canada to assert their views. Issues traditionally promoted by middle powers such as human rights, environmental protection, and human security assumed a higher profile, and that suggests to middle power theorists that these countries could increase their international role.

This sense of the growing importance of middle powers even spawned another interpretation: that Canada made the transition to being a "foremost" (Eayrs 1975), "major" (Lyon and Tomlin; Gottleib 1987) or "principal" power (Dewitt and Kirton 1983). Kirton argued that despite the apparent rise of the United States during the 1990s, as the only superpower, the Asian financial crisis of 1997–1999 affirmed Canada's position as a principal power. According to Kirton "In the diplomacy behind the Hong Kong reform package, Canada acted as an equal member of the G7 concert in which different members lead on specific issues and mutually adjust to create a new and effective consensus" (Kirton 1999:607). Thus Canada's diplomacy during the financial crisis is said to call into question traditional interpretations of Canadian foreign policy. The crisis, he argues, demonstrated that Canada remains a global player, rather than one forced by diminishing relative capabilities in the 1990s to turn to a more restricted, niche-based, regional focus (Kirton 1999:624).

However, there are strong arguments against this growth industry celebrating a middle or principal power role for Canada. Participation in U.S. organised military ventures such as the Gulf War and Kosovo (Allen 1999; Phillips 1999) in the later Cold War and post-Cold War period has seen Canada operating very much an agent of American foreign policy. That stance is consistent with the continentalist orientation of economic foreign policy. For example, Webb (1992) held that small and medium sized countries were ineffective in multilateral settings and that was why Canada turned to a bilateral agreement with the United States — not from strength but rather from weakness. Despite the arguments suggesting middle or principal power status, an alternative interpretation portrays Canada as a dependent, satellite state. By the late 1960s, the middle power image of Canada was already greeted with scepticism by some and complete rejection by others (Nossal 1997:60). In this view, Canada's capacity for independent and autonomous action in international affairs had been eliminated by its successive membership in the British and American empires. Canada went from colony to nation to colony, so "what for some marked the emergence of a middle power in world politics was, for others, merely a transfer of dependent orbit, with Canada consigned to the periphery — or at best the 'semiperiphery' of the world economy" (Nossal 1997:60–61; see also see Hawes 1984; Clarkson ed. 1968; Lumsden ed. 1970).

That view, too, has deep roots. Historian A.R.M. Lower, in 1946, described Canada as a "subordinate state" and declared that it was a "complete satellite of the United States" (quoted in Resnick 1970:99).[1] Minifie, concerned over Canada's ability for independent action in international politics, rejected the notion of Canada as a middle-power peacemaker and concluded that Canada's "close association with policies of military and economic imperialism … makes Canada the choreboy of the Western world, [and] returns Canada from colony to satellite in three generations" (Minifie 1960:52).

Later, when, after the election of the Mulroney government in 1984, Canada pursued a policy of loyal and uncritical alliance with the Americans, this interpretation found new currency. The pro-American policy was pursued overtly and, to critics, on occasion obsequiously. That stood in partial contrast to policy, and more particularly in contrast to the political optics of the Trudeau era. The shift from Trudeau to Mulroney has been represented as a redefinition of Canada's middle power role — from one that was partially exercised in a "counter-consensus" direction to one that was "limitationist," reflecting "an orientation more in keeping with existing power and privilege in Canadian society and in the global order" (Neufeld 1995:22).

Thus the foreign and domestic policy response of the Mulroney government gave fresh impetus to the view that Canada was part of the American imperialist orbit (Nossal 1997:62). The policy record of the Mulroney years — the Canada–U.S. Free Trade Agreement, the pursuit of deregulation, the elimination of some of the key elements of the welfare state, and the embrace of a more hawkish foreign policy — were clear signs that Mulroney had "closed down the Canadian dream" of autonomy and independence (Martin 1993:272–73). Yet, even under Mulroney, it has been argued that there were examples of an independent course being followed — on the Strategic Arms Limitation Treaty, on central America, Cuba, and South Africa (Clarkson 2002:387–388).

September 11 was to bring the scale of the underlying attitudinal shift of Canada's elite into the open. Here I am addressing elite attitudes which, of course, can rarely be gleaned by survey research.[2] Two aspects of elite opinion are probed: that ascribed to the business elite as represented by speeches and reports of business-friendly think tanks; and that of the media elite through a content analysis of editorial and columnists' articles in the three months following September 11. Based on that material it seems that, although the Canadian elite may have been bidding goodbye to a lingering sense of nationalism for some time, after September 11 the farewell was definitive.

In making this argument I am, of course, conscious of the fact that the demise of Canadian nationalism has been lamented many times before but has reappeared in some form to confound those gathered for the wake. John A. Macdonald's National Policy was a reaction to being rebuffed in an effort to revive Reciprocity. Trudeau's mild 1970s nationalism and pursuit of the "Third Option" represented a desire to "lessen the vulnerability of the Canadian economy to external factors, in particular the impact of the United States" (Sharp 1972). But it was stimulated as much by domestic U.S. politics as by Canadian preferences. Under Richard Nixon the U.S. signalled that self-interest, narrowly defined, would be the determining factor in American economic policy. Henceforth any "special relationship" for Canada — the de facto "preferred option" — would be hard to achieve. And it is certainly possible that concerns about U.S. unilateralism may trigger greater caution about the American embrace than seemed likely in analysing the immediate response of Canada's economic and media elite to the September 11 events[3] (Clarkson 2002:405). Certainly in retrospect it seems that the aggressiveness of the Bush Administration's response to September 11 has cooled somewhat the ardour of Canada's elite for closer integration with the U.S.

Business Opinion after September 11

Canadian business was the chief architect of deep integration with the United States and tirelessly promoted the original free trade agreement with the U.S. and its NAFTA successor (see McBride 2001:Ch. 3). Unsurprisingly, therefore, a desire not to see this undone by stringent border controls and reduced access to the American market looms large in the business response to September 11. In business speeches and publications there are, of course, expressions of sympathy, solidarity, and outrage to the events. But the focus is on how to ensure that economic integration continues in the post-September 11 environment. The responses range through technical measures to ensure the flow of goods continues, to more ambitious projects, "big ideas," to use the opportunity presented by American attention to North American security, to forge ahead with a deeper form of integration than is represented by NAFTA. In advancing both projects considerable attention is paid to depicting Canadian sovereignty as lying in the pursuit of deeper integration rather than in resisting the process.

Noting that the Business Council on National Issues (BCNI) had been at work for the two previous years in developing the next "big step forward" in Canada–U.S. relations, Thomas D'Aquino, its President and CEO, emphasized U.S. Ambassador Cellucci's warning that there was no guarantee of an open southern border unless Canada was able to convince the U.S. of the integrity of its external perimeter. Thus, issues like defence, policing, customs and immigration were tightly linked to the relationship with the U.S. and, therefore, to Canada's economic prosperity. Two alternative approaches were highlighted: "In developing Canada's strategy, we will need to consider where the security of Canadians can best be enhanced through greater cooperation and collaboration with the United States and where we should engage in more fundamental harmonization and integration" (D'Aquino 2001:7). No sacrifice of sovereignty would be involved since such measures would enhance the security of Canadians and their quality of life.

Conference Board of Canada publications adopted a similar position. For example, Shea argued for a "fundamental re-evaluation of how security and economic interests can best be served" (2001:1). That led to development of several scenarios, ranging from better processing methods at the border, through rethinking border management such that "Canada and U.S. law enforcement agencies would work more closely away from the ... border to mitigate the need for intensive inspections at the border itself," to "comprehensive harmonization of all policies, laws and agencies dealing with security issues." Shea takes pains to point out that discussions of such measures should not be sidetracked by considerations of sovereignty. Sovereignty was not the issue because early post-September 11 polling data indicated Canadians' willingness to sacrifice some sovereignty to achieve greater security, and because "in a globalized, interdependent world the concept of sovereignty is not black and white, it is not a debate of sovereignty versus free trade; it is about balancing the need for trade and security" (Shea 2001:3). This depiction shows in equal measure the sensitivity of the business sector to the sovereignty issue, and also its willingness to define it largely in economically reductionist terms.

Dobson (2002) advances the proposition that because of the September 11 events, the U.S. attitudes are open to its friends and allies and that Canada should seek to take advantage of this by securing better access to the American market. That is essential to Canadian economic performance but less assured than formerly because of the U.S. preoccupation with border security and defence. The paper argues that only a "big idea" will capture the attention of U.S. decision-makers and make it possible to address U.S. objectives while creating better economic opportunities for Canada. Having noted that "We are now deeply integrated with our large neighbour to the south through market forces and through policies of openness, such as those reflected in the Canada–U.S. Free Trade Agreement (FTA) and the North American Free Trade Agreement (NAFTA)," Dobson goes on to argue that September 11 showed that openness can create vulnerability and that U.S. reactions to those events could damage Canada economically. She concludes that "Today, even more than in the past, removing barriers to deeper bilateral integration should be high on Canada's list of interests" (Dobson 2002:1). But to achieve that will require generating U.S. interest in a North American economic security pact — "cooperation between neighbours to produce the public goods of homeland security and economic stability that neither country can produce on its own" (Dobson 2002:5). That must be achieved on Canadian terms: "without sacrificing political independence or distinctive institutions, such as public services, and our own approaches to labour market issues and immigration" (ibid., 7–8). Dobson then advances three examples of a "big idea" that might generate the necessary agreement — customs union, a common market, or a strategic bargain which would be preferable since it would comprise "a package of initiatives, some of them radical ones, that Canada might take in exchange for what it wants. Canada's goal should be to achieve customs-union and common-market-like integration without full-scale harmonization and the resulting erosion of political independence" (Dobson 2002:25).

What then would be the trade-offs in such a strategic bargain? Based on Dobson's text the following table presents a summary.

Table 1: Dobson's Strategic Bargain

Canada Initiates:

- More border security [more infra-structure; point of origin, rather than border crossing registration and inspection]
- Immigration from 3rd countries cooperation [bilateral working groups; common training programs for officials; mutual recognition]
- Energy supplies [Canada proactively works out what it will be able to deliver]
- Anticipates and works out what it can do to help with demand pressures on other natural resources such as water

U.S. Will Demand:

- Ending supply management boards in agriculture and the Canada Wheat Board
- Pressure on state trading practices
- Modification of Canadian content and cultural policies
- Modification of intellectual property policies

Canada Achieves:

- Removal of obstacles to freer flow of goods, services, capital, technology and people within North America
- Modification of U.S. agricultural policies and subsidies
- Eliminate U.S. trade remedy laws
- Strengthen dispute settlement procedures
- Common competition policy
- Possible creation of common institutions such as:

    Training school for customs and immigration personnel

    A North America Commission to plan for the integration and development of the continent

    A parliamentary group

    A permanent court on trade and investment

    Regular institutionalized meetings of cabinet members from each country

It might be objected that guaranteed access to the U.S. market was the purpose behind both the FTA and NAFTA. Now it appears more concessions are necessary to achieve what was supposed to have been achieved a decade and a half ago. The strategic bargain proposal is framed as a way of exercising Canada's sovereignty rather than eroding it: "a nation that merely reacts to events is likely to see its sovereignty erode and its future determined by others. A nation that exercises its sovereignty anticipates change, prepares options that promote the key interests of its partner, but channels actions in ways that best serve its own interests" (Dobson 2002:18). This assessment rests on an earlier elaboration of sovereignty which suggests that in surrendering (some) sovereignty to international regimes governments gain since they now have leverage against the actions of *other* governments. Moreover, "International regimes tie governments' hands in beneficial ways, such as to prevent backsliding on domestic reforms. In other words, sovereignty is not just about what a country gives up but also about what it gains in more efficient production, larger markets, freer flow of investment, swift resolution of disputes, and greater protection of intellectual property, to name a few of the benefits" (Dobson 2002:3).

In a second C.D. Howe report, Granatstein (2002) notes that economically Canada is inextricably linked to the U.S. As a result, refusing support for U.S. ventures such as the war on terrorism would have major costs, not least in economic terms. That leads to the proposition that Canadian sovereignty would seriously diminish if the Unites States acted to protect itself from attack without working with the Canadian government and the Canadian Forces. But since the United States *will* defend itself, whether or not Canada cooperates fully, supports the NMD (National Missile Defence) scheme, and backs an expanded anti-terrorist war, the only question is how best to protect Canadian sovereignty: by joining in or hanging back? This paper argues that there is no choice at all: Canada must cooperate with the United States in its own interest (Granatstein 2002:1). The notion that Canadian sovereignty consists of recognizing the inevitable, or of the recognition of necessity, is reinforced when Granatstein observes that: "Canada's links with the United States are key to our survival as an independent and sovereign state.... Washington's capacity to inflict pain and enforce compliance on Canada is boundless. Canadian policy must be devoted to keeping the elephant well fed and happy" (Granatstein 2002:15).

Apart from the fact that sovereignty disappears to the point of invisibility in Granatstein's formulation, the use of the September 11 to pursue a pre-existing agenda of deeper integration with the United States is striking in both these reports.[4]

Media Opinion after September 11

This part of the paper summarizes the results of a content analysis of editorial, columnist, and op-ed page material pertaining to Canada–U.S. relations in the post-September 11 period. Analysis is limited to two national newspapers, the *Globe and Mail,* and the *National Post.* That material is taken as representative of the positions adopted on the issue by Canada's media elite. A search of editorial material in these newspapers dealing with Canada–U.S. relations and relating to trade, security or terrorism yielded 190 documents or articles (82 *Globe and Mail*, 108 *National Post*). The search covered two days a week of these newspapers in the period between September 12 and December 31 and, thus, amounts to one-third of the total coverage in that period. Although computer-assisted content analysis can be used to yield sophisticated quantitative results, it has been used here rather as a text management system. That is, a few simple frequencies are reported in Table 3 below. However, the aim was simply to manage and identify themes in a large volume of text. Wherever a choice had to be made between simplification (to achieve greater quantitative precision) and retention of text and context (to capture the nuances of what was being said in the articles) the latter won out.

The general question related to the media's interpretation of the significance of these events for the Canada–U.S. relationship. An initial reading produced a number of detailed "nodes" identifying types of reaction. These were subsequently combined into summary nodes (see Table 2, next page).

Table 2: Nodes Used to Code Documents

Node	Description
Outrage	September 11 events as an attack on justice, civilization, democracy, economic freedom, capitalism.
Solidarity	Admiration for America(ns); U.S. as closest friend, best ally; shared common heritage.
Prudence	Concerns over damage to economy, trade, border access.
Self-criticism /Self-flagellation	We (Canada) have failed our friends because of: lax border controls, sloppy immigration procedures; underfunding the military and other defence shortcomings; anaemic and embarrassing response to September 11; need to be better friends to U.S.
Hurt	Not mentioned in Bush speech; U.S. does not appreciate us.
Criticism of U.S.	U.S. foreign policy; middle east policy; lax U.S. border and immigration controls.
Sovereignty concerns; need for Canadian independence	Need to retain sovereignty/independence, draw the line between cooperation and harmonization.
Civil Liberties concerns	Scope of anti-terrorism legislation.

Over two-thirds of the documents were coded into these categories (80.5 percent in the case of *Globe and Mail* material; 59.5 percent in the case of the *National Post*). The lower number in the *National Post* is explained by the larger number of documents on business and economic issues generated — many of these were on more technical issues and made little reference to the consequences of September 11.

The next section of the paper consists largely of extracts from the press coverage. Partly the extracts serve as examples of what is meant by the coding entries. More importantly, however, as the immediate memory of the reaction to September 11 fades, these quotations provide the texture of the responses. They give voice to the media elite and recall the tone and intensity of the immediate reactions. The extracts are, of course, selections from a much wider range of available text. Some attempt was made both to represent a wide range of responses whilst ensuring that the sample is not unrepresentative of the whole.

Outrage

It would be unreasonable to suppose that the media elite would be immune from the general public and human reaction to the events of September 11. Outrage was one widespread reaction and it is reflected in the media coverage. Within the category, as these two extracts illustrate, there are differences of degree of outrage, and in the attempted linkage between outrage and a broader political agenda.

Diane Francis, "We must hunt and eliminate these monsters: America falls victim to vicious attacks over ideology," *National Post*, 15 September 2001:

> This week ... America became an ideological victim. A handful of fanatical Moslems — who believe capitalism, globalization and free trade are the roots of all evil — killed themselves and thousands more. They equate America with Satan because it is the biggest and best example of free enterprise at work, the World Trade Center towers its ultimate symbols. Free enterprise and the rule of law are humanity's only hopes.
>
> Bin Laden, and his accomplices and assets, must be eliminated. They are throwbacks, unevolved and delusive re-creations of the worst ideological monsters in history. They must be destroyed. Anything less leaves the globe and the world's economy increasingly exposed and impedes the eventual eradication of poverty.

Gordon Gibson, "Canada's Free Ride ended September 11," *National Post,* 29 September 2001: "Terrorism is not simply an attack on this or that target. It is an attack on civilization. It is the cutting edge of a revolution not merely against some government, but against innocents."

Solidarity

Many expressions of solidarity with the U.S. took the opportunity to revisit and condemn what the authors regarded as an unhealthy anti-Americanism within the Canadian body politic.

Edward Greenspon, "Debunking the Myths about post-September Canada" *Globe and Mail,* 2 October 2001:

> The myth of Canadian ambivalence toward the United States: While listeners and viewers of the CBC may have cause to wonder, most Canadians are at peace with their southern cousins. Our similarities greatly outweigh our differences, starting with our common embrace of such values as freedom, democracy, tolerance and order — shared beliefs directly attacked by the terrorists on Sept. 11.

National Post editorial, 9 October 2001:

> What possible need could there be for Canada to be independent of a U.S. led effort to fight international terrorism?... this is no time for aloofness or equivocation. America's actions are just. Canada's interests and security needs are virtually identical to America's interests and security needs.

Prudence

Canada's dependence on U.S. export markets understandably gave cause for concern about the effects of impeded, or even closed, border crossings.

William Watson, "Good fences make good neighbours but dead economies" *National Post,* 29 September 2001:

> "Good fences may make good neighbours," as Robert Frost said, but they kill economies. If the U.S.–Canadian border is permanently subject to long lines and arbitrary delays or even closures, that's equivalent to tariff barriers going back up.

Gordon Gibson, "Perimeter is no threat to our security," *National Post*, 3 November 2001:

> What matters is our great neighbour, our customer for almost all of our exports, has taken a position on perimeter security that it considers fundamental to its national interest. Now what do we do? Intelligent people weigh the costs and benefits. If we don't go along with the Americans the costs of a significantly tightened U.S.–Canadian border will be clear.

Self-Criticism/Self-Flagellation

The former term best describes *Globe and Mail* articles in this node; the second was coined to describe many *National Post* entries. In both cases, though there is an undertone that Canada's response is deficient. The size of this theme was something of a surprise. It appears that the volume of entries was connected to pre-existing political agendas, including an unsavoury obsession with "immigrants" and "refugees," which were vigorously revisited in the aftermath of September 11, together with initial rumours, subsequently refuted, that some of the terrorists had crossed into the U.S. from Canada.

Edward Greenspon, "The Measure of a PM" *Globe and Mail,* 22 September 2001:

> What counts in the U.S. capital is the contribution that countries can and are willing to make in this war on terrorism. On that score, Canada comes up short.... Passive is the best word to describe Canada's policy response over the past 10 days. European countries already have introduced tougher law-enforcement measures to combat terrorism. The best we've done is order the cockpit doors locked.

James Bissett, "Immigration Security: From Bad to Worse: Our New Immigration Bill poses an even greater risk of abuse by asylum seekers than the old one.) After September 11 that's a scandal" *Globe and Mail* 16 October 2001:

> Government spokesmen are hailing the new immigration bill now before the Senate as being tough on terrorists and criminals. Yet the new bill, C-11, does not address the one area where Canada is most vulnerable — our inadequate and overly generous asylum system. Bill C-11 will make it easier for asylum seekers to enter Canada and much more difficult to remove them after they get in. In normal circumstances, this failure would be deplorable. After Sept. 11, refusal to implement immediate reform of our asylum system borders on criminal irresponsibility.

Diane Francis, "Canada Back Door to America: Bush Snubs Chrétien in U.S. anger over our border security" *National Post* 23 October 2001:

> Canada is a major security risk to the Americans and Ottawa is the problem..., here are the questions Canadians and Americans deserve answers to:
>
> - Last year, 26,564 "refugees" were let into Canada, some with and some without identification. Where are they? Who are they?
>
> - For the past decade, an average of 26,000, or 71 "refugees" a day, have been let into this country, some with and some without identification. That's 260,000 strangers, many of whom have disappeared or become a police, housing, welfare, medical, educational or terrorist burden on our society. Where are they? Who are they?
>
> - Why hasn't Ottawa arrested and removed the three dozen dangerous Algerian terrorists (linked to Osama bin Laden) living in Montréal after I reported they were here as fake refugees in 1997? One was caught in 1999 on his way to blow up Los Angeles

International Airport. Where are the others? Why haven't they been arrested?

- Why did Ms. Caplan, in December, 1999, use her special powers to let 3,000 Muslims from Afghanistan and Somalia into the country without identification? Where are they? Who are they?

- Why has Canada allowed Québec to dictate immigration policy, which has facilitated the arrival of hundreds of questionable and potentially dangerous francophone Muslims into Montréal as "students?" Where are these people? Who are they? Why aren't they checked thoroughly?

- Why does Canada allow in as refugees, and even immigrants, persons with non-treatable tuberculosis and who are HIV positive? Why does Canada let people pick their own doctors to examine them? Does Canada not realize that by doing so it is also exposing Americans to health hazards because the border is so easily crossed?

Michael Bliss, "Well that was obvious: Nothing very wrong, nothing very right from a party adrift," *National Post*, 11 December 2001:

> ... it cannot yet be said that the government of Canada has fully accepted the new continental realities. We are working hard to convince the Americans, and ourselves, that we're serious about fighting terrorism, protecting air travel and keeping the border open, but most of yesterday's announcements were just the obvious, stopgap measures.
>
> The serious policy issues swirling around continental integration have yet to be faced by a government unable to make up its mind about Canada's North American future.
>
> The government isn't ready to grapple with the range of harmonization issues — tariffs, visas, refugees, security arrangements — let alone the fundamental question of whether our military should be a peacekeeping force or a fighting component of the North American military machine. The $1.2-billion increase for the military over

five years is unexpectedly small, little better than derisive tokenism. Canada's fundamental defence policy remains unchanged: Let the United States protect us.

Criticism of the U.S.

The sense that the U.S. was going "too far" and was inaccurate in its diagnosis of the problem did lead to some muted criticism.

William Watson. "Good fences make good neighbours" *National Post* 29 September 2001:

> Attorney-General John Ashcroft didn't actually mention Canada by name in his prepared remarks to Congressional committees this week, but he did spend a lot of time on the border and how it needs to be beefed up.
>
> Let's get a few things straight about the border. To begin with, it's the Americans' border, too. It may be the entry of choice for terrorists and criminals, as a Maine senator told CNN, but if some Sept. 11 terrorists did slip into the United States via this country, they slipped in past U.S. border guards, not Canadian ones. We're the first line of defence, not the last....

Editorial, *Globe and Mail*, 4 December 2001:

> Canada is not a threat to the United States, and it is unfair for U.S. critics to make sweeping statements about a "porous" Canadian border ... there is no evidence of a flood of terrorists crossing the border.

Sovereignty Concerns

Long-standing concerns about Canada's ability to sustain a desirable degree of independence vis à vis the U.S. surfaced from time to time.

Editorial, *Globe and Mail*, 2 October 2001:

> Canada cannot simply abandon its independence to control its borders; nor should it enact U.S. rules or policies wholesale. Despite our common interest in fighting terrorism and ensuring national security, there are still good reasons for Canada to maintain the independence to manage immigration and foreign policy.... The solution is voluntary cooperation and a decision to create similar standards where useful. It is not an abandonment of sovereignty.

Edward Greenspon, "When the 800-pound gorilla shifted position," *Globe and Mail*, 1 December 2001:

> Canadians will be challenged to think through what sovereignty really means. We will have to explore the true boundaries of our nationalism and determine the acceptable trade-offs between our desire for maximum prosperity and our desire for minimum disruption to our value system. So far, this has proved to be relatively easy. Sharing airline manifests with the Americans—their biggest demand up to now—hardly offends anyone's sense of sovereignty. But would the same be said for issues not yet on the table, such as the future of our dollar or the creation of a customs union? Where will we draw the line on immigration and refugee policies? What does this all mean for NAFTA and a Free Trade of the Americas—or are we back to worrying about just us and them?

Civil Liberties Concerns

The draconian nature of Canada's anti-terrorism legislation triggered concerns about civil liberties.

Editorial, *Globe and Mail*, 6 November 2001: "The danger is that public support for heightened security will be used to allow law enforcement authorities to overstep reasonable boundaries."

Karen Selick, "Be very afraid of the anti-terror bill" *National Post*, 30 October 2001: "In seeking to ensure no borderline crime escapes the net, (Bill C-36, the proposed *Anti-Terrorism Act*) casts its net broadly. The result I fear, is that many innocent people will be ensnared by its provisions...."

The percentage of documents coded by these nodes, are given in Table 3, which also identifies differences between the *Globe and Mail* and the *National Post.*

Table 3: Frequencies

NODE	Percentage of total documents coded	Percentage of *Globe and Mail* documents coded	Percentage of *National Post* documents coded
Outrage	4.7	1.2	7.4
Solidarity	6.9	6.1	7.4
Prudential	7.4	7.3	7.4
Self criticism/flagellation	30.0	25.6	33.3
Hurt	1.1	2.4	0
Criticism of U.S.	7.9	15.9	1.9
Sovereignty concerns	6.9	15.9	0
Civil Liberties concerns	3.7	6.1	1.9
Percentage of documents coded into these nodes	68.6	80.5	59.5
	n=190	n=82	n=108

The frequencies do capture important aspects of the coverage. There is an obvious difference of emphasis and tone between the two newspapers. Criticism of the U.S. (typically very mild) and expression of concern about the sovereignty implications of post-September 11 developments are very largely confined to the *Globe and Mail* but, as a percentage of total documents, these concerns are weakly represented.

The most common story line related to Canadian failings. In some cases these attributed responsibility to Canada (lax immigration, border controls etc.) summed up in the (presumably) satirical *National Post* column headlined "Thousands Die: Blame Canada" (*National Post* 18 December 2001). Satire or spoof it may be, the headline does capture the flavour of much of the *National Post's* coverage coded under self-flagellation. In other cases this node captured dissatisfaction with Canada's reaction to the September 11 events — slow moving, insufficiently sympathetic, lack of military resources to contribute to the coming battle etc. The *Globe and Mail's* more moderate entries are of this type and better described as self-criticism.

Conclusion

In terms of the familiar interpretation of Canadian history that runs from colony to nation to colony, the largest single type of media response could be marshalled as evidence of a colonial mentality on the part of Canada's media elite. This is reinforced by something not captured by the numbers — the visceral pro-Americanism of many of the contributions, especially those coded under outrage or solidarity. This is personified in the title of a Christy Blatchford, *National Post* column, titled "Emotionally I'm flying the American flag" and is characteristic of many of Margaret Wente's columns in the *Globe and Mail.*

Emerging from the content of the material rather than its summary, it is clear that pre-existing domestic agendas were fuelled by the events. That is particularly evident in the case of the *National Post's* anti-immigrant and anti-refugee columnists, notably Diane Francis. Outside the media, but emerging from the business elite, the pursuit of deeper integration with the U.S. fits the same profile. There is little challenge to the notion that Canada has no option but to get enthusiastically onside with U.S. actions after September 11. The implications of that for sovereignty are mentioned on occasion but receive no serious analysis. There is every indication that these elites have given up on Canadian nationalism and opted for ever deeper integration inside a North American entity. Based on this evidence, any defence of Canadian sovereignty or nationhood would come from other, non-elite, social groups, or be dependent on American actions and attitudes reigniting the flame of Canadian nationalism.

Notes

1 For an earlier version of the argument see Keenleyside 1927.
2 Although see Ornstein and Stevenson 1999.
3 Canada's non-participation in the U.S. war against Iraq might be taken as an illustration of this point. However, the decision to participate in the U.S.'s missile defence system indicates a price being paid for this brief demonstration of independence.
4 In retrospect the push for a grand bargain or big idea approach to Canada–U.S. relations has given way, in the face of U.S. indifference, and some Canadian second thoughts, to an incremental approach. Nevertheless, in April 2003, the *Financial Post* reported that Ottawa's Policy Research Institute, a federal agency devoted to studying emerging policy issues, was planning an 18-month study to explore the merits of a full customs union with the United States as part of a future "NAFTA-plus" agreement. But mostly, the post-September 11 reality is somewhat more prosaic than the grand bargain approach. One aspect is incremental moves to a "smart border," with greater collaboration on security and immigration issues.

References

Allen, Bob. 1999. "Why Kosovo? Anatomy of a Needless War." Ottawa: Canadian Centre for Policy Alternatives.

Axworthy, Lloyd. 1997. "Canada and Human Security: The Need for Leadership," in *International Journal* 52 (2).

Baillie, Charles. 2001. "Smart Nationalism: An Agenda for Canada's Future," 17 December, 2001. at: http://www.td.com/communicate/speeches/17dec01.html.

Canada 21 Council. 1994. *Canada and Common Security in the Twenty-First Century.* Toronto: Centre for International Studies.

Clarkson, Stephen. 2002. *Uncle Sam and Us: Globalization, Neoconservatism, and the Canadian State.* Toronto: University of Toronto Press.

——. 1968. *An Independent Foreign Policy for Canada?* Toronto: McClelland and Stewart.

Clarkson, Stephen, and Christina McCall. 1990. *Trudeau and Our Times. Volume 1: The Magnificent Obsession.* Toronto: McClelland and Stewart

——. 1994. *Trudeau and Our Times. Volume 2: The Heroic Delusion.* Toronto: McClelland and Stewart.

Cooper, Andrew, Richard Higgot, and Kim Richard Nossal. 1993. *Relocating Middle Powers: Australia and Canada in a Changing World Order.* Vancouver: UBC Press.

Cutler, A. Claire, and Mark W. Zacher eds. 1992. *Canadian Foreign Policy and International Economic Regimes.* Vancouver: UBC Press.

D'Aquino, Thomas. 2001. "Beyond September 11: A Time for Prudence, Creativity and Unity of Purpose." Presentation to the Standing Committee on Finance, House of Commons, Parliament of Canada, September 25, 2001. Found at: http://www.bcni.com.English/Media/speeches/sept25-01htm, or http://www.bcni.com/en/view/?document_id=114

Dewitt, David, and John Kirton. 1983. *Canada as a Principal Power: A Study in Foreign Policy and International Relations.* Toronto: John Wiley and Sons.

Dobson, Wendy. 2002. *Shaping the Future of the North American Economic Space: A Framework for Action.* Toronto: C.D. Howe Institute.

Eayrs, James. 1975. "Defining a New Place for Canada in the Hierarchy of World Powers," in *International Perspectives.* May/June.

Gotlieb, Allan. 1987. "Canada: A Nation Comes of Age." In the *Globe and Mail,* October 29 A7.

Granatstein, J.L. 2002. "A Friendly Agreement in Advance: Canada–U.S. Defence Relations Past, Present and Future." Toronto: C.D. Howe Institute

Hawes, Michael K. 1984. "Principal power, middle power, or satellite?" Toronto: York Research Programme in Strategic Studies.

Keenleyside, Hugh L. 1929. *Canada and the United States: Some Aspects of the History of the Republic and the Dominion.* New York: A.A. Knopf.

Lower, A. quoted in Phillip Resnick. 1970. "Canadian Defence Policy and the American Empire." In Ian Lumsden (ed.) *Close the 49th Parallel Etc: The Americanization of Canada.* Toronto: University of Toronto Press.

Lumsden, Ian. 1970. *Close the 49th Parallel, etc: the Americanization of Canada.* Toronto: University of Toronto Press.

Lyon, Peyton, and Brian Tomlin. 1979. *Canada as an International Actor.* Toronto: Macmillan of Canada.

Martin, Lawrence. 1993. *Pledge of Allegiance: The Americanization of Canada in the Mulroney Years.* Toronto: McClelland and Stewart.

McBride, Stephen. 2001. *Paradigm Shift: Globalization and the Canadian State.* Halifax: Fernwood.

Minifie, James. 1960. *Peacemaker or Powermonkey: Canada's Role in a Revolutionary World.* Toronto: McClelland and Stewart.

Morton, Desmond 1988. "Defence Policy." *The Canadian Encyclopedia* v. 1 Edmonton: Hurtig 2nd ed.

Neufeld, Mark. 1995. "Hegemony and Foreign Policy Analysis: The Case of Canada as Middle Power," *Studies in Political Economy 48* (Autumn), 7–29

Nossal, Kim Richard. 1997. *The Politics of Canadian Foreign Policy.* Scarborough, Ontario: Prentice-Hall Canada Inc.

Ornstein, Michael, and H. Michael Stevenson. 1999. *Politics and Ideology in Canada.* Montréal: McGill-Queen's University Press.

Phillips, Paul. "Why Were We Bombing Yugoslavia?" 1999. *Studies in Political Economy.* Autumn.

Sharp, Mitchell. 1972. "Canada–U.S. Relations: Options for the Future." *International Perspectives. Special Edition* Oct. 17.

Shea, Andrew. 2001. "Border Choices: Balancing the Need for Security and Trade." Conference Board of Canada Special Report. October.

Webb, Michael. 1992. "Canada and the International Monetary regime" in Cutler and Zacher eds. 1992.

PART VI

PLENARY DISCUSSIONS: THE POLITICS OF IN/SECURITY

19

The Politics of In/Security: Summary of a Discussion by a Panel of Distinguished Individuals

Panellists: John Brewin, Rollie Keith,
Peter Stursberg, Colonel Richard Williams
Chair: Dave Barrett (former Premier of
British Columbia, 1972–75, MP, 1988–1993)

John Brewin

Barrett introduced Brewin as a former caucus colleague and as MP for Victoria from 1988 to 1993, in which capacity he had been the New Democratic Party's critic for the Solicitor General and CSIS. He currently practices labour law in Toronto and recently completed a Master's degree in theological studies.

At a narrow level, the effect of the so-called security crisis since 9/11 has been to put pressure on the "fault lines" of Canada's three major parties. Although the Liberals retain a "faint memory" of being a nationalist progressive party, they have become increasingly vulnerable to the American corporate agenda, a situation exacerbated by the post-9/11 world. The Alliance has strong, right wing, pro-American impulses, yet has attempted to break out of that, which is causing tensions. Within the NDP, tension exists between a pacifist tradition that has developed into skepticism of anything American and a tradition of collective security that is torn between connecting with social movements, on one hand, and broadening mainstream support for the party, on the other hand.

From a broader socialist perspective, the issue can be oversimplified by saying "there's Tony Blair and there's everyone else," he said. Not very many democratic socialists are fans of Tony Blair, yet he may reflect an increasingly mainstream form of democratic socialism. Brewin noted that he was recently "struck" when he heard an Alberta conservative on CBC commentary saying he was "indignant" about all the people lining up behind Bush because "they've got it all wrong." The true conservative position would oppose a war in Iraq. The attitude at the end of the First and Second World Wars was: if countries get together and fight a war then maybe they can get together to do some other things. "The left needs to take a look at that," he said.

That said, there are some reasons to support Blair's position. Intervention in Iraq could be justified using the same principles as were used to intervene in Kosovo: there must be persuasive evidence and it must be done through the UN Security Council. Democratic socialists hold basic values regarding equality, security, sustainability, and a belief in "a good state." They are also generally internationalists. If the evidence demonstrates that Saddam Hussein is in breach of international law, that law must be enforced through any means necessary. If the UN chooses to act in that way, the international community will have set a precedent that can be used when a nation threatens to deploy nuclear weapons, fails to treat its citizens appropriately, or fails to protect them. We intervened in Rwanda and Kosovo, and so, arguably, we should also intervene in Iraq. Yet, such intervention could challenge the security of the world.

In closing, Brewin commented, "Adam Smith and Karl Marx had it right." Capitalism is a social and environmental disaster and an alternative has to be found. The kind of democratic socialism we need will build an international order, legislate international laws, and create international institutions to enforce them. That is what will help us build the kind of "New Jerusalem" that Tommy Douglas talked about.

Peter Stursberg

Barrett introduced Stursberg as a most distinguished individual with years of experience as a war correspondent and Canadian writer. His latest book No Foreign Bones in China *was published by the University of Alberta Press in 2002.*

We've heard a lot about the War on Terrorism, yet it's not really a war, said Stursberg. "It's a police action at best, and colonialism at worst." Another police action, the Korean War, was supposed to be a UN action but was actually a U.S. action. The U.S. had its entire 8th Army in Korea, including a Commonwealth Division with 25,000 Canadian soldiers. That conflict was about defeating North Korea, which borders on Chinese territory, but the two countries together were able to push the U.S. troops back. "That was unexpected, but then you can never be sure about the outcome of war." The First World War was successful in many ways, yet it gave rise to a sinister by-product: Communism. Noting that he covered the World War II for the CBC, he commented that the British were victors, yet also losers: within a few years afterward, they lost India—"the jewel in the Crown"—and within a few more years, all of their colonies were gone. Stursberg also covered the Greek Civil War in 1947, which he described as similar to the War on Terrorism in that the army was incapable of fighting the guerrillas, who were also known as terrorists, and who called themselves freedom fighters.

Since 9/11, terrorism has become a synonym for subversion, and terrorists are anyone who is anti-American, especially if they are of Arab background. The Israelis call the Palestinians terrorists for their use of suicide bombers, yet this is not a new phenomenon—think back to the Japanese kamikaze pilots, Stursberg said. What it is, is an act of desperation. Canada has had its own terrorists in the form of the FLQ. When the FLQ kidnapped James Cross and Pierre Laporte, Prime Minister Pierre Trudeau proclaimed the *War Measures Act*. Amid hysterical images of thousands of armed, revolutionary separatists roaming the streets of Montréal, Trudeau's actions garnered him 80 percent approval, which is about the same as George Bush is enjoying now. Yet it was the RCMP who insisted that the WMA be proclaimed so they could execute predawn raids on the homes of suspected terrorists. In all, they arrested

400 people, not one of whom belonged to the FLQ. In fact, it turned out that the FLQ consisted of only 12 people in two cells. In the end, ten of these were exiled to Cuba while the two responsible for Laporte's death were tried for murder.

What does history tell us? In terms of guerrilla wars, it shows us that a whole army is less effective than a number of independent, commando-type units. But in the end, negotiation is still the best option. Or, said Stursberg, as Winston Churchill put it, "jaw, jaw is better than war, war."

Richard Williams

Barrett introduced Colonel Williams as Director of Western Hemisphere Policy for the Canadian Forces, with responsibility for defence policy in the U.S. and in Central and South America. Educated at Carleton, Williams has been in the armed forces for 30 years. After talking to him for a while, said Barrett, "I feel better about our national security knowing that people like this are in charge."

Williams began by noting that, as a uniformed officer, he could not speak to the "politics" of "In/Security." Instead, he wished to highlight the complexity of decisions made for security reasons, and the need to bring balance to decision-making. He referred to a model called Truman's Triangle, which has key attributes at each of its corners. In terms of a product like computers, the three attributes might be good, cheap, and fast. Truman's Triangle states that it is only ever possible to possess two out of three of these attributes.

Put in the context of national security, the three attributes or goals might to be (1) free and sovereign, (2) safe and secure, and (3) not overtaxed. If Canadians want to be (1) free and sovereign, and (3) not spend too much money, they will have to sacrifice (2) safety and security, because it requires a certain amount of money to be able to defend ourselves against threats if and when they arise. This is not far-fetched when we consider neighbourhoods in the country that are beset by gangs, because that is exactly what's happening.

On the other hand, if Canadians want to be (2) safe and secure, and (3) not spend too much money, we will have to focus on security at the expense of personal freedoms, which can lead to manifestations of prejudice such as racial profiling. An example occurred in Florida recently when someone of Asian background was arrested by police because a stranger overheard him say "something bizarre." Then again, if Canadians want to be (1) free and sovereign, and (2) safe and secure, it won't be cheap. As much has been said by Prime Minister Chrétien, but many Canadians will not willingly accept the expense.

Moreover, actions that affect one attribute of the triangle often affect another. For example, if Canada chooses not to side with other nations but "goes it alone" in pursuit of freedom and sovereignty, how does that feed into our sense of safety and security in the world? Are safety and security even the same? The U.S. has a system of red and yellow alerts regarding threats to national security. Should we respond by sharing U.S. information about credible threats with Canadians? If we don't, it could easily come back to haunt us. Canada is not directly threatened by terrorism now. If we isolate ourselves, we could become vulnerable, but if we work closely with the U.S., we could be targeted.

"Every decision regarding national security must be considered in balance with the urgency of the situation and the long-term results," said Williams, concluding that the only way to do this is for Canadians to become involved in informed debate.

Rollie Keith

Barrett introduced Captain Keith [Canadian Armed Forces-ret.] as a long-time NDP activist who had served with the OSCE Kosovo verification mission in 1997, and had recently visited Baghdad as a private citizen. Keith was present at the birth of the peacekeeping project at Suez in 1956 and served in a wide variety of roles during his military career.

Canadians want a peaceful and secure world. Canada is involved in trade, international discourse, and humanitarian missions. Social democrats and other progressive movements believe in internationalism as a way to keep the world secure. The world has avoided nuclear warfare since 1945, and has avoided World War III. "It was clear to me as a youth that if we had taken a more active role against the Spanish fascists, World War II wouldn't have been what it was," said Keith. "But when we did take up against Hitler, we did so very enthusiastically." Canada came out of that war as the fourth or fifth most powerful military force of the time, and went into the post-war world with a commitment to internationalism. We supported the UN and NATO because Canada, as a middle power working with other small and middle powers, could restrain American, British, and French adventurism.

As a young soldier, Keith was involved in "cleaning up" the Suez Canal crisis and separating Egyptian and other forces in the region. At that time, the whole world had changed: the creation of the State of Israel (1948) and the Hungarian Revolution (1956) had surely made British concern about security of "Passage to India" historically irrelevant. He went off not knowing what peacekeeping was going to be and arrived to find a conflict that had gone badly for the superpowers. "In hindsight, Gamal Abdel Nasser is one of my heroes," he said, because Nasser was promoting pan-Arabism, socialism, and nationalism, and trying to bring an aspect of restraint to the polarized world we were in.

[A historically very controversial figure, Nasser was a secular pan-Arabist who was the first republican leader of post-colonial Egypt. *Ed.*]

Then in the post-Cold War world, we ended up with a NATO that had been designed to defend us against a Soviet nation that now no longer exists. That led to some immoral and illegal actions, such as our intervention in the Balkans. Noting that he had been in the Balkans as a civilian observer, he said he quickly found that what the media were saying "was not only incorrect but a complete misinterpretation of the facts." Canada was monitoring the Yugoslav government and the Serbian police and talking to Albanian insurrectionists. The goal was to avoid war, but the Americans were also there, and they had a different agenda: to help the Albanians and punish the Serbs. "There were grievances and injustices that needed to be dealt with diplomatically and weren't."

Turning to present-day Iraq, Saddam Hussein is being unfairly demonized, Keith said. Keith made clear that he is not a supporter of

Saddam, but the alternatives were very unclear, the old royalist and Communist leadership factions having long since been destroyed under Baathist Party rule. "He is not a nice man," he said. "But no president of Iraq would survive if he were nice because it's an area of thuggery." If he were removed, who would replace him, and would replacing him avoid war? Unlikely. As a person with an interest in Middle East security if not political affairs, Keith's opinion of Saddam is that he's "a paper tiger with tenth-rate forces." He's not a threat to the region and certainly not to the United States. If we want to punish people for UN Security Council violations, Israel should be punished because they've been getting away with technical and other violations for 30 years.

More importantly, dealing with countries like Iraq is taking energy away from other concerns like North Korea and Asia Pacific concerns. The Canadian Defence Minister sends forces into Afghanistan but apparently cannot sustain a battalion there, a vivid contrast to Canada's sustained involvements overseas dating back to World War II and West German defence during the Cold War. In closing, Keith noted that although he agrees that "jaw, jaw" is better than "war, war," he also believes that we must spend enough money on the Canadian military to be a credible player on the international stage.

[Keith's fellow partisans in the New Democratic Party, members of the Liberal Party, and many others then agreed to disagree on this vital point. The Afghan contingent was later replaced or reinforced. On Iraq, members the government heeded the voice of anti-war dissenters as opposed to left-wing "hawks" like John Brewin, all for their own reasons. *Ed.*]

Discussion

A participant commented that when Stursberg referred to a sinister by-product of World War I, he thought he was going to say the fascists and the Nazis, not the Communists. Stursberg responded that all three came out of World War I, but the Nazis and fascists came later, whereas the Communists came directly out of World War I. In this context, Barrett recommended a book called *Hitler and Stalin: Parallel Lives.*

[Whether Communism, as such, was a sinister force in twentieth-century history was a matter of widespread debate in Russia, the U.S. and elsewhere at this particular time, before President Putin restored a small measure of economic and administrative order on the truly chaotic post-Communist regime. Communism in China had been all but abolished by the authoritarian Communist Party itself under the slogan of "socialism with Chinese characteristics" and only a few other remnants of Stalin's legacy remained. *Ed.*]

A participant asked Keith to clarify his comments about the American agenda in Kosovo, and why he felt that repressive regimes are necessary to maintain stability in the Middle East. Keith replied that when Canadians arrived in the Balkans, they took over a hotel where American diplomats had been staying for some weeks. "I quickly learned that these people were out talking to the KLA and supplying the KLA with arms that were used to kill Serbs," he said. "I thought, 'Here we are, our purpose is conflict resolution, yet Madeleine Albright is determined to go to war and morality be damned.'" He fears the same thing is happening with the demonization of Saddam. In answer to the second question, Keith said that, if the West had supported Nasser, the world could have avoided Middle Eastern governments filled with "thugs and dictatorial characters." We need to go to some other vision of Arab nations, he said.

[The KLA—Kosovo Liberation Army—was being reigned in to some extent by NATO forces at the time, but wreaked true havoc on the Belgrade state and various security forces at the time of Keith's observations there. *Ed.*]

A participant asked Brewin why Iraq should be held to account for Security Council violations when Israel has not been. Brewin responded that the will of the international community should be enforced in both cases. Just because it has not been enforced against Israel does not mean it should not be enforced against Iraq, and taking action against Iraq might strengthen the position for enforcement against Israel.

A participant commented that the rationale for undertaking certain foreign actions— such as a war on Iraq— is to reinforce domestic policy on other issues, such as supporting a resolution to Canada–U.S. trade disputes. Yet the U.S. is unlikely to change its position on softwood lumber dispute because we side with them against Iraq. One of the factors in whether or not we support the war is the U.S. reaction to what we do, said Williams, but there are also other questions, such as whether we have the capability and whether it's in our best interests. History will place the decision to put Canadian forces in Kandahar in a much more balanced light. But to those who think the U.S. will be so grateful that they'll flip strategies on the softwood lumber issue, he said, "It doesn't work that way."

Douglas Ross noted that European countries are not eager to create a security force, but the U.S. wants them to do so, and asked what the context is for the U.S. wanting that. Keith noted that the Germans, who were the driving force behind creating the European Union, want to see a peaceful union with shared foreign policy and defence policy. The U.S. does not want to lose control of NATO but does want Europe to take control of its own affairs in a way that it was unable to do in the Balkans. Therefore, what the U.S. wants is for the EU to take responsibility. It is not concerned about the EU becoming an opposing military power.

Colonel Williams noted that the U.S. pushed the EU to develop its defence capabilities but did not accomplish its goals because there was no political structure for decision-making and no ability to deploy forces. NATO provides Canada with a way to contribute in Europe, which is advantageous to the U.S. However, even if the EU has forces, it needs political will, "and that's not always there." Brewin added that there are two considerations— military and political. Canada got out of any serious military role in NATO a long time ago, but still has a modest political role. However, we need to begin looking at other military roles for Canada, such as intervening when nations are failing in their obligations to protect their citizens.

Recalling that Williams had talked about the possibility of enhanced cooperation with the U.S. making Canada a more likely target, a participant noted that during the Cold War, Canadian and U.S. security could not be separated. He asked if a case could be made for creating a maritime equivalent to NORAD, or if Canada would be less of a target if we distanced ourselves from the U.S. Williams replied that Canada has moved beyond the Cold War model. Threat assessment is now done on two levels, strategic and domestic. The aim of terrorists is to spread mass terror and they can do that without setting a foot in the U.S. because Canada and the U.S. have so much shared infrastructure. "We cannot be complacent about Canada being unchallenged by terrorism," he said. He predicted an expansion of shared military capacity and said that probably would occur in a maritime context.

Professor Ross noted that when Brewin was talking about the fault lines in the three major parties, he did not refer to Lester Pearson and the commitment to security, and he asked if this concept has been utterly banished. Brewin commented that Pearson generally fits within the progressive tradition of Liberalism. "Although I don't want to romanticize him," he said, "the memory of Pearson still faintly beats in Liberal hearts."

Dave Barrett closed the session by expressing appreciation for the panelists, each of whom had shared some views he agreed with, and some that surprised him; and all interveners who had made for a most revealing dialogue on the politics of security.

20

Plenary Discussion: Terror, Democracy, and National Identity

Panellists: Gregory S. Kealey, Andrew Parnaby, Douglas Ross, Stephen McBride
Chair: Robin Mathews (author, poet, and playwright, and a founding figure in the discipline of Canadian Studies)

The Times They are a-Changing (Back): Canada's "War on Terrorism" in Historical Perspective

by Kealey and Parnaby

Mathews introduced Gregory Kealey as a long time leader of the Canadian Committee on Labour History who is working behind the scenes to publish a history of CSIS; Andrew Parnaby, who will soon be taking up a post at Trent University, is his collaborator in this stealthy endeavour.

Kealey and Parnaby briefly summarized the main points of their paper (see Chapter 5), which are that the Canadian security system was rooted in the British Imperial response to Irish and South Asian independence movements that spilled over into nineteenth and early twentieth-century Canada in many different ways. Bolshevism, U.S. guidance, and many other issues would follow, but the important point is that Canada's system has long crossed many borders and has a history older than Confederation itself.

Weapons of Mass Destruction, Canadian Political Inertia, and the Threat to Human Rights in Canada

by Douglas Ross

Mathews introduced Professor Douglas Ross, a faculty member at Simon Fraser University who has undertaken significant research on nuclear issues, environmental degradation, international conflict, and has contributed to a wide range of journals.

There is currently no effective Canadian diplomacy or foreign policy regarding major crises, said Ross in briefly summarizing his paper (see Chapter 3). Current foreign policy is simply rhetoric that panders to Canadian voters. Most Canadians oppose intervention in Iraq, which may simply be because Bush is the least-liked American president in years. About 12 leading international relations specialists have said no to war in Iraq because it would destabilize the region, is not in American interests, and would alienate Europe. In addition, with a new fundamentalist government in Pakistan, the possibility of their involvement looms large, and given the fact that it is a nuclear power with bombs larger than China's, conflict takes on alarming potential. It is also argued that political engagement might still work if sanctions are tightened. Saddam Hussein was willing to sell off Iraq's nuclear weapons if the price was high enough, but the U.S. did not want to set that precedent.

The Long Goodbye: Elite Nationalism in the Era of Globalization

By Stephen McBride

Mathews introduced Professor Stephen McBride, who has been chair of SFU's political science department twice. Widely published, he has written several books, including one on the globalization of the Canadian state and one on neo-conservatism in Canada.

"Now for the good news," joked McBride in summarizing his paper (see Chapter 18). September 11 is taken as a seminal event, yet in reality it did not change much but did reveal the degree to which Canadian nationalism, as characterized by the media and business elites, has eroded. Another seminal event in Canada a year earlier was the death of Pierre Trudeau. That evoked a sense of nostalgia for when Canada was still a middle power in pursuit of autonomy. Trudeau's career spanned a period when continentalism became entrenched. The roots of that run deep: economically before World War II and during World War II with defence cooperation. However, during the Trudeau era Canada gained some sense of distance from the U.S., particularly through the creation of independent institutions. Most of these came to an end in the 1980s. This fading of our nationalism was obscured by persistent nationalism among the older elites, a multiplication of purely symbolic displays of nationalism such as the "I am Canadian" commercial, and reduced efforts at soft diplomacy. At the same time, there was a drift of events in the opposite direction during the Mulroney era, such as the FTA and NAFTA.

Dialogue

In regard to the Parnaby and Kealey paper, a participant noted that he (typically) had no knowledge of these historical issues and how they connected to present-day multicultural politics and relations with the USA. The authors responded by stating that Canada's relations with Britain were "more organic" than any present-day relations; the Governor General, for example, would never dream of serving as direct conduit for intelligence information from Washington DC. Victorian Canadians feared American Manifest Destiny and acted accordingly. Projecting forward in time, the RCMP maintained its own "spies" or agents in the United States for many years — activity coordinated with the FBI only in the 1930s. The technique of "fingerprinting" arose in British India and was smuggled into the United States by a British constable who helped pioneer this science.

In answering related questions Parnaby emphasized that assessing the effectiveness of intelligence is always difficult. The Fenian Raiders of 1860s were driven back in open combat but successfully formed a secret network in the Dominion that greatly affected the repressive policies of the Macdonald government in Manitoba and elsewhere. Later, British-Canadian collusion fuelled the fires of anti-British radicalism in India and among Indo-Canadians as well. "I am more struck by how often intelligence efforts are counterproductive," he observed.

Kealey added that "we" have not recovered from Cold War habits of thought; there is a serious lack of agents with an understanding of the wider range of issues and cultures involved in the War on Terror. Foreign visitors and others are "easy" targets: "I actually think that the treatment of refugees who come under suspicion is outrageous and violates their civil rights" he concluded.

Turning to McBride's presentation of content-analysis of the press, Allen Seager noted that the *National Post* (successor to the *Financial Post*) and the *Globe and Mail* have, indeed, strong ties to the business and investment communities, as both papers are essentially built around their authoritative reports on business and investment news. He also added that Elizabeth Nickson, a well-known political columnist for the *Post*, had been invited to speak at the conference and would have had interesting comments to make on the relationship, no doubt, between business and political reportage in the paper, had she been able to attend. But he questioned if these papers really reflected the opinions of "non-business" Canadians and wondered if an analysis of other press sources, such as the *Toronto Star*, might yield different results. McBride agreed that the present study was not regionally comprehensive but suggested that further research might only nuance the main argument. Seager responded by calling for team-based research using the new computer tools employed by McBride, including attention to Canada's French-language media.

Reg Whitaker noted that McBride had not talked about the *political* elite and offered an alternative explanation of the findings. He suggested that the immediate political response to 9/11 surrounded discussion of common-entry and immigration policies, which suggested a loss of Canadian sovereignty. In the second wave, there was more to do with seizing opportunities to further continental integration. However, the Canadian government responded by engaging the U.S. in a series of incremental negotiations about details. As that happened, everyone lost sight of the big picture, which was actually a good strategy. "It's not exactly nationalism," he said, "but it reduces the element of alarm." The politics of small differences can be important, said McBride, and small differences add up. But he did not look at the political elite, and indeed there are political choices to be made. But if we look at the kind of pressures currently facing the political elite, they circumscribe a narrow range of options. So the focus was on how the options of the political elite are conditioned by the opinions of the business and media elites.

A participant referred to a radio piece in which an Iraqi speaker advised Condoleeza Rice that the wisest course of action would be to take an enlightened approach toward the reconstruction of Iraq, and wondered if this might be an influential avenue to pursue in the post-9/11 Middle East. Ross responded that Canadian foreign policy and security matters under Chrétien are no different from what they were under Mulroney: there is rhetorical support for the UN masking efforts to disengage. Foreign policy has been turned into a border management issue, when in fact there is a war going on and the U.S. is concerned. The kind of small bomb he referred to is not only an option for terrorists but for many small governments. "Ottawa doesn't see this," he said, noting, "99 per cent of our policy is on trade." As far as the suggested enlightened approach, Condoleeza Rice is more likely to pursue stability in Turkey than Iraq. If we "do" Iraq first, we'll have to do Iran next because they are the next biggest threat, which is why the Israelis fear them.

Another participant asked if Mexico figured in the 9/11 issue and whether Canada and Mexico have the potential of working together. Over six or seven years, said Ross, security regarding Mexico has been a focal point. If a half-million Mexicans are crossing the U.S. border illegally compared with a few Canadians, why spend millions tightening up security at the Canadian border? Yet, the U.S. still has the perception that Canada attracts a huge pool of immigrants from the Middle East and North Africa. "We have 140,000 untracked refugees and the U.S. sees this as a real threat, and sees us as part of the problem," he said. There is no such threat from Mexico. The U.S. feels that for 40 years Canada has spent nothing on security while it has spent everything, he said, "so it's time for us to ante up." A participant added the U.S. probably does not care as much about the Mexican border because those illegal immigrants form a large, cheap labour pool. That is not so with Canada, so the U.S. will expect greater border security.

A participant commented that the number of Middle Eastern people in Canada is fewer than in the U.S. and suggested that we're "playing with numbers" as an aspect of the post-9/11 self-criticism that McBride referred to. Regarding Perez's letter to Kofi Anan, he said the Israelis do their best to project the Palestinian question elsewhere. Yet, if Israel solved its problems with the Palestinians, Syrians, and Lebanese, there would be no more problems in the Middle East. Iran is not capable of doing any real harm to Israel; it actually fears Israel because Israel has threatened to destroy its nuclear reactor. Ross responded that while that may be true, Iran is not weaponless. The Israelis are as vulnerable as New York to the kinds of attacks he described. The Palestinians are not going to blow up an area they want to take over, but bin Laden might. For the Israelis to harm Iran, he concluded, would be "a huge mistake."

Regarding the business elite and the crystallization of its agenda, a participant noted that that agenda was being worked on for years prior to 9/11. Ironically, a meeting was held in New York on 9/10 regarding how to launch that agenda, although at that point, Mexico was the bigger concern. "Don't be fooled," she said, "we are working to move NAFTA forward trilaterally." McBride clarified that when he used the word crystallized, he did not mean "created" but "made clearer."

A participant expressed her "overall frustration with the world. We're all talking about mass destruction. We all know that Israel is the fourth or fifth most-armed country in the world. Now we need more money to create weapons that will fight the biological threat. Yet it would only take $40 billion to solve the world's health problems, bring clean water to poor areas, and so on." There will always be Hitlers, Saddams, and bin Ladens, she said, and we're not going to solve the world's problems by continuing to devote so much energy to these kinds of people at the expense of all the other good we could do.

Professor Ross was asked if he could sum up the argument for not going to war with Iraq. Ross answered that many U.S. politicians believe containment would work as long as they're not trying to depose anyone, and the nay-sayers believe the U.S. is not positioned to depose Saddam Hussein anyway. More importantly, the Middle East is a major source of oil for Europe and Japan, but less for the U.S., so there is no national interest in a war on Iraq. Even if the worst-case scenario arises in the Middle East, there is no point in increasing U.S. involvement in the Middle East because the more involved the U.S. becomes, the more people hate them and the more of a target they become. Iraq is trying to obtain weapons-grade uranium, but nobody knows if it has been successful. Some say it actually set off its first nuclear bomb in the 1970s, but nobody knows for certain.

A participant commented that there is an argument to be made that what the U.S. is doing will create a massive cultural clash that will last for generations and asked if that creates an interest for Canadians in distinguishing our foreign policy and ourselves. Ross agreed there is a compelling argument to be made in favour of the isolation, diplomacy, and constraint that characterized Canadian involvement in the Cold War. However, he added, "we're not in the bull's eye but we are in the inner rings and pretending that a threat doesn't exist is irresponsible and self-deluded."

Mathews thanked participants for attending and members of SFU's Centre for Canadian Studies and Department of Political Science for their assistance. He noted that it is part of a pattern of symposia on issues related to globalization organized by Stephen McBride. Several books of proceedings are available — details are below:

Related Publications

Stephen McBride, John Wiseman, eds., *Globalization and Its Discontents.* London: Macmillan, 2000.

Theodore Cohn, Stephen McBride, and John Wiseman (eds.) *Power in a Global Era: Grounding Globalization.* London: Macmillan, 2000.

James Busumtwi-Sam and Laurent Dobuzinskis, eds. *Turbulence and New Directions in Global Political Economy* Basingstoke: Palgrave Macmillan 2003. Included in the *International Political Economy* Series, ed. Tim Shaw.

Marjorie Griffin Cohen and Stephen McBride eds. *Global Turbulence: Social Activists' and State Responses to Globalization.* Aldershot: Ashgate 2003. Included in *The International Political Economy of New Regionalisms* Series, ed. Tim Shaw.

Stephen McBride, Laurent Dobuzinskis, Marjorie Griffin Cohen and James Busumtwi-Sam eds. *Global Instability: Uncertainty and New Visions in Political Economy.* Dordrecht: Kluwer 2002. Included in *The Social Indicators Research Series,* ed. Alex Michalos.

21

List of Contributors

Dave Barrett is social and political activist. Mr. Barrett served as a member of the British Columbia Provincial Parliament from 1960–1984. First elected in 1960, he became leader of the Provincial New Democratic Party (NDP) in 1970 and Premier of the Province of British Columbia from 1972 to 1975. After leaving provincial politics in 1984, Mr. Barrett was an NDP MP from 1988–1993. Two years later Dave Barrett published his memoirs, *A Passionate Political Life* (Douglas & McIntyre) with William Miller. In 1998 he was appointed by the provincial government to head an inquiry into the "leaky condos" affair in Vancouver, B.C.

John Brewin is a political activist and lawyer. He was the Member of Parliament for Victoria B.C. from 1988–1993, and acted as the New Democratic Party (NDP) critic for the Solicitor General and the Canadian Security Intelligence Service (CSIS). He currently practices labour law in Toronto and recently completed a Master's degree in theological studies.

Louis-Blaise Dumais-Lévesque (B.Sc. Political Science, Université de Montréal; M.A. Political Science, McGill University) is a Ph.D. candidate in political science at the University of Virginia. His work focuses on theories of hegemony.

Anne-Marie Durocher (B.Sc. Political Science, Université de Montréal; M.A. Political Science, McGill University). She is currently enrolled in the Ph.D. program at the University of Virginia. She is interested in great powers' strategic overextension and the notions of great powers' credibility and reputation.

Lisa L. Ferrari is an assistant professor in the Department of Politics and Government at the University of Puget Sound where she teaches courses on international relations and ethics. Her research interests include moral authority, U.S.–Canadian relations, and the Catholic Church as a political actor.

Karl Froschauer is Director of the Centre for Canadian Studies and Assistant Professor in Sociology at Simon Fraser University. His main publications include the book *White Gold: Hydroelectric Power in Canada* (1999) and international articles in the *Zeitschrift für Kanada-Studien* (1997), *Journal of Ethnic and Migration Studies* (2001), *Energy Policy* (2004), and *Comparative Political Studies* (2004). He is currently working on another book, *Immigrant Entrepreneurship in Canada.*

Samir Gandesha is an Assistant Professor in the Humanities Department at SFU. He is currently working on a book that examines Theodor W. Adorno's critique of Martin Heidegger's "fundamental ontology."

Houchang Hassan-Yari is Professor and Head of the Department of Politics and Economics, Royal Military College of Canada. He is a specialist on the Middle East and Canada's foreign and defence policy. Recent publications include *Le processus de paix au Moyen-Orient, Paris, L'Harmattan* (2001), "Khatami's Lebanon Policy," in *Houchang Chahabi, Distant Relations Iran and Lebanon in the Last 500 Years* (2003), and "Perspectives de changements pour la défense et les forces armées du Canada," in Charles-Philippe David et la Chaire Raoul-Dandurand, *Repenser la sécurité. Nouvelles menaces, nouvelles politiques*, Montréal (2002).

Gregory S. Kealey is Vice-President Research and Professor of History at the University of New Brunswick. The Editor of University of Toronto Press' Themes in Canadian Social History Series and founding editor of *Labour/le Travail*, which he edited for 26 years, he also authored prize-winning works in social history. More recently he has published numerous articles in Canadian Security and Intelligence History and co-edited, with Reg Whitaker, eight volumes of RCMP Security Bulletins from 1919–45. His current project with Whitaker and Parnaby is *A History of the Canadian Secret Police.*

Roland Keith is a career soldier, educator, administrator, and political activist. His military career spanned three decades and extensive participation in Canadian Peacekeeping Missions. After military service, Rollie did graduate studies in History, taught, and then took the position as Chair of a regional health authority in British Columbia. Throughout, Rollie Keith has been a long term activist on international justice issues. In 1999 he was a Director of the Kozsovo Polje Field Office of the Kosovo Verification Mission. More recently, he has been a critic of the war against Iraq.

Ayla Kiliç teaches in the Department of Politics at the University of Winnipeg. Professor Kiliç's research interests are: international and domestic dimensions of ethnic conflict management; human rights, democratization, and globalization in the developing world; and comparative study of the principles and practices of human security. Her field of study is the Middle East and North Africa with a special emphasis on Turkey. She has published articles and book reviews on human rights, democratization, and ethnic nationality. Her works have appeared in several publications, including the *Journal of Muslim Minority Affairs* and the *Canadian Journal of Political Science.*

Peter Karl Kresl is Professor of Economics and International Relations at Bucknell University in Lewisburg Pennsylvania. He teaches courses on Canada–U.S. relations, the EU, cities, and international economics. In addition to articles in the *American Review of Canadian Studies*, *Urban Studies*, and several other journals, his recent publications include *France Encounters Globalization* (Elgar, 2002, co-authored with Sylvain Gallais) and *The Urban Response to Internationalization* (Elgar, forthcoming, co-authored with Earl Fry). He has been a Seagram Fellow at the McGill Institute for the Study of Canada.

David MacAlister is an Assistant Professor in the School of Criminology at Simon Fraser University. He currently teaches courses on Criminal Procedure and Evidence, the Philosophy of Law, Human Rights and Civil Liberties, Advanced Criminal Law, and Sentencing. His research interests centre on the above areas, and especially include analyses of the exercise of police powers, legal responses to terrorism, the conduct of Crown prosecutors, and current sentencing practices.

Robin Matthews was born in Smithers, British Columbia, and attended the University of British Columbia, Ohio State University in the United States, and the University of Toronto in Ontario. He has lectured in Canada, the United States, Britain, France, and Finland. He has been instrumental in the development of Canadian Studies as a discipline, and was active during the 1970s in nationalist causes, particularly, national recruitment for Canadian universities. His publications include books of poetry, plays, and short stories, as well as books on the universities, library criticism, Canadian identity, Canadian intellectual history, and Canadian cultural ideals. He lives in Vancouver and is an adjunct professor at Carleton University in Ottawa and Simon Fraser University in Burnaby, British Columbia.

Stephen McBride is Professor of Political Science and Director of the Centre for Global Political Economy at Simon Fraser University. He specializes in political economy, comparative public policy, and Canadian politics. His current research is focused on the impact of globalization on the state.

Denis Michaud is a Ph.D. candidate at the University of Ottawa. His research interests include regional economic integration, monetary policies, and the study of political élites. He was a visiting scholar at Université de Paris 1 Panthéon Sorbonne in 2003 and has been teaching various undergraduate classes for over two years at the School of Political Studies, University of Ottawa.

Matthew S. Mingus is Associate Professor of Public Administration and Doctoral Director at Western Michigan University. Mingus received his Ph.D. from the University of Colorado at Denver and his MPA from the University of Victoria. His primary research agenda is U.S.–Canada comparative administration, and he has published in the *Journal of Borderlands Studies, Public Administration Quarterly*, the *Journal of Comparative Policy Analysis*, the *International Journal of Public Administration*, and elsewhere, as well as several edited volumes

Desmond Morton holds the Hiram Mills chair in history at McGill University. His most recent book is *Understanding Canadian Defence* (Toronto: Penguin Canada, 2003).

Shaun Narine is an Assistant Professor of International Relations at St. Thomas University. He primarily studies institutions and economic/security relations in the Asia Pacific, but his interests include global security relations and political economy. He has published articles in *Asian Perspective, Global Governance*, the *Pacific Review, Pacific Affairs* and elsewhere. His book *Explaining ASEAN – Regionalism in Southeast Asia* was published by Lynne Rienner in 2002.

Alexander Netherton is an adjunct professor in the Department of Political Science and a Research Associate with the Institute of Governance Studies and the Centre for Canadian Studies at Simon Fraser University. He is the author, with Michael Howlett and R. Ramesh, of *The Political Economy of Canada – An Introduction*, 2nd Edition. He has published on social democracy, continental integration, Manitoba politics, and energy policy.

Abdelkérim Ousman is Assistant Professor and co-Chair of the Defence Management and Policy Program at Royal Military College in Kingston Ontario. His research interests centre on the revolution in military affairs, Canada–U.S. military relations, and Islamist terrorism. During the last year he has published in *Geopolitical Perspectives on World Politics*, the *International Journal of Politics, Culture and Society*, and *Le nouvel environnement de la sécurité internationale: Acteurs et défis.*

Andrew Parnaby is an assistant professor in the Department of History at the University College of Cape Breton in Nova Scotia. He has published in the areas of labour history and state security. His Ph.D. thesis, which examined Vancouver's waterfront workers in the 1920s and '30s, won the Eugene A. Forsey Prize in Canadian Labour History. He is currently researching aboriginal people and wage labour and co-authoring, with Gregory Kealey and Reg Whitaker, *A History of the Canadian Secret Police*.

Avery Plaw is an Assistant Professor of Political Science at Concordia University in Montréal. He specializes in Contemporary Political Theory, the History of Political Thought, and International Relations. He received his Master's Degree at the University of Toronto and his Doctorate at McGill (2002). He is the Editor of a volume coming out this summer from Rodopi Press entitled *Frontiers of Diversity: Essays in Contemporary Pluralism*.

Darren Prokop is an Assistant Professor of Logistics in the College of Business and Public Policy at the University of Alaska, Anchorage. He specializes in transportation economics and international trade. Dr. Prokop's applied research examines government policy as related to transportation and non-tariff trade barriers. His theoretical research concerns the microeconomic foundations of logistics and models of secure supply chains. Dr. Prokop's publications cover international taxation of transportation, cabotage regulations, and air cargo logistics.

Douglas A. Ross is a Professor of Political Science at Simon Fraser University. His research interests include Canadian Foreign Policy, Strategy and Arms Control, and International Conflict and Conflict Resolution. He was a founding director of the Canadian Centre for Arms Control and Disarmament in 1983, and served on the national policy advisory group for the Canadian Ambassadors for Disarmament from 1986–1993. He is at present on the editorial board of *International Journal*. Recent work includes four edited collections of papers concerning security and arms control in the North Pacific. Current research interests include Canada–U.S. aerospace defence relations and the relationship between environmental crisis and national security policy-making.

Allen Seager is an Associate Professor of History at Simon Fraser University. His areas of interest are social democracy, culture and labour history, and the radical movement in Western Canada. He has coauthored and contributed to several collections on Western Canada and labour history and published extensively in *Histoire Sociale/Social History, Labour/le Travail, Labour History,* the *Beaver, Prairie Forum* and the *Journal of the Canadian Historical Association.*

Patrick J. Smith is the Director of the Institute of Governance Studies and Professor of Political Science at Simon Fraser University. Professor Smith has written on political parties, elections, urban governance, aboriginal issues, labour market policy, public sector ethics, global cities, planning, anti-terrorism legislation, and human rights in such journals as *Canadian Journal of Political Science, International Political Science Review, Canadian Journal of Urban Research, BC Studies, International Journal of Canadian Studies, Canadian Public Policy, Planning and Administration, Representation, International Journal of Canadian Studies*, and related books.

Christopher Spearin is an Assistant Professor of National Security Studies at the Canadian Forces College in North York, Ontario. His research interests pertain to the privatization of security, non-state actors and conflict, human security, and Canadian foreign and defence policies.

Peter Stursberg is a writer and journalist. He was the first Canadian Broadcasting Corporation (CBC) war correspondent, covering the Canadian troops in Sicily and was the only Canadian journalist to enter both Rome and Berlin with the Western Allies. As a political journalist he wrote books on both Prime Ministers Diefenbaker and Pearson. Peter was also active with the Centre for Canadian Studies at Simon Fraser University during the 1980s and was named to the Order of Canada in 1996. The author of more than a dozen books, the most recent is the award winning *No Foreign Bones in China*, University of Alberta Press, 2002.

Colonel Richard Williams is the Director of Western Hemisphere Policy for the Canadian Forces, with responsibility in Ottawa. Williams has been in the armed forces for 30 years.